Information Technology and Changes in Organizational Work

IFIP – The International Federation for Information Processing

IFIP was founded in 1960 under the auspices of UNESCO, following the First World Computer Congress held in Paris the previous year. An umbrella organization for societies working in information processing, IFIP's aim is two-fold: to support information processing within its member countries and to encourage technology transfer to developing nations. As its mission statement clearly states,

> IFIP's mission is to be the leading, truly international, apolitical organization which encourages and assists in the development, exploitation and application of information technology for the benefit of all people.

IFIP is a non-profitmaking organization, run almost solely by 2500 volunteers. It operates through a number of technical committees, which organize events and publications. IFIP's events range from an international congress to local seminars, but the most important are:

- the IFIP World Computer Congress, held every second year;
- open conferences;
- working conferences.

The flagship event is the IFIP World Computer Congress, at which both invited and contributed papers are presented. Contributed papers are rigorously refereed and the rejection rate is high.

As with the Congress, participation in the open conferences is open to all and papers may be invited or submitted. Again, submitted papers are stringently refereed.

The working conferences are structured differently. They are usually run by a working group and attendance is small and by invitation only. Their purpose is to create an atmosphere conducive to innovation and development. Refereeing is less rigorous and papers are subjected to extensive group discussion.

Publications arising from IFIP events vary. The papers presented at the IFIP World Computer Congress and at open conferences are published as conference proceedings, while the results of the working conferences are often published as collections of selected and edited papers.

Any national society whose primary activity is in information may apply to become a full member of IFIP, although full membership is restricted to one society per country. Full members are entitled to vote at the annual General Assembly, National societies preferring a less committed involvement may apply for associate or corresponding membership. Associate members enjoy the same benefits as full members, but without voting rights. Corresponding members are not represented in IFIP bodies. Affiliated membership is open to non-national societies, and individual and honorary membership schemes are also offered.

Information Technology and Changes in Organizational Work

**Proceedings of the IFIP WG8.2
working conference on information
technology and changes in organizational
work, December 1995**

Edited by

Wanda J. Orlikowski
Massachusetts Institute of Technology
Cambridge, USA

Geoff Walsham
Lancaster University
Lancaster, UK

Matthew R. Jones
University of Cambridge
Cambridge, UK

and

Janice I. DeGross
University of Minnesota,
Minneapolis, USA

Published by Chapman & Hall on behalf of the
International Federation for Information Processing (IFIP)

CHAPMAN & HALL
London · Glasgow · Weinheim · New York · Tokyo · Melbourne · Madras

Published by Chapman & Hall, 2–6 Boundary Row, London SE1 8HN, UK

Chapman & Hall, 2–6 Boundary Row, London SE1 8HN, UK

Blackie Academic & Professional, Wester Cleddens Road, Bishopbriggs, Glasgow G64 2NZ, UK

Chapman & Hall GmbH, Pappelallee 3, 69469 Weinheim, Germany

Chapman & Hall USA, 115 Fifth Avenue, New York, NY 10003, USA

Chapman & Hall Japan, ITP-Japan, Kyowa Building, 3F, 2-2-1 Hirakawacho, Chiyoda-ku, Tokyo 102, Japan

Chapman & Hall Australia, 102 Dodds Street, South Melbourne, Victoria 3205, Australia

Chapman & Hall India, R. Seshadri, 32 Second Main Road, CIT East, Madras 600 035, India

First edition 1996

© 1996 IFIP

Printed in Great Britain by Hartnolls Ltd, Bodmin, Cornwall

ISBN 0 412 64010 4

A catalogue record for this book is available from the British Library

∞ Printed on permanent acid-free text paper, manufactured in accordance with ANSI/NISO Z39.48-1992 and ANSI/NISO Z39.48-1984 (Permanence of Paper).

Contents

Contents

Preface

The papers in this volume are the proceedings of a working conference organized by IFIP's Working Group 8.2 whose brief is "The Interaction of Information Systems and the Organization." The conference, entitled *Information Technology and Changes in Organizational Work,* was held from 7-9 December 1995 at the Judge Institute of Management Studies, University of Cambridge, Cambridge, UK.

The Call for Papers received a total of 64 submissions. Of these, nineteen papers and three panels were finally selected for presentation at the working conference. The submissions were selected through a blind review process involving three reviewers per paper (two per panel), and authors of selected submissions were requested to revise their contributions in accordance with reviewers' and the editors' comments. The editors would like to thank all the members of the program committee and the additional reviewers who participated in this reviewing process.

The selected contributions have been complemented by two invited papers, provided by the plenary speakers at the conference: Bruno Latour (Ecole des Mines: Paris, France) and Shoshana Zuboff (Harvard University: Boston, USA). An introductory paper by the editors provides an overview of the papers in this volume.

The editors would like to take this opportunity to thank all the contributors to this volume. We would also like to acknowledge the assistance provided by the Judge Institute of Management Studies and Department of Engineering at the University of Cambridge, and the support of Lancaster University (UK) and the Massachusetts Institute of Technology (USA).

Wanda J. Orlikowski
Geoff Walsham
Matthew Jones
Janice I. DeGross

Program Committee

Program Co-Chairs:

Wanda Orlikowski   Massachusetts Institute of Technology, USA
Geoff Walsham   University of Lancaster, UK

Organizing Chair:

Matthew Jones   University of Cambridge, UK

Program Committee:

Lynda Applegate   Harvard University, USA
Claude Banville   Université Laval, Canada
Niels Bjørn-Andersen   Copenhagen Business School, Denmark
Susanne Bødker   Aarhus University, Denmark
Richard Boland   Case Western Reserve University, USA
Claudio Ciborra   THESEUS Institute, France
Andrew Clement   University of Toronto, Canada
Kevin Crowston   University of Michigan, USA
Guy Fitzgerald   Birkbeck College, UK
Robert Galliers   University of Warwick, UK
Lynda Harvey   Griffith University, Australia
Rudy Hirschheim   University of Houston, USA
Suzanne Iacono   Boston University, USA
Bonnie Kaplan   Quinnipiac College, USA
Kenneth Kendall   Rutgers University, USA
Heinz Klein   Binghamton University, USA
Rob Kling   University of California at Irvine, USA
Allen Lee   Cincinnati University, USA
Kalle Lyytinen   University of Jyväskylä, Finland
Shirin Madon   London School of Economics, UK
M. Lynne Markus   Claremont Graduate School, USA
Lars Mathiassen   Aalborg University, Denmark
Enid Mumford   University of Manchester, UK

Faith Noble	UMIST, UK
Brian Pentland	Michigan State University, USA
Daniel Robey	Georgia State University, USA
Gunter Schäfer	Commission des Comniroutes, Luxembourg
Hugh Willmott	UMIST, UK
Steve Woolgar	Brunel University, UK
Chee Sing Yap	National University of Singapore, Singapore

Additional Reviewers

David Avison	University of Southampton, UK
Richard Baskerville	Binghamton University, USA
Brian Bloomfield	UMIST, UK
Michael Gallivan	Massachusetts Institute of Technology, USA
Mike Hales	University of Brighton, UK
Paul Hart	Florida Atlantic University, USA
Sue Holwell	University of Lancaster, UK
Juhani Iivari	University of Jyväskylä, Finland
Julie Kendall	Rutgers University, USA
Frank Land	London School of Economics, UK
Jonathan Liebenau	London School of Economics, UK
David Meader	University of Arizona, USA
Ramiro Montealegre	University of Colorado, USA
Ken Peffers	University of Hong Kong, Hong Kong
Vicky Russell	Darwin College, UK
Susan Leigh Star	University of Illinois at Urbana-Champaign, USA
Steve Smithson	London School of Economics, UK
Eileen Trauth	Northwestern University, USA
Duane Truex	Georgia State University, USA
Dave Wastell	University of Manchester, UK
Leslie Willcocks	University of Oxford, UK
Elaine Yakura	Michigan State University, USA,

Information Technology and Changes in Organizational Work: Images and Reflections

Wanda J. Orlikowski
Massachusetts Institute of Technology

Geoff Walsham
Department of Management Science
The Management School
Lancaster University

Matthew Jones
Management Studies Group
Department of Engineering
University of Cambridge

The papers appearing in this volume are the collection of articles and panels presented at the 1995 IFIP 8.2 Working Conference on *Information Technology and Changes in Organizational Work.* It is widely accepted that work and work-life in the industrialized societies of the late Twentieth Century are undergoing a profound transformation in terms of aspects such as the nature of work and job security at the personal level, changes in practice and instability of structures at the organizational level, and increasing interconnection and globalization at the national and international levels. Information technologies are deeply implicated in these transformations, and the papers in this volume explore some of the relationships between these information technologies and the ongoing and possible future changes in organizational work.

The papers present a more complex picture of the relationship(s) between information technology and new forms of organizational work than has typically been the case. This comes from critical, empirically-based analyses of practice, and the innovative application of a range of theoretical approaches (both new and more established), enabling us to move beyond traditional technocentric narratives to reveal other stories. These stories are not univocal but present multiple perspectives which are sometimes complementary, sometimes contradictory. Further, many of the papers seek to locate changes in organizational work within a broader context of social transformation and social discourses. These papers illustrate historical precedents for current changes, but also offer a picture of possible new forms of working and organizing.

Taken as a whole, the papers do not offer, either singly or collectively, any definitive conclusion about the relationships between IT and organizational work. Instead, they offer an array of accounts, concepts, and critiques which more than anything reveal the particular intellectual and pragmatic sensibilities underlying our current discourse on these relationships. This discourse is animated both empirically and conceptually, and we can read in it both images and reflections on the nature of organizational work as approached from the analytic and practical lens of information technology. The *images* offered by these papers focus on organizational practices around information technology including both technological development and the creation of new kinds of organizational work and processes. These images provide critical, empirically-grounded analyses of the role of information technology in a range of contemporary and situated work practices. The *reflections* embedded in these papers concern the theoretical concepts and approaches we, as researchers, use to make sense of and investigate organizational practice around information technology. They reflect on us as scholars and the particular ways we see, understand, and act toward our phenomena of interest.

1. IMAGES OF PRACTICE

One major set of papers in this volume focuses our attention on the practices of designing and using information technology in organizations, and on the assumptions, ideologies, motivations, methodologies, omissions, and implications of such practice. Three broad categories of practice emerged from the set of papers accepted for the conference. The first category comprises the production of new forms of work, and whether, how, and with what implications information technology plays a role in facilitating this creation. The second category concerns the practice of business process reengineering, the most recent in a line of managerial approaches intended to reform organizational work and to create innovation and flexibility through the deployment of information technology. The papers raise a number of important questions about this practice, questions involving its conceptual contradictions and its mixed results in implementation. The third category involves systems development, the process responsible for the design, construction and deployment of information technology in organizations. Reviews of the practices employed by systems analysts and designers, as well as their expertise, methodologies, and techniques reveal a range of unarticulated and questionable assumptions about the nature of work and the process of organizational change. They also point to some significant omissions in the conception and conduct of systems development, most notably the exclusion of nonhuman stakeholders and human bodies.

1.1   New Forms of Work

Zuboff argues that despite the many calls for new organizations and new forms of work, the possibilities for transforming organizations remain severely limited by assumptions and imaginations locked in a prior discourse of industrialization, control, and hierarchy. She argues that current attempts at "changing" organizations have focused on reengineering, downsizing, and obtaining operational efficiencies, rather than on fundamentally challenging and reinventing the nature of work and organization. She points to a contemporary absence of "moral leadership" in organizations, and suggests that notions of an information economy and informated organizations will remain illusory if traditional assumptions about work and control are simply repackaged in new ways.

Zuboff's critique of contemporary managerial practice is continued by a number of authors who critically examine the role of information technology in the workplace and the ideological nature of knowledge work, business process reengineering, and information technology itself.

Fuller, Hartman, and Raman deconstruct the nature of "knowledge work" and reveal how it embodies a set of assumptions, ideologies, and illusions about professional labor, intellectual skills, and expertise which are contradicted in practice. In the various empirical cases they consider, a range of possibilities are seen to characterize the application of information technology to knowledge work — displacement, visibility, reskilling, deskilling, control, accountability, and outsourcing.

The use of computer-based information systems has been seen as an essential feature of the organizational changes introduced in the UK National Health Service since 1990. *Louw* argues, however, that much of the resulting investment in healthcare computerization has been ineffective. Invoking a distinction between proceduralized (structured) and interpretative (semi-structured and unstructured) information, she argues that computerization is unsuitable for systems that use information primarily of the latter type. Drawing parallels with recent developments in cellular manufacturing, Louw suggests that it may be better to reduce information processing needs, by, for example, creating self-contained organizational units. She uses a case study of the planning of a patient-focused care system in a British hospital to illustrate the advantages of this approach.

1.2   Business Process Reengineering

Business process reengineering — both in practice and theory — is subject to critical examination by four of the papers in this volume, and found wanting. Conceptual critiques reveal its utopianism, its contradictions, and its lack of novelty. Assessments of business process reengineering initiatives indicate that organizational members report conflicting interpretations and experiences, as well as decreased organizational commitment and job satisfaction after the initiative has ended.

Grint, Case and Willcocks analyze the practice of reengineering using the results of a survey of UK companies claiming to be engaged in reengineering initiatives. The results suggest that these companies were less radical in their approach than reengineering's proponents advocate, and that they achieved less dramatic outcomes. Given these results, Grint, Case and Willcocks question reengineering's popularity, and why companies seek to ally themselves with its prescriptions even if their practice is different. The authors identify an important dimension of reengineering's attraction to be its politics. Reengineering, they argue, both denies politics and advocates a form of organizational utopianism, but also proposes a directly political, top-down model of organizational change. They identify information technology as one of the "actors" in this political process, and suggest that part of the effectiveness of reengineering rhetoric lies in its encouragement of a selective amnesia about previous failures of IT-led organizational change. In the light of this assessment, the chances that reengineering will learn from previous experience, as Hamilton and Atchison propose, would seem to be low.

Willmott and Wray-Bliss seek to locate reengineering within a broader discourse of enterprise and to consider the implications for the employees of companies that adopt its prescriptions. They also critically examine the rhetoric of reengineering through an analysis of its claims to establish an "empowered" form of accountability. They argue that the characteristics of reengineering bear little resemblance to those of socializing systems of accountability, and that reengineering remains essentially hierarchical in its approach to organizational control. This exemplifies tensions and contradictions within the concept or reengineering which are likely to give rise to difficulties in its implementation. Such contradictions, however, may also provide opportunities for resistance to the discourse of which it is seen to be a part.

Hamilton and Atchison argue that reengineering has many similarities to earlier IT-led change initiatives, and illustrate this with a case study of a large-scale IT project in Telecom Australia in the 1960s and 1970s, the COMIS plan. They see reengineering as sharing two key assumptions with this earlier initiative: that IT has reached a stage of development such that it fundamentally alters the logic of business process design; and secondly, that existing processes are so inefficient as to require radical restructuring. In the absence of reliable empirical evidence of the long-term implications of reengineering, Hamilton and Atchison propose that the experience of these earlier initiatives may provide insights into the limitations and dangers of such a model of organizational change.

Gallivan describes a case study of a large telecommunications utility company in the USA which had initiated a major reengineering and reskilling program. He examines the perceptions and attitudes of three stakeholder groups, namely the change management specialists, IS managers and employees, and outsiders to the reskilling initiative. Results from the study demonstrate strong differences of view among the stakeholder groups, and Gallivan explains these in terms of the different cognitive frames they hold with respect to the anticipated technological changes, as well as to their assumptions about organizational changes that must accompany technological change to achieve the desired outcomes. Gallivan argues that, where possible, organizations should seek to reorient members' frames to more congruent positions, although he recognizes the problematic nature of such an endeavor.

Guimaraes examines how the job perceptions of organizational members change following the implementation of a business process reengineering initiative in one manufacturing company. Applying the Job Characteristics Model to this question, Guimaraes assessed a range of attitudinal variables before and after the BPR initiative. He found that while the BPR initiative created a richer overall work environment, as measured by variables such as task identity, skill variety, and job autonomy, employees reported lower job satisfaction and organizational commitment after the business processes were reengineered. Guimaraes suggests that more effort by both researchers and practitioners should be devoted to exploring the negative perceptions employees have of initiatives such as business process reengineering.

1.3   Systems Development

The contributions on systems development raise a variety of critical issues about the efficacy and appropriateness of the processes, methodologies, concepts, and expertise prevailing in the practice of information systems development. Some call for greater integration of approaches from other disciplines into systems development, others argue that the very notion of systems development needs to be problematized, and some urge the reconstruction of systems development approaches in the light of organizational shifts toward new forms of work and organizing.

Westrup calls for an examination of developers' practices to reveal the ways in which these actively constitute the organizations for which they build information systems. That is, analysts construct representations of organizations that require the use of information technologies. In addition, their practices constitute developers as competent and authoritative, and configure users as passive participants. Westrup argues that without an investigation of how developers' practices abstract, simplify, and rationalize organizational work, calls for greater social analysis skills by analysts are misguided.

Kuutti further critiques the assumptions embedded in the work of systems designers, pointing to their implicit notions of routinization and automation, and hence their inadequacy in the context of new work practices and structures. However, in contrast to Westrup, he proposes that the integration of approaches from information systems and computer-supported cooperative work can inform and elaborate the practices of systems designers. Such connections can help designers integrate the post-Fordist and collaborative work notions characterizing the new forms of organizational work emerging today.

Scarbrough examines the influence of IS specialist expertise on the social construction of IT systems as strategic or non-strategic, which has consequent implications in shaping information technology and organizational work. He describes the results from an empirical research study of six IT projects in Scottish-based financial institutions, and shows, using paired comparisons, that the strategic classification of particular projects did not depend primarily on the technology deployed, but rather on the way that the IS function enlisted both the immediate contingencies of the project at hand, and the wider institutional context, in advancing its classificatory claims. Scarbrough cautions that resultant classifications will, however, remain tentative and uncertain, since they do not represent timeless and universal representations of IS activities.

Gasson and Holland report on a survey of senior information technology managers which found that the majority of tools and techniques applied to information technology-based organizational change projects were oriented toward technical/functional, rather than business, issues. In examining user participation, these authors found that such involvement was heavily skewed toward the implementation stage where most of the requirements had already been "frozen" so that user involvement had little impact. In addition, they found a significant lack of user participation in third party systems development. These findings point to the continued difficulty of changing systems development practices and approaches so as to integrate both a business orientation and user contributions throughout the systems development life cycle.

Baskerville, Fitzgerald, Fitzgerald, and Russo challenge the widespread belief that methodologies can improve the practice of systems development. They question this assumption by contrasting the experiences of developers with the prescriptions of their methodologies, and expose some critical inconsistencies. They argue for the importance of moving to a new systems development paradigm which better accommodates the new organizing assumptions and practices emerging today.

Baskerville raises the issue of security in information systems and shows how mechanisms aimed at reducing direct threats against systems such as software unreliability or physical abuse (first order security issues) have unintended consequences for the organization (second order security issues). In particular, Baskerville argues that the first order safeguards embedded in information technologies reduce the capacity for organizations to be adaptable and flexible. He recommends that systems developers include a consideration of second order security issues when developing new systems, and proposes some mechanisms and safeguards for implementing adaptive security.

Finally, the work of Vidgen and McMaster and that of Mingers force us to reconsider the very objects we choose to incorporate in our systems design practices and methodologies. *Vidgen and McMaster* argue that our tendency to separate nature and society creates problems in systems development, in particular, the elision of nonhuman stakeholders from the analysis. They propose a view of information technology as quasi-object, a representation that captures organizational context *and* technology without privileging either. They illustrate their ideas using a case study of an innovative car parking system which was both an information system and an access control system. They carry out a stakeholder analysis of both human and non-human interests, and describe how the attempted translation of these interests into the black box of a hard(ened) fact was not achieved in this case due to weaknesses in the network of associations between stakeholders.

Mingers argues that most contemporary work in artificial intelligence and information systems perpetuates the Cartesian dualism of mind and body. He draws on a range of theoretical writers to emphasize the embodied nature of human communication and action. He concludes that traditional disembodied artificial intelligence will shed little light on embodied human intelligence, and he calls for the development of AI systems with embodied characteristics. With respect to information systems, Mingers argues for the development of technologies that make more use of people's bodies, and for the need to consider seriously the impacts on human society of disembodying technologies such as the Internet.

2. REFLECTIONS OF RESEARCH

As researchers studying information technology and organizational work we have shared in and contributed to the modernist narrative that technology is a powerful agent of change in human history. Yet, as the papers in this volume reveal, there is disquiet about the implicit determinism underlying accounts of technology as a dominant force in organizational life. The assumptions, approaches, and analyses proffered by the papers in this volume, while acknowledging a central role for technology in human history, focus more intently on human doings and institutional influences. By explaining the influence of technology in organizations through the power of social action, whether intended or unintended, these papers reveal their authors' belief in human agency, as expressed in learning and participation, as well as in institutionalization, as evident in the inscriptions, classifications, and narratives, of, for example, reified accounting methods, standards, and medical ideologies.

2.1 Inscription

Latour raises our awareness of the multiple and interdependent inscriptions that exist in the various systems with which humans interact in daily life. He further highlights the process of delegation in which non-human actors represent, define, act on behalf of, and delimit human behavior. Latour identifies two earlier broad approaches to understanding information technology in human society: first, the rationalist approach which treated humans as largely irrelevant and, second, the humanist backlash which tried to restrict and circumscribe the role of non-humans. Newer approaches such as actor-network theory recognize the weakness of both these earlier approaches, and treat human and non-human actors as part of a network bound together by a set of heterogeneous associations. In this paper, Latour discusses the limitations of trying to identify all such associations. He proposes instead a supplement to actor-network theory involving examining networks by tracing how an indefinite number of entities grasp one another in a limited number of ways. He illustrates this idea with an amusing example of Anglo-French cooperation.

A number of authors seek to apply Latour's concepts, and consider in some detail how the various inscriptions, classifications, and narratives constructed in everyday practice constitute and control ways of thinking, acting, and developing information technology.

Boland and Schultze examine the role of activity-based costing as an exemplar of the use of information technology for inscribing and representing organizational work. They consider the truth claims of those arguing in favor of activity-based costing as a more faithful representation of work than prior systems of cost accounting, by examining the role of a narrative of factory life and its use as a rhetorical device. Boland and Schultze undermine this approach by constructing an anti-narrative in which additional events are added, a later story is told, and the conclusions on the merits of activity-based costing are reversed. The purpose of their analysis is not to argue for the use of a particular system of accounting. Rather, as a more interesting way to think about the organization, ethics, and aesthetics of work, the authors suggest the need to consider multiple narratives which give voice to and allow the construction of multiple inscriptions and representations of organizational work through information technology.

Monteiro and Hanseth continue the focus on inscription and consider the role of standards, particularly those embedded in infrastructures, in prescribing and proscribing forms of interaction with information technology. They describe two examples in the Norwegian health sector, using actor-network theory as an analytic approach. The first example concerns the definition of an EDI message standard for describing the identifiers of a drug prescription, and illustrates how the standard represented a translation and inscription of the pharmacies' interests. The second is an EDI system for the exchange of test results from laboratories to general medical practitioners, the standard for which was initially developed in line with the interests of a particular laboratory. This created problems for other laboratories, and the development of a broader standard to meet all their needs was a radically more difficult translation task.

Bowker, Timmermans and Star explore the ways in which the apparently simple process of designing a classification scheme contributes to the restructuring of work practices and knowledge production and inscribes a moral order. In particular, they describe how classification schemes involve tradeoffs between three areas: comparability, visibility and control. Focusing on the design of a classification scheme for understanding the nature of nursing work, they illustrate how these areas are addressed in practice and the dilemmas that this gives rise to. Bowker, Timmermans and Star's analysis provides an interesting background to that of Louw, where the adoption of standardized nursing protocols is seen as a necessary and desirable part of the development of patient-focused care systems.

Bloomfield and McLean examine and disclose the ideologies underlying technological interventions to promote empowerment within the UK National Health Service. In an empirical examination of a psychiatry department, the authors show how empowerment of actors, such as patients and health care workers, is not a consequence of information technology introduction and use, but is implicated in the particular psychiatric and technological practices used to develop and implement the technologies. Through their participation in such practices, patients and health care workers are constituted as empowered subjects, and particular forms of organizing are produced and reinforced.

2.2   Learning

The "Learning Organization" is widely promoted, but what this means in practice is much less frequently discussed. *Ciborra, Patriotta and Erlicher* address this question through an analysis of the operation of Fiat's new Melfi plant, where a semi-autonomous work-team structure has been adopted. They propose a model of the firm as a learning organization which they describe as the "learning ladder." This seeks to integrate different learning processes at the strategic, capability and routine level. The authors pay particular attention to the way in which the organizational context both shapes and is created by the learning process. For example, they highlight the way in which interpretive schemes and organizational routines developed in traditional assembly lines, and instantiated in the design of the information systems, hamper the effectiveness of the work-teams. They propose an audit methodology to evaluate the effectiveness of learning processes and describe its application in the new Fiat factory.

Continuing the focus on learning as a central organizing practice, *Beuschel, Van den Besselaar, Krogh and Gowlland* discuss the challenge and opportunity of tele-learning. The technologies available for tele-learning are developing at a considerable pace, but relatively little attention has been paid to complex social and organizational issues. Management issues include leadership, access, control, coordination and the balancing of the different needs of companies, end-users, and the providers of learning materials and technology. Other issues include the economics of tele-learning, and questions of appropriate modes of interaction related to different theories of learning.

2.3   Participation

Mumford explores the ideas of Mary Parker Follett on freedom, and in this empathetic review, revisits the principle of participation and her own work in that area. Follett emphasized the importance of organizational integration, and believed that freedom for the individual and the group were mutually supportive and enhancing. She accepted the traditional concepts of power, authority and leadership, but redefined them as power *with*, *joint* responsibility, and *multiple* leadership. Mumford's own work on participative approaches to systems design draws heavily on Follett's ideas, and her objective has always been to increase the user group's freedom to choose the organizational and technical systems that they prefer. Mumford argues that Follett's ideas remain a relevant vision for designing in the technologically-based worlds of today and tomorrow. Indeed, these ideas may embody some of the "moral leadership" called for by Zuboff.

3. IMAGES AND REFLECTIONS: CONCLUSION

Collectively, the set of papers in this volume represent a significant critique of contemporary practice with and through information technology, and pose a substantial challenge to those who would do otherwise. One challenge which arises from the contributions in this volume is how to replace or modify current management ideologies concerning information technology as a support for hierarchy and control with alternative ideologies concerned with using information technology to enable human agency and augment human capacity. A more specific challenge is to consider the role of business process reengineering, and how it reflects prevailing management approaches of top-down control as a means of bringing about organizational change. The papers also challenge the modes and practices of systems development, reflecting and reinforcing as they do, particular views of management, technology, work, and organizing. A contemporary challenge for design practice is how to account for and facilitate non-traditional views of work and work-organization. These papers also represent some challenges for the practice of research, and the need to look beyond simple technocratic explanations of organizational change, and to develop theoretical approaches that engage the complex interaction of social, technical, institutional, and interpretive influences that shape organizational changes in specific contexts.

The ubiquity of information technology in today's organizations and the central role that it plays in the transformation of work give a particular significance to the images and reflections expressed in these papers. They paint a picture of where we have been and where we may be heading, both at the level of practice and that of theory. This picture connotes some of the ambivalence and ambiguity we share about information technology and its relationship to changes in organizational work. We know there is a relationship, indeed, many relationships, but their contours, the what, why, when, where, and how of those interactions elude easy characterization and categorization. Perhaps that is how it should be. The very nature of information technology shifts and changes, historically and contextually, conceptually and empirically. Organizational work too, is a multi-valenced concept as well as a multi-dimensional practice. It has included and continues to cover much territory: clerical, artistic, managerial, craft, supervisory, production, professional, routine, knowledge, symbolic, emotional, informal, technical, individual, and collaborative. Animating both technology and work is the human capacity to act in the world, to construct and use information technology, to define, control, and modify work. Human agency is routine and innovative, mindless and reflective, planned and improvisational. It has both intended and unintended consequences. Most importantly, the assumptions, interests, concepts, approaches, and theories that we use, shape and refine our views of the world and of ourselves.

As views and mirrors, the papers in this volume inscribe, construct, delegate, inform, constrain, enable, highlight, critique, provoke, and promote particular forms of information technology, particular changes in organizational work, and particular understandings of them. We believe that this rich collection of images and reflections offers much to think about as we grapple — intellectually and practically — with the ongoing issues of inventing and reinventing work and our concepts of work through the particular lens of information technology.

About the Authors

Wanda Orlikowski is the Gordon Y. Billard Career Development Associate Professor of Information Technologies at the Massachusetts Institute of Technology, Sloan School of Management. She received her Bachelor and Master of Commerce degrees from the University of the Witwatersrand, and her M.Phil. and Ph.D. degrees in Information Systems from New York University. Her primary research interests focus on the organizational change implications of information technology, with particular emphasis on organizational dimensions such as structure, culture, work practices, knowledge, communication, control mechanisms, and social cognition.

Geoff Walsham became Professor of Information Management at Lancaster University in 1994, after nineteen years at Cambridge University. Prior to that, he was a lecturer for four years at the University of Nairobi in Kenya, and he also worked for a similar period as an operational research analyst for BP Chemicals. His work over the last ten years has been concerned with computer-based IS and their implications for organizations and society, and he has published on a wide range of IS topics. His current research interests include IS strategy and implementation, GIS, and IT in developing countries.

Matthew Jones is a University Lecturer in Information Management in the Department of Engineering and Judge Institute of Management Studies at the University of Cambridge, UK. He previously held postdoctoral positions at the Universities of Reading and Cambridge where he was involved in the development of computer-based models for public policy decision-making. His current research interests are concerned with the social and organizational aspects of the design and use of information systems and the relationship between information technology and social and organizational change.

PART ONE

Images of Practice:
New Forms of Work

The Emperor's New Information Economy

Shoshana Zuboff
Benjamin and Lilian Hertzberg Professor
of Business Administration
Harvard Business School

According to the U.S. Commerce Department, 1990 was the first year in which capital spending relevant to the information economy (computers and telecommunications) exceeded capital spending on the more traditional aspects of the industrial infrastructure (plant, equipment, physical transportation, etc.). Many scholars and business-oriented commentators have greeted these data as evidence that the U.S. economy is now firmly rooted in the information age, that a new "information economy" has replaced the industrial economy that dominated most of the twentieth century.

This is a conclusion from which I heartily dissent. An information economy requires more than infrastructure investment. It requires a new social contract derived from a new moral vision, binding members of the firm together in ways that contrast profoundly with the well worn emotional pathways of the industrial hierarchy. Until these matters are seriously engaged by the leadership in a majority of our business organizations, the notion of an information economy is much like the foolish emperor of fairy tale fame, naked and very much at risk.

In an information economy, information is the core resource that firms exploit in order to create the value their customers seek. While businesses are generously investing in the information infrastructure to make this possible, they show little evidence of a commitment to creating the forms of organization and developing the people that can exploit that new infrastructure for value creation. Organization is a methodology for responding to complexity. The nature and degree of complexity in a globally integrated information-rich marketplace is exponentially greater than anything we have known. Organizational methodologies, however, are evolving far more slowly than the markets they endeavor to serve.

Considered in historical perspective the problem becomes more clear. In the early decades of the twentieth century, a new organizational form was invented and continued to be perfected over several decades. Known as the functional hierarchy, it was characterized by a number of brilliantly inventive features designed to meet the challenges of complexity associated with the new mass markets of that period. Strategically, firms concentrated on increasing throughput and lowering unit costs. Wealth derived from the coupling of physical products with new domestic channels of distribution, enabled by the then new modes of transportation and communication, rail and truck, telegraph and telephone. The organizational inventions of the early twentieth century constitute just about everything that has come to be regarded as definitive of modern work. These include the mass production techniques of the factory and office based on the separation of execution and conception, the fragmentation of tasks or minute division of labor, the professionalization of management and the growth of the managerial hierarchy to scrupulously standardize and control operations, the simplification and delegation of administrative functions to a newly contrived clerical workforce. These and many other features of the emerging industrial workplace proved to be incredibly successful, producing unprecedented wealth through productivity gains that were, over time, widely shared. They came to define the modern workplace, born in the USA, a colossus that reigned over the industrial life of the century.

Now, at the century's end, the structure of the marketplace and the technological infrastructure upon which it depends have changed yet again. The globalization of markets and the conditions of hypercompetition thus created have accelerated the commoditization of products in virtually every industry. Mass market approaches have been forced to give way to a highly differentiated and often information-saturated marketplace in which firms must distinguish themselves through the value-added they can create along the dimensions their customers deem important. New information technologies now provide the means through which these processes of value creation can occur. But this new infrastructure is not benign. It has profoundly altered the operational and managerial systems of the firm, and in so doing has transformed the nature of work at every level of the organization. The new work depends upon a radically different approach to the distribution of knowledge and authority within the organization, according to principles of equal access and equal opportunity. New organizational methodologies are required that allow complexity to be effectively managed at the point where it enters the organization. This would enable the identification and exploitation of opportunities for the creation of added-value at any point in the value chain. The transformation of information into wealth means that more members of the firm must be given opportunities to know more and to do more.

The problem is this: the brilliant inventions of the early twentieth century workplace are now the barriers that inhibit the next great leap forward. The successful reinvention of the firm consistent with the demands of an information economy will continue to be tragically limited as long as the principal features of modern work are preserved. Unlocking the promise of an information economy now depends upon dismantling the very same functionalized managerial hierarchy — with its moral vision, social system, entrenched interests, and vertical focus —that once spelled greatness.

In order to grasp the roots of these developments it is necessary to consider the nature of work, how it has changed, and the vast implications of this poorly understood transformation. The agony and the ecstasy of work have been the great story of the human spirit. Work was heroic. It meant physical sacrifice, exertion, and depletion. But the same physical engagement with work that put the body at risk was also the means by which precious skills of know-how and craft were developed. For all of human history, most people have had to work in this way — giving up their bodies in the service of production, often in sorrow, sometimes with skill.

This is the immanent context in which humans have developed their tools and technologies. The universal logic of these developments has been to design tools that substitute for the human body, extending and amplifying its capabilities while saving it from ruin. This developmental process has not been a straight linear function. There have been eras and industries in which machinery has served to increase the agony of work. However, the overall historical pattern is one in which mechanization and later automation have served to marginalize the worker from the physical aspects of work. This pattern, most prominent in the twentieth century, has been coupled with a general shift in employment that absorbed more of the laboring population in "white collar" knowledge-oriented activities whose demands on the human body have tended to be of a very different nature. Indeed, the twentieth century is the first in human history in which it can be said of any society that a majority of the working population was exempt from the excesses of physical exertion and sacrifice that have been work's implacable companion.

This century's long trend toward the abstraction of work has been dramatically accelerated since the early 1980s by the adoption of information technologies. These new technologies were widely regarded as simply the next phase of automation. The logic of their development and deployment hardly varied from the ancient impetus toward labor substitution. But we have learned that these technologies are different, that the intelligence at their core provokes a discontinuity in the history of technological development. This is because even when information technologies are applied to automate, they simultaneously set into motion an entirely unique set of reflexive processes, translating newly automated activities into data and information for wide-ranging display. Information technologies symbolically render processes, objects, behaviors, and events so that they can be seen, known, and shared in a new way. In other words, these technologies codify and illuminate interior detail, creating transparency where there was opacity, an explicit public text where there was once fragmentation, privacy, and intuition. The organization, its internal processes and exchange relationships, becomes visible in a wholly new way, whether that pertains to thousands of newly codified variables in the production process or the global flow of cash tracked on an hourly basis. The word I coined to capture this unique capacity of information technology is "informate." These technologies informate as well as automate, and as they do, the organization is increasingly imbued with an electronic text, its mysteries surrendered to anyone with the skills to access and understand the relevant information.

Under these conditions what does it mean to work? Work is now an abstraction. It depends upon an understanding of, responsiveness to, and ability to manage and create value from information. It is in terms of its informating capacity that information technologies represent a radical discontinuity in the history of work and the evolution of industrial technology. Earlier generations of machines in the workplace tended to decrease the complexity and substantive content of work tasks, making it possible to employ people with ever lower levels of skill and wages. In contrast, informating technologies frequently increase the substantive complexity and intellectual content of work at all levels of the organization. This presents a profound challenge to the functional hierarchy and its management. It also brings us to the moral center of current debates about the information-based organization.

The essential logic of the managerial hierarchy rests on the premise that complexity can constantly be removed from lower level jobs and passed up to the management ranks. Automation has been a primary means of accomplishing this. An iron curtain was drawn between those whose tasks were simplified and through mechanization stripped of substantive content, and those who received that content and were expected to preside over it. Indeed, the management cadre was invented for this purpose. Over the course of the century, the manager's role evolved as guardian of the organization's knowledge base. The manager's legitimate authority derived from being credited as someone fit to receive, interpret, and communicate orders based on the command of information.

We have come to accept that the managerial hierarchy operating in this way reflects a reasonable division of labor, a neutral concept denoting efficiency and rationality. We are less comfortable discussing the moral vision at the heart of this arrangement, something I call the "division of love." Here I mean to suggest that the managerial hierarchy drew life not only from rational considerations of efficiency, or differences in the political power of its constituents, but importantly from the ways in which some organizational members were valued and others were devalued.

But why worry now about the emotional wounds of these hierarchical divisions, just as we are entering the brave new age of the information economy? The reason is this. The new information infrastructure creates an opportunity for firms to deal with complexity at the point where it enters the organization, whether that is the customer interface, the point of production, or in the act of service delivery. That capacity, or methodology, implies speed, informed action, and efficiency in the process of problem solving and value creation. These in turn are precisely the methodological features associated with the success of firms challenged by the current conditions of hypercompetition and hypercomplexity. But for firms to avail themselves of such opportunities, they must be prepared to drive a stake into the heart of the old division of labor and the division of love from which it continues to draw sustenance. Exploiting the newly informated environment means opening up the information base of the organization to members at every level, assuring that each level has the knowledge and skills to productively engage with that information, and endowing all members with the authority to express and ultimately act on what they can know. It implies a new social contract that redefines who people are at work, what they can know, and what they can do.

Lamentably, most of what has passed for transformational change in business organizations over the past decade remained formally indifferent to this moral heart of the matter. Most efforts at restructuring and downsizing have been aimed at slenderizing the managerial hierarchy without questioning its fundamental purpose and function. The widespread interest in reengineering has allowed firms to focus obsessively on operational efficiencies while ignoring the many necessary dimensions of change that would lead to a reimagining of the moral fabric and emotional texture of the firm, thus providing the basis for the serious work required to implement a new social contract.

Every powerful legacy harbors the secret of its own demise, and the mighty force that was the industrial workplace is no exception. The division of labor and division of love that characterized modern work have been the source of almost miraculous efficiency, but as we confront a new era of discontinuity they have taken on a rigidity that desecrates the very spirit of inventiveness and adaptation from which they were derived. The moral, social, and emotional requirements of adaptation to an information economy have been badly underestimated. By the end of this economic transition, in twenty five years or so, the managerial hierarchy as we know it will have been dismantled and the purposes and functions of organizational membership will have been profoundly reconfigured. During this period of transition, environmental conditions will select for success firms that proactively adapt their organizational methodologies to the moral, social, and psychological requirements of an information economy. However, proactive adaptation requires the kind of moral leadership that can articulate new values and embed them in a complex and long-term process of change. Such leadership is rare. Without it, most firms will fall prey to the slow grind of the global marketplace. Many will die a long and painful death, while others wend their way, kicking and screaming across the decades, to a new moral universe. Only then will the promise of an information economy come true. Only then will the emperor come in from the cold, because we have found the way to clothe him.

About the Author

Shoshana Zuboff is the Benjamin and Lilian Hertzberg Professor of Business Administration at Harvard University, Graduate School of Business Administration. She earned her Ph.D. in Social Psychology from Harvard University and her undergraduate degree from the University of Chicago. Her pioneering research, *In the Age of the Smart Machine,* was aimed at understanding the implications of the massive diffusion of information technology for the nature of work, organization, and management. Professor Zuboff's continuing research focuses on the challenges of historical adaptation as firms confront the social, moral, and economic discontinuities associated with the shift to an information-based economy.

PANEL

Bell Meets Taylor: Demystifying Knowledge Work

Participants

Steve Fuller
University of Durham, UK

Amir Hartman
University of Pittsburgh, USA

Sujatha Raman
University of Pittsburgh, USA

1. INTRODUCTION

The theme of this panel is *the impact of information technology on information work.* The well-known debate on the relation between new electronic technologies and skill initially turned on the dichotomy of massive upskilling versus deskilling of work. For Bell, work in different sectors was increasingly becoming knowledge-based, hence high-skilled. For Braverman, both blue-collar and white-collar work was becoming routinized with the application of Taylor's scientific management principles. The mental component of work (knowledge functions) was being separated from the manual and taken over by managers.

The large scholarly literature following these predictions has generally noted that the empirical evidence is mixed, with the outcome depending on type of job, organization, industry, technology, or national context. So, it is quite common to hear that we must distinguish between say, electronic cash registers and flexible manufacturing systems (FMS). The mixed-effect view when applied to information technology (IT) has resulted in predictions of a dual workforce —

with high-skilled information or knowledge producers at the top and low-skilled information handlers and processors at the bottom.

The panelists take issue with the core assumption of this claim for a dual info-workforce — namely, that information production work or "expertise" is inherently high-skilled and complex, immune to a division into smaller routine tasks. Collectively, they argue that IT makes it possible to deskill the most mystified types of cognitive work, while simultaneously elevating the importance and skill of hitherto "lowly" support work. Contrary to Braverman, the outcome of the Taylorization of Bell's knowledge-workers could actually be progressive in the sense of subverting traditional hierarchies. Where the panelists vary is in their vision of the difference between potential and actual outcomes in the ongoing transformation of information work.

The panel is therefore set up to bring out what might happen in actual organizational settings from the confrontation of Bell's information work with the deskilling tendencies of Taylorism, mediated by information technology. Drawing on historical trends, Steve Fuller lays out the "strong" argument for a radical demystification of expert work, a deskilling that is socially progressive from his standpoint. Amir Hartman and Sujatha Raman each take up a specific case — audit work and academic work, respectively — to show how the actual outcomes will depend on the struggles (or lack thereof) in these settings. Drawing on the social constructionist position, they explore how particular occupational groups could represent their work as high-skilled even in the face of "actual" deskilling. On the other hand, actually upskilled work can continue to be devalued or subject to intensified control from above.

2. PAPER ABSTRACTS

Through an exploration of the possible impact of expert-systems on scientific and technological work, Steve Fuller will make the case for "Why the Post-Industrial Society Never Came." Fuller will argue that expert systems contain the radical *possibility* of diminishing the mystique of expertise and intelligence through automation and deskilling. Rather than bemoaning this trend as the *elimination* of human expertise, Fuller notes that expert-systems *displace* particular groups of experts in the hierarchy of cognitive labor and make currently "invisible" and under-valued tasks, such as those performed by technical support personnel, more valuable.

Amir Hartman will take us through the wonderful world of Big 6 Accounting. Describing empirical work which investigates the notion of the "postindustrial" organization, Hartman will make visible the *realities* of computerization and the day-to-day worklives of audit profession-als. In his discussion of "The Alienated Auditor," Amir Hartman will make the case that both utopian and dystopian notions of work computerization are inadequate. Rather than wholesale deskilling or enskilling of audit work, what he finds is a combination of both. Following up on Fuller's claim that expert systems displace traditional "winners" and benefit the "losers" in the occupational distribution, he shows why it has **not** happened so far in this instance.

Can academic research be "offshored" to Third World countries or otherwise "outsourced," much like production processes for goods ranging from automobiles to computer software? Sujatha Raman will explore this reflexive question in her description of the "Brave New Academy — Downsized." She will first outline instances that show how academic research has already become routinized. Word processors and the Internet enable the break-down of text production into tasks that can be performed by different people in different places. In the context of the privatization of universities and a continued demand for symbolic capital (information), this could make the outsourcing of academic work feasible. How the strain of competition, plus the increasing pressures for accountability, will affect our own work becomes a moot question.

Each panelist will speak for no more than fifteen minutes in order to give sufficient time for audience discussion of the two key issues they are raising: (1) the possibilities for the transformation of knowledge work in general, entailed by different ways in which IT could be successfully constructed and institutionalized, and (2) the transformation of our own (i.e., academic) work through similar processes.

Reducing the Need for Computer-Based Information Systems in Healthcare Through the Use of Self-Contained Organizational Units

Gail Louw
Institute of Cancer Research
Royal Cancer Hospital

Abstract

The relentless move to computerization in the UK National Health Service (NHS) is challenged in this paper. The distinction between two types of information is defined: proceduralized and interpretative. An alternative to the use of computerized information systems for the latter is presented that relies on a change in organizational structure in the form of a self contained unit. This effectively reduces the need to process information. The unit, based on the principles of Patient Focused Care, provides multiskilled teams using a combination of multi-disciplinary documentation and protocols of care to ensure effective communication takes place without the use of interpretative information systems.

1. INTRODUCTION

The National Health Service in the United Kingdom (NHS) is in the throes of much change. The workforce in the NHS is becoming increasingly familiar with on-going change as initiatives are introduced at regular intervals. The NHS is central to the agenda of all the major political parties in the UK and is consequently prone to influence by political fluctuations and the whims of social and media pressure. The costs of introducing change are enormous in terms of money, resources and human endeavor, yet the effects are often variable. The introduction of computerized information systems have accounted for a significant proportion of these costs and much scepticism exists as to the benefits that are said to accrue from these investments.

A recent initiative introduced in most of the hospitals in the NHS is the Resource Management Initiative. The Initiative, which introduced organizational as well as cultural change, was deemed incapable of working successfully without an extensive commitment to computerized information systems. Indeed, the initial funding from the Department of Health was given with the proviso that a considerable proportion was spent on purchasing substantial and expensive Clinical and Nursing Information Systems.

The enthusiasm on the part of the Department of Health for systems that were largely untried and unevaluated has been criticized (Health Economics Research Group 1989) . Yet the underlying belief that computerization was the answer to the information needs of the organizations was essentially accepted, and indeed, considered unremarkable. This shift in thinking that has developed over the last two decades or so is relatively unchallenged. In the NHS, although computerized information systems are still somewhat undeveloped and untried, the essential belief is that "the future is in the technology." There are few instances where the perceived need is ever questioned, only the availability of resources to acquire them.

In this paper information systems are categorized into two types: *proceduralized* and *interpretative*. The need for the latter is questioned.

2. PROCEDURALIZED VERSUS INTERPRETIVE INFORMATION SYSTEMS

Proceduralized and interpretative information systems are two ends of a continuum that stretches from purely technical, formalized systems that are bound with structure, measurements and data, to those systems that are derived from, and based on, the skills of people in interrelationships. The former are systems that rely on technical measures and indices and are, of necessity, formalized ways of measuring procedures. The latter are based on the interpretations that people apply to interactions, needs or influences. They are bound up with communication and the communicative process and are interpretations or evaluations based on the skills and tacit knowledge that people apply to their work.

Proceduralized systems are defined as those which benefit from the computer's ability to process vast quantities of data in order to arrive at data that can be used by people or other machines. The computer's greatest attribute is its ability as a superb number crunching tool. Thus its value as a database, able to process data for other purposes and outputs, is without question. Within the NHS context, the Patient Administration System (PAS), where demographic data is input and accessed periodically as well as being used for reports and management information, provides an example of an effective and useful proceduralized information system.

Interpretative information systems, on the other hand, are defined here as developing systems that use information that is acquired by human intuition and tacit knowledge. An example of this is computerized care plans. In brief, care plans are produced by nurses showing a plan of action and goals for the delivery of nursing care based on a problem solving approach. They are produced based on depth of nursing experience as well as intuitive and experiential knowledge of the unique features of the individual patient.

A greater likelihood of information systems being appropriate and useful will result if design is developed using an approach that takes into account the social relations between the participants, the infrastructure which supports the computerized system, and the previous history of commitments to computer-based technologies within the organization. In short, the social context has to be defined. An effective model covering many of these aspects is provided by Kling's (1987) "web model."

In addition, to ensure that the knowledge necessary for effective systems development is utilized, users must be significantly involved in the design of the systems (Mumford 1983). The need for user involvement is considerably greater than that incorporated into traditional systems analysis and design methodologies. Users need to be involved from the outset of the project, indeed from the point where the need for a change is recognized, right through the design and implementation stages. Conventional analysis and design systems involve users but confine them to a supporting role rather than focusing the "professional" activity in support of them. The need for greater involvement is recognized, however, and recent extensions of SSADM are beginning to address this.

To function at its optimum, it is necessary to contain the users to a relatively small group that is able to interact effectively. This group would have a level of tacit knowledge such that a deep, situated knowledge of actual work processes would be available to them. They are then capable of designing systems that incorporate accurate, necessary and useful features that would be difficult to emulate without the use of computers.

3. AN ALTERNATIVE TO INTERPRETIVE INFORMATION SYSTEMS

The value of computerized information systems for those systems which have been defined as *proceduralized* is undeniable. For those which have been defined as *interpretive* , however, the value of computerized information systems is far less obvious. This paper offers an alternative to such systems by reducing the need for having information systems at all. Following Galbraith (1977), it is argued that an effective means of meeting information needs is to reduce the need to process information. One way of achieving this, through the creation of self-contained organizational units, is elaborated in this paper.

The paper therefore focuses on the design of a self-contained unit in the NHS, showing how a multi-disciplinary group of people collaboratively designed an integrated, self-regulating unit. This unit seeks to ensure effective communication and documentation procedures without the use of computerized *interpretive* information systems, but does not preclude the use of networked data processing systems, the *proceduralized* systems distinguished earlier, to access demographic data, clinical and laboratory reports, or management information that is available from databases within the hospital.

The group's methods did not consist of devising efficient manual information systems to simply replace computerized information systems, but rather a redesign of work processes. As a result, the organizational design of their work unit is radically different from anything else that exists in the NHS (other than similar projects which are being developed in several pilot sites across the country).

It is argued that there are no significant inadequacies that *interpretive* systems could have bettered, yet many of the problems and wastage in resources that have tended to occur when computers have been introduced in the NHS have been avoided. Additionally, the benefits gained by collaboratively designing the various features of the unit's work are potentially enormous.

4. BACKGROUND TO THE CASE STUDY

This case study describes the principles underlying the planning of Patient Focused Care (PFC) in a hospital on the south coast of England. The hospital was one of seven pilot sites in Britain to introduce PFC, or Integrated Patient Care (IPC) as it was described.

PFC's introduction coincided with a significant capital redevelopment at the hospital of around £75 million. The implications of this simultaneous development were enormous as PFC challenged not only work processes, and organizational culture and structure, but also the physical design and layout of the buildings. A successful implementation of PFC would help ensure that the redevelopment program at the hospital would be based on PFC principles.

PFC was first proposed by the management consultants, Booz Allen Hamilton (Lathrop, Krauss and Shows 1988). They argued that the general focus on specialization found in hospitals was inefficient and costly and proposed a more appropriate organizational system whereby self-contained, or partially self-contained, units would be established.

Originating in the USA, which has a sophisticated and well-established market approach to health services, the concept was imported into the UK as part of the internal market reforms of the NHS. This paper does not seek to address the financial changes, the impact of separating the purchasers and providers, contracts, competition and so on associated with these developments, but focuses on the information processing aspects of PFC.

The PFC design process involved workshops with members of staff from Gastroenterology, the proposed specialty for the new PFC unit. The initial workshop defined the hospital's vision of how best to deliver care to patients, the groups of staff that would enable the delivery of such care, and the key indicators which could be used to measure the success of the new method of care delivery. This was deemed crucial as the basis for much of the later work.

A significant innovation that PFC intended to introduce was the concept of multiskilling and cross training. The human resource implications of these were significant and much of the intended changes in personnel policy were to be introduced on the back of PFC. The need for a reduction in the number of specializations and categorizations in jobs within hospitals has been recognized and is discussed in the Patient Focused Care literature (e.g., Lathrop 1993). The proposed PFC care center unit would therefore be staffed by multiskilled, trained carers able to perform some of the functions and duties they now normally require from others. Examples include phlebotomy (the taking of blood) and simple chest physiotherapy.

A crucial development in PFC was the introduction of protocols of care for documentation and audit purposes. These are also known as Clinical Care Pathways or Anticipated Recovery Pathways. These guidelines were devised and owned by multidisciplinary teams. Once a pathway, or protocol, was identified and care agreed, it could be used as a care plan. Only the individual patient's deviations from the protocol would be recorded, thus potentially reducing the extensive amount of time spent by nurses and other professionals acting as scribes. It could also be used as a powerful audit tool as the deviations, or variances, could be analyzed. This form of *variance reporting* was expected to reduce drastically the excessive time spent on documentation, without the use of computers. As Lathrop argues:

> The time devoted to documentation is reduced by as much as 75 percent. One particular hospital has reduced documentation time for nurses from more than two hours per nurse per day to less than fifteen minutes (for surgical patients). This saving was accomplished without the use of computer systems: a manual process was simply dramatically improved.

In addition to the protocols, a PFC working group developed an Integrated Care Plan for patient notes. The relevant factor in this development was the move away from individual notes for different professional groups to one multidisciplinary care plan. The various professions should thus be able to relate their care to other professionals' care. Patients should thus avoid the current necessity of repeatedly providing details about their demographics and medical history.

By having documentation that provides a mutual focus for all carers, and by reducing the extent of the documentation by using protocols and exception reporting, a powerful alternative to using computerized information systems will be achieved. Proceduralized information systems that could compute the variances were seen to be useful, however, as an aid to the processing of data from the audit. These various changes may therefore be seen to illustrate the fundamental principle that there are alternative means of dealing with an organization's interpretative information problems or requirements and that effective information processing can be designed into an organization and structure by means other than computerization.

5. PARALLELS WITH DEVELOPMENTS IN MANUFACTURING INDUSTRY

A shift from rigid, bureaucratic organizational forms toward more flexible modes of production and reduced division of labor is seen increasingly in manufacturing industry, as Bessant (1991) describes. This move toward "networking and decentralization" is emulated in the developments discussed in this paper. PFC bears a striking resemblance to *"cellular manufacturing"* which, it is claimed (Ingersoll Engineers 1993), now extends to 73% of UK companies. This involves the creation of "product-focused cells" which are self-sufficient in "all four key dimensions of engineering, logistics, people and accountability." The deployment of such cells is said to nurture productivity gains and cost reduction as well as "commitment, teamworking and empowerment." Other benefits reported include quicker throughput, reduced work-in-progress, improved control, improved quality, better service and better skills.

Kaplinsky (1994) discusses the introduction of a cellular layout in an organization and suggests there was a shift in production philosophy from "the old objective of 'efficiency' to the new objective of 'effectiveness'." As with PFC, the new organizational structure also lead to "multitasking and multiskilling work practices." "All cell-workers...were given a variety of tasks to perform, and were trained in a range of skills." Kaplinsky describes the consequence of this being a "significant flattening of the decision hierarchy" from seven layers down to three.

This case also highlights the problems of communication prevalent in the management of change. Kaplinsky describes the previous unidirectional information flows as "focused on the settlement of conflict rather than the communication of information relevant to effective production." The new strategy included cell managers communicating with their work team for the first ten minutes of each shift, videos, slides, newsletters and courses on continuous improvement as well as other meetings and forums.

Bessant (1994) uses a different term to evoke a similar development. He talks of "focused factories" that "identify a clear business segment which manufacturing can then support in a coherent fashion." These may develop, it is argued, "either by dedicating factories to particular businesses or by grouping resources within a factory into areas or cells dedicated to particular businesses." The development of "process innovation," which Bessant (1994) defines as "the set of radical changes and incremental improvements which a firm makes to the ways in which it produces its outputs," is reflected in the development of "process redesign" or "process reengineering." These latter terms are also well entrenched in the philosophy of PFC.

The traditional organizational structure of a hospital in which the functions of individual specialities and departments are extensive and based on bureaucratic, organizational arrangements may thus be seen to have many similarities with the organization of the Fordist factory. The intense specialization and compartmentalization that this can give rise to is illustrated by Lathrop, who quotes an example of a typical 500 bed hospital where, with a total of 2,756 employees, there were 388 job classifications, of which 314 had fewer than six employees, and the average number of employees per classification was 7.1.

Another feature of Fordist manufacturing is the focus on "economies of scale." This principle, that greater capacity leads to greater efficiency, is seen as fundamental to increasing productivity. While this may be appropriate for high-volume, low-variety production, Marsh (1989) argues that "increased competition and more fragmented markets have in the past few years forced the industry to steer toward more specialized product sectors in which the focus is on tailoring goods to customers needs." The principle in PFC of focusing services, resources and skills around the needs of the patient thus bears striking similarities to these developments in industry.

Kaplinsky's case also introduces the principle of "families-of-parts" where the factory was broken down into three "sub-factories" with a physical redesign, each cell having "an almost complete range of machinery." This provides an interesting comparison with PFC and the dilemma associated with the extent of decentralization of equipment or services. While the philosophy of PFC would suggest locating satellite pathology laboratories, X-rays, physiotherapy and occupational therapy areas within each self-contained unit, economies of scale are likely to lead to a sharing of resources and expensive items of equipment among smaller units. There is, therefore, a need to balance issues of economies of scale with alternative means of providing decentralized services. One solution adopted in the case study was the intelligent vacuum tube system installed throughout the hospital to transport tests and specimens to the various laboratories located around the hospital. This avoided the need for satellite laboratories in the self-contained units.

Finally, the movement toward self-containment and Schumacher's principle of "small is beautiful" is reflected in PFC.

6. GALBRAITH'S STRATEGY AND PFC

The development of self-contained units as a means of reducing the need to process information was proposed by Galbraith as a strategy for effective information processing. Less information processing is required, it was argued, once there is a reduction in resource sharing. This could be achieved in two main ways: reducing output diversity and reducing the division of labor. Thus, "reduced diversity reduced the information processing needed to schedule and reschedule the demands for shared resources [and] there is usually a reduction in the division of labor and therefore fewer distinctly different resources whose work needs to be coordinated and scheduled" (Galbraith 1977).

Both these methods were seen as important aspects of PFC. In practice, this included grouping patients with similar needs thus reducing output diversity, and developing a multiskilled workforce, thereby lessening the division of labor and reducing specialization. Zuboff (1988) also discusses the necessity of introducing new divisions of labor in a flexible organizational structure. She considers this essential so that all workers at all levels are able to develop their intellectual skills in a continuous learning process. Multiskilling, and its concomitant cross training, are seen as means of maintaining a continuous learning process.

Further effects of self-containment on information processing are identified by Galbraith as being that "exceptions have to travel through fewer levels before reaching a shared superior" and that "decisions can be taken at lower levels while supported with local information...self-contained groups permit local discretion based on local information only" (Galbraith 1977).

Three particular issues are highlighted Galbraith's analysis:

- Local decision making and the team structure
- Decision making and information based on the concept of exception reporting
- Decision making based on empowerment and a sense of team ownership.

7. LOCAL DECISION MAKING AND
THE TEAM STRUCTURE

The PFC structure will be focused on multiskilled bedside teams comprising nurses and carers and a team leader. There are other teams, including the core team with specialist skills and a team providing administrative support. The core team includes the relevant consultants, physiotherapist, dietitian, radiotherapist, occupational therapist and social worker. The administrative support includes ward clerks, secretaries and administrative clerks. A bedside team of two is responsible for six patients, or four responsible for four high dependency patients. High dependency patients require more intensive caring. Six such teams comprise a larger team with a team leader. The bedside teams are placed in close geographical proximity to each other as they are on a ward, or ward-like area. The unit comprises around thirty inpatient beds as well as endoscopy suites and outpatient facilities. The management structure consists of the team leaders and a care center manager who is on site and has overall responsibility for the unit.

This small team-based structure facilitates the communication process. Information is based locally and there is little in the way of waiting for information to arrive, be retrieved or processed. Much of the processing will be done on the unit by decentralized services, or by improved facilities, such as the intelligent vacuum tube movement of pathology tests.

The information pertinent to the individual patient will be contained within the unit and among the people dealing with them on a daily basis. Clinical decisions are made by individual carers within the context of the team, as well as with team leaders, on the basis of information available and immediately accessible. The self-contained nature of the unit provides an in-built control mechanism in that team members are able to communicate and obtain information when necessary. This seeks to ensure an integration of information that was not possible in the pre-PFC gastroenterology wards. This was mainly because gastroenterology was not seen as an entity with defined boundaries. It was fragmented over various wards as well as different specialities.

This lack of clear boundaries affected the position of the consultants as well. Gastroenterologists are normally general surgeons as well as specialists in gastroenterology, and the delineation between gastroenterology and general surgery is fine. Both groups of consultants do "on take" sessions in emergency wards dealing with all general surgery and gastroenterology. By removing all the gastroenterology to a separate unit, therefore, the general surgeons would have the variety of their workload diminished. There was consequently much displeasure among the general surgeons at the prospect of a PFC center. They felt their professional positions were threatened by a removal of such an important section of their workload — important in terms of interest rather than quantity. The situation unearthed a deep-seated problem that had not been resolved through the years: "What is a general surgeon and is there a role for them?" The movement to specialists that is gathering pace is a movement away from generalists. These boundary issues were important ones that were not resolved for the consultants in the debate about a PFC center, but were rather exacerbated.

8. DECISION MAKING AND EXCEPTION REPORTING

Galbraith argues that decreasing information processing in a self-contained unit has the effect of reducing the levels through which exceptions have to travel, thus ensuring more efficient, effective and appropriate decision making. This concept is enhanced in the PFC context for not only are exceptions passed on rather than produced as a mass of data, but exception reporting is introduced at the initial stages of documentation. This is done by using protocols of care rather than documenting care given for each patient in minute detail. Decisions about patient care are then made either by those producing the information or by others further up the hierarchy, such as team leaders or clinical advisors. Control is maintained by stringent audit procedures.

It must be understood that documentation is a feature that affects all professional carers. Everything that is done is documented by all professions, for caring and informing as well as litigation purposes. In the vast majority of hospitals and departments, medical record documentation is unidisciplinary. All professions produce and carry their own notes. These are not, as a matter of course, made available to other professions. The potential problems of duplication or missing information are enormous.

The primary need for multidisciplinary sets of medical notes, with ease of access and uniformity, was made apparent and was seen as an essential prerequisite to any change introduced by PFC. However, multidisciplinary notes are the starting point rather than the whole story and, to complete the change, protocols need to be introduced.

Protocols define "the usual care requirements for a particular episode of care [and are] designed to record actual individualized care against agreed best practice" (Sparks 1994). They are in pro-forma and diary form. The pro-forma is designed to record actual individualized care against agreed best practice. The protocols are being developed by the clinical team who use them and team involvement helps ensure a strong sense of ownership of the protocol. They are, necessarily, supported by policies and guidelines. The normally slow development progress for each protocol is problematic as initial protocols may take several months to develop. However the speed is invariably quickened after a number have been produced.

The protocol is seen as a dynamic working document and, as such, is updated to "incorporate improvements resulting from concurrent clinical audit and changing practice based on ongoing research into best practice" (Sparks 1994). Care is delivered to a patient according to the protocol with very little text added other than in cases of variance where the exception is noted. This provides a powerful tool for audit where individual action or the protocol procedure can be questioned.

9. DECISION MAKING, EMPOWERMENT AND TEAM OWNERSHIP

The need for ownership and empowerment has been identified as crucial to the successful introduction of Patient Focused Care in hospitals both in the UK and the USA. Lathrop suggests that "empowerment is inherent in any notion of ownership."

There was an attempt to ensure empowerment in this project by making decisions in workshops with multidisciplinary attendances. This intention was set as a benchmark for the entire project in the initial visioning process. However, decision making in workshops is only viable if the workshops are attended by those who will be responsible for making the relevant decisions. In many of the workshops that took place, many of the decision makers were not included. Thus, at the personnel workshops where jobs were redesigned, the porter, housekeeper, secretaries and nurses were included, but the consultant did not take part (although he was invited), neither did a doctor (other than one initial meeting), nor the secretarial manager.

The team structure of the proposed self-contained unit was organized to facilitate decisions being made about patient care and need by the carers themselves. Thus, at an elemental level, stock for the unit could be ordered by the team who were aware of unit requirements rather than centrally on a fixed time basis by others removed from daily activities.

Other Patient Focused Care hospitals in the UK focused on different aspects of empowerment. At one PFC hospital, for example, team leaders were chosen by team members, thus instituting democracy-in-action which may contribute to sustained empowerment of team members. Although the changes that were being designed at the case study hospital were certainly significant and, indeed, radical, they never intended to reach the limits that were being discussed in at least one other hospital. There, the aim for PFC is for developing self-directed work teams. This far-reaching aim is beyond the scope of, or indeed recognized goal for, PFC at the case study hospital. Although the need for "cultural change" is recognized, it is within the confines of "team work, trust and ownership" (Integrated Patient Care Team 1993). This may be seen as the initial point on a continuum that develops into self-directed work teams and the implied diminishment of a hierarchical structure. The failure to recognize the need to extend the ambit and encompass self-direction marks an unfortunate deficiency in the project.

10.   REDESIGN: PROCESS REDESIGN

A major principle of PFC is that, by redesigning work processes within a self contained unit, many of the benefits of improved efficiency are attainable with or without the need to incorporate extensive computerized information systems. This is possible by:

- integrating and co-ordinating process changes with care protocols
- reducing complexity of processes
- improving effective utilisation of all resources strengthening team work and improving job satisfaction
- reducing handovers [Integrated Patient Care Team 1993]

The diversity of the above ideas, all part of process reengineering, indicate the inter-connectivity between the four main facets of PFC. Thus, although "process redesign" was not developed in the workshops, the other areas of role redesign, physical redesign and documentation redesign were all based on changes devised by reviewing work and practice processes.

A small amount of operational analysis was undertaken in the early stage of the project by the management consultants to attain base line data for evaluation. Much of it was based on work undertaken by them at a different hospital.

One area the management consultants analyzed was the processes involved in a simple "Urea and Electrolytes" blood test. This is a routine test given to around 80 percent of patients. The analysis provided data showing inefficient and wasteful usage of resources. The analysis found that it took eleven people to process the test, eighteen hours turnaround time and sixty-four actual process steps. Other data acquired illustrated the excessive time wasted by junior doctors walking from place to place within the hospital as opposed to being in a self-contained unit. They attached pedometers to a number of doctors and found that, on average, they walked up to sixteen miles during the course of their work day, substantially more than would be necessary in a self-contained unit.

11. REDESIGN: PHYSICAL REDESIGN

The multidisciplinary workshops brainstormed their vision of the *ideal care center*. The requirements, in many instances, were aligned to a necessary physical restructuring of the unit in accordance with the principles of PFC. Gastroenterology, in its original state, was far re-moved from the ideal of an integrated self-contained unit in that it was dispersed over thirteen wards and departments based in three of the four hospital sites.

The ideal Gastroenterology unit that was defined in the multidisciplinary workshops included in-patients, out-patients and the endoscopy suite. By including both medical and surgical patients, it aimed to span all the demarcated boundaries established in the hospital, i.e. the separation of in/out patients and medical/surgical patients.

Many of the design features identified as desirable or necessary by the multidisciplinary work group were included in the initial design stage. These would have ensured a high level of comfort as well as good patient care. They included a diet kitchen for education purposes, single rooms for infection control and privacy, adequate waiting areas for out-patients and visitors, diagnostic services and a business center with a library and seminar rooms.

An important means of enabling a unit to be self-contained is by devolving services onto the unit from the center. The extent of the devolvement was discussed in detail. It was considered important to balance the arguments of economies of scale with those of efficiency and accessibility. The hospital-wide intelligent vacuum tube processor for pathology was pro-posed as one means of continuing to use a central service.

Some existing centralized services were clearly inappropriate to support the envisioned center. Porters and domestic cleaners or housekeepers, for example, were to be part of the care team and, as such, were to be dedicated to the unit. However, a back-up, though reduced, centralized service of porters and cleaners was still required to provide cover when necessary.

12.   REDESIGN: MULTISKILLING AND ROLE REDESIGN

Role redesign leading to multiskilling is a principle of PFC that has profound implications on major developments leading to an implemented PFC center and the process of accepting change. In addition, it will be argued that it was a crucial factor in ensuring that the self-contained unit communicates effectively because of its reduced information processing needs.

Multiskilling is a means of ensuring that, once people are able, or trained, to do particular jobs, they can do them without relying on other specialists. It is diametrically opposed to the traditional division of labor or *compartmentalization* that is so predominant in many hospitals around the world. The syndrome of "I'll get someone to do that for you" typifies the reaction of many carers when asked to do something for a patient which is not strictly within the boundaries of their remit, or perceived remit.

The excesses of compartmentalization are exemplified in the numbers of people involved in performing simple activities. Lathrop produces evidence from research in American hospitals to suggest that it takes six people between thirty and forty minutes to produce a chest X-ray. This activity entails "a few minutes of a technologist's time and less than a minute of a radiologist's reading time." The resource implications of scheduling and monitoring the various discrete tasks are huge and not reflected in corresponding service levels. Reducing the number of job categories is a preliminary stage in the introduction of multiskilling.

The term *multiskilling* is resonant with threat to many health care professionals. The need to identify the fears and establish their legitimacy or otherwise was deemed essential in the early phases of the project. At an early workshop, for example, the participants brainstormed their views on the hopes and fears associated with multiskilling. The group's hopes related to an improved service for patients, including an improved information service, improved professional morale and greater job satisfaction. Their fears were summed up in one word: deskilling. They also feared a decrease in quality and more mistakes being made, more work being generated, and a demise of the professions.

A set of principles was agreed by the workshop members to relate to developing and implementing multiskilling throughout the hospital.

13.   COMMUNICATION AND INFORMATION
IMPLICATIONS

Multiskilling also has considerable implications for communication strategies. The issue of multiskilling adds a further dimension to the self-contained argument that information processing can be reduced. It adds a dimension that Galbraith considers only partially, yet it contains within it the potential for dramatically improving communication by the expedient of reducing numbers of people to whom information needs to be communicated.

Galbraith suggests that self-contained units usually result in "a reduction in the division of labor and therefore fewer distinctly different resources whose work needs to be coordinated and scheduled." However, reducing the division further by having a multiskilled workforce minimizes to an even greater extent the amount of coordination and rescheduling necessary. Together with the team structure it creates a highly efficient communication structure. The ability to communicate verbally about issues that directly affect immediate work processes to a small team, with whom constant contact exists, ensures that little is ignored. The chances of missing data or care processes is negated, or certainly minimized, by the use of protocols. The legal considerations of documenting all care undertaken are recognized as the protocols are individualized documents. Protocols also ensure that the team is aware of activities performed to their patients by other professionals — something that tends not to happen with multiple, uniprofessional clinical notes

The importance of producing documentation that is valid, relevant and useful was a crucial requirement for PFC. The inadequacies of the current method of producing medical records have much in common with other hospitals. "Writing things down has become the biggest single activity in our hospitals" (Lathrop 1993). All professions keep individual records which lead to fragmentation and ineffective communication. Medical notes by doctors are kept separately from those used by other professions. Physiotherapists and dietitians keep discrete notes which are not filed in the medical record. Nursing notes are stored apart from the medical record during the time of patient admission and filed in the record at the time of discharge. However, they are relegated to a multipurpose storage section at the back of the notes and remain there with various charts and papers. The perception that very little of significance is in the nursing notes is in sharp contrast to the length of time and effort that is expended on producing them.

There is much duplication of professional effort with each group asking repetitive questions leading to frustration and lack of trust among patients. Documentation can be split into two categories: medical and institutional. Lathrop suggests that 19% of personnel time is devoted to medical documentation and 11% to institutional documentation. However, Lathrop's evidence is based on research undertaken in the USA and as such is not entirely valid in the UK context. Much of his "institutional" documentation relates to billing individual patients, a practice which is not yet politically acceptable in the UK.

Research taking place at the hospital in the form of a clinical audit suggests that the time taken in documenting medical and clinical details is excessively high. It was found that nursing time spent on documentation equates to the equivalent of three full-time staff (or the term commonly used in the NHS "whole time equivalents") per week for a sixteen bed ward. This is time that could be used for direct care of patients. Additionally, there is the problem of duplicated questioning. From discussions with patients it emerges that it is common for patients to be asked their medical history by six different professional groups before they receive an initial treatment.

One objective for PFC was to produce a single, integrated record that was applicable and appropriate for all the various professions dealing with the particular patient group. A survey was conducted among junior doctors (all doctors apart from consultants are grouped together as "junior doctors," whether they are House Officers, Senior House Officers or Registrars) to assess their commitment to the concept of one integrated care plan. There was significant acceptance of it with 55% agreeing or strongly agreeing with it, 14% disagreeing and 31% neutral.

The inevitable cultural obstacles, prevalent in the complex organization that is a hospital, had to be overcome so that the inherent lack of trust among the different professions could be overcome. Unless each professional group were confident that the plan was able to accommodate their requirements, they would be reluctant to use it and the fragmented status quo of duplication and repetition would continue. There was never any suggestion that the record would be anything other than a paper document. The working group considered that an integrated, multidisciplinary care plan could be developed collaboratively that would meet the divergent needs of the user groups. They felt that it could be done without computer support.

14. EVALUATION

Patient Focused Care is in its very early stages and it is difficult to assess accurately its effect on real change and development. Thus Kelly, Rawlinson and Whittlestone (1993) argue that "because of its comparative novelty, the balance of costs and benefits accruing to patient-focused care is not fully known." They also claim, however, that "there is a general consistency regarding benefits that have been reported, including: reduced length of stay, improved patient and staff satisfaction, better clinical outcomes and improved process efficiency."

The NHS has long been considered sluggish and traditional in its organizational development. Indeed, hospital management does not generally show many signs of great innovation and radical restructuring. PFC is one area that seems to have taken many of the radical developments from industry and used them specifically to provide real improvement in patient care.

Self-contained patient-focused care units exist both in the UK and the USA. The effectiveness of the strategy to reduce information processing by having self-contained units remains unproven, however. No conclusive research studies have been undertaken, and certainly there is no statistically valid evidence to support the theory. There would therefore appear to be a need for a greater research effort to address this important question.

15. CONCLUSIONS

The reformist ideas discussed above are being introduced into the NHS, albeit slowly. The development has become possible through the change in culture that has progressed systematically over the previous few years.

This paper has introduced two terms to distinguish categories of information systems: *proceduralized* and *interpretative* information systems. The lack of such a distinction in traditional information systems design can lead to generic design methods being used with little recognition of varying requirements. An alternative to interpretative information systems has been presented based on Galbraith's strategy for reducing information systems by having self-contained units.

The proliferation of patient-focused care principles, including process reengineering and protocols, within the NHS ensures the need for the development of this debate. Managers, with the remit of designing or procuring information systems, need to be offered different frames to view their requirements. Instead of thinking solely in terms of computerized information systems, they must be shown alternative perspectives to enable them to make effective choices.

16.   REFERENCES

Bessant, J. *Managing Advanced Manufacturing Technology.* Oxford: NCC Blackwell, 1991.

Bessant, J. "Innovation and Manufacturing Strategy." In M. Dodgson and R. Rothwell (Editors), *The Handbook of Industrial Innovation.* London: Edward Elgar, 1994, pp.393-404.

Galbraith, J. R. *Organization Design.* Reading, Massachusetts: Addison-Wesley, 1977.

Health Economics Research Group. "Mapping RM." *Health Services Management*, December 1989.

Ingersoll Engineers. *The Quiet Revolution Continues: A Survey of Implementation and Performance of Cell Manufacture across British Engineering.* Ingersoll Engineers, 1993.

Integrated Patient Care Team. *Integrated Patient Care at Brighton Health Care: Bringing Care to your Bedside Planing and Design: Phase End Report.* Brighton: Brighton Health Care, 1993.

Kaplinsky, R. *Easternisation: The spread of Japanese Management Techniques to Developing Countries.* Institute of Development Studies. London: Frank Cass, 1994.

Kelly, J.; Rawlinson, C.; and Whittlestone, P. "Patient-Focused-Care: Built to Last or this Year's Model." *British Hospital Management 1994: The Annual Review of British Hospital and Health Care Planning and Development.* 1994.

Kling, R. "Defining the Boundaries of Computing across Complex Organizations." In R. Boland   and R. Hirschheim (Editors), *Critical Issues in Information Systems Research.* Chichester: Wiley, 1987, pp. 307-362.

Lathrop, J. P. *Restructuring Health Care: The Patient Focused Paradigm.* San Francisco: Josey-Bass, 1993.

Lathrop, J. P.; Krauss, K. R.; and Shows, G. P. "Operational Restructuring: A Recipe for Success." *Health Care Viewpoint.* London: Booz Allen Hamilton, 1988.

Marsh, P. "Big Supplier Starts to Think Small." *Financial Times*, May 9, 1989, p. 8.

Mumford, E. *Designing Participatively.* Manchester: Manchester Business School, 1983.

Sparks, D. *The Care Management Pathway: Notes from the IPC Project Team.* In-house paper, Brighton Health Care, 1994.

Zuboff, S. *In the Age of the Smart Machine.* Oxford: Heinemann Educational, 1988.

About the Author

Gail Louw is currently the clinical research coordinator at the Institute of Cancer Research. She obtained her Ph.D. in 1994 in the field of organizational informatics specifically within health care.   Her research interests include process reengineering within healthcare organizations, issues around success and failure of nursing information systems, and the role of IT in organizational development.

PART TWO

Images of Practice:
Business Process Reengineering

5

Business Process Reengineering Reappraised: The Politics and Technology of Forgetting

Keith Grint
Fellow in Organizational Behaviour
Templeton College, University of Oxford

Peter Case
Senior Lecturer in Management
Oxford Brookes University

Leslie Willcocks
Fellow in Information Management
Templeton College, University of Oxford

Abstract

In this paper, we reappraise the phenomenon of business process reengineering through our own recent case study and survey findings, and through developing an interpretivist account of its appeal and content. A preliminary assessment questions what is actually being achieved under the label of BPR and the efficacy of the methodologies and tools available. We then argue that its claims to radicalism and novelty are exaggerated, provide an externalist account for part of its appeal, together with locating BPR as a form of utopian thought applied to work organizations. We then deepen the analysis by suggesting how its essentially political origins, aims and characteristics link inextricably with the high importance management commentators give to the role of information technology as a catalyst and consolidator of radical change in how work is organized and performed. A key concept throughout is that of deracination — the rooting out of the past. In the view that we develop, a significant impetus within BPR is toward a technology-supported deracination that requires a collective forgetting.

This forms both an essential part of its appeal, but also creates a number of major difficulties for BPR as a set of actioned organizational practices.

On his return from Troy, Odysseus' ship became separated from the rest of the Greek fleet and ended up on the coast of Libya. There, a group of inhabitants known as "the lotus eaters" existed whose consumption of the flowers of the Lotus plant made them forget everything except the desire to eat more Lotus flowers. Some sailors succumbed to the temptation and had to be forcibly returned to the ship. [Story in Homer's *Odyssey*]

1. INTRODUCTION

There can be no doubting the popularity of Business Process Reengineering (BPR), though a variety of different terms are in use to describe BPR activities, including for example process innovation (Davenport 1993), business process redesign (Short and Venkatraman 1992), business reengineering (Spurr et al. 1993) and combinations of such terms. In the United States, a 1993 Deloitte and Touche survey found the average Chief Information Officer involved in 4.4 reengineering projects (Moad 1993). In the United Kingdom, a 1995 survey found some 59% of UK organizations planning or undertaking something called BPR, and all surveys showed increasing BPR activity throughout the 1993-1995 period (see for example Preece and Edwards 1993; Price Waterhouse 1994; Willcocks 1995b). Allied to this popularity are some startling claims for what BPR must, and can, achieve. For Hammer and Champy (1993b), BPR is nothing less than "a reversal of the Industrial Revolution....It isn't about *fixing* anything [it] means starting all over, starting from scratch...the alternative is for Corporate America to close its doors and go out of business." Again, the new approach will, we are told,

drive down the time it takes to develop and deliver new products, dramatically reduce inventory and manufacturing time, slash the cost of quality and win back market share....The following changes are possible: 30-35 percent reduction in the cost of sales; 75-80 percent reduction in delivery time; 60-80 percent reduction in inventories; 65-70 percent reduction in the cost of quality; and unpredictable but substantial increase in market share. [Ligus 1993, p. 58]

Most commentators add that information technology is, or should be, a critical enabler, in some cases a major driver, of radical reengineering projects (see for example Bartram 1992; Davenport 1993; Hammer and Champy 1993a, 1993b; Heygate 1993, 1994). However, despite some high profile cases of success, these claims are as immodest as the reliable data is difficult to find.

In this paper, we reappraise the phenomenon of business process reengineering through our own recent case study and survey findings, and by consolidating and developing several strands of our own thinking. In a preliminary assessment, we question what is actually being achieved under its name and evaluate both the nature of the phenomenon and why it is so popular. We argue that its claims to radicalism and novelty are exaggerated and locate part of its appeal as a form of utopian thought applied to work organizations. We then deepen the analysis by suggesting how its essentially political origins, aims and characteristics link inextricably with the high importance management commentators give to the role of information technology as a catalyst and consolidator of radical change in how work is organized and performed. A key concept throughout is that of deracination — the rooting out of the past. In the view that we develop, a significant impetus within BPR is toward a technology-supported deracination that requires a collective forgetting. This forms both an essential part of its appeal, but also, if actioned, creates a number of major difficulties that inhibit the regaining of the business paradise so manifestly lost, at least according to BPR's main progenitors such as Champy (1995), Hammer and Champy (1993a, 1993b), and Johanssen et al. (1993).

2. REVIEWING BPR: A PRELIMINARY CRITIQUE

BPR is usually described as a means of facilitating significant, even fundamental, change in the way an organization operates. A key element is a focus on process, usefully defined by Davenport as a structured, measured set of activities designed to produce a specified output for a particular customer or market. The BPR activity described in the literature varies in the scale and type of change contemplated (Jones 1994). Central to BPR practice is a holistic approach to strategy, structure, process, people and technology.

BPR as an analysis, a set of prescriptions for management, and as practice can be assessed in several ways and at several different levels. One concern is to compare the exhortations against what managers claim to have achieved in BPR programs. Hammer and Champy estimated a 70% failure rate for the radical reengineering efforts they had observed, though this figure was not rigorously arrived at, and "implied nothing about the expected rate of success or failure of subsequent reengineering efforts" (Hammer and Stanton 1994). Two US studies show most reengineering projects consistently falling well short of their expected benefits (Hall, Rosenthal and Wade 1993; Moad 1993). In the UK, recent case study research found dramatic improvements in some companies, but documents these examples as few and far between (Bartram 1992; Harvey 1994).

Our own 1995 research in 168 UK-based organizations adds to this picture. High risk, radical BPR approaches were generally not being taken. One indication of this was the low size of spending, with 43% of medium and large organizations each incurring BPR related expenditures of under £1 million. Many of the processes being reengineered seemed to be existing ones to which improvements were being sought rather than those identified as a result of a radical rethink of how the organization needed to be reconfigured and managed. Radical BPR is portrayed as achieving sizeable job losses yet we found that, for all completed BPR projects and all types of process, staff redundancies averaged less than 5% of total BPR costs (see Willcocks [1995a, 1995b] for detailed reviews of the survey data). Generally, whatever the process being reengineered, organizations did not seem to be aiming high when they looked for improvements from BPR. There may well be a cause and effect here, with organizations aiming low and hitting low, because the actual improvements being achieved were also relatively low. The best claimed performance on actual improvements were found to be with core processes. Support, management and cross-boundary process reengineering produced consistently lower improvements than these. Very few organizations were achieving what could be called "breakthrough" results. Thus, of the organizations that had completed BPR programs, if a relatively conservative benchmark of significance of 20% profitability gain, 20% revenue gain and 10% decrease in costs of doing business is used, only 18% of organizations had achieved significant financial benefits from BPR on all three measures. Organizations were achieving, and in most cases aiming for, tangible improvements rather than radical change. The picture of discontinuous change represented in the BPR literature is not clearly underscored in the reported BPR practice.

A second approach is to assess the means by which BPR programs are meant to be accomplished. A prime question raised by the multidisciplinary holism at the heart of BPR study and practice is whether there are robust methodologies and tools available to facilitate the outcomes required from BPR activities. Certainly there are plenty available, including methodologies for developing the enabling role of IT and ones developed from diverse disciplines such as industrial engineering, software development, operational research and systems analysis, change management and the quality movement (as examples only, see Barrett 1994; Belmonte and Murray 1993; Couger, Flynn and Hellyer 1994; Davenport 1993; Harrington 1991; Jacobson, Ericsson and Jacobson 1995; Morris and Brandon 1993). The conclusion has been that there are many approaches, methodologies and tools more or less useful, but that bringing together the offerings from such diverse fields has so far proved difficult and adds up to an immaturity and a lack of integratedness on the methodological front (Earl and Khan 1994; Klein 1994) This is complemented by our own findings. Respondents registered considerable difficulties in finding a methodology that worked for BPR design phases and listed weaknesses in redesign methodologies as one of the main barriers in BPR programs. In particular, formal methodologies were often found less than helpful, likewise what were cited as "methodology vendors" (Willcocks 1995a).

A range of commentators point to the rigor and structure that methods can bring, but also to a number of downsides relative to other approaches (see for example Earl 1993; Mintzberg 1994; Peters 1987). Goals can become easily displaced into serving the method. Often the adoption of methods, together with external consultants, is a sign of an immaturity in the organization's ability to manage change projects. Methods-driven approaches can also encourage inflexibility and one-off, "initiative" approaches, and push out the learning and incrementalism and attention to social and political processes identified as vital where new and radical change is being undertaken (Craig and Yetton 1994; Davenport and Stoddard 1994). In case study research in four organizations, we found the methodologies adopted were often partial and handled some aspects of what should be a holistic approach better than others (Willcocks and Smith 1995). Frequently, IT-based change activities have utilized methodologies that focus on information flows and processes, and are based on systems analysis techniques, but in such a way as to marginalize human, social and political processes and issues (Clegg, Waterson and Carey 1994; Walsham 1993). Our own UK survey found such predilections often flowing into how the increasing number of IT-enabled or IT-driven BPR projects were being handled (Willcocks 1995a). Indeed, what emerges from the BPR literature itself is the frequency with which failure is related, among other reasons, to mismanagement of human, social and political issues and processes (for examples only, see Belmonte and Murray 1993; Moad 1993; Thackray 1993). We will argue later that the reasons for these failures may well be imbedded not just in the methodologies adopted, but also in the political resonances and ramifications inherent in how BPR is conceptualized, constructed as a change process, and operationalized.

2.1 Toward an Interpretivist Account

A further, less instrumentally-orientated, approach to assessing BPR is to investigate the claims of BPR and the analysis and interpretation in which these claims are set. Much of the rationale for BPR has been developed initially in a North American context, then generalized across the developed economies. The focus can be summarized as: How did corporate America lose its way in the business Paradise and how can that business Paradise be regained? The argument underlying much of the BPR management literature suggests that current failure is a direct result of previous success under Taylorite and Fordist work regimes, and a radical break from current managerial practices is required (Hammer and Champy 1993b; Harrington 1991; Johanssen et al. 1993). The BPR approach is presented as simultaneously necessary, radical, holistic and novel.

We have argued elsewhere that the eleven individual changes that make up BPR, at least as detailed by Hammer and Champy, are hardly novel — each has previously appeared, if in a different guise (Grint 1994). As one pertinent example they list "developing IT as an essential enabler of the reengineering process"; however, the concern to exploit IT has grown in importance on the management agenda over two decades along with increasing technological capability and price/performance (Grint and Woolgar 1995). Earl and Khan and Willcocks and Smith, in case study research on IT-enabled reengineering, also support the case that there is much that is not so new in BPR, although there are some novel combinations of old elements. In practice, as we will argue, it may not be the novelty of BPR in terms of a practice, but its stress on transformation and difference that more fully explains its appeal to, and modified adoption by, a corporate audience.

An externalist account is useful here, in that it focuses attention less on whether the *content* of reengineering is radically different *and* demonstrably superior to anything that went before, and rather more on *why* the package is effective in its particular envelope of space and time. That is, why has reengineering taken off at the beginning of the 1990s and why is it even more popular in the USA than anywhere else? BPR's popularity, of course, has precedents as far as managerial philosophies are concerned. Moving through Taylorism and Fordism, human relations and neo-human relations, each finding a resonance with external events, and for each of which an externalist account can be given, one can posit the arrival of a fourth wave, the culture of excellence approach where the limits of modernism and Fordism are perceived as the stimulus of change. Reengineering, in this perspective, is the summation of the fourth wave, and BPR can be read as portraying an external and internal crisis to which BPR can provide a manageable, "clean-slate," response (for a detailed exposition, see Grint 1994).

The neatness of BPR as a rhetorical explanation and, on our reading, what partly accounts for its phenomenal popularity, lies in how, as a self-presented "new" organizational and management idea, it renders an account of both problem and solution and sets up sympathetic "resonances" with related developments in and beyond the world of business. Furthermore a particular appeal lies in juxtaposing the washing of hands inherent in the "clean slate" approach, together with a representation of the novelty element in BPR as, paradoxically (and paradox also has its attractions), historically rooted in American culture. Success can be achieved not through breaks with tradition but through a radical return to tradition. That the USA's retrospective ideals, manifest in such rhetorical calls as "back to basics," "stick to the knitting" and "protect the core business," appears to have had only limited success can then be read as a result of either not being radical enough, not reengineering properly (Hammer and Stanton 1994), or of not returning to the roots of American tradition. Hence:

> [BPR] isn't another imported idea from Japan...[it] capitalizes on the same characteristics that made Americans such great business innovators: individualism, self reliance, a willingness to accept risk and a propensity for change...unlike management philosophies that would have "us" like "them," [it] doesn't try to change the behavior of American workers and managers. Instead, it takes advantage of American talents and unleashes American ingenuity. [Hammer and Champy 1993b]

To arrive at this conclusion, a certain amount of cultural manipulation is required if the resonances between the idea and the particular culture concerned are to be clear. For example: BPR is supposed to be about teamwork not (American) individualism; it is supposed to be about starting to risk change — so how can change be an element of the US culture; it is supposed to be about radically increasing the level and content of supportive social networks, not about American individual self-reliance. In effect, what counts as important aspects of culture can be interpreted afresh by those who seek to change it.

On this reading, reengineering, at least as represented in the main populist accounts, rests on an interpretation and use of the rhetoric and practice of reengineering that is fundamentally political. Reengineering attempts to provide a new discourse with which contemporary developments can be simultaneously explained and controlled. Following Foucault, one can preface the argument developed below by suggesting that the process of discursive formation necessarily implicates both knowledge and power, theory and practice (Foucault 1980; Wolin 1991). This raises a prime issue: the extent to which the "back to basics" and "return to the roots" movements also implies a "back to politics" movement. As with "culture" and "excellence" in the 1980s BPR rhetoric and practice emerge as ways of talking about and conducting political activity by seemingly other, more acceptable, means. Below we will develop further three aspects of this theme: the political resonances of BPR as deracination; the role of technology in this and how its analysis can be developed; and finally, how BPR's appeal and purpose can be interpreted as essentially about an IT-enabled politics of collective forgetting.

3. BPR AND DERACINATION AS POLITICAL INTERVENTION

In this section, we use the idea of deracination — to pull up by the roots or to remove from a natural environment — to consider BPR. Like so many forms of organizational change, BPR is sometimes premised upon deracination in its assumption that the uprooting of organizational norms and traditions is a necessary prerequisite for radical increases in productivity. This uprooting not only relates to the organizational form — whether it be flattened hierarchies or teams or whatever — but also to the displacement of "normal" management practices. In effect, BPR is adopted and deployed as if office politics either do not, should not or will not exist in the reengineered corporation. In the words of Johansson et al., for example:

[Managers] should measure everything they can....Once managers know what changes have to take place...they will start to influence the behavior of staff, focus on results, and release their creative talent. They also start changing their roles becoming less concerned with control and instruction, and more concerned with challenge and discussion....With this change of management style, *organizational politics can be cast aside*. [p. 202, quoted in Padulo 1995, p. 305, emphasis added]

From the beginnings of industrial capitalism in the late eighteenth century in Britain, management tasks and causal explanations have been locked into models of rational behavior ultimately embedded in the operations of the market: managers do what they do because the imperatives of the market require that it be done. According to Hales (1986), managers achieve this by leading, liaising, monitoring, allocating resources, maintaining production, maintaining peace, innovating, planning and controlling. In other words, managers manage the organization for the benefit of all or for the benefit of the shareholders or for the benefit of stakeholders. Whichever beneficiaries spring to the fore, there is often one group singularly missing — the managers themselves.

At the same time, there have long been arguments that management is as much a political process as a rational one. From both descriptive and critical perspectives, management as a political activity has a considerable and well-documented history (as examples see Bendix 1956; Baldamus 1961; Child 1972; Dalton 1959; Jay 1967; Hannaway 1989; Marx 1954; Stewart 1983). If organizational life is as Machiavellian as some of the literature suggests, then attempting to inhibit this is clearly a difficult task. On our reading, BPR is an essentially political intervention — normative, metaphorical, and practical — into work organizations.

That the conceptualization and analysis of power are important in studying BPR emerges strongly from our recent survey work. Four of the top five, and seven of the top ten, most significant barriers to BPR reported by the respondents related to human and political issues, broadly conceived. As far as interest groups were concerned, lower level employee fear and resistance were rated by managers themselves as much less significant barriers to BPR than middle and senior management. This seemed to be related to the relatively greater power middle, line and senior managers claim to have in the prevailing cultures and political structures in the organizations under review. The finding on the criticality of political/human issues in BPR was endorsed when we asked respondents to identify the critical success factors and what they would have done differently in their BPR programs. Six of the nine top critical success factors related to human/political issues: top management support, gaining employee buy-in, project management, implementation style, communication processes and establishing the need and the levers for change. The strongest single finding when respondents were asked what they had learned from their BPR experience can be summarized as pay much earlier, focused attention to the human and political issues inherent in BPR (see Willcocks 1995a).

Despite this, most conventional perspectives on organizational decision making and action, including those of the main BPR progenitors in the management literature, are predicated upon a very traditional theory of power. These perspectives tend to imply that where organizational power is in the hands of an individual or a small elite, then power emanates from the center to the periphery with the causal influence similarly centrifugal (see Handy 1985). In practice, if subordinates themselves do not act, then a leader has little power; only as a *consequence* of subordinate actions can leaders be deemed to have power. Our own evidence suggests the difficulty that a BPR program can then run into: middle and line management resistance was the first, and the prevailing culture and political structure the fourth most significant barrier experienced in BPR programs. Even assuming senior management support for BPR, it inevitably runs into political problems. Power, in this perspective, therefore, is contingent upon the production and reproduction of a network of associations that facilitates "acting at a distance" (Latour 1986). Thus, power is a consequence of action, rather than a cause of action.

This shift from the "principle" of power to the "practice" of power, as Latour (1986) calls it, or from power as a possession to power as a relationship, as Foucault's writing implies (1980), also suggests that subordinate action only occurs through the interpretation of self-advantage by the subordinate: subordinates obey because they consider it to be in their self-interest to obey. In turn, it is likely that the command of the leader will become distorted through what Latour calls the "translation" process: not only are leaders dependent upon their subordinates but a subordinate's translation of the edict may well prove to be a distortion of the leader's intention. The implication of this is that, rather than the rays of power spreading out from the center to the periphery in a determinate and unmediated fashion, they are both highly contingent and the subject of constant interpretation and renegotiated. Such a revision in this context implies that the existence of policies or rules does not ensure the enacting of such policies or commands. Moreover, difficulties in BPR initiatives may lie in the misrecognition of power: if subordinates are ultimately in control of their own destinies, then whether BPR — or any change program — fails or succeeds is ultimately dependent upon them being persuaded to act in particular ways. In practice, as Giddens (1984) describes, a dialectic of control operates. It is also useful, following Foucault (1988), to refer to power as a relationship, and therefore to power relations in which resistances are formed right at the point where relations of power are exercised (Foucault 1980). Following these considerations, the power of the deracination concept imbedded in BPR becomes more clear, but so also do the difficulties which come with trying to operationalize the uprooting of the past and planting of the new.

All this brings a great deal of weight to bear on winning the hearts as well as the minds of stakeholders. In the BPR case, rhetoric and emotional appeal become a highly important power resource (Grint 1994; Jones 1994).Rhetoric is implicated in power relations to the degree to which it supports the legitimacy of change. On a broader front, legitimacy is tied in with politics as the management of meaning (Pettigrew 1985; Willcocks, Currie and Mason 1996). The dimensions of the political appeal of deracination concept has even further dimensions when reengineering in its radical versions is located as a particular form of utopian thought applied to work organizations. On this reading, reengineering's innovation is in the idea that only an attack upon all fronts simultaneously in which every possible institution, ritual, practice and norm is subject to critique and reconstruction, is likely to succeed. The premise of the radical argument is that incrementalism is itself a barrier to change. This does not imply that *all* attempts to change should be utopian in their scale and direction (see Yin 1994) but rather that utopian thought here should be considered rather differently from its traditional role, in More's Utopia and Huxley's Island for example, as fit only for dreamers, fit for "nowhere" (see Grint [1995] for a detailed account).

Thus reengineering can be located as a utopian form of thought, necessarily political in its use during interventions to galvanize organizational practice. However, our own evidence (see above) suggests that the radical extent of the change required explains both the wide rhetorical (but few practical) successes *and* the many relative disappointments with reengineering. On this interpretation, the high degree of uncertainty and risk involved unhinges the nerves of those attempting to reengineer so that they seek more conservative and instrumental approaches to change that appear both less risky and more plausible. This, of course, is precisely the argument made over thirty years ago by Lindblom's (1959) account of "disjointed incrementalism" or "muddling through" and the prior "satisficing" behavior described by Simon (1947). These incisive critiques of rational decision making imply that decision-makers do not approach organizational problems with a clean sheet of paper and an ideal, but with a pre-folded piece of paper and in the light of existing structures and policies (see Jabes 1982).

Of course, such political and organizational realities have already been recognized in several revisionist alternatives to the utopian version of BPR (see for example Heygate 1993; Craig and Yetton 1994; Davenport and Stoddard 1994). Our own survey evidence shows a complementary picture. Politics intrudes in another way. Even if the form and extent of the change is as utopian in its radical result as reengineering suggests, it is unlikely that the end product will emerge as a depoliticized island of paradise in a Machiavellian sea but, rather, as an island where managerial life may have changed but it remains essentially political: there are still careers to be carved out, clans to join and gangs to avoid. Indeed, in the revitalized, dynamic and slimmed down reengineered organization, the transparency of the operations may mean that political life has to be, if anything, more subtly handled than before, but handled nonetheless. If Morris's "News From Nowhere," and the works by More and Huxley were utopian, nevertheless they represented visions where political ideas, interests and actions were strongly represented. In practice, and as our survey evidence suggests, there is nothing inherent in BPR as a process or outcome that depoliticizes organizational life; if anything, politics breed in times of major, IT-enabled change (Pettigrew 1985; Willcocks, Currie and Mason 1996; Willcocks 1995a).

4. TECHNOLOGY IN THEORY AND AS POLITICS

In the management literature, information technology is also a highly significant element in how the Utopia that could be ushered in by BPR would be constructed and run. If most commentators point in BPR theory to IT as a critical enabler of business process reengineering then, notwithstanding the limits of the survey, the data can be interpreted as supporting the claim that IT also emerges from self-reported managerial practice as an important enabler of BPR activity and support for redesigned processes. Thus, in our 1995 survey, 58% of respondents rated the IT role in enabling radical process redesign as "critical," 32% rated the IT role as "marginal," while 10% said IT had no role to play in their BPR projects. For even more organizations, IT played an important role in supporting redesigned processes: 68% of respondents rated IT process support for BPR as "critical" in their organizations. IT, or rather its management, also figured as one of the top ten critical success factors for BPR programs, while technical deficiencies, together with poor IT management, were also experienced as seventh out of the ten most significant barriers to BPR. IT represented between 24% and 45% of total spending on each of the BPR programs we reviewed.

IT was regarded as a critical element in the success of the top "best performers" that had completed BPR programs. This group consisted of the "breakthrough" organizations and the organizations claiming significant profitability, revenue and cost reduction improvements as a result of BPR. In practice, over 75% of the top 30% "best performers" in BPR did see IT as critical in both enabling radical process redesign and supporting redesigned processes. Over half of the top best performers were incurring over 40% of their total BPR spending on IT, though for the others IT spending was average or below for the type of process being reengineered. This finding is based on a small sample but supports research findings elsewhere that there tends to be little or no correlation between size of IT spending and organizational performance (Willcocks 1994; 1995a).

In our reading of the BPR message and the degree of IT utilization, IT has a highly significant role in how BPR is constructed and operationalized. One highly political employment — IT's role in collective forgetting and remembering — is dealt with in the next section. As a precursor, in this section we reconsider perspectives on technology in organizational settings, with a view to reconstructing the relationship between technology and politics, and indeed the possibility of technology as politics.

One common understanding of technology is as the BPR "black box": the mysterious and complex amalgam of metal and plastic into which pass problems and out of which flow solutions in a manner both impressive and relatively easy to measure, and therefore understand. In effect, technology is seen as really the only objective, solid, dependable and measurable thing in a world of dynamic change and subjective confusion. Moreover, technology — or at least contemporary information technology — offers a powerful solution to the "reverse salient" (Hughes 1987) which has hitherto inhibited organizational change. The consequence of apprehending technology in this way is to make it impervious to social analysis, to make social analysts "forget" that what the technology is, what its capacities and consequences are, can be the subject of considerable dispute. In fact, one might want to suggest that what counts as the role played by technology is the upshot of a contingent negotiation, not something which can be derived from close perusal of the technology or its human supporters.

This common, and traditional, approach to technology is premised upon an acceptance of one or another statement of the technical capabilities of technology. Sometimes the view accepts that there may be disagreements and ambiguities as to what precisely the technical capacity of any artefact or system is, but holds to the view that some objective view of technical capacity is in principle available and this technical capacity is viewed as inherent to the technology (artefact or system). For this reason, the perspective will be referred to as *essentialist*: technical attributes derive from the internal characteristics of the technology. Moreover, these internal characteristics are (often) supposed to have resulted from the application of scientific method or from the linear extrapolation and/or development of previous technologies.

But what happens if we reconsider technology as no more nor less of a black box than any other element in the BPR equation? This general approach has been referred to as *anti-essentialist* (see Grint and Woolgar for an extended review of this approach). This encompasses a broad church of perspectives, including "social shaping" (e.g., MacKenzie 1990), "social construction of technology" (e.g., Bijker, Hughes and Pnich 1987; Bijker and Law 1992) and what has been called "designer technology." These otherwise different approaches share the view that the nature, form and capacity of a technology is the upshot of various antecedent circumstances involved in its development (mainly taken to include design, manufacture and production). These antecedent circumstances are said to be "built into" and/or "embodied in" the final product; the resulting technology is "congealed social relations" or "society made durable." Differences between anti-essentialists turn on the specific choice of antecedent circumstances — between for example, "social interests," the "solutions sought by relevant social groups" and "social structure and the distribution of power." Although anti-essentialism is characterized by some heated internal disputes, all parties share the aim of specifying the effects of these circumstances upon technological capacity.

One particular approach within the broad anti-essentialist model that seems worth exploring here in detail is Actor-Network theory. Actor-Network theory seems to imply three critical issues need to be "remembered" rather than forgotten. First, the world is composed of "hybrids" (Latour 1993) rather than discrete elements of the social and non-social. In effect, a world full of naked and isolated humans is as unviable as one full of autonomous technologies. There are virtually no conditions under which humans exist except within networks of other humans and non-humans. These "hybrids" or "Monsters" (Law 1991b) run counter to the analytic tradition set up under the procedures and rules of the Enlightenment philosophies (Latour 1993) and pose formidable problems of analysis since our understanding of the world is premised upon divisions between people and things not the agglomerations. They are also problematic because our tradition has been one in which the specific "effect" of any variable can be readily assessed.

However, when we reconsider the world of hybrids, attempting to measure effects becomes extraordinarily difficult. One problem that is particularly pertinent here has already been alluded to: how can we differentiate between the "effect" of IT in the reengineering process and the "effect" of all the other elements? Since BPR is, by its very nature, a holistic hybrid, it becomes an impossible task to evaluate the significance of the discrete elements. Traditionally, of course, we persuade ourselves that, because we can assess the capacity of a technology, we can assess its impact. Relatedly, while we can grasp an objective view of technology we are forced to remain with subjective views of the human element. Thus we are forced to conclude with only tentative evaluations of the whole even if we accept that the result is a consequence of the mixture of human and non-human.

However, as a second point, Actor-Network theory suggests not just that a holistic analysis is necessary but also that we should avoid "switching registers" (Law 1991a, p. 8) when we move from analyzing the human and the non-human. This symmetry of analysis runs not just counter to the entire Enlightenment but has profound implications for understanding the significance of both the human and the non-human. Callon (1986), for example, in his account of certain French scallops, poses it in a counter-intuitive form that talks of the "interests" of the scallops in aligning themselves to one particular actor-network rather than another. The significant point here, for our purposes, is not whether he *really* means that scallops can have interests or whether this is a mere rhetorical flourish but the impact of this approach on our understanding of the human. We may dismiss Callon's seemingly arrogant attribution of interests to scallops but might this merely reflect our more traditional — and equally arrogant — attribution of interests to other humans on the basis of a similarly thin veneer of knowledge and understanding? That is, since we probably know as much about the *real* interests of scallops as we do about those of other people, perhaps we can learn from Actor-Network approaches both by discarding the different registers that inhibit understanding and by reconsidering our universally all too easy attribution of interests, cause and effect.

The third aspect of Actor-Network theory that is relevant to our discussion is the notion of the network's strength being derived from the robustness of the links rather than the "inherent" strength or power of any discrete element. This idea of technology being "society more durable" (Latour 1991), or political amber, is especially relevant to BPR's radical claim to enhanced performance since it asserts that the holistic union of the social and technical is the key to the strength and influence of the approach. But to what extent is the radical garnering of a heterogeneous network within BPR premised upon taken-for-granted claims about the capacity and effects of its component parts, when the capacities and effects of both human and non-human elements are themselves the result of constructive, or constitutive, rather than descriptive efforts?

In general, the anti-essentialist approach, and particularly Actor-Network theory, has enormous policy implications for technology design, development and use and this, in turn, may be critical for explaining the success or failure of various BPR initiatives. However, it is important to note that three key features of the general anti-essentialist approach threaten to compromise its radical potential. The first is the ambivalence associated with the idea of antecedent circumstances being "built in," since this seems to imply that a technology is "neutral" and can be objectively evaluated until such time as the politics or values are built in. Since, to borrow a phrase from Levi-Strauss, technologies always arrive "cooked" and never "raw," it is difficult to accept that a non-evaluative account is plausible. In other words, only if we can forget the political dimension of technology will we be able to analyze it. Yet, since we can only know the technology through the evaluative interpretation such a "raw" analysis is illogical. The second problem is the difficulty in specifying the nature of these "antecedent circumstances." In short, this is to problematize the assumption that "interests" are transparently available to the analyst and do not require considerable interpretive activity. Unless we can be certain that we can "read" the interests of various groups into various technologies, we might be chary of this. The third stems from the view that technologies, albeit those at the end of a cycle of embodying antecedent circumstances — the final stabilized technological products — are still capable of having effects; that is effects which, again, do not require interpretive action — they speak for themselves (see Grint and Woolgar for a detailed critique).

In sum, Actor-Network and other anti-essentialist approaches to technology can offer a more heuristic purchase on the significance of technology to the success of BPR, although they bring a number of compromising problems with them. Only in Actor-Network theory do the "things" appear to have the same status as "humans" in the development of interests. In radical versions of BPR, as among our survey respondents, there is high stress on redesign through the notion of process with IT as critical enabler. We would argue that artefacts — in the BPR case information-based technologies and redesigned processes — can themselves be interpreted as having political properties (see also Winner 1985). Clearly as part of the politics of BPR, "things" as well as people need to change radically, and in doing so the Actor-Network that results can make concrete the repoliticized, reengineered organization. In the next section, we explore more fully how the

Actor-Network can be conceived as being formulated politically in the context of supporting the deracinating thrust in BPR toward collective forgetting and remembering.

5. TOWARD FURTHER INTERPRETATION: DERACINATION AS COLLECTIVE FORGETTING

The process of political deracination finds its ultimate expression in BPR's rhetorical attitude toward organizational culture and history. Indeed, it is in statements and inferences made about the past that analytical elements — such as utopias, non-rational decision making and psychological abdication of responsibility — combine to produce a rhetorical effect of sweeping proportions. While this effect is most apparent in the radical "breakthrough" claims of certain BPR proponents (Hammer 1990; Hammer and Champy 1993b; Harrington 1991; Johanssen et al. 1993), it may also be discerned in the "incremental" prescriptions of various revisionists (Heygate 1993 1994; Davenport 1993). The rhetorical trope in question is BPR's exhortation to audiences that they, and with them entire corporations, forget the past. Before we examine the nature of this appeal in full, however, it is necessary to establish clear conceptual links between espoused "forgetting" and other forms of deracination.

On the basis of a participant observation study of a computer installation, Case (1995) documents an emergent, repeated and prominent pattern of behavior; that is, the failure of designers, programmers and operators to meet deadlines and, ultimately, their inability to deliver a working computer system. The study details a complex interplay of "technical" and micro-political factors which combined to produce an accelerating cycle of "investment without result." During development of the system under scrutiny, there was repeated "frustration" experienced by participants as various software and hardware elements were deemed to have malfunctioned. Frequently, however, it was not "technical problems" which prevented successful operation, but deliberate political strategies on the part of individuals or coalitions within the host institution and supplying organization. Much empirical and theoretical work supports this finding (Coombs, Knights and Willmott 1992; Markus 1983; Pettigrew 1973, 1985; Pfeiffer 1992; Robey and Markus 1988; Willcocks, Currie and Mason 1996). Our own survey also confirms this general observation and underlines the political dynamics of BPR implementation (see also Belmonte and Murray 1993; Moad 1993; Thackray 1993).

The means by which participants (project managers, systems analysts, consultants, programmers, operators) constructed and rationalized "failure" ranged from momentary expressions of cynicism and sarcasm through to "organizational amnesia" (Case 1995). Metaphorically adapted from psychiatry, this latter notion intentionally invokes an image of "traumatized" individuals turning away from their experience, both mentally and socially. The *Longman Dictionary of Psychology and Psychiatry* defines amnesia as

> a partial or complete, temporary or permanent loss of memory due to (a) organic factors....(b) psychogenic factors, as in unconscious repression of painful or traumatic experiences. In the latter case...it serves as a *defense against anxiety and distress*, or as a way of *escaping from specific situations*. [1984, p. 37, emphasis added]

The pathological image of a distressed and anxious person seeking to escape the guilt and pain of their history resonated strongly with observed conduct. Individuals who attempt to flee an unpleasant organizational reality do so through a process of motivational "substitution." In accordance with Freud's Pleasure Principle, such socio-emotional flight becomes a form of self-protective rejection (Board 1978; Kets de Vries and Miller 1984). The participant denies an "unfavorable" interpretation of past events and simultaneously replaces it with a more "favorable" account, accompanied by an optimistic set of future organizational possibilities.

The American philosopher and literary critic Kenneth Burke identifies this process of motivational substitution as a generic rhetorical strategy found in many forms of textual expression and hortation. He refers to the phenomenon as "secular futurism" (Burke 1969, pp. 333-335), a notion which is particularly helpful in apprehending BPR's master trope. Rhetorical moves employed by BPR proponents bear more than a passing resemblance to the patterns of conduct described above. In short, we encounter a peculiar cocktail of cultivated "amnesia" and "utopianism." The following represents a typical passage:

> Reengineering is about beginning again with a clean sheet of paper. It is about rejecting the conventional wisdom and received assumptions of the past. Reengineering is about inventing new approaches to process structure that bear little or no resemblance to those of previous eras. [Hammer and Champy 1993b, p. 49]

Why are BPR proponents so eager to encourage a radical denial and renunciation of the past? As we have noted, much of the literature of the protagonists and commentators points to the potential benefits of "IT-enabled" BPR. Where such an intimate link does exist, it could be suggested that BPR is being sold as an IT solution to an IT debacle. In these cases BPR's overriding justification derives from the construed failure of past IT investment to deliver promised productivity improvements. Viewed from this perspective, furthermore, BPR literature offers cathartic absolution of the guilt associated with past IT "mismanagement."

While BPR's rhetoric demands that its audience forget the past, protagonists themselves are by no means enthusiastic to do so. On the contrary, BPR relies fundamentally on a careful and purposeful reconstruction of the past; one which makes implicit reference to its "sinful" and abhorrent nature. Churchward and Bennett (1993), in their report on BPR and "Work Flow" techniques, for example, cite "spectacular" levels of US expenditure ($1 trillion) on IT in the period 1980-1989 and question the efficacy of such investment. The management consultant John Pearson (1993), in his BPR sales pitch, quotes US Bureau of Labor Statistics to demonstrate that, despite high levels of "per-information-worker" investment, overall white collar productivity has fallen in the period 1970 to 1992. Likewise, Heygate begins in his paper on IT-enabled restructuring with a direct reference to the failure of past IT promises:

> The failure of computer technology to deliver on ambitious promises of bottom-line value, together with a number of conspicuous systems disasters, has led many top managers to question the notion that IT can be used to gain competitive advantage. [1994, p. 137]

In each of these cases the intention is to emphasize how IT solutions have failed to fulfil their promise. Pearson intimates, for instance, that a shared intuition of this painful truth is now being "rationally" borne out. As he puts it, "The gut feeling that despite all these investments in technology, we have not really become more productive; is now supported by various studies" (1993, p. 2).

Such observations focus on the pain of the past in order to set the stage for its victimization and the cathartic appearance of a secular savior — BPR. History is reconstructed so that its various agents (both human and non-human) may be roundly scapegoated by managers in the present. Through their implicit "confession" to having played a part in this despicable drama, audiences are simultaneously offered absolution and a chance to partake of the new technological sacrament.

Nowhere is this logic more plainly evident than in the work of Hammer and Champy (1993b, pp. 49-50). In typically immodest fashion, they contrast their "Manifesto for Business Revolution" with Adam Smith's *Wealth of Nations*. What they refer to as Adam Smith's "paradigm" is construed as the embodiment of all that is "evil" about the industrial/commercial past; a kind of secular Satan whose memory has to be exorcized and whose material legacy annihilated. Hammer and Champy "reject" the assumptions of Smith's "industrial paradigm," referring to such notions as the division of labor, economies of scale, hierarchical control, and so forth. Such "nasties" are without exception characteristics of a modern, or in their terms "early-stage," Fordist industrial era. The reader who, likely as not, will recognize within themselves and their organizations a strong commitment to "Adam Smith's industrial paradigm" is then offered secular absolution and salvation in the form of BPR.

By scapegoating a collective organizational past and recommending collective amnesia, proponents of BPR make available *collective* absolution. IT managers are invited to reestablish their "innocence" and sense of identity through a ritual transference of guilt. What guilt? The guilt accruing from decades of costly errors in decision and implementation. In sum, the billions (pounds, dollars, yen, etc.) "squandered" on IT solutions that have been seen to "fail" or otherwise not lived up to their initial performative "promises." Would-be believers are being invited, as it were, to be "born again" and to cleanse themselves of taints associated with past managerial misdeeds. The collective forgetting of histories, "amnesia writ large," thus performs a central role in this rhetorical calculus of "vicarious atonement." It operates, as in general with political manifestos, to "configure" the past for present rhetorical purposes (Chapman, McDonald and Tonkin 1989). Most conveniently for the priestly suppliers of new "solutions," it disassociates them from involvement with snake oil remedies of the past, which otherwise might look uncannily like those panaceas presently on offer. All may happily be forgotten and forgiven: "Reengineering is a new beginning" (Hammer and Champy 1993b, p. 2).

We are reminded of a parallel in Greek mythology recorded by Homer in his epic the *Odyssey*. On his return from Troy to Ithaca, Odysseus is blown off course by a tempest and separated from the rest of the Greek fleet. In due course, he arrives at the coast of Cyrene (present-day Libya) where he encounters the legendary Lotophagi — the Lotus-eaters. The peoples of Cyrene are addicted to eating lotus fruit, consumption of which results in their losing all memory save that of the desire to eat more fruit (see Guerber 1994). The hero of the epic, while fortunately not succumbing to the temptation himself, experiences enormous difficulties tearing his companions free from the seductive malaise of the lotus induced amnesia. Analogously, Heygate (1994, p. 137) refers to "IT's troubling lack of business value" and has no hesitation in suggesting that managerial consumers invest in "new intelligent applications," promising to make good the faults of the old. This logic would presumably extend reflexively to BPR (whether IT-enabled or not). If it has not yet delivered the expected results, it is because consumers have not yet forgotten enough; a malady that is best remedied by ever more copious and conspicuous consumption (see, for example, Grint and Case 1995).

6. CONCLUDING REMARKS : (RE)ENGINEERING FORGETTING

The appearance of the "(re)engineering" metaphor in BPR guise is historically distinct from earlier manifestations of mechanistic imagery in managerial innovations. Even though there are obvious parallels, BPR does not simply replicate the nineteenth century "engineering" spirit of Taylorism. Contemporary (re)engineering takes place in an era of silicon innovation and, correspondingly, derives inspiration from the new technological wave. It is thus not so much a question of *engineering* business processes as *re*engineering them in accordance with the connotations of a post-mechanistic metaphor. In many ways, the micro-electronic revolution heralded an intensification of the spirit of calculation and measurement inherent in earlier clockwork models of the universe. Advances in micro-circuitry supply the material means by which accelerating computational speed and accuracy can be accomplished. These technologies, in turn, have acted as post-Fordist *mise-en-scene* for the development of managerial interventions in the organizational realm.

We have already noted that, in collapsing the common-sense dichotomy between "technology" and "society," Latour (1991, p. 129) suggests that "technology is society made durable." It would be no contradiction, however, to reverse this proposition when we consider how these durable technologies turn back reflexively on their co-creators. Conforming with the demands of a post-mechanistic metaphor, BPR implies that "society is technology made malleable." "Starting from scratch" might thus be apprehended mimetically as, say, the reformatting of a PC hard drive — wiping the memory with a push of the button. In the nomenclature of MSDOS: BPR = del *.*, the implication being that entire complex organizations may purge their collective memories and practices with the same ease as dropping a few file addresses.

The image of BPR's espoused intent to "scratch" or "delete" memory seems all the more ironic given IT's role as facilitator of data storage and retrieval. The increasing "power" of information and communications technology resides in its ability to store ever denser new forms of digitized information at ever lower costs and process it at ever faster rates. An unintended corollary of the enhancement of artificial memory, however, may be a proportionate reduction in the importance of sheerly human memory, culture and history. Viewed in this light, BPR is contributing to the institutionalization and rationalization of a much wider form of memory loss in post-industrial societies. As we have seen, proponents of BPR certainly prescribe a form of "ahistoricity" and organizational erasure. In effect, they entice managerial audiences to indulge in acts of cultural-historical nihilism with little or no regard to the wider consequences.

In his concluding remarks concerning the application of IT-enabled BPR, the protagonist Heygate tacitly acknowledges many of these points:

There is, of course, no way to know for certain how these challenges will play out in any particular case. In an environment shaped by intelligent technology, there are few, if any, hard-wired solutions. Managers will not discover what to do by deducing proper courses of action from first principles. Instead, they will need to experiment and prototype and pilot-test — proactively, aggressively, repeatedly. [1994, p. 147]

In this statement, then, we glimpse the envisioned effects of BPR induced, IT-enabled amnesia. Uncertain, displaced and deracinated entities wander aimlessly in worlds void of organizational and cultural meaning. Their only *raison d'etre* is that of commercial necessity. Stripped of volition, their "repetitive" actions merely mimic the quasi-random heuristics of the "intelligent" machines with which they form partial cybernetic connections (Haraway 1991; Strathern 1991). In the absence of a richer social milieu, expression becomes purely one-dimensional, undirected yet emotive. Entities in competition need no other response than naked aggression:

"Don't automate, obliterate!" [Hammer 1990, p. 104]

"On this journey... we shoot the dissenters." [Hammer 1993, p. 71]

This final reading perhaps helps to explain, and also provides further insight into the many ramifications and consequences of, the corporate lotus-eating inducements presented in the BPR literature. While organizational politics can be quietly forgotten, it is clear that Machiavelli will still live on.

7. REFERENCES

Baldamus, W. *Efficiency and Effort.* London: Tavistock, 1961.

Barrett, J. "Process Visualization: Getting the Vision Right is Key." *Information Systems Management,* Spring 1994, pp. 14-23.

Bartram, P. *Business Reengineering: The Use of Process Redesign and IT To Transform Corporate Performance.* London: Business Intelligence, 1992.

Belmonte, R., and Murray, R. "Getting Ready For Strategic Change: Surviving Business Process Redesign." *Information Systems Management,* 1993, pp. 23-29.

Bendix, R. *Work and Authority in Industry.* New York: John Wiley, 1956.

Bijker, W. E.; Hughes, T.; and Pinch, T. J. (Editors). *The Social Construction of Technological Systems.* Cambridge: MIT Press, 1987.

Bijker, W. E., and Law, J. (Editors). *Shaping Technology/Building Society.* Cambridge: MIT Press, 1992.

Board, de R. *The Psychoanalysis of Organization.* London: Tavistock, 1978.

Burke, K. *A Grammar of Motives.* Berkeley: University of California Press, 1969

Callon, M. "Some Elements Of A Sociology Of Translation: Domestication of the Scallops and the Fishermen of St Brieuc's Bay." In J. Law (Editor), *Power, Action and Belief: A New Sociology of Knowledge.* London: Routledge, 1986.

Case, P. "Reengineering the End of History." *CRICT Discussion Paper.* London: Brunel The University of West London, 1995.

Champy, J. *Reengineering Management.* London: Nicholas Brealey, 1995.

Chapman, M.; McDonald, M.; and Tonkin, E. "Introduction." In E. Tonkin, M. McDonald and M. Chapman (Editors), *History and Ethnicity.* London: Routledge, 1989.

Child, J. "Organizational Structure, Environment And Performance." *Sociology,* Volume 6, Number 1, 1972, pp. 1-22.

Churchward, M., and Bennett, J. *A Guide to Workflow and Business Re-engineering.* London: Olivetti UK Limited, 1993.

Clegg, C.; Waterson, P.; and Carey, N. "Computer Supported Collaborative Working: Lessons From Elsewhere." *Journal of Information Technology,* Volume 9, Number 2, 1994, pp. 72-86.

Couger, J.; Flynn, P.; and Hellyer, D. "Enhancing The Creativity Of Reengineering." *Information Systems Management,* June 1994, pp. 24-29.

Coombs, R.; Knights, D.; and Willmott, H. "Culture, Control And Competition: Towards A Conceptual Framework for the Study of Information Technology in Organizations." *Organization Studies,* Volume 13, Number 1, 1992, pp. 51-72.

Craig, J., and Yetton, P. "The Dual and Strategic Role of IT: A Critique of Business Process Reengineering." *Working Paper 94-002 Australian Graduate School of Management.* Kensington: University of New South Wales, 1994.

Dalton, M. *Men Who Manage.* New York: McGraw-Hill, 1959.

Davenport, H. *Process Innovation: Reengineering Work Through Information Technology.* Boston: Harvard Business Press, 1993.

Davenport, T., and Stoddard, D. "Reengineering: Business Change Of Mythic Proportions?" *MIS Quarterly,* Volume 18, Number 2, 1994, pp. 121-127.

Earl, M. "Experiences In Strategic Information Systems Planning." *MIS Quarterly,* Volume 17, Number 1, 1993, pp. 1-24.

Earl, M., and Khan, B. "How New Is Business Process Redesign?" *European Management Journal*, Volume 12, Number 1, 1994, pp. 20-30.

Foucault, M. *Power/Knowledge: Selected Interviews and Other Writings, 1972-77.* Edited by Colin Gordon. Brighton: Harvester Press, 1980.

Foucault, M. "The Ethic Of Care For The Self As A Practice Of Freedom." In J. Bernauer and D. Rasmussen (Editors), *The Final Foucault.* Cambridge: MIT Press, 1988.

Freud, S. *The Complete Psychological Works of Sigmund Freud*, Volume 1. London: Hogarth, 1966.

Giddens, A. *The Constitution of Society.* Cambridge, England: Polity Press, 1984.

Grint, K. "Reengineering History." *Organization*, Volume 1, Number 1, 1994, pp. 179-202.

Grint, K. "Reengineering Utopia." *Management Research and Discussion Paper.* Oxford: Templeton College, February, 1995.

Grint, K., and Case, P. "Now Where Were We? BPR as Espoused Corporate Amnesia." Paper for the *Workshop On Critical Studies Of Organizational and Management Innovations*, European Institute for Advanced Studies In Management, Brussels, May, 1995.

Grint, K., and Woolgar, S. *Deus ex Machina.* Cambridge, England: Polity Press, 1995.

Guerber, H. A. *Greece and Rome.* London: Senate, 1994.

Hales, C. P. "What Do Managers Do?" *Journal of Management Studies*, Volume 23, 1986, pp. 88- 115.

Hall, G.; Rosenthal, L.; and Wade, J. "How To Make Reengineering Really Work." *Harvard Business Review*, November-December 1993, pp. 119-131.

Hammer, M. " Don't Automate — Obliterate." *Harvard Business Review*, July-August 1990, pp. 104-112.

Hammer, M. Quoted in *Forbes Magazine*, Summer 1993, p. 71.

Hammer, M., and Champy, J. "Reengineering the Corporation." *Insights Quarterly*, Summer 1993a, pp. 3-19.

Hammer, M., and Champy, J. *Reengineering the Corporation: A Manifesto for Business Revolution.* London: Nicholas Brealey, 1993b.

Hammer, M., and Stanton, S. "No Need For Excuses." *Financial Times*, October 5, 1994, p. 20.

Handy, C. *Understanding Organizations*. London: Penguin, 1985.

Hannaway, J. *Managers Managing*. New York: Oxford University Press, 1989.

Haraway, D. "A Cyborg Manifesto — Science, Technology and Socialist Feminism in the Late Twentieth Century." In D. Haraway (Editor), *Simians, Cyborgs and Women — The Reinvention of Nature*. London: Free Association Books, 1991.

Harrington, H. *Business Process Improvement*. New York: McGraw-Hill, 1991.

Harvey, D. *Re-engineering: The Critical Success Factors*. London: Business Intelligence/ Financial Times, 1994.

Heygate, R. "Being Intelligent About 'Intelligent' Technology." *The McKinsey Quarterly*, Volume 4, 1994, pp. 137-147.

Heygate, R. "Immoderate Redesign." *The McKinsey Quarterly*, Volume 1, 1993, pp. 73-87.

Hughes, T. P. "The Evolution of Large Technological Systems." In W. E. Bijker, T. P. Hughes and T. Pinch (Editors), *The Social Construction of Technological Systems*. Cambridge: MIT Press, 1987.

Jabes, J. "Individual Decision Making." In A. G. McGrew and M. J. Wilson (Editors), *Decision Making: Approaches and Analysis*. Manchester: Manchester University Press, 1982.

Jacobson, I.; Ericsson, M.; and Jacobson, A. *The Object Advantage: Business Process Reengineering with Object Technology*. New York: Addison Wesley, 1995.

Jay, A. *Management and Machiavelli*. New York: Benton Books, 1967.

Johansson, H.; McHugh, P.; Pendlebury, A. J.; and Wheeler, W. A., III. *Business Process Reengineering: Breakpoint Strategies for Market Dominance*. Chichester: John Wiley, 1993.

Jones, M. "Don't Emancipate, Exaggerate: Rhetoric, 'Reality' And Reengineering." In R. Baskerville, S. Smithson, O. Ngwenyama and J. I. DeGross (Editors), *Transforming Organizations with Information Technology*. Amsterdam: North Holland, 1994.

Kets de Vries, M., and Miller, D. *The Neurotic Organization*. London: Jossey-Bass, 1984.

Klein, M. "Reengineering Methodologies And Tools. *Information Systems Management*, Spring 1994, pp. 31-35.

Latour, B. "The Powers Of Association." In J. Law (Editor), *Power, Action and Belief: A New Sociology of Knowledge*. London: RKP, 1986.

Latour, B. *"The Prince* for Machines As Well As Machinations." In B. Elliott (Editor), *Technology and Social Process.* Edinburgh: Edinburgh University Press, 1988.

Latour, B. "Technology Is Society Made Durable." In J. Law (Editor), *A Sociology of Monsters.* London: Routledge, 1991.

Latour, B. *We Have Never Been Modern.* Hemel Hempstead, England: Harvester Wheatsheaf, 1993.

Law, J. (Editor). "Introduction: Monsters, Machines And Socio-technical Relations." In J. Law (Editor), *A Sociology of Monsters.* London: Routledge, 1991a.

Law, J. (Editor). *A Sociology of Monsters.* London: Routledge, 1991b.

Ligus, R. G. "Methods to Help Reengineer Your Company fr Improved Agility." *Industrial Engineering,* January, 1993.

Lindblom, C. "The Science of Muddling Through." *Public Administration Review,* Volume 19, 1959, pp. 79-99.

Longman Dictionary of Psychology and Psychiatry. London: Longman, 1984.

MacKenzie, D. *Inventing Accuracy: a Historical Sociology of Missile Guidance.* Cambridge: MIT Press, 1990.

Markus, M. L. "Power, Politics and MIS Implementation." *Communications of the ACM,* Volume 26, Number 6, 1983, pp. 430-444.

Marx, K. *Capital,* Volume 1. London: Lawrence and Wishart, 1954.

Mintzberg, H. "The Fall And Rise Of Strategic Planning." *Harvard Business Review,* January-February 1994, pp. 107-114.

Moad, J. "Does Reengineering Really Work?" *Datamation,* August 1, 1993, pp. 22-28.

Morris and Brandon. *Reengineering Your Business.* London: McGraw Hill, 1993.

Padulo, R. "Reengineering Management Learning." *Templeton College Management Research Paper.* Oxford: Templeton College, 1995.

Pearson, J. "Business Process Management." Unpublished lecture notes, Pearson Associates, Old Shire Lane, Chorley Wood, Hertfordshire, 1993.

Peters, T. *Thriving on Chaos.* New York: Harper and Row, 1987.

Pettigrew, A. *The Awakening Giant: Continuity and Change in ICI.* Oxford: Blackwell and Sons, 1985

Pettigrew, A. *The Politics of Organizational Decision-Making.* London: Tavistock, 1973

Pfeiffer, J. *Power in And Around Organizations.* New York: Free Press, 1992.

Preece, I., and Edwards, C. *A Survey of BPR Activity in the United Kingdom.* Unpublished Research Paper. Cranfield: Cranfield University Business School, 1993.

Price Waterhouse. *Price Waterhouse Review, 1994/5.* London: Price Waterhouse, 1994.

Robey, D., and Markus, M. L. "Rituals In Information System Design." In J. Wetherbe, V. Dock and S. Mandell (Editors), *Readings in Information Systems.* St. Paul: West Publishing, 1988

Short, J., and Venkatraman, N. "Beyond Business Process Redesign: Redefining Baxter's Business Network." *Sloan Management Review,* Fall 1972, pp. 7-21.

Simon, H. A. *Administrative Behavior.* New York: Macmillan, 1947.

Spurr, K.; Layzell, P.; Jennison, L.; and Richards, N. *Software Assistance for Business Re-Engineering.* Chichester: John Wiley and Sons, 1993.

Stewart, R. "Managerial Behaviour." *Templeton College Research Paper* MRP94/1. Oxford: Templeton College, 1993.

Strathern, M. *Partial Connections.* Baltimore: Rowman and Little, 1991.

Thackray, J. "Fads, Fixes and Fictions." *Management Today,* June 1993, pp. 41-43.

Walsham, G. *Interpreting Information Systems in Organizations.* Chichester: Wiley and Sons, 1993.

Willcocks, L. "Business Process Reengineering: A Survey of Current Practice." In D. Harvey (Editor), *Reengineering: The Critical Success Factors,* Second Edition. London: Business Intelligence, 1995a.

Willcocks, L. "False Promises or Delivering the Goods? Recent Findings on the Economics and Impact of Business Process Reengineering." Paper in *The Second IT Evaluation Conference,* Henley: Henley Management College, July, 1995b.

Willcocks, L. *Information Management: Evaluation of Information Systems Investments.* London: Chapman and Hall, 1994.

Willcocks, L.; Currie, W.; and Mason, D. *Information Politics: People and Technology in the Workplace.* Henley: Alfred Waller, 1996.

Willcocks, L., and Smith, G. "IT-Enabled Business Process Reengineering: Organizational and Human Resource Dimensions." *Journal of Strategic Information Systems*, Volume 4, Number 2, 1995 (forthcoming).

Winner, L. "Do Artifacts Have Politics?" In D. MacKenzie and J. Wajcman (Editors), *The Social Shaping of Technology*. Milton Keynes: Open University Press, 1985.

Wolin, S. "On The Theory And Practice Of Power." In J. Arac (Editor), *After Foucault — Humanistic Knowledge, Postmodern Challenges*. New Brunswick: Rutgers University Press, 1991.

Yin, J. Z. "Managing Process Innovation Through Incremental Improvements: Empirical Evidence in the Petroleum Refining Industry." *Technological Forecasting and Social Change*, Volume 47, 1994, pp. 265-76.

About the Authors

Keith Grint is a lecturer in Management Studies at Oxford University and a Fellow in Organizational Behaviour at Templeton College, Oxford. His previous publications include *The Sociology of Work* (1991) and *Management: A Sociological Introduction* (1995), both published by Polity Press, and *The Gender-Technology Relation* (edited with Ros Gill) (1995), published by Taylor and Francis. He is currently editing a book on leadership for Oxford University Press.

Peter Case is a Senior Lecturer in Management at the School of Business, Oxford Brookes University. His Ph.D. in Organizational Behaviour (University of Bath) was based on an ethnographic study of a blue chip company's attempt to install a mainframe computer system. Developing out of that work, his current research interests and publication activities are concerned with the human impact of IT implementations, critical studies of management innovations, issues of employing qualitative and reflexive methods in organizational research, and the study of organizational culture and symbolism.

Leslie Willcocks is Fellow in the Oxford Institute of Information Management and University Lecturer in Management Studies at Templeton College, University of Oxford. He is also Editor in Chief of the *Journal of Information Technology* and visiting professor at the University of Amsterdam. His co-authored books include *Computerising Work* (1987), *Information Management* (1984), *A Business Guide to IT Outsourcing* (1994), *Investing in Information Systems* (1995), *IT Outsourcing: Theory and Practice* (1996) and *Information Systems at Work* (1996). He has published numerous academic and refereed papers in such journals as *Harvard Business Review, Journal of Management Studies, Journal of Strategic Information Systems*, and *Long Range Planning* and has produced several research reports for major government institutions.

6

Process Reengineering, Information Technology and the Transformation of Accountability: The Remaindering of the Human Resource?

Hugh Willmott
Edward Wray-Bliss
UMIST
Manchester School of Management

Business Process Reengineering (BPR) is set to become the most influential management idea, or fad, of the 1990s.[1] Most commentaries on Business Process Reengineering are written by enthusiasts, consultants or journalists in the business and computing journals (see Grey and Mitev [1994] and Jones [1994a] for extensive citations of these). When, more rarely, BPR is subjected to critical scrutiny, attention has been focused upon such questions as its distinctiveness (e.g., Rigby 1993; Grint 1994), its practical application (e.g., Taylor and Williams 1993) or its relevance and implications for specific practices (e.g., Computer Supported Cooperative Work: Pycock et al. 1993) and specialisms (e.g., Human Resource Management: Willmott 1994). In this paper, we are more concerned with the *ethos and ideals* favoured, conveyed and promoted by leading proponents of BPR.

A focus upon BPR's ethos and ideals locates our analysis in an emergent literature that examines the disciplinary significance of management theories, programs and techniques (e.g., Rose 1990; Willmott 1993) — theories that involve not only "the re-imagination of the organization" (du Gay and Salaman 1992, p. 616) but also the re-imagination of the employee. Whatever view is taken about its distinguishing features or its effectiveness, BPR contributes to a climate of thinking about, accounting for, and mobilising people and change in organizations and society:

> Much of the current hysteria over labels such as "the new organization" and "empowerment" can be seen as an attempt to lend new energy to the collective

---

[1]Jones (1994a, p. 1) reports that it has ben described in *Business Week* as "the hottest management concept since the quality movement" and that the *Financial Times* quotes forecasts of a worldwide market for BPR products growing at a rate of 46% per annum to reach $2.2 billion by 1996.

enterprises that have recently found themselves in a period of doubt and realignment. In their daily practice, managers *use* labels and concepts as they see fit, as part of their ongoing use of language to coax, inspire, demand and otherwise produce action in their organizations. [Eccles and Nohria 1990, pp. 29-30]

The study of how ideas are translated, through the media of managerial and organizational ideologies, into actions is an important focus for empirical research into how BPR is being interpreted and applied in organizations. As we note in our concluding remarks, there is a need for in-depth empirical research on the application of BPR — especially studies that are attentive to how its claims and prescriptions are interpreted within the social and organizational aspects of its use, and which can thereby provide a critical perspective upon its effects upon people as well as its consequences for social and cultural development as well as for productivity and employment. However, it is also important to scrutinise the contents of new ideas or fads, not least because they at once articulate, amplify and influence broader process of social and economic development. In effect, the gurus and consultants are the policy advisors of the modern corporation. The prognostications, prescriptions and presentations of gurus and consultants provide a major resource of meaning, identity and power for the managers of modern corporations (Knights and Morgan 1991; Hucyzynski 1993). In addition to proffering a language for interpreting what "is" happening, they prescribe for what "should" happen. It is with these ideas that academics must engage if they are to participate in the equivalent of policy debates in the field of management and organization.

To this end, the intention of this paper is to contribute to a process of reflection upon the assumptions and prescriptions contained within BPR, focusing specifically upon the claims of its leading proponents, notably Michael Hammer, to promote a new form of employee accountability. We begin by locating BPR within the culture of enterprise, including its advocacy of IT to secure dramatic, revolutionary change that liberates work from bureaucratic custom and practice. Drawing upon a framework developed within the work of du Gay and Salaman, we consider BPR's technological, political and ethical dimensions. We then utilise the distinction between hierarchical and socializing accountability, devised by Roberts (1991) and elaborated by Munro and Hatherley (1993), to scrutinise BPR's claims to establish a new and seemingly empowering form of accountability. Returning to the work of du Gay and Salaman, we then identify a number of internal contradictions within BPR which suggest that the translation of its prescriptions into practice is likely to encounter unanticipated difficulties and resistance. Such "problems" arise, we argue, not only from the endemic difficulty of providing a complete or comprehensive representation of the complex, politically-charged world of organizations but, more importantly, because the realization of BPR's ambitions is contingent upon employees' unequivocal identification with the values of a putative culture of enterprise. However, enterprise culture is increasingly a target of critique as diverse social and economic problems are traced to its unbridled and uncaring reliance upon market mechanisms in the name of "meeting the demands of the 'sovereign' consumer" (Keat 1991, p. 3). In a situation of high unemployment that is likely to continue, in part as a consequence of reengineering programs, employees may be frightened into complying with the radical changes advocated by leading BPR gurus, especially if, paradoxically, these changes are perceived to secure their prospects of employment. However, BPR requires more than compliance: it demands a commitment from staff to realize organizational objectives that are assumed to be shared, unproblematically, by all employees.

1. BPR AND THE CULTURE OF ENTERPRISE

The domain of management and organization has been repeatedly assailed by prescriptions for change — sometimes characterized as fashions and fads — that revolutionize the organization of collective productive activity or, at least, to replenish the portfolio of managerial rhetoric. Historically, each new prescription for enhancing the efficiency and/or effectiveness of productive activity leaves an imprint upon our thinking about management and organizations. "Scientific management" (Taylor 1911) encouraged and legitimized the idea that employees should be understood and treated as rational economic beings who willingly execute instructions so long as a rational schedule of material rewards activated their compliance. "Human relations" ideas (e.g., Mayo 1949) have suggested that productive activity is impeded so long as the design of work disregards the sentiments of employees. Subsequently, interpersonal processes and sociotechnical arrangements were identified as a neglected area of managerial surveillance and expertise (e.g., Likert 1961; Trist et al. 1963). More recently, the advocates of Corporate Culturism have sought to confine or sequester (Giddens 1991) the possibilities for self-actualization (e.g., McGregor 1960) within a single, uniform culture in which each employee is encouraged to identify with, and demonstrate a commitment to, values ascribed by top management (e.g., Peters and Waterman 1982; see Willmott 1993).

Current managerial thinking and theorizing has been distinguished by an emphasis upon the development of organizational cultures and personnel that are "enterprising" in the sense that they are geared to meeting the demands of the sovereign consumer who is deemed to be increasingly knowledgeable, discerning, and spoiled for choice. Free markets, flexibility, the freedom of capital to introduce new technologies and shed labor, the right of employers to use workers free from "archaic" restrictions from unions, legislation, or bureaucracy, and the search for individual satisfaction through competition — these are the slogans that resonate strongly with the neo-liberal, non-interventionist governments of most advanced capitalist societies, especially the US and the UK. The enterprise politics of the New Right and managerial developments such as Excellence, TQM and, most recently, BPR are inseparably linked and mutually reinforcing. Only a free market system allows purchasers (customers buying products, organizations buying supplies, or producers buying labor) to secure the best possible deal. Regulations impose restrictions and inhibit flexibility, a point made by Hammer in relation to the need for a "free" labor market: "I don't want to have to write a job description for a position in order to get it by some government bureaucrat to make sure I am being fair in its application. I don't want to define what the job requires" (Hammer in Karlgaard 1993, p. 74). Within this political framework of unrestricted competition and free markets, the Customer Is King; and there is no bigger customer than the mass purchaser of labor and supplies: the reengineered organization.

With regard to contemporary recipes and programs of organizational change, du Gay and Salaman note how they are permeated by the idea of the sovereign consumer:

The common element of these programs is that they argue the need to impose the model of the customer-supplier relationship on internal organizational relations, so departments now behave as if they were actors in a market, workers treat each other as if they were customers, *and customers are treated as if they were managers.* [1992, p. 619, emphasis added)]

TQM, the widely adopted recipe for organizational change prior to the advent of BPR, celebrates the sovereignty of the external customer as employees are enjoined continuously to develop ways of improving the quality of products or services. Within its recipe, TQM urges employees to look upon each other as links in a customer-supplier chain, with each "customer" monitoring the quality of its "supplier," including the demands that employees make upon employers. The customization of work is reaffirmed in BPR:

The conflict is now between labor and the customer. In the old days, when you had the company — the supplier — controlling the market, Samuel Gompers could go to the manager and get red in the face and say, "Damn it, give me more or I'm going to fight you." That was reasonable. Today, the manager says, "What are you arguing with me for. Go talk to the customer. If I give you more, I have to raise prices, and the customer will leave us both. [Hammer quoted in Kiely 1994]

In a global market, where only the fittest are deemed to survive, the retention of practices that deny the sovereignty of the customer is said to spell death for corporate dinosaurs: there is always another company waiting to "build a wall" in front of you to leave you "lying injured on the ground" (Hammer and Champy 1993, p. 35). Managers are told that they simply *must* reengineer. Organizing around processes of value to the customer, in contrast, it is claimed, eliminates all the old problems as it improves "innovation, speed, service and quality," the corporate "watchwords of the new decade" (Hammer 1990, p. 104).

1.1   The Accountability Revolution?

The most recent and currently fashionable recipe for managerial success is Business Process Reengineering (or Redesign/Transformation, etc.). The promise of BPR, as articulated by Michael Hammer, is to achieve revolutionary organizational change. This it aspires to realize by reintegrating and compressing work that is fragmented within a specialized, bureaucratic division of labor. According to its leading proponents, BPR heralds a "new beginning."[2]

For two hundred years people have founded and built companies around Adam Smith's brilliant discovery that industrial work should be broken down into its simplest and most basic *tasks*. In the postindustrial age we are now entering, corporations will be founded and built around the idea of reunifying those tasks into coherent business *processes*. [Hammer and Champy 1993, p. 2]

---

[2]As the advocates of BPR attempt to out-hype their predecessors and rivals, they place themselves, in effect, *outside of history* (see Grint 1994).

Reengineering, its advocates contend, is not just another short-lived management fad (Hammer and Champy 1993, Filipowski 1993). Nor is it a continuation of historically rooted industrial practice. Rather it is *the* "radical," "fundamental," and "dramatic" solution to corporate under-competitiveness (Hammer and Champy 1993, p. 33). Continuing compliance with the principles established by Adam Smith, albeit with incremental improvements secured by the likes of TQM and JIT, is identified as the principal cause of competitive decline since they cannot deliver the "quantum leaps in performance" (Hammer 1990, p. 105) necessary to compete successfully. Organizing around tasks, it is argued, can only perpetuate endemic problems of sectarian thinking, inflexibility, blurring of accountability, hierarchy, bureaucracy and poor service. As Hammer has reportedly encapsulated the philosophy of BPR: "Its basically taking an ax and a machine gun to your existing organization" (*Computerworld*, 24 January 1994 cited in Strassmann 1994, p. 37).

By obliterating established divisions of labor in favor of a "process-oriented" approach, BPR claims to provide the ultimate solution to the perennial managerial problem of employee recalcitrance: the inclination of employees to define and pursue their own (sectional) goals and interests rather than realize the goals that are ascribed to them by corporate management. In the traditional organization, Hammer declares,

> people tend to substitute the narrow goals of their particular department for the larger goals of the *process as a whole*. When work is handed off from person to person and unit to unit, delays and errors are inevitable. *Accountability blurs, and critical issues fall between the cracks.* [1990, p. 108, emphasis added]

To repeat, Hammer is dismissive of efforts to make incremental improvements in established work practices, as commended by the purveyors of TQM, or even of using new technology to automate such practices, as widely advocated by (J)IT specialists. By harnessing the power of information and communication technologies (ICTs), *BPR envisions a completely new approach to the organization of work in which employee accountability changes from hierarchy to collegiality, and in which outputs are governed by processes that are geared exclusively to the "needs" of customers.* In the reengineered organization, the substitution of narrow goals for larger ones is no longer deemed to be a problem because work is (re)designed around the process as a whole rather than around individual tasks. In principle, at least, the work of each employee is then totally integrated into the business process so that s/he is by definition creating "an output that is of value to the customer" (Hammer and Champy 1993, p. 35). Organizational redesign around processes places "accountability to the customer" right at the heart of work.

In response to the claims made for BPR by its leading advocates, various commentators have suggested that they are absurdly inflated and grandiose. For example, Rigby (1993, p. 25), argues that BPR is not so much "a spanking new discovery" (any pun intended?) as a re-invention and recombination of elements of the managerial imagination — notably, the idea that successful operation in a turbulent, uncertain environment requires a more organic, flatter organization and, relatedly, that in a world of saturated markets and excessive productive capacity, companies must become more customer-focused. Grint identifies historical examples of all of Hammer and Champy's professedly "revolutionary" proposals, finding that "few, if any, are actually innovations, least of all radical innovations that would support the hype" (1994, p. 191). We are also persuaded that there is nothing radically new about the elements of BPR. However, we suggest that the *combination and thrust* of its elements is distinctive and challenging, not least because BPR (I) makes central the role of information and communication technology in programs of organizational change that emphasize the importance of "customer focus" and (ii) bucks the recent trend toward an ideology of increased employee involvement in organizational change (e.g., in Excellence and TQM) as it reaffirms a Taylorist or Fordist ideology in which employees are slotted into reengineered systems — an interpretation that is supported by commentators who usefully identify links between BPR and the tenets of Industrial Engineering (e.g., Wilkinson 1991). A further differentiating feature of BPR, at least in the work of (aptly named) Hammer is the use of aggressive and violent language to communicate the message (see Strassmann 1984). We now seek to expand upon this claim by examining BPR in the light of the "technological," "political" and "ethical" dimensions of enterprise culture identified by du Gay and Salaman (p. 630).

1.2   Technology in BPR

Du Gay and Salaman draw upon the work of Laclau (1990) to suggest that the discourse of enterprise emerged during the 1980s as a "nodal point" which simultaneously brought together and served to articulate diverse complaints about social institutions and offered a program for remedying their deficiencies. By forging a series of linkages between the "technological, the "political" and the "ethical," enterprise discourse is understood to provide "a seemingly coherent design for the radical transformation of social, cultural and economic arrangements, and a seductive ethics of the self" (du Gay and Salaman 1992, p. 630). By focusing in turn upon the "technological," the "political" and the "ethical," we suggest that, in the sphere of work and organization, BPR operates in a similar fashion.

When exploring the technological dimension of enterprise culture within organizations, du Gay and Salaman (pp. 624, 629; see also du Gay 1991, p. 50) refer exclusively to social technologies, such as de-layering, the creation of project teams, quality circles, assessment centers, appraisal systems and so on. We have already noted that BPR incorporates or accommodates many of these technologies. In addition, it identifies *information technology* as the facilitator of innovation and change. In contrast to the champions of Excellence and TQM who identify *social* technologies as principal means whereby "various authorities seek to shape, normalize and instrumentalize the conduct of persons in order to achieve the ends they postulate as desirable" (du Gay and Salaman 1992, p. 629), much of the BPR literature adopts an "essentially technical model of IS and organizations" (Jones 1994b, p. 357),[3] in which *ICTs* basically drive the reengineered effort. Hammer for instance elevates ICTs to the status of being *"the* critical enabler" of reengineering (Hammer in Karlgaard 1993, p. 74, emphasis added). It is information

---

[3]It should be noted that some authors have identified various "strands" of BPR (e.g., Jones 1994b); not all BPR proponents, for instance, stress the role of ICTs to the same degree. BPR is not a perfectly coherent ideology, and contradictions can be found between different accounts of BPR and even within one account or book (e.g., Hammer and Champy 1993) and certainly between different "reengineered" organizations. However, despite the differences in emphasis between different accounts, we believe that the ethos and ideals of BPR can still be identified and that these ethos and ideals are a product of, and contributor to, the wider "culture of enterprise" within which BPR is inescapably bound. For the purposes of such an analysis of the ideals and ethos of BPR, therefore, we treat BPR as consistent.

technology, not workers, managers or customers etc, which "*permits* companies to reengineer business processes" (Hammer and Champy 1993, p. 83).

For Hammer (1990, p. 104), information technology and reengineering are virtually synonymous: reengineering means using "the power of modern information technology to radically redesign our business processes," an equivalence that is not entirely surprising given Hammer's background in Computer Science and the suggestion that the IT industry created the BPR market (Earl and Khan 1994, p. 22). Technology, rather than the interpretation of its value and role developed by human beings, is identified as the principal driver of change — a view that is most forcefully expressed in an interview with Hammer published in *Forbes Magazine* (Karlgaard 1993, p. 75):

> It is my firm belief that we have not even scratched the surface of what informa-
> tion technology is going to do to organizations and businesses. We're going to
> look back 50 years from now and laugh at everything that's been done with
> computers today. We're going to say, That's what they thought computers were
> for? What simpletons!

For the leading advocates of BPR, the development and application of Information and Communication Technologies (ICTs) is productive of new ways of organizing that elicit, or at least provide the conditions of possibility for, the full emergence of (more) enterprising employees who are liberated by ICTs from the (bureaucratic) custom and practice that, Hammer and Champy contend, has dominated work organization since Adam Smith established the principle of the division of labor in the *Wealth of Nations*.

> When a process is reengineered, jobs evolve from narrow and task-orientated to
> multidimensional. People who once did as they were instructed now make
> choices and decisions on their own instead. Assembly-line work disappears.
> Functional departments lose their reasons for being. Managers stop acting like
> supervisors and behave more like coaches. Workers focus more on the custom-
> ers' needs and less on their bosses'. Attitudes and values change in response to
> new incentives. Practically every aspect of the organization is transformed, often
> beyond recognition. [Hammer and Champy 1993, p. 65]

Of course, the idea that ICTs are capable of transforming work has stimulated the managerial imagination for a decade or more. By suggesting how the power of ICTs might be harnessed to secure this transformation, BPR appeals to, and inflates, this element of the imagination in a way that resonates strongly with contemporary anxieties and opportunities. Instead of pursuing productivity and flexibility gains incrementally through the refined management of people, for example, through "better human relations" or the development of a "stronger culture," radical improvements are promised primarily through the effective use of ICTs — the technical fix — to reengineer business processes. In sum, BPR is presented/marketed as the vanguard of a revolution that mobilizes the power of ICTs to liberate organizations from "the assumptions inherent in Adam Smith's industrial paradigm" (Hammer and Champy 1993, p. 49). Instead of promoting "Human Relations" and "Corporate Culturism" to produce incremental gains in competitive advantage, elements of their philosophies are appropriated as a means of realizing the full potential of BPR once the reengineered systems have been designed and "put in place."

1.3   Politics in BPR

In common with other strands of contemporary managerial theory, such as Excellence and TQM, BPR celebrates the idea of free markets and unrestricted competition. The unconstrained discipline of the market is assumed to be most compatible with the full flowering of enterprise culture to which reengineering is intended to make a "quantum leap" contribution. According to Hammer, "You are forced to do reengineering because of your competition, your customers and where your market is headed" (Hammer in Karlgaard 1993, p. 74). This quote highlights the importance of competition and markets to BPR. However it should not be thought that BPR is a passive follower of competition. Nor is competition regarded as an unfortunate evil that must be accommodated. Reengineering professes to address, and even solve, the problems organizations currently face as a consequence of (destructive and inefficient) restricted competition. For BPR, competition is unquestionably *desirable* (Grey and Mitev 1994) since it means that only the worlds best organizations survive: "Good performers drive out the inferior, because the lower price, highest quality, the best service available from any one of them soon becomes the standard for all competitors" (Hammer and Champy 1993, p. 21).

To realize this vision, markets must be cleansed of bureaucracy, legislation and other controls. Just as individual consumers in this "age of the customer" (Hammer 1990, p. 104) tell suppliers "what they want, when they want it, how they want it, and what they will pay" (Hammer and Champy 1993, p. 18), so too should the leaders of organizations decide *unilaterally* how work is to be organized, who stays and who goes, and how those that stay are to be rewarded. Control over the big issues of organizational life (such as who is to have a job, what job, and for how long) is unequivocal, non-negotiable and *rightfully* (we might also add "tyrannically") vested in senior positions within the hierarchy.

At the same time, the individualizing ethic promoted by the management techniques of the 1980s — notably TQM, which institutionalizes employee self-surveillance, and Corporate Culturism, which expects each individual to exercise discretion in ways that are consistent with a set of corporate values — is consolidated and extended in BPR by its professedly revolutionary approach to organization in which such virtues can, at last, be fully realized. In common with previous techniques, BPR aspires to reinforce the (bourgeois humanist) representation of individuals as essentially free agents who crave greater freedom for self-expression and autonomy by equating the satisfaction of these cravings with unconditional commitment to, and participation in, the realization of its Brave Productive Regime. Becoming a "better" person is equated with becoming a more fulfilled employee and becoming a more fulfilled employee is conditional upon embracing the new working practices of BPR. In BPR, self-realization is represented as a process in which individual employees identify themselves as sovereign consumers of employment opportunities that can "better" the individual self.[4]

---

[4] Or, as du Gay and Salaman (p. 627) put it, "The employee, just as much as the sovereign consumer, is represented as an individual in search of meaning and fulfilment, looking to 'add value' in every sphere of existence."

BPR is a radical intensifier of competition which owes its existence and appeal to a broader enterprise discourse that celebrates unrestricted, free market, competition. It is the claim to provide such "benefits" that, perversely, endows BPR with the moral authority to impel managers to use unbridled managerial control to impose its requirements. As du Gay and Salaman (p. 623) note, corporations become truly enterprising only when they fully adhere to "the moral obligation...to become obsessed with staying close to the customer, and thus with achieving continuous business improvement." The champions of BPR endorse this view but argue that *only the reengineering* of business processes enables the managers of modern corporations to discharge their "moral obligations." In sum, and in common with other contemporary management techniques, it mobilizes the language of markets to intensify competitive pressures within as well as between organizations. Reengineering, done well, is understood to transform the basis of competition in an industry (Hammer in Filipowski 1993, p. 48L) and a prime reason for reengineering is the creation of a business environment that will intimidate prospective new entrants and severely disadvantage established competitors.

1.4   Ethics in BPR

The "politics" in BPR is aligned with a particular representation of people's desires, values, actions and relationships: the dimension of "ethics." In BPR, workers are understood to occupy a position subservient to the needs of the market and the need of the organization to be competitive. In this way the "75% reduction in head count" at Ford can be celebrated and justified because it benefits the customer and meets the organization's need to be competitive more effectively than the mere 20% redundancies conventional programs would have provided (Hammer 1990, p. 106). This suggests that BPR represents employees principally as a cost to be cut. However, as we shall see, BPR also represents workers as autonomous individuals who find fulfilment, satisfaction and a sense of meaning through work in the reengineered firm. Indeed, employee empowerment and satisfaction are claimed to be "unavoidable consequences of reengineered processes" (Hammer and Champy 1993, p. 71).

When addressing the issue of employment (in)security, which is a consequence of many reengineering programs, individuals are informed that they can reduce the risk of redundancy by ensuring that they acquire the attitudes (e.g., flexibility, mobility) and skills (continuous extension and retraining) relevant for reengineered organizations. The message to remaining staff is that the redundancy of fellow employees is not problematic because that is some *other person's* plight; it doesn't, or shouldn't, affect their *personal* situation (indeed, it may be construed to enhance it) any more than the failure of another consumer to buy an item affects *their* capacity to purchase. The positive relationship between workers and work, like the "need" to make redundancies is represented in terms of the atomized yet equitable operation of the market. Empowerment, autonomy and a sense of identity are treated as commodities, offered for sale by the gurus of reengineering and the leaders of reengineering programs, purchasable by the worker's labor, and purchased *individually*: work in the reengineered firm is an individual act of acquiring skill and deriving meaning. As Grint (1994, p. 198) has observed, the world of reengineering presents golden "opportunities for bootstrappers": "The reengineered future is not the land of the sullen or lethargic employee but the dedicated corporate warrior; it is a reengineered neo-feudalism, a total way of life."

Those who are "reengineered out" get little attention from the proponents of BPR. According to its market logic, the "rejects" simply failed to make the grade: they failed to acquire what the reengineered organization wanted to buy. Those who can sell what the organization wants to buy are valued, but all others are marginalized and excluded. The marginalization of the "value-less" — those lacking the requisite purchasing power — is shamelessly displayed in Hammer's characterization of those made redundant by reengineering as "semiliterate" and/or "lazy" (Hammer in Karlgaard 1993, p. 70).

1.5   Discussion

Like enterprise discourse, BPR collects elements of the technological, political and ethical into a "powerful critique of contemporary institutional reality" (du Gay and Salaman 1992, p. 630) as it purports to present a new and radical challenge to the bureaucratic principles and practices that, since Adam Smith's *Wealth of Nations*, have dominated the organization of work. However, BPR does not seek to challenge Smith's liberal political philosophy in which the ends of increased productivity, cheaper products and greater profits justify the means of skill fragmentation and degradation. Rather BPR promises to revitalize the means of finally fulfilling Smith's agenda by using a combination of new technology, integrated work processes and "empowered" employees to obliterate inefficiencies incurred by highly fragmented and specialized divisions of labor.

The vision of BPR is totalizing. It aspires to realize a complete transformation of the world of work. In this process, the culture of enterprise is boosted by BPR's obliteration of elements that currently moderate and impede entrepreneurialism and the dynamic operation of markets. Overcoming the lack of reengineering is deemed to provide the means of perfecting the system so that contradictory elements are finally eliminated. Or, as Hammer (1990, p. 112) champions the BPR case for revolutionary change:

> We must have the boldness to imagine taking 78 days out of an 80-day turn-around time, cutting 75% of overhead, and eliminating 80% of errors. These are not unrealistic goals. If managers have the vision, reengineering will provide a way.

However, an unimpeded realization of the BPR vision is improbable on two counts — one transcendental, the other immanent. The transcendental reason is that reengineering discourse will never overcome its partial and perspectival quality. What du Gay (1990) has said of the enterprise discourse in contemporary society can be applied to BPR discourse: namely, that "lack of re-engineering" appears to be "a foreign body introducing corruption into the pure, sound social fabric" (p. 57). Drawing upon the ideas of Lacan, du Gay observes that "the Real" — in this case, the complexity and perversity of organizational relations — defies all attempts to represent and control it.[5] There is always a residue, or surplus, which is routinely disregarded or displaced — a residue which continuously threatens to unsettle its plausibility.

However, the lack of reengineering can also be interpreted as indicative of the limits of its fulfilment within a system where labor is treated as a disposable commodity and employees commitment to "reengineering" practices is likely to be, at best, ambivalent. The focus here is upon the immanent — *historically and materially contingent* — nature of the discourse of enterprise — a contingency which opens upon "the possibility of its transformation" (du Gay and Salaman 1992, p. 631). In this analysis, it is not simply that change is made possible by the (transcendental) impossibility of closure. In addition, the authority of a discourse is deemed to be contingent upon the context of its emergence — for example, the ascendence of enterprise discourse is deemed to be "predicated upon the visible failure of the welfare state's own utopia" (du Gay and Salaman 1992, p. 631). If this is so, then it is to be anticipated that any perceived failure of the enterprise (or reengineering) discourse to realize its own utopia will actively support the emergence, and boost the credibility of, an alternative discourse that might attribute failure to "a lack of community." This possibility is nicely illustrated in Watson's (1994) *In Search of Management*, where one manager reports that he had no answer to an operator who asked how he (the operator) is expected to give of his best when he could be made redundant at any minute. As the manager recounted this episode to Watson:

> How the hell can you preach this flexibility, this development, at the same time as you are getting rid? As someone said to me yesterday — an operator — "Why am I in here now doing the best I can, getting this product out, when tomorrow morning you can give me a brown envelope." I had no answer. [Watson 1994, p. 125]

In the following section, we seek to make more transparent and accessible for debate the formulation and treatment of people by BPR. We take this as a focus because, in common with previous programs for organizational change, this is where the realization of the pristine technicist vision is most likely to encounter stubborn "residues" (see above) that it will struggle to neutralize or absorb. BPR purports to advance a shift away from hierarchical toward more horizontal and egalitarian forms of accountability, where managers are "coaches" not bosses. But, as we shall see, for all its shimmering humanistic rhetoric of empowerment, Hammer's formulation of BPR is founded upon an authoritarian negation of any shift in which employees are identified and treated as factors of production who must simply accede to the "obliteration" of established practices (Hammer 1990, p. 105), including their jobs. Even for those remaining in employment, there is the prospect of an intensification of effort as elements of supervisory activity are (re)integrated into their work and the (relative) security provided by contracts tied to specific jobs is eroded by pressures to work more flexibly and cooperatively. Indeed, as we noted earlier, the BPR call to obliterate established practices includes the obliteration of regulations that provided employees with a valued measure of security and predictability.

---

[5]Every attempt to reflect the "Real" is thwarted by what Laclau and Mouffe (1985) and Laclau, (1990) term an antagonism — a kernel at the heart of such efforts to reflect the "Real" that is resistant to "symbolic integration-dissolution" (Žižek 1989, p. 3, cited in du Gay 1991, p. 57; see also Žižek 1990 in Laclau 1990). It is this antagonism, they argue, that is productive of residues that make possible the co-existence and plausibility of other counter discourses.

2. ACCOUNTABILITY IN THE REENGINEERED CORPORATION

The nature of employee accountability, according to the BPR gurus, is radically changed in a reengineered organization. These "radical" changes in accountability threaten to transform not just organizational structure, patterns of authority, or even managerial thinking, but also the "economic citizenship" of the worker (Miller and O'Leary 1993, p. 197). It is claimed that the reengineered corporation frees workers from the outdated, constraining practices of traditional organizations. Employees are co-equal rather than coerced. Employees control their own work and support their teams of co-equal colleagues. Few managers exist, and those that do act as coaches, helping teams and individuals to achieve the best results they can. Workers are not accountable to managers, but instead have a responsibility to the team. By promoting such changes, BPR's new ideal of accountability can be seen to provide "an organizing rationale that seeks to link together the opportunities and demands of new technology with a revised perception of the relationship that individuals are to have with their productive activity" and an image of organizations where "workers and managers alike are to have an *active and engaged* relationship with the productive machine" (Miller and O'Leary 1993, p. 199, emphasis added).

A casual reading of the writings of BPR gurus, and a cursory examination of the "active" and "engaged" relationships which these writings espouse, might suggest a degree of rapprochement with progressive or even leftist critiques of work organization (e.g., Benson 1977; Heydebrand 1983). Certainly, there is some shared usage of key terms: Hammer and Champy's text is subtitled *"A Manifesto for Business Revolution"* (emphasis added), and unsparing use is made of emancipatory/egalitarian sounding terminology, such as "radical change," "fundamental transformation," "empowered workers," etc. However, the similarities are deceptive. To elaborate this claim, it is helpful to draw upon Roberts' distinction between two ideal-typical systems of accountability: hierarchical and socializing. By doing this, it will be argued that BPR contains the trappings of the latter but without abandoning, or even re-assessing, its commitment to reproducing the former.

2.1   From Hierarchical to Socializing Accountability?

Hierarchical accountability, Roberts argues, is associated with the creation and maintenance of an instrumental and individualistic relationship between employees. Within a system of hierarchical accountability, each employee is encouraged to show their value as a productive force; to engage in a competition for recognition and reward; and to compare and differentiate him/herself from others on the strength of productive ability or use value. The polar alternative to individualizing, hierarchical accountability is "socializing accountability." Distinguished by a strong sense of interdependence between employees — a sense that is fostered where accounts of events and actions are *collectively interpreted* rather than hierarchically imposed (Roberts 1991, p. 362). In such a system, there is a "much richer and fuller source of recognition and identity, with the relatively unguarded flow of talk drawing us into a much deeper form of mutual engagement and reciprocal recognition than a calculated conformity with others' wishes can ever secure" (Roberts 1991, p. 362).

Ethically and managerially, hierarchical accountability is problematical. It frequently operates, in unintended ways, to frustrate cooperation and mutual learning upon which a premium is placed in turbulent environments where rapid responses to changing conditions are demanded: each employee becomes preoccupied with demonstrating his or her *individual* value to the neglect of the contribution that s/he can make to the development of reciprocal understanding and collaboration. To take Adam Smith's example of pin-making, hierarchical accountability induces each employee to concentrate on increasing the speed of particular, atomized operations without regard for the overall design of the process, the quality of the product or the interdependent nature of productive activity. And, of course, it is precisely a reversal of the division of labor (with the organization of work around separate tasks and departments) and the rejection of the premise of hierarchical control (with the channeling of information, decision making and control up the hierarchy) that BPR claims to achieve (see Hammer and Champy 1993, p. 49). As Obeng and Crainer have recently written, using an exceptionally colorful metaphor

> Re-engineering seeks to solve the problems created by functional organization. It replaces the vertical axis of the hierarchy....Traditional hierarchies fall away under the burden of self-examination...the goal of re-engineering is not to flatten structures. *Talk of flat or horizontal structures still assumes the existence of a hierarchy. Instead, re-engineering produces a fist-full of dynamic processes more akin to writhing snakes.* [Obeng and Craner 1994, pp. 92-93, emphasis added]

Indeed, when reading BPR texts with their emphasis on "unavoidable empowerment," "self-disciplined workers," "teams of coequal colleagues," and accountability only to each other and the customer (Hammer and Champy 1993), it might well seem that BPR heralds the replacement of hierarchical accountability with socializing accountability. However, it is necessary to exercise a degree of reflective scepticism (Thomas 1993) on this issue before concluding that BPR broadly shares the concerns and agenda of critical studies of accountability (e.g., Roberts 1991; Miller and O'Leary 1993; Munro and Hatherley 1993; Schweiker 1993). In particular, it is relevant to take note of two conditions identified by Roberts for the development of socializing accountability. Socializing accountability, he contends, "is easiest between individuals of equal status, where hierarchy does not intervene [and it] inevitably flourishes where there is regular face-to-face contact" (p. 362).

In other words, according to Roberts, the following conditions are necessary for the development of socializing systems of accountability:

(i)   The non-intervention of hierarchy in employee relations

(ii)   Unsurveilled, face-to-face communication between employees

Likewise, Munro and Hatherley deem the replacement of hierarchical accountability to be contingent upon employee values that are not manipulated from above. Otherwise, it is possible to envisage a situation where "giving customers what they want" would stand "as a slogan, involving managers in no more than a process of imposing more "decisions" on employees in the name of consensus and in the name of the customer" (Munro and Hatherly 1993, p. 385). Thus, in addition to those conditions identified by Roberts, Munro and Hatherly identify two further conditions for the development of non-hierarchical accountability:

(iii)   No coercive manipulation of workers attitudes and beliefs to secure cultural conformity or shared values.

(iv)   No imposition of "knowledge of the customer" upon workers by management

Here, again, it might seem that these conditions are met by BPR. On the question of who has knowledge of the customer, BPR's answer is that workers have it: this knowledge is available via customer satisfaction surveys, the number and profitability of finalized deals and other measurements instantly accessible on the IT network (Hammer and Champy 1993, p. 73). On the question of shared values, it could be argued that employees are under no obligation to work for reengineered companies or to share their values. Rather, such values are voluntarily embraced, assisted by the skillful use of selection procedures, measurement schemes and payment systems. By examining more closely BPR's claims and capacity to meet the conditions for socializing accountability identified by Roberts and by Munro and Hatherly, the remainder of this section suggests why such a view cannot be sustained. As the difficulties associated with meeting the first two conditions have been repeatedly signaled in earlier sections, we revisit these very briefly before giving rather more attention to the latter two conditions.

(i)   The non-intervention of hierarchy in workers relations

Upon closer examination, BPR fails to meet the condition of non-intervention by the hierarchy in workers' relations. It is fundamentally top-down in conception and application (Hammer and Champy 1993, p. 207): the idea for reengineering is "always born in the executive suite" (p. 213) and implementation of BPR depends entirely upon the role played by senior managers: "If reengineering fails, no matter what the proximate cause, the underlying reason can invariably be traced to senior managers' inadequate understanding or leadership of the reengineering effort" (p. 213).

BPR must be imposed upon workers by those at the top of the hierarchy. There is absolutely no scope for negotiation: reengineering "never, ever happens from the bottom up" (p. 207). Resistance by workers to BPR is anticipated, as are the job losses occasioned by its implementation. But any recalcitrance must be managed and checked so that the advance of reengineering is not set back (p. 212). To use one of Michael Hammers favorite analogies, senior management may carry those wounded by reengineering for a little while but they must "shoot the dissenters" (Hammer in Karlgaard 1993, p. 71).

Nor are process teams free from the interference of hierarchy. While the relations *within* process teams are supposed to be those of "friends" of "coequal status," hierarchical interventions that determine the scope of their actions severely limits the ability of these "self-directing process teams" to actually "self-direct." The autonomy of the team is subjugated to the "boundaries of their obligations to the organization" defined by Hammer and Champy as "agreed upon deadlines, productivity goals, quality standards, etc" (1993, p. 71). However, as we will elaborate in *(iii)* below, the process of "agreeing" to these constraints occurs in an environment where managers are encouraged to allow no disagreement and to "break eggs" where necessary in order to make the "omelette" of reengineering (p. 212). The contradiction — of self-determination by hierarchical control — is articulated most explicitly by Johansson et al. (1993, p. 197) who write that "self-managing" teams "will not create and direct their own efforts; rather they will understand the role they are to play in the overall effectiveness of the process" — a process which is, of course, reengineered by those higher in the hierarchy. Despite the fine words about empowering employees, it is hard to envisage a recipe for change that is *more* in breach of the condition of "non-intervention of the hierarchy in workers relations" than BPR.

The hierarchy is perpetuated by the promotion of the values of the "self-disciplined" and "responsible" worker. Even though one of the main reasons for promoting these values is to "minimize the necessary amount of management" (Hammer in Karlgaard 1993, p. 70), thus enabling organizations to strip out managers in layers (Hammer 1990, pp. 111, 112), delayering, it is worth stressing, does not involve an attack upon the principle of hierarchy. It is, instead, an attack upon the cost of labor, albeit that this (managerial and supervisory) labor has occupied a relatively privileged and expensive position within the hierarchy. As Roberts (1991, p. 366) has noted, the hierarchy is safe in the hands of"the super individual — the leader/hero."

(ii) Unsurveilled, face-to-face, communication between workers

With regard to the second condition of socializing accountability, Roberts (1991, p. 362) highlights face-to-face communication as a condition for the emergence of socializing accountability. Hammer fails to acknowledge how communication becomes more transparent, and more open to surveillance, when it is reduced to textual or numerical images. It becomes less the product of the worker and his/her colleagues when instead it stands "autonomously over and against [the worker] who engages with them" (Zuboff 1988, p. 131). Teleconferencing, and oral/visual communication technology proposed by BPR also lacks the interpersonal, private quality of face-to-face communication. As Hammer and Champy (1993, p. 89) themselves acknowledge, "the medium is too cool, and teleconferencing is no substitute for hand-to-hand combat." There is a real and symbolic distance between the speakers which inhibits what may be said, and which generates the ever present possibility of someone "listening in" to communications. The increasing prospect of covert surveillance where new communication technologies are used has major implications for accountability.

Instantaneous and simultaneous information on workers performance, available via ICTs (and celebrated by BPR proponents — see, for example, Hammer and Champy 1993, p. 92), aligned with intense individualizing pressures, is more likely to subvert socializing systems of accountability than it is to facilitate face-to-face communication. The principle of "unsurveilled communication between workers' is most unlikely to be met in the reengineered organization. Instead, the widespread use of ICTs make it likely that hierarchical surveillance — or its internalization through processes of self-disciplining and peer monitoring of behavior — will be increased as the hierarchy uses "technology to reproduce itself" (Zuboff 1988, p. 392).

(iii)   No coercive manipulation of workers attitudes and beliefs to secure cultural conformity or "shared values"

The issue of shared values is an important one for the possibilities of accountability as well as for BPR. The removal of hierarchical accountability depends upon employees developing their own understandings in a way that is free (or as free as possible) from coercive manipulation of beliefs and values. One value that BPR requires workers to hold is the belief in the fundamental importance of the customer: "Reengineering demands that employees deeply believe that they work for their customers, not for their bosses" (Hammer and Champy 1993, p. 74).

Outside of work, employees are routinely constituted as consumers. The idea of pleasing the customer may therefore strike a responsive chord. Potentially, the belief that employees work for their customers, not for their bosses, could foster a system of accountability in which employees are more aware of the effects of their actions (e.g., psychological, ecological, etc.) upon their fellow human beings who consume what they produce, assemble and provide. However, in BPR, the justification given for employees paying more attention to customers' views is a purely instrumental, materialistic and individualistic one — namely, that "Customers pay all our salaries: I must do what it takes to please them" (p. 76).

The propensity of employee and customer to affiliate with each other (Munro and Hatherly 1993, p. 385) is not the intended effect, nor is it likely to be the most frequent consequence, of BPR. More probably, because employment relations continue to constitute employees as commodities that are purchased and disposed of by employers, employees who are disciplined and rewarded by management will try and find ways to "get around" the customer just as they used to "get around" the boss. This is because, within the enterprise discourse of BPR, the customer "is not a concrete person whose aims the (worker) is interested to satisfy" but is "an object to be manipulated" (Fromm 1942, p. 102). Exhortations to "value the customer" in the reengineered firm are liable to reinforce instrumentalism and individualism.[6] This is not least because, in BPR, pay is deemed to be the primary inducer of value-change rather than any more fundamental belief in its virtues: "the ways in which people are paid, the measures by which performance is evaluated, and so forth — are the primary shapers of employees' values and beliefs" (Hammer and Champy 1993, p. 75).

New payment and measurement systems focus upon the results of an activity (the value added to the customer) rather than the activity itself. Employees become directly accountable to customers as IT provides continuously up-dated information about "the number and profitability of finalized deals and by the quality, as reflected in customer satisfaction surveys" (p. 73). In short, the objectives and values promoted by BPR, and the methods proposed to instill them, involve the coercive manipulation of attitudes and beliefs to secure cultural conformity. They certainly do not enable employees to develop their own priorities and values. In BPR, it is management's job to "reengineer values" and to "refashion...people to enjoy the new realities" (Leigh 1994, p. 51). Or, as Hammer and Champy delineate the role of management, their task is to "educate"

---

[6]The customer focus also instilled by symbolic gestures made by senior management. To show just how committed they are to the "values by which they expect everyone to live," the "leader" should spend "an hour a week on the phone with customers" (Hammer anc Champy 1993, p. 75). This hour may well serve to reinforce values, but will it be the values proposed by Hammer and Champy? Just as likely is the response that such gestures involve a cynical, manipulative and wasteful purpose. Indeed, Hammer and Champy themselves admit that such gestures may be of little actual value to the customer.

employees "so that they can discern for themselves what the right thing is" (1993, p. 71), and make "others want what he or she [the management] wants" (p. 105).

(iv)   No imposition of "knowledge of the customer" upon workers by management

The final condition for the emergence of alternative, socializing accountability concerns "knowledge of the customer." We have just noted how, in BPR, knowledge of the customer drives and directs work. "Customers now tell suppliers what they want, when they want it, how they want it, and what they will pay" (Hammer and Champy 1993, p. 18).

Such information assumes customers comprise a homogeneous group whose "preferences" and "needs" can be sensibly generalized and summarized. However, BPR also identifies the customer as a unique individual when it demands that employees identify with, embrace and exploit this representation:

> There is no longer any such notion as *the* customer; there is only *this* customer, the one with whom a seller is dealing at the moment and who now has the capacity to indulge his or her own personal tastes....Individual customers... demand they be treated individually. [Hammer and Champy 1993, p. 18]

If each customer has his/her own individual "needs," the meaning of aggregate measures is tenuous. At the very least, it exposes the created and contestable nature of "knowledge of the customer'. More fundamentally, a system based upon responding to customers' "needs" denies the role that producers play in *creating* needs. The conception of the "sovereign consumer" "overlooks the extent to which consumers' preferences are generated and structured by the producers themselves" (du Gay and Salaman 1992, p. 619).[7] The recognition that customer "needs" are created by producers presents a considerable problem for a production system based on the idea of presenting customers with "what they want, when they want it, how they want it" (Hammer and Champy 1993, p. 18). There is also the irony of treating the customer as an atomized, sovereign consumer when BPR simultaneously commends the replacement of systems based upon a specialized division of labor in which each individual performs a specific task, with systems designed around processes and team working. An atomized representation of people is recognized by the champions of BPR as problematic and destructive when applied to the process of production where an appreciation of interdependence and, at least some form of, collectivity is instrumentally valued. But it is unblinkingly applied by BPR to customers in a way that inhibits any understanding of how "needs" are socially organized, ascribed and represented.

To conclude this section, many of the tensions and contradictions identified in BPR are common to other approaches to the (re)design of work organization that are not self-professedly "revolutionary." However, BPR presents one of the most advanced formulations, and perhaps the apotheosis, of management thinking in which "customers are made to function in the role of

---

[7]Perversely, Hammer and Champy (1993, p. 87) recognize this possibility in relation to the development of technology where they note that, "in many situations, supply creates its own demand. People do not know they want something until they see that they can have it; then they feel they can't live without it." But the insight is not translated into the sphere of mass consumption.

management" (du Gay and Salaman 1992, p. 612). The idea of consumer sovereignty legitimizes the shedding of staff and increases the vulnerability of those who remain in employment to an intensification and casualization of their work (see Frances and Garnsey [1995] for an empirical example of this in the UK supermarket sector). In the following section, we briefly examine some of the possibilities for the resistance and transformation of BPR. Rather than being a plan for resistance or a complete catalogue of the possibilities in BPR for workers and society, this section takes a brief look at some of the spaces in BPR, and in social and organizational life, where resistance can occur — spaces that remind us of the more or less conscious ability of people to, as Hammer and Champy (1993:213) put it, "drop the ball" of reengineering as we resist and disrupt the exercise of its control over our lives.

2.2 Discussion

The implications of BPR for employees today are a cause for considerable concern. In addition to the significant effects upon employee accountability and identity, there is the prospect of continuing redundancies and an intensifying spiral of competition fueled by organizational changes promoted or legitimized by the advocates of BPR (Grey and Mitev 1994). The retention of (veiled) hierarchical accountability, combined with the customerization of work, courts the danger of *the idea* of consumer sovereignty and comes to provide what Munro and Hatherly (1993, p. 385) describe as a "chopping block for harassing employees."

We have noted how BPR contains strong individualizing pressures, which are liable to be corrosive of collectivity. There are, however, also pressures that could promote an opposite reaction. BPR is presented to employees in terms of the values of *individual* empowerment and of achieving satisfaction and personal development through work.[8] However, the tensions between an espoused concern for the welfare of the individual employee and the unbridled and unapologetic use of hierarchical control to secure the brave new world of the reengineered corporation may "sensitize" employees to the *created* nature of individualism; and it may also heighten awareness of BPR's embodiment of instrumentalism and individualism rather than any other more collective or value-rational thinking. In turn, the sensitizing of employees to tensions within BPR can stimulate further reflection upon the possibility and desirability of collective organization and resistance (on the possibility of conflicts leading to reflection and change in consciousness (see Alvesson 1991, especially pp. 220-221).

Resistance may also be fostered by BPR's focus upon processes rather than tasks. When employees are responsible for performing individual tasks, the relationship between the producer and the consumer of the good or service is loosely coupled. By tightening this coupling, BPR makes the effect of any resistance more transparent and potent. When workers perform a whole process, which "by definition produces a result that somebody cares about" (Hammer and Champy 1993, p. 69), an awareness of the importance of their work for the organization is fostered, and with it an awareness of the damage that resistance (e.g., non-performance of this

---

[8]This individualized focus in BPR is not necessarily refuted by the existence of the process "team." These teams, "of one person or several" (Hammer and Champy 1993, p. 71), do exist in the reengineered firm. These teams are represented as comprising atomized individuals who each give individual effort, interact purely in terms of the process to be performed, and then disband, taking with them only what individual recognition or reward they have secured.

work) could cause. One important political benefit of a highly fragmented division of labor, as commended by Smith, Taylor and Ford, is the relative ease with which substitute factors of production can be trained,"slotted in" and, if necessary, replaced. BPR champions the loss of such benefits but continues to assume that employees will willingly operate its systems or, at least, will be persuaded by strong leadership from senior managers to do so; and that they will not, in time, deploy the increased dependence of employers upon staff to fight for an increased share of the surplus produced and/or for the extension of control over the production process.

Critical and active solidarity is by far the most effective strategy employees have devised for resisting unwelcome change, including the effects of reengineering upon employment and conditions of work. For those who remain in employment, BPR's emphasis upon "real work" — that is, work which creates value for customers, and a "work-oriented culture" (Hammer in Karlgaard 1993, p. 70) — may paradoxically enable employees to demonstrate their value and worth to the organization, and to use this to push for higher status, recognition, and reward. The emphasis upon "direct" work also places the onus upon managers to justify *their* status, authority and rewards in terms of the "value" which they "add" to the final product or service. Arguably, the position of (middle) management, at least, is considerably weakened in a climate where it is openly said that a "customer never buys a product because of the caliber of management" (p. 70) and "the last thing in the world that reengineering does is to enhance the manager's sense of self-importance, because *one of the things that reengineering does says is that managing isn't so important*' (Hammer quoted in *Across the Board*, cited in Strassmann 1994, p. 37, emphasis added). Without denying the disadvantages of reinforcing the idea of consumer sovereignty in support of demands for improved rights and recognition, the challenge to the "self-importance' of managers presents an opportunity for employees to challenge the organization of work that strict managerial prerogative or "management by right" systems do not.

However, resistance from within the reengineered organization in itself is unlikely to be sufficient to stem the tide of similar managerial techniques. Distancing from work, maximizing performance rewards, or presenting alternative definitions of "real work" or "customers needs" are unlikely significantly to affect reengineering programs.[9] Indeed, such individual strategies of resistance may be counterproductive (see Knights and Collinson 1987). If the possibilities of resistance to BPR (such as those mentioned above) are to be translated into effective opposition, individual and localized resistance must be supported by wider opposition to the discourse of enterprise.

During the 1980s, the culture of enterprise was widely championed as the way of addressing and redressing diverse, uncoordinated grievances about contemporary institutional reality, especially the lack of entrepreneurialism and the use of (slow, unresponsive) bureaucracy, rather than (speedy, adaptable) markets, to govern economic life. While the values of enterprise culture have been progressively institutionalized in numerous organizational practices that individualize employees (e.g., performance related pay) and privilege the customer (e.g., customer care programs), there is a growing sense of disenchantment with, and cynicism about, its unintended consequences (e.g., the divisiveness of performance related pay and the superficiality of such

---

[9]The limited effect of localized resistance to, and failure of, BPR can be seen in Hammer's confidence of being able to go public with the news that "70% of reengineering projects fail" without expecting this to harm BPR's start-up rate (see Moad 1993, p. 22).

"care") that are magnified in respect of the wider corrosive effects of "enterprise" and "deregulation" upon standards in public life, the additional pressures and costs placed upon families and communities, and the widespread perception that the quality of life for a majority of the customers of society, previously known as citizens, has deteriorated.

Currently, in the UK, there is widespread public unease about the restructuring of many public services and utilities — such as the health service, water, education and the postal service — around "market" lines. At the time of writing (late 1994), there has also been an (often unreported in the popular media) upsurge in strike action (for instance, among hospital staff, fire fighters, college lecturers and signal workers). These developments lend support to the view that the discourse of enterprise is not totalizing, and that spaces are forming that are hostile to its ethos and agenda. Instead of acting as a "nodal point" which connects and catalyzes a critique of contemporary institutional reality (e.g., consensus politics, lackluster economic performance), enterprise discourse is itself becoming a target of criticism by other discourses that serve to expose its "lack" and limits. Of course, it remains the case that discourse does not have to be loved for it to be hegemonic (Leys 1990 cited in du Gay and Salaman 1992, p. 630); and that, despite its partial slide from grace as a *discourse*, it has become, and continues to be, widely institutionalized in social and organizational practices. Nonetheless, there is mounting evidence of disillusionment with the fruits of the Enterprise Decade — a disillusionment that is accompanied by a degree of nostalgia for the values of "impartiality, complex equality and pluralism" (du Gay 1994, p. 144) that are attributed to more socially accountable forms of political and economic organization. Whether this disenchantment can become translated into effective political demands for a new organizational order committed to socializing accountability remains to be seen. But one thing is certain: it does not *have* to be a "reengineered future." One the other hand, without the active development of an counter discourse that questions the "truths" distilled in the received wisdom of the "enterprise culture," there is little prospect of effectively challenging its aspirations and claims, let alone translating a critical consciousness into the realization of some alternative agenda.

3. CONCLUDING REMARKS

Our concern has been to stimulate debate about the nature and value of Business Process Reengineering. Studies that associate current developments in management theory and practice with enterprise discourse and culture have been applied to show how BPR exemplifies and intensifies their technological, political and ethical aspects. Building upon this analysis, we then focused upon BPR's claims to transform processes of accountability within organizations. There we noted how BPR deploys much of the language of "socializing" accountability (Roberts 1991). Yet, upon close examination, it was found to be firmly wedded to a top-down philosophy of organizational change in which self-styled experts design the systems which employees are then expected to operate. Ideas about "empowerment" and "teamworking" are repeatedly invoked by BPR gurus. But they are employed instrumentally as a means of deriving legitimacy for a philosophy that, paradoxically, marks a reassertion of classical, mechanistic thinking as it calls for a focus upon business processes. In sum, the paper has provided analytical support for the claim, made most forcefully by the consultant Meg Wheatley, that reengineering is simply the latest "attempt, usually by people at the top, to impose new structure over old — to take one set of rigid rules and guidelines and impose them on the rest of the organization" (Wheatley in Brown

1994, p. 20). She continues: "Its a mechanical view of organizations and people — that you can 'design' a perfect solution and then the machine will comply with this new set of instructions."

BPR appropriates and reengineers the humanist rhetoric of empowerment, etc., as it reverses the nostrum that jobs should be (re)designed and improved around"the new employee" or "human resource." For BPR, the design of business processes should be determined entirely by senior managers, acting as a surrogate of the customer, who are urged to enforce their designs through strong leadership.

Other contemporary recipes for corporate success (e.g., TQM and Corporate Culturalism) share BPR's top-down belief that top management must oversee the process of culture strengthening or programs of quality management. But they also recognize that winning the hearts and minds of employees is a *precondition* of lasting organizational change. In contrast, BPR assumes that the key to increased performance is revolutionary change in the *(re)structuring* which, if it is to succeed, must be introduced rapidly and decisively in advance of securing the understanding and consent of employees; and that, with strong, determined leadership from top management, employee involvement and commitment is the inevitable outcome of the opportunities provided by the new structures. In this respect, BPR is closer to the philosophy of Taylor and Ford in its philosophy and practice of organizational change: "Don't try to forestall reengineering. If senior management is serious about reengineering they'll shoot you" (Hammer quoted in *Management Review*, cited in Strassmann 1994, p. 37). In post-Human Relations prescriptions for change, the iron fist of intensification and job insecurity is softened as well as strengthened by the velvet rhetoric of "self-actualization" and the opportunity to work for "meaning as well as money" (Peters and Waterman 1982, p. 323). In BPR, elements of this rhetoric operate very much as a supplement to, rather than an integral part of, its radical recipe for change. Humanistic elements are present in BPR not because of any commitment, however naive, to humanist values which, arguably, is evident in the writings of Peters, Kanter, Pascale, Handy, etc. Rather, they are present simply because there is an (instrumental and untheorized) awareness that the effective operation of reengineered processes depends upon the constitution of "responsible," empowered employees. But, to repeat, instead of developing a genuinely socializing approach to employee empowerment and accountability, it is assumed that manufacture of "responsible," empowered employees can be engineered, post "Revolution,"[10] by fiat.

Revitalizing the overtly coercive tradition of Taylorism, BPR expects the worker (now the employee) to adapt to the system, with the additional twist that s/he must derive satisfaction primarily from pleasing the customer (rather than from any monetary or symbolic – self-esteem – reward that working life might bring). For those remaining in employment post reengineering, there is the prospect of an intensification of effort, an impersonalization of communication required and/or a casualization of employment. For those made redundant, job prospects deteriorate and the capacity to influence the system, even as customers, is diminished. What will the next step in this discourse require in order to satisfy demands for change that seemingly are as insatiable as they are unquestioned? As Grey and Mitev (1994, p. 8) have remarked, the unquestioned God of competition

---

[10]The allusion here is to the subtitle of Hammer and Champy: "A Manifesto for Business Revolution."

locks us into a frenzied cycle of growth with desperate environmental consequences...competition does not just exist as some transcendental condition but is
the outcome of practices, of which BPR is the latest variant. It is as if a person
were running on a treadmill being constantly encouraged to run faster to keep up
with the wheel.

The gurus of BPR celebrate, yet do not acknowledge, their role in promoting enterprising
discourse and intensifying the cycle of competition. When exploring claims made by leading
advocates of BPR in relation to the development of enterprise culture and the transformation of
(employee) accountability, we noted their common appeal to the customer as the primary
justification for the imposition of market disciplines. Likewise, the additional stress, ecological
and social costs, waste and redundancies that follow from BPR's radical prescriptions for change
are all justified in the name of the sovereign consumer sovereignty. If the influence of BPR upon
the discourse of enterprise goes unchallenged, then the development of society will follow in the
wake of the reengineered organization, and the attitudes and values of BPR will become
increasingly enshrined in our social institutions and indeed in our consciousness. The prospect,
then, is of a reengineered future comprising of an increasing emphasis upon technology, markets,
competition, individualism, and hierarchical control at the expense of an appreciation of
interdependence and community: a future with spiraling numbers of people redundant and
unemployed; with people having even less control over their work and lives; and the continual
restructuring of commercial and public institutions around market lines, resulting in the near total
exclusion of all those without purchasing power: a future where the mystification of hierarchical
control and hierarchical accountability as "the customer," in the guise of the Chartered Citizen,
plays the role of surrogate manager and developer.

However, as we have argued, the discourse of BPR is unlikely to go unchallenged. Competitive
pressures and the resources mobilized by business leaders may remorselessly stimulate and fulfill
the idea of enterprise. But the politics and practices that comprise the culture of enterprise
necessarily rely upon employees, academics, politicians and consultants legitimizing and
reproducing their development or challenging their value and discrediting their application.
Fortunately, the culture of enterprise in general, and BPR's contribution to it, is not irresistibly
produced by market forces or imposed by business leaders. Academics, in particular, are in a
position to stimulate debate upon the political and ethical foundations of BPR, and their
implications for the quality of life. Given the influence of the guru literature in guiding and
legitimizing management practice, it is disappointing to note the reluctance of management
academics to engage *critically* with their ideas. With few exceptions (e.g., Huczynski 1993;
Wilkinson and Willmott 1994), their ideas have not been the subject of sustained conceptual or
empirical research and participate in discussion of what are effectively policy issues within the
sphere of work.

This silence, which may be taken as indifference if not approval, is not without its consequences.
As du Gay and Salaman (1993, p. 630, quoting Leys 1990, p. 127) have ruefully observed "in
order for an ideology/discourse to be considered hegemonic it is not necessary for it to be loved.
Rather, "it is merely necessary that it has no serious rival." For academics and practitioners who
are concerned about the current direction and probable consequences of such discourse, the

limitations and failures associated with enterprise culture and BPR open spaces for the development of rival discourses. The challenge is to contribute to a process of debate that can serve to expose and redress the absence of "a serious rival." This paper has sought to make such a contribution upon which it is hoped that others will build by undertaking empirical studies of efforts to operationalize the ideas of BPR gurus as well as by subjecting other aspects of their thinking to critical scrutiny.

4. REFERENCES

Alvesson, M. "Organizational Symbolism and Ideology." *Journal of Management Studies*, Volume 28, Number 3, 1991, pp. 207-225.

Benson, K. "Organizations: A Dialectical View." *Adminstrative Science Quarterly*, Volume 22, 1977, p. 1-21.

Brown, T. "Interview with M. Wheatley: *De*-engineering the Corporation." *Industry Week*, April 1994, pp 18-26.

du Gay, P. "Enterprise Culture and the Ideology of Excellence." *New Formations*, Volume 13, 1991, pp. 45-61.

du Gay, P. "Colossal Immodesties and Hopeful Monsters: Pluralism and Organizational Conduct." *Organization*, Volume 1, Number 1, 1994, pp. 125-148.

du Gay, P., and Salaman, G. "The Cult[ure] of the Customer." *Journal of Management Studies*, Volume 29, Number 5, 1992, pp. 615-633.

Earl, M., and Khan, B. "How New is Business Process Redesign?" *European Management Journal*, Volume 12, Number 1, 1994, pp. 20-30.

Eccles, R. G., and Nohria, N. *Beyond the Hype: Rediscovering the Essence of Management.* Boston: Harvard University Press, 1990.

Filipowski, D. "Is Reengineering More Than a Fad?" Interview with Michael Hammer, *Personnel Journal, Special Report*, December, 1993, p. 48L.

Frances, J., and Garnsey, E. "Re-Engineering the Food Chains: A Systems Perspective on UK Supermarkets and BPR." Paper presented at *EIASM Workshop on Critical Studies of Organizational and Management Innovations*, Brussels, May 8-9, 1995.

Fromm, E. *The Fear of Freedom.* London: Ark Paperbacks, 1942.

Giddens, A. *Modernity and Self-Identity: Self and Society in the Late Modern Age.* Cambridge: Polity, 1991.

Grey, C., and Mitev, N. "Reengineering Organizations: Towards a Critical Appraisal." Working Paper, Department of Management, University of Leeds, 1994.

Grint, K. "Reengineering History: Social Resonances and Business Process Reengineering." *Organization*, Volume 1, Number 1, 1994, pp. 179-201.

Hammer, M. "Reengineering Work: Don't Automate, Obliterate." *Harvard Business Review*, July/August, 1990, pp. 104-112.

Hammer, M. "ASAP Interview with Michael Hammer." *Forbes*, September 13, 1993, pp. 69-75.

Hammer, M., and Champy, J. *Reengineering The Corporation: A Manifesto for Business Revolution*. London: Nicholas Brealey, 1993.

Heydebrand, W. "Organization and Praxis." In G. Morgan (Editor), *Beyond Method*. Beverly Hills: Sage, 1983.

Hucyzynski, A. A. *Management Gurus*. London: Routledge, 1993.

Johansson, H.; McHugh, P.; Pendlebury, A. J.; and Wheeler, W. *Business Process Reengineering: Breakpoint Strategies for Market Dominance*. Chichester: John Wiley and Sons, 1993.

Jones, M. "The Contradictions of Business Process Reengineering." Paper presented at the Management Challenges in Information Systems Conference, Cranfield, July 12-13, 1994a.

Jones, M. "Don't Emancipate, Exaggerate: Rhetoric, Reality and Reengineering." In R. Baskerville, S. Smithson, O. Ngwenyama, and J. I. DeGross (Editors), *Transforming Organizations with Information Technology, IFIP Transactions 1994*. Amsterdam: North Holland, 1994b.

Karlgaard, R. "ASAP Interview with Michael Hammer." *Forbes*, September 13, 1993, pp. 69-75.

Keat, R. "Introduction: Starship Britain or Universal Enterprise." In R. Keat and N. Abercrombie (Editors), *Enterprise Culture*. London: Routledge, 1991.

Kiely, T. "A Heretics Convention." *CIO*, Volume 7, Number 19, 1994, pp. 81-86.

Knights, D., and Collinson, D. "Disciplining the Shopfloor: A Comparison of the Disciplinary Effects of Managerial Psychology and Financial Accounting." *Accounting, Organization and Society*, Volume 12, Number 5, 12,5, 1987, pp. 457-477.

Knights, D., and Morgan, G. "Strategic Discourse and Subjectivity: Towards a Critical Analysis of Corporate Strategy." *Organization Studies*, Volume 12, 1991, pp. 251-273.

Laclau, E. *New Reflections Upon the Revolution of Our Time*. London: Verso, 1990.

Laclau, E., and Mouffe, C. *Hegemony and Socialist Strategy: Towards a Radical Democratic Politics*. London: Verso, 1985.

Leigh, A. "How to Reengineer Hearts and Minds." *Management Consultancy*, May, 1994, pp. 51-54.

Leys, C. "Still a Question of Hegemony." *New Left Review*, Volume 180, 1990, pp. 119-128.

Likert, R. *New Patterns of Management*. New York: McGraw-Hill, 1991.

Mayo, E. *Social Problems of an Industrial Civilisation*. London: Routledge, 1949.

McGregor, D. *The Human Side of Enterprise*. New York: McGraw-Hill, 1960.

Miller, P., and O'Leary, T. "Accounting Expertise and the Politics of the Product: Economic Citizenship and Corporate Governance." *Accounting, Organizations and Society*, Volume 19, Number 2/3, 1993, pp. 187-206.

Moad, J. "Does Reengineering Really Work?" *Datamation*, August 1, 1993, pp. 22-28.

Munro, R., and Hatherly, D. "Accountability and the New Commercial Agenda." *Critical Perspectives on Accounting*, Volume 4, 1993, pp. 369-395.

Obeng, E., and Crainer, S. *Making Re-engineering Happen*. London: Pitman, 1994, pp. 92-93.

Peters, T. J., and Waterman, R. H. *In Search of Excellence: Lessons from America's Best-Run Companies*. New York: Harper and Row, 1982.

Pycock, J.; King, V.; Calvey, D.; Sharrock, W.; and Hughes, J. "Present in the Plan: Process Models and Ethnography." Working Paper, Department of Psychology, University of Manchester, 1993.

Rigby, D. "The Secret History of Process Reengineering." *Planning Review*, March/April, 1993, pp. 24-27.

Roberts, J. "The Possibilities of Accountability." *Accounting, Organizations and Society*, Volume 16, Number 4, 1991, pp. 335-368.

Rose, N. *Governing the Soul: The Shaping of Private Self*. London: Routledge, 1990.

Schweiker, W. "Accounting For Ourselves: Accounting Practice and the Discourse of Ethics." *Accounting, Organization and Society*, Volume 18, Number 2, 1993, pp. 231-252.

Strassman, P. A. "The Hocus-Pocus of Reengineering." *Across the Board*, Volume 34, Number 6, 1994, pp. 35-38.

Taylor, F. W. *Principles of Scientific Management*. New York: Harper, 1911.

Taylor, J. A., and Williams, H. "The Transformation Game": Information Systems and Process Information in Organizations." *New Technology and Employment*, Volume 9, Number 1, 1993, pp. 54-65.

Thomas, A. B. *Controversies in Management*. London: Routledge, 1993.

Trist, E.; Higgin, G.; Murray, H.; and Pollock, A. *Organizational Choice*. London: Tavistock, 1963.

Watson, T. *In Search of Management: Culture, Chaos and Control in Managerial Work*. London: Routledge, 1994.

Wilkinson, R. "Reengineering: Industrial Engineering in Action." *Industrial Engineering*, August 1991, pp 47-49.

Wilkinson, A., and Willmott, H. C. (Editors). *Making Quality Critical*. London: Routledge, 1994.

Willmott, H. C. "Strength is Ignorance; Slavery is Freedom: Managing Culture in Modern Organizations." *Journal of Management Studies*, Volume 30, Number 4, 1993, pp. 515-552.

Willmott, H. C. "Business Process Reengineering and Human Resource Management." *Personnel Review*, Volume 23, Number 3, 1994, pp. 34-46.

Žižek, S. *The Sublime Object of Ideology*. London: Verso, 1989.

Žižek, S. "Beyond Discourse-Analysis" in E. Laclau (1990), *New Reflections Upon the Revolution of Our Time*. London: Verso, 1990.

Zuboff, S. *In the Age of the Smart Machine*. London: Hieneman Professional Publishing Limited, 1988.

About the Authors

Hugh Willmott is Professor of Organizational Analysis in the Manchester School of Management, having previously worked at Aston Business School and Copenhagen Business School. His work has appeared in a wide range of leading management, accounting, finance, and social science journals. With David Knights, he co-founded the International Labour Process Conference, which he organized for a number of years. He is currently working on a number of conceptual and empirical projects whose common theme is the critical examination of the changing organization and management of work in modern society. His most recent books are *Labour Process Theory* (Macmillan, 1990, co-edited with David Knights), *Critical Management Studies* (Sage, 1992, co-edited with Mats Alvesson), *Skill and Consent* (Routledge, 1992, co-edited with Andrew Sturdy and David Knights), *Making Quality Critical* (Routledge, 1995, co-edited with Adrian Wilkinson), and *Managing Change, Changing Managers* (CIMA, 1995, co-authored with M. Ezzamel, S. Lilley, and C. Green). *Making Sense of Management: A Critical Introduction* (Sage, co-authored with Mats Alvesson) is to appear early in 1996.

Edward Wray-Bliss is a postgraduate researcher in the Manchester School of Management. For his Ph.D., he is developing a critique of business ethics, drawing upon Marxist and other critical theories of capitalism, structure and self, combined with an extensive critical ethnography of a well-known UK "ethical" organization. He has produced/presented papers (written jointly with Professor Hugh Willmott and jointly with André Nihjof) at the EIASM workshop and the EBEN conference. In addition to research, he runs a seminar program on an undergraduate course (directed by Professor Willmott) which critically examines current management theory and practice. Mr. Wray-Bliss is also actively involved in socialist politics, both within and outside the academic community.

7

The COMIS Plan: IT-Mediated Business Reengineering in Telecom Australia during the 1960s

Doug Hamilton
Martin Atchison
Department of Information Systems
Monash University, Caulfield Campus

Abstract

The authors suggest in this paper that the understanding of business reengineering as a current discipline can be enhanced by research into past process redesign initiatives which appear to be based on similar assumptions, particularly in relation to the role of IT as the essential enabler of change. As an instance of this approach, the paper deals with a business reengineering plan developed by Telecom Australia during the 1960s. After several years of implementation activities, the plan was abandoned in 1972. The authors conclude that the assumptions made in preparing the plan effectively precluded adequate consideration of the practical issues involved. They suggest that business enterprises undertaking major reengineering initiatives in the 1990s may be at risk of underestimating the difficulties involved for essentially the same reason.

1. INTRODUCTION

Business reengineering has been widely canvassed as a means of achieving radical change in business structures and processes. Some dramatic claims have been made for the power of reengineering concepts. Hammer and Champy (1993) state that "most companies have no choice but to muster the courage to do it [reengineer]. For many, reengineering is the only hope for breaking away from the ineffective, antiquated ways of conducting business that will otherwise inevitably destroy them." In their view, business processes are currently institutionalized in fragmented, disjunct forms that are inimical to the effective management of business as a whole. Their recommended alternative is a business redesign based on the reintegration of underlying logical processes, enabling a better focus on customer service and business performance.

Much of the reengineering literature is extremely positive in tone. A leading theorist comments that

> in some companies, I have encountered situations where managers invoked flimsy and unsubstantiated excuses – "we tried something like this and it didn't work" or "we can't afford to make such changes now" – to prevent initiation of the higher levels of transformation. [Venkatraman 1994]

We take the management comments in this quotation to represent legitimate practical concerns, however. Research into a related area of IT application shows that a longer-term perspective can cast doubt on the validity of strong claims made for the benefits of assigning IT a central role in the development of corporate strategies. In a study of "classic cases" of strategic information systems, Kettinger, Grover and Segars (1995) found that the business advantages identified as deriving from the successful application of IT to achieve strategic business goals could not in all cases be confirmed by objective performance measures. Merrill Lynch, CIGNA and Citicorp were, for example, among a number of "high-profile" case study firms that showed reduced profitability relative to industry averages over an extended period following the implementation of a strategic system. The authors concluded that "too often, decisions concerning the introduction of strategic IT have been based on management's ability to make a leap of faith" (Kettinger, Grover and Segars 1995). We infer that a company investing time and resources in applying business reengineering concepts may well be making just such a leap of faith.

The problem for empirical research into the business value of reengineering in its current form is that there is as yet a shortage of case material from which to develop a long-term perspective on the full practical implications of applying the concepts. We suggest that one way of supplementing research into examples of reengineering as a contemporary phenomenon is to investigate earlier approaches to IT-mediated organizational change deemed to embed analogous principles. To this end, we examine the aims and effects of a major corporate IS plan (known as COMIS – Computer Operations and Management Information System) developed during the 1960s in Telecom Australia. Comprehensive in its scope, the plan was intended to provide a framework for the development of an integrated structure of programs and files able to be reconfigured as required to support changing organizational process structures. Activities to implement the plan were undertaken and pursued for some years, but abandoned when a number of major practical difficulties were encountered.

The suggestion that a parallel can be drawn between COMIS and contemporary business reengineering theory is based on our view that the key concepts underpinning reengineering are a set of assumptions analogous to those deemed to provide the basis for the development of the COMIS plan. Broadly speaking, these assumptions are taken to be, first, that information technology has evolved to a level of power and sophistication sufficient to alter the fundamental logic of business process design and, second, that existing business processes are inefficient enough to warrant redesign. On the basis of this perspective we suggest that the ultimate failure of COMIS has implications relevant to the further development of reengineering theory.

2. BUSINESS REENGINEERING THEORY

Based on a review of four years' experience with the application of business reengineering principles in a number of companies, Davenport and Stoddard (1994) identify five concepts as constituting the basic theory:

1. A clean slate approach to organizational design and change.
2. An orientation to broad, cross-functional business processes, or how work is done.
3. The need for, and possibility of, radical change in process performance.
4. Information technology as an enabler of change in how work is done.
5. Changes in organizational and human arrangements that accompany change in technology.

Davenport and Stoddard suggest that these concepts can all be found in previous theories of organizational change, and that business reengineering is new only to the extent that well-established concepts have been "combined in a new synthesis." While other theorists make stronger claims for the novelty of reengineering as an approach to organizational change (Hammer 1990; Hammer and Champy 1993; Venkatraman 1991, 1994), the synthesis of a process orientation with the concept of modern IT as the enabler of change is the common thread running through different representations of the approach.

Implicit in the view of IT as the "essential enabler of process change" (Hammer and Champy 1993) is the assumption that it is IT which has changed the logic of doing business sufficiently to generate a need for fundamental change. In general the nature of this assumption is not explored in detail. Hammer and Champy do not, for instance, indicate whether in their opinion the possibility of radical change through business process redesign has been inherent in the business environment since the first emergence of powerful new information technologies such as telegraphy, or alternatively whether the continuing evolution in both computing and telecommunications technologies has resulted in a qualitative change in the ways in which the technology can be applied.

Yates and Benjamin (1991) provide a specific rationale at least for a claim that there has been a qualitative change in the power of IT. They identify the four key functions of IT as information conversion, information storage, information processing and information communications, and state that in their view a major turning point has been reached with the possibilities for the integration of communications and data processing capabilities raised by the convergence of computing and telecommunications technologies. The example quoted is one in which the four key functions can be integrated in relation to a specific business activity at one workstation. Venkatraman cites this research as support for the view that IT "can be thought of as a new engine for the organization" and that IT is now at a point where it renders "some modes of organizing relatively inefficient" (Venkatraman 1991).

We take the assumption that modern IT has effectively changed some of the rules for doing business to be extremely strong. Proponents of reengineering do not simply suggest that the organizational structures supporting business processes should be redesigned to accommodate the incorporation of IT in those processes, but claim instead that the logical basis for redesign has changed (Hammer and Champy 1993, Venkatraman 1994). In our view this assumption is implicitly based on an abstract view of IT as a "given" in the business environment, or in other words on the idea that IT considerations can for the purposes of redesign be considered as a separate issue. We discuss later whether adopting this view might have a tendency to mislead planners and designers as to the true complexity of process issues in a dynamic business environment, where the logic of existing structures is continually being challenged by changes in the competitive situation. At this point however, it is relevant to point out that the technology itself remains problematic to some extent; in common with Keen (1991), Yates and Benjamin strike a strong note of caution, pointing out that integration techniques are still quite immature and face a number of compatibility problems. Keen makes the additional point that firms face "many technical uncertainties as they try to balance conflicting demands for efficiency now and integration tomorrow."

To provide a background to our discussion of the case, we suggest that the view of integrated IT as an "essential enabler of change" is strongly paralleled by views on the promise of computing for business during the 1960s. In the first flush of enthusiasm for computing, there seemed no real limit to its potential. A leading theorist of the time commented in 1960 that "within the very near future — much less than twenty-five years — we will have the technological capability of substituting machines for any and all human functions in organizations" (Simon 1970). Weizenbaum notes that the computer was viewed as "the ultimate abstract tool" and that a view emerged in the years after World War II that it had providentially arrived to rescue industry from problems caused by the failure of existing organizational systems to keep up with the increasing pace of business:

> managers and technicians agreed that the computer had come along just in time
> to avert catastrophic crises; were it not for the timely introduction of computers,
> it was argued, not enough people could have been found to staff the banks, the
> ever increasingly complex communication and logistic problems of armed forces
> spread all over the world could not have been met, and trading on the stock and
> commodity exchanges could not have been maintained. [Weizenbaum 1976]

3. METHODOLOGY

The case discussion is based on qualitative data from a study of the information systems (IS) function in Telecom Australia (referred to in the rest of this paper simply as Telecom) during the period 1960-1995. The COMIS plan discussed in this paper emerged during the course of the study as an activity that played a significant role in shaping future IS directions in the company, and was consequently made a specific study focus. The primary source documentation available on COMIS was extensive and was the major source of data. Supporting data was obtained from the five (of more than forty) people interviewed in the course of the total study who had direct experience of COMIS. Part of the interview in each of these five cases was devoted specifically to COMIS and its repercussions.

A constructivist approach to the study was adopted. The constructivist paradigm implies that it is the researcher's job to provide sufficient contextual information in the form of "thick description" (Geertz 1973) for a reader to make an individual assessment of the relevance of the findings within the reader's frame of reference (Firestone 1990). Thus while a number of parallels between COMIS concepts and those underpinning business reengineering became apparent during the course of the analysis, the changes in business, technology and terminology that have occurred since 1970 were deemed sufficient to render direct comparisons and evaluations redundant. The analytical method used instead was to examine the data for evidence of prejudgments and expressed intents which appeared to be strongly analogous to those being presented in the context of business reengineering, to analyze the findings in the light of IT experience over the subsequent years, and to identify what in our view are the implications for reengineering theory.

4. THE COMIS PLAN IN TELECOM AUSTRALIA 1960-1972

During the period from 1960 to 1972, Telecom Australia (Telecom) was responsible for administering a national monopoly in the telecommunications industry. Charged with a number of social responsibilities, including the development of the telephone network as a key national asset, the organization had a strong vested interest in the fully planned and managed introduction of new technology.

There was a strong technological strain in the Telecom culture during that time. The key corporate values were derived from engineering considerations of efficiency and quality of workmanship, and a belief in the efficacy of technology as a solution for social as well as technical problems. Moyal (1984) records that Telecom staff were in general well aware of the social roles played by telecommunications in a sparsely populated country such as Australia, and that there was considerable corporate pride in the technical achievements that had been required to build the cable networks linking remote rural areas with the rest of Australia, and Australia with the rest of the world. The result was an organizational environment extremely receptive to the introduction of new technology.

A number of small computer applications were developed in Telecom during the late 1950s. These were deemed by management to have been sufficiently successful to warrant an in-depth exploration of the possibilities of the new technology, and a major planning study was initiated in 1959. In its final form, the COMIS plan for the development of a set of integrated applications was the result of this initial study, complemented by a further study during 1967 and 1968.

4.1   The ADP Exploratory Study 1959-1960

The Telecom documentation indicates that the application of computers to business processes was already being considered in strategic terms late in the 1950s. The report from the 1959 study group stated that "the Post Office is ready for A.D.P. and...its introduction is as necessary and inevitable as was the introduction of automatic telephony fifty years ago. It only remains for us to plan to introduce the best system as efficiently and speedily as possible" (Australian Post Office 1961). The concept of an integrated system which would automate many of Telecom's business processes was introduced at this time, when it was thought it would handle all of the "business processes susceptible to electronic data processing" (Australian Post Office 1959).

There is little indication in the study group report of serious consideration having been given to the full range of organizational impacts contingent on the widespread introduction of computing technology. There was instead a tendency throughout the report to identify the proposed applications with the technology, as evidenced in a discussion of the benefits expected to be achieved. These were listed as:

(1) The ability of the equipment to hold very large volumes of records at a central point;
(2) The ability of the equipment to extract from these records, with practically no expenditure of human effort, information in any desired form;
(3) The ability of the equipment to make logical decisions in conformity with predetermined rules;
(4) The ability of the equipment to print out information based on its records without significant human effort;
(5) The fact that the equipment rarely makes mistakes. [Australian Post Office 1961]

The planning orientation was at this stage largely toward the automation of existing processes. Interviewees put forth the view that Telecom planners were just commencing to consider the possibilities of the technology in more radical terms. This can be detected in the study group report as a view that systems integration could enable the organization to rationalize clerical activities in specific areas.

> In order to obtain maximum use from the input data, and to obtain the benefits of an integrated system, the central computer should process all the work within a specific geographical area for which the system as a whole is designed. The use of one computer [i.e., application or system] to handle, say, telephone accounts, another to handle payroll work and so on would not be as economical or efficient as the integrated system envisaged in this report. It is probably true that such a course of action would permit the introduction of A.D.P. on a limited scale earlier than would otherwise be the case. [Australian Post Office 1961]

The initial scope of the system was specified in this study. Work commenced on the first application (the Telephone Accounting or TEL/DRS system) in 1963, which was released into production in suburban Melbourne in 1967. In 1968, the term COMIS (Computer Operations and Management Information System) was introduced to refer to the integrated system, and its scope was considerably expanded in another major study.

4.2   The Study Group on Application of Computers 1967-1968

The Telecom IS area had gained considerable experience in the construction of computer applications for business by 1967, when the second major systems study was commenced. The TEL/D.S. application already in production was a large system, with more than $3M invested in it by 1966 (Australian Post Office 1966). The study group report was much more sophisticated in its analysis of IS issues than its predecessor, with a specific focus on the capabilities for computing to facilitate radical change. The two major emphases were, first, on the potential for computing to enable the organization to stay in control of evolving business requirements and, second, on a perceived opportunity to develop a system that could be reconfigured as required to meet changing organizational needs. The approach was, however, not based specifically on theoretical considerations and justification for the proposal was couched in terms of quantified capital and operational costs savings rather than more abstract strategic considerations.

A significant aspect to the expanded COMIS plan was the conceptualization of Telecom's set of business processes as an engineered structure forming a network in principle little different from any other network. The inference drawn was that the application of IT to business processes could be treated as primarily an abstract engineering design issue. The planners viewed the process structure as "wide-ranging and complex; it is comprehensive in its way though heavily compartmentalized and limited by the means it employs" (Australian Post Office 1968).

In addressing the issue of change, the report noted that

> telecommunications is a key activity for all economic and social progress, requiring capital investment at a rate that greatly exceeds the economic growth-rate of the community as a whole....There is often a temptation to believe that some sort of a plateau of expansion is being reached; subsequent events invariably disprove this. [Australian Post Office 1968]

The report went on to an analysis of the implications of the rates of change then being experienced and concluded that an integrated system was required to deal with the likely effects. For the time, the system envisaged was huge:

> the complete COMIS will be a vast system catering for the information needs of practically all Departmental activities. It will include on-line storage of some 20,000 million characters, high capacity processors with security back-up and a communications network giving access to some 5000 Departmental stations including terminal equipment ranging from teleprinters to visual displays. The capital cost of such a system would be around $90M....System design and implementation would amount to some 1500 man-years. Nevertheless the system would be highly profitable and would, in fact, represent the only feasible solution to the immense management problems of scale and complexity that will confront the Department in the future. [Australian Post Office 1968]

The planners addressed a number of data issues in the development of COMIS. While the comments were somewhat scattered, taken as a whole they were sufficiently comprehensive to form the basis for what would be a data management policy in more recent terminology. Recommendations included the standardization of codes and terminology, the once-only rendering of information in permanent store, and the high-priority restructuring of the telephone service occupancy file so that it could support the full range of business processes requiring occupancy data.

The integrated system was no longer seen simply as an end in itself, but as a means of restructuring the organization's business processes along more flexible lines. An interviewee working in a business unit at the time said that "we were finally getting round to some idea of commercialization and the customer. It was very early days though and most of the engineers wouldn't have a bar of it." The implications of a more commercial approach were, however, recognized by the study group:

> where the increase [in information requirements] is purely in volume, it may be practicable to meet it by corresponding expansion of existing methods. However, more typically there is an increase in complexity....Increasing emphasis on the Department as a business enterprise is generating demands for information needed to exercise new controls....For these new methods must be found. [Australian Post Office 1968]

The solution proposed was an almost seamless collection of sharable files and processes. The fundamental concept was that the structure of files and programs would be designed so that it could be dynamically reconfigured to form new applications as needs changed. To a very considerable extent, the study group was constrained to speak in terms of fixed applications and functions for the report to be generally intelligible within Telecom, but the report notes that where applications were mentioned this was "only a means of study and reporting" and that the referents were not to be taken to be self-contained systems. Overall there was a clear process orientation to the plan. The stated intention was to do away with the "compartmentalization" of manual processes mentioned earlier and to use IT to establish a highly flexible structure. The long-term objective for the IS area was to be

> a comprehensive COMIS, which would provide a framework within which all future applications should be considered. In this development, program and file strategies as well as codes and terminology should take account not only of contemporary applications but also needs envisaged for the future. [Australian Post Office 1968]

An interviewee who was subsequently a senior IS executive for many years commented that "COMIS was more about reengineering the business than anything I've seen since. Some of the people on COMIS were quite radical and would have gone further but felt you couldn't get away with changing too much at once." .

It is noteworthy that the planning report deals with the issues involved almost exclusively in technical terms. The report does not contain any form of risk analysis, nor any significant reference to potential problems in relation to the management of separate but logically dependent projects. The report conveys no sense at all that the development of COMIS was expected to be anything more than a straightforward technical exercise.

4.3   The COMIS Review 1971

With the TEL/DRS system discussed earlier providing a foundation, the first major step in realizing the "ultimate system" (Australian Post Office 1968) was to be the development of an application to automate telephone directory compilation in conjunction with a redevelopment of TEL/DRS to form an integrated suite of programs and files. A number of problems were encountered and in 1971 a major review of COMIS activities resulted in the conclusion that "although considerable benefits in accuracy, control and economy could be obtained through a total integrated system, the conclusion has been reached that it is probably beyond the resources, experience, management and technical capability of the Department [to achieve] at this stage" (Australian Post Office 1971).

The review team identified a number of practical problems. Most significant was that of dealing simultaneously with the difficulties of building two large systems, as well as managing the interactions between them. It was commented that

> the extended system development periods associated with the comprehensive nature and considerable resource requirements for system testing were not previously appreciated and are seen as major difficulties. It must be appreciated also that large scale systems tend to be fairly rigid and do not permit changes to be made easily for changed user needs either during development or subsequently. [Australian Post Office 1971]

A related issue was a "snowball" effect on resource and management overhead requirements as the business environment continued to evolve and new requirements for systems support emerged. The review report notes that

> since the original COMIS study was completed, computer controlled telecommunications equipment has been introduced to the APO [Australian Post Office]....The impact of these developments has resulted in the diversion of significant ADP and user resources to plan and design systems to produce outputs originating from the use of this equipment. [Australian Post Office 1971]

Interviewees discussed a range of detailed difficulties with a long-term senior executive commenting that, "We just couldn't construct a model that worked under test. File conditions were too complicated and too volatile. In reality most of the systems we were building were at least partly out of date before they hit production. COMIS testing showed me that integrated systems weren't on." This reference to data issues was echoed in other interviews; there was strong agreement that despite the planners' recognition of data issues, the most intractable practical difficulties in synchronizing the two initial systems developments were those of aligning file structures and conditions (Australian Post Office 1971). Interviewees reported a range of problems stemming particularly from difficulties in developing data structures capable of supporting multi-stage processes comprising a number of distinct functions.

The review did not formally signify the end of COMIS, but references to the integrated system and its reengineering intents were quietly dropped. A subsequent major strategic planning document (Telecom Australia 1977) contained no reference to COMIS.

5. INTERPRETATION OF THE CASE STUDY FINDINGS

With a further twenty years of IS theory and research as a foundation for 20/20 hindsight, it can be concluded that COMIS was an extremely optimistic plan which had virtually no chance of success.

While COMIS was specified in concrete terms, and at a level of detail sufficient to provide a basis for the development of implementation plans, the study showed that a number of the key issues were discussed solely in abstract terms and without specific consideration of the practical issues involved. This was particularly so first in relation to the view that Telecom's organizational structures were unduly rigid, compartmentalized and suitable for redesign and second in the discussion of data design and management issues.

5.1   Computing Technology and Business Process Redesign

Interviewees confirmed the view that COMIS was intended to provide a blueprint for a series of steps in which computing technology would enable the restructuring of what were seen to be, particularly in the engineering areas, the excessively bureaucratic processes associated with functions such as billing, service provisioning, service restoration, stores management and network planning. One of the striking things about the study group's report is that the planners did not feel the need to qualify any of their remarks in these respects. An interviewee commented that the preparation of COMIS was an unusually harmonious activity for Telecom, and that this reflected a strong sense in the technical arms of the organization that the advent of computing had fundamentally "changed the rules."

Weizenbaum has commented on the tendency for the power of new technology to "blind" people to its limitations. In our interpretation, the technological bias within Telecom's organizational culture was a significant factor which predisposed planners to believe in the efficacy of technology-mediated solutions to business problems generally. Interviewees commented to the effect that this predisposition was being reinforced during this period by the awareness in technical areas of the world-wide explosion of interest in computing as a business technology (discussed in Gibson and Nolan 1974). We infer that, from a technological perspective, the potential for the application of computers to alleviate existing and anticipated business problems was perceived to be so great as to preclude a critical evaluation of the full range of issues involved in reorganizing process structures.

The result in our view was an implicit but powerful assumption that a computing-mediated restructure of existing inefficient business processes was both desirable and fundamentally unproblematic. The exclusively technical focus identified earlier suggests both a lack of awareness of, and perhaps a lack of interest in, the true complexity of the business issues involved. In the final analysis, the result was a highly detailed and specific plan designed to solve a number of "engineering" problems perceived to exist in organizational structures on the basis of a superficial and very high-level analysis.

5.2   Difficulties in Implementing COMIS

The case discussion highlighted the problems encountered in attempting to implement COMIS. In retrospect, most of those now look to have been inevitable. It is, however, of value to consider some specific issues in more detail as follows:

1. Managing business support requirements in an evolving environment.
2. Planning and managing corporate data.

Managing Business Support Requirements in an Evolving Environment. The COMIS Review report noted that the difficulties of building and implementing large systems had been underestimated (Australian Post Office 1971). As already discussed, the plan for automating the set of business processes was treated as essentially an engineering issue, and not a particularly difficult one at that. Despite this, it is difficult to criticize the planners for what has only since been recognized as an ongoing problem for the IS industry. Even now, the problems of managing and stabilizing user requirements in a dynamic business environment remain a major issue for systems analysts and designers (for instance, Curtis et al. 1988; Wastell and Newman 1993; Brooks 1987).

A point made in the COMIS Review, and strongly supported by interviewees, was that the technology itself was a major contributor to the environmental volatility which proved so difficult to manage. The introduction of computers into the business and into the telecommunications network led to almost constant rearrangements of business processes such as the collection of network usage details for billing purposes. Benjamin and Blunt (1992) suggest a general recursive relationship between IT and business processes when they point out that

> the technology is allowing us to build ever larger and more complex systems, and supporting interdependent business processes will require those larger and more complex systems. Thus IT will continue to be involved in a change process that at the same time it makes more complex.

Although as discussed above the planners were well aware that changes, including the widespread introduction of computing, would occur in the business environment, they evidently failed to anticipate the extent of the effects. The discussion in the COMIS Review report (Australian Post Office 1971) on staffing and resource impacts makes it clear that there were continual conflicts between requirements based on emerging needs to apply computing technology in a specifically business support role and those based on the wish to apply it in the interests of enabling process integration and restructure. The result in effect was a dynamic, constantly moving target for systems development. A concluding comment in one interview was that, "Finally we had to face the fact that the systems we were developing were out of date before they hit production. Things were even worse when we tried to match systems up."

Planning and Managing Corporate Data. Broadly speaking, the data concepts in COMIS were consistent with the philosophy underpinning information engineering. This has been defined as the view that systems should be designed "with the total organization's information needs in mind and based on an assumption that a relatively stable group of data entities lies at the center of an organization's information processing needs" (Goodhue et al. 1992). In recent years, this idea has been used to ground the development of a number of planning methodologies (for instance, Martin 1982, 1990).

In our view, the data problems experienced in attempting to implement COMIS are a particularly valuable illustration of the risks involved in assessing specific practical issues at an abstract level. When considering data requirements such as standardized code-sets, corporate data definitions and common data structures, the planners were in a sense unfortunate to have few if any precedents on which to base an assessment of possible problems and inhibitors. Extensive subsequent research indicates that similar problems to those encountered with COMIS have been experienced by almost all firms committing to corporate data planning (for instance, in Allen and Boynton 1991; Goodhue et al. 1992; Earl 1993). A common finding from these studies is that very careful and detailed planning and management is required even for limited progress to be made in developing implementable corporate data structures.

The level of abstraction in the COMIS analysis was such that data consistency was viewed simply as a necessary precondition for the development and implementation of an integrated structure, and therefore as something which had to occur. In effect, issues of a fundamental nature from a practical perspective remained below the planners' threshold of attention. Yet in the event the problems of defining generally usable structures, reconciling conflicting views and dealing with the dynamics of business change proved insuperable even in the context of the first two applications.

6. THE IMPLICATIONS OF COMIS FOR BUSINESS REENGINEERING THEORY

We believe that Telecom's experience with COMIS suggests the desirability of critically examining the assumptions underpinning any concept of IT-mediated organizational change.

In our understanding, reengineering theory in its current formulation embeds an equivalent broad assumption to that underpinning COMIS; i.e., that the effects of IT on the business environment have "changed the rules" of business organization in fundamental ways. The leading claim for the desirability of reengineering is that current business processes are inefficient or obsolete because they are based on principles of organization which became relevant during the industrial revolution but are no longer applicable due primarily to the effects of modern IT (Hammer 1990; Hammer and Champy 1993; Davenport and Short 1990; Venkatraman 1991, 1994). One problem is that it is difficult to discern what the existing principles of organization are being taken to be. Venkatraman, for instance, states that

> the current business processes subscribe to a set of organizational principles that responded to the industrial revolution. Organizational concepts such as centralization versus decentralization, span of control, line versus staff, functional specialization, authority-responsibility balance, and administrative mechanisms for coordination and control are all derived from the general principles. Although these concepts are still valid, IT functionality can significantly alter some of these "first principles" of business process redesign. [Venkataraman 1994]

A difficulty is that neither here nor in context are these first principles fully explicated, nor is it clear why the derived concepts would remain valid if the principles change, though a related comment to the effect that IT can "shrink the effects of time and space" (Venkatraman 1994) suggests perhaps that it is the organization of process support structures according to the principle of the division of labor which is in doubt.

Hammer and Champy in their turn identify IT as a "powerful solution" and recommend that companies should "seek the problems it might solve." While this seems to be good general advice, it does not present as a rigorous justification for the claims made for reengineering as a specific theory. At a more detailed level of discussion they adopt a "broad brush" approach similar in principle to that of Davenport (1993) and identify a number of IT capabilities with specific relevance to process redesign. Much of this material is based on the view that technology can be used to disrupt inappropriate "rules" of organizational behavior and a number of largely independent examples of rule transformations are presented. The connecting link again appears to be that IT has reduced the relevance of specialization and hence of process structures based on different functional domains of skill and expertise. Again, however, there is little or no attempt at formal justification. To take a specific example, one "old rule" is presented as "only experts can perform complex work"; the disruptive technology recommended is expert systems and the new rule as "a generalist can do the work of an expert" (Hammer and Champy 1993). This totally ignores a large body of literature indicating that reliable and organizationally valuable expert systems are still very rare and that in practice the search for, and definition of, expertise is extremely problematic (see Eaves [1993a, 1993b] for an overview of the literature and a discussion of the issues involved).

We take the overall justification for the claim that basic organizational principles have changed to be that IT has developed to a point at which it can be effectively applied in a general integrative role within a large organization. It seems correct to argue that large organizations have traditionally been able to survive only on the basis of task and skill specialization, and we agree with the view that there is usually an increase in overhead staff performing integrative functions as an organization grows larger, a problem which integrated IT *may* be able to alleviate to an extent (Hammer and Champy 1993). It also seems correct to infer that process design must take into account the full range of possible roles IT can play in process support, up to and including the automation of all steps.

It still seems to us that a leap of faith is required to assume that there is a new *basis* for process design. Findings from studies into the effects of automation on work practices do demonstrate that skill sets are changing in complex and difficult to manage ways but not that requirements for skill and task differentiation are being reduced (Zuboff 1988). The rate of environmental change is such that the optimization of structures and processes seems inherently unachievable. In a detailed analysis of the issue, Bergquist (1993) comments that the problem of scale is a major issue in the analysis of large organizations. He suggests that process and structural inefficiencies which are "obvious" at a high level cease to be obvious as a finer grain of analysis is undertaken, and the impacts of requirements to change and stabilize new arrangements become apparent.

In our interpretation, COMIS provides a clear illustration of the risks involved in taking a highly abstract view of organizational change. The COMIS analysis was conducted at a level that helped to conceal the real issues of dealing with the application of computers in a dynamic rather than static environment. We suggest that a similarly high-level view of process problems in modern business is to be found in reengineering theory, and that a convincing case has yet to be made for the claim of a change in the principles of process design. While it is obvious that both IT and the business environment have changed dramatically in the years since 1970, it seems by no means equally clear that there has been any qualitative change in the relationship between IT and business processes.

COMIS indicates that issues affecting the role of IT in an organization particularly tend to arise at the nexus of business and functional planning, where long-term structural objectives need to be evaluated in the light of support for shorter term business strategies and requirements, a finding substantially supported by other research (for instance, Allen and Boynton 1991; Keen 1991). The types of systems and data problems encountered appear to be analogous with those still unresolved in current IS and IT theory. The implication in our view is that the effective application of IT in a large enterprise is a multi-dimensional activity and that it over-simplifies the situation to conceive the role of IT in relationship to process design as an enabler of change.

7. CONCLUSION AND SUGGESTIONS FOR FURTHER RESEARCH

A tendency has emerged in the reengineering literature to downplay the view that process redesign should be undertaken in the interests of radical change. It has, for instance, been suggested by one of the original proponents of reengineering that the movement has already "peaked" and that business process redesign is in the throes of being combined with other process-oriented approaches in an "integrated process management approach" (Davenport and Stoddard 1994). In our view, this effectively begs the question as to the substance in re-engineering theory.

A relevant background consideration in our view is that business management is becoming increasingly concerned with IT costs. There appears to be a significant business risk involved when the implications of adopting a business reengineering approach to organizational change are primarily worked out on the basis of practice. In reviewing the issues involved in the management of IT economics, Keen comments that evaluations of IS function effectiveness in business tend to be generally negative. He deems this unsurprising on the basis that "with costs growing far faster than business profits, evidence of pay-off limited or absent, and small sanctioned increases in annual budgets generating long-term expenses, it is no wonder that corporate IS units are under siege." The growing trend toward outsourcing has been interpreted as a reaction to recurring failures by IT units to deliver on the promise of technology, and in this context has been described as "the revenge of the business manager" (Fitzgerald 1994).

COMIS, in our view, is simply one instance of a past IT failure deriving to a considerable extent from an excessively abstract analysis of the issues involved. Our concern here is that the widespread application of reengineering principles by companies which have failed to appreciate the magnitude of the tasks involved will add to the list of such failures. In this regard, Davenport and Stoddard's comment that "the popular management literature, by relying too much on hype and too little on research, common sense and the lessons of the past, has created more myth than methodology" is indicative of the problems for business. The danger is that companies confronting the problems imposed by the complexity of modern business will be misled by the simplicity of a statement such as "don't automate, obliterate" (Hammer and Champy 1993) as to the likely benefits of reengineering. Such detailed case study literature as is available suggests that, even where reengineering concepts have been applied purely in the interests of incremental process improvement, the costs are high, the learning curve steep and the risks significant (Caron, Jarvenpaa and Stoddard 1994).

It seems clear, however, that reengineering is here to stay as an approach to planned process redesign. Based on our analysis of COMIS, we believe that the key research requirement is to build up a body of case studies of sufficient depth to illustrate the full organizational implications of applying reengineering principles in a range of different enterprises and industries. Areas for examination would include the impacts on staff training, skills development and job structures, the direct costs of action, the impacts on existing systems, the need for new systems, data structure requirements and the time frames required to specify, develop and then implement changed business processes. We believe that it is only through detailed research into major reengineering initiatives that an adequate understanding of the validity of the assumptions involved will be developed.

8. REFERENCES

Allen, B. R., and Boynton, A. C. "Information Architecture: In Search of Efficient Flexibility. *MIS Quarterly*, Volume 15, Number 4, 1991.

Australian Post Office. *A.D.P. Project: Exploratory Study Terms of Reference.* Melbourne: Australian Post Office, 1959.

Australian Post Office. *A.D.P. Project: Exploratory Study – Report.* Melbourne: Australian Post Office, 1961.

Australian Post Office. *Joint Committee of Public Accounts Inquiry into Automatic Data Processing: Submission by Postmaster-General's Department.* Melbourne: Australian Post Office, 1966.

Australian Post Office. *Report of the Study Group on Application of Computers.* Melbourne: Australian Post Office, 1968.

Australian Post Office. *COMIS Review.* Melbourne: Australian Post Office, 1971.

Benjamin, R. I., and Blunt, J. "Critical IT Issues: The Next Ten Years." *Sloan Management Review*, Volume 34, Number 1, 1992.

Berquist, W. *The Postmodern Organisation: Mastering the Art of Irreversible Change.* San Francisco: Josey-Bass Publishers, 1993.

Brooks, F. P. "The Silver Bullet: Essence and Accidents in Software Engineering." *Computer*, April 1987.

Caron, J. R.; Jarvenpaa, S. L.; and Stoddard, D. B. "Business Reengineering at CIGNA Corporation: Experiences and Lessons Learned from the First Five Years." *MIS Quarterly*, Volume 18, Number 3, 1994.

Curtis, B.; Krasner, H.; and Iscoe, N. "A Field Study of the Software Design Process for Large Systems." *Communications of the ACM*, Volume 31, Number 11, 1988.

Davenport, T. H. *Process Work: Reengineering Work Through Information Technology.* Boston: Harvard Business School Press, 1993.

Davenport, T. H., and Short, J. E. "The New Industrial Engineering: Information Technology and Business Process Redesign." *Sloan Management Review*, Volume 32, Number 1, 1990.

Davenport, T. H., and Stoddard, D. B. "Reengineering: Business Change of Mythic Proportions." *MIS Quarterly*, Volume 18, Number 2, 1994.

Earl, M. J. "Experiences in Strategic Information Systems Planning." *MIS Quarterly*, Volume 17, Number 1, 1993.

Earl, M. J. "The New and the Old of Business Process Redesign." *Journal of Strategic Information Systems*, Volume 3, Number 1, 1994.

Eaves, D. "Experts, Expertise and Professionals' Explanations." Monash University Department of Information Systems Working Paper Series, Number 19, 1993a.

Eaves, D. "Professionals, Professions and the Curiosities of Clinical Practice." Monash University Department of Information Systems Working Paper Series, Number 20, 1993b.

Fitzgerald, G. "Outsourcing of IT in the United Kingdom: A Legitimate Strategic Option?" *Proceedings of the Fifth Australian Conference on Information Systems*. Melbourne: Monash University, 1994.

Firestone, W. A. "Accommodation: Towards a Paradigm-Praxis Dialectic." In E. G. Guba (Editor), *the Paradigm Dialog*. Newbury Park, California: Sage Publications, 1990.

Geertz, C. *The Interpretation of Cultures*. New York: Basic Books, 1973.

Gibson, C. F., and Nolan, R. L. "Managing the Four Stages of EDP Growth." *Harvard Business Review*, January-February 1974.

Goodhue, D. L.; Kirsch, L. J.; Quillard, J. A.; and Wybo, M. D. "Strategic Data Planning: Lessons from the Field." *MIS Quarterly*, Volume 16, Number 1, 1992.

Hammer, M. Reengineering Work: Don't Automate, Obliterate." *Harvard Business Review*, Volume 68, Number 4, 1990.

Hammer, M., and Champy, J. *Re-engineering the Corporation: A Manifesto for Change.* London: Nicholas Brealey Publishing, 1993.

Keen, P. G. W. *Shaping the Future: Business Design Through Information Technology.* Cambridge: Harvard Business School Press, 1991.

Kettinger, W. J.; Grover, V.; and Segars, A. H. "Do Strategic Systems Really Pay Off?" *Information Systems Management*, Winter 1995.

Martin, J. *Information Engineering: Planning and Analysis*. Englewood Cliffs, New Jersey: Prentice-Hall, 1990.

Martin, J. *Strategic Data-Planning Methodologies*. Englewood Cliffs, New Jersey: Prentice-Hall, 1982.

Moyal, A. *Clear Across Australia: A History of Telecommunications*. Melbourne: Thomas Nelson Australia, 1984/

Simon, H. A. "The Shape of Automation." In Z. W. Pylyshyn (Editor), *Perspectives on the Computer Revolution*. Englewood Cliffs, New Jersey: Prentice-Hall, 1970.

Telecom Australia. *Information Systems Strategic Plan 1977-1987*. Melbourne: Telecom Australia, 1977.

Venkatraman, N. "IT-Enabled Business Transformation: From Automation to Business Scope Redefinition." *Sloan Management Review*, Winter 1994, pp. 73-87.

Venkatraman, N. "IT-Induced Business Reconfiguration." In M. S. Scott Morton (Editor), *The Corporation of the 1990s*. Oxford: Oxford University Press, 1991.

Wastell, D., and Newman, M. "The Behavioral Dynamics of Information System Development: A Stress Perspective." *Accounting, Management and Information Technology*, Volume 3, Number 2, 1993.

Weizenbaum, J. *Computing Power and Human Reason: From Judgment to Calculation*. San Francisco: W. H. Freeman and Company, 1976.

Yates, J., and Benjamin, R. I. "The Past and Present as a Window on the Futur." In M. S. Scott Morton (Editor), *The Corporation of the 1990s*. Oxford: Oxford University Press, 1991.

Zuboff, S. *In the Age of the Smart Machine: The Future of Work and Power*. New York: Basic Books, 1988.

About the Authors

Doug Hamilton spent twenty-seven years in industry as an IS professional. He worked as a programmer, systems analyst, systems designer and project manager. During the 1980s and early 1990s, he was involved in IS strategic planning in Telecom Australia. Executive assignments have included management of the applications integration function, coordination and management of IS strategic plan implementation, management of the corporate MIS and EIS initiatives and management of the internal business consultancy function. He has been engaged in higher degree studies at Monash University since 1993 and is now enrolled as a doctoral student in the Information Systems Department. Mr. Hamilton's primary research interest currently is strategic information systems planning.

Martin Atchison has worked variously as an engineer, town planner, and systems analyst. Currently employed as a lecturer in Information Systems at Monash University, his primary research interests are in information systems strategic planning and geographical information systems.

8

Contradictions among Stakeholder Assessments of a Radical Change Initiative: A Cognitive Frames Analysis

Michael J. Gallivan
Sloan School of Management
Massachusetts Institute of Technology

Abstract

This paper explores the concept of frames of reference by examining stakeholders assumptions regarding but transcending their technological frames. Specifically, the concept of technology frames (Orlikowski and Gash 1994) is expanded in order to identify stakeholders' assumptions regarding the complementary organizational changes necessary to implement successful technological change. Through analysis of data from a case study, the paper identifies inconsistencies among various stakeholders' reports of a change initiative and then identifies a possible resolution to these discrepant reports through an analysis of how stakeholders develop characteristic frames which shape how they understand the goals of the technological change efforts, the set of complementary organizational changes that are required, and their assumptions about what constitutes progress toward achieving these goals.

1. INTRODUCTION

Organizations today recognize the importance of simultaneously harnessing new technologies and changing the organizational parameters in order to support more streamlined, effective operations (Hammer and Champy 1993; Henderson and Venkatraman 1993). For example, many firms today have heeded the call for business processing reengineering, investing significant efforts to achieve radical changes, while recognizing that the required changes will be neither painless nor fast. The increasing popularity of business process reengineering coincides with managers becoming increasingly skilled at implementing technology-based change, reflecting a more sophisticated understanding that assimilating new technology involves much more than physically installing new hardware and software and then training workers to operate it (Walton 1989). Instead, organizations increasingly recognize that changes in technology and work processes are, fundamentally, cultural changes, and that preparing organizational members for such cultural changes is a long-term undertaking that can best be accomplished in stages over time. Furthermore, some change managers recognize that users' and managers' expectations must be set during the preliminary phases of technology assessment and evaluation *prior* to formal adoption and, even then, the values and assumptions that users and managers have toward their own roles, their co-workers, and the clients they serve will influence how they assimilate these technological changes.

Yet not all managers and employees in a given organization will share the same beliefs about a given technology, nor about how a major technological and organizational initiative should be implemented. Various stakeholder groups, by virtue of their position in the organization (Isabella 1988), their education and prior socialization (Van Maanen and Schein 1979) will embody different expectations for organizational change and may, in fact, perceive and interpret the same events as signifying different — even contradictory — implications for the organization. For example, IS developers, given their distinct job duties and the knowledge about technical issues, may perceive progress where users see inaction, or they may perceive success where line managers see failure.

2. PRIOR RESEARCH ON TECHNOLOGICAL FRAMES

A recent contribution to social cognitive theory by Orlikowski and Gash (1994) has offered the concept of a technological frame as a way of characterizing the mental models that organizational members hold about specific technologies. They define a technological frame as "that subset of members' organizational frames that concern the assumptions, expectations and knowledge they use to understand technology in organizations." Although frames are mental models that exist at the individual level, they are often shared across groups, based on similar professional training, socialization experiences (Van Maanen and Schein 1979) and career stage (Isabella 1988).

The concept of frames both supports and extends research by other authors which has shown that diverse stakeholder groups hold divergent concepts about information technology. In particular, Kling and Gerson (1978) developed their social world of computing theory to illustrate that system developers, users, and line managers each hold unique assumptions about information technology (Zuboff 1988). Orlikowski and Gash expand on this concept by showing evidence from an empirical study of the adoption of Lotus Notes that three sets of assumptions about technology are important in shaping group members' behavior. "Domains of technological frames" is the label they introduce to describe these sets of assumptions, which include individuals' beliefs about the technology itself, about the firm's technology strategy, and about technology-in-use. The latter domain (technology-in-use) refers to users' beliefs about "how the technology will be used on a day-to-day basis, and the likely or actual conditions and consequences associated with such use." Such domains of assumptions shape members' interactions with, expectations for, and evaluation of these new technologies. These authors conclude that the notion of technology frames is useful because these shared frames exert a powerful influence on people's behavior — not only in terms of how they learn to use a technology, but under what conditions they regard it as appropriate to use, and their anticipated outcomes for doing so.

In particular, it is useful to understand the frames held by various individuals and shared across stakeholder groups because it is possible for these frames to be incongruent with the technology itself — that is, members' frames do not accurately reflect the technology — or they may be inconsistent across groups. For example, diverse stakeholder groups may have inconsistent frames, which may lead to difficulties in implementing or using the technology. When this occurs, some technologies may fail to achieve the intentions held by technology designers or management sponsors (Orlikowski 1992a), as shown by a case study of one firm's adoption of the Lotus Notes groupware product (Orlikowski 1992b). The concept of technological frames is useful for both researchers and practitioners because it allows them to predict and explain the likely outcomes of technological implementation and, in principle, to take action to avert potential problems (Ginzberg 1981).

In addition to describing three domains of frames, Orlikowski and Gash show that the use of certain technologies may require changes to users' frames of reference, specifically first-order and second-order changes — that is, minor efficiency changes, or major transformation changes, respectively (Bartunek and Moch 1987). In fact, it is this difficulty in implementing technologies that require radical, second-order, or paradigm change which may, at least partially explain the failure of users to assimilate a new technology into their daily routines (Orlikowski 1992b). In contrast, achieving first-order or incremental change is far easier (Bartunek and Moch 1987), since it requires no major realignment of frames. Such an approach can help to explain successful outcomes, whether the implementation represented a simple, first-order change (Gallivan et al. 1993) or a radical change approached through gradual, phased implementation (Gallivan, Hofman and Orlikowski 1994; Ettlie 1986).

This paper will borrow the concept of frame from Orlikowski and Gash as an analytic construct which shapes meaning and behavior. Since the purpose of this research was not to investigate individuals' understanding of a new technology itself but rather their notions of the organizational change processes required to effectively deploy the new technology, this research will expand on the concept of a *technological* frame to consider respondents' understanding of the broader set of organizational changes necessary for IS developers and managers to harness the potential of a new technology (client/server).

There are three reasons for our modification of the original domains of technological frames to include complementary organizational changes. First, this construct emerged from the field study described below. Second, this introduces a broader range of assumptions that matter to organizational members and which appear to influence their beliefs about the likely outcomes of change. Third, understanding stakeholders' frames surrounding the required organizational changes can facilitate a comparison of such frames *prior* to actual implementation, or *in the absence of* an actual implementation altogether. Such a comparison of members' assumptions about the required, organizational changes that must accompany technology deployment may identify inconsistent expectations for change, and may serve as a caution light before significant resources are invested in implementing the technology (Ginzberg 1981).

3. PRIOR RESEARCH ON RESKILLING IS PROFESSIONALS

This paper describes a case study conducted as part of a larger research project examining the organizational and technological change processes within the information systems (IS) departments of four firms with regard to their adoption of new software process innovations (Fichman and Kemerer 1993). This larger research project has investigated the hiring, training and other learning approaches necessary to ensure that IS developers can employ a set of software process innovations including client/server technology, object-oriented development, and graphical user interface (GUI) development tools. These changes have often been described in the computer trade press using colloquial terms such as *retooling* or *reskilling* (Ziff 1993). These terms suggest that what is required is the replacement or realignment of existing IS staff resources. Given their implicit emphasis on hiring and training, these labels suggest a relatively straightforward approach to upgrading a firm's human resources. The metaphor is one of replacing an old machine component with a new one whether this means replacing an old developer with a new one, or replacing obsolete technical tools with new ones (while retaining the same people). Such mechanistic images of change belie the complexity of the organizational changes that must occur in order to fully exploit the potential of the software process innovations, since many other changes must occur at the individual, department, and organizational levels. Although several authors have suggested that the culture of the IS organization must change (DeFiore 1995), to date there has been little empirical research to demonstrate how such fundamental changes can actually be made. Instead, the widespread metaphors of retooling IS professionals create a one-dimensional image of change — that of firms using hiring and technical skills training with none of the upheaval experienced with other radical change initiatives. Such images are oversimplified, and possibly misleading to IS practitioners, since research on a prior generation of software innovations (CASE tools) has shown changes in the culture, skills, roles, and work processes of IS departments are difficult to achieve (Orlikowski 1993).

Perhaps, because these metaphors for changing IS departments are so simplistic and due to the ease with which those firms profiled in the computer trade press made these changes, the true challenges that organizations face when implementing these software innovations have not been examined in depth, either in the trade press or the academic literature. Ironically, it is the IS consultants who have focused significant attention on these issues, both in practitioner-oriented journals and on the lecture circuit (DeFiore 1995; Swanborg 1993; Raphaelian 1993; Stokes 1993a, 1993b; Farwell et al. 1992), rather than IS academics, with the exception of some recent work by Nance (1994, Nance and Sessions 1994).

Another relevant line of research to implementing radical change in the IS organization is that of business process reengineering, since we can consider these challenges to the skill requirements, roles, work processes and culture to represent a reengineering of the IS function. Yet this literature, too, has not shed light on understanding how radical change actually gets implemented. As suggested by several recent critiques of the rhetoric of the BPR literature (Craig and Yetton 1994; Jones 1994; Keidel 1994; O'Neill 1994), this literature has focused almost exclusively on the ideal, end state of reengineering, rather than on the processes required to transform the organization to be able to achieve the new ideal. Craig and Yetton have portrayed this as a preoccupation with "design" over "implementation" issues. There has been little emphasis on explaining how the mental frames of employees are changed or how their skill sets are upgraded to prepare for their new jobs. The only reference to "skills" or "training" found in either of the two reengineering bibles (Hammer and Champy 1993; Davenport 1993) focus on selecting the right people to participate in the reengineering design, rather than on the skills and training of employees that must be considered during implementation. Ironically, the basic tenets of reengineering are premised on radical changes to managers' and employees' skills and work processes. While creating a good design is, admittedly, an important component of reengineering, it is during implementation that the mettle of this design will be tested and, more importantly, it is at this stage that the importance of individual, group, and organizational learning can become the primary barriers to success (Craig and Yetton 1994).

The literature on managing technology implementation has paid somewhat more attention to those influences which shape outcomes (Orlikowski 1993; Leonard-Barton 1988a, 1988b; Ettlie 1986; Gallivan, Hofman and Orlikowski 1994), although it generally notes only the presence or absence of a formal user training program during technology implementation, without explaining the *nature* of the training approach nor the mechanisms though which new skills are reinforced on the job, outside the classroom. A few exceptions (Orlikowski 1992b; Olfman and Mandviwalla 1994) have remarked on the nature of the training approach, demonstrating that the training approach can shape (or *fail* to shape) users' frames regarding a new technology. These researchers also provide a possible explanation for users' subsequent behavior, both in terms of *how much* they use a new technology and *how differently* they use it (compared to prior work methods) to streamline or to transform their work processes. As suggested earlier, this challenge is significantly greater when the technology calls for second-order change than for first-order change (Gallivan, et al. 1993).

Research on the implementation of new technologies (such as groupware) has shown that, in the absence of *conceptual* training (which attempts to shape users' frames around a particular model of a new technology), users will simply attach a familiar technology frame to the system (Orlikowski 1992b; Bullen and Bennett 1990). Where the goal of technology implementation calls for transformation or radical change, the outcomes of this inability to reshape users' frames may lead to results that differ from the designer's or management sponsor's intentions (Kraut, Dumais and Koch 1989). In general, the shortcomings of training that focuses on teaching mechanical or procedural routines may result in users' inability to grasp the larger purpose and significance of the technology. Users may thus be unable to transfer their rote skills to new problems and scenarios (Sein and Bostrom 1990). Empirical studies have shown that both procedural and conceptual training may be required for new patterns of behavior to consolidate over time (Olfman and Mandviwalla 1994).

This study sought to understand how various stakeholders understood the process of organizational change surrounding the adoption of new software process innovations in the firm (client/server development) and how their respective frames influenced their beliefs about the activities that constituted progress toward achieving the objectives of the change effort. Results from the study demonstrate extreme differences among the various stakeholder groups over seemingly trivial issues as to whether there exists an IS reskilling initiative. Such contradictory stakeholder views of the change initiative might suggest that some parties had withheld critical information during the field study — an interpretation that might call for more interviews to isolate the source of the missing, erroneous, or inconsistent data. Yet another way to understand this quandary, and the primary insight of this paper, is that a more fruitful way of analyzing the contrasting information gathered from the various stakeholder groups is to consider the different frames they hold with respect to the anticipated technological changes, as well as their assumptions about organizational changes that must accompany technological change to achieve the desired outcomes. This concept of organizational *complements* emerged from the field study analysis that follows, and coincidentally, reflects the key assumptions of a new theory called business value *complementarity* (Barua, Kreibel and Mukhopadhyay 1995; Barua, Lee and Whinston 1994; Barua and Whinston 1994), which proposes a set of organization design decisions (or variables) that must accompany technological change in order to achieve a set of objectives.[1] Whereas stakeholder experiences with the results of the change initiative do appear to be directly contradictory with each other, the analysis of their experiences through the perspective of technology frames — particularly stakeholders' assumptions about organizational complementarities — thus allows for the coexistence of divergent views of the technological change and IS reskilling initiatives.

4. RESEARCH QUESTIONS AND METHODOLOGY

The research presented here was conducted as part of a larger study on the implementation approaches used for "reskilling" IS professionals to perform systems development work using a set of software development process innovations (Fichman and Kemerer 1993) such as client/server technology, object-oriented development, and GUI development tools. Field studies were conducted in four companies that were in the process of implementing these innovations and modifying the skill set of their IS staff to utilize these new tools and methods. One of these field studies, TechCo, is presented here. TechCo was the first case study completed and, for this reason, the framework that emerged is a preliminary one. The research questions that motivated the study were:

- What types of learning processes do IS developers engage in to acquire new skills for performing systems development work (e.g., formal classroom training, self-study)?

- How do IS developers experience these different learning activities (in terms of usefulness for learning to perform client/server development)?

- Do IS developers' roles change as new technologies for performing system development are implemented and what are the drivers behind such role changes?

Data were collected through semi-structured interviews with twelve respondents drawn primarily from the IS organization of a single case site, TechCo (a pseudonym). Since the study focused on reskilling IS professionals, most respondents were IS developers or first-level managers within the IS organization itself (seven out of twelve). The remaining respondents were from functions closely related to IS, such as technical training and change management (two from each, respectively), and one user analyst from a system implementation project. Each respondent was interviewed once for 60 to 90 minutes and questions were tailored to individual respondents based on their organizational level, job duties, and specific involvement in the process of implementing client/server development and the organization's IS reskilling initiative.

---

[1] The notion of complementarities is derived from economic theory (Edgeworth 1881) and has been empirically demonstrated in research on information technology investments (Milgom and Roberts 1990).

Due to the framing of this research as a study of IS reskilling, the initial interview was conducted with the staff manager responsible for TechCo's IS reskilling initiative and she served as the primary contact person for the study. Six of the remaining respondents were IS developers and project managers suggested by her. The last five respondents were based on referrals made during the first set of interviews. The interviews were not tape recorded, but detailed notes were recorded during each interview, then reviewed and analyzed at the conclusion of each day. This analysis summarized each respondent's knowledge and exposure to the IS reskilling initiative and any other experience with client/server technology (e.g., participation on project teams using the technology, individual reading, or classes taken outside the firm). Beyond the interviews, additional materials about TechCo and its IS department were collected through public sources (such as online databases) and proprietary sources (such as company reports and IS department newsletters).

Data were analyzed through qualitative analysis techniques, first by developing a chronological history of the IS organization, including the structure, technologies used, relationships between the IS and business groups, the culture, and events leading up to the current change initiatives both at the firm level and within the IS organization.

Individual respondents were aggregated into subgroups for more detailed analysis, based on functional boundaries, using the notion of "critical social groups" (Kling and Gerson 1978). Rather than using a traditional clustering of respondents into managers, users, and technologists as the critical groups, because this study focused on the implementation of a reskilling program, the relevant stakeholder groups were 1) managers of the reskilling initiative, 2) prospective participants in the reskilling initiative, and 3) other IS stakeholders not directly affected by the reskilling initiative.

Based on this initial grouping of stakeholders, a more in-depth analysis into the experiences and attitudes of each respondent was conducted. This analysis was not entirely inductive or grounded (Strauss and Corbin 1990); instead, it used a set of pre-existing categories (Orlikowski and Gash's three domains of technology frames) but supplemented with an inductive analysis of respondents' responses which did not fit into one of these prior domains. Once the concept of *organizational complements to technology change* emerged as an additional frame that shaped respondents' perceptions of the reskilling initiative, the specific organizational activities that respondents believed were required to successfully harness the potential of client/server technology were mapped to an existing set of categories suggested by Leavitt (1965) and subsequently expanded by Rockart and Scott Morton (1984). These categories are individual skills, roles, management processes, organizational structure, strategy, culture, and technology.[2] These themes were contrasted among the three stakeholder groups, using cross group comparison techniques suggested by Eisenhardt (1989, p. 540), which draw on the cross case analysis techniques from Miles and Huberman (1994), although the comparisons were for different stakeholder groups *within* the same case study.

---

[2]Note that the categories Rockart and Scott Morton use are similar to the seven organization design variables identified by Barua and Whinston (1994) in their theory of business value complementarity. The latter theory includes seven "organizational design variables" — organizational structure, decision authority structure, coordination mechanisms, incentive and reward systems, business processes, management processes, and information technology.

The remainder of the paper is structured as follows. First, background information about the context in which the technological and organizational changes occurred is described, followed by the results from the three stakeholder groups. For each group, their intentions and expectations for the IS reskilling initiative, for technological change, and for the organizational complements to these changes are described. Following this, the discussion section will first identify the contradictions between these diverse accounts and then, by incorporating the notion of stakeholders' frames, will seek to resolve the inconsistencies between them.

5. RESULTS

5.1   Organizational History and Context

The field study was conducted at TechCo, a large telecommunications utility which operates in one region of the U.S. TechCo was formerly one of the regional Bell telephone operating companies. Both the regulated utility industry in which TechCo competes and the firm itself are undergoing tremendous change. Impending competition with new service providers is driving TechCo to remake itself from a sluggish, oversized, monopoly into a smaller, more agile, market-oriented competitor. In the past, service rates (prices) were determined by a regulatory commission, based on formal rate requests submitted by TechCo, and the firm held a monopoly in one of the most heavily populated regions of the country. Given this lack of competition, market sensitivity and cost controls were not important drivers.

5.2   Corporate Culture

Historically the corporate culture was paternalistic and rule-bound.[3] Several respondents described the firm as "a pension company," implying that it provided lifelong employment for its workers, with several respondents adding that "there is the belief that the company owes me something." Many of the management nostrums of the previous decades did little to invigorate the firm. For example, one manager described the efforts to introduce then-fashionable notions of *empowerment* to the firm; unfortunately, the concept was interpreted to mean *entitlement*. According to this manager, employees believed they were *entitled* to job security, excellent fringe benefits, and the expectation that their salaries — like the regulated service rates — would rise over time, since both were protected from market forces. There was a well-established hierarchy, and people knew their position within it. One respondent said, "This firm was designed as a cross between the Catholic church and the Prussian Army. I am serious — we have levels of management like you wouldn't believe."

In addition to being hierarchical and a protected monopoly, there were well-established procedures for everything. One IS manager said, "In the past, things changed much more slowly. Our culture was 'you don't rattle anybody's cage'." One colorful catch phrase describing employee resistance

---

[3]In addition to the interviews, some of the information in this section was drawn from sources about the company that were in the public domain. This includes a set of articles written about the company and published in a national outlet and excerpts from the CIO's speeches that appeared in the computer trade press. Publication sources are omitted to protect the firm's confidentiality.

to change was the phrase *bell-head mentality* — a twist on the pejorative term "blockhead" and simultaneously a reference to the firm's origin as one of the regional Bell telephone operating companies. Stability, hierarchy, and lifetime employment characterized the nature of the employee-employer bond at TechCo.

5.3 Recent Company Changes

Rapid change is now the order of the day at TechCo. Regulatory changes scheduled for 1996 will permit other new competitors to enter TechCo's former monopoly service market and TechCo has recently engaged both a premier strategy consulting and systems integration firm to drive a series of reengineering projects, with substantial anticipated headcount reductions on the order of 20% of the firm's total workforce. TechCo is trying to make the layoffs painless at first by offering a *carrot,* in the form of generous voluntary retirement to more senior employees and managers, with the veiled threat of a *stick,* forced layoffs, which may soon follow if insufficient numbers of employees choose the voluntary severance offer.

Not only are the long-term consequences of the reengineering and downsizing anticipated to be dramatic, many respondents in the study were living with its repercussions on a daily basis. Almost every respondent interviewed for this study had experienced one or more of the following changes within the weeks prior to their interviews; some had experienced all three:

- they began reporting to new bosses,
- new subordinates began reporting to them,
- they assumed job duties from departing co-workers.

The general perception of respondents was that the bond of paternalism which had been symbolized through the promise of lifetime employment had clearly been severed and employees were fearful of the changes that were to follow with the reengineering and downsizing. In the words of one employee, "We've had more change than we can handle. Senior management says 'we don't have the time to go slowly.' But people can't adjust to change that rapidly. We are changing the culture of the company overnight."

5.4 Overview of IS Organization

The IS organization is itself divided into several autonomous groups or *portfolios,* each reporting to a functional business department of the company (Finance, Engineering, Customer Service). Historically, the work of IS professionals was focused on technology rather than on understanding the users' business needs, and this bias is still reflected today by the fact that developers call themselves "programmers," despite the fact that their titles were changed years ago to "systems analysts." The IS employees have historically been buffered from users by the existence of a separate career path called "methods analysts," who assumed responsibility for business analysis, procedure writing, and user training related to system implementation. In effect, the creation of the "methods analyst" role at TechCo shielded the "programmers" from users, permitting them to focus on technology issues.

At TechCo, the IS organization traditionally suffered from a poor reputation of being slow, overly bureaucratic, technically-oriented and isolated from the business divisions. One senior IS executive drew an analogy between the weak relationship IS has with its internal customers (users) and the company's poor communication with *their* customers:

> I've been surprised by the distance between the IS organization and the customer....As for our culture, the IS organization is like a monopoly within a monopoly....Everything I could say about TechCo, I could say about the IS function in the company. We're both facing the same challenges — a super-high novelty rate, unprecedented change, regulatory issues, and new lines of business.[4]

Several respondents said that "the IS group was not fast enough in the past," nor were they customer oriented. Many respondents faulted the IS department for using technology standards — including their structured systems development life cycle — as a barrier to being more customer-oriented or efficient. Several other respondents validated this perception of "the IS organization being unable to deliver," which resulted in many business departments deciding to bypass them by hiring their own IS contractors to develop systems for them. This was exacerbated in the late 1980s, when the IS organization lagged in responding to the PC revolution. With IS still mired in a mainframe mentality, these business divisions increasingly bought their own workstations, software, and consultants to develop their systems, but without following any standards. Such systems were designed as standalone, departmental systems, yet when the need arose for data integration across functions, this lack of adherence to standards led to fingerpointing and recrimination between IS and the business groups. The IS department refused to support systems that had been developed by outside consultants.

5.5   Precursors to Adoption of Client/Server Development

Until very recently, the skill base of the IS workforce at TechCo was exclusively mainframe-oriented. At the time of the field study, nearly all production systems were IBM mainframe applications written in COBOL or PL/1, using either IMS or DB-2 databases. Some respondents mentioned efforts to standardize on new methodologies and tools during the late 1980s (such as data modeling and Knowledgeware's *Information Engineering Workbench* CASE tool), but after some initial enthusiasm, these efforts were abandoned. There was no standard set of tools or system development methodology in use across the IS groups.

Four important events occurred in 1992 that set the stage for the department's subsequent move toward client/server technology. First, the IS department replaced the 3270 "dumb" terminals on every programmer's desk with new workstations, but this was neither preceded nor accompanied by any training program. As a result, several programmers lacked any knowledge of or incentive for using the new workstations. One IS manager recalled how the hardware was rolled out to IS developers: "They said 'there you are, go to town.' They wanted you to get on board with using the PC, but they didn't tell you how."

---

[4]This quote is borrowed from a 1993 speech presented by the CIO shortly after his arrival and is excerpted from an IS industry newsletter. It is titled "Meeting the Challenge of Rapid Change: The Evolving Role of IS in Telecommunications."

The second event occurred later in the year, when a series of videotaped training classes were made available to IS employees. These classes covered a variety of personal productivity software packages, including several software packages that could be substituted for each other.[5] These training classes were voluntary, although some IS managers encouraged their staff to take as many of them as possible. During this time, IS still continued to build systems in traditional ways, with developers using terminal emulation with their workstations to connect to the mainframe.

Third, a new CIO was hired to lead the firm. In an unusual move, the firm hired an outsider, a fairly young, aggressive executive with significant experience in the for-profit sector. The fourth event was the administration of a skill survey to IS staff, which was conducted to gather data to validate the new CIO's concern that the IS staff was lagging behind in its knowledge of emerging technologies — such as distributed hardware and client/server development. The results of the survey confirmed the CIO's misgivings and led to an increased reliance on hiring outside consulting firms and individual contractors to supply the necessary skills in emerging technologies.

5.6   Adoption of Client/Server Development and IS Reskilling

In the next subsections of the paper, the contrasting perspectives from three stakeholder groups will be presented regarding the goals and progress achieved to date in implementing client/server development and IS reskilling. The three stakeholder groups are the Change Management specialists, IS employees and managers, and a miscellaneous group of respondents who are outside of the group of IS staff targeted for reskilling.

Stakeholder Group 1: Change Management Specialists. The first stakeholder group consisted of members of TechCo's *Change Management Group*, an internal staff function within the IS organization charged with overseeing the reskilling of TechCo's IS staff. The very existence of a separate Change Management Group reporting directly to the CIO revealed a positive and progressive approach toward IS reskilling. Furthermore, the names of the sub-departments within Change Management highlighted the intended approach to managing change. Within the Change Management Group are the Employee Investment Group and the Communication Group. The very title *employee investment group* was carefully chosen to signify that reskilling should be an investment in each employee. Similarly, the Communication Group was created to foster two-way communication between the CIO and the IS staff. The latter department published a monthly newsletter which one respondent dubbed "the mouthpiece of the CIO."

The Change Management specialists envisioned their mission as facilitating a cultural change within IS and doing so through a partnership with each IS department manager and his or her staff. Part of the cultural change meant breaking away from the paternalistic notion that "the company will take care of me," by instead creating a sense of shared responsibility among the Change Management Group and each IS manager and employee. The firm's investment in new skills was something that could benefit each employee and thus each employee was expected to be an active participant in it. The reskilling initiative was a change management program directed at every

---

[5]These included two word processing packages (Microsoft Word for Windows and WordPerfect); two spreadsheet packages (Microsoft Excel and Lotus 1-2-3); two graphics packages (PowerPoint for Windows and Harvard Graphics); and Lotus Notes.

member of the IS organization — managers in particular — and the key mechanisms for achieving a reskilled technical and managerial force relied on individual mentoring and skills assessment conducted with one's immediate supervisor, followed by training.

Most importantly, the managers in the Employee Investment Group recognized that the change being introduced at TechCo transcended a simple change in the technology for producing software. Instead, the effort encompassed a broader set of cultural changes. These managers described a broad transformation of the IS organization, including the opportunity to become more customer-oriented, for the employees to learn new technical skills, software development life cycle skills, project management skills, and new approaches for collaborating with users.

Finally, the Employee Investment Group, which was overseeing the reskilling program, was neither a technology standards group nor a training department, since TechCo already had departments dedicated to both of those functions. According to one respondent, the purpose was not to administer a training program, but rather "to create the [career] development opportunity to happen by figuring out the skills gaps that exist and allowing project team training to occur at the right time."

It was the intention of the Change Management Group to fulfill this vision by creating a process in which career mentoring could occur and to disseminate a set of structured tools to facilitate the skills assessment process, in particular a skills assessment database. This database was an important tool in the process, since it would allow IS managers to "inventory their employees" by creating a database containing information both about current skills and future skill requirements. The database was envisioned to serve as a tool to facilitate identification of any resulting gap and to document remedial actions to fill these gaps.[6]

Stakeholder Group 2: IS Managers and Employees. TechCo's second stakeholder group consists of IS staff and first-line managers. A total of seven interviews with these IS stakeholders were conducted between one and three months after the interviews with the Change Management Group. The experience and outlook of six of these IS members are summarized here.[7] In contrast to the image of *partnership*, communication, and mentoring portrayed by the previous stakeholder group, a major surprise was encountered with this second stakeholder group. These respondents were either completely unaware or skeptical about the existence of a Change Management Group addressing the issue of reskilling and, secondly, they had their own definition and approach to reskilling that differed from that of the first stakeholder group.

---

[6]The skills database was purchased in mid-1993 and scheduled to be implemented in late 1993. Due to the changes occurring within the IS organization — notably the voluntary layoff (spring 1994) and subsequent forced layoff (scheduled for fall 1994), a decision was made to delay implementation of the skills database in order to avoid having employees equate the skills inventory with the layoffs. IS management also recognized that they could minimize their implementation effort by postponing implementation until after the layoffs, since this would result in a reduced employee population size for whom skill profiles would be developed.

[7]One additional IS respondent had recently been relocated from the IS organization to a special strategic reengineering project. Due to her experience and outlook, which diverged quite dramatically from the six respondents described in this section, she is incorporated into the third stakeholder group. These differences may have resulted from her access to confidential information about the corporation's goals due to her involvement in the reengineering team and exposure to working directly with both strategy and systems integration consultants.

Of the six IS members in the second stakeholder group, only two were even vaguely familiar with the fact that plans for an IS reskilling initiative were "in the works" within the Change Management Group. A more common stance among these stakeholders when they were questioned about the reskilling initiative was either ignorance or disbelief. One manager, in fact, commented, "I don't believe that TechCo has a grand plan to reskill its IS workforce. I don't believe that TechCo is taking reskilling seriously."

Furthermore, when asked about the career counseling process that managers were expected to engage in with their staff, responses were inconsistent regarding whether IS managers traditionally had engaged in such mentoring activities, or whether managers were themselves prepared to offer such direction and advice to their subordinates regarding personal development. Given that most IS managers had spent even more years in the rule-bound hierarchy at TechCo, some were in greater need of skill development than their subordinates. Several respondents suggested that IS managers could not be counted on themselves to fulfill the mentoring role envisioned by the change management specialists.

Instead, most IS staff defined reskilling to be their own autonomous efforts to learn about, and experiment with, anything related to developing systems on distributed hardware — whether experimenting with front-end GUI-based application development tools (such as PowerBuilder) or back-end server software (such as SQL). In the absence of any firm-defined standards for developing client/server systems, IS employees had broadly defined client/server reskilling as anything related to PC-based system development.[8] In the absence of any firm-sponsored standards or mandate to reskill, IS employees were engaging in two types of reskilling, both in a bottom-up mode, with little direction or structure from their division's IS management or from the Change Management Group.

There were two types of reskilling occurring within the IS organization which are labeled here *project-driven* and *career-driven*. Neither resembled the vision described by the Change Management Group of top-down, goal-directed, standards-compliant training. Furthermore, none of this training was in response to skills assessment or career mentoring that had been conducted with the person's supervisor (as envisioned by Change Management), because such skills assessments were not being conducted.

•   *Project-driven* reskilling occurred where developers had been assigned to new projects where they were expected to evaluate, recommend for adoption, and learn to use new client/server tools, yet where they lacked previous experience or formal training. In such cases, IS staff were engaged in a self-directed program of reading, hands-on practice, and trial-and-error learning about the new hardware and software development approaches.

---

[8]This contrasts with the traditional definition of client/server technology, which requires a specific configuration of computer processes that is divided between a user workstation (the client) and a central database management system (the server). Normally the user interface and application programming logic reside on the "client" workstation and the database resides on the server. Most personal computer workstations, even those connected by a LAN, are thus not client/server systems.

- *Career-driven reskilling.* The second type of reskilling was also initiated by the individual, but it differed in purpose and form. The purpose, in this case, was a more general desire to keep up with changes in emerging technology; the form was through taking a course outside the workplace, through a local university's extension program. This is labeled *career-driven reskilling,* since the IS respondents pursuing this option explained their reskilling motives in terms of their desire to keep their resumes up-to-date. For example, when asked why he was taking the six-month part-time university extension course on client/server development, one IS manager replied "just open up the newspaper," referring to the wealth of help-wanted advertisements requiring skills in client/server development. Whether or not these respondents fell victim to future layoffs, the new skills would help to bolster the demand for their skills (and likely salary) in the future job market.

Despite some obvious differences between the *project-driven* and *career-driven* reskilling efforts, they share four common features. The first is that employees are *able to* reskill themselves without any explicit direction from the firm, that is without the firm needing to identify a set of standards to follow for client/server hardware, software, or methodology. The second shared feature is the belief that motivated IS employees are *better off* reskilling without explicit direction about corporate standards, specific skills, and required training courses. Several respondents ascribed a "survival of the fittest" motif to reskilling, suggesting that the very initiative shown by an IS employee to reskill can serve as evidence of his or her dedication. This image alone may boost the employee's long-term job prospects at TechCo. For example, one IS manager, when asked her opinion about the Change Management Group's proposed structure and skills database for identifying skills gaps, said:

> *Fearless*people are those who will roll up your sleeves and go. People who want to be fearless don't need someone telling them what types of skills they need to have. The employees [their co-workers] don't want someone who is too passive either [in terms of requiring specific direction].

The third shared feature is the IS developers' belief that reskilling is about learning new *technical* skills, and does not extend to the more fundamental transitions regarding the roles, culture, structure, or business skills of IS employees. Given this assumption regarding reskilling, their chosen path made sense (individual, bottom-up learning) because reskilling is synonymous, in their minds, with new technical skills, which may be learned through hands-on, individual effort. Reskilling is not a broad cultural transformation of the work process, which would certainly require some top-down vision, leadership and coordination. Finally, reskilling should serve short-term objectives (such as completing a required project or updating one's resume with marketable skills), rather than being part of a broader, long-term transformation of how the firm would develop information systems in the future.

Stakeholder Group 3: "Outsiders" to the Reskilling Initiative. The third set of stakeholders consisted of a variety of respondents who were involved with TechCo's IS organization, but were not intended subjects for the reskilling initiative. In terms of research chronology, these respondents were the last ones interviewed, having been recommended to the researcher by stakeholders in group two. Given the range of respondents in this stakeholder group (two technical trainers, one user analyst, and one IS manager involved in the strategic reengineering project) and their status as outside of the intended audience for the IS reskilling initiative, the term "outsiders" will be used to refer to them collectively, indicating that they were beyond the intended target population for the IS reskilling initiative.

The "outsider" stakeholder group held one set of expectations in common with each of the other stakeholder groups, while also offering divergent views of what IS reskilling would require. The commonalities are identified first, followed by the differences. Like the members of the first stakeholder group (Change Management), the outsiders suggested a vision of a radically transformed IS function — one where the culture, skills, roles, and structure of the IS function would be radically different than they exist at present. Like the members of the second stakeholder group (IS members), they were unfamiliar with the vision for skills assessment and top-down culture change within the IS group that had been conceived by the Change Management Group. When questioned about this initiative during these interviews, they were bluntly skeptical, as revealed by the earlier quote: "I don't believe that TechCo has a grand plan to reskill its IS workforce. I don't believe that TechCo is taking reskilling seriously." Yet, despite these similarities, the area in which this third stakeholder group diverged from the previous two groups was truly quite shocking. They believed there would be little or no in-house IS development at TechCo in the future, and that most IS staff would see their present jobs eliminated in the near future. The stark predictions for the IS organization held by these stakeholders was revealed by the following statement: "There is no future for IS in this company. I don't see one. There may be a small portion of people with very specific skills, [but] I can't tell you [what those will be]."

A second respondent confirmed this prediction, describing that "traditional IS work as we know it today [applications development and maintenance] will no longer exist." These stakeholders described a radically downsized IS organization where application packages are purchased, then external consultants with expertise in reengineering and systems integration will modify and implement the packages. Their vision left little room for the legions of existing IS staff who currently perform system development and maintenance work. One of these respondents was able to envision a limited role for TechCo's in-house IS staff, who will become *system baby-sitters* — basically a deskilled (not reskilled) role of operations support. These system baby-sitters will monitor the operation of packaged application software on distributed systems and will simply relay any problems to the application software's vendor, who will, in turn, diagnose and resolve these problems.

Based on the input from these stakeholders, it was unclear whether they had some "inside scoop" on the plans and visions of TechCo's senior IS management, or whether they had simply acquired a pessimistic outlook about TechCo's long-term commitment to its IS staff. It is also unclear whether these stakeholders' expectations about how reskilling would be implemented differed so dramatically from the other stakeholder groups because they knew that senior IS management lacked faith in the ability of IS staff to learn and change, or whether they believed that senior management wanted to simply take the easy route of relying on outsourcers, with the uncertain implications for TechCo's long-term human resource policies.

There is limited evidence for the "inside scoop" explanation (i.e., that the "outsider" stakeholders had inside information that others lacked). One informant, the IS manager who described her experience working on the reengineering project with strategy consultants, explained TechCo's need to hire external consultants because TechCo "didn't have people that could talk to users to get the requirements from them." Moreover, after spending a year on the reengineering project, this thirteen year IS veteran added that "I acquired most of my present skills from the consultants." Her comments underscored the fundamental challenge of trying to develop these communication and business analysis skills among an entrenched workforce that perceives its role as limited to technology. Obviously, it is a much quicker solution for a business that must change technology direction suddenly to simply buy the necessary skills from external consultants.

6. DISCUSSION: THE RESKILLING PROGRAM — PHANTOM OR FACT?

The three stakeholder views of TechCo's plan for implementing client/server development and for reskilling its IS staff are, at best, inconsistent and, at worst, contradictory. The first stakeholder perspective (that of the Change Management Group) describes a reskilling initiative that will rely on a three-way partnership among themselves, the IS managers, and the developers. This vision for IS reskilling seeks a major *transformation* in the skills and roles of developers, as well as changes in the organizational culture such as how developers interact with users, are rewarded, learn new skills, etc. Their vision for how this radically new strategy will be implemented featured both centralized and decentralized attributes. The centralized attributes were the purchase and planned deployment of a skills assessment database to create an inventory of skill information and to identify remedial actions required. The decentralized attributes were the mentoring and career development activities, which they expected would occur within every IS workgroup, with no oversight from the Change Management group.

The second stakeholder group's perspective suggests a narrower view of changes that are required to *update* the skills of IS — basically limited to technical skills — without any broader implications for changing the culture, roles, or developer interaction with users. These stakeholders' assumptions about the strategy for achieving these skill changes are that these modest changes can occur through a fragmented series of bottom-up, individual efforts to experiment with and learn new technologies. It ignores changes other than technical skills and changes that are more long-term in nature. While this second stakeholder vision of reskilling (to *update* technical skill sets) is not mutually exclusive with the first vision (to transform the IS culture), since one is really a subset of the other, nevertheless there is a fundamental irony. Was there a reskilling initiative and, if so, why did no one outside of the Change Management Group know about it?

The third perspective, that of describing a vision of transformation largely achieved through increased reliance on external consultants, combined with dramatic layoffs and new, deskilled roles for existing IS staff, is also inconsistent with the spirit of the reskilling initiative envisioned by the Change Management Group. The only way this discrepancy could be reconciled is to assume that the "career development counseling" and "skills assessment" that IS managers will conduct for their staffs are largely to prepare them for their transition to unemployment, or to provide assistance in finding a job elsewhere. Yet, could this truly be what the Change Management Group had in mind when they spoke of broad-based career development counseling between each manager-subordinate dyad? Was the real purpose behind the Employee Investment Group merely softening the blows that would result from future lay-offs, the group's title notwithstanding? In fact, there is tremendous irony in the organization creating an "Employee Investment Group," when the third stakeholder perspective is that the firm plans to *divest* itself of nearly all its IS development staff. Similarly, one might question the sincerity of organizational units with names such as "Communications Group" or "Change Management Group" when, from the perspective of the IS respondents, there has been little either communicated or changed by these respective staff groups.

7. EXAMINING STAKEHOLDERS FRAMES

Although the preceding discussion highlighted the contradictions between the various perspectives of change offered by the three stakeholder groups, it is possible, through examining more carefully the language that various stakeholders use and the beliefs they hold in talking about the impending change effort, to show that these perspectives appear to be contradictory because they are grounded in different assumptions, each of which can be traced to distinct experiences and historical precedents across the stakeholder groups. Here we can invoke the concept of members' frames of reference, not only to characterize their beliefs about technological change, but to capture their assumptions regarding the organizational *complementarities* required to achieve technological change (Barua, Kriebel and Mukhopadhyay 1995; Barua and Whinston 1994).

The Change Management specialists used the term reskilling to refer to a host of organizational changes, of which migrating to new technology was merely one small part. Instead, their frames of what "IS reskilling" constituted is a much broader set of changes, beginning with new ways of organizing and serving users, and pervading all the constructs of the Rockart and Scott Morton framework, including organizational culture, technical and non-technical skills, roles, technology, management processes, and strategy. Furthermore, their assumptions about the mechanisms required for implementing this vision were to create a shared partnership with all the members of the IS function and then allow career mentoring activities to cascade down the organization through a series of face-to-face meetings, beginning with the most senior IS executives on down to the junior programmers. Given their assumptions about reskilling IS — that it requires a broad, cultural transformation — then any efforts which may facilitate this transformation, such as preparing IS managers for the impending cultural shift, would constitute progress toward the goal of reskilling, even if the objectives of the change and detailed implementation plans were not communicated to the IS workforce.

In the second stakeholder group, the members' frames for understanding IS reskilling suggested that it is merely an updating of technical skills, one involving a *substitution* of new technical skills for old ones (e.g., replacing COBOL with *PowerBuilder* as the programming language and replacing IMS with SQL as the database). In fact, given this framing of reskilling as a simple *substitution* of new technical skills for old, there are few complementary changes required to achieve it. For example, there are no required changes in the communication skills or industry knowledge on the part of IS employees, nor in such intangibles as their individual roles, interactions with users, the department's culture, management strategy, etc. There is further evidence that the IS stakeholders' assumptions about what constitutes reskilling and how each employee should approach it are based on their prior experiences at TechCo with learning technical skills — specifically, their experience with learning to use PCS and personal productivity software, both of which occurred in 1992. As described above, the 1992 roll-out of PCS was characterized by the absence of any mandates to learn the new tools and the individual autonomy to select which software packages to learn (from the multiple "standards" that had been identified for word processing, spreadsheets, etc.) The underlying message that had previously been communicated was that it was not necessary to have a uniform set of technology standards or a mandated set of training courses. Furthermore, the prior adoption of PCS had reinforced to IS developers that learning need not be coordinated — either across various subgroups within the IS department or across the knowledge domains for learning (the various skills to be learned). Each employee could simply do it on his or her own, learning whatever new technical skills they desired, and in whatever sequence they chose. Given this prior experience of what reskilling is about (substitution of new technical skills for old) and how it is accomplished (through individual autonomy and initiative), the IS stakeholders later recognized that they were free to reskill — *or not* — as they saw fit. Due to this frame about how reskilling occurs, the IS stakeholders interpreted any learning attempt — such as reading a trade magazine or hands-on practice with any PC tool — as progress on their part, regardless of whether the learning was related to client/server, as narrowly defined, or related to a tool that had been — or would ultimately be — designated a standard for the firm. Since multiple PC and software standards had been acceptable in the recent past, respondents perceived that any tool learning they engaged in was a form of reskilling.

Finally, the description of the perceptions of the third stakeholder group (the "outsider" group) suggests that they share some assumptions with the Change Management group — namely, that some radical transformation is required, but with diametrically opposite beliefs about *how* this transformation would be achieved. The issue of whether the members of this "outsider" stakeholder group were actually "insiders" in terms of knowing something more about senior management's true intentions for investing in or *divesting* IS employees is a moot question. It was not possible, during the course of this research, to corroborate the suspicions of this stakeholder group. Perhaps more importantly, the question that matters is not simply "was the outsider stakeholder group *more accurate* than the other stakeholder groups?" but rather "how were the frames they held regarding senior IS manager's likely course of action consistent with their own experiences of how radical change gets implemented at TechCo?"

Like the other stakeholder groups, these members' own prior experiences were the key to their future expectations, since their assumptions about the future were shaped by their own past experiences. These stakeholders had each observed that the outsourcing of work to consultants was feasible, fast, and a likely-to-be-repeated option. Each of these stakeholders had also experienced first-hand the outcomes of outsourcing as a short-term success in project milestones and reduced headcount costs, accompanied by dramatic layoffs and uncertain implications for human resources long term.[9] Thus, these stakeholders had concrete experience with senior management's increased reliance on outsourcing and lay-offs as the route to change, which shaped their beliefs that management would accomplish the challenge of reskilling IS through similar tactics.

---

[9]Specifically, the two IS training department members had watched their department reverse, over a period of three years, from a training portfolio where "70% of the training classes were taught in-house and only 30% outsourced to a situation where nearly everything 100% was outsourced." They had also experienced, over the weeks preceding our interviews, the dramatic layoffs in their own department, amounting to what one called "the virtual decimation of the IS training department." The other two stakeholders here (the user and the IS manager on the reengineering project) had recently completed a successful project that relied on systems integration consultants. Each of these projects was anticipated to streamline business operations, thus reducing the workforce in a specific business unit.

8. LIMITATIONS AND CONTRIBUTIONS OF THE RESEARCH

Further research is required to understand how each set of stakeholder frames will play out in the future, since we lack information about which of these different perspectives on TechCo's reskilling initiative will become the reality. One of the limitations of this research is that it was conducted without input from the CIO or other senior IS executives. Senior IS management represents a fourth important stakeholder group, with frames about IS reskilling that very likely differ from the other stakeholders. Furthermore, senior IS management, by virtue of being the *dominant coalition* (Child 1972) in the firm, differs from the other stakeholder groups in terms of having the formal authority to impose their vision of change over the others. While the absence of this powerful stakeholder perspective clearly leaves us with many questions, it also has created the paradoxical benefit that by *not* knowing which scenario of IS reskilling will likely occur, we are able to examine the evidence for each of the other stakeholders' frames of reference and, by identifying past experiences which shape and reinforce them, to explain their present expectations and behavior. If instead, this field study had begun by querying the CIO and other senior IS executives about their assumptions and intentions for IS reskilling, then this may have biased the research, since the presumption would be that senior management's plan would be implemented. Thus, by not gaining this senior management perspective, the research was free to carefully analyze the frames of the less-powerful stakeholder groups.

Given this constraint and the opportunities it has facilitated, there are four contributions that this paper offers. The first is a contribution to theory, namely, expanding upon Orlikowski and Gash's concept of technological frames to illustrate stakeholders' frames about the set of organizational complementarities necessary to successfully implement technological change. As discussed previously, certain stakeholders perceived a great number of complements as necessary to benefit from new technology while others perceived none. The second contribution is a reiteration of Orlikowski and Gash's theoretical statement: that participants in a change initiative will bring to bear their previous experiences with developing frames of reference around organizational change, and that in the absence of any clear, concrete message or vision from the organization which alters these frames of reference, that stakeholders will continue to *act toward* and *evaluate* the firm's progress toward its goals, based on the initial frames they hold.

The third contribution is the corollary to this; that, where possible, organizations should seek to reorient members' frames regarding the goals of change to ensure that these frames are consistent with the frames held by senior management, organizational change specialists, technology designers, etc. For example, in the case of TechCo, the Communication Group within Change Management could have more effectively communicated their views about the extent of the anticipated transformation. By communicating their assumptions about the organizational complements required for the reskilling initiative to succeed, the Change Management Group may have better shaped the frames and expectations of IS staff and managers regarding the goals of the change effort and the sacrifices required of them.

There may be times when achieving such a reorientation is difficult or impossible. For example, the literature on organizational change is replete with scenarios where individuals, groups, and organizations as a whole have been unable to question and change their frames where necessary (Bolman and Deal 1991; Starbuck 1989; Dougherty 1992). Yet there have been some success stories where frames have been altered or "realigned" (Nadler and Tushman 1989; Bartunek 1987; Poole, Gioia and Gray 1989; Isabella 1990). As discussed above, specific types of training have been successfully shown to shape the frames of potential users so that they can better learn to use new technologies (Santhanam and Sein 1994). Similarly, organizational development consultants have used a variety of techniques to prepare organizational participants for major changes, such as "frame-bending" exercises (Nadler and Tushman 1989) and identifying individuals' threshold for change through measuring their personal resilience profile (Conner 1992).

Fourth, while this paper describes only one case study, it was conducted as part of a larger study of organizational change around IS reskilling to understand how skill and role changes are experienced by members of an organization. This paper has suggested that such changes are defined in terms of the frames that stakeholders hold about the goals of the change effort and that their evaluation of progress toward these goals rests upon their implicit understanding of what types of skill changes are necessary (e.g., whether technical, interpersonal, project management, or business-related), and how broad are the organizational complementarities required. The insights offered in this paper may help to shed light on different stakeholders' divergent explanations of whether there exists a change initiative at all, which activities are within the scope of the initiative, and whether the organization has made progress toward achieving its goals.

9. REFERENCES

Bartunek, J. "Changing Interpretive Schemes and Organizational Restructuring: The Example of a Religious Order." *Administrative Science Quarterly*, 29, 1987, pp. 355-372.

Bartunek, J., and Moch, M. "First Order, Second Order and Third Order Change and Organization Development Interventions: A Cognitive Approach." *Journal of Applied Behavioral Science*, Volume 23, 1987, pp. 483-500.

Barua, A.; Kreibel, C.H.; and Mukhopadhyay, T. "Information Technologies and Business Value: An Analytical and Empirical Investigation." *Information Systems Research,* Volume 6, Number 1, 1995, pp. 3-24.

Barua, A.; Lee C.-.H. S.; and Whinston, A.B. "The Calculus of Reengineering." Working Paper, Center for Information Systems Management, University of Texas, Austin, 1994.

Barua, A., and Whinston, A. B. "The Art of Managing Organizational Design Dynamics." Working Paper, Center for Information Systems Management, University of Texas, Austin, 1994.

Bolman, L. G., and Deal, T. E. *Reframing Organizations: Artistry, Choice and Leadership.* San Francisco: Jossey-Bass, 1991.

Bullen, C. V., and Bennett, J. L. "Groupware In Practice: An Interpretation of Work Experience." MIT Center for Information Systems Research Working Paper 205, October, 1990.

Child, J. "Organization Structure, Environment and Performance: The Role of Strategic Choice." *Sociology,* Volume 6, 1972, pp. 2-22.

Conner, D. R. *Managing at the Speed of Change: How Resilient Managers Succeed and Prosper Where Others Fail.* New York: Villard Books, 1992.

Craig, J. F., and Yetton, P. W. "The Dual Strategic and Change Role of IT: A Critique of Business Process Reengineering." Paper presented at Academy of Management Meeting, Dallas, August, 1994.

Davenport, T. H. *Process Innovation: Reengineering Work through Information Technology.* Cambridge: Harvard Business School Press, 1993.

DeFiore, D. "Changing the Culture of IT to Ensure Client/Server Success: The Opportunity for IT Training." Keynote Address, Information Technology Training Conference, Newport, Rhode Island, June 28-30, 1995.

Dougherty, D. "Interpretive Barriers to Successful Product Innovation in Large Firms." *Organization Science*, Volume 3, Number 2, 1992, pp. 179-202.

Edgeworth, F. Y. *Mathematical Psychics: An Essay on the Application of Mathematics to the Moral Sciences.* London: K. Paul, 1881.

Eisenhardt, K. M. "Building Theories form Case Study Research." *Academy of Management Review*, Volume 14, Number 4, 1989, pp. 532-550.

Ettlie, J. E. "Implementing Manufacturing Technology: Lessons from Experience." In D. Davis (Editor), *Managing Technological Innovation.* San Francisco: Jossey-Bass, 1986, pp. 72-103.

Farwell, D. W.; Kuramoto, L. W.; Lee, D.; and Trauth, E. M. "A New Paradigm for IS." *Information Systems Management*, Spring 1992, pp. 7-14.

Fichman, R. G., and Kemerer, C. F. "Adoption of Software Engineering Process Innovations: The Case of Object Orientation." *Sloan Management Review,* Winter 1993, pp. 7-23.

Gallivan, M. J.; Goh, C. H.; Hitt, L. M.; and Wyner, G. "Incident Tracking at InfoCorp: Case Study of a Pilot Lotus Notes Implementation." *MIT Center for Coordination Science Technical Report* 149, July 1993.

Gallivan, M. J.; Hofman, J. D.; and Orlikowski, W. J. "Implementing Radical Change: Gradual versus Rapid Pace." In J. I. DeGross, S. L. Huff, and M. C. Munro (Editors), Proceedings of the Fifteenth International Conference on Information Systems, Vancouver, British Columbia, December 1994, pp. 325-339.

Ginzberg, M. J. "Early Diagnosis of MIS Implementation Failure: Promising Results and Unanswered Questions." *Management Science,* Volume 27, Number 4, April 1981, pp. 459-478.

Hammer, M., and Champy, J. *Reengineering the Corporation: A Manifesto for Business Revolution.* New York: Harper Business Press, 1993.

Henderson, J. C., and Venkatraman, N. "Strategic Alignment: Leveraging Information Technology for Transforming Organizations." *IBM Systems Journal*, Volume 32, Number 1, 1993, pp. 4-16.

Isabella, L. A. "The Effect of Career Stage on the Meaning of Key Organizational Events." *Journal of Organizational Behavior*, Volume 9, 1988, pp. 345-358.

Isabella, L. A. "Evolving Interpretations as a Change Unfolds: How Managers Construe Key Organizational Events." *Academy of Management Journal*, Volume 33, Number 1, 1990, pp. 7-41.

Jones, M. "Don't Emancipate, Exaggerate: Rhetoric, Reality and Reengineering." In R. Baskerville, S. Smithson, O. Ngwenyama, and J. I. DeGross (Editors), *Transforming Organizations with Information Technology*. Amsterdam: North Holland, 1994, pp. 357-377.

Keidel, R. W. "Rethinking Organizational Design." *Academy of Management Executive*, Volume 8, Number 4, 1994, pp. 12-30.

Kling, R., and Gerson. E. "Patterns of Segmentation and Intersections in the Computing World." *Symbolic Interaction*, Volume 1, 1978, pp. 24-43.

Kraut, R. E.; Dumais, S. T.; and Koch, S. "Computerization, Productivity and Quality of Work-Life." *Communications of the ACM*, Volume 32, Number 2, February 1989, pp. 220-238.

Leavitt, H. "Applied Organizational Change in Industry." *Handbook of Organizations*, Chapter 27. Chicago: Rand-McNally, 1965.

Leonard-Barton, D. "Implementation Characteristics of Organizational Innovations: Limits and Opportunities for Management Strategies." *Communications Research*, Volume 15, Number 5, 1988a, pp. 603-631.

Leonard-Barton, D. "Implementation as Mutual Adaptation of Technology and Organization." *Research Policy*, Volume 17, 1988b, pp. 251-267.

Miles, M., and Huberman, M. *Qualitative Data Analysis: An Expanded Sourcebook*. Newbury Park, California: Sage Press, 1994.

Milgrom, P., and Roberts, J. "The Economics of Modern Manufacturing: Technology Strategy and Organization." *American Economic Review*, June 1990, pp. 511-528.

Nadler, D.A., and Tushman, M.L. "Organizational Frame Bending: Principles for Managing Reorientation." *Academy of Management Executive*, Volume 3, Number 3, 1989, pp. 194-204.

Nance, W. D. "Growing Pains in IS: Transforming the IS Organization for Client/server Development." In J. W. Ross (Editor), *Proceedings of the ACM Special Interest Group on Computer Personnel Research Conference*, Alexandria, Virginia, March, 1994, pp. 78-86.

Nance, W. D., and Sessions, R. T. "Releasing the Hostages: Experiences in Client/Server Development and Organizational Change." In R. Baskerville, S. Smithson, O. Ngwenyama, and J. I. DeGross (Editors), *Transforming Organizations with Information Technology*. Amsterdam: North Holland, 1994, pp. 451-481.

O'Neill, H. M. "Restructuring, Re-Engineering and Rightsizing: Do the Metaphors Make Sense?" *Academy of Management Executive,* Volume 8, Number 4, 1994, pp. 9-11.

Olfman, L., and Mandviwalla, M. "Conceptual versus Procedural Software Training for Graphical User Interfaces: A Longitudinal Field Experiment." *MIS Quarterly,* Volume 18, Number 4, 1994, pp. 405-426.

Orlikowski, W. J. "CASE Tools as Organizational Change: Investigating Incremental and Radical Changes in Systems Development." *MIS Quarterly,* Volume 17, Number 3, 1993, pp. 309-340.

Orlikowski, W. J. "The Duality of Technology: Rethinking the Concept of Technology in Organizations." *Organization* Science, Volume 3, Number 3, 1992a, pp. 398-427.

Orlikowski, W. J. "Learning from Notes: Organizational Issues in Groupware Implementation." In J. Turner and R. Kraut (Editors), *Conference on Computer-Supported Cooperative Work,* Toronto, Canada, 1992b, pp. 362-369.

Orlikowski, W. J., and Gash, D. "Technological Frames: Making Sense of Information Technology in Organizations." *ACM Transactions on Information Systems,* Volume 12, Number 2, 1994, pp. 174-196.

Poole, P. P.; Gioia, D. A.; and Gray, B. "Influence Modes, Schema Change, and Organizational Transformation." *Journal of Applied Behavioral Sciences."* Volume 2, Number 3, 1989, pp. 271-289.

Raphaelian, G. "Making the Business Case for Reskilling IS." Retooling '93 Conference Proceedings, Atlanta, Georgia, Ziff Institute, December, 1993.

Rockart, J. F., and Scott Morton, M. S. "Implications of Changes in Information Technology for Corporate Strategy." *Interfaces,* Volume 14, Number 1, January 1984, pp. 84-95.

Santhanam, R., and Sein, M. K. "Improving End-User Proficiency: Effects of Conceptual Training and Nature of Interaction." *Information Systems Research,* Volume 5, Number 4, 1994, pp. 378-399.

Sein, M. K., and Bostrom, R. P. "An Experimental Investigation of the Role and Nature of Mental Models in the Learning of Desktop Systems." In K. M. Kaiser and H. J. Oppelland (Editors), *Desktop Information Technology*. Amsterdam: North-Holland, 1990, pp. 253-276.

Starbuck, W. H. "Why Organizations Run into Crises...and sometimes Survive Them." In K. Laudon and J. A. Turner (Editors), *Information Technology and Management Strategy.* Englewood Cliffs, New Jersey: Prentice-Hall, 1989, pp. 11-33.

Stokes, S. L. "Managing IS Personnel: Blueprint for Business Literacy." *Information Systems Management*, Spring, 1993a, pp. 73-76.

Stokes, S. L. "Reengineering IS Professionals." *Information Management,* 1993b, pp. 1-13.

Swanborg, R. "Strategies for Redesigning IT Processes." Retooling '93 Conference Proceedings, Atlanta, Georgia, Ziff Institute, December, 1993.

Strauss, A., and Corbin, J. *Basics of Qualitative Research: Grounded Theory Procedures and Techniques.* Thousand Oaks, California: Sage, 1990.

Van Maanen, J., and Schein, E. "Toward a Theory of Organizational Socialization." *Research in Organizational Behavior*, Volume 1, 1979, pp. 209-264.

Walton, R. E. *Up and Running: Integrating Information Technology and the Organization.* Boston: Harvard Business School Press, 1989.

Yin, R. K. *Case Study Research: Design and Methods.* Thousand Oaks, California: Sage, 1994.

Ziff Institute. *Retooling '93: Wanted — Leaders to Plan Future of Corporate Computing.* Proceedings Book, Retooling '93 Conference, Atlanta, Georgia, December 1-3, 1993.

Zuboff, S. *In the Age of the Smart Machine: The Future of Work and Power.* New York: Basic Books, 1988.

About the Author

Michael Gallivan is currently finishing his Ph.D. in Information Technologies from the Sloan School of Management at MIT. He has prior industry experience working as a systems consultant for Andersen Consulting and holds a B.A. degree in Psychology from Harvard and an M.B.A. from the University of California, Berkeley. His research is on the topic of implementing technological and organizational change within IS departments, in particular the learning activities and attitudes to change that lead to successful adaptation. Mr. Gallivan will be a Visiting Assistant Professor at New York University's Stern School of Business beginning January 1996.

9

Assessing Employee Turnover Intentions Before/After BPR

Tor Guimaraes
J. E. Owen Chair of Excellence
Tennessee Technological University

Abstract

Many BPR related people problems have been mentioned in the literature: communications barriers between functional areas, difficulty having the changes accepted by the employees affected, disruption to the company as a social system, and the elimination of positions and worker anxiety over losing jobs. The importance of gaining a better understanding of the factors related to the retention of manufacturing employees is underscored by rising personnel costs and high rates of turnover. Researchers have established the important determinants of employee turnover. The major purpose of this study was to test several hypotheses which compare employee turnover intentions and its antecedents before and after BPR projects. Employees from a manufacturing plant were randomly selected before and after the BPR project was completed. BPR does have significant impact on personnel attitudes toward their jobs and their organizations. The results show that the BPR project significantly affected the average employee ratings for eight of the thirteen major variables studied. Furthermore, the BPR project has produced a significantly wider difference of opinion among employees along nine of these variables.

As pointed out by Willcocks and Smith (1994), Business Process Reengineering (BPR) is being widely adopted by organizations in the 1990s, and a variety of different terms are used to describe BPR activities: process innovation (Davenport 1993), business process redesign (Short and Venkatraman 1992), business reengineering (Spurr, et al. 1993) and combinations of such terms. A 1993 Deloitte and Touche survey found that, in 1992, American Chief Information Officers, on the average, are involved in 4.4 reengineering projects (Moad 1993). From the consulting companies' perspective, BPR activity is also quite brisk with an Anderson Consulting representative estimating his firm's worldwide income from BPR in 1992/93 as close to $700 million (Thackray 1993).

While the number of BPR projects continues to go up (Cafasso 1993b), the literature on the topic continues to proliferate into an abundance of articles criticizing the problems or extolling the benefits of BPR. Despite the confusion, there is increasing consensus about the primary features of BPR: (1) it involves breaking outdated paradigms and making radical changes to one or more business processes affecting the whole organization; (2) it calls for a cross-functional effort usually involving innovative applications of technology; (3) it is not evolutionary change over time; (4) it is not a quick fix solution to business problems; (5) while technology is a critical ingredient for innovation (Guimaraes 1993), BPR is not merely applying new technology to existing business processes.

BPR projects vary widely in terms of their scope. A project may address anything from one business process to the entire organization and its many processes. A wide variety of business processes are potential targets for reengineering: customer service, sales and order entry, invoicing and billing, purchasing, etc. The primary objective of the BPR process is to make business organizations more competitive by improving quality, reducing costs and shortening product development cycles (Dagres 1993; Grover, Teng and Fiedler 1993). The change process itself should emphasize the value-added element for every activity, recognizing time as a competitive weapon, focusing on end results and objectives, ensuring quality at the source, planning for an end-to-end solution, challenging the old ways and proposed new ways, using the right technology, empowering people and building consensus on making changes, and setting aggressive goals for the new process (Stadler and Elliott 1992). The right idea for BPR is to look at the end-to-end processes that are really important to a company's success, then rapidly redesign who does what and give workers new tools to get more done (Moad 1993).

Many organizations that have undertaken reengineering projects reported significant benefits from their BPR experience (Cafasso 1993a) in several areas such as customer satisfaction, productivity and profitability (The Economist 1993; Goll and Cordovano 1993). The expected improvements vary dramatically by company: productivity, quality, profits and customer satisfaction are expected to improve from 7 percent to 100 percent, depending on where the company is starting from and the extent of its efforts. Improvements forecast in costs, inventory, cycle time and response time range from 10 percent to as much as 400 percent. Other benefits include reduced floor space requirements; reduced labor requirements, particularly indirect labor; reduced material handling; improved employee empowerment and morale; improved communications between operations; and improved quality (Farmer 1993).

While the promises from BPR implementation seem impressive, the problems are also numerous. Although many firms have implemented a variety of reengineering programs over the past years, few have reaped the benefits they expected (Cummings 1993). According to CSC Index, approximately one fourth of 300 reengineering projects in North America are not meeting their goals and the authors speculated that the figure may be closer to 70 percent (Cafasso 1993c). Many CIOs say that the actual benefits of the projects fall short of their expectations along the dimensions of customer service, process timeliness, quality, cost reduction, competitiveness, new/improved technology and sales/revenues (Hayley, Plewa and Watts 1993). A Deloitte and Touche survey showed reengineering projects consistently fall short of their expected benefits (Moad 1993). The up-front costs are high, particularly in the areas of training and consultant fees, with a time consuming learning curve (Bozman 1992).

1. BPR AS HUMAN RESOURCES ISSUES

For some companies, creating an environment in which reengineering will succeed may be exceedingly difficult (Grover, Teng and Fiedler 1993). Some argue in favor of more gradual departures from traditional practices since managerial innovations take time and induce substantial strain on the organization (Brown 1993). As discussed by Guimaraes, Bell and Marston (1993) in the context of organizational change in general, there is much business organizations can do to reorganize for fast changing environments. The changes often fail because worker habits are not addressed during implementation (Grover, Teng and Fiedler 1993). Succumbing to the pressure to produce quick results, many managers who implemented BPR tend to ignore the massive changes in organizational structure, have misused and alienated middle managers and lower level employees, sold off solid businesses, neglected important research and development, and hindered the necessary modernization of their plants (Cascio 1993).

While downsizing may be done strictly for cost cutting and does not necessarily imply process reengineering, in many cases BPR leads to downsizing. In such cases, the human resources tend to suffer strong setbacks (Ehrbar 1993) and much can be learned from the literature and practical experience in company downsizing. More than half the 1,468 restructured companies surveyed by the Society for Human Resource Management reported that employee productivity either stayed the same or deteriorated after the layoffs. A four-year study of thirty organizations in the automobile industry revealed that very few of the organizations implemented downsizing in a way that improved their effectiveness. Most deteriorated relative to their "pre-downsizing" levels of quality, productivity, effectiveness, and human relations indicators (Cascio 1993). In many cases, massive layoffs of middle managers have led to fewer layers of management but left in place the essence of the same organizational structure (Brandt, Byrne and Port 1993). Another problem is that, unwilling or unable to cope with the changes, many long-time workers have left the company (Moad 1993). Many studies show that surviving employees become narrow-minded, self-absorbed, and risk averse. That, in turn, results in sinking morale, productivity drops, and distrust of management (Cascio 1993).

Many other important people problems associated with BPR implementation have been mentioned in the literature: communications barriers between functional areas (McKee 1992); lack of leadership and inability to properly handle personal risk and confrontations (Stadler and Elliot 1992); difficulty having the changes accepted by the employees affected (Ryan 1992); the unexpected enormity of the undertaking and the disruption to the company as a social system (Huff 1992); the elimination of positions and worker anxiety over losing jobs are tough problems (King 1993); and lack of communication between CIOs and CEOs (McPartlin 1992).

While "dramatic business changes" and/or major job losses (which are not necessarily associated with process reengineering) have attracted most of the attention in the literature, the importance of well trained and motivated employees is universally recognized as key for increasing company competitiveness. Nevertheless, lessons in this area do not seem to sink in. For example, US companies have experienced an estimated 50 percent to 75 percent failure rate while implementing advanced manufacturing technologies, mostly due to neglect of human factors (Saraph and Sebastian 1992). The need for increased research on human resource management issues has been emphasized in a number of recent studies (Allen and Katz 1986; Badawy 1988; Brooks and Wells

1989; Chan 1989; Garden 1989; Saleh and Desai 1990; Sherman 1986). The importance of gaining a better understanding of the factors related to recruitment, motivation, and retention of employees is further underscored by rising personnel costs and high rates of turnover (Badawy 1988; Basta and Johnson 1989; Garden 1989; Parden 1981; Sherman 1986). With increased competitiveness on a global scale, human resource departments in many organizations are experiencing greater pressure from top management to improve employee recruitment, selection, training, and retention. Reducing employee turnover intentions is important to reduce the loss of skilled workers, as well as to identify and check loss of employee motivation in general.

Researchers have learned about the important relationships between personnel costs and turnover (Badawy 1988; Garden 1989; Sherman 1986), and that for one to reduce excessive turnover it is necessary to understand the reasons behind it. A review of the literature reveals a growing research interest in investigating the linkages among diverse variables posited to be predictors of turnover among a wide variety of employee types (Baroudi 1985; Bartol 1983; Chan 1989; Garden 1989; Parden 1981; Sherman 1986). Given the importance of the topic, it is surprising that no study has explored turnover and its antecedents among employees who survived the dramatic changes to their organizations from BPR projects.

Even more important than turnover behavior (which is dependent on extraneous variables such as economic conditions and alternative job opportunities) is employee turnover intentions which provides a measure of employee morale and motivation. Needless to say, disgruntled employees who can't find employment elsewhere are probably just as harmful to the company as the loss of skilled personnel. The major purpose of this study was to test several hypotheses which compare employee turnover intentions and its antecedents before and after BPR projects.

2. THE CONCEPTUAL FRAMEWORK AND HYPOTHESES

Current empirical research provides strong support for Fishbein and Ajzen's (1975) proposition that behavioral intentions constitute the most immediate determinant of actual behavior, in this case employee turnover (Bluedorn 1982; Cotton and Tuttle 1986; Hom, Katerberg and Hulin 1979; Michaels and Spector 1982; Williams and Hazer 1986). Given the modest costs associated with collecting turnover intentions statements compared to generating data about actual turnover, and the problem of temporarily dispersed leaving episodes typically found in most studies using an individual level predictive design, Bluedorn (1982) and Coveradale and Terborg (1980) have recommended using intent to leave attitudes rather than actual staying or leaving behavior as a criterion variable. Steel and Ovalle's (1984) meta-analysis suggested that turnover intentions and turnover are related, and that turnover intentions is a better predictor of turnover than affective variables such as job and career satisfaction, and organizational commitment. Last, but extremely important operationally, collecting data on employees' turnover intentions is much easier than observing turnover behavior. For all these reasons, turnover intentions was used in this study instead of actual turnover.

The four sets of variables addressed in this study are (a) two role stressors: role ambiguity and role conflict; (b) five task characteristics: variety, identity, significance, autonomy, and feedback; (c)four indicators of work-related attitudes: job involvement, job satisfaction, career satisfaction, and organizational commitment; and (d) turnover intentions.

2.1   Role Stressors

Two role-based stressors were included in this study: role ambiguity and role conflict. Role ambiguity refers to the difference between what people expect of us on the job and what we feel we should do. This causes uncertainty about what our role should be. It can be a result of misunderstanding what is expected, how to meet the expectations, or the employee thinking the job should be different (Kahn, et al. 1964; Muchinsky 1990). Insufficient information on how to perform the job adequately, unclear expectations of peers and supervisors, ambiguity of performance evaluation methods, extensive job pressures, and lack of consensus on job functions or duties may cause employees to feel less involved and less satisfied with their jobs and careers, less committed to their organizations, and eventually display a propensity to leave the organization.

Role conflict can develop when two or more conflicting job requirements occur together so that complying with one would make doing the other more difficult (Kahn, et al. 1964). This could occur in a variety of ways. It might be a function of conflicting messages, a request for a high quality work within a very short period of time, or splitting loyalties between co-workers and the organization. It has been reported that role conflict is negatively associated with job satisfaction, and organizational commitment, and positively associated with intention to leave (Baroudi 1985; Bedeian and Armenakis 1981; Chan 1989). Badawy (1973, 1988) found that satisfaction is negatively correlated with role conflict among scientific professionals and R&D personnel. Saleh and Desai also reported that role stressors could affect satisfaction among plant managers. Similar results were found among programmers and other technical professionals (Baroudi 1985; Goldstein and Rockart 1984). As discussed earlier, BPR projects tend to create considerable turmoil within organizations and affect how employees perform their business tasks, relate to peers, superiors and subordinates, and feel about their organizations. Therefore, the ratings for role stressors are expected to be considerably higher after BPR. The following hypothesis is proposed:

H1:   Role stressors will be higher after BPR.

2.2   Task Characteristics

Task characteristics have been found to be potential determinants of turnover among engineering and technical personnel (Couger 1988, 1990; Couger and Zawacki 1980; Garden 1989; Goldstein and Rockart 1984). These include the five core job characteristics identified by Hackman and Oldham (1975, 1980): (1) skill variety, which refers to the opportunity to utilize a variety of valued skills and talents on the job; (2) task identity, or the extent to which a job requires completion of a whole and identifiable piece of work — that is, doing a job from beginning to end, with visible results; (3) task significance, which reflects the extent to which the job has a substantial impact on the lives or work of other people, whether within or outside the organization; (4) job autonomy, or the extent to which the job provides freedom, independence, and discretion in scheduling work and determining procedures that the job provides; and (5) job feedback, which refers to the extent to which the job provides information about the effectiveness of one's performance. Task characteristics have been found to influence turnover intentions through their relationships with job satisfaction and organizational commitment (Michaels and

Spector 1982; Steers 1977). Furthermore, the engineering and MIS literature has focused extensively on the importance of a job which permits people to work on challenging and interesting tasks (Badawy 1978, 1988; Couger 1988, 1990; Garden 1989; Sherman 1986). It was suggested that if the job provides technical professionals, including plant managers, the opportunity to engage in challenging and exciting jobs, they will be more involved and satisfied in their jobs, more committed to their organizations, and finally, less likely to leave the organization. Task characteristics have also been found to be positively related to job satisfaction and organizational commitment and have direct and indirect effects on turnover intentions through satisfaction and commitment among technical professionals (Igbaria 1991; Parasuraman 1989). Note that the job design literature suggests that motivators (e.g., job challenge, autonomy, responsibility, and achievement) lead to satisfaction and commitment and eventually reduce employee's intention to leave the organization (Hackman and Oldham 1980).

BPR calls for dramatic changes to business processes and the business tasks involved. However, no literature presently exists suggesting whether task characteristics as defined in this study will improve. In BPR, the emphasis is on performing tasks which build added value to customer, and on doing whatever it takes to achieve predefined results (Gulden and Reck 1992). Thus, we propose the following hypothesis:

> **H2:   Task Characteristics will be different before and after BPR.**

2.3   Job Involvement

Job involvement describes an individual's ego involvement with work and indicates the extent to which an individual identifies psychologically with his/her job (Kanungo 1982). It is also suggested that involvement refers to the internalizing values about the goodness or the importance of work and it was found that job involvement is related to task characteristics. Workers who have a greater variety of tasks and who deal with other people at work may feel more involved in the job. Involvement was also found to influence job satisfaction and organizational commitment. Employees who are more job involved are more satisfied with their jobs and more committed to their organization (Blau and Boal 1989; Brooke and Price 1989; Brooke, Russell and Price 1988; Kanungo 1982). Job involvement has also been found to be negatively related to turnover intentions (Blau and Boal 1989). Given the established relationship between task characteristics and job involvement, and the poorly understood impact of BPR on task characteristics, the following hypothesis is proposed:

> **H3:   Job involvement will be different before and after BPR.**

2.4   Job/Career Satisfaction, Organization Commitment and Turnover Intentions

Job satisfaction, career satisfaction, and organizational commitment reflect a positive attitude toward the organization, thus having a direct influence on employee turnover intentions. Job satisfaction, job involvement and organizational commitment are considered to be related but distinguishable attitudes (Brooke and Price 1989). Satisfaction represents an affective response to specific aspects of the job or career and denotes the pleasurable or positive emotional state resulting from an appraisal of one's job or career (Locke 1976; Porter, et al. 1974; Williams and Hazer 1986). Organizational commitment is an affective response to the whole organization and the degree of attachment or loyalty employees feel toward the organization. Job involvement represents the extent to which employees are absorbed in or preoccupied with their jobs and the extent to which an individual identifies with his/her job (Brooke, Russell and Price 1988).

Several studies have focused on the relationships between job satisfaction and organizational commitment, and intention to leave (Baroudi 1985; Bartol 1983; Bluedorn 1982). It was suggested that job satisfaction and organizational commitment were related but distinguishable attitudes, in that commitment is an affective response to the entire organization, whereas job satisfaction represents an affective response to specific aspects of the job (Locke 1976; Porter, et al. 1974; Williams and Hazer 1986). Moreover, the findings of Dougherty, Bluedorn, and Keon (1985), of Cotton and Tuttle, and of Michaels and Spector provide evidence that job satisfaction has a direct effect on turnover intentions as well as an indirect effect through organizational commitment. In addition, it is reasonable to expect that high levels of career satisfaction would enhance organizational commitment since employees who are satisfied with their careers should perceive greater benefits in retaining membership in their organizations than employees whose careers have been less gratifying.

A number of empirical studies confirm the important role of organizational commitment in influencing turnover intentions (Baroudi 1985; Bartol 1983; Steers 1977). Employees who are highly committed to their organization are less likely to leave than those who are relatively uncommitted. It has also been reported that organizational commitment is more strongly related to turnover intentions than to job satisfaction (Baroudi 1985; Shore and Martin 1989).

Following the same line of reasoning behind the previous hypothesis, the following hypotheses are proposed:

    H4:   **Job satisfaction will be different before and after BPR.**
    H5:   **Career satisfaction will be different before and after BPR.**
    H6:   **Organizational commitment will be different before and after BPR.**
    H7:   **Turnover intentions will be different before and after BPR.**

3. METHODOLOGY

3.1 Sampling Procedure

In September of 1993, the President and the Human Resources Manager for a Fortune 500 manufacturing company's plant with 654 employees located in the Southeastern portion of the U.S. agreed to a study of the determinants of turnover intentions among its employees.

A random sample of two hundred employees produced 116 usable survey questionnaires, after discarding the ones containing invalid (seven) or missing data (twelve), with sixty-five non-respondents. Approximately four months later, the company embarked on a corporate-wide BPR program which has created substantial changes to some of its business processes and employees. Eleven months later, the BPR implementation was completed and the new processes were operational. In February of 1995, two months later, the same data collection instrument was used to assess the impact of the BPR changes on employee turnover intentions. In this case, the 116 respondents to the first survey (before-BPR) were used as the starting point. Of these, fourteen could not be reached because they had resigned (five) or been laid off (nine). Twenty-two did not respond in time for this study, resulting in a sample of eighty usable after-BPR responses.

In both data collection efforts, participation was voluntary and the same survey instrument was accompanied by a cover letter from the researchers which explained the study and assured that individual responses would be treated as confidential. Also, on both occasions a postage-paid envelope was provided so that respondents could return their completed surveys directly to the researchers.

3.2   The Organizational Setting and BPR Project

The plant involved in this study produces world-class electronic equipment for a global and hyper-competitive market. Aware of the need to keep ahead of the competition, top mangers decided to engage the regional office of a major consulting company to help them evaluate the need, redesign any process improvements, and help implement the changes. While the BPR project was initiated from the top and was closely watched by the top managers, the consulting company and the managers agreed on the need for direct employee participation in process redesign and implementation. There were numerous meetings to communicate to the employees the nature of the project and its importance, as well as presentations designed to allay possible employee feelings of insecurity about their jobs and quality of life. While the effectiveness of such meetings may be questioned, substantial time and effort was spent in this area.

The plant-wide project substantially changed several processes, including product design/development and manufacturing, and brought several of the large customers directly into the product design/development process. While at first many employees seemed to take the project as a fad, the process of redesigning major business processes and the job change implications soon created a serious atmosphere. At the end of the project, the layoffs and resignations were part of the changes created by the project.

3.3   Variable Measurement

As demographic information, participants were asked to indicate their level of formal education: (1) high school; (2) bachelor's degree; and (3) graduate or professional degree. Organizational tenure was measured by the number of years an individual had been employed in the organization. Level in the organization hierarchy consisted of five tiers: (1) line employees; (2) professionals; (3) first level supervisors; (4) middle management; and (5) strategic management (top executives).

Role stressors.   Role stressors consist of role ambiguity and role conflict. They were operationally defined using a combined index of role ambiguity (three items) and role conflict (three items) adopted from Kahn, et al. and from Rizzo, House, and Lirtzman (1970). Each scale was scored using a five-point response mode ranging from (1) very false to (5) very true. The role conflict and role ambiguity items were reverse-scored so that the greater the score, the greater the perceived stress. These scales were chosen because of their established psychological properties (Schuler, Aldag and Brief 1977; Van Sell, Brief and Schuler 1981) and their wide usage in role theory research. The three items of role ambiguity were averaged to obtain an overall index of role ambiguity. The Cronbach's Alpha coefficient of internal consistency reliability (alpha) for this scale was .69. Similarly, the three items of role conflict were averaged to develop the role conflict score (alpha = .75).

Task Characteristics. Task characteristics reflecting the five core task attributes of skill variety (alpha = .66), task identity (alpha = .90), task significance (alpha = .73), job autonomy (alpha = .70), and job feedback (alpha = .84) were measured by the Hackman and Oldham (1975) Job Diagnostic Survey (JDS), with some modification of the reverse-scored items following Idaszak and Drasgow's (1987) findings. The reliability and validity of the revised JDS have been well established and documented (Kulik, Oldham and Langner 1988). Dunham (1976) felt that all five dimensions could be subsumed in a single dimension reflecting job complexity without losing the meaning of enriched work. That is, it could be said that an enriched job is simply more complex than a routine job. Following Michaels and Spector in their test of the Mobley, et al. (1979) model and Dunham, the motivating potential score (MPS) was computed from the five task characteristics (alpha=.83) using the formula proposed by Hackman and Oldham (1975, 1980):

$$MPS = \ (Skill \ variety + Task \ Identity + Task \ Significance)/3 \ x \ Autonomy \ x \ Feedback$$

Job involvement. This was measured using a four-item scale based upon Kanungo's study. Job involvement is defined as the extent to which an individual identifies psychologically with his/her job. A Likert-type response format was provided with response options ranging from (1) strongly disagree to (5) strongly agree. These four items were averaged to obtain an overall index of job involvement. The internal consistency reliability of the scale was .86.

Career satisfaction. This was measured by a five-item scale adapted from prior research (Greenhaus, Parasuraman and Wormely 1990), with appropriate changes to make the items more relevant to the present study. Individuals were asked to indicate their agreement or disagreement with each statement on a five point Likert-type scale ranging from (1) strongly disagree to (5) strongly agree. Responses to the five items were averaged to create a career satisfaction score (alpha = .83).

Job satisfaction. This was operationalized by the six-item scale developed by Hackman and Oldham (1975). Each item required the respondents to indicate their agreement or disagreement on a five-point scale ranging from (1) strongly disagree to (5) strongly agree. Responses to the six items were averaged to produce a total job satisfaction score (alpha = .75).

Organizational commitment. This variable, defined as the identification with a particular organization and the desire to maintain membership in the organization, was measured by an abbreviated version of the Organizational Commitment Questionnaire (OCQ) developed by Porter, Crampon, and Smith (1976). The nine items used to construct the scale tap two of the three dimensions of commitment included in the longer version of the OCQ: (1) a strong belief in and acceptance of the organization's goals and values; and (2) a willingness to exert considerable effort on behalf of the organization. In order to avoid concept redundancy (Morrow 1983), the six items reflecting a strong desire to maintain membership in the organization were excluded from the measure of commitment because they overlapped with the measure of turnover intentions. Thus the shorter version of the scale used in this study represents a more "pure" measure of the affective dimensions of commitment to the employing organization. The response options to the items ranged from (1) strongly disagree to (5) strongly agree. The reliability and validity of the nine-item version have been found to be acceptable (Brooke, Russell and Price 1988; Price and Mueller 1981). The items were recoded such that high scores reflected more commitment to the organization. The coefficient of reliability of this measure was .89.

Intention to leave. This was measured by two items. One asked participants: "Given everything you know about the company in which you are employed and the type of work you like to do, how long do you think you will continue to work at this company?" The response options were anchored on a time-linked five-point scale ranging from (1) one year or less to (5) eleven years or more, or until retirement. The responses were reverse coded such that high scores reflected stronger intentions to leave the organization. The second item asked: "If you expect to leave this company before retirement, please indicate whether you expect to be forced out or to quit voluntarily." Since only one respondent expected to be forced out before-BPR and two after-BPR, this item was not used. The efficacy of a single-item measure of intention is supported by the findings of Kraut (1975) and others.

3.4   Validity of Measures and Research Design

The measures used in this study were chosen because they have been previously used and their psychometric properties are relatively well known. Factor analysis showed that the items for each scale loaded unambiguously ($\geq$.50 into one factor and $\leq$.30 into the others) thus indicating construct unidimensionality, a requirement for computing the Cronbach's Alpha. The internal consistency reliability coefficients (alpha) for the constructs in this study are all well above the level of .70 acceptable for social sciences studies (Nunally 1978).

The quasi-experiment design (one-group, pretest-posttest) used in this study "is one of the more frequently used designs in the social sciences" (Cook and Campbell 1979). It also has major potential weaknesses which must be guarded against. Of the many potential problems discussed by Cook and Campbell, "history," "statistical regression," "maturation," "testing," and "instrumentation" threats, only the first is plausible in this case. History in this case stands for the possibility that extraneous events might have happened during the BPR project period. For example, besides the BPR project, the employees participating in this study may have received a substantial pay raise which changed perceptions of their jobs and company. Similar possibilities are related to other changes in the work environment, company policies, or the layoffs which have occurred after the BPR project. While no relevant changes extraneous to the BPR project are apparent, this possible threat to the results validity can not be completely discarded.

Except for the last item which will be addressed later, the importance of these potential threats can be minimized to some extent by the very nature of the BPR project. In this case, not uncommon in practice, the BPR project represents such massive change to the organization, in such a relatively short period of time, that in preparation for the project other initiatives were put on hold. For example, training programs, quality improvement programs, and any changes to policies and business processes all came to a standstill pending the redesign, planning, and implementation phases of the BPR project. Only then were these other initiatives allowed to proceed and become part of the BPR project implementation process, or to proceed separately and co-exist with the new business processes, or were terminated indefinitely.

The layoffs and resignations (fourteen people), and non-respondents (twenty-two people) significantly reduced the number of participants to the after-BPR data collection. These two non-respondent groups must be discussed separately. The employee layoffs or resignations associated with the BPR project were expected to affect the attitude of employees responding to the after-BPR questionnaire. To detect this and other such effects from the BPR project was the very objective of the study. The second group, non-respondents to the after-BPR questionnaire still with the company, is expected to have been affected by the project in a similar fashion. While measuring this effect is not possible, based on a set of independent-sample t-tests comparing this group to the other respondents to the before-BPR questionnaire, no significant differences exist along the thirteen major variables in this study. For all these reasons, the one-group pretest-posttest design employed in this study is thought capable of supporting the "reasonable causal inferences" made in this report (Cook and Campbell 1979).

3.5   Data Analysis

Given the exploratory nature of this study, the statistical techniques used are fairly simple. To test the proposed hypotheses, two-tailed t-tests (with paired samples) were used to identify any differences in employee turnover intentions and its determinants before and after the BPR changes. Pearson correlation coefficients were used to examine the hypothesized relationships between the major constructs in this study.

4. RESULTS

Table 1 presents selected demographic information on the study participants. The sample is comprised of approximately one third females and two third males, mostly married people with at least a bachelor's degree and several years working for the host organization.

4.1   Regarding the Relationships Among Major Variables

Table 2 shows the statistical relationships among the major study variables. The results corroborate the literature proposing the direct impact of the MPS construct on career satisfaction, and organization commitment, and its inverse relationship with turnover intentions. However, the impacts of MPS on job satisfaction and job involvement are not statistically significant. Except for an inverse relationship between role ambiguity and organization commitment, the importance of role ambiguity and role conflict as determinants of any of the other major variables is also not significant. A possible explanation is that employees in this organization have performed in a hyper-competitive environment before and after BPR and have grown accustomed to the stressful environment, thus minimizing the impact of role stressors on job satisfaction, organization commitment, and the other major variables in this study. The importance of task characteristics, career satisfaction, job satisfaction, job involvement, and organization commitment as determinants of employee turnover intentions is supported by the results.

Table 1: Sample Demographics (n=80)

Variables	Frequency	Percent
Gender:		
Male	55	68.8
Female	25	31.3
Marital Status:		
Single	21	26.2
Married	59	73.8
Education Completed:		
High School	6	7.5
Bachelor's Degree	48	60.0
Graduate/Professional	26	32.5
Level in Organization Hierarchy:		
Line Employee	53	66.3
Professional Staff	2	2.5
First Level Supervisor	23	28.8
Middle Management	2	2.5
Number of years employed with this Company:		
Less than 5 years	8	10
5-9 years	28	35
10-14 years	16	20
15-19 years	22	27.5
20 or more years	6	7.5

Table 2: Intercorrelation Matrix for Major Study Variables

Variables	AVG	ST.D.	1.	2.	3.	4.	5.	6.	7.
1. Role Ambiguity	3.17	.70	1.0						
2. Role Conflict	3.57	.74	.48**	1.0					
3. Task Characteristics (MPS)	107.35	56.68	NS	NS	1.0				
4. Career Satisfaction	3.25	.78	NS	NS	.20**	1.0			
5. Job Satisfaction	3.53	.67	NS	NS	NS	.40**	1.0		
6. Job Involvement	3.21	.91	NS	NS	NS	.14	.34**	1.0	
7. Organization Commitment	3.14	.51	NS	NS	.24**	.32**	.63**	.46**	1.0
8. Turnover Intention	3.15	.94	NS	NS	-.31**	-.33**	-.49**	-.37**	-.55**

* Significant at the .05 level or better.
** Significant at the .01 level or better.

4.2   Regarding the Proposed Hypotheses

Table 3 presents the results used in testing the hypotheses proposed in this study. Based on the significant differences between the arithmetic means (AVG) before and after the BPR project, the following hypotheses are supported at the .01 level or better:

H2:   Task characteristics will be different before and after BPR.
H4:   Job satisfaction will be different before and after BPR.
H6:   Organizational commitment will be different before and after BPR.

In the case of task characteristics, the differences are significant for the MPS construct as a whole, as well as for every one of its major sub-components. In every case, based on employees' perceptions, the impact of the BPR project seems to have increased the task characteristics addressed in this study. However, on the average, the employees' perceptions suggest that the BPR project has decreased the level of job satisfaction among employees and their commitment to the organization. A possible explanation is that task characteristics such as task variety and task autonomy went up because fewer people are doing more work, and job satisfaction went down because people are working harder and may be exhausted. Another explanation is that many employees may just want to keep their jobs as simple as possible, finish the work and go home, instead of the job enrichment they apparently have received.

Table 3: Comparing Employees Before/After BPR Along Study Variables

Variables	Before BPR		After BPR		* (**)
	AVG	ST.D.	AVG	ST.D.	
1. Role Ambiguity	3.10	.70	3.23	.73	.26 (.75)
2. Role Conflict	3.61	.63	3.51	.85	.38 (.01)
3. Task Characteristics (MPS)	88.95	29.34	138.33	70.73	.00 (.00)
-Skill Variety	4.6	.77	5.15	1.00	.00 (.02)
-Task Identity	4.37	1.14	4.91	1.32	.01 (.19)
-Task Significance	4.38	.89	5.07	.90	.00 (.95)
-Job Autonomy	4.53	.78	5.10	.97	.00 (.06)
-Job Feedback	4.39	1.02	4.97	1.10	.00 (.57)
4. Career Satisfaction	3.25	.75	3.31	.83	.61 (.36)
5. Job Satisfaction	3.44	.53	3.17	.86	.01 (.00)
6. Job Involvement	3.18	.81	3.14	.87	.71 (.53)
7. Organization Commitment	3.14	.45	2.98	.56	.05 (.10)
8. Turnover Intention	3.18	.81	3.11	.13	.71 (.00)

   * Significance level for two-tailed t-tests comparing means (AVG) of paired samples.
  ** Significance level for F test comparing standard deviations (ST.D.).

The reader is cautioned that, given the relatively small sample size, the power of the t-tests producing non-significant results may be too low for rejecting some of the hypotheses. Using Cohen's (1988) methodology, the power levels for the respective hypotheses were calculated as role ambiguity (0.26), role conflict (0.24), job involvement (0.63), career satisfaction (0.40), and turnover intention (0.17). Based on the results in Table 3, the following hypotheses can not be accepted:

He: **Role stressors will be higher after BPR**
H3:   **Job involvement will be different before and after BPR.**
H5:   **Career satisfaction will be different before and after BPR.**
H7:   **Turnover intentions will be different before and after BPR.**

It is interesting to note that while the results show no significant difference in role ambiguity and role conflict before/after BPR contrary to stated expectations, on the average respondents reported lower role conflict after the BPR project. A possible explanation is that the BPR project may have resulted in more streamlined personnel roles (task combinations) with individual employees performing a less conflicting mix of tasks.

4.3   Results Regarding Differences in Standard Deviations

Table 3 also presents the results from F tests regarding differences in the standard deviations for the major variables and the major sub-components for role stressors and MPS. The F tests indicated some before/after BPR differences significant at the 0.05 level or lower. Based on the employees' perceptions, the BPR process seems to have had a significant impact on the standard deviations of five of the thirteen variables in Table 3: role conflict, MPS, skill variety (one of the MPS components), job satisfaction, and turnover intentions. In summary, as discussed in the context of hypotheses testing, on the average the personnel attitudinal changes from the BPR process were apparent only in terms of improved task characteristics, lower job satisfaction, and lower organizational commitment. Besides that, not originally proposed, the employees' perceptions suggest that the BPR process has also significantly increased difference of opinion along the five study variables mentioned above.

5. CONCLUSIONS AND MANAGERIAL IMPLICATIONS

As previously warned by some authors, BPR does seem to have significant impact on personnel attitudes toward their jobs and their organizations. This single company field test reveals that their BPR project has significantly affected the average employee ratings for eight of the thirteen variables studied, but showed no apparent difference in the consequent variable, employee turnover intentions. Furthermore, the employees' perceptions suggest that the BPR project has produced a significantly wider difference of opinion among employees along five of these variables, including turnover intentions.

Despite the organization turmoil which many authors have associated with large BPR projects such as the one studied here, the change process on the average seems to have had no significant impact on role conflict. Employees' opinions suggest that the BPR changes apparently also resulted in a richer overall job environment, with significant improvements in the skill variety used, task identity and significance, job autonomy and performance feedback. However, despite these improvements, on the average employees reported lower job satisfaction, without any significant differences in job involvement and intentions to leave. Furthermore, based on the employees' opinions, the BPR project has significantly reduced employee job satisfaction and organization commitment. A possible explanation is that task characteristics such as task variety and task autonomy have increased because fewer people are being forced to perform more tasks. That, in turn, may be leading to overwork and lower satisfaction with the job. It is also possible that employees lower "job dissatisfaction" may be temporary and due primarily to the organizational turmoil commonly associated with BPR projects. Another likely explanation is that other job related factors such as pay and job security play an important role in determining job satisfaction and commitment. Psychological factors, such as the degree of "ownership" employees feel regarding the changes to their jobs, are also likely to play an important role in determining attitudes toward the job and the organization. The latter is particularly important for large BPR projects with wide organization impact such as the one studied here. Such projects normally require top management control for effective implementation. Without management sensitivity to the importance of employee project ownership, workers are likely to express lower job satisfaction and organization commitment with the required job changes.

On the average, the results have shown no significant change in employee job involvement or turnover intentions. Nevertheless, BPR project managers must carefully understand and hopefully contain the apparent employee attitude polarization from the project. While on the average the BPR project did not seem to produce significant changes along some variables, the attitude of many employees seems to have been negatively affected to a significant extent. To improve employee morale and performance, and to pre-empt future personnel problems, it is important that managers understand the reasons why some employees may see the BPR changes (or the BPR process itself) in a negative light. As cautioned by previous authors, some effective employee training about the nature and objectives of the BPR project seems advisable.

6. STUDY LIMITATIONS AND RESEARCH OPPORTUNITIES

This study has several limitations which can be viewed as opportunities for further research. The complexity of the issues addressed in this paper would greatly benefit from larger sample sizes able to support multivariate statistical techniques. It is also important that other major constructs addressing the BPR implementation process (including employee participation, degree of empowerment, management support for the project, communication), and the job changes (including rewards for performance, future job security, organization support for the employee) be added to the conceptual framework underlying this study.

Besides a larger sample size, to ensure a more general application of the results, it is also important that the hypotheses proposed here be retested with data from several companies and industry sectors. Very likely, intercompany differences will significantly affect the results. Finally, it may be important to include certain characteristics of the BPR project such as the degree of organization downsizing involved, the presence of external change agents (i.e., consultants and benchmarking organizations), and the financial strength of the organization immediately before the BPR project. These desirable improvements and extensions to this study do not in any way diminish its contribution as the first attempt to formally test human resources management issues surrounding the implementation of BPR projects.

7. REFERENCES

Allen, T. J., and Katz, R. "The Dual Ladder: Motivation Solution or Managerial Delusion." *R&D Management*, Volume 16, Number 2, 1986, pp. 185-197.

Badawy, M. K. "Bureaucracy in Research: A Study of Role Conflict of Scientists." *Organization*, Volume 32, Number 3, 1973, pp. 123-133.

Badawy, M. K. "One More Time: How to Motivate Your Engineers." *IEEE Transactions of Engineering Management*, Volume 25, Number 2, 1978, pp. 37-42.

Badawy, M. K. "What We've Learned about Managing Human Resources in R&D in the Last Fifty Years." *Research Technology Management*, Volume 31, Number 5, 1988, pp. 19-35.

Baroudi, J. J. "The Impact of Role Variables on Is Personnel Work Attitudes and Intentions." *MIS Quarterly*, Volume 9, Number 4, 1985, pp. 341-356.

Bartol, K. M. "Turnover among DP Personnel: A Causal Analysis." *Communications of the ACM*, Volume 26, Number 10, 1983, pp. 807-811.

Basta, N., and Johnson, E. "Ch.E.s are Back in High Demand." *Chemical Engineering*, Volume 96, Number 8, 1989, pp. 22-29.

Bedeian, A. G., and Armenakis, A. A., "A Path-Analytic Study of the Consequences of Role Conflict and Ambiguity." *Academy of Management Journal*, Volume 24, Number 2, 1981, pp. 417-424.

Blau, G., and Boal, K. "Using Job Involvement and Organizational Commitment Interactively to Predict Turnover." *Journal of Management*, Volume 15, Number 1, 1989, pp. 115-127.

Bluedorn, A. C. "A Unified Model of Turnover from Organizations." *Human Relations*, Volume 35, 1982, pp. 135-153.

Bozman, J. S. "Downsizing, Rightsizing, Somethingsizing." *ComputerWorld*, December 28, 1992, pp. 6-10.

Brandt, R.; Byrne, J. A.; and Port, O. "The Virtual Corporation." *Business Week*, February 3, 1993, pp. 99-102.

Brooke, P. P., and Price, J. L. "The Determinants of Employee Absenteeism: An Empirical Test of a Causal Model." *Journal of Occupational Psychology*, Volume 62, 1989, pp. 1-19.

Brooke, P. P.; Russell, D. W.; and Price, J. L. "Discuss Validation of Measures of Job Satisfaction, Job Involvement and Organizational Commitment." *Journal of Applied Psychology*, Volume 73, Number 2, 1988, pp. 139-145.

Brooks, L. S., and Wells, C. S. "Role Conflict in Design Supervision." *IEEE Transactions on Engineering Management*, Volume 36, Number 4, 1989, pp. 271-281.

Brown, W. B. "Leading the Way to Faster New Product Development." *Academy of Management Executive*, Volume 7, Number 1, 1993, pp. 36-47.

Cafasso, R. "Jean Genies." *ComputerWorld*, June 14, 1993a, pp. 99-102.

Cafasso, R. "Rethinking Reengineering." *ComputerWorld*, March 15, 1993c, pp. 102-105.

Cafasso, R. "Reengineering Projects: Up, Up, and Away." *ComputerWorld*, March 29, 1993b, pp. 92.

Cascio, W. F. "Downsizing: What do We know? What have We learned?" *Academy of Management Executive*, Volume 7, Number 1, 1993, pp. 95-104.

Chan, M. "Intergroup Conflict and Conflict Management in the Division of Four Aerospace Companies." *IEEE Transactions on Engineering Management*, Volume 36, Number 2, 1989, pp. 95-104.

Cohen, J. *Statistical Power Analysis for the Behavioral Sciences*, Second Edition. San Diego: Academic Press, 1988.

Cook, T. D., and Campbell, D. T. *Quasi-Experimentation: Design and Analysis Issues for Field Settings*. Chicago: Rand McNally College Publishing Company, 1979.

Cotton, J .L., and Tuttle, J. M. "Employee Turnover: A Meta-Analysis and Review with Implications for Research." *Academy of Management Review*, Volume 11, Number 1, 1986, pp. 55-70.

Couger, D. J. "Motivating Analysts and Programmers." *ComputerWorld*, Volume 14, Number 3, 1990, pp. 73, 76.

Couger, D. J. "Motivators vs. Demotivators in the IS Environment." *Journal of Systems Management*, Volume 39, Number 6, 1988, pp. 36-41.

Couger, D. J., and Zawacki, R. A. *Motivating and Managing Computer Personnel*. New York: Wiley, 1980.

Coverdale, S., and Terborg, J. R. "A Reexamination of the Mobley, Horner and Hollingsworth Model of Turnover: A Useful Replication." Paper Presented at the Fortieth Annual Meeting of the Academy of Management, Detroit, Michigan, 1980.

Cummings, J. "Reengineering Falls Short of Expectations, Study Finds." *Network World*, March 22, 1993, pp. 27.

Dagres, T. "Network Reengineering for Competitive Advantage." *White Paper*, 1993.

Davenport, H. *Process Innovation: Reengineering Work Through Information Technology*. Boston: Harvard Business Press, 1993.

Dougherty, T. W.; Bluedorn, A. C.; and Keon, T. W. "Precursors of Employee Turnover: A Multi-Sample Causal Analysis." *Journal of Occupational Behavior*, Volume 6, 1985, pp. 259-271.

Dunham, R. B. "The Measurement and Dimensionality of Job Characteristics." *Journal of Applied Psychology*, Volume 61, 1976, pp. 404-409.

The Economist. "Take a Clean Sheet of Paper." Volume 327, May 1, 1993, pp. 67-68.

Ehrbar, A. "Reengineering Gives Firms New Efficiency, Workers the Pink Slip." *The Wall Street Journal*, Volume 221, Number 51, March 16, 1993.

Farmer, J. R. "Reengineering the Factory." *APICS*, March 1993, pp. 38-42.

Fishbein, M., and Ajzen, I. *Belief, Attitude, Intention and Behavior: An Introduction to Theory and Research*. Reading, Massachusetts: Addison-Wesley Publishing Company, 1975.

Garden, A. M. "Correlates of Turnover Propensity of Software Professionals in Small High Tech Companies." *R&D Management*, Volume 19, Number 4, 1989, pp. 325-334.

Goldstein D. K., and Rockart, J. F. "An Examination of Work-Related Correlates of Job Satisfaction in Programmer/Analysts." *MIS Quarterly*, Volume 8, Number 2, 1984, pp. 103-115.

Goll, E. O., and Cordovano, M. F. "Construction Time Again." *CIO*, October 15, 1993, pp. 32-36.

Greenhaus, J. H.; Parasuraman, S.; and Wormley, W. M. "Effects of Race on Organizational Experiences, Job Performance Evaluations, and Career Outcomes." *Academy of Management Journal*, Volume 33, Number 1, 1990, pp. 64-86.

Grover, V.; Teng, J. T. C.; and Fiedler, K. D. "Information Technology Enabled Business Process Redesign: An Integrated Planning Framework." *OMEGA*, Volume 21, Number 4, 1993, pp. 433-447.

Guimaraes, T. "Managing Expert Systems Technology and Business Process Re-engineering." Symposium of the Information Processing Society of Japan, Tokyo, June 19, 1993.

Guimaraes, T.; Bell, R. E.; and Marston, R. "Organizing for Innovation." Fourth International Forum on Technology Management, Berlin, Germany, October 18-20, 1993.

Gulden, G. K., and Reck, R. H. "Combining Quality and Reengineering Efforts for Process Excellence." *Information Strategy: The Executive's Journal*, Spring 1992, pp. 10-16.

Hackman, J. R., and Oldham, G. R. "Development of the Job Diagnostic Survey." *Journal of Applied Psychology*, Volume 60, 1975, pp. 159-170.

Hackman, J. R., and Oldham, G. R. *Work Redesign*. Reading, Massachusetts: Addison-Wesley, 1980.

Hayley, K.; Plewa, J.; and Watts, M. "Reengineering Tops CIO Menu." *Datamation*, April 15, 1993, pp. 73-74.

Hom, P. W.; Katerberg, R.; and Hulin, C. L. "Comparative Examination of the Three Approaches to the Prediction of Turnover." *Journal of Applied Psychology*, Volume 64, 1979, pp. 280-290.

Huff, S. L. "Reengineering the Business." *Business Quarterly*, Winter 1992, pp. 38-42.

Idaszak, J. R., and Drasgow, F. "A Revision of the Job Diagnostic Survey: Elimination of a Measurement Artifact." *Journal of Applied Psychology*, Volume 72, 1987, pp. 69-74.

Igbaria, M. "Job Performance of MIS Employees: An Examination of the Antecedents and Consequences." *Journal of Engineering and Technology Management*, Volume 8, 1991, pp. 141-171.

Kahn, R. L.; Wolfe, D. M.; Quinn, R. P.; Snoek, J. D.; and Rosenthal, R. A. *Organizational Stress: Studies in Role Conflict and Ambiguity*. New York: Wiley, 1964.

Kanungo, R. "Measurement of Job and Work Involvement." *Journal of Applied Psychology*, Volume 67, 1982, pp. 341-349.

King, J. "Reengineering Repercussions." *ComputerWorld*, June 28, 1993, pp.149-150.

Kraut, A. I. "Predicting Turnover of Employees from Measured Job Attitudes." *Organizational Behavior and Human Performance*, Volume 13, 1975, pp. 24-33.

Kulik, C. T.; Oldham, G. R.; and Langner, P. H. "Measurement of Job Characteristics: Comparison of the Original and the Revised Job Diagnostic Survey." *Journal of Applied Psychology*, Volume 73, 1988, pp. 462-466.

Locke, E. "The Nature and Causes of Job Satisfaction." In M. D. Dunnette (Editor), *Handbook of Industrial and Organizational Psychology*. Chicago: Rand McNally, 1976, pp. 1287-1349.

McKee, D. "An Organizational Learning Approach to Product Innovation." *Journal of Product Innovation Management*, Volume 9, 1992, pp. 232-245.

McPartlin, J. P. "Seeing Eye to Eye on Reengineering." *Information Week*, June 15, 1992, p. 74.

Michaels, C. E., and Spector, P. E. "Causes of Employee Turnover: A Test of the Mobley, Griffeth, Hand, and Meglino Model." *Journal of Applied Psychology*, Volume 67, 1982, pp. 53-59.

Moad, J. "Does Reengineering Really Work." *Datamation*, August 1, 1993, pp. 22-28.

Mobley, W. H.; Griffeth, R. W.; Hand, H. H.; and Meglino, B. M. "Review and Conceptual Analysis of the Employee Turnover Process." *Psychological Bulletin*, Volume 36, 1979, pp. 493-522.

Morrow, P. "Concept Redundancy in Organizational Research: The Case of Work Commitment." *Academy of Management Review*, Volume 8, 1983, pp. 486-500.

Muchinsky, P. M. *Psychology Applied to Work: An Introduction to Industrial and Organizational Psychology*, Third Edition. Pacific Grove, California: Brooks/Cole Publishing Company, 1990.

Nunally, J. C. *Psychometric Theory*, Second Edition. New York: McGraw-Hill, 1978.

Parasuraman, S. "Nursing Turnover: An Integrated Model. *Research in Nursing and Health*, Volume 12, 1989, pp. 267-277.

Parden, R. J. "The Manager's Role and the High Mobility of Technical Specialists in the Santa Clara Valley." *IEEE Transactions on Engineering Management*, Volume 28, Number 1, 1981, pp. 2-8.

Porter, L. W.; Crampon, W. J.; and Smith, E. J. "Organizational Commitment and Managerial Turnover: A Longitudinal Study." *Organizational Behavior and Human Performance*, Volume 15, 1976, pp. 87-98.

Porter, L. W.; Steers, R. M.; Mowday, R. T.; and Boulian, P. V. "Organizational Commitment, Job Satisfaction, and Turnover Among Psychiatric Technicians." *Journal of Applied Psychology*, Volume 59, 1974, pp. 603-609.

Price, J. L., and Mueller, C. W. "A Causal Model of Turnover for Nurses." *Academy of Management Journal*, Volume 24, 1981, pp. 543-545.

Rizzo, J. R.; House, R. J.; and Lirtzman, S. I. Role Conflict and Ambiguity in Complex Organizations." *Administrative Science Quarterly*, Volume 15, 1970, pp. 150-163.

Ryan, H. W. "Managing Change." *Information Systems Management*, Summer 1992, pp. 60-62.

Saleh, S. D., and Desai, K. "An Empirical Analysis of Job Stress and Job Satisfaction of Engineers." *Journal of Engineering and Technology Management*, Volume 7, Number 1, 1990, pp. 37-48.

Saraph, J. V., and Sebastian, R. J. "Human Resource Strategies for Effective Introduction of Advanced Manufacturing Technologies (AMT)." *Production and Inventory Management Journal*, First Quarter 1992, pp. 64-70

Schuler, R. S.; Aldag, R. J.; and Brief, A. P. "Role Conflict and Ambiguity: A Scale Analysis." *Organizational Behavior and Human Performance*, Volume 20, 1977, pp. 111-128.

Sherman, J. D. "The Relationship Between Factors in the Work Environment and Turnover Propensities among Engineering and Technical Support Personnel." *IEEE Transactions on Engineering Management*, Volume 33, 1986, pp. 72-78.

Shore, L. M., and Martin, H. J. Job Satisfaction and Organizational Commitment in Relation to Work Performance and Turnover Intentions." *Human Relations*, Volume 42, Number 7, 1989, pp. 625-638.

Short, J., and Venkatraman, N. "Beyond Business Process Redesign: Redefining Baxter's Business Network". *Sloan Management Review*, 1992, pp. 7-21.

Spurr, K.; Layzell, P.; Jennison, L.; and Richards, N. *Software Assistance for Business Re-Engineering*. Chichester: John Wiley and Sons, 1993.

Stadler, D. A., and Elliot, S. A. "Remake Your Business." *Inform*, February 1992, pp. 12-17.

Steel, R. P., and Ovalle, N. K. "A Review and Meta-Analysis of Research on the Relationship Between Behavioral Intentions and Employee Turnover." *Journal of Applied Psychology*, Volume 69, 1984, pp. 673-686.

Steers, R. M. "Antecedents and Outcomes of Organizational Commitment." *Administrative Science Quarterly*, Volume 22, 1977, pp. 46-56.

Thackray, J. "Fads, Fixes and Fictions." *Management Today*, 1993, pp. 41-43.

Van Sell, M.; Brief A. P.; and Schuler, R. S. Role Conflict and Role Ambiguity: Integration of the Literature and Directions for Future Research." *Human Relations*, Volume 34, Number 1, 1981, pp. 43-71.

Willcocks, L., and Smith, G. "IT-Enabled Business Process Reengineering: From Theory to Practice." Unpublished Paper. Oxford: Oxford Institute of Information Management, 1994.

Williams, L. J., and Hazer, J. T. "Antecedents and Consequences of Satisfaction and Commitment in Turnover Models: A Reanalysis Using Latent Variable Structural Equation Methods. *Journal of Applied Psychology*, Volume 71, Number 2, 1986, pp. 219-231.

About the Author

Tor Guimaraes is the director of the Institute for Technology Management and holder of the J. E. Owen Chair of Excellence at Tennessee Technological University. He has a Ph.D. in MIS from the University of Minnesota and an M.B.A. from California State University, Los Angeles. Dr. Guimaraes was a Professor and Department Chair at St. Cloud State University. Before that, he was Assistant Professor and Director of the MIS Certificate Program at Case Western Reserve University. He has been the keynote speaker at numerous national and international meetings sponsored by organizations such as the Information Processing Society of Japan, Institute of Industrial Engineers, American Society for Quality Control, IEEE, ASM, and Sales and Marketing Executives. Dr. Guimaraes has consulted with many leading organizations including TRW, American Greetings, AT&T, IBM, and the Department of Defense. Working with partners throughout the world, Dr. Guimaraes has published over one hundred articles about the effective use and management of Information Systems and other technologies.

PART THREE

Images of Practice:
Systems Development

10

Transforming Organizations Through Systems Analysis: Deploying New Techniques for Organizational Analysis in IS Development

Chris Westrup
Department of Accounting and Finance
University of Manchester

Abstract

It has become conventional wisdom that information systems have the capacity to transform the workings of organizations and large numbers of information systems are being developed on that premise. As information systems move to center stage in making possible organizational activity, the capacities for organizational analysis of those developing these systems has come into question. Calls have been made for systems developers to acquire "refined skills in organizational analysis" (Kling 1993, p. 72) and similar appeals for the development of "hybrid" managers have been made in the UK. This paper argues that much of existing technique in requirements analysis is based on limited organizational theory and that moves to enrich that theory by means of improved techniques for organizational analysis are themselves *problematic* for three reasons. They abstract and simplify organizational theories while downplaying critiques of those theories; second, those techniques move unquestioningly from descriptive organizational theory to prescriptive practices; and third, they neglect the practices of systems developers that may embody sophisticated organizational awareness but which are not apparent in explicit development techniques. Finally, the paper argues that focusing on the practices of system developers suggests that developers *actively construct* representations of organizations that are rational, coherent and amenable to computerization and, by implication, they are not just engaged in passive representation. From this perspective, calls for "refined social analytical skills" are misplaced as developers are constituting the organizations they seek to develop information systems for and what will be fruitful is investigation of the practices of developers themselves.

1. INTRODUCTION

> Without a *disciplined skill* in analyzing human organizations, computer scientists'
> claims about the usability and social value of specific technologies is *mere
> opinion*, and bears a significant risk of being misleading. Further, computer
> scientists who do not have *refined social analytical skills* sometimes conceive and
> promote technologies that are far less useful or more costly than they claim.
> Effective CS [Computer Science] practitioners who "compute for the future" in
> organizations need *refined skills* in organizational analysis to understand
> appropriate systems requirements and the conditions that transform high-
> performance computing in high-performance organizations. [Kling 1993, p. 72,
> emphasis added]

There appears to be a paradox in the current development of advanced computerized information
systems. On the one hand, it is recognized by academics and practitioners that these information
systems have the capacity to transform the workings of an organization (Keen 1991; Scott
Morton 1991; Tapscott and Caston 1993; Zuboff 1988). This produces greater efficiency and
effectiveness and the likelihood of novel forms of working that may lead to new organizational
opportunities in different markets (Porter and Millar 1985). On the other hand, there is unease
that those developing these systems and, in particular, those developing the software do not have
the requisite skills and techniques in organizational analysis that may enable them to attain the
expectations of organizational transformation through the deployment of information systems.
Much of the literature on organizational transformation using information technology ignores the
issue of *how* organizational transformation is to be accomplished. Indeed, it is easy to fall for
some form of technological determinism that the deployment of advanced information systems,
of itself, will transform/revolutionize organizational practices and structures. Although this
argument may propel senior managers to invest in information technology, the introduction into
organizations and the outcome of its deployment is not clear-cut as well publicized information
systems failures demonstrate. Taking a different position, we argue that, in systems development,
the role and nature of technology and of organization is constituted. Neither technology nor
organization have an essential quality so that we can talk about social and technical factors.
Rather, what becomes social and what becomes technical is an outcome of a systems development
process.

In this paper, I wish to focus on the techniques available for organizational analysis that
developers can call on so as to construct systems that "transform organizations." In the field of
requirements analysis for software development, public soul-searching is evident so as to improve
techniques of requirements analysis and their adoption by development practitioners (Davis and
Hsia 1994; Hsia, Davis and Kung, 1993, 1994). The need for "refined skills in organizational
analysis" as proposed by Kling seems to be a pressing concern. The aim of this paper is to
explore this issue in three areas: first, to examine those current techniques in organizational
analysis and their inadequacies within requirements specification; second, to consider two novel,
less widely used approaches to organizational analysis that draw on organizational theory and
assess the problems they raise; third, to consider the import of this appeal for improved
organizational analysis when a constructivist approach to systems development is adopted. The
thrust of this paper is to enter into a critical appraisal of current techniques and practices within

systems development in the spirit of calls made by Preston (1991) for a questioning of problems posed within MIS. Therefore this paper does not seek to present a "better" approach to educating systems developers in organizational analysis; rather, it points to the difficulties that beset such a venture and how it downplays the considerable tacit skills in organizational analysis that developers use in making new systems work. Of course, it is tempting to see systems developers as being the key players in IS development; this is often far from the truth as many other groupings are involved but we wish, in this paper, to consider their role in particular.

2. IS ORGANIZATIONAL ANALYSIS A PROBLEM?

The short answer for systems developers appears to be yes. An issue that haunts software and information systems development is the continuing problem of failure. The cases of Taurus in the City of London and SOCRATES in France are but two high profile examples; many projects do end in failure even though there remains scholarly disagreement as to how many (Davis et al. 1992; Lyytinen and Hirschheim 1987). The question is how many of these failures can be laid at the door of inadequate organizational analysis? Hsia, Davis and Kung, in a review of requirements engineering[1] have few doubts on this matter:

> Many large projects have failed in spite of using modern requirements-engineering techniques. Currently, there is no convincing evidence that modern requirements engineering improves productivity and quality, although the goal of understanding user needs early is obviously a worthy one. [1993, p. 76]

A second difficulty is the paucity of material on organizational analysis for those training to be computer scientists or, more importantly, software engineers. This point has been made eloquently by Kling although there are courses that attempt to address this problem.[2] A more pressing aspect from this perspective is the numbers who develop information systems but have limited or no formal training in this area at all.

A third perspective on this issue comes from those engaged in research into information systems (IS). It has been recognized for many years (cf. Mumford et al. 1985) that IS researchers have tended to emulate canons of scientific method in their research and the fruits of this approach have permeated the formulation of methodologies of IS development (Orlikowski and Baroudi 1989; Hirschheim and Klein 1992). The widespread appeal of this approach has fostered the development and use of quantitative techniques for requirements elicitation and representation which has been shown, using a well known framework in sociological analysis (Burrell and Morgan 1979), to be a subset, albeit a significant one, of a plethora of approaches to organizational analysis (cf. Hirschheim and Klein 1989). This has led to the explicit formulation of

---

[1] I propose that organizational analysis can be equated with requirements analysis as both are concerned with the collection and analytical formulation of information relating to an organization or organizations.

[2] For example, in the UK, there are several innovative courses that link computer science and social science (Murray and Woolgar 1991, p. 21). The socio-technical approach to organizational analysis is a notable exception to a lack of organizational theory for computer scientists.

methodologies that use differing forms of organizational analysis (Hirschheim and Klein 1994; Nissen, Klein and Hirschheim 1991).

Finally, academics who teach systems analysis are troubled. A recent panel was summed up by the succinct statement,

> We [academics] teach c**p" and the observation that "more on business, organizations and people [is needed] in our courses....Systems analysis is the most important thing we should be teaching our students about otherwise they will be coding a lot of rubbish. [Galliers 1995]

These issues point to a problem with organizational analysis within systems development. However, the identification of a problem is one thing, the resolution of that problem is quite a different matter. The next section explores some of the common techniques currently used in organizational analysis in the development of IS before moving on to novel techniques that are being proposed.

3. ORGANIZATIONAL ANALYSIS TECHNIQUES: CURRENT ORTHODOXY

Pick up any textbook on requirements analysis or systems development and an assortment of similar techniques meet the eye; in the newer editions, it object oriented analysis while the older ones (and often discretely inserted in the newer editions) present structured analysis based on one or several well known methodologies (Davis 1990, 1993; Firesmith 1993; Laudon and Laudon 1994; Layzell and Loucopoulos 1989). It was not always so; indeed a convincing argument could be made that requirements analysis itself was "invented" in the late sixties from a position when the purpose and requirements of a proposed system was seen as self evident or, if not, could be gleaned from managers (Ackoff 1967; Daniels and Yeates 1969; Friedman 1989; Hirschheim and Klein 1992). Variants of structured analysis (cf. DeMarco 1979; Gane and Sarson 1979) probably remain the dominant technique and certainly they are the techniques best known by those practicing systems development.

Structured analysis sets out to analyze an organization in terms of its information processes and its information usage. Commonly, it seeks to link these two activities with overall objectives that have been set for the organization. Usually data flow diagrams are used to successively decompose an overall function of an organization into discrete subfunctions that ultimately may be expressed in algorithmic form using pseudo-English or decision tables. Information usage generally proceeds from a different basis. Entity relation diagrams are constructed from information on data used in specific functional areas of an organization. An overall pattern of information usage and relationship can be produced by merging the specific entity relationship diagrams, a process known as view integration with the removal of homonyms and synonyms. The representations of both techniques may be matched by cross tabulating entities and processes to form life histories of information entities.

As a technique of organizational analysis, structured analysis clearly focuses on functions. It represents an organization in terms of information entities and the processes that occur to these entities. The assumption is that these processes are systematic, that is, they form (or should form) a coherent whole in which all processes and data interlock to perform the requisite functions that enable the (knowable?) objectives of the organization to be attained. At the same time, it is assumed that each process is algorithmic and can be explicitly represented as such without recourse to the skills or expertise of those who perform these procedures. In short, these techniques conjure up a tidy world of functionality, harmony and clarity in which Occam's razor[3] holds sway; one that is far removed from the muddle, conflict and short-termism so common to much experience in systems development (Curtis, Krasner and Iscoe 1988) let alone organizations in general. This helps explain its attraction to management and systems developers and also its prime failing (Boland 1987). In a review of industrial sociology (now more fashionably called organizational analysis), Brown (1992) describes the 1950s as the decade of the application of systems theory to organizations. It appears no coincidence that this is the period when computers first found their application outside the military. However, this phase of organizational analysis floundered on two key points. First, there appears to be no *a priori* reason why an organization should be systemic. Second, and perhaps more crucially, systems theory fails to explain the conflicts and differing objectives that appear to be endemic in descriptions of organizational life (March and Olsen 1976; Mintzberg 1989).

The emerging move toward object-oriented analysis, though radical in its implications for programmers and analysts, has many more similarities than differences as organizational analysis when contrasted with structured analysis. Object oriented analysis seeks to describe the organization in terms of entities that may be subdivided using detailed inheritance criteria. Each entity has specified activities that it may initiate or be subjected to and these actions are assigned to individual entities. Hence the encapsulation of data and process in objects (entities) and the potential for the abstraction of complexity in analysis giving an equivalent to decomposition from the general to the specific as found in structured analysis.

When we move beyond the textbook examples of lift control mechanisms and library renewals, do we find much difference in organizational analysis? Well, not really. In this representation, the organization is composed of discrete entities that may be combined if needed and which perform specific (and algorithmic) actions. We have substituted a world of entities and processes for one akin to a complex game of billiards where the moves allowable and the properties of each ball are essentially knowable. The belief in the systemicity of the organization is retained and the expectation of an objective and mechanistic organization is taken for granted. In other words, we have a change in the formulation of the analysis but the rules of the game remain the same.

These techniques are powerful and cannot be dismissed lightly even though their analysis of organizations does not accord with representations of organizational life drawn from other sources such as ethnographic accounts. In fact, it is precisely this appeal to the analysis and uncovering of objective structures of entities, processes and the like that is their greatest strength (Bloomfield and Vurdubakis 1994). These techniques appear to cut through the muddle of organizational contingency and show management what is "actually" happening by representing the organization in a rational, structured form. The deployment of these techniques in any

---

[3]Occam proposed that "entities should not be multiplied beyond necessity.

organizational context will always come up with an analysis. They are techniques for all seasons. The downside of this universality of application is that their representation of the organization does not, and can not, map out how to reach this objective state of grace. Put differently, a mechanistic and holistic conception of an organization has nothing to say about activities that are non-algorithmic and that relate to tacit knowledge or "forms of life." Hence the difficulty in the implementation of computer systems when a move is made from objective analysis to the deployment of these systems into the bustle and muddle of organizational life.

In general, these "orthodox" forms of analysis have come under attack on two flanks; on one, there are those arguing for more sophisticated forms of organizational analysis that reflect changes in social theory while, on the other, there are those decrying the laxity of currently used techniques. Let us turn to the latter assailant and leave the former to the next section.

Within software development there is a vociferous lobby that rails against programming which cannot be formally proven through mathematics and extends this critique to nonformal approaches in the analysis of organizations (Hoare 1984). Arguably, the end point of their approach leads from a formal requirements specification to the largely automated production of the requisite computer systems (cf. Couger, Colter and Knapp 1982; Balzar 1985). In requirements engineering, a recent review makes this case plain.

> Formal methods are used to ensure an unambiguous description of requirements. Without them, requirements engineering will remain an ad hoc practice [p. 9].... What industry uses extensively are the methods developers *think* are modern (structured and object-oriented analysis). Projects that rely on either of these technologies for requirements engineering will probably increase the likelihood of failure. [Hsia, Davis and Kung 1994, p. 8, emphasis in original]

This is strong stuff and takes the assumption of organizations being capable of description as objective, rational, unambiguous and consistent entities to its logical endpoint where it wrestles with the difficulties of the divergent practices of requirements engineers. As Hsia reports elsewhere:

> Sadly, today we [software engineers] report only the success stories and bury the failures [p. 14]....Can we enforce better practices through process engineering? Can we change common practices through software-engineering education? Can we modify a software-engineer' behavior through better tools? The answer to all these three questions is yes, but only to a certain extent. *But the real answer is to change the hearts of software professionals.* [Hsia 1993, pp. 16-17, emphasis added]

This contemporary formulation of the confessional is unexpected in the midst of formalist concerns but gives an insight into the difficulties that formal approaches to software development and, in our case, organizational analysis, find themselves. A more positive and upbeat alternative comes from reformers on the other flank of orthodox technique in which they seek to apply more recent forms of organizational analysis to information systems development.

4. DEPLOYING RECENT ORGANIZATIONAL THEORY IN IS DEVELOPMENT

One point has to be made clear early on. An orthodoxy in organizational theory does not exist and many competing forms of theory are to be found that vary from abstruse formulations deriving in part from philosophical considerations to more pragmatic varieties of analysis (Tsoukas 1994). Anyone seeking to apply different forms of organizational theory to IS development faces an immediate difficulty in determining which theory to use followed by the still more difficult problem of how to package that theory in the form of practical technique. Perhaps fortunately, few seem to work in that methodical fashion and the application of social theory in systems development has tended to be less self conscious of its origins and remit.

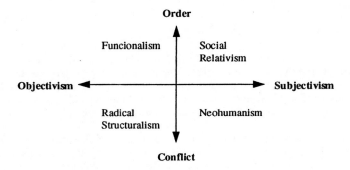

Figure 1: Information Systems Development Paradigms
(after Hirschheim and Klein 1989, p. 1202)

A popular point of departure has been to critique existing theorization and practice in systems development mining a similar vein to the previous section. Many regard the existing orthodoxies in organizational analysis as "positivistic," "Cartesian," "functionalism," or "scientistic" (Ehn 1988; Hirschheim and Klein 1989; Klein and Lyytinen 1985; Orlikowski and Baroudi 1989)., although, as we will argue later, the practices of systems developers in organization analysis are more accomplished than their techniques would imply. Apart from this critique, a well known approach has been to use classificatory systems that demonstrate the partiality of current theorization. Orlikowski and Baroudi drawing on Chua (1986) use a tripartite division of positivist, interpretivist and critical to show that most research work in IS is in the first category to the detriment of the, by implication, other two equally important categories. From this approach, it follows that organizational analysis is similarly suspect as reflecting but one of three possible viewpoints. A differing analysis but using a similar technique has been adopted by Hirschheim and Klein (1989, 1992, 1994). They use Burrell and Morgan's well known classification that categorizes social theory by its epistemological (way in which it produces knowledge) and ontological (its assumptions about reality) premises. A neat four boxed diagram can be produced (Figure 1) in which the majority of current theorization and once again, by implication, current practice is found in just one quadrant labeled functionalism.[4] But if a space is made to legitimate other social theory/organizational analysis, which one is to be chosen?

In this paper, I wish to focus on two contenders, "neohumanism" and ethnography, to exemplify the difficulties in applying social theory and developing "refined skills in organizational analysis." The nub of the argument is that operationalizing social theory to develop organizational analysis runs risks in, first, abstracting and limiting the theory that is appropriated through its incorporation in technique and, second, that well founded critiques of the deployed theory will be ignored. In conclusion, an incorporation of novel forms of organizational analysis into IS development is at the mercy of the technique that it is encapsulated within and there is no guarantee that the usage of that technique will be in accordance with the intentions of those deploying this organizational analysis. Let us examine this argument in relation to those examples, "neohumanism" and ethnography.

Hirschheim and Klein (1994, p. 109) propose that

> [The] *neohumanist* paradigm seeks change, emancipation, and the realization of human potential and stress the role that different social and organizational forces play in understanding change. It focuses on barriers to emancipation — in particular ideology (distorted communication), power and psychological compulsions, and social constraints — and seeks ways to overcome them.

In this formulation, the neohumanist approach is both descriptive in characterizing organizations in terms of ideology, power and so on as well as being prescriptive in "seeking change." Hirschheim and Klein (1994) draw on the work of Habermas (cf. 1984) as critical social theory and on Alvesson and Willmott (1992) for its application to organizations. To make the move from grand social theory à la Habermas to its use in IS development, Hirschheim and Klein formulate an emancipatory methodology that seeks to institute this form of organizational analysis. Hirschheim and Klein appear to be aware of the tightrope they walk when they seek to institute self reflection and self transformation as part of their approach toward awareness of the power relations in organizations. However, the solutions remain unconvincing, relying on essentially technical means (diary keeping and possibly electronic meeting systems [p. 88 note 2]) to support these activities.

A second example is found in "perform[ing] a diagnosis to assess the degree to which distortions are present in a given situation" (Hirschheim and Klein 1994, pp. 89-90). This form of organizational analysis sets out a checklist of four conditions and uses a rationalist basis to assess power relations; that is, is x present and so on. However, while presuming that an IS "help to overcome communicative distortions" (Hirschheim and Klein 1994, p. 88), this institutionalization of rational discourse relies on the curious mix of methodological caveat and the presence of an enlightened steering group and facilitator. It is arguable that the technical forms imposed by the methodology could lead away from communicative rationality as expected and foster technical rationality: the very opposite of what is being sought. In other words, it appears likely that the

---

[4]This classification has itself been critiqued (cf. Hassard and Pym 1990) as being too simplistic and by others (Tinker and Yuthas 1994) as being overly philosophical.

methodological encapsulation of the emancipatory form of social theory can lead to a limiting of its potential through the institution of specific forms of power relations.

Turning to the second issue, Hirschheim and Klein do point towards critiques of the emancipatory form of organizational analysis and in particular the presumption of an "ideal speech situation" where no power distortions are present (1984, p. 89, note 3) though they conclude that the exploration of these critiques is "beyond the scope of this paper." However, the critiques of this approach to social theory are many and have formed some of best known debates in the social theory literature without, as one might guess, either side winning the argument (cf. Dallmeyr 1991). It is unlikely that the user of this methodology will be aware of these debates let alone their detail and yet they go to the heart of the analyses that Hirschheim and Klein propose. For instance, one key issue is whether an interpretative approach, which recognizes that an individual has prejudgements in whatever situation that individual interacts within can be reconciled with the explicitly rationalist forms of argumentation and resolution that Habermas proposes (cf. Francis 1994).[5]

The use of ethnography forms our second example. Ethnography, that is, the use of participant observation of organizational life, is becoming better known in IS development and this is in part due to the work of Suchman (1987) and the CSCW movement. Within IS development and the field of organizational analysis, ethnography promises to give insight into the micropractices of everyday working life and to shed light on the tacit knowledge and "ways of life" of users and potential users of IS systems. Randell, Hughes and Shapiro (1991) provide a useful introduction to ethnographic practice in requirements analysis. They consider that ethnography describes an organization not simply in terms of tasks but shows the skills that those in organizations bring to work, the ways in which those skills are utilized and the ways in which "patterning of interests" is manifested in organizations. This careful use of ethnography makes it difficult for those not skilled in ethnographic work to accomplish this activity. Indeed, Randell, Hughes and Shapiro use of ethnography within a multidisciplinary team with representation from both sociologists and computer scientists/software engineers. In this example, a nuanced approach such as ethnography cannot, it appears, be framed in a technique that IS professionals can use but, even so, the shortcomings of ethnography may not be evident to those professionals when they work along side others using ethnography. It cannot be taken as a method without a careful awareness of the problems it raises within social theory in general and anthropology in particular in which it has been the dominant form of fieldwork (Clifford and Marcus 1986; Fabian 1991; Hammersley 1992). There is an increasing recognition that ethnography does not provide an unvarnished picture of an organization and that ethnography, leaving aside critiques raised from a quantitative viewpoint (cf. Benbasat, Goldstein and Mead 1987), faces difficulties of its own. Essentially, these arise from the reliance on an author presenting an ethnography of a situation and critiques center on issues of who chooses what to present, what to leave out and how this is chosen — issues about which ethnographic texts are often silent. A second problem derives from the structural issues: how was access gained and under what conditions; how is confidentiality to be reconciled with presenting a complete picture? In social science and organizational analysis, the

---

[5]Habermas' proposition that both labor and power are extralinguistic categories, and therefore separate spheres from interpretative process, gives the possibility of "real factors" being present but this defense is also vigorously disputed (cf. Dallmeyr 1991, pp. 15-24).

role of ethnography is being reappraised (Hammersley 1992; Brewer 1994) and ironically this appears to be occurring just as this form of analysis is gaining adherents within IS development (Sommerville et al. 1993).

These two examples show some of the difficulties that were faced in attempting to import novel approaches from organizational and social theory into IS development. It is not easy to encapsulate within a technique new approaches from organizational theory especially when those who will use it are likely to apply them uncritically as a resource no different than data flow diagrams. A different path out of this impasse is to use multidisciplinary teams for the analysis and development of information systems. Such an approach has much to commend it and is recommended by some within requirements engineering (Potts 1993) and by those in the social sciences interested in this area (cf. Murray and Woolgar 1991). Its major advantage is that it assumes that specialists within the team are familiar with the techniques and skills within their own discipline and are unlikely to misuse an approach to, say, organizational analysis. But it also shares a problem with the call for those within IT to develop refined skills in organizational analysis, namely, that no matter who performs the analysis, a social theory must be transformed into an analytical tool and an IT system must be predicated on basic consent from those that will use it. In other words, no matter what other objectives are present, the thrust behind developing an IS is to construct a system that users will use even if they use it to disagree. To reach this point, an analysis has to take place to transform current discourse into one that may take place using the IS.

5. DISCUSSION

The argument so far has centered on the relative poverty of existing techniques of organizational analysis, within IS development and the difficulties that arise in the deployment of novel forms of analysis. However, despite the calls for development of skills in organizational analysis those arguing that technology transforms organizations have retained quite simplistic models of organizational activity (Scott Morton 1991). For example, Hammer (1990) argues that the automation of existing practices is part of the problem; what is required is a thorough analysis of the processes that the organization must undertake. In other words, detailed user participation and nuanced social theory is unnecessary for organizational analysis, the main analytic tool is a focus on organizational processes that is not dissimilar to process analysis in current systems analysis coupled with an awareness of the capabilities of technology. Scott Morton (p. 18) goes further and proposes that new technologies change organizational structures completely with a move toward "networking" organizations that rely on IT to link groups of workers to perform specific projects. In this approach, the role for organizational analysis is limited once an organizational strategy has been put in place because the ways that the organization will work in future will be qualitatively different.

A common thread running through all these forms of organizational analysis, be they traditional, novel, or attempting "transformation," is a limited or nonexistent consideration of the activities of systems analysts. The performance of analysts and their understanding of organizations is generally richer than the analysis techniques would indicate. Hsia (p. 14) decries this gap between theory and practice: "The truth is that most companies have two sets of practices; one real, the other recommended." We can argue that this is actually a positive accomplishment and that systems analysts are not simply engaged in analyzing an organization (using traditional or refined tools) but use analysis as a resource to construct a representation of the organization that *requires* the use of an information system.[6] This implies that systems development is actively constituting the organization while analyzing requirements. Any analysis technique arrives at a representation of the organization that, by definition, is different from prior understandings of it and the application of a technique creates an ordered representation in place of other understandings of the organizational members. The efficacy of the analysis is governed not by intrinsic "refinement" in the technique but by the ability of those applying it to convince others that the analysis is correct. This requires those being persuaded to accept the need for a particular technique, to acquiesce to requirements being formulated in this format, and for subsequent alteration to occur in that format. So, for example, a manager has to be convinced that data flow diagrams are a valid technique for organizational analysis (by appeals to its widespread use, previous successes, its rigor and so on) and then for requirements to be expressed in this form and alterations to be restricted to amending the data flow diagrams.

An important appeal by those using organizational analysis techniques is to the "rationality" of the organization (Bloomfield and Vurdubakis 1994) and the resulting analysis often requires existing practices to be reformulated in a systematic form. For example, the introduction of resource management (mediated through IS) in the UK National Health Service has led to clinicians being required to classify their medical diagnoses and interventions in a standard national format. Likewise, nurses are in the process of producing a classification of their practices (Westrup 1994). Those proposing that organizations be transformed through IS require similar changes. For instance, Haeckel and Nolan (1993) propose that the future for organizations is to computerize their functions so that they may "fly by wire" like jet fighters, but to do this they consider that the enterprise model of the organization, a result of organizational analysis, should be in a "business language" and that "a *common* business language is required" (p. 132, emphasis added).

A constructivist perspective does not take either the organization or technology for granted but proposes that they are constituted and reconstituted through the activities of various agents. The problem for IS developers is to constitute the organization in such a way that the a new technology may be introduced, stabilized and utilized so that it becomes successful. Resources that persuade others of the efficacy of and need for IS are important for IS developers. Techniques for organizational (and requirements) analysis are important resources that are deployed in this regard and what becomes interesting is not just the strengths or weaknesses of the techniques themselves but the practices of developers in utilizing these resources in developing IS and convincing others of the need for information systems.

From this, several consequences flow. First, the concern of academics teaching systems analysis techniques can be reformulated. The problem is not one of the techniques being inadequate *per se*, rather it is encapsulated by a rhetoric plea of an academic at ECIS: "how to become relevant once again in how we [academics] approach the subject of analysis" (Cornford 1995). We can see such a call for relevance as going to the heart of the issue of how to produce analyses that

---

[6]This is not meant as a pejorative statement that condemns developers for their instrumentality. Instead, it points to an exploration of *how* IS practitioners actually enable IS systems to work in different situations.

demarcate roles for organizations (and technologies) which are plausible and therefore convincing to others, particularly managers. To do this, developers seek to link analysis techniques with current formulations of the organization and in this process they may claim to be capable of putting flesh to the bones of "organizational transformation" concepts. For example, a senior IT consultant working for one of the big six consultancy firms put it like this:

> How do business and IT systems analysis relate?....Management are disinterested in business processes...their eyes go blank [when they are discussed and]...the processes are soft, if you touch it, it moves....[With] data it is difficult to be precise....There is a need to integrate business and IT analysis....There is no silver bullet [and] no seamless link between the enterprise analysis domain and the IT analysis domain. [Braithwaite 1995]

In this respect, disappointment with existing techniques is misplaced. Techniques are necessary otherwise, in the absence of accepted forms of accreditation, how are we to recognize systems analysts? So, analysis techniques are useful to analysts in demonstrating their role and expertise as analysts. But the search for "relevant" techniques continues.

Second, what is a relevant and therefore useful analysis technique? We can see that relevance is relative; different parties in systems development may have differing perspectives. In this case, calls for relevance are not directed to the "needs" of systems developers, or users for that matter, but to management. Bjørn-Anderson (1995) makes this clear in a recent rallying call: "Our [IS academics/IS developers' challenge is to identify our role in relation *to management strategies* on the route to the 21st century organization" (emphasis added).

From this we would expect that "better" techniques are those that persuade managers more fully and that they must be congruent with current managerial ideas of the primacy of strategy and of organizational transformation. Hence the curiosity of managers aware of the "pivotal role" of information technology and the scramble for techniques by systems developers that represent themselves, organizations, and technologies in those terms. As Bjørn-Anderson put its: "We [IS academics/developers] have not been good at *capturing* organizational strategy" (emphasis added).

Third, a constructive approach casts light on the roles of actors in the systems development process. The very idea of a process of systems development is questioned. Arguably, the construction of a process of development with timescales, resource inputs and deliverables is very much an accomplishment by developers using methodologies as technical resources. The creation of a plan of development, a systems development process, is an initial and important step that creates a representation of what will happen and what will be regarded as normal in a specific situation.[7] As we know, this creation of order is important for management control so that there is something to manage with specific inputs, outputs and timescales. This leads to a second point that, paradoxically, rather than management (and other actors) becoming able to exercise their

---

[7]So, for instance, it may become normal for developers to work through the night to meet specific deadlines set by the representation of the development process — the project plan. See Boland (1979) for a discussion of the work of systems designers and the construction of organizational worlds.

roles in this process through these techniques, their roles are actually constructed through techniques and, of course, systems developer practices.

Put differently, prior to "systems development," no users or developers are to be found; their roles are constructed in relation to a development process. So, to talk about user participation already implies a development process in which certain parties have been construed as users. User participation is, in a sense, a tautology as to become a user involves a role that requires a relationship with computers and therefore participation is already implied. We may find in different situations that users are being "configured" in systems development (Woolgar 1991). For example, Woolgar shows how activities in the design of personal computer hardware configure certain roles for users. To be a user involves using a keyboard and mouse but does not include changing hardware cards, which is done by maintenance engineers, and so on.

Developers must also construct their role. They have to be seen as authoritative, competent, experienced and practices will be used to create these impressions. This will come as no surprise to academics who encounter situations where they have to speak with authority about issues they know little about. For systems developers, one knack is an ability to translate "problems" into development activities that they can undertake and produce swift results. Management may appear to be a different category than either developers or users because the expertise of management is always with us in modern organizations. Nonetheless, a similar argument holds. In systems development, management is often constituted in relation to the project through the creation of management teams and the like. The literature abounds in stories of management who become "project champions" and so create glittering careers for themselves and also make the project a success. In other words management roles in relation to a project are constructed and then enacted so that success in one is linked with success in the other. Even if management is not set up for a specific systems development project, the practices and rhetoric of systems development lead to a reinforcement of their role of managers. For example, witness the primacy accorded to management and managerial decision making in relation to IS deployment for organizational transformation in texts such as Scott Morton's.

In short, a constructive approach to systems development does not take the roles within systems development as given, which even much empirical work in information systems would lead us to believe. Rather, a consequence is that we should treat these roles as accomplishments and look to the resources mobilized by systems developers and others so that these groupings are produced and related.

As a final point, a consequence of a constructive approach is a questioning of the tenets of much of the empirical work in systems development. We have already argued as much above, but let us illustrate this with a different example. Most empirical work, such as a processual approach, tends to presume a division between context and content. Once again, a proposal of a constructive approach is that these are constructed rather than pregiven (Callon and Law 1991). In developing information systems, developers must do considerable work to create a context in which they may "develop" the information system. Management may have to be made a context rather than content so that they may only become involved in certain instances. From this perspective, system development plans do not simply enable managerial control but, for developers, it enables them to restrict managerial involvement to certain predefined situations when they may review deliverables. In other words, management is moved from the content of the project into a context of development work for much of the time. Conversely, one of the developer's worst nightmares is continual managerial involvement/interference which breaches this division between context and content. Similarly developers strive to construct stable requirements as a context for the development work. When requirements are acknowledged to be continually in flux, then that division between the content of the project and the context of organization is removed and development is put in jeopardy.[8]

6. CONCLUSION

Despite confident assertions that information systems transform organizations, how this is to be done remains problematic. We have notable successes and many unsung failures. In this paper, we have sought to show that a search for "refined social analytical skills" runs the risk of turning into a Holy Grail for systems development distracting attention from the affairs of those engaged in development. This claim was illustrated in three ways. First, we concur that conceptions of organizations in much of current methodology is problematic but consider that the simplicity of organizational representation is often an asset, not a weakness. It provides an apparently rational mirror for management to see its domain reflected but it is less forthcoming as to how organization may be transformed. Second, we argue that deploying novel approaches drawn from organizational and social theory is not a simple answer. In particular, encapsulating social theory as refined analytic technique is fraught with difficulty. Is it possible to shoehorn the complexity of often descriptive social theory into technique? Which organizational theory should be chosen and why? How are critiques of these approaches within the social sciences to be accommodated in systems development technique? What certainty is there that these techniques will be applied as intended in their use? To illustrate these concerns, we briefly considered two recent examples that use neohumanism and ethnography within systems development.

Third, we argue that a constructivist approach to systems development is useful in focusing attention on the practice of systems developers and how they utilize techniques as resources to construct organizational representations, be they traditional, novel or "transformatory." The activity of systems development is one in which organizational and technological identities are constructed that demonstrate the requirement for information systems. Nowhere is this clearer than in current debates and exhortations to use information technology to transform organizations. Adopting a constructivist stance to systems development may lead to several advantages though it is unlikely to afford the luxury of yet a "better" technique of systems development. Arguably, it shows how all forms of systems analysis are useful in development despite the handwringing of academics teaching this material. The relevance of techniques becomes important and not regarded as self evident and how analysis techniques are made relevant by systems developers becomes an important question. A constructivist approach opens up the complexities of development by not assuming roles in this process are pregiven. Instead, it becomes interesting to see how the roles themselves of managers, developers and users are constructed and sustained in development. In a similar vein, this approach questions some of the accepted wisdom of other empirical approaches such as the division between the content and

---

[8]Curtis, Krasner and Iscoe, in their study of system development processes, illustrate many of these issues.

context of systems development. Finally, it alerts researchers to what developers no doubt have known all along: that the practices of development are complex and skilled accomplishments that seek to produce stable relationships while constructing technologies and organizations.

7. ACKNOWLEDGMENTS

I would like to thank Mike Newman, Francis Wilson and the anonymous reviewers for their useful comments on a previous draft of this paper. I would also like to thank participants at the ECIS '95 conference in Athens where a draft of this paper was presented.

8. REFERENCES

Ackoff, R. "Management Misinformation Systems." *Management Science*, Volume 14, Number B, 1967, pp. 145-156.

Alvesson, M., and Willmott, H. (Editors). *Critical Management Studies*. London: Sage, 1992.

Balzar, R. "Software Technology in the 1990s: Using a New Paradigm." *Computer*, November 1985, pp. 39-45.

Benbasat, I.; Goldstein, D.; and Mead, M. "The Case Research Strategy in Studies of Information Systems." *MIS Quarterly*, Volume 9, Number 3, 1987, pp. 369-386.

Bjørn-Andersen, N. "The Role of IT in Creating the 21st Century Organization." *Third European Conference on Information Systems*, Athens, June 1-3, 1995.

Bloomfield, B., and Vurdubakis, T. "Visions of Organization and Organizations of Vision: The Representational Practices of Information Systems Development." *EIASM Workshop on Writing, Rationality and Organization*. Brussels, March 21-22, 1994.

Boland, R. "The In-formation of Information Systems." In R. Boland and R. Hirschheim (Editors), *Critical Issues in Information Systems Research*. Chichester: Wiley, 1987.

Boland, R. "Control, Causality and Information Systems Requirements." *Accounting, Organizations and Society,* Volume 4, Number 4, 1979, pp. 259-272.

Braithwaite, M. Presentation at Panel, "Whatever happened to Systems Analysis." *Third European Conference on Information Systems*. Athens, June 1-3, 1995.

Brewer, J. "The Ethnographic Critique of Ethnography: Sectarianism in the RUC." *Sociology*, Volume 28, Number 1, 1994, pp. 1, 231-244.

Brown, R *Understanding Industrial Organizations: Theoretical Perspectives in Industrial Sociology*. London: Routledge, 1992.

Burrell, G., and Morgan., G. *Sociological Paradigms and Organizational Analysis.* London: Heinemann, 1979.

Callon, M., and Law, J. "On the Construction of Sociotechnical Networks: Content and Context Revisited." *Knowledge and Society: Studies in the Sociology of Science, Past and Present,* Volume 8, 1991, pp. 57-83.

Chua, W. "Radical Developments in Accounting Thought.." *The Accounting Review,* Volume 61, 1986, pp. 601-632.

Clifford J, and Marcus, G. *Writing Culture.* Berkeley: University of California Press, 1986.

Cornford, T. Presentation at Panel, "Whatever happened to Systems Analysis." *Third European Conference on Information Systems.* Athens, June 1-3, 1995.

Couger, J. D.; Colter, M.; Knapp, R. *Advanced System Development/Feasibility Techniques.* New York: Wiley, 1982.

Curtis, B.; Krasner, H.; and Iscoe, N. "A Field Study of the Software Design Process for Large Systems." *Communications of the ACM,* Volume 31, Number 11, 1988, pp. 1268-1286.

Dallmeyr, F. *Life-World, Modernity and Critique.* Cambridge, England: Polity Press, 1991.

Daniels, A., and Yeates, D. (Editors). *Basic Training in Systems Analysis.* London: Pitman, 1969.

Davis, A. *Software Analysis and Specification.* Englewood Cliffs, New Jersey: Prentice Hall, 1990.

Davis, A. *Software Requirements: Objects, Functions and States.* Englewood Cliffs, New Jersey: Prentice Hall, 1993.

Davis, A., and Hsia, P. "Giving Voice to Requirements Engineering." *IEEE Software,* March 1994, pp. 12-15.

Davis, G.; Lee, A.; Nickles, K.; Chatterjee, S.; Hartung, R.; and Wu, Y. "Diagnosis of an Information System Failure: A Framework and Interpretative Process." *Information and Management,* Volume 23, 1992, pp. 293-318.

DeMarco, T. *Structured Analysis and Systems Specification.* Englewood Cliffs, New Jersey: Prentice Hall, 1979.

Ehn, P. *Work-Oriented Design of Computer Artefacts.* Stockholm: Arbetslivscentrum, Stockholm, 1988.

Fabian, J. *Time and the Work of Anthropology*. Chur, Switzerland: Harwood Academic Publishers, 1991.

Firesmith, D. *Object-Oriented Requirements Analysis and Logical Design*. Chichester: Wiley, 1993.

Francis, J. "Auditing, Hermeneutics and Subjectivity." *Accounting, Organizations and Society*, Volume 19, Number 3, 1994, pp. 235-270.

Friedman, A. (with D. Cornford). *Computer Systems Development: History, Organization and Implementation*. Chichester: Wiley, 1989.

Galliers, R. Closing Statement at Panel, "Whatever Happened to Systems Analysis." *Third European Conference on Information Systems* Athens, June 1-3, 1995.

Gane, C., and Sarson, T. *Structured Systems Analysis: Tools and Techniques*. Englewood Cliffs, New Jersey: Prentice Hall, 1979.

Habermas, J. *The Theory of Communicative Action: Reasons and the Rationalization of Society*. Boston: Beacon Press, 1984.

Haeckel, S., and Nolan, R. "Managing by Wire." *Harvard Business Review*, September-October 1993, pp. 122-132.

Hammer, M. "Reengineering Work: Don't Automate, Obliterate." *Harvard Business Review*, July-August 1990, pp. 104-112.

Hammersley, M. "A Myth of a Myth: An Assessment of Two Ethnographic Studies of Option Choice Schemes." *British Journal of Sociology*, Volume 42, 1992, pp. 61-94.

Hassard, J., and Pym, D. *The Theory and Philosophy of Organization: Critical Issues and New Perspectives*. London: Routledge, 1990.

Hirschheim, R., and Klein, H. "Four Paradigms of Information Systems Development." *Communications of the ACM*, Volume 32, Number 10, 1989, pp. 1199-1216.

Hirschheim, R., and Klein, H. "Paradigmatic Influences on Information Systems Development Methodologies: Evolution and Conceptual Advances." In M. Yovits (Editor), *Advances in Computers*, Volume 34, 1992, pp. 294-392.

Hirschheim R., and Klein, H. "Realizing Emacipatory Principles in Information Systems Development: The Case for ETHICS." *MIS Quarterly*, Volume 18, Number 1, 1994, pp. 83-109.

Hoare, C. "Programming, Sorcery or Science?" *IEEE Software*, April 1984, pp. 5-14.

Hsia, P. "Learning to Put Lessons into Practice." *IEEE Software* September 1993, pp. 14-18.

Hsia, P.; Davis, A.; and Kung, D. "Status Report: Requirements Engineering." *IEEE Software*, November 1993, pp. 75-79.

Hsia, P.; Davis, A.; and Kung, D. "Reply." *IEEE Software*, March 1994, pp. 8-9.

Keen, P. *Shaping the Future: Business Design through Information Technology.* Cambridge: Harvard Business School Press, 1991.

Klein, H., and Lyytinen, K. "The Poverty of Scientism in Information Systems." In E. Mumford, R. Hirschheim, G. Fitzgerald, and A. Wood-Harper (Editors), *Research Methods in Information Systems.* Amsterdam: North Holland, 1985.

Kling, R. "Organizational Analysis in Computer." Science *Information Society*, Volume 9, Number 2, 1993, pp. , 71-87.

Laudon, K., and Laudon, J. *Management Information Systems: Organization and Technology.* London: Macmillan, 1994.

Layzell, P., and Loucopoulos, P. *Systems Analysis and Development*, Third Edition. Lund, Sweden: StudentLitteratur, 1989.

Lyytinen, K., and Hirschheim, R. "Information Systems Failures: A Survey and Classification of the Empirical Literature." *Oxford Surveys in Information Technology*, Volume 4, 1987, pp. 257-309.

March, J.,and Olsen, M. *Ambiguity and Choice in Organizations.* Bergen, Norway. Universitisforlaget, 1976.

Mintzberg, H. *Mintzberg on Management: Inside our Strange World of Organizations.* New York: Free Press, 1989.

Mumford, E.; Hirschheim, R.; Fitzgerald, G.; and Wood-Harper, A. *Research Methods in Information Systems.* Amsterdam: North Holland, 1985.

Murray, F., and Woolgar, S. *Social Perspectives on Software: A Preliminary Report.* CRICT Discussion Paper, Brunel University, London, 1991.

Nissen, H.; Klein, H.; and Hirschheim, R. (Editors). *Information Systems Research: Contemporary Approaches and Emergent Traditions.* Amsterdam: North Holland, 1991.

Orlikowski, W., and Baroudi, J. "Studying Information Technology in Organizations: Research Approaches and Assumptions." *Information Systems Research*, Volume 2, Number 1, 1989, pp. 1-28.

Porter M., and Millar, V. "How Information Gives You Competitive Advantage." *Harvard Business Review* May-June 1985.

Potts, C. "Software Engineering Research Revisited." *IEEE Software* September 1993, pp. 19-28.

Preston, A. "The 'Problem' in and of Management Information Systems." *Accounting, Management and Information Technology*, Volume 1, Number 1, 1991, pp. 43-69.

Randell, D.; Hughes, J.; and Shapiro, D. "Systems Development — The Fourth Dimension: Perspectives on the Social Organization of Work." *SPRU CICT Conference*, Sussex University, July 18-19, 1991.

Scott Morton, M. (Editor). *The Corporation of the 1990s: IT and Organizational Transformation.* Oxford: Oxford University Press, 1991.

Sommerville, I.; Rodden, T.; Sawyer, P.; Bentley, R.; and Twindale, M. "Integrating Ethnography into the Requirements Engineering Process." *Proceedings of International Symposium on Requirements Engineering.* Los Alamitos, California: IEEE CS Press, 1993, pp. 165-171

Suchman, L. *Plans and Situated Actions: The Problem of Human-Machine Communication.* Cambridge, England: Cambridge University Press, 1987.

Tapscott, D., and Caston, A. *Paradigm Shift: The New Promise of IT.* New York: McGraw Hill, 1993.

Tinker, T., and Yuthas, Y. "Social Change and Theoretical Structures in MIS." *Fourth Interdisciplinary Perspectives on Accounting Conference.* Manchester, England, July 11-14, 1994.

Tsoukas, H. *New Thinking in Organizational Behavior.* Oxford: Butterworth-Heinemann, 1994.

Westrup, C. "Something That Makes the Job Potentially Exciting: Costing Health Care and the Work of Nurses and Accountants." *Fourth Interdisciplinary Perspectives on Accounting Conference.* Manchester, England, July 11-14, 1994.

Woolgar, S. "Configuring the User: The Case of Usability Trials." In J. Law (Editor), *A Sociology of Monsters: Essays on Power, Technology and Domination.* London: Routledge, 1991.

Zuboff, S. *In the Age of the Smart Machine: The Future of Work and Power.* Oxford: Heinemann, 1988.

About the Author

Chris Westrup is a lecturer in the Department of Accounting and Finance at the University of Manchester. His interests are in the development of information systems and, in particular, the processes of requirements analysis and the use of information systems development methodologies.

11

Debates in IS and CSCW Research: Anticipating System Design for Post-Fordist Work

Kari Kuutti
Department of Information Processing Science
University of Oulu

Abstract

The field of the study is challenges posed to Information Systems research by emerging new forms of work organization. The concepts used for analyzing work in a routine automation context are insufficient when analyzing new work situations and new conceptual tools are needed.

The characteristics of post-Fordist work are identified and compared with issues raised in recent discussions in Information Systems and Computer-Supported Cooperative Work research. It is found that there is a remarkable overlap. Based on such findings, it is claimed that the emergence of new organizational forms may have influenced the occurrence of the debates more than was expected or was documented in the literature. This connection greatly increases the importance of the theoretical debates, but also increases the pressure to produce results of practical relevance.

1. INTRODUCTION

This paper is an attempt to connect debates in Information Systems (IS) and Computer-Supported Cooperative Work (CSCW) research with emergent new work organization forms in order to identify the direction in which our conceptual tools for analysis and design should be augmented.

It not an exaggeration to say that IS research throughout the 1980s was characterized by a growing discussion and criticism of the prevailing way of understanding the system to be designed and the "normal" ways of studying the use of computer applications. The discussion is still going on. This paradigmatic discussion will be used here as one indication of the ongoing change in IS. The discussion is characterized by Klein and Hirschheim, for example, in the following way:

> It is possible, therefore, to speak of an IS orthodoxy, one where fundamental
> tenets are shared and form a general conception of how information systems can
> and should be developed. Recently, however, it is possible to note the emergence
> of some radically different approaches to ISD, ones which do not share the same
> paradigm, which possess an underlying philosophy that is quite different from the
> orthodoxy, and which challenge the basic assumptions, values and beliefs of the
> past. [Klein and Hirschheim 1987, p. 275-276]

Another issue interpreted as an indication of change is the emergence of CSCW as a relatively
independent field of study. Although there are few direct links from the IS tradition to CSCW,
the latter can be seen as a continuation of the former. On one hand, central parts of CSCW
research clearly fall within a broad definition of "Information Systems research" because the main
emphasis is also put on the use of computer applications. On the other hand, CSCW research
addresses many of the same questions as are raised in IS paradigmatic discussion. This can also
be seen in the closing paper of the European CSCW conference in 1991, "CSCW: Discipline or
Paradigm?" by Hughes, Randall and Shapiro (1991), who give it the subtitle "A Sociological
Perspective."   They question the general characterization of CSCW as a separate, new
subdiscipline among others studying the development and use of computer artefacts and suggest
that it should be interpreted more as a shift in the prevailing paradigm, a change of emphasis in
the way we as designers see the world around us:

> Our view is simple but with far-reaching consequences, namely that CSCW should
> be viewed not as a specialized subdiscipline but as a general shift in the perspec-
> tive from which computer systems — all computer support systems — are
> designed.

Could this striking similarity in opinions within two separate communities that are working within
the same broad field be merely a coincidence? Hardly so. This paper attempts to connect both
claims with a broader change going on in society, the change toward a "post-Fordist"
organization of work. An extensive discussion exists in the work sociology, management and
organizational literature on emerging new forms of work organization. Organizational forms in
which workers possess more actorship and take the initiative and responsibility in cooperative
settings are being presented as the major alternative to recent dominating practices.

> Moreover, in a post-industrial society, adaptability is the characteristic of the
> modern enterprise (private or public). Mass production with economy of scale is
> giving way to flexible adaptation to the market or community's needs, as the
> guiding principle of organizational strategy. Organizations are becoming flatter,
> project groups tending to replace permanent departmental structures; information
> systems must keep pace with these and other new organizational demands.
> [Stamper et al. 1991, Introduction, p. xi]

One of the distinguishing features of the new work organizations — emphasized in this paper —
is that participants in cooperative work processes have to be treated as active subjects who make
sense of situations, take responsibility and make decisions and judgements, detect and correct
errors and solve problems, overcome and circumvent obstacles, negotiate and reorganize their

cooperation and innovate and reconstruct their ways and means. These features themselves are nothing new: all work has always contained some aspects of them. What is changing is the attitude toward them: previously exceptions were considered harmful and were to be eliminated if possible by the careful design of processes, whereas now they are becoming accepted as an essential part of work. In other words, the "emergent" features of work are becoming visible and crucial — and thus something one has to prepare for in the terms of support, as well.

Here we come to the pivotal element in the line of argument to be pursued in this paper: that if work is developing along "post-Fordist" lines and if we want to utilize the available potential of information technology to support the emergent features of this new work, then the concepts generally used in the design of the systems of the "old type" (and, correspondingly, research into them) will be inadequate for the new purposes, and new conceptualizations are needed. This paper suggests that this need is actually one major factor motivating IS discussion, and one of the major reasons for the emergence of CSCW.[1]

2. DEBATES IN INFORMATION SYSTEM RESEARCH AND CSCW

2.1 The IS Debate on Methodologies

One of the notable events in the paradigmatic discussion was without doubt the Manchester colloquium organized by IFIP WG 8.2 in 1984 — a manifestation of the existence of an opposition against the positivistic mainstream within the IS research community. The name of the colloquium was deliberately polemic: "IS research — a dubious science?" The ISRA-90 conference held in Copenhagen six years later was intended by the organizers to be a direct continuation of the discussion of the themes raised in Manchester. In the opening article of the proceedings of the Copenhagen conference the organizers return to the elaboration of "dubiousness." They define a dubious branch of science in the following way:

> A science is dubious if it either lacks meaningful problems or effective, reliable methods for solving them. An example of a dubious science is alchemy: it had meaningful problems like producing gold from lead but lacked effective methods for addressing them. [Nissen, Klein, and Hirschheim 1991, p. 4]

The authors do not actually ask whether IS research lacks meaningful problems, but they do concentrate on methods and the justification of their existence.

It is clear that the authors were striving more after eloquent writing than scientific accuracy, but their example gives a good starting point for the purposes of this paper. If we look at the nature of alchemy from the viewpoint of the history of science, it is quite easy to see that the borderline between a "dubious" science (alchemy) and a "real" one (chemistry) is not so easy to draw and may not be possible to draw at all using the criteria mentioned above. The history of science

---

[1] The theme is also relevant to other branches studying systems and their design, i.e., Human-Computer interaction (see Bannon 1991; Kuutti and Bannon 1991) or Software Engineering (Floyd 1988), which have engaged in a very similar debate of their own.

usually looks on alchemy as an immediate precursor of chemistry, the methods of which were carried over without any break to become standard methods of chemistry, some of which are still in use in modern laboratories. Thus alchemy actually had quite efficient methods.

On the other hand, founding the definition of a science on "meaningful problems" may not be very fruitful. "Meaningful problems" — such as they appear in everyday life — are meaningful only within a limited historical horizon. Framed differently, it may transpire that the question has been formulated partially or even totally in the wrong manner and that the actual point lies elsewhere. Everyday "meaningful problems" belong to the "appearance" side of reality, whereas science should be devoted to revealing the "essence" beyond the appearance. Alchemy, too, had to reject totally its "meaningful problem" before it was able to be transformed into chemistry. Thus the alchemy example is unfortunately lame in both legs.

How was "dubious" alchemy able to be transformed into "real" chemistry? Only with its capability to identify and define a research object of its own. Because in the old philosophy of nature mixed phenomena were not classified, it was necessary to rule out both the purely physical and the purely biological and concentrate on the area "between" them. Only after this area had been defined was it possible to start groping for theories to explain it — chemical theories.

The alchemy example may give us an idea of where to look when observing the paradigmatic discussion within IS research. I would like to claim that one of the major factors behind the methodological debate is the lack of certain ontological foundations — what is the nature of the object of study? Of course, the answer to the ontological question may also have a strong impact on methodological questions. If we are hunting, our methods will most certainly differ depending on whether we are hunting whales, flies or microbes.

The ontological questions are much less visible in discussions than the methodological ones. For example, at the above mentioned Manchester symposium (Mumford et al. 1985), the main concern was clearly "to oppose positivism," the legitimation of studies that use approaches other than traditional "scientific method." The question "What is the object that should be studied?" is discussed amazingly little and only superficially. Six years later, the organizers of the ISRA-90 conference started with a greater sense of purpose:

> No field can avoid assumptions on the nature of its research approaches. These approaches tend to deal with two basic issues: (I) the nature of what is investigated (ontology) and (ii) the nature of human knowledge and understanding that can possibly be acquired through different types of research and the appropriateness of the methods of investigation (epistemology). [Klein, Hirschheim, and Nissen 1991, pp. 4-5]

Unfortunately, this remains about the only point upon which ontological questions are touched. This is a consequence of the relativistic "methodological pluralism" adopted by the organizers: "Each method defines the objects to be studied differently...each method constructs the very situation that it is trying to address" (Klein, Hirschheim and Nissen 1991, p. 7). Thus their main emphasis is directed away from the object of research.

2.2 A "Social System" as the Object

The major issue in the debate, as emphasized by several authors (Banville 1991; Boland and Hirschheim 1987; Lyytinen 1986), is the question of whether the object of research (and finally design) is of a technological or a social nature, where the meaning of "social" is often explained as being that used in sociological analysis, the main emphasis thus being on social relations between people (Klein and Hirschheim 1987; Lyytinen 1986).

The primacy of the "social system" aspect means that it should be the determining factor in information system design. This puts a heavy load on the practical applicability of "social system" concepts in design.

Against the background of the IS research debate it is easy to understand why the importance of the "social" has been so greatly emphasized: it has been the strongest argument in the legitimation of any "social" research approaches. This attitude has led to some harmful distortions, however, such as a sort of "system-centrism" in which the information system appears as a self-sufficient entity which forms a "social system" of its own. In practice, observable "social systems" are not mainly formed according to information systems which are so deeply embedded and intertwined into work practices that it makes no sense at all to try to separate them. The relationship between the social and the technical in design is not as easily resolved as the promoters of the "social" aspect in IS debates have been proposing.

Since there is little coherence or consensus between the different voices in the paradigmatic debate, it is impossible to find a coherent and generally accepted set of features that should be better taken into account. It is possible to collect a list of separate issues emphasized by different approaches, however. Besides the generally accepted importance of the "social system," at least the following can be identified:

- The importance of subjective interpretation and cultural factors, emphasized especially by researchers using phenomenology and hermeneutics (e.g., Boland 1984, 1987, 1991, 1985; Rathswohl 1991).

- The importance of communication, emphasized especially by researchers using the Critical Social Theory of Habermas (e.g., Lyytinen and Klein 1985; Klein 1986; Lyytinen 1986, 1990b; Hirschheim, Klein, and Newman 1987; Lyytinen and Hirschheim 1988; Hirschheim and Klein 1989; Dietz and Widdershoven 1991; Lyytinen, Klein, and Hirschheim 1991; Ngwenyama 1991; Perrole 1991).

- The importance of the construction of structures, emphasized especially by researchers using the structuration theory by Giddens (e.g., Poole and DeSanctis 1989; Robey and Zmud 1990; Walsham and Han 1990; Lyytinen 1990a; Orlikowski 1992; Orlikowski and Robey 1991; Lyytinen and Ngwenyama 1992).

- The importance of emancipation, emphasized specially both by those using Habermas and those belonging to the Scandinavian critical tradition (e.g., Bjerknes, Ehn and Kyng 1987; Ehn 1988; Greenbaum and Kyng 1991).

2.3   The Emergence of CSCW

During the 1980s, a new approach emerged within the broad area of computer systems use and design under the title CSCW (Computer-Supported Cooperative Work). The term was first used in a workshop in 1984, and the first open conference under the same name was organized in 1986, in Austin, Texas. This started a series of biannual conferences organized by ACM: 1988 in Portland, 1990 in Los Angeles, 1992 in Toronto, and 1994 in North Carolina. Europe followed a little later: the first European conference was held at Gatwick, England, in 1989, the next one in Amsterdam in 1991, the third in Milan in 1993, and there will be one in Stockholm in 1995. Besides these larger events, there have been a number of smaller ones, and sections devoted to CSCW have been established in other conferences, such as those devoted to HCI, computer networks, etc. Beginning in the late 1980s, the publication of books on CSCW topics has increased and it has been recognized in professional journals (e.g., thematic issues in *Byte* in 1988, in *IEEE Computer* in 1991, in *Communications of the ACM* in 1992). Two new journals addressing CSCW topics have started up: the *Journal of Organizational Computing* (1991) and the *Journal of CSCW* (1992). Thus, CSCW has established itself as a recognized research area in less than ten years — quite an achievement.

From the very beginning, CSCW has been a broad, diversified field, consisting of varied approaches from multiple disciplines. The available space does not allow further elaboration of its different subfields: it can be only mentioned that research emphasizing the social aspects of cooperative work settings is the most relevant from the viewpoint of this paper.

2.4   Characterization of CSCW

Although there may not been any conscious attempt involved, the very name CSCW is the antithesis of traditional information systems: instead of automation, support is emphasized; instead of predetermination, active cooperation is emphasized; and instead of a concentration on systems, work is emphasized.

When it comes to issues considered important by CSCW researchers, many of them are very similar to those expressed in IS debates. Thus CSCW research also emphasizes communication as a fundamental prerequisite for organizing cooperation, situationality, subjective interpretations and cultural factors shaping the interpretations, e.g., those using ethnomethodology (see Hughes, Randall and Shapiro 1992; Suchman 1989), and local innovation leading to the construction and reconstruction of elements of the work environment (see Hughes, Randall and Shapiro 1991; Lyytinen 1990a).

The issues of power, control, conflicts and emancipation have received less attention than in IS discussions, however, and his has been criticized, e.g., by Howard (1987) and Kling (1991).

Besides the important issues similar to those in IS discussions, CSCW research has found some of its own:

- CSCW research has emphasized objects of work. The concept of a *shared object* is central to many of the types of suggested systems.

- It also recognizes two levels in work: "real" work and "*articulation*" work, the overhead necessary to create the "real" work and to keep it running, i.e., organization, negotiation, coordination, etc. (Schmidt and Bannon 1992).

- Much emphasis is placed on tools and their mediatory character between the worker and the object of the work (Suchman 1989).

- The *integrity* of work situations has been recognized, in that technological, psychological and social aspects "amalgamate" together (Moran and Anderson 1990).

To summarize, CSCW research sees work as cooperatively done by multiple active subjects at both "real" and "articulation" levels. It has an object which is manipulated and transformed by mediating tools, and it is situational and local so that active subjects have to interpret and make sense of situations, this interpretation being shaped by the culture and history of the corresponding community of practice. The workers involved in the work process are able to detect and solve problems, circumvent obstacles and innovate improvements. They are continuously constructing and reconstructing their sphere of work.

3. A CHANGE IN WORK

According to many writers, we are living in critical times, a critical period in the history of developed countries when well-established truths and patterns in production and in the economy are being shattered and new ones formed. A general outline of this change and its relation to information technology can be condensed as follows:

1) The developed countries are moving toward a "post-industrial," "post-Fordist" organization of work or at least this is emerging as a viable alternative to the traditional organization. This change is embedded in a wider restructuring of society.

2) The central features of the new organization of work are flexibility and intensive growth instead of extensive — a more efficient use of both material and human resources. This means that workers must become more active subjects in their work, more knowledgeable and aware of the whole of the "production" — whatever it is — and cooperative within the whole, more capable of taking part in and being responsible for the planning, design and error recovery tasks that formerly belonged to the managerial level. This organization of work has to be shaped in order to reap the benefits of active, cooperative workers. This will have deep impacts on training, commitments, rewards and the social relations system as a whole.

3) Information technology is a key element in the change in two senses: on the one hand, it is the crucial enabler for many of the flexibility features and, on the other hand, the design and implementation of information systems is perhaps the most common of all the processes in which work and its organization are changing nowadays — although not always consciously.

3.1　The "Post-Fordist" Organization of Work

How can this ongoing change in society and organizations be characterized? Jones (1991), in his comprehensive review, develops two broad perspectives on the changes at both the societal and the organizational level, a "post-industrial " and a "post-Fordist" one. The "post-industrial" perspective puts emphasis on technology and sees information as the source of power in the future. It takes an optimistic view of the social impacts of such change and is in general rationalistic and technocratic in outlook, while the "post-Fordist" perspective as defined by Jones has arisen largely as a reaction to the straightforward optimism of the post-industrialist perspective. Under it, Jones groups viewpoints such as information society "pessimists" and "sceptics" like Hamelink and Miles and Gershuny, Piore and Sabel's Second Industrial Divide, flexible accumulation by Aglietta and Boyer, post-modernism at the societal level, and Piore and Sabel's flexible specialization and post-Fordism within organizations (Jones 1991, p. 174).

This paper is based on Jones' "post-Fordist perspective" on change in organizations. "Flexible specialization" is part of the theory of the Second Industrial Divide put forward by Piore and Sabel (1984). The areas of change are summarized by Phillimore (1989) as follows: the economics of scale will give way to the economics of scope; technology will move toward more flexible instead of dedicated machinery; niche markets will replace standardized products, products will become more information-intensive; task flexibility will replace fragmentation and standardization of work processes and skills; networks will replace managerial hierarchies; linkages with customers and suppliers will become tightly integrated; and competition based on capacity will be replaced by competition by innovation. Wood (1989) characterizes post-Fordism as follows: product variability and the division of labor will change significantly, product innovation and improved design capability will be emphasized, and close links with suppliers and responsiveness to the market will become important. What are the characteristic features of such a work organization as faced by the workers?

One of them is obviously the active, innovative and responsible role of workers: people will have to take the initiative, detect and solve problems, deal with unforeseen contingencies and work around breakdowns (Drucker 1991; Seely Brown 1991; Watson 1980).

Another distinguishing feature will be the strong emphasis on active cooperation in teams, groups, networks and the like (Drucker 1992; Hughes, Randall and Shapiro 1991; Savage 1990).

The changing environment of organizations and their dynamic and emergent features has also been emphasized by many writers talking about the new forms of work organization (Hedberg 1991; Schmidt 1991; Stamper et al. 1991).

Noikka, Norros, Hyötyläinen, and Kuivanen (1991) present among their stages of developmental orientation (Table 4, pp. 38-40) a good description of the change toward the "new production worker." Their lowest stage (1) is called "withdrawal from disturbance handling" and the highest stage (5) "design oriented operation." They base the distinctions between the stages on differences in four domains: "thinking and learning," "work culture and motivation," "cooperation and communication" and "coping with stress." When a work organization moves from stage 1 toward stage 5, they expect the following changes:

Thinking and learning

From: Algorithmic models of normal operations, reactive thinking, experimental learning: adopting algorithms, routinization.

To: Dynamic system model for systematic and cooperative development of system, planning through continuous system design, theoretical-practical experimental learning.

Work culture and motivation

From: "Alienated" wage labor, responsibility for normal operations and given tasks.

To: A new production culture, responsibility for system development as a condition for individual development.

Cooperation and communication

From: Individual decisions, a rigid division of labor, one-way transitory communication.

To: Cooperation within design and cooperation through new organizational forms, horizontal and vertical communication based on common models.

Coping with stress

From: Withdrawal from activity in disturbance situations, disturbances as rest.

To: Elimination of stress factors and creation of new resources through cooperative system development.

This direction toward "design oriented operation" is shared by many writers. Drucker (1992) wants workers to see themselves as "executives," Scott Morton (1991) sees that they are changing from "doers" to "analyzers," Ciborra and Schneider (1992) demand a situation in which "Everybody is a Designer," and Howard (1987) talks about "organizational reflexivity" as an overall term pointing to learning about an organization and its possibilities and knowing how to influence them.

3.2   Information Technology and New Forms of Working

The emergence of the new forms of organization is largely connected in one way or another with information technology. Networking capability, in particular, and also information producing facilities, are seen as crucial enablers for the new forms of organization. A picture is outlined in which the new work organization, multiskilled and active workers, and advanced information technology become inseparably and harmoniously connected.

The picture painted this far looks neat — too neat to be accurate. Nothing is so straightforward in reality. Many of the issues and relationships are complicated and are being debated within their home disciplines. It is very plausible that there will be no automatic development toward the new forms of work described above. Instead, they represent just one potential development path among many alternatives in an area where different forces and pressures are present and are changing dynamically. This is clearly expressed by Hughes, Randall and Shapiro (1991) and Orlikowski and Robey.

3.3   Features Relevant to the Discussion

It still seems to be difficult to evaluate the conditions on which the new forms can be successful, and it is perhaps still too early to make any final judgement whether there is a fundamental change going on — as some researchers suggest — or whether the new forms of work organization are but one more choice among many alternatives.

In any case, it seems clear that there are situations where the new ways of organizing work offer a promising potential and we can expect them to increase — in the form of either a radical redesign or a more subtle, partial change in the existing way of work. In both cases the need for computer support for the new features in work will increase. Although the talk of a "new industrial revolution" is probably an exaggeration, it is clear that enough interest has been shown in such features to warrant their use in searching for solutions to work organization problems. It is also plausible that there will be cases in which economically viable alternatives will emerge to the old forms of work organization. Even if "complete" versions of these forms were to be slow to spread, we can expect some features characteristic of them to start to penetrate the old forms anyway.

To summarize, what will be the characteristic features of work under new the organization?

1) The work will be done by active subjects who will take initiative, make decisions, reflect on their work and can change some aspects in it.

2) The work will be done cooperatively by the actors. Some aspects in this cooperation may need the generation of mutual understanding, planning and negotiation of the necessary division of labor and active coordination in order to link individual actions into the process.

3) The work will take place in a turbulent environment in which actors will have to make sense of unforeseen situations and redirect and reorganize their work as the process goes on.

4) Conflicts and controversies at places of work will not disappear.

To put it briefly, the process nature and emergent aspects of the work become more important.

3.4 Connection Between IS and CSCW Debates and New Forms of Work

If we compare the features of work presented above with the list of "important issues" raised in both IS and CSCW debates, it is easy to see a remarkable similarity between them. All the topics considered important in the discussions would be useful and important when analyzing a work situation of a new type.

• Because of the situational character of the work and the necessity to make sense of it, and because workers belong to particular communities of practice, it is necessary to pay attention to issues of personal interpretation and cultural factors.

• Because situations emerge in the course of a work process in an unforeseen way and it is thus impossible to plan or organize everything beforehand, it is necessary to pay attention to articulation aspects.

• Because work is done by several active subjects who have to share viewpoints, negotiate, make decisions and coordinate their actions, it is necessary to pay attention to communication aspects.

• Because work has to be continuously adapted to the changing environment, it is necessary to pay attention to aspects of learning, construction and reconstruction.

• Because, in the new forms of work organization, the scope of a worker's actions will be broader, new skills will be needed and the worker's responsibility will increase, it will be necessary to pay attention to aspects of power, control, conflict and emancipation.

It can thus be concluded that the IS discussion has already been raising questions that will be essential for dealing with the new work forms of organization. In many cases, however, these questions are either raised at a "macro" level, without any direct, intimate connection with actual work processes where systems are used, or different aspects are studied separately, without any attempt to deal with reality in all its richness. The discussion within CSCW research has been much more comprehensive and systematic where it comes to studying the issues in actual work processes at a "micro" level.

This difference is easy to see by comparing what these communities deem to be worth publishing, e.g., in the relatively recent proceedings of the Ann Arbor conference (Baskerville et al. 1994) and CSCW'94 (*Transcending Boundaries* 1994). There are many themes discussed in both of the collections and related to the issues raised in this paper, but the treatments are vastly different. The former publication is full of theories, frameworks and organizational-level issues such as power and control, but there is only one paper discussing these issues at the detailed level of actual work processes (Zimmerman, Grande and Johnston 1994), while the CSCW'94 publication contains just a couple of "framework" papers and almost all the rest deal extensively with the processes in which work is actually done or systems are used. Correspondingly, the CSCW volume is thin indeed on "macro" or organizational issues and, where these are touched upon, the "organization" is more likely to be interpreted as the immediate environment of the users rather than any larger structure or change process.

4. DISCUSSION

The connection recognized between the IS and CSCW debates on the one hand and emerging new forms of work organization on the other sounds plausible and is, after all, not very surprising. What is surprising is that it is hardly ever even mentioned in IS debates, let alone elaborated further. CSCW research has a slightly richer record in this respect, but no substantial attempt has been made to study the connection there, either — despite the fact that CSCW systems are sometimes even seen as "archetypes" for the emerging new work forms (Hughes, Randall and Shapiro 1991). How is it that both communities have developed this blind spot — especially when emphasizing the connection would have been beneficial for both of them in terms of legitimation of the approach?

4.1   IS and Work as an Object of Analysis

It has not been popular at all to use the concept of work and work processes in information system research beyond the Scandinavian critical tradition (Bansler 1989). As shown above, even those challenging the mainstream concept have been happy with "social systems" and not really interested in "work systems." A couple of explanations can be suggested.

Historically, information systems research has based its identity on the concept of information and the use of information in organizations. The system is seen as a means of providing the information. The archetypal user of an information system is someone who, when performing something (it is very rare that this "something" is called "work"), develops an "information need" which has to be satisfied by the system: a decision-maker in a smaller or larger scale. The viewpoint of the Management Information Systems tradition has remained central even though the tradition itself has been diminishing in importance. Rob Kling is one of the few researchers within the IS tradition who has clearly indicated this difference:

> We view organizations as work systems in which participants make decisions about their work rather than as decision systems in which work is incidentally done. This apparently academical distinction is of far-reaching importance. While many people make decisions in the course of their work, most jobs result in a set of actions based on whatever decisions are made by the actor or others. In organizational life, the physical work with and around computers influences what is done and what is used. [Kling 1987, p. 321]

Another possible reason is that there has been a conscious or unconscious reluctance to become involved in the controversies raised in studying working life in general and wage labor in particular. It has been more convenient to use neutral concepts and not ones that might arouse controversies. The concept of work obviously does not belong to this neutral class. Given the increased interest in the issues of power and control (e.g., Baskerville et al. 1994), this barrier seems to be lowering, however

Yet another reason may be an attitude of mind adopted from the organizational-level frameworks and grand social theories used in research efforts which maintains that grass-root work processes are hardly visible and are uninteresting in any case.

4.2   CSCW and Organizational Change

The CSCW community has a totally different problem. It has neither been nor is it now oriented toward organizational change. If we divide the community coarsely into two groups — "technical tinkerers" and "social scientists" — the former are interested in the implementation of their own system and the latter in how people use or misuse systems, are disturbed by them in their work or are able to circumvent their problems. Both groups are largely lacking a perspective and interest in design in general and in changing work processes or organizations by using systems. Thus the perspective that work processes themselves might be undergoing a change remained unnoticed. There is just one paper in the CSCW'94 proceedings (Hughes et al. 1994) discussing CSCW design in general — and none discussing it as a means for planned organizational change.

4.3   Explaining the "BPR Failure"

The rise of BPR (Business Process Reengineering) may be one of the most notable features in the whole system design area during the last few years. BPR as a term was invented about five years ago, and the expansion of its popularity and spread of its use is without doubt one of the success stories of the 1990s. Hundreds, if not thousands, of articles have been written; tens, if not hundreds, of books have been published, and a whole consultation industry has arisen to exploit the business potential BPR seems to offer. What is the secret — what is new in it? It is not so easy to say, but one has a certain deja-vu feeling when reading BPR books, a feeling of having seen one idea or another earlier in some other context. It is not surprising that several IS writers analyzing BPR (e.g., Earl and Khan 1994; Galliers 1994; Jones 1994) are slightly bitter, as they think that BPR is reinventing some old stuff already discussed within IS long ago. They are correct, in fact, for when it comes to ingredients, BPR could well have been initiated by the IS community. There is a crucial difference, however, from the viewpoint elaborated in this paper. Unlike the IS community, which has tried to understand the world through concepts such as "organization" and "social system," the initiators of the BPR movement were bold enough to redefine the unit of analysis and development as the "business process," thus coming much closer to the demands of the new forms of work organization. On the other hand, unlike the CSCW community, which was already studying work practices at the level of actual processes, the promoters of BPR had a clear agenda of organizational change. It did not matter that the concept of "business process" itself was and is weakly defined and in fact insufficient to define the unit of analysis and development, as Earl and Khan and Galliers correctly note in their papers. It was a promising enough step in the right direction, and thus people struggling with organizational change and information technology have followed it.

5. CONCLUSIONS

Three suggestions can be made to the IS research community regarding the relation between IS and new forms of work organization. The first and most fundamental is that we should start a theoretical discussion about the proper unit of analysis and design. If an organization is too broad and vague, an information system too narrow, and a social system too hazy and one-sided, then what is it that we are actually going to analyze and change in this newly organized work? We can use the "business process" as a starting point for this purpose, and in fact both Earl and Khan and Galliers have already opened up a discussion on how to go beyond "business processes." I believe that the IS research community, with its rich tradition, would be much better armed for such a task than the more practically oriented BPR community itself, for example.

The second suggestion is that we should revive interest in the methods and methodologies of system design, for if the object of design is changing, a methodical arsenal has to be created that can cope with it. The scope of the analysis has to be broadened and methods enriched. If the ideals of the new work forms are going to be realized, tasks that have been separated in hierarchial work organizations — planning and design, decision-making and the execution of plans — will merge together, and in ways that cannot be predetermined. Additionally, when we have several active planners and decision-makers working together, the "overhead" work that is necessary to get the "real" work done becomes highly visible and important. This overhead or "articulation work" contains all activities such as the generation of a mutual understanding of the object and the transformation procedures, tools, etc., among the participants involved, the planning and negotiation of the necessary division of labor, the coordination of individual actions to form the necessary cooperative procedures, etc. This type of work is local and situational, and thus it has been invisible in all analyses searching for permanent, well-defined routines.

The active actors have to cope with what comes, and in order to do so they could be helped by tools, something that is deliberately used in a particular emergent situation for a desired effect. Thus methods are needed for identifying and for designing tools for different purposes, as for transformation and manipulation, for communication and for sense-making. As we are dealing with emergent processes that cannot be prescribed, it would also be necessary to enable the construction of new tools to cope with the unforeseen situations.

For successful design, we would need new methods to identify the potential support available for the work practices and knowledge of how such methods could be organized to deal systematically with problems in designing the new forms of work. Hence there is a need for reopening the methodological discussion.

The third suggestion to be made to the IS community is that it might be worthwhile to seek cooperation with the CSCW community. The IS community has a strong orientation toward design and organizational change and a rich tradition in understanding organizational-level problems in designing and implementing systems, but it is relatively weak in dealing with work processes. CSCW has made clear progress in understanding work processes, but it is lacking an orientation toward design and organizational change and it has little experience of problems of organizational implementation. Both sides could learn from each other, and a dialogue between these two relatively separated communities should be opened — the sooner the better.

6. ACKNOWLEDGMENTS

The constructive comments to the earlier version of this paper given by Wanda Orlikowski and the three anonymous referees have been very helpful, and Malcolm Hicks has assisted in editing the English. The work has been financially supported by the Finnish Centre for Technological Development (TEKES) as a part of CEC ESPRIT project 6225 COMIC.

7. REFERENCES

Bannon, L. J. "From Human Factors to Human Actors: The Role of Psychology and Human-Computer Interaction Studies in System Design." In J. M. K. Greenbaum (Editor), *Design at Work: Cooperative Design of Computer Systems*. Hillsdale: Lawrence Erlbaum, 1991, pp. 25-44.

Bansler, J. "Systems Development Research in Scandinavia: Three Theoretical Schools." *Scandinavian Research in Information Systems*, Volume 1, Number 1, 1989, pp. 3-20.

Banville, C. "A Study of Legitimacy as a Social Dimension of Organizational Information Systems." In H.-E. Nissen, H. K. Klein, and R. Hirschheim (Editors), *Information System Research: Contemporary Approaches and Emergent Traditions*. Amsterdam: North-Holland, 1991, pp. 107-129.

Baskerville, R.; Smithson, S.; Ngwenyama, O.; and DeGross, J. I. (Editors). *Transforming Organizations with Information Technology (IFIP Transactions A-49)*. Amsterdam: North-Holland, 1994.

Bjerknes, G., Ehn, P., and Kyng, M. (Editors). *Computers and Democracy — A Scandinavian Challenge*. Aldershot: Avebury, 1987.

Boland, R. J. "The In-formation of Information Systems." In R. J. Boland and R. A. Hirschheim (Editors), *Critical Issues in Information Systems Research*. Chichester: John Wiley and Sons, 1987, pp. 363-379.

Boland, R. J. "Information Systems Use as a Hermeneutic Process." In H.-E. Nissen, H. K. Klein, and R. Hirschheim (Editors), *The Information Systems Research Arena of the 1990s: Challenges, Perceptions and Alternative Approaches*. 439-458). Amsterdam: North-Holland, 1991, pp. 439-458.

Boland, R. J. "Sense-Making of Accounting Data as a Technique of Organizational Diagnosis." *Management Science*, Volume 30, Number 7, 1984, pp. 868-882.

Boland, R. J. "Phenomenology: A Preferred Approach to Research on Information Systems." In E. Mumford, R. Hirschheim, G. Fitzgerald, and A. T. Wood-Harper (Editors), *Research Methods in Information Systems.* Amsterdam: North-Holland, 1985, pp. 193-203.

Boland, R. J., and Hirschheim, R. A. (Editors). *Critical Issues in Information Systems Research.* Chichester: John Wiley and Sons, 1987.

Ciborra, C. U., and Schneider, L. S. "Transforming the Routines and Contexts of Management, Work and Technology." In P. S. Adler (Editor), *Technology and the Future of Work.* New York: Oxford University Press, 1992.

Dietz, J. L., and Widdershoven, G. A. M. "Speech Acts or Communicative Actions." In L. J. Bannon, M. Robinson, and K. Schmidt (Editors), *Proceedings of the Second ECSCW.* Amsterdam: Kluwer, 1991.

Drucker, P. F. "The New Productivity Challenge." *Harvard Business Review*, Volume 69, Number 6, 1991, pp. 69-79.

Drucker, P. F. "The New Society of Organizations." *Harvard Business Review*, Volume 70, Number 5, 1992, pp. 95-104.

Earl, M., and Khan, B. "How New is Business Process Redesign?" *European Management Journal*, Volume 12, Number 1, 1994, pp. 20-30.

Ehn, P. *Work-Oriented Design of Computer Artifacts.* Stockholm: Arbetslivscentrum, 1988.

Floyd, C. "Outline of a Paradigm Change in Software Engineering." *ACM SIGSOFT Software Engineering Notes*, Volume 13, Number 2, 1988, pp. 25-38.

Galliers, R. D. "Information Systems, Operational Research and Business Reengineering." *International Transactions on Operational Research*, Volume 1, Number 2, 1994, pp. 1-9.

Greenbaum, J., and Kyng, M. (Editors). *Design at Work.* Hillsdale, New Jersey: Lawrence Erlbaum, 1991.

Hedberg, B. "Imaginary Organizations." In R. Stamper, P. Kerola, R. Lee, and K. Lyytinen (Editors), *Collaborative Work, Social Communications and Information Systems. Proceedings of the IFIP TC 8 Working Conference COSCIS'91* Amsterdam: Elsevier/North-Holland, 1991.

Hirschheim, R., and Klein, H. "Four Paradigms of Information Systems Development." *Communications of ACM*, Volume 32, Number 10,

Hirschheim, R., Klein, H., and Newman, M. "A Social Action Perspective of Information Systems Development." In J. I. DeGross and C. H. Kriebel (Editors), *Proceedings of the Eighth International Conference on Information Systems.* Pittsburgh, Pennsylvania, 1987.

Howard, R. "Systems Design and Social Responsibility: the Political Implications of 'Computer-Supported Cooperative Work'." *Office, Technology and People,* Volume 3, Number 2, 1987, pp. 175-187.

Hughes, J.; King, V.; Rodden, T.; and Anderson, H. "Moving Out from the Control Room: Ethnography in System Design." In *Proceedings of the CSCW'94.* New York: ACM Press, 1994, pp. 429-440.

Hughes, J.; Randall, D.; and Shapiro, D. "CSCW: Discipline or Paradigm? A Sociological Perspective." In L. J. Bannon, M. Robinson, and K. Schmidt (Editors), *Proceedings of the Second ECSCW.* Amsterdam: Kluwer, 1991, pp. 309-323.

Hughes, J. A.; Randall, D.; and Shapiro, D. "Faltering from Ethnography to Design." In J. Turner and R. Kraut (Editors), *CSCW'92. Proceedings of the Conference on Computer-Supported Cooperative Work.* New York: ACM, 1992.

Jones, M. "Don't Emancipate, exaggerate: Rhetoric, Reality and Reengineering." In R. Baskerville, S. Smithson, O. Ngwenyama, and J. I. DeGross (Editors), *Transforming Organizations with Information Technology (A-49).* Amsterdam: Elsevier Science, 1994, pp. 357-378.

Jones, M. R. "Post-Industrial and Post-Fordist Perspectives on Information Systems." *European Journal of Information Systems,* Volume 1, Number 3, 1991, pp. 171-182.

Klein, H. K. "Organizational Implications of Office Systems: Toward a Critical Social Action Perspective." In A. A. Verrijn-Stuart and R. A. Hirschheim (Editors), *Proceedings of the IFIP TC8 Conference on Office Systems.* Amsterdam: North-Holland, 1986.

Klein, H., and Hirschheim, R. "Social Change and the Future of Information Systems Development." In R. Boland and R. Hirschheim (Editors), *Critical Issues in Information Systems Research.* Chichester: John Wiley and Sons, 1987, pp. 275-305.

Klein, H. K.; Hirschheim, R.; and Nissen, H.-E. "A Pluralist Perspective of the Information Systems Research Arena." In H.-E. Nissen, H. K. Klein, and R. Hirschheim (Editors), *Information System Research: Contemporary Approaches and Emergent Traditions. Proceedings of the IFIP Conference ISRA'90.* Amsterdam: North-Holland, 1991, pp. 1-20.

Kling, R. "Cooperation, Coordination and Control in Computer-Supported Work." *Communications of ACM,* Volume 34, Number 12, 1991, pp. 83-88.

Kling, R. "Defining the Boundaries of Computing across Complex Organizations." In R. J. Boland and R. A. Hirschheim (Editors), *Critical Issues in Information Systems Research.* London: Wiley, 1987, pp. 307-362.

Kuutti, K., and Bannon, L. J. "Some Confusions at the Interface: Re-conceptualizing the 'Interface' Problem." In G. R. S. Nurminen (Editor), *Human Jobs and Computer Interfaces.* Amsterdam: North-Holland, 1991, pp. 3-19.

Lyytinen, K. *Computer-Supported Cooperative Work — Issues and Challenges. A Structurational Analysis.* Manuscript, University of Jyväskylä, Department of Computer Science, 1990a.

Lyytinen, K. *Information Systems and Critical Theory — A Critical Assessment.* Working Paper No. WP-13. University of Jyväskylä, Department of Computer Science, 1990b.

Lyytinen, K. *Information Systems Development as Social Action: Framework and Critical Implications.* Doctoral Dissertation, University of Jyväskylä, Jyväskylä, Finland, 1986.

Lyytinen, K., and Hirschheim, R. A. "Information Systems as Rational Discourse: An Application of Habermas' Theory of Communicative Action." *Scandinavian Journal of Management,* Volume 4, Number 12, 1988, pp. 19-30.

Lyytinen, K., and Klein, H. K. "The Critical Theory of Jürgen Habermas as a Basis for a Theory of Information Systems." In E. Mumford, R. Hirschheim, G. Fitzgerald, and A. T. Wood-Harper (Editors), *Research Methods in Information Systems.* Amsterdam: North-Holland, 1985.

Lyytinen, K.; Klein, H. K.; and Hirschheim, R. A. "The Effectiveness of Office Information Systems: A Social Action Perspective." *Journal of Information Systems,* Volume 1, Number 1, 1991, pp. 41-60.

Lyytinen, K. J., and Ngwenyama, O. K. "What Does Computer Support for Cooperative Work Mean? A Structurational Analysis of Computer Supported Cooperative Work." *Accounting, Management and Information Technology,* Volume 2, Number 1, 1992, pp. 19-37.

Moran, T. P., and Anderson, R. J. "The Workaday World As a Paradigm for CSCW Design." In *Proceedings of CSCW'90.* New York: ACM, 1990, pp. 381.393.

Mumford, E.; Hirschheim, R.; Fitzgerald, G.; and Wood-Harper, A. T. (Editors). *Research Methods in Information Systems.* Amsterdam: North-Holland, 1985.

Ngwenyama, O. "The Critical Social Theory Approach to Information Systems: Problems and Challenges." In H.-E. Nissen, H. K. Klein, and R. Hirschheim (Editors), *The Information Systems Research Arena of the 1990s: Challenges, Perceptions and Alternative Approaches.* Amsterdam: North-Holland, 1991.

Nissen, H.-E.; Klein, H. K.; and Hirschheim, R. (Editors). *The Information Systems Research Arena of the 1990s: Challenges, Perceptions and Alternative Approaches.* Amsterdam: North-Holland, 1991.

Orlikowski, W. "The Duality of Technology: Rethinking the Concept of Theory in Organizations." *Organization Science*, Volume 3, Number 3, 1992, pp. 398-427.

Orlikowski, W., and Robey, D. "Information Technology and the Structuring of Organizations." *Information Systems Research*, Volume 2, Number 2, 1991, pp. 143-169.

Perrole, J. A. "Conversations and Trust in Computer Interfaces." In C. Dunlop and R. Kling (Editors), *Computers and Controversy*. New York: Academic Press, 1991.

Phillimore, A. J. "Flexible Specialization, Work Organization and Skills: Approaching the 'Second Industrial Divide'." *New Technology, Work, and Employment*, Volume 4, 1989, pp. 79-91.

Piore, M. J., and Sabel, C. F. *The Second Industrial Divide: Possibilities for Prosperity*. New York: Basic Books, 1984.

Poole, M. S., and DeSanctis, G. "The Use of Group Support Systems as an Appropriation Process." In *Proceedings of the Twenty-Second Annual Hawaii International Conference on System Sciences*. New York: ACM, 1989.

Rathswohl, E. J. "Applying Don Idhe's Phenomenology of Instrumentation as a Framework for Designing Research in Information Science." In H.-E. Nissen, H. K. Klein, and R. Hirschheim (Editors), *The Information Systems Research Arena of the 1990s: Challenges, Perceptions and Alternative Approaches*. Amsterdam: North-Holland,. 1991, pp. 421-438.

Robey, D., and Zmud, R. "Research on End-User Computing: Theoretical Perspectives from Organization Theory." In K. M. Kaiser and H. Oppelland (Editors), *Desktop Information Technology*. Amsterdam: North-Holland, 1990, pp. 15-36.

Savage, C. M. *Fifth Generation Management: Integrating Enterprises through Human Networking*. Bedford, Massachusetts: Digital Press, 1990.

Schmidt, K. "Computer Support for Cooperative Work in Advanced Manufacturing." *International Journal on Human Factors in Manufacturing*, Volume 1, Number 4, October 1991, pp. 303-320.

Schmidt, K., and Bannon, L. "Taking CSCW Seriously. Supporting Articulation Work." *Computer Supported Cooperative Work (CSCW)*, Volume 1, Number 1-2, 1992, pp. 7-40.

Scott Morton, M. S. (Editor). *The Corporation of the 1990s: Information Technology and Organizational Transformation*. New York: Oxford University Press, 1991.

Seely Brown, J. "Research that Reinvents the Corporation." *Harvard Business Review*, Volume 69, Number 1, 1991, pp. 102-111.

Stamper, R.; Kerola, P.; Lee, R.; and Lyytinen, K. (Editors). *Collaborative Work, Social Communications and Information Systems. Proceedings of the IFIP TC 8 Working Conference COSCIS'91.* Amsterdam: North-Holland, 1991.

Suchman, L. *Notes on Computer Support for Cooperative Work.* Working Paper No. WP-12, University of Jyväskylä, Department of Computer Science, 1989.

Toikka, K.; Norros, L.; Hyötyläinen, R.; and Kuivanen, R. *Häiriönhallinta joustavassa valmistuksessa (Disturbance management in flexible manufacturing. In Finnish).* Publication Number A14, Work Environment Fund, 1991.

Transcending Boundaries. Proceedings of the *Conference on Computer Supported Cooperative Work,* Chapel Hill, North Carolina, 1994.

Walsham, G., and Han, C. K. "Structuration Theory and Information Systems Research." In J. I. DeGross, M. Alavi, and H. Oppelland (Editors), *Proceedings of the Tenth Annual International Conference on Information Systems.* Copenhagen, Denmark, 1990.

Watson, T. J. *Sociology, work and industry.* London: Routledge and Kegan Paul, 1980.

Wood, S. "The transformation of Work?" In S. Wood (Editor), *The Transformation of Work?* London: Unwin Hyman, 1989, pp. 1-43.

Zimmerman, J.; Grande, S.; and Johnston, S. "Adding Value by Working Differently: Enabling the Learning Culture." In R. Baskerville, S. Smithson, O. Ngwenyama, and J. I. DeGross (Editors), *Transforming Organizations with Information Technology (IFIP Transactions A-49).* Amsterdam: North-Holland, 1994, pp. 437-450.

About the Author

Kari Kuutti has a position of senior research scientist at the Department of Information Processing Science, University of Oulu, Finland. He is currently working as the principal researcher on the Finnish portion of a multinational European Union funded research project (ESPRIT COMIC) on Computer-Supported Cooperative Work. He holds a Ph.D. in Information Systems from the University of Oulu. Dr. Kuutti has published in the areas of Information Systems, Human-Computer Interaction, Computer-Supported Cooperative Work, and computer-supported learning. His current research focus is on the computer support of organizational learning.

12

Strategic Change in Financial Services: The Social Construction of Strategic IS

Harry Scarbrough
Warwick Business School
University of Warwick

Abstract

This paper is based on empirical research into the role of IS functions in shaping strategic changes in a sample of financial institutions in the late 1980s and early 1990s. It argues that the implications of IT for organizational redesign are worked through the social construction of different classificatory systems; "strategic versus non-strategic IS" being an important example of such a system. The construction of these classifications encompasses wider institutional factors, the competitive relations between different expert groups, and the unfolding characteristics of IS projects. In this competitive arena, constructing IS as a strategic concern within the business depends on IS functions enlisting both the immediate contingencies of the project at hand and the wider institutional context..

1. INTRODUCTION

How do certain IS projects or activities come to be seen as "strategic," while others are viewed as merely "operational"? Although these terms are extensively employed in the literature on information systems management to denote differing approaches to planning and implementation, this question is rarely addressed in any depth. Instead, a "common sense" epistemology tends to prevail in which the strategic character of certain tasks and activities is either taken as given or is established through logical induction from their effects on business goals or competitiveness. In contrast, this paper views strategic IS not as a self-evidently important task domain but as the outcome of organizational processes of classification based on the strategic/non-strategic schema. Systems of classification are powerful methods of ordering organizational realities. They not only shape the management of particular activities — cueing particular decision criteria and development techniques — but also supply retrospective legitimation. A project which is defined as strategic, for instance, will be managed quite differently from its operational counterpart, and the label itself will serve to retrospectively justify its existence as well as the relaxation of the usual controls on development and resources.

Although the strategic/non-strategic continuum (Hirschheim 1982) is typically defined in purely cognitive terms, this paper will argue that these categories are neither robust nor self-evident in the emergent context of new IS projects. Rather, the inductive exercise involved in labeling a project strategic or operational is heavily shaped by the organizational context and, in particular, by social and institutional processes of classification. As the allocation of IS activities to either strategic or operational categories has emerged as a key element in IS management practice (Wilson 1989; Niederman, Brancheau and Wetherbe 1991), it has become increasingly important to understand the social construction of these categories within organizations.

The following study addresses these social processes of classification through an empirical account of the emergence of strategic and non-strategic IS projects in the financial services sector if the UK. This study tracked the design and development of a number of IS projects, some of which had been designated as strategic by senior IS management and others which were viewed as more routine. Instead of taking the concepts of "strategic" and non-strategic as *a priori* or ontological categories, the study concentrated on the way in which these labels were selectively applied to the management of particular projects and the organizational processes involved in developing and securing this labeling.

2. MAKING IS STRATEGIC

Using Whittington's (1993) terminology, views of strategy can be broadly assigned to two different schools of thought. In the still-dominant "classical" perspective, organizations are seen as basically market-driven and having to constantly adapt to the changes and contingencies of the external environment. IT is seen as a resource to be deployed according to the needs and pressures of that environment. Strategy has the job of transmitting such pressures by forging links between internal structure and resources, on one hand, and external product-market moves, on the other. In brief, this perspective sees the relationship between strategy and IS as essentially having to do with recognizing the contingencies of the technology and the product-market environment (Premkumar and King 1994) and relating these factors to business objectives.

In contrast, the "processual" approach (Pettigrew 1985) rejects formal plans and methodologies as simply the tip of the organizational iceberg. It delights in exposing the hidden world of the organization, where social values, political interests and structural inertia shape the formal instruments of rationality. It rejects the idea that organizations are engaged in a ceaseless struggle to adapt to changing environments. Its focus is more on the ceaseless struggle within the organization, as different groups within the structure of the business compete for power.

In contrast to these established schools of thought on strategy, the social constructionist view (Berger and Luckmann 1967) challenges the fundamental assumption that there is a singular external reality confronting organizations. It is skeptical about the ability of organizations to rationally identify relevant contingencies in their environment (Smircich and Stubbart 1985). Equally, it does not subscribe to the view that the internal reality is the dominant one. Rather, its concern is not with the focal organization adapting to its environment but on the way in which social groups within and across organizations actually construct the realities which seem to confront them. In this context, the notion of strategy is neither a concrete reality in its own right nor an outcome of political bargaining, but a resource which groups use to construct reality. To say that the concepts and classifications employed in organizations are socially constructed is to make an important epistemological point: a distinction between correspondence and consensus views of truth (Knights and Murray 1994). Substantiating this point, however, involves developing an empirically grounded understanding of the social structures and processes which shape organizational cognition. In particular, the social construction of strategic IS draws attention to organizational processes of classification which are a central element in the way organizations order reality.

Viewing strategic IS in these terms demonstrates that it is only one of many possible schemas that can be applied to IS work. The management of IS is characterized by a proliferating variety of typologies and other frameworks — for example, the "stages" model and its many variants. Even within the literature of strategic IS, it is possible to discern different approaches to categorizing IS work. There are, for instance, both internally and externally derived classifications. The internal arguments focus on the top-down ordering of organizational goals through planning mechanisms (Premkumar and King 1994) while the external arguments highlight the competitive advantage to be derived from IS (Kettinger, Grover and Segars 1995). In both variants, however, the emphasis is firmly on the cognitive domain of classification. Sweeping assumptions of managerial rationality allow writers to pursue elaborate forms of classification based purely on "objectively" defined business and technological contingencies. The oft-cited McFarlan and McKenney (1983) matrix is the locus classicus for this form of classification.

However, as Farbey, Land and Tagett (1995) have noted of the evaluation of IS investments, the content of these schemas is less important than their social context. If we wish to understand why certain classificatory systems are implemented and others not, we had better unpack these matrices and ask what institutional codes underpin their axial principles. Douglas (1987) in explaining the different classifications of wine used in the French and Californian vineyards (the French based on region, the Californian on types of grape) shows how different institutions produce different classificatory styles. She argues: "Institutions bestow sameness. Socially based analogies assign disparate items to classes and load them with moral and political content.." (Douglas 1987, p. 63).

In turn, King et al. (1994) have identified a number of institutions which may produce such classificatory effects on "IT innovations." These include government agencies, universities, banks and trade unions, and, most importantly, the role of "trend setting corporations." As subsequent cases will show, many of the crucial institutional influences on IS in financial services emanate from the sectoral context. Business strategies are heavily influenced by the "recipes" defined by leading firms within the sector (Child and Smith 1987). Likewise, the spread of the strategic IS label can be related to the demonstration effect of the small number of cases which "have become the models of how to use information technology to improve a firm's competitive advantage" (Kettinger, Grover and Segars 1995, p. 35). Significantly, these cases typically demonstrate the strategic character of IS through a retrospective account of impacts and benefits, providing few clues for a prospective pursuit (Kini 1993).

3. THE INSTITUTIONAL EFFECTS OF EXPERTISE

What distinguishes the construction of classificatory systems in the technology field is their greater reliance on professional expertise. Where folk classifications lean heavily on analogies with nature (Douglas 1987), the frameworks applied to IS work show the imprint of an evolving knowledge-base. Networks of researchers and practitioners are constantly engaged in producing new frameworks and new ways of classifying reality. This activity, moreover, is self-conscious in its intentions, if not sociologically conscious in its effects.

This being said, the influence of IS expertise on the classificatory systems of IS practice is partial and constrained. IS specialists are in constant competition with other occupational groups, such as accountants and marketing specialists, to promote classificatory world-views in which their own expertise is central. IS specialists promote taxonomies based on information processing while accountants map organizational processes through financial measures and labels. Organizations become, in effect, a contested terrain across which these different classificatory systems slug it out. For example, the classificatory system defining strategic IS cuts directly — and not coincidentally — across the categories and criteria defined by accountancy expertise. The stakes are high since the victory of one system over another will determine both winners and losers. As Kettinger, Grover and Segars (1995) note wistfully of the heyday of strategic thinking: "Strategic information technology was once viewed as the catalyst to propel IS managers from the back room into the corporate suite. Many consultants and researchers still push strategic IT" (p.35).

Note here the close relationship between the concepts and categories of strategic IS and the interests of occupational groups and institutions. This way of classifying IT serves to "propel" IS managers and it is "pushed" by related interest groups. However, at the same time as IS groups promote a strategic framework for their work, other groups such as accountants and marketing specialists are also laying claim to the strategic high ground, but with different criteria and arguments. The strategic category of IS work has to be socially constructed in an arena where the claims of IS specialists are competing with the clamoring voices of senior managers from other functions and interests. From that competition of concepts and occupational groups emerges the dominant classificatory systems for interpreting the realities facing the business.

4. THE EMPIRICAL STUDY

Research was carried out in the period 1989-1991.[1] It focussed on IT projects in six Scottish-based financial institutions spanning the insurance and retail banking sectors. The account begins with a survey of the sectoral and institutional context in which these case-study firms were located.

---

[1]The study was carried out by a multidisciplinary team drawn from the universities in Edinburgh, Stirling and Warwick. It was supported by a grant from the Joint Committee on the Economic and Social Research Council and the Science and Engineering Research Council. Its detailed findings are reported in Fincham et al. (1994).

4.1   Sectoral Context

The evolution of financial institutions in the UK has typically involved the elaboration of branch networks controlled from a central headquarters. This in turn established the classic infrastructural patterns for computing and IT, where large mainframes served a large number of branch systems. IS expertise inevitably developed around this pattern, with consequences — notably, the development of sizeable central Information System functions — which are still being felt today.

These sectoral factors not only shaped IS expertise, however. They had equally important repercussions for the emergence and subsequent pecking-order of many other forms of specialist expertise. In particular, sectoral evolution helped to establish the centrality of financial intermediary roles which came to be occupied by specialist bankers, accountants and actuaries. The latter have in turn inhibited the emergence of other forms of expertise, notably in the areas of general management, marketing and corporate planning (Dalbey 1986).

Against the dominance of these established professions, technological trends in the 1980s and 1990s promised to increase the centrality of IS expertise (Scarbrough 1992). As financial services are information-based, there seemed to be ample opportunities for new product development and the creation of new electronic delivery systems. Equally, the power of IT to appropriate the expertise of specialist groups seemed to presage greater consumer accessibility to once esoteric intermediary skills. As Child and Loveridge (1990) note:

> The ability to rationalize service provision through the application of new technology depends upon an ability to codify transactional information which consumers can then use to make their own choices, in principle on a self-service basis. [pp. 36-37]

However, there were also important constraints on the pervasiveness and centrality of IT in financial services. These included the continuing importance of financial intermediary roles in profit generation and more generally the weakness of IS professional groupings. Equally, it would be a mistake to see the role of IS functions as being wholly oriented toward product marketing and innovation. Much IT investment and IS expertise was still dedicated to the maintenance and development of infrastructural technologies for funds movement or shared ATM networks, which had little direct connection with product-market competition. Even in the highly fragmented US banking industry, around 65% of systems expenditure in banking was going to supporting "invisible" functions such as funds transfer with only 10% going into potentially competitive product-market areas. In short, it seemed that "the vast bulk of systems investments support products or services that are commodities throughout the industry" (Steiner and Teixeira 1990, p. 45)

Although these factors limited the extension of IS expertise into other fields, the nature of IS work itself continued to preserve IS autonomy from deskilling and the detailed specialization of jobs. Both the proliferation and the nature of IT applications limited the incorporation of IS skills into hardware. Moreover, the uncertainty generated by the spread of innovative applications effectively inhibited the routinization of IS work. As Friedman and Cornford note,

Technical progress...which arises from the cumulation of individually minor improvements is also important today. What distinguishes computer systems development is the extent to which technical change of this...type occurs. This is, in turn, dependent upon the inherent creativity which still characterizes systems development. [Friedman and Cornford 1989, p. 360]

If IS expertise was sustained by constraints on management deskilling and rationalization, its position was also underpinned by the inability of other organizational groups — specifically users and accounting professionals — to exercise effective control over IS work. This is not to say that IS expertise was blissfully unaffected by these groups' expectations and pressures. The growth of distributed IT and the waning of the mainframe, for instance, had greatly boosted the role and knowledge of user groups in shaping IT developments. Indeed, the 1980s were dubbed the era of "user relations" constraints by Friedman and Cornford. However, given the integrated and centralized character of IT systems in financial services, this shift effectively gave a new twist to the tensions between centralized control and user demands. In our sample organizations, this tension expressed itself in the work organization of IS staff and in the allocation of IS resources. For example, while IS personnel typically worked in teams that shadowed user departments, they were not devolved to those departments but were managed from the central IS function. Similarly, while IS work was largely driven by user demands, IS expertise was effectively rationed through systems of project prioritization. Revealing asides from IS staff — "priority 4 never gets done" or "it's the greeting wean that gets fed" — demonstrated that prioritization was as much a question of political expediency as of the rational allocation of resources. These tensions might have ultimately been resolved in favor of user control, but this decentralizing tendency was countered in most of our sample firms by the continued need for a centralized IS resource to sponsor and develop organization-wide IT projects.

The politics of IS expertise were also shaped by the role of the accounting functions in our case-study organizations. The IS function poses a particular set of problems for the application of financial controls and hence for the way in which it can be structured. These problems relate to the "tyranny of shared costs" noted earlier: the difficulty of apportioning the central mainframe costs of development, maintenance and processing to user departments. In this period, our sample firms typically handled such accounting issues through cost-center and budgetary controls for IS functions. The infrastructural and integrated nature of IS technology created significant constraints on the allocation of IS costs to users. At one bank, for instance, progress in linking IS projects to costs had only been made in the last three years: "Three years ago...you didn't know if it would cost you £1/4 million or £10 million...we know the basics of the technology, but it didn't necessarily translate into the bottom line of cost."

Even accountants acknowledged the difficulty of achieving a precise breakdown of costs:

> You can look at an engineering factory and you can see the product being built and you can say "well that should not have taken twice as long as that," except maybe there is a bit more stress or a bit more sophisticated welding in doing that. It's very difficult to do that with a development project when it is all done on a computer....If you can record your man-hours on the project, you have still got this problem with processing capacity. Its difficult to isolate completely.

4.2   Case Studies

The cases[2] have been organized so as to provide paired comparisons. The aim of these pairings is three-fold. First, coupling projects involving similar tasks, technologies or product-market contexts helps to highlight the influence of the politics of expertise on the management of IS projects. Second, the distribution of strategic and non-strategic projects between the different pairings sheds much light on the distinctively organizational processes underpinning the development of strategic concepts and categories. Taken together, these comparisons then help to reveal the different classificatory systems applied to these projects.

- Bank of Scotland VISA CENTRE and Premier Financial Service* (PFS) INDEX: customization of card processing packages.

- Clydesdale Bank's TELEBANK and Royal Bank of Scotland's ROYLINE: remote banking systems.

- Bank of Scotland's CABINET and Home & Auto Ltd's* MIS: a Branch Information Network and a Corporate MIS (Management Information System) respectively.

Although a number of the projects were deemed strategic by IS management, the focus in our research was not on a predefined conception of what constituted strategic IS, but on the social processes involved in constructing such concepts and categories. In that sense, the local meanings attached to strategic IS were the end-point rather than the starting-point of our study.

VISA CENTRE and INDEX

This first pairing of cases brings together two projects where the main IS developments involved the acquisition and maintenance of software packages for the processing of credit card accounts. Although there were important issues to do with customization, the technology was well-defined and the IS development process itself was reasonably routine. These features corresponded closely to the "factory" category of IS defined by McFarlan and McKenney. That model suggests that the key decision criteria for these projects would not be strategic but rather operational goals of cost and efficiency.

However, this contingency-based classification was only partly reflected in the development processes for these projects. Certainly, the acquisition of the software packages was largely governed by operational issues of cost, reliability, and processing efficiency. But, in the PFS case the organizational context for the project gave it an added political significance that pre-empted a "factory" style treatment. Although the INDEX package was a routine card-processing technology, its acquisition for PFS was complicated by that company's status as a recently acquired subsidiary of a larger clearing bank group — ScotBank Group. In the previous year, the diversification of the Group had prompted the establishment of a "Group Services" function,

---

[2]Whenever possible, actual company names have been used. In some instances, which are asterisked, pseudonyms have been used.

which was dedicated to maximizing the effective use of the Bank's technical resources. As control of IS developments in the Group had previously rested almost exclusively with the in-house IS function of the clearing bank part of the Group, this aim brought Group Services into direct conflict with the management of that function. The acquisition of INDEX became a key issue in that conflict.

Group Services saw IS developments at PFS as a unique opportunity to establish their influence over the allocation of IS resources. Exploiting their new mandate to the full, they were able to insist that both the customization and the maintenance of the new package be turned over to the software supplier. Since both of these tasks would normally have been the responsibility of ScotBank's in-house IS function, the effect of this decision was to establish an important precedent for the future organization of IS resources. Thus, the political significance of the project effectively overrode the more immediate concerns of efficiency and practicality. Indeed, the technologically routine nature of the project only made it a more important precedent for such decisions in the future. One member of the Group Management team hinted at the possible repercussions:

> I think what we're really talking about here is power. We're talking about a historical environment where nothing, but nothing, would happen in a computer development unless it was done either directly or under the control of IS Division. Now the implications of a user getting a system in and running without ever going anywhere near Management Services...if you were in IS Division in a senior position, you would say, "Wait a minute!"

The political nature of the PFS case is highlighted by the comparison with the Bank of Scotland Visa Centre project. Although the technological component of both projects was very similar — the acquisition of a credit-card processing package — the Bank of Scotland had not followed a diversification strategy of the kind pursued by ScotBank. Consequently, there was no need for a Group Management function nor the attendant conflicts. When the Bank established its new Visa processing center in 1988, it did so very largely under the auspices of its in-house Management Services Division (MSD). Although labor market factors led to the Centre being located a few miles away from the Bank's Computer Centre, its senior management were in the main transferees from MSD and the Visa Centre itself drew heavily on the Division's technological resources. With no structural conflict to darken the mood, the decision-making processes around the Visa Centre's systems were placid and uncontentious; the outline organization chart, for example, was reputedly drawn up in a local hostelry over a quiet drink. The same untroubled calm pervaded the decisions on the processing systems which would be the technological core of the new Centre. The selection, customization and maintenance of the supplier package were all handled by MSD itself, with none of the obtrusive interventions that marked the ScotBank case.

Two points emerge from the comparison between the PFS and Visa Centre cases. First, it shows that contingencies such as the routineness of a technology are not exogenous determinants of the classificatory moves around a particular project. Rather such contingencies stand to be enlisted, or ignored, in the active construction of a classificatory schema that respects organizational politics as much as it does technical characteristics. Interestingly, the deployment of the Factory

IS classification was not a product of the technological routineness or otherwise of the projects but of the organizational context in which they were being applied. This is not to say, however, that technological or business contingencies have no effect upon the way projects are classified: the INDEX development was not managed as a Factory IS project, but there was no question of it being classed a strategic project either.

TELEBANK and ROYLINE

Our second paired comparison shows how organizational politics can help to sustain a strategic classification for a project if it is actuated by the advancing claims of a powerful expertise. The relevant comparison here is between the development of two remote banking systems. At Clydesdale Bank, the in-house IS function conceived (and subsequently justified) the TELE-BANK remote banking system as a strategic project. They argued from the evidence of market and technological trends that remote delivery systems would play an increasingly important part in the Bank's future product range. TELEBANK was conceived as one element in a range of remote banking products and as an important competitive response in a rapidly changing market-place. One senior IS manager claimed:

> So we had made greater sense of home and office banking; we'd taken it a lot further than anyone else had. We'd moved from being second to Bank of Scotland, and through the use of this telephone system which was innovative, we've moved ourselves to being market leaders in the UK.

In contrast, at the Royal Bank of Scotland there was no attempt by the in-house IS function to classify their ROYLINE system as strategic, even though in purely technological terms it was a more sophisticated remote banking system. Significantly, the impetus for ROYLINE came from senior management who were aware of similar developments in the USA and were concerned to extend the range of services available to business customers. Far from playing up the strategic or competitive aspects of the new technology, however, IS management took a decidedly pragmatic view: "There are business requirements for which we are finding technological solutions....You can't utilize technology for its own sake."

Again, neither the technological characteristics of the projects, nor the features of comparable market contexts, can explain the variation in the way the projects were managed and developed. Although both projects clearly derived from a new sectoral recipe centered on remote delivery systems, the conceptual frameworks within which they were designed and justified were markedly different. In the Clydesdale Bank case, we found an IS function that was increasingly unhappy with its role. Clydesdale was a relatively small subsidiary of a larger banking group — Midland Bank — and in recent years ScotBank-style controls had begun to impinge on the autonomy of its IS function. In this context, TELEBANK not only represented a way of securing greater autonomy within the group structure, but also of securing a lead role in any future technological developments in that area. This was described by one of the system's major proponents. TELEBANK, he said,

> is not highly important in terms of our own systems; though, remember, it was extremely important at the time. Politically, it was immensely important

politically. It was incredibly important that people here could see that we had something outwith the Midland Bank. Because beyond that point we were able to persuade Midland Bank that we should project manage the Group developments in home and office banking.

Apart from showing the political interests behind TELEBANK's strategic status, this quote also hints at the way such interests are not given by structural position alone but also reflect the collective identity or self-image which its managers are seeking to cultivate. Clydesdale's IS specialists had been involved in a number of important innovations in the preceding decade, including the development of a unique branch network, and also of a prototype EFTPOS (Electronic Funds Transfer at Point Of Sale) system. To develop a crude typology here, the IS specialists at Clydesdale Bank seem to have seen themselves as *Innovators*, with a responsibility for expanding the role of IS in the bank's services. They were therefore much more inclined toward exploiting the rhetorical and conceptual resources offered by strategic IS. Conversely, IS management at the Royal Bank of Scotland saw themselves as *Professionals*, emphasizing the need to serve specific needs of the Bank and priding themselves upon achieving the closest possible relationships with user groups. Given this image, they eschewed the pursuit of strategic projects, but viewed remote banking as a pragmatic and incremental response to customer needs.

Bank of Scotland CABINET and the Home & Auto MIS

In this pairing, we have a comparison of two important projects which were both labeled strategic by their respective IS managements, but which produced very unequal outcomes. In broad terms, one might say that CABINET was a successful project which validated the classificatory system propounded by IS management, while the Home & Auto MIS (Management Information System) was a comparative failure which actually undermined the credibility and claims of the in-house IS function.

The success and failure of these projects has much to tell us about the social construction of strategic IS. First, these projects suggest that success in developing a strategic category of IS has little to do with strategic rhetoric alone. Such rhetoric was a feature of both cases — if anything, more explicitly in the Home & Auto MIS case which was termed the "strategy project" by management themselves. On the other hand, the contingent features of the projects themselves do seem to have exerted a powerful influence. Even in its embryonic stages, the CABINET (Customer and Branch Information Network) project had all the McFarlan and McKenney hallmarks of a strategic project. As designed by the in-house Management Services Division, this was to be the major infrastructural investment for the Bank's branches well into the 1990s. It would provide on-line customer-based information to branches, replacing a current account-based information flow which involved the daily updating and despatch of thousands of microfiches. Moreover, it not only involved the development of a new information network connecting the bank's several hundred branches to its central mainframes, but also required the integration of existing account records into a central customer database. This last feature was particularly important because the Bank of Scotland, like most UK clearing banks to that date, had only recorded information on its many millions of branch-based accounts. There was no centralized record of its customers — many of whom might have a number of different accounts and contacts with the Bank.

For all of these reasons, CABINET was widely hailed as a major part of the Bank's product strategy for the coming decades. Said one senior manager: "CABINET itself is not a product. CABINET is a strategy. It's a strategy to attack the market place in the 1990s."

The Bank's Chief Executive was equally convinced of its importance, even while recognizing the risks: "The danger with CABINET is that you go down a blind alleyway from which you cannot escape. The danger of not doing it is that you go out of business."

With top management's backing, CABINET was firmly located in the strategic category of IS projects. Nothing illustrated this better than the Board's willingness to relax the usual accounting criteria in the face of the project's massive capital outlay. In their dealings with colleagues from the Accounting function, IS management had been able to argue successfully that the singular character of CABINET freed it from the need for detailed cost-benefit justification:

> We knew that if we tried to cost justify each application as it came up, we would never be able to do it...because the infrastructural costs would always be too high. We had to take on a longer-term marketing view and accept that we would have to implement one project that was actually not going to be cost justified...provided we were sure it was taking us in the right direction.

Even a management accountant was prepared to accept that CABINET was "a strategic decision, and the cost of not doing it was more important than the cost of doing it."

Viewed retrospectively, the CABINET project seems to deserve its strategic classification simply by reason of its innate characteristics. However, this post-hoc rationalization — the project is long-term and requires massive expenditure therefore it must be strategically important — too easily neglects the preceding hard work of the IS function in creating the categorical possibility of such a strategic project. In the first instance, the very fact that the Bank selected this project from many other possible investment opportunities serves to highlight the role of MSD itself in making IS a strategic item in the deliberations of top management. In part, MSD's success here involved mobilizing sectoral recipes emphasizing quality of customer service which happened to dovetail neatly with the operational facilities offered by new database technologies. However, it also rested on the role which MSD had carved out for itself within the Bank. The early 1980s had seen important structural changes in the IS area, with first a small strategic planning unit being established and then the merger of what had been separate (sometimes squabbling) divisions of Management Services and Computer Services. The new amalgamated Management Services Division succeeded in establishing a unified mandate for interpretation and action in relation to the changing technological environment. That new mandate was simultaneously reflected in an outpouring of project proposals — CABINET being only one of a series of innovative projects — and the fostering of a self-consciously strategic identity to define the Division's role in the Bank's affairs.

Given its mandate and self-image, the MSD function was keen to use a strategic system of classification to finesse the problems raised by new technological developments. Such problems came in two forms. First, new technologies — such as customer database systems — tended to generate significant managerial and technical uncertainties. The latter, in fact, were less the result of intrinsic technical features than of the degree of fit between the new technology and the existing competencies of the IS function. The greater the gap between the two, the more useful the interpretive flexibility of strategic IS in patching over the resulting uncertainty. Second, one of the key problems raised by new technologies was the troubling effect they tended to have on the definition of task domains. Large-scale IS projects such as CABINET could not easily be accommodated within the established borders between IS and Accounting functions. Where previous "back office" systems had been efficiency-oriented and therefore amenable to the routine accounting criteria of payback or discounted cash flow, these new systems were predicated on less quantifiable gains in market share and customer loyalty. Hence, the deployment of a strategic category of IS investment not only helped to circumvent the standard accounting criteria, but also secured a new space for IS development less subject to accounting controls.

These steps in the social and organizational construction of strategic IS can be usefully contrasted with parallel developments at Home & Auto Ltd. Although its development of a Corporate Management Information system did not approach the levels of capital expenditure required by CABINET, it did offer important, if again relatively intangible, benefits. This was a system which promised to rationalize and improve what were hitherto rather patchy and sporadic information flows to product managers. The pay-off was to come through improving the quality and responsiveness of product managers' decisions on premium rates.

From the outset, the MIS project was classed as a strategic initiative. This was reflected particularly in the development methodology employed. By adopting, in almost textbook fashion, the complete paraphernalia of a methodology termed Business Systems Planning (BSP), the director of the IS function sought to ensure that the project was responsive to the long-term needs of the organization, as a whole. This approach involved taking an holistic view of information needs, moving in logical sequence from corporate goals, as identified through interviews with senior managers, to the technical features of the operational system. The adoption of BSP was partly a reaction to an earlier abortive attempt by the rival "Statistical Services" function to develop a workable system. This had ultimately foundered when it was belatedly discovered that supposedly up-to-the-minute MIS reports could take days of mainframe run-time to produce. BSP would avoid such oversights by beginning with a detailed assessment of information needs and then moving logically and carefully onto the possible IS solutions for those needs.

Like the CABINET project, one of the principal implications of the Corporate MIS' strategic status was the relaxation of the standard financial criteria. The project report's one and only statement of financial cost-benefits claimed it would produce a "decrease in claims ratio which in turn will be reflected as benefit on the Underwriting profit/loss in a year." Noting as a conservative estimate that a 1% reduction in the claims ratio would lead to a £5 million benefit across all classes of business, the report did not even attempt to substantiate the relationship between the MIS and the quality of rate-setting within the company. One of the report's authors noted of the 1% estimate: "There was no grounding for that really. It was just a figure that everyone accepted would be the case."

However, despite — or because of — this rigorous attempt to drive the Corporate MIS from strategic business needs, the project quickly encountered problems. This was partly because the MIS project depended from the outset on the local knowledge and cooperation of a wide range of user groups. Eliciting the information needs of the different groups involved proved to be no easy matter. Also, another major barrier was the complexity of the existing process and its dependence on the tacit knowledge of those setting premium rates. All of these problems were further exacerbated because the IS function — located in the basement of the headquarters building — lacked the necessary status and credibility to gain the active commitment of the top management team, who were located on the top floor. One of the youthful team of systems developers noted: "The topmost level was banned from us, perhaps because we were pretty scruffy."

Not surprisingly, the IS developers were unable to squeeze these complex and ambiguous features of organizational life into their formal BSP model:

> We produced organization charts but this was one of the more difficult tasks. In a complex business you may leave areas of responsibility slightly grey. Like the individual Product Managers formally had some responsibilities, but they varied in their approach to product pricing and left different decisions to their product managers....That was the first big hole we fell down.

The Home & Auto MIS project thus offers a stark contrast to the CABINET project. The latter attained strategic status through MSD's mandate and its infrastructural implications. Moreover, as it involved a product innovation, it did not have the same need to map existing norms and practices. Its early stages were therefore relatively independent of the local knowledge and cooperation of the user groups in the branches. In contrast, the Home & Auto project rapidly fell into the "big hole" of existing organizational practices. The complexity and time demands of the project were further compounded by political pressures from impatient user departments. There was a feeling that the IS function had "analyzed it to death." Ultimately, this combination of political pressures and technical failure prompted a change both in the personnel and policy of the IS function. This involved a switch to a more "realistic" and pragmatic approach: "evolution not revolution" as the new IS manager put it. The holistic, strategic approach was abandoned and the MIS design was simply tailored to the specific needs of the largest (and most vociferous) user department.

The contrast between the CABINET and Home & Auto Ltd. cases is revealing. It suggests, for example, that mapping a strategic methodology onto a development process is not in itself enough to construct a robust classificatory system. Instead, factors to do with the internal distribution of expertise and the scope of the project at hand seem to play a crucial role. These include the credibility of the IS function itself, especially in the top management arena; the function's basic competences in making the technology work; and the characteristics of the project, most notably dependence on user groups.

5. DISCUSSION

Each of these case pairings tells us something about the social construction of strategic IS. Even the first pairing (of non-strategic projects) has some counter factual relevance and usefully underscores the importance of the IS project itself to the management process. At the same time, though, the PFS case challenges the contingency model of IS management by demonstrating that expert groups are not passive in the face of the tasks which they are set, but actively seek to exploit them in ways that enhance their own stature. However, if this leads in turn to the political aspirations of expert groups, the pairing of TELEBANK and ROYLINE also reminds us that such aspirations are malleable and closely related to the collective identity which such groups construct for themselves.

Our final pairing of cases shows that making IS strategic is a more complex construction than narrowly rational or political models would suggest. Although the structural power-bases of the IS functions involved were certainly relevant, broader questions of expertise were revealed by the unfolding of project development. For example, the distribution and range of knowledge enlisted by each project was a uniformly important factor in constructing a strategic system of classification. Thus, to cite one example, CABINET's strategic standing was more easily secured because the Bank's MSD function controlled so much of the relevant knowledge. Conversely, the strategic failure at Home & Auto was closely implicated with the distribution of relevant knowledge among user groups over whom the IS function had no control.

6. CONCLUSIONS

This study has focussed on the role of IS functions in constructing new ways of classifying IS activities in a context of organizational and technological change. Along the way, rational and political models of change have been contrasted with the ability of IS functions to project a compelling world-view in which the strategic possibilities of IS are central. Although it obviously helps if such a world-view is supported by wider sectoral features, the contingencies of the immediate environment are probably secondary to the way in which they are interpreted. In this process, the IS function's expertise, status and self-image are important factors.

For IS functions in general, though, the construction of a classificatory system based on business strategy remains a tentative and uncertain project. Although such a system presents itself as a timeless and universal representation of IS activities, its self-referential logic needs to be enshrined in institutional codes and organizational processes to become as fully metabolized (and therefore as powerful) as it aspires to be. As the rise and fall of normative systems such as strategic IS and Business Process Reengineering demonstrates, nothing is more ephemeral than a timeless system, nor as contrived in its appeals to logic and nature.

7. REFERENCES

Berger, P., and Luckmann, T. *The Social Construction of Reality: A Treatise in the Sociology of Knowledge.* New York: Doubleday Anchor Books, 1967.

Child, J., and Loveridge, R. *Information Technology and European Services: Towards a Microelectronic Future.* Oxford: Blackwell., 1990.

Child, J., and Smith, C. "The Context and Process of Organizational Transformations — Cadbury Limited in its Sector." *Journal of Management Studies*, Volume 24, Number 6, 1987, pp. 565-593.

Dalbey, H. "Planning on Both Sides of the Atlantic." *The Banker's Magazine*, March-April 1986, pp.33-46.

Douglas, M. *How Institutions Think*. London: Routledge and Kegan Paul, 1987.

Farbey, B.; Land, F.; and Targett, G. *It Investment: A Study of Methods and Practice*. London: Butterworth-Heinemann, 1985.

Fincham, R.; Fleck, J.; Procter, R.; Scarbrough, H.; Tierney, M.; and Williams, R. *Expertise and Innovation: IT Strategies and Financial Services*. Oxford: Oxford University Press, 1994.

Friedman, A. L., and Cornford, S. D. *Computer Systems Development: History, Organization and Implementation*. Chichester: Wiley and Sons, 1989.

Hirschheim, R. "Information Management Planning in Organizations, Part One: A Framework for Analysis." LSE Working Paper, London: London School of Economics, 1982.

Kettinger, W. J.; Grover, V.; and Segars, A. H. "Do Strategic Systems Really Pay off." *Information Systems Management*, Winter 1995, pp. 35-43.

King, J. L.; Gurbaxani, V.; McFarlan, F. W.; Raman, K. S.; and Yap, C. S. "Institutional Factors in Information Technology Innovation." *Information Systems Research*, Volume 5, Number 2, 1994, pp. 136-169.

Kini, R. J. "Strategic Information Systems: A Misunderstood Concept." *Information Systems Management*, Volume 10, Number 4, 1993, pp. 42-45.

Knights, D., and Morgan, G. "Corporate Strategy, Organizations and the Subject." *Organization Studies*, Volume 12, Number 2, 1991, pp. 251-273.

Knights, D., and Murray, F. *Managers Divided: Organisational Politics and Information Technology Management*. Chichester: Wiley, 1984.

McFarlan, F. W., and McKenney, J. L. *Corporate Information Systems Management: The Issues Facing Senior Executives*. New York: Dow Jones Irwin, 1983.

Niederman, F.; Brancheau, J.; and Wetherbe, J. C. "Information Systems Management Issues for the 1990s." *MIS Quarterly*, Volume 15, Number 4, 1991, pp. 475-500.

Pettigrew, A. M. *The Awakening Giant: Continuity and Change in ICI.* Oxford: Basil Blackwell, 1985.

Premkumar, G., and King, W. R. "Organizational Characteristics and Information Systems Planning: An Empirical Study." *Information Systems Research*, Volume 5, Number 2, 1994, pp. 75-109.

Scarbrough, H. (Editor). *The IT Challenge: IT and Strategy in Financial Services.* Hemel Hempstead: Prentice-Hall, 1992.

Smircich, L., and Stubbart, C. "Strategic Management in an Enacted Environment." *Academy of Management Review*, Volume 10, Number 4, 1985, pp. 724-736.

Steiner, T. D., and Teixeira, D. B. *Technology in Banking: Creating Value and Destroying Profits.* Homewood, Illinois: Business One Irwin, 1990.

Whittington, R. *What Is Strategy — and Does it Matter?* London: Routledge, 1993.

Wilson, T. D. "The Implementation of Information Systems Strategies in UK Companies: Aims and Barriers to Success." *International Journal of Information Management*, Volume 9, 1989, pp. 245-258.

About the Author

Harry Scarbrough is Lecturer in Industrial Relations and Organizational Behaviour, Warwick Business School. His consultancy and research work encompasses a variety of firms in the car industry and the financial services sector. His research interests lie in the interface between Information Technology and organizations, especially the role of expert groups in that context. Dr. Scarbrough's latest publication is *The Management of Expertise* (Macmillan 1995), but he is also co-author of *Technology and Organizations: Power, Meaning and Design* (Routledge 1992), *Expertise and Innovation* (Clarendon Press 1994), and Editor of *The IT Challenge: Strategy and IT in Financial Services* (Prentice Hall 1992).

13

The Nature and Processes
of IT-Related Change

Susan Gasson
Information Systems Research Unit
Warwick Business School
University of Warwick

Niki Holland
Transition Partnerships

Abstract

This paper presents the findings of an empirical survey of senior IT managers' perceptions of their company's approach to IT-related change in the UK. The survey was based upon a theoretically-derived framework for the classification of information systems development approaches; this is used to map trends in development approaches graphically. The findings of this study are also used to examine the feasibility of academic, business-process oriented approaches to IT-change strategies, which encourage high degrees of user-participation in the change process — an examination that has largely been missing from contemporary discussions of IT-related organizational change.

The paper thus has important implications for research and practice. Specifically, the findings suggest that the overall management approach to IT-related change is less critical to the extent of user-participation in the overall change-process than is the question of whether system development is performed in-house or by a third party. Additionally, these findings demonstrate the overriding preponderance of technical/functional approaches to IS development during the system design stage of development, regardless of whether a business/organizational or a technical/functional emphasis is given to the IT-related change overall.

1. INTRODUCTION

The academic community has recently been the center of a debate about the nature of IT-related change. While academics would see IT-related organizational change as being most closely aligned with the organization's business processes and strategic direction (Galliers 1987; Scott Morton 1991), IT-related change is thought to be perceived, within organizations, as a primarily technical task (Hornby et al. 1992; Hopker 1994). The study described here set out to explore this perception. Do managers see IT-related change as primarily a technical problem? Do the tools and approaches used to support IT change-analysis and IT system development support a business-oriented or a functional/technical approach to change? To what extent do users participate in the processes of IT-related change?

2. THE THEORETICAL FRAMEWORK

Much of the prior research in approaches to IT-related change has either treated the organizational and social factors of IT change as a "black box," concentrating upon exploring what methods are used and how these methods are applied (Wynekoop and Russo 1993; Hornby et al. 1992; Hopker 1994; Hardy, Thompson and Edwards 1994) or has treated the development approach as a "black box," examining social and organizational factors, such as user-participation (Kappelman and McLean 1992; Morley 1993), developer attitudes to users (Hedberg and Mumford 1975), work-group organization (Mumford and Henshall 1983; Heller 1987), or the politics of interest-groups (Markus and Bjørn-Andersen 1987). Little empirical work can be found investigating the middle-ground: that bifurcation of interest between organizational behaviorists and computer-scientists, which lies in the interactions of methods, processes and organization. This paper addresses that middle ground by discussing the results of an exploratory survey into the relationship between approaches to IT-related change, the methods used to develop the Information Systems involved in the change, and the extent to which users of the target system participate in the processes of change.

This investigation was based upon a framework for the classification of approaches to Information System (IS) development which attempts to bring together the elements of both technical and organizational change. This framework, shown in Figure 1, was presented in detail in an earlier paper (Gasson 1994). The theoretical background to the framework is summarized briefly below.

The framework in Figure 1 was derived from Leavitt's (1972) "diamond" model of organizational change. Leavitt presents the four factors of the model as the objects of organizational change and sees them as interdependent: change in any one results in changes in the others. If information systems development is seen as organizational change, then the four factors of this model can be seen as the objects of information systems development. Choices between pairings of these objects may thus be helpful in characterizing differing approaches to systems development; an interpretation of this is shown in Figure 2. The interactions between the four factors of Leavitt's model form six "dimensions" of action along which information systems development approaches may be modeled: technology-structure, technology-people, technology-task, task-people, structure-people, and task-structure.

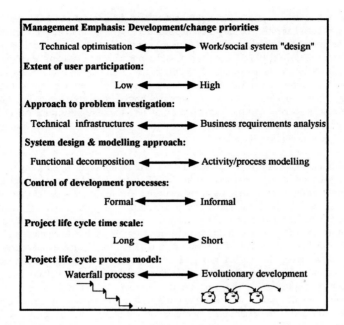

Figure 1: Framework for the Classification of Approaches To IS Development

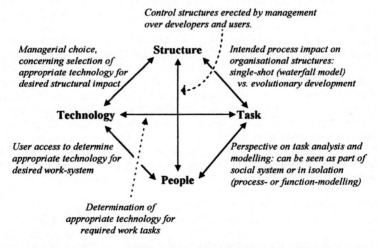

Figure 2: Approaches to Information Systems Development as Organizational Change
(adapted from Leavitt 1972)

A previous dichotomy of systems development between datalogical and infological perspectives (c.f. Methlie 1980) has more recently been expanded to a trichotomy between the organizational context, the conceptual/infological (or language) context and the datalogical/technical context (c.f. Lyytinen 1987; Iivari 1987). Lyytinen models approaches to systems development as lying on the spectra between the extremes of contexts: for example, life-cycle models are shown as lying between the language and technical contexts. Lyytinen's language context can be seen as embodying both modeling conceptual/cognitive knowledge and signifying human action. Although crude, the terms "people" and "task" may be used to represent the dual objects of this language context; the framework can thus be seen to fit with existing thinking about the domains of information systems development.

Coupled with the above interpretation was a need to encompass the dichotomy between "hard" and "soft" systems thinking proposed by Checkland (1981). Hard systems thinking, typified by systems engineering or structured systems analysis, sees the system development problem as relatively well-defined: the methodological objective is to satisfy the given requirements through the technical implementation of a closed system. In contrast, soft systems thinking sees the problem situation as ill-defined: the target object system is perceived as part of a wider, social and political system and the task of the analyst is to determine desirable and feasible change by exploring and expressing the problem situation. In hard systems thinking, the concern is with the properties of a physical (technical) system and it is believed that human behavior can be modeled using rule-based systems, so the problem is *analyzed*, by defining system objectives and requirements. In soft systems thinking, the concern is with a system of human activity, so the problem is *expressed*, by examining elements of structure and process and their mutual relationship.

The six dimensions of the framework were operationalized, using constructs from systems development practice, in such a way that one extreme of each dimension represented hard systems thinking and the other extreme represented soft systems thinking (the framework has been constructed so that hard approaches align with the left axis of the model spectra and soft approaches align with the right axis). The resulting dimensions are given in Figure 3.

When the framework was applied in a pilot study, it was discovered that the long, systems life-cycle approach versus the short, evolutionary approach was insufficient to define all projects, as some were long, evolutionary projects (corresponding to staged functional delivery, rather than an evolutionary approach where the structural impact of the system may change with evolution) and some were short waterfall approaches (where the system development did not have significant impact on the organization). To remove ambiguity from the application of the framework in practice, it was decided to split this element into two dimensions, the time dimension and the process-model dimension, giving seven dimensions to the framework.

The expected relationships (from the literature) between these variables are shown in Figure 4. In most of the literature in this area, two of the seven development approach framework dimensions are singled out for special attention: the management approach to IT-related change (c.f. Galliers 1987; Checkland and Scholes 1990; Scott Morton 1991; Benjamin and Levinson 1993) and user participation in the processes of IT-related change (c.f. Kappelman and McLean 1992; Morley 1993; Hirschheim and Klein 1989, 1992, 1994).

Leavitt's Model	Operationalized Concepts	
	hard	*soft*
technology-structure	technical optimization ↔	work & social system design
technology-people	low user participation ↔	high user participation
technology-task	top-down, technical approach to problem investigation ↔	bottom-up, task approach to problem investigation
task-people	function-oriented approach to system design ↔	work-process orientation to system design
structure-people	formal, system specification orientation to development project management ↔	informal user-satisfaction orientation
task-structure	long, waterfall approach to systems development ↔	short, evolutionary approach to systems development

Figure 3: The Six Dimensions of the IS Development Approach Framework,
Operationalized from the Interactions of Leavitt's (1972) Diamond Model

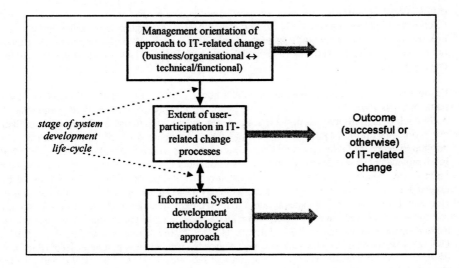

Figure 4: Proposed Relationships among Research Variables

The other five dimensions can be considered representative of the factors considered in the literature on development methodologies (c.f. Boehm, Gray and Seewalt 1984; Boehm 1988; Avison and Fitzgerald 1988; Avison and Wood-Harper 1990; Jayaratna 1994). The shadowed lines show relationships which were not investigated by this study, but justify the selection and separation of these variables. The dotted lines show a *modifying* influence: the stage of the system development life-cycle (SDLC), as it was discovered in a previous case study (Gasson 1995), that the extent of user-participation in information system development was likely to vary with the stage of the SDLC. The SDLC was split according to the three stages given in Budde and Zullighoven (1983): requirements specification, systems design, coding and implementation.

Jayaratna (1988) argues that process-oriented methods are appropriate for less well-structured organizational contexts. It can be argued that, as organizations have to increasingly respond to highly complex and turbulent product-market environments, all organizational contexts are becoming less well-structured and a functional/technical orientation is no longer appropriate. Argyris (1987) argues that designing for adaptive behavior is central to any effective approach to information system development. One would thus expect managerial approaches to IT-related change to be primarily business and process oriented.

Kumar and Bjørn-Andersen (1990) state that the prescription of a particular methodology incorporates into the design process "the ontological assumptions about what constitutes reality and the epistemological assumptions about how to conduct the ISD enquiry." They proceed to argue that the designers' value-systems are largely influenced by the choice of ISD methodology. This methodological determinism is challenged by Markus and Bjørn-Andersen, who argue that designers' existing value systems influence the selection of development methodologies. IS development methods are largely based upon a waterfall model and emphasize technical/functional optimization because technical expertise is the basis of IS professionals' power (Markus and Bjørn-Andersen 1987; Hornby et al. 1992). If managers' approaches emphasize a business orientation, one would expect the emphasis taken by system development approaches to be in conflict with that taken by organizational managers and to lack direct influence from the management approach.

Eason (1982) and Corbett, Rasmussen and Rauner (1991) argue that the extent of user-participation is directly influenced by the methodological approach taken to IS development. A traditional, (waterfall process-model based) development methodology excludes users, as their only contact with the process is via the validation of documents which they may not be in a position to understand fully. An evolutionary, prototyping approach to development, on the other hand, provides users with learning opportunities throughout the development process, permitting them to contribute to design decisions in an informed and powerful way. Thus it could be expected that the extent of user-participation is directly related to the type of methodology in use. However, in practice methodologies are not often used in the manner intended: IS professionals use tools and methods from a variety of methodologies, adopting a contingency approach to method customization (Vitalari 1984; Hornby et al. 1992; Hardy, Thompson and Edwards 1994). Users may be permitted to participate to a high degree in system development projects which use traditional methodologies (Hardy, Thompson and Edwards 1994; Hopker 1994) and may be excluded from system development which uses evolutionary prototyping approaches (Gasson 1995). A more detailed framework than is provided by a description of the methodology is therefore required to examine the overall *approach* to IS development. There is a need for a bridging framework between theory and practice (Keen 1987) which assesses the approach to information systems development and enables a comparison of the actual development approach to that intended by the methodology.

3. RESEARCH METHOD

An initial case study investigation (Gasson 1995) supported the findings of Hornby et al. and of Hopker that prevailing approaches to IS development were driven by technical considerations and that user participation in these technically-driven processes was problematic. An exploratory questionnaire was devised to explore current approaches to Information System development as part of strategic IT-related change, to investigate the relationships shown in Figure 4 and to test the utility of the research framework, given in Figure 1, for the classification of approaches to IS development. This survey is part of a wider exploration of these issues which adopts methodological pluralism (Hirschheim 1992) in order to obtain a multi-perspective understanding of IS development in an organizational context.

The survey method was used to determine senior management perspectives across a wide range of organizations, to ascertain whether development practice is changing to a more business/process oriented approach and the impact that this has upon user participation in IS development processes. While a survey was judged the best method to collect data from a large number of organizations, the research instrument was not intended to be used for quantitative measurement, but as a qualitative framework for assessing IS development practice in the UK. The data collected represents a subjective, single stakeholder perspective on the practices of IS development, rather than a quantitative assessment of IT change approaches.

When piloting the questionnaire, it was found that the framework permitted ambiguities and some questions (pertaining to the system development life-cycle model and the extent of user-participation) were rephrased to use clear examples of meaning — this necessarily compromised the use of a consistent scale for all dimensions of the framework. The survey questions are given in the appendix. As this study formed part of a larger questionnaire on management aspects of IT-related change, it was not possible to actively seek comments from respondents. However, managers did make comments freely in the spaces on the questionnaire, providing useful feedback on the utility of the terms used to interpret the research framework. Three questionnaires were sent to large UK companies: to a senior human resource manager, to a senior line manager and to a senior IT-function manager. This paper examines the responses of the senior IT-function managers to those questions pertaining to the approach used to accomplish IT-related change.

Managers were asked to classify their seniority in the function they represented on a scale of 1 to 7, where 1 was a junior manager/specialist and 7 was the head of the function. The average management level given was 5.59, with 81% (26) of the respondents being at management level 5 or above. Respondents at level 3 or below were excluded from the study, as a strategic overview was required. However, there is the danger that senior managers may not know what methods and approaches were taken, in detail. When the data was judged to be insufficiently detailed, or when sections were left blank (or returned marked "don't know"), that response was excluded from the analysis. We received 49 valid responses. Of these, only 32 companies had performed Information System development as part of the change process; 17 companies had contracted-out IS development to a third party.

For the purposes of this study, the system development life-cycle was split into three phases: system requirements analysis, system design and modeling, and system implementation and testing. The Information System development approach was determined using the classification framework given in Figure 1. Responses to questions 1 and 2 (Appendix) were used to classify the companies with respect to the six-stage model of stage of growth with respect to IT (Galliers and Sutherland 1991). This was a fairly subjective assessment, determined from the organization's current use of IT and was performed with less detail than that recommended by Galliers and Sutherland, as the need to keep the survey of manageable length indicated a focus on the primary interest of the survey, which was the processes of IS development in the context of IT-related organizational change. However, it was required to determine that the respondents were at a relatively advanced stage of growth, in order to determine whether their responses represented companies that have a reasonable extent of *experience* with IT-related change and could therefore be considered representative of "good practice" in the UK. This was found to be so: 86% of all responses were from companies at stage 4 to 5, the other 14% were from companies considered to be at an advanced point in stage 3 — the transition-point between managing the technology and managing corporate information (Galliers and Sutherland 1991). Responses to questions 3 to 7 were used to classify responses according to the research models given above.

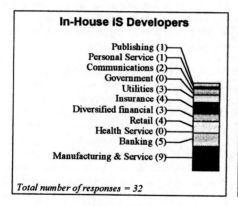
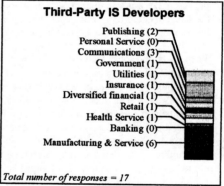

Figure 5: Profile of Survey Respondents (Number of Firms
in Each Category in Brackets)

A postal survey is not ideal for this type of study: it provides a wide picture without providing a rich picture. However, it does have the advantage that a relatively large amount of data may be collected fairly quickly, for an investigative study. For this reason, the survey method was used to investigate whether perceptions of the IS development process acquired through the earlier case study applied to a wide range of contemporary UK practice. Because the research instrument was subjective, no advanced statistical analysis was performed: the results presented here are summary results and exploratory, rather than confirmatory, in nature. The findings do, however, provide a rich and interesting picture of IS development in large UK companies.

4. FINDINGS OF THE SURVEY

A higher proportion of those companies that contracted out their IS development to a third party (76%) took an evolutionary approach to IS development than the proportion of those companies that performed their own IS development in-house (59%). This may be because companies that perform their own development do so for more complex IT change — it was not possible to ascertain if this was the case from the responses available. However, the companies that contracted out IS development had comparable average project duration (2.76 years) to those companies that performed their own development (2.47 years), so the project complexity of the two groups' development projects is likely to be comparable, as the time scales are comparable.

Respondents were asked what methods and tools were used for project management and for system development, at the requirements analysis, system design and implementation stages of the system development life-cycle. Responses from this, open, question were coded: the results from the sub-population who performed in-house IS development are given in 6. There was a high level of non-reporting for the sub-population which contracted out IS development — presumably they did not know what tools had been used.

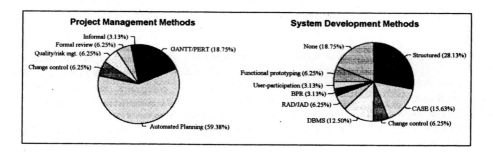

Figure 6: Tools Used For Project Management and For System Development

It is noticeable that 78% of respondents reported the use of an automated or manual project-scheduling tool. The functions of project management have so clearly become synonymous with scheduling and resource-allocation that managers do not use any tools to support other areas of responsibility such as facilitating and recording user-input to the development process. Even when asked to identify tools used for system development purposes, only one company reported using a tool which supported user-participation. This finding would tend to reinforce previous findings in this area, which report that IS development is largely seen as a scheduling management problem and as a functional/technical responsibility (Hornby et al. 1992).

One of the main findings, which supports previous studies performed in this area (c.f. Hornby et al. 1991; Hopker 1994), is that the approach to system design and modeling is significantly "harder" (i.e., with a more functional/technical orientation than a business/process orientation) than the management approach or the approach to problem investigation. Respondents were asked to rate their approach to the overall emphasis of the change (the management approach of the research framework), the approach to system requirements definition (the problem investigation approach of the research framework) and the approach taken to system design and modeling (the system design and modeling approach of the research framework). The results are presented in Table 1, where the given figures are for respondents who rated their approach at level 5, 6 or 7 on a 7-point scale for the three emphases (i.e. those respondents who took a more business/process orientated approach to change than a functional/technical orientated approach).

	Overall Emphasis of Change	Approach to System Reqs. Definition	Approach to System Design & Modeling
In-house IS Development: *32 valid responses*	22 (69%)	28 (87%)	9 (28%)
Third-Party IS Development: *17 valid responses*	6 (35%)	11 (65%)	5 (29%)

Table 1: Proportion of Respondents Taking a "Soft" Management, Problem Investigation and System Design Approach

The proportion of companies taking a business/process orientation to IT change declined markedly at the system design and modeling stage of the system development life-cycle, for both companies who performed in-house IS development and companies who contracted IS development to a third-party. Another interesting finding is that the proportion of companies who contracted out their IS development which took a business/process oriented approach to managing IT-related change is almost half the proportion of companies who performed their own IS development.

To provide a consistent assessment of the extent of user-participation between responses, respondents were asked whether certain mechanisms had been used to involve users in the IS development process. These mechanisms are listed in question 7 (Appendix); of these, the mechanisms which encourage the highest degree of user participation are given in Table 3. Although this type of question is still open to interpretation, it does remove a level of subjectivity associated with a "high-low" scaling response mechanism. The extent of user-involvement varied, as predicted, with the system development life-cycle, with the lowest reported involvement being at the system design and modeling stage. Table 2 summarizes the responses: a "high" level of user involvement is ranked as a company using one of the two user-participation mechanisms that most permit users to participate meaningfully and equally in the IS development process, at various stages of the system development life-cycle.

	System Requirement Analysis	System Design & Modeling	System Implementation & Test	System Operation
In-house IS Development: *32 valid responses*	28 (88%)	17 (53%)	27 (84%)	21 (66%)
Third-Party IS Development: *17 valid responses*	8 (47%)	1 (6%)	5 (29%)	9 (53%)

Table 2: Proportion of Respondents Reporting a High Level of User Participation at Various Stages of System Development Life-Cycle

What is particularly significant about these results is the very high level of user-participation shown by users in companies performing their own IS development and the relatively low levels shown in companies that contracted out IS development to third parties. The proportion of companies using the two highest-ranked mechanisms for user-involvement at each stage of the system development life cycle are shown in Table 3. Of companies that performed IS development, 81% reported having users as members of the IS development team at the system requirements analysis stage, although only 34% of these companies reported that users had been trained in the use of development tools at the system design and modeling stage.

	IS Developers	Third-Party Development
Participation of users as development team members	81%	47%
Joint design with users	63%	6%
User training in development tools	34%	6%
Use of evolutionary systems prototypes	31%	0%
User workshops to discuss design changes	50%	18%
User-directed testing schedules	75%	18%
User-redesign of work processes	28%	18%
Modifications to system design to support business applications	63%	47%

Table 3: Proportion of Respondents Using Highest-Ranked User-Participation Tools at Each Stage of System Development Life Cycle

One of the most interesting findings of the survey as a whole was that 88% of the sample responded that user-consultation and involvement helped a great deal (i.e., ranked this factor as 5, 6 or 7 on a 7-point scale), whereas only 72% of the sample responded that approaches to planning and project management helped a great deal; these findings are shown in Table 4. This is significant, as it contradicts the finding that IT-related change is mainly driven by functional/technical considerations (Hornby et al 1992), in which case one would expect planning and project management approaches to be valued more highly than user-involvement. Additionally, both user-consultation and planning and project management were rated less highly by companies that contracted-out IS development, perhaps reflecting both the lower levels of user-participation discussed above and also the higher degree of delegation of planning and project management which is performed by companies who contract-out system development.

	User-Consultation	Planning & Project Management
In-house IS Development: *32 valid responses*	28 (88%)	23 (72%)
Third-Party IS Development: *17 valid responses*	11 (63%)	11 (65%)

Table 4: Proportion of Respondents Ranking User-Consultation or
Planning and Project Management as "Helped a Great Deal"

We is intend to explore whether the development methods used also affected the degree of user-participation in more detailed investigations; it is probable that many more tools and methods are used in support of development processes than are known to senior IT managers.

5. REFLECTIONS ON THE USE OF THE RESEARCH FRAMEWORK

The research framework (given in Figure 1) was useful in that it helped to structure areas for exploration in the questionnaire and gave a reasonably consistent analysis tool with which to classify approaches to IT change and system development. Figure 7 shows the research findings mapped onto the framework.

This framework gives a clear, graphical comparison of the two sub-populations: those companies who developed Information Systems in-house and those companies who contracted IS development to third-parties. It also clearly illustrates variations in companies' approach to IS development at various stages in the system development life-cycle — there is a clear swing to the left of the model (the "hard" side of the continuum) at the system design and modeling stage. It can also be seen that project control approaches are much harder than the emphasis intended for the overall IT-related change. However, it should be noted that the project control measure is the least reliable of this study — it was obtained from analysis of the reported methods for project management and of answers to open questions as to what the respondent felt that they did well or badly. The process-model dimension was also a blunt tool, as applied in this survey, as respondents were asked to select one of two alternatives: single-stage or evolutionary.

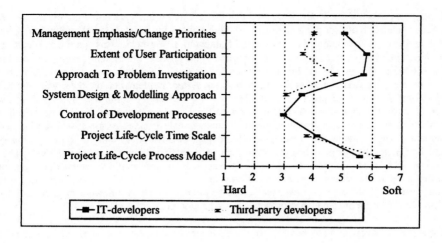

Figure 7: Research Findings Mapped onto the Research Framework

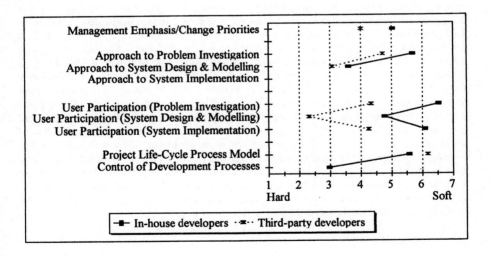

Figure 8: Research Findings Mapped onto Revised Research Framework

During the design of this study, it was felt that the research framework could be revised to give a better indication of user participation at different stages of the system development life-cycle. The results have been mapped on the revised framework in Figure 8. This is more informative, as the extent of user-participation can be compared to the approach to system development at the same stage of the system development life-cycle. (It was originally intended to use the overall management emphasis as a proxy for the approach to system implementation; there was later felt to be insufficient justification for this). The patterns are telling: both the "soft-ness" of the approach to development and the extent of user-participation in that stage of development decline rapidly from the problem investigation/requirements analysis stage to the system design and modeling stage of the system development life-cycle. This is true for both in-house developers and third-party developers. However, while user-participation for in-house developers is higher than would be predicted from the softness of the approach to information systems development at that stage of the system development life-cycle, user-participation for development that was contracted to third parties is lower than could be predicted. This framework gives a helpfully clear identification of trends in approaches to IS development.

The research framework described has provided a clear visual representation of overall trends in Information System development practice; however, the operationalization of the framework needs further work in the context of case study investigations. The framework is not considered complete. The duration of the project did not prove helpful in gauging whether the project was evolutionary in the sense that user-feedback was used as input to the next evolution or evolutionary in the sense that technical developers delivered an incremental set of system functions; this dimension has been removed from the revised model. One of the survey respondents commented that "we involved the users in the selection of new systems and implementation, which is unique in my experience." A feeling of pride or uniqueness in permitting user-participation in various ways was quite frequent among respondents' comments and raises the issue (also identified in Gasson 1995) of the perceived *legitimacy* of user-participation in information systems development processes. This dimension could be helpful in identifying the "theory-in-use" rather than the "espoused theory" (Argyris and Schon 1978) of information systems development. It was also felt, following the survey, that the dimension of project control was ambiguous — it may be more useful to split this into two dimensions: (I) a Loose-Rigid control dimension and (ii) a Devolved-Centralized organizational structure dimension. However, with these modifications, the framework provides a clear structure for the classification of development approaches and it is felt that this will prove of immense use when using interview techniques and case study observations, especially as it is can be used as a diagram-based method of communication — IT professionals are accustomed to using such methods and this framework may elicit richer communication than verbal research instruments; it also communicates results to the IT profession much more clearly than numerical analysis, so may permit a higher transfer of research recommendations to industry practice.

6. CONCLUSIONS

It was discovered that the overall management perspective of IT-related change is to see it primarily as a business/organizational change, with the exploitation of technology as a secondary consideration. While the initial driver may be a change in technology, the system requirements analysis stage of the system development life-cycle is overridingly seen as being pertinent to business requirements rather than to technical infrastructures. However, once the system design and modeling stage begins, this business process emphasis is subsumed by the technically-driven approaches used by IS professionals.

User-participation varied significantly at different stages of the system-development life-cycle. Users are involved heavily at the implementation stage of the IT change. However, research in the area of user participation has shown that user involvement at this stage is mainly token: the system design will, by this point, have become "frozen" and the system requirements will have been specified formally at a much earlier stage (Eason 1982). The user therefore has little influence, except to change small, operational aspects of the system. Its scope and its effect on their work and their experience of the business/process support from the IT system cannot be affected at this stage in the change process. However, the findings were positive, in that attitudes to users are positive: 88% of respondents felt that user-involvement in the change had helped a great deal — a higher percentage than those who felt that project management and planning had helped a great deal.

Users of systems which were developed in-house stood a much higher chance of being permitted to participate in system development than potential users of systems developed by a third party. However, as for the development approach, user-participation declined markedly during the system design and modeling stage — the stage when their input could most affect the form of the new system and its impact upon the way in which their work is structured.

If one looks at the tools used for system development, these are overwhelmingly geared toward the control and support of technical aspects of the system under development, which could explain the low level of user-participation at this stage of the system development life-cycle.

There did appear to be a link between the orientation of the approach emphasized by the senior IT manager and the degree of user-participation, as predicted in the research model. With a subjective research instrument, it is not feasible to attempt to quantify the strength of this link, but there is sufficient evidence to suppose that there is a dependency relationship. This would also be supported by the ranking of user-involvement as "helping a great deal" by a significantly higher proportion of respondents than that which ranked planning and project management approaches as "helping a great deal."

7. IMPLICATIONS FOR FUTURE RESEARCH AND ORGANIZATIONAL PRACTICE

This study did not analyze in detail the type of Information System that formed the basis of the "major IT-related organizational change" about which respondents were asked to provide information. There may be a link between the type of system being changed or introduced and the approach taken to manage that change: this needs further investigation. There was a high degree of variation in IT managers' interpretations of the phrase "major IT-related organizational change," so the organizational impact of the reported IT-related change would have been much greater for some organizations than for others.

The two most significant findings are that the level of user-participation is markedly higher at all stages of development for in-house Information System development than for third-party development and that both the degree of user-participation and the extent to which organizational and business factors are considered as high priority decline significantly at the system design and modeling stage of the system development life-cycle.

The first of these findings needs further investigation in terms of the type of system under development. Are users permitted to participate less in third-party IS development because their participation would be inappropriate for this type of system (which perhaps requires little human interaction) or are users excluded because of geographical constraints? At a superficial level, it would appear that the types of system where development was contracted out to third parties were more concerned with IT-infrastructure reorganization, whereas those developed in-house were more concerned with the reorganization of business processes. From an analysis of the brief system and impact details given by respondents, there is some evidence to support the theory that contracted-out systems were less radical in terms of their impact on the organization than those developed in-house and often took the form of a purchased package or a new IT infrastructure which was implemented by specialists in that technology. Given that the nature of many of the systems whose development was contracted out was a change in internal communications or software infrastructures, such as new electronic-mail systems, it would be expected that users would be encouraged to participate more, not less, than for the changes reported for those companies developing systems in-house. If user-participation is limited to applications that directly affect users' day-to-day tasks and not seen as legitimate for infrastructure systems which indirectly affect them, there may be adverse implications for the supportiveness and productivity of the working environment. It may be that the issue of legitimacy is critical here and the respondent who proclaimed his company's uniqueness in involving users in the selection of new systems *is* an exception. Most organizations may see IT-related change as driven by technical considerations and involve users only when radical business or organizational change is required as a pre-requisite to technical change.

The second finding confirms trends found in previous studies of the system design stage of the system development life-cycle, when examined in isolation from other stages (c.f. Hedberg and Mumford 1975; Curtis, Krasner and Iscoe 1988). An examination of changes in approach over the system development life-cycle is required in far more detail. Again, the issue of legitimacy is seen as critical: Gasson (1995) found that both developers and users perceived information system design and modeling to lie in the technical domain, excluding the infological and organizational domains, even when the development process had been designed explicitly around emancipatory, evolutionary prototyping. System requirements are only partially known at the start of the design and modeling stage: they are explored and may be discounted or redefined through the processes of system design. Any definition of the system which emerges from this stage may be very different from that intended by users, but users have the least input to the processes of exploring and understanding system requirements at the design stage. While the overall system *objectives* are defined during the problem investigation/system requirements stage, the *form* of the eventual system, determining its impact upon users and organizational effectiveness, is decided during the system design and modeling stage. Exclusion of users at this stage must be detrimental to the system outcome: even if users are permitted to participate in system implementation and testing, the design has been frozen by this point and users' scope for change of the system will be limited to requesting changes to system functions that do not work, rather than those that do not work in a manner supportive of their desired work environment.

However, the overall business/organizational emphasis accorded to IS development by senior managers gives hope for those academics who have been attempting to "convert" IT managers to a business/organizational orientation! It is clear that there is a "take-over" of the processes of IT-related change at the system design stage by IT-professionals (analysts, designers and programmers), which gives functional/technical factors higher priority than business/organizational factors. There follows a set of research questions about how this process happens, which domains and objects of IS development are considered legitimate by different development stakeholders and whether the outcome is less effective, in matching organizational requirements, than if business/organizational factors had been prioritized. It is probable that the trend to a hard development approach during the system design stage of the system development life-cycle is undesirable, in terms of outcome. These areas needs further investigation in more detailed studies.

8. REFERENCES

Argyris, C. "Some Inner Contradictions In Management Information Systems'." In R. D. Galliers (Editor), *Information Analysis*. Reading, Massachusetts: Addison-Wesley, 1987.

Argyris, C., and Schon, D. A. *Organizational Learning: A Theory of Action Perspective*. Reading, Massachusetts: Addison-Wesley, 1978.

Avison, D. E., and Fitzgerald, G. *Information Systems Development: Methodologies, Techniques and Tools*. Oxford: Blackwell Scientific Publications, 1988.

Avison, D. E., and Wood-Harper, A. T. *Multiview: An Exploration In Information Systems Development*. Oxford: Blackwell Scientific Publications, 1990.

Benjamin, R.I., and Levinson, E. "A Framework for Managing IT-Enabled Change." *Sloan Management Review*, Summer 1993, pp. 23-33.

Boehm, B. W. "A Spiral Model Of Software Development And Enhancement." *IEEE Computer Journal*, May 1988.

Boehm, B. W.; Gray, T. E.; and Seewalt, T. "Prototyping Versus Specifying: A Multiproject Experiment." *IEEE Transactions on Software Engineering*, Volume SE-10, Number 3, 1984, pp. 290-302.

Budde, R., and Zullighoven, H. "Socio-Technical Problems of System Design Methods." In U. Briefs, C. Ciborra, L. Schneider (Editors), *Systems Design For, With and By The Users*. Amsterdam: North-Holland Publishing Company, 1983.

Checkland, P. *Systems Thinking, Systems Practice*. Chichester: Wiley, 1981

Checkland, P., and Scholes, J. *Soft Systems Methodology in Action.* Chichester: Wiley, 1990.

Corbett, J. M.; Rasmussen, L. B.; and Rauner, F. *Crossing The Border: The Social and Engineering Design of Computer Integrated Manufacturing Systems.* London: Springer-Verlag, 1991.

Curtis, B., Krasner, H., and Iscoe, N. "A Field Study of the Software Design Process for Large Systems." *Communications of the ACM*, Volume 31, Number 11, November 1988.

Eason, K. D. "The Process of Introducing Information Technology." *Behavior and Information Technology*, Volume 1, Number 2, April-June 1982. Reprinted in R. Paton, S. Brown, R. Spear, J. Chapman, and J. Hamwee (Editors), *Organizations: Cases, Issues and Concepts.* London: Paul Chapman Publishing, London, 1984.

Galliers, R. D. "An Approach to Information Needs Analysis." In R. D. Galliers (Editor), *Information Analysis.* Reading, Massachusetts: Addison-Wesley, 1987.

Galliers, R. D., and Sutherland, A. R. "Information Systems Management and Strategy Formulation: The 'Stages Of Growth' Model Revisited." *Journal of Information Systems*, Volume 1, 1991, pp. 89-114.

Gasson, S. "Managing Organizational Change: The Impact of Information System Development Methods." In N. Jayaratna, G. Paton, Y. Merali, and F. Gregory (Editors), *Proceedings of the Conference of the BCS Information Systems Methods Specialist Group.* Heriot-Watt University, Edinburgh, September 1994.

Gasson, S. "User Involvement In Decision-Making In Information Systems Development." *Proceedings of IRIS 18*, Gjern, Denmark, August 1995.

Hardy, C.; Thompson, B.; and Edwards, H. "Method Use and Customization in the UK: A Preliminary Survey." In N. Jayaratna, G. Paton, Y. Merali, and F. Gregory (Editors), *Proceedings of the Conference of the BCS Information Systems Methods Specialist Group*, Heriot-Watt University, Edinburgh, September 1994.

Hedberg, B., and Mumford, E. "The Design of Computer Systems: Man's Vision of Man as an Integral Part of the System Design Process." In E. Mumford and H. Sackman (Editors), *Human Choice and Computers.* Amsterdam: North-Holland, 1975.

Heller, F. A. "The Technological Imperative And The Quality Of Employment." *New Technology, Work and Employment*, 1987.

Hirschheim, R. A. "Information Systems Epistemology: An Historical Perspective." In R. D. Galliers (Editor), *Information Systems Research: Issues, Methods and Practical Guidelines.* Oxford: Blackwell Scientific, 1992.

Hirschheim, R. A., and Klein, H. K. "Four Paradigms of Information Systems Development." *Communications of the ACM*, Volume 32, Number 10, 1989.

Hirschheim, R. A., and Klein, H. K. "Realizing Emancipatory Principles in Information Systems Development: The Case for ETHICS." *MIS Quarterly*, March 1994, pp. 83-109

Hirschheim, R. A., and Klein, H. K. "A Research Agenda for Future Information Systems Development Methodologies." In W. W. Cotterman and J. A. Senn (Editors), *Challenges and Strategies for Research in Systems Development*. New York: John Wiley and Sons Ltd., 1992.

Hopker, O. "Evaluation and Choice of Information Systems Methodologies — A Welsh Perspective." In N. Jayaratna, G. Paton, Y. Merali, and F. Gregory (Editors), *Proceedings of the Conference of the BCS Information Systems Methods Specialist Group*, Heriot-Watt University, Edinburgh, September 1994.

Hornby, P.; Clegg, C. W.; Robson, J. I.; Maclaren, C. I.; Richardson, S. C.; and O'Brien, P. "Human and Organizational Issues In Information Systems Development." *Behavior and Information Technology*, Volume 11, Number 3, 1992.

Iivari, J. "A Methodology for IS Development as Organizational Change: A Pragmatic Contingency Approach." In H. K. Klein and K. Kumar (Editors), *Systems Development for Human Progress, Proceedings of IFIP WG8.2*. Amsterdam: North-Holland, 1987.

Jayaratna, N. "Guide To Method Understanding In Information Systems Practice." *International Journal of Information Management*, August 1988.

Jayaratna, N. *Understanding and Evaluating Methodologies: A Systemic Framework*. New York: McGraw Hill, 1994.

Kappelman, L. A.; and McLean, E. R. "Promoting Information System Success: The Respective Roles of User Participation and User Involvement." *Journal of Information Technology Management*, Volume 3, Number 1, 1992, pp. 1-12.

Keen, P. G. W. "MIS Research: Current Status, Trends and Needs." In R. A. Buckingham, R. A. Hirschheim, F. F. Land, and C. J. Tully (Editors), *Information Systems Education* Cambridge: BCS, 1987.

Kumar, K., and Bjørn-Andersen, N. "A Cross-Cultural Comparison of IS Designer Values." *Communications of the ACM*, May 1990, Volume 33, Number 5, 1990, pp. 528-538.

Leavitt, L. *Managerial Psychology*. Chicago: University of Chicago Press, 1972.

Lyytinen, K. "A Taxonomic Perspective Of Information Systems Development Theory." In R. J. Boland, and R. A. Hirschheim (Editors), *Critical Issues In Information Systems Research*, London: Wiley, 1987.

Markus, M. L., and Bjørm-Andersen, N. "Power Over Users: Its Exercise By System Professionals." *Communications of the ACM*, Volume 30, Number 6, June 1987.

Methlie, L. B. "Systems Requirements Analysis — Methods And Models." In H. C. Lucas Jr., F .F. Land, J .J. Lincoln and K. Supper (Editors), *The Information Systems Environment*, Proceedings of IFIP TC8.2 Working Conferences, Bonn 1979. Amsterdam: North Holland Publishing Company, 1980.

Morley, C. "Information Systems Development Methods and User Participation: A Contingency Approach." In D. Avison, J. E. Kendall, and J. I. DeGross (Editors), *Human, Organizational and Social Dimensions of Information Systems Development: Proceedings of IFIP WG8.2 Conference*, Noorwijkerhout, The Netherlands. Amsterdam: North Holland, 1993.

Mumford, E., and Henshall, D. *Designing Participatively*. Manchester, England: Manchester Business School, 1983.

Scott Morton, M. S. "Introduction." In M. S. Scott Morton (Editor), *The Corporation of the 1990s*. New York: Oxford University Press, 1991.

Vitalari, N. P. "A Critical Assessment of Structured Analysis Methods: A Psychological Perspective" In T. M. A. Bemelmans (Editor), *Beyond Productivity: Information Systems Development For Organizational Effectiveness*. Amsterdam: North-Holland, 1984.

Wynekoop, J. L., and Russo, N. L. "System Development Methodologies: Unanswered Questions and the Research-Practice Gap." In J. I. DeGross, R. P. Bostrom, and R. D. Robey (Editors), *Proceedings of the Fourteenth International Conference on Information Systems*. Orlando, Florida, December 1993.

About the Authors

Susan Gasson is a Lecturer in Information Systems at Warwick Business School. Her research interests include software development process modeling, the development of human-centered approaches to information system design, and the impact of IT on effective organizational work. Prior to joining Warwick Business School she worked as a data communications consultant, specializing in the design of Open Systems.

Niki Holland is a founding consultant of Transition Partnerships, a consultancy which helps people and organizations to manage their own change. It has developed its own approach to managing IT-related change which integrates IS design with the design of work and organizational systems, facilitating user commitment to change.

APPENDIX: SURVEY QUESTIONS

1. How would you describe the system architecture in your organization? (Tick as many as apply).

   1. Stand-alone PCS
   2. Workstations – connected by a Local Area Network
   3. Workstations – connected by a Wide Area Network
   4. Minicomputer – with dumb terminals

   5. Client/server architecture
   6. Mainframe – with PC links
   7. IT links to customers
   8. IT links to suppliers

2. To what extent are the following true of your organization?

	False				True
Business functions can access applications from a network	1	2	3	4	5
Business functions can extract data from central databases to use local applications	1	2	3	4	5
Business functions have access to integrated office systems	1	2	3	4	5

3. Think about the main IT development project as a whole. What did it most resemble?

   1. A single, staged life-cycle.   2. A Set of evolutionary developments

4. What was the duration of the main IT development project?

1.	< 1 year	5.	- 4 years
2.	- 2 years	6.	- 6 years
3.	- 3 years	7.	> 5 years

5. Now think about the approach to system development during the main IT development project. How would you rate the following factors?

The overall emphasis was on:	*Exploiting technical opportunities*	1 2 3 4 5 6 7	*Supporting organizational changes*
The approach to system requirements definition stressed	*Business requirements*	1 2 3 4 5 6 7	*Technical infrastructures*
The approach to system design and modeling stressed:	*Financial requirements decomposition*	1 2 3 4 5 6 7	*Modeling work processes*

6. Think of the methods and tools used in the main IT development project for project management and system development. What tools were used at each of the following 3 stages?   *(Open question)*

   ### A. Requirements Analysis

Project Management	System Development

   ### B. System Design

Project Management	System Development

   ### C. Implementation

Project Management	System Development

7. Think about the approach to business needs definition. Which of the following mechanisms were used to match IS needs to business needs?

(N.B. Mechanisms were derived from the first author's experience as a System Designer).

A. During system requirements analysis
1. Validation and sign-off of specifications by users
2. Participation of users at requirements "walk throughs"
3. User-participation workshops
4. Interviews with users to elicit requirements
5. Joint design (using groups of users to design work processes)
6. Participation of users as development team members.

B. During system design
1. User validation and sign-off of design documents
2. User attendance at design "walk-throughs"
3. Use of experimental system prototypes (to try out ideas)
4. Use of evolutionary system prototypes (incorporated into system)
5. Formal user training in use of development tools

C. During system implementation and testing
1. Provision of user manual s
2. Provision of help-desk facilities to support user problems
3. Formal user training in use of the new systems
4. User workshops to discuss design changes
5. User-directed testing schedules
6. Modifications to system design to support business applications

D. During ongoing operation of system
1. User manuals describing advanced system features
2. Formal advanced training in use of the system
3. Use of methods to help users re-design work processes
4. Modifications to system design to support business applications.
5. User-support mechanisms for dissemination of information about the new system.

8. Think about the overall change of which this project was a part. To what extent did the following factors get in the way of, or help the success of, the change?

| User consultation and involvement | *Really got in the way* | 1 2 3 4 5 6 7 | *Helped a great deal* |
| Approaches to planning and project management | *Really got in the way* | 1 2 3 4 5 6 7 | *Helped a great deal* |

9. Think about the IT aspects of the change process. What do you feel . . .
   A. . . . you did well?
   B. . . . you should do differently next time?
   C. . . . are the aspects of a well-managed change process that you missed altogether?

14

PANEL

Beyond Systems Development Methodologies: Time To Leave the Lamppost?

Participants

Richard Baskerville
Binghamton University, USA

Brian Fitzgerald (Chair)
University College Cork, Ireland

Guy Fitzgerald
University of London, UK

Nancy Russo
Northern Illinois University, USA

1. INTRODUCTION

The importance of successful systems development persists as an issue of central significance and concern in the IS field, especially in light of the well-documented problems associated with system development which have given rise to what has been termed the "software crisis." However, many methodologies in use today are derived from practices and concepts relevant to a very different organizational environment. There is a need to reconsider their role in view of changes in organizational forms and work practices and the increasingly-complex applications that need to be developed to suit the faster "metabolism" of today's complex organizational environment. Given the significant "push" factor that this environment represents, there is an urgent need to leverage new developments, both technological and in organizational work practices, which enable new development approaches more appropriate to this organizational climate.

This climate requires that organizations act more effectively in shorter time frames. There is a need for more rapid systems delivery than that which is currently being achieved with the monolithic development approaches inherent in traditional system development methodologies (SDMs). In fact, the latter impose a considerable degree of inertia on the development process. Thus, the current development environment is much different than the one faced by developers in the past and development practices must change accordingly. Also, given the strong arguments in favor of informating the workplace and empowering employees, the expectation implicit in many methodologies, that developers will plod robotically through standardized checklists, is not valid.

However, many researchers and practitioners continue to see the solution to the software crisis in terms of increased control and the more widespread adoption of methodologies. Indeed, some significant arguments and pressures support the use of such methodologies. However, the problems associated with the use of methodologies have not, perhaps, received adequate attention in the literature. Thus, the assumption that increased adoption of methodologies would help address the problems inherent in systems development is by no means proven. In fact, it is possible that methodologies are best used as suggested frameworks, or guidelines, rather than as dogma, and that one methodology is not sufficient for all development situations.

We use a lamppost metaphor here to illustrate the central problems, both in SDM research and in practice, with the traditional view which advocates the use of methodologies. Following this we argue for the need to leave the lamppost and move to a new paradigm and modes of development which would better complement the new organizational forms and leverage the technological facilitators that now exist.

2. SDM RESEARCH: A CASE OF LOOKING UNDER THE LAMPPOST?

Given the inconclusive nature of the vast body of research that has focused on evaluating and comparing system development methodologies, an analogy could be drawn with that of the drunk losing his watch in the street and moving to look for it under the light of a lamppost because the light is best there, even though it had been lost somewhere else. Likewise, it is perhaps easier to conduct research on existing methodologies as the light is best there, rather than to investigate the real complexity of systems development, since the latter requires consideration of a host of organizational and political issues which are much more difficult to illuminate.

3. SDM PRACTICE: A CASE OF LEANING AGAINST THE LAMPPOST?

In relation to system development practice, the use of methodologies may be a case of leaning against the lamppost for support rather than for illumination; that is to say, while methodologies may contribute little to either the process or product of systems development, they continue to be used in organizations, principally as a "comfort factor" to reassure all participants that "proper" practices are being followed in the face of the stressful complexity associated with system development. Alternately, they are being used to legitimate the development process, perhaps to win development contracts with government agencies, or to help in the quest for ISO-certification. In this role, methodologies may be more a placebo than a panacea, and there is a danger that developers, particularly inexperienced ones, may fall victim to goal displacement, that is, blindly and slavishly following the methodology at the expense of actual systems development. In this mode, the vital insight, sensitivity and flexibility of the developer may be replaced by automatic, programmed behavior.

4. THE FUTURE: BEYOND METHODOLOGIES

Research is therefore needed which would investigate the true nature of the current systems development environment in real organizational situations and on real development projects. Practitioners have in many cases assimilated good practices and techniques and may be rejecting methodologies for pragmatic reasons rather than due to ignorance as has been suggested. The "renaissance" developer is using technology innovatively to overcome some of the problems inherent in system development. Specifically, developers are leveraging electronic mail and Groupware databases to help structure and share development knowledge. These technological advances are also being used to facilitate the rapid creation and disbandment of development teams. These teams are remarkably fluid in the manner in which different development personnel assume principal roles at different stages according to their expertise. Also, there is a need to build learning into the development process rather than tagging it on at the end as part of a post-implementation audit phase. These initiatives contribute to the acceleration of the development process, which is necessary to suit the needs of the systems development environment currently faced in organizations.

5. PANEL DISCUSSION FORMAT

The panel chair will frame the issues to be discussed with a short introduction. This will be followed by a five minute presentation by each panelist. Each panelist will consider explicitly the role of methodologies in the context of current organizational trends.

Richard Baskerville will consider the concept of "method" as a synonym for "exemplar." To a large degree, the method concept is simply the lens through which many systems development experts view their subject. They seek criteria for classifying activities and products and then work to improve the various things discovered in their abstract categories. These experts have created a veritable panoply of methods that are suggested to systems practitioners. Most experienced system developers recognize that these methods are indeed a set of idealized activities and products that could proceed from a problem setting that exactly matches the expert's notions. These experienced developers adapt some, skip some, and invent some of their activities and products each time a system is developed. From this perspective, a method is a singular example of how a system might be developed. A method is a case study. It has limited generalizability. Experts and naive students may fail to realize that a method cannot be applied in a literal sense. Attempts to apply a method in an exact sense can be very destructive. Since methods cannot be applied in a literal sense, the organization and its actors must "learn" how to develop each system in an ideographic sense.

Guy Fitzgerald will discuss systems development in the context of outsourcing. Some organizations are outsourcing some or all of their IT, including systems development activities. This is in some cases due to poor experiences of internal systems development, including an inability to develop systems quickly enough to respond to organizational needs. There is a need to consider the ways in which outsourcing affects the development process and what are the organizational implications. For example, outsourcing focuses extra attention on the contractual issues of systems development, on the implementation stage including successfully bringing the development back in house, and the relationship with users. There is also the necessity of dealing with vendors, contracts, and negotiations. These are all skills in which IS practitioners have not historically excelled.

Nancy Russo will argue that existing methodologies are unable to support the needs of the current development environment. Although changes in technologies, economies, organizational structures, and competitive environments are causing fundamental changes in the both the types of information systems that are developed and the process by which they are developed, there is little evidence to indicate that methodologies are keeping pace with these changes. Current research indicates that a large percentage of organizations continue to use traditional structured, linear methodologies. However, these same organizations report that adherence to the methodology is lax. The degree of adherence to the methodology typically varies from project to project. Decisions to use, modify, or ignore the methodology standard often are made on an ad hoc basis. Few organizations have formal guidelines in place to guide developers in their decisions regarding methodology use. A new paradigm for methodology research and development is needed in order to understand the complexities of the development process and to design methodologies and tools that are relevant in the current environment.

After the panelists have presented, the audience will be invited to ask questions and join in the discussion. To stimulate this discussion, a series of key issues will be posed:

- What is the profile of the development environment (e.g., outsourcing, in-house development, integration of packages) currently faced in organizations?

- What role, if any, do methodologies play given the various modes of development that may apply in different development environments?

- What are the broad factors which need to be leveraged if development approaches are to meet current organizational demands?

This discussion will last for about thirty minutes. In the final ten minutes, the chair will briefly summarize the main issues raised during the discussion and ask the panelists for a final reaction to these issues.

15

The Second-Order
Security Dilemma

Richard Baskerville
Institute of Computer and Systems Science
Copenhagen Business School
(On leave from The School of Management
Binghamton University)

Abstract

Security is an important aspect of information systems. However, much of the current work in this area is concerned with first-order issues of the security problem. These first-order issues regard the direct threats against systems such as computer abuse, software unreliability, and natural disasters. These issues also regard the safeguards that may be deployed to protect systems from these direct threats. The second-order issues regard the impact of these safeguards on the organization. In particular organizational flexibility and adaptability may be affected. This is because predictability is an attribute of security, and organizational spontaneity implies a large degree of entropy. The paper discusses issues and aspects of managing adaptive systems security including adaptive safeguard techniques.

The purpose of this paper is to analyze a fundamentally different perspective on the nature of information systems security safeguards. These safeguards often constitute highly constraining organizational structures that can become costly burdens. Typically, security managers and safeguards designers only consider the surface security issues, i.e., the first-order security problems. Deeper analysis reveals broad organizational implications that could strike in surprising ways at the core of organizational flexibility and survival.

1. FIRST ORDER SECURITY

The security of our information systems is an issue of growing importance in our field. In its broadest perspective, it encompasses the integrity and reliability of information systems, computer crime and abuse, and data privacy. Each of these elements is an area of increasing concern as our society grows ever more dependent on computer-based information technology:

> As computer systems become more prevalent, sophisticated, embedded in physical processes and interconnected, society becomes more vulnerable to poor system design, accidents that disable systems, and attacks on computer systems. [National Research Council 1991, p.1]

The issue of integrity and reliability is closely aligned with the development of information systems. Errors and oversights in analysis, requirements definition, systems design and implementation will open vulnerabilities for operating errors, system crashes, and inadequate performance (Baskerville 1993). The issue of computer crime and abuse regards the ease with which many information systems may be assaulted. According to Neumann (1995) the major techniques for this abuse include external misuse, hardware misuse, masquerading, pest programs, controls bypass, active misuse, passive misuse, and misuse by inaction. The issue of privacy regards the protection of sensitive personal computer-based data. This issue has gained importance steadily as computer growth enabled organizations to amass, sometimes unintentionally, remarkable dossiers on private individuals. Major concerns regard trans-border data flows, financial secrecy, medical data, police files, marketing data and work-place monitoring. The concern has precipitated a maze of international, national, provincial and professional laws, regulations and guidelines (Madsen 1992).

These issues regard the "first-order" security problem. These are the problems against which systems security designers seek to protect systems. Based on his collection of "risks to the public" via a computer newsgroup, Neumann classifies these problems into the following categories: intentional misuse, security accidents, spoofs and pranks, intentional denials of service, unintentional denials of service, financial fraud by computer, accidental financial losses, risks in elections, jail security, and privacy. System designers prescribe security safeguards or controls with the intention of protecting information systems against these problems.

There are many types of first-order safeguards. These are sometimes classified as deterrent, preventative, detective, and corrective (Baskerville 1988). Examples include (1) additional management policies and procedures such as access control, backup procedures and password management schemes; (2) additional hardware and software such as data or communications encryption, call-back modems and smart cards; and (3) additional organizational resources such as disaster recovery services, backup sites, and insurance.

The primary analytic concept underlying the management of this first order security problem is risk analysis. This is a form of cost-justification procedure used in the selection decision for information systems security safeguards. It is an open debate whether risk analysis is really very practical for information systems (Baskerville 1991). However, it is clear that the simple risk analysis formula that arose in early computer security management literature is still a mode of thinking that permeates practice today (*cf.* Courtney 1977; U.S. Department of Commerce 1979). This mode of thinking centers on the formula for risk (r) as the product of probability (p) and cost of damage (c) when a threat occurs:

$$r = p \cdot c$$

This formula summarizes the first-order security management problem. Safeguards can be put in place to reduce either the probability of a threat's occurrence (preventive or deterrent safeguards) or the cost of the threat's occurrence (corrective or detective safeguards). Reducing either or both of these components of risk is seen to drive down the risk profile of the organization's information system. Strong proponents of risk analysis have developed elegant mechanisms for modeling this first-order problem, for example using Bayesian statistics and nationalized databases of threats and safeguards (*cf.* Ozier 1989) while opponents object to the critical reliance on irrational, "guessworked" data points and the ethics of quantifying public risk using monetary units (*cf.* Parker 1990). To a certain degree, this debate parallels the quantitative-qualitative debate in many research method circles.

2. SECOND ORDER SECURITY

A central problem with this simple first-order formula is its limited scope. The formula is incomplete and addresses only part of the decision that security designers and managers actually undertake. The question posed by the simple formula above is quite limited: "What is the risk that my organization is confronting?" The decision faced by the security manager is actually quite different: "Does the risk to my organization justify the investment in the safeguard?" This more relevant issue is properly modeled as

$$c_s \leq p_t \cdot c_t$$

Which is to say, the cost of the safeguard c_s should be less than, or at least equal to the risk confronted (threat probability p_t times the cost of a threat occurrence c_t). Currently all of the attention and debate is paid to the right-hand side of this formula. Increasingly, security managers in distributed systems must consider the left hand side of the formula. In the past, it may have been felt that the cost of the safeguard c_s is so low that it was not worth considering. In highly flexible or adaptive systems the cost of the safeguard c_s becomes complex because the safeguard s could limit or constrain the flexibility or adaptivity that might otherwise be present in the information system. In such situations, the costs of safeguard c_s might be higher — maybe dramatically higher — than the total risk faced from threat t.

This safeguards-cost is the second order security problem. The problem that arises when security measures throttle the information system that they are deployed to protect. From a socio-technical perspective, such controls are easily discovered in practice: password expiration schemes that are so tricky that the users become discouraged and stop using the system; building or system access restrictions that are so cumbersome that it becomes impossible for users to access the system in unusual or exceptional situations; or encryption techniques that make it impossible to use versatile system utility programs when a business opportunity rises suddenly and demands information processing that is not provided by existing applications.

For example, many organizations are currently very concerned about protecting organizational computing access from abuse through Internet connections. System designers can specify an assortment of safeguards that offer varying levels of security. The least security would be provided by a simple router that transfers any and all communications packets between the local network and the Internet. Any Internet client or server, such as world-wide-web or telnet programs, could run on any local computer. Increasing the security necessarily adds constraints, for instance, by adding "firewall" functions to the router. Such functions could prevent establishing inbound ftp or telnet sessions and stave off many kinds of attacks from the network. However it also makes it more difficult to establish servers (like web servers) in the local network. Establishing such a server requires costly reprogramming in the firewall, and approval from the security authorities in charge of the firewall. With the safeguard in place, there is a security technocracy that must be negotiated each time certain types of Internet communication are needed.

In this example, the costs of the control certainly include the firewall technology and its maintenance. But these costs also include the organization's inability to act quickly and flexibly when the need arises. For example, suppose an airline finds itself deluged with e-mail inquiries from its agents owing to a bad snowstorm and many flight cancellations. If the scheduling department attempts to innovate by creating an emergency web server on a local machine, they could find their attempts defeated by the firewall. Getting the firewall reprogrammed, or moving the web site to an established server, will add time, labor and cost to the effort when both time and labor are in short supply. The security not only eliminates certain kinds of attacks, it eliminates certain kinds of flexibility and opportunity.

As another example, an organization concerned about persons scavenging sensitive data from its computers may design certain safeguards into a local area network. These safeguards might include eliminating diskette drives from most desktop computers, placing all printers in supervised locations, and blocking ftp packets from Internet transfer. These safeguards create new (or reinforce old) power structures in the organization which regard such issues as whose office supervises printers, who is authorized to have a diskette drive, and who has access to the Internet. The system safeguards define who gets to carry on what kinds of activities and when these may be done. These structures erect technical roadblocks before the underprivileged members of the organization. These structures may effectively prevent flexible work schedules, telecommuting, Internet experimentation and other forms of innovative activity that characterize highly adaptive organizations.

3. PREDICTABILITY AS AN ATTRIBUTE OF SECURITY

To understand the issues that we now raise over many taken-for-granted security safeguards, we must understand the essential purpose of these safeguards. The common purpose of all security safeguards across the broad spectrum of information system elements is to constrain the information system to legitimate, allowed behavior. This means that the role of security safeguards is to prevent the system from accidentally or deliberately working to illegitimate purposes. Above all else in the system, security defines many of the ultimate boundaries of any information system function. This is the essence of security safeguards: to prevent unpredicted, disallowed system behavior.

The essential components of most security safeguards are order and structure. When software engineering or procedural standards fail to protect information assets, the order imposed by security safeguards constrain the system from severely damaging the organization. When the electricity fails or an employee attempts to cheat, the structure imposed by security safeguards should contain the damage to some reasonable extent.

It is an unstated tenet of the IS security profession that a system constrained to "allowed behavior" is of greater benefit to an organization than an uncontrolled system. But there is an underlying assumption of this tenet that make these objectives increasingly anachronistic in many highly competitive organizations. This assumption states that we are capable of predicting the allowed behavior for an adequate period of time. This assumption reveals the essence of the second order security problem, and may be faulty to the assumed degree in certain kinds of organizations. The next section will consider this potential fault in depth.

4. ORGANIZATIONAL UNPREDICTABILITY

Rapid adaptation is fast becoming one key characteristic for the management of commercial success. The adapt-or-die concept underlies many of the trends that have washed over modern IS management in recent times, such as fast-changing, strategic information systems (*cf.* Rockart 1988; Eisenhardt 1989, 1990) and business process reengineering (Hammer 1990; Davenport and Short 1990). This concept prescribes an increasing need for IS security managers to cope with unpredicted change in their organizations. The growing importance of organizational adaptability and the consequent organizational unpredictability are intensifying the second order security problem.

Adaptive organizations represent a radical transformation in the context for information systems (Smithson, Baskerville and Ngwenyama 1994). An adaptive organization will be able to change its own forms in response to rapid shifts in the nature of its market and its economic or political environment. From the security viewpoint, it is important to note that this adaptability is organizationally distributive. It materializes as a trend in an organization for its entire cadre of elements to independently seek to become more flexible and adaptive (Florida 1991; Kraft and Truex 1992).

Adaptive organizational forms are not conducive to centralized control. They are characterized by loose and shifting internal structures; diffused autonomy; fuzzy boundaries with trading partners, governments, and services; and strategic plans that swell from within the organization rather than being rationally dictated from the CEO.

Information systems spontaneity is a consequence of this rapid-paced organizational adaptivity. For flexibility, organizations must create spontaneous information systems that can be quickly reshaped to provide different processing and structures for data. In some cases, information technology may be the very "stuff" of these new organizational forms — the underlying, enabling factor that triggered the volatile environment in the first place (*cf.* McFarlan 1991). At the very least, rapid-paced change in information technology is an important consequence of these new organizational forms (*cf.* Blackler 1988).

This spontaneity materializes in reoriented IS development paradigms and technologies. Flexible development paradigms revolve around prototyping, end-user development and packaged software. Flexible information technologies include "downsizing" to smaller, cheaper computers, the drive for open systems and interconnectivity between heterogenous computing machinery, highly flexible client-server architectures, and local area networks. Hypertext and hypermedia, perhaps the most flexible information resources on the market, are among the fastest-growing technology segments (especially on the Internet).

Taken as a whole, the trends to new organizational forms that are rapidly adaptive, to decentralized and small-scale information systems development, and to easily-reconfigured open systems and flexible technologies represent no less than a complete revolution for the security and control of organizational computing assets. That is, the central data processing management must yield direct control over these corporate assets to line management (Rockart 1988). Attempts by information systems staff to regain centralized control over these systems could very well represent a threat to organizational survival. It is in this regard that many aspects of current centralized computer security practice are becoming part of the anachronism of monolithic computing resource management in adaptive organizations.

5. SECURITY AS ENTROPY: COPING WITH ORGANIZATIONAL CHANGE

The second-order costs of information systems security are illustrative of a class of inhibitive organizational structures that constrain adaption. Inhibitive structures, like the firewall and scavenging safeguards described earlier, increase the amount of work within the organization under conditions of change. From a systems science viewpoint, we could say that the human organization or its environment are changing around a set of fixed structures. These structures may not have been inhibitive originally, but may become so because they do not exactly match the "new" organization or its "new" environment. Consequently, additional work is required to convert input or output forms such that they match the new requirements and to cope with the inhibitive aspects of the structures.

From a strictly systems perspective, we could consider an organization as a complex social system. The inhibitive structures and the additional work constitute incoherent energy, since their outputs are not discharged from the system and their collective activities could be eliminated completely without any impact on the system outputs. Leifer (1989) modeled organizational change on cycles of rising "entropy," a term he uses to describe energies such as an increase in inhibitive and coping activities under conditions of organizational change.

Security safeguards, in situations of rapid and unpredictable organizational change and adaption, can contribute to organizational entropy by creating unnecessary coping activities. The cost of these safeguards is, to a certain degree, the cost of the related entropy. Unacceptably high entropy related to inhibitive safeguards constitutes the second-order security dilemma.

6. ISSUES OF SECOND-ORDER INFORMATION RISK IN ADAPTIVE ORGANIZATIONS

An understanding of this second-order problem in information systems security raises at least two groups of important interlinked practical and research issues. First, the linkage of second-order costs with entropy suggest that security managers in adaptive organizations need new security management models and techniques. Second, the IS field needs new system safeguards that are less inhibitive in situations of rapid or unpredictable change.

There are at least three aspects of security management that need further investigation. These aspects include needs assessment models for determining the degree of flexibility required in security, organizational models for security roles and activity models for security organizations.

Under current models, security management is primarily seen as a technical problem. Recognition of the second-order dilemma implies thematic changes in the way organizations manage their security and design their safeguards. The security management process may require a basis in a review of overall organizational trends, considering if the organization is exhibiting characteristics of adaptive behavior. This means that security management might begin by reviewing indicators of key adaptive characteristics in the organization such as cross-functional teams, downsizing, product specialization, or an increasing dependence on virtual organizations. Such indicators could be evidence of the distribution of authority downward in the organization. Security management might also require studies of the role of information assets in the organization, looking for patterns of almost continuous change in the methods or procedures for information processing. Based on such indicators and studies, security management might be able to determine the degree of flexibility required in security.

A second aspect requiring further investigation is the need for new security organizational models. For example, can additional staff can be "co-opted" from other organizational elements to undertake cross-functional security teams? Could the security organization function as a network throughout the corporate organization? Can security authority be dispersed throughout the organization? Given that centralized control over security is impractical in highly flexible distributed systems, perhaps even the tiniest distinct group of system users should have a designated security manager responsible for ensuring the protection of the information assets controlled by the group. Under such a model, the professional security staff would no longer be the entire organizational security team, but rather would be the apex of a much larger, possibly informal organizational security contingent.

The third aspect regards new activity models for the professional security staff. With regard to adaptive elements in the organization, perhaps the major role of the professional staff would shift away from enforcing controls and auditing operations toward training and consulting. This may be required because users will start making key decisions about how to safeguard and protect information. Consequently the security training mission may have to expand to support end-users and co-opted security managers who will be making final decisions about information safeguards under their authority. Such co-opted security managers might need to be regularly exposed to both new and existing techniques which they might be able to employ for their local information security.

A second group of practical and research issues arises in the need for less-inhibitive system safeguards. This need can be illustrated by considering three potential aspects of such safeguards.

One aspect is the possible increased reliance on people for safeguards rather than complete reliance on rigid technologies. This might involve the use of manual procedures and policies as the basis for safeguards under the assumption that human behavior is more flexible and more easily adaptable than programs or machinery. Proper user conduct can effectively prevent privacy violations (e.g., abstain from and report browsing behavior), virus infections (e.g., protect against and report foreign executables), fraud (e.g., maintain separation of functions), and denial of resources (e.g., careful user password management) without intruding in any severe way on system flexibility.

A second aspect of adaptive security could involve increasing the dependence on logical safeguards. Logical safeguards, especially where these are data-oriented, are thought to be more flexible than physical safeguards (Baskerville 1988). This may not only improve organizational flexibility, but also systems security because physical safeguards may be the easiest to be circumvented when the system no longer matches its environment. For example, embedded control fields and check digits can remain effective even when the data procedures, technology or personnel are changed.[1] Other examples include data classification schemes, non-transparent file encryption, and password/passphrase enforcement.

A third aspect would be the potential for temporary, throw-away security. This might involve the use of small-scale physical or logical safeguards and technology that could be changed piecemeal with increasing frequency in highly adaptive environments. For example, an organization might choose to protect access to its network by controlling access to each desktop system individually. This might prove less expensive and more flexible than centralized accounts using elaborate server software. By minimizing the investment in expensive, highly structural security elements, the security might come to rely on cheap, flexible elements that can be discarded sooner (or redeployed elsewhere). This throw-away safeguard proclivity could also involve an increased use of software-based rather than hardware-based safeguard elements. These disposable safeguards could include security elements for encryption, communications firewalls, user identification, and access control.

7. DEALING WITH PRACTICAL IMPLICATIONS

These issues illustrate the fundamental practical implications that arise from an understanding of the second order security problem. There is clearly a need for empirical research and practical experimentation with such alternative models of security management and safeguards design.

---

[1]It is an established tenet in information engineering that data is more stable than processing (Finkelstein 1989). This means that controls primarily based on data tend to be flexible across more volatile process changes.

Although security is a sensitive and difficult area for practical experimentation, useful progress is being made.

For example, the Canadian Computer Security Establishment developed a focus on flexibility and localized autonomy out of its process for setting a federal guideline for risk management of computer information systems in the Government of Canada. The working group that regarded managerial considerations became particularly concerned with adopting a risk management methodology that was flexible enough to be applied in large, complex installations (e.g., a large air base), as well as small, simple installations (e.g., a small, remote police post).

Rather than seek a single method, dictated from the central government security establishment, the working group concentrated on distributed security decision-making. That is, instead of completely defining the risk assessment process to be universally applied throughout the Government of Canada, the exact decision would be deferred to the localized agencies responsible for the computing elements. The summary of the recommendations appear in Verrett and Hysert (1993).

The approach recommended by the working group was oriented toward centralized standard-setting, rather than centralized control. The central authority would set the criteria for the process of risk assessment, and defer the determination of the exact process to the local agency. Even the specification of a range of techniques together with criteria for choosing among these techniques was seen to exclude the use of ideal, unique approaches that might occur to managers "on the scene." Instead, the recommendations suggest the criteria by which a trusted local manager might determine whether the risk management process was successful. While examples of risk assessment techniques may be suggested, it would not be mandatory to choose one of the examples. The local manager would be free to innovate in situations where such innovation, in the judgement of that local manager, seemed to be required.

8. CONCLUSION

It is the nature of information security safeguards to be stable, constraining structures in organizations. These security structures should match the organization and its environment. Where the environment changes rapidly and the organization becomes highly adaptive, organizational elements must engage in coping activities to compensate for mismatches between the safeguard structures and the organization's changed needs. In such situations, the safeguards and the coping activities constitute one component of organizational entropy. If the change is unpredictable and fast-paced, security can magnify the entropy and help destroy the organization. This is the second-order security dilemma: strong security (severe constraints) may damage the organization which it is intended to protect.

Security management and safeguards design could more closely consider this second-order problem. Such considerations raise issues of security organization and flexible safeguard design. There is potential for improving the security in rapidly adapting and spontaneous information systems, while reducing organizational entropy and improving performance. Early experiments with such second-order thinking are possible, as illustrated by the Canadian Computer Security Establishment example.

9. REFERENCES

Baskerville, R. *Designing Information Systems Security.* Chichester: J. Wiley, 1988.

Baskerville, R. "Information Systems Security Design Methods: Implications for Information Systems Development." *Computing Surveys,* Volume 25, Number 4, December 1993, pp. 375-414.

Baskerville, R. "Risk Analysis as a Source of Professional Knowledge." *Computers & Security,* Volume 10, Number 8, December 1991, pp. 749-764.

Blackler, F. "Information Technologies and Organizations: Lessons from the 1980s and Issues for the 1990s." *Journal of Occupational Psychology,* Volume 61, 1988, pp. 113-127.

Courtney, R. "Security Risk Assessment in Electronic Data Processing." *AFIPS Conference Proceedings NCC,* Volume 46, 1977, pp. 97-104.

Davenport, T., and Short, J. "The New Industrial Engineering: Information Technology and Business Process Redesign." *Sloan Management Review,* Volume 31, Number 4, Summer 1990, pp. 11-27.

Eisenhardt, K. "Making Fast Strategic Decision in High-Velocity Environments." *Academy of Management Journal,* Volume 32, Number 3, (September 1989, pp. 543-576.

Eisenhardt, K. "Speed and Strategic Choice: How Managers Accelerate Decision Making." *California Management Review,* Volume 32, Number 3, Spring 1990, pp. 39-54.

Finkelstein, C. *An Introduction to Information Engineering: From Strategic Planning to Information Systems.* Sydney: Addison-Wesley, 1989.

Florida, R. "The new industrial revolution." *Futures,* July/August 1991, pp. 559-576.

Hammer, M. "Reengineering Work: Don't Automate, Obliterate." *Harvard Business Review,* Volume 90, Number 4, July-August 1990, pp. 104-112.

Kraft, P., and Truex, D. "Postmodern Management and the Modern Industrial Corporation." Annual Meeting of the Society for the Study of Social Problems, Pittsburgh, Pennsylvania, August 1992.

Leifer, R. "Understanding Organizational Transformation Using a Dissipative Structure Model." *Human Relations,* Volume 42, Number 10, 1989, pp. 899-916.

Madsen, W. *Handbook of Personal Data Protection.* New York: Stockton Press, 1992.

McFarlan, F. W. "The Expert's Opinion — Keynote Speech for the 1991 Information Resources Management Association International Conference in Memphis, Tennessee, May 1991." *Information Resources Management Journal*, Volume 4, Number 4, Fall 1991, pp. 39-41.

National Research Council. *Computers At Risk: Safe Computing in The Information Age.* Computer Science and Telecommunications Board, System Security Study Committee. Washington: National Academy Press, 1991.

Neumann, P. G. *Computer Related Risks.* New York: ACM Press, 1995.

Ozier, W. "Risk Quantification Problems and Bayesian Decision Support System Solutions." *Information Age*, Volume 11, Number 4, October 1989, pp. 229-234.

Parker, D. "Seventeen Information Security Myths Debunked." In K. Dittrich, S. Rautakivi, and J. Saari (Editors), *Proceedings of The Sixth IFIP International Conference on Computer Security and Information Integrity in Our Changing World.* Amsterdam: North-Holland, 1990, pp. 363-370.

Rockart, J. "The Line Takes the Leadership — Is Management in a Wired Society." *Sloan Management Review* Volume 29, Number Summer 1988, pp. 57-64.

Smithson, S.; Baskerville, R.; and Ngwenyama, O. "Perspectives on Information Technology and New Emergent Forms of Organizations." In R. Baskerville, S. Smithson, O. Ngwenyama and J. DeGross (Editors), *Transforming Organizations with Information Technology*. Amsterdam: North-Holland, 1994, pp. 3-13.

U.S. Department of Commerce, National Bureau of Standards. *Guideline for Automatic Data Processing Risk Analysis*, Federal Information Processing Standards Publication FIPS 65, August 1979.

Verrett, R., and Hysert, R. "Summary of Findings, Working Group 2, Managerial and Structural Issues in the Draft Risk Management Framework." In *Proceedings Fifth International Computer Security Risk Management Workshop*. Ottawa: National Institute of Standards and Technology and Communications Security Establishment, 1993, pp. 7-9.

About the Author

Richard Baskerville is a visiting associate professor at Copenhagen Business School, on leave from the School of Management at Binghamton University. His research focusses on security and methods in information systems, their interaction with organizations and research methods. He is an associate editor of *MIS Quarterly* and *The Information Systems Journal*. Baskerville's practical and consulting experience includes advanced information system designs for the U.S. Defense and Energy Departments. He is vice chair of the IFIP Working Group 8.2, and a Chartered Engineer under the British Engineering Council. Baskerville holds M.Sc. and Ph.D. degrees from the London School of Economics.

16

Black Boxes, Non-Human Stakeholders and the Translation of IT Through Mediation

Richard Vidgen
Tom McMaster
Information Systems Research Centre
University of Salford

Abstract

The adoption of technological determinism or social constructivism (or a dialectical combination of the two) is considered to be problematic due to a lack of symmetry between organizational work and technology. Latour's notion of quasi-objects is introduced to mitigate the limitations of an artificial distinction between object and subject worlds that results from the adoption of a dualistic approach. The idea of a mediated network of technology and organizational context is proposed, in which Information Technology implementations become black boxes as a result of dissemination through space and time. This process requires that allies be enrolled and controlled, which in turn indicates a need for the interests of relevant stakeholders (human and non-human) to be understood. The ideas of quasi-objects and mediated networks are applied to a case study of an automated access control system for a car park. The case study demonstrates the potential impact of (information) technology on organizational work through physical and informating changes in a pluralistic situation.

1. INTRODUCTION

Methods used in support of Information Technology (IT) have a long tradition of separating "what" and "how" issues. For example, in SSADM (Structured Systems Analysis and Design Method) there is a clear distinction, in theory at least, between analysis, which addresses *what* is needed, and design, which is concerned with *how* requirements are to be met (CCTA 1990). In the life-cycle model (Boehm 1976), these stages are then followed by detailed physical design and construction, testing, implementation, and maintenance. However, in practice it is difficult to separate the issues of what and how into successive time periods and the two can only be separated with any confidence once a computer system has been built (Budde, et al. 1992); while a computer system is being constructed, what and how issues are co-present. Furthermore, the presence of ongoing maintenance to computer systems suggests a process of continuous (re)building in which what and how issues reach temporary rather than final separation. A soft systems approach, such as SSM (Soft Systems Methodology), avoids the means-ends limitation by widening the debate to include issues associated with "why" and a recognition that although change should be systemically desirable, it must be culturally feasible (Checkland 1981; Checkland and Scholes 1990). In the Information System development process, neither the hard approach typified by structured methods nor soft approaches such as SSM gives a symmetrical weight to the organizational work to be supported and the IT that might be deployed. For example, in SSADM Version 4, specific technologies and platforms that might be used are not addressed until stage 4, Technical System Options. Stages 1, 2, and 3 of SSADM address Investigation of Current Environment, Business System Options, and Requirements Definition respectively. These stages focus on understanding and specifying real world business requirements. With SSM, the exhortation is to think conceptually and to avoid contamination from the real world when constructing human activity system models. SSM conceptual models are then placed in a dialectical relationship with a real-world problem situation.

This paper is concerned with a symmetrical treatment of organizational work and IT and we seek to avoid the limitations of an artificial distinction between technological determinism and social constructivism (Woolgar 1994). To do this, we will draw principally from Latour (1987, 1993). The structure of the paper is as follows. In section two, the notions of mediation, networks, and black boxes are introduced. Section three explores stakeholders and interests. The ideas from sections two and three are then applied to a case study in section four, followed by a discussion of the findings in section five. Section six contains conclusions and thoughts on further research.

2. QUASI-OBJECTS, NETWORKS, AND BLACK BOXES

Information System (IS) development methods that adopt a separation of what and how reflect a dualism that can lead to a separation of analysis and design, organizational work (context) and technology. An ontological distinction that pervades IS development methods is objectivism and subjectivism. When combined with epistemological issues, this distinction leads to a seemingly implacable dualism of scientism and interpretivism. Burrell and Morgan (1979) used the objective/subjective distinction and a radical change/regulation distinction to derive four paradigms. They consider that these paradigms should be closed:

> We firmly believe that each of the paradigms can only establish itself at the level of organizational analysis if it is true to itself. Contrary to the widely held belief that synthesis and mediation between paradigms is what is required, we argue that the real need is for **paradigmatic closure**....the paradigms reflect four alternative realities. They stand as four mutually exclusive ways of seeing the world.
> [Burrell and Morgan 1979, pp. 397-398, emphasis added]

The four paradigm model has been taken up in IS research, particularly by Hirschheim and Klein (1989). Willmott (1990) has reported on developments that go beyond paradigmatic closure, highlighting the work of Berger and Luckman (1966) and structuration theory (Giddens 1984). An implication of structuration theory is that the objective and subjective can be seen as a duality, in which structures of signification constrain action while at the same time those very structures can be changed by action. A critique of dualistic thinking is provided by Latour (1993), whose analysis directly addresses the relationship between *object* worlds, such as the technical artefacts of IT, and the *subject* world of society. This analysis is described in overview in the next section.

2.1   Quasi-Objects

Latour argues that one aim of the modernist project is purification: the separation of an objective and given natural world from a socially-constructed subject world. Modernism contains a paradox insofar as it espouses separation of natural and social worlds while relying upon their inseparability for its successes. However, the middle ground is more than a meeting place of natural and social worlds:

> We do not need to attach our explanations to the two pure forms known as the Object or Subject/Society, because these are, on the contrary, partial and purified results of the central practice that is our sole concern. The explanation we seek will indeed obtain Nature and Society, but only as a final outcome, not as a beginning. Nature does revolve, but not around the Subject/Society. It revolves around the collective that produces things and people. The Subject does revolve, but not around Nature. It revolves around the collective out of which people and things are generated. At last the Middle Kingdom is represented. Natures and societies are its satellites. [Latour 1993, p. 79]

With respect to IT, the quest for purification leads us to make artificial distinctions, such as the separation of context from technology, conceptual model from real-world, incremental change from radical change, analysis from design. The tendency is toward purified subject and object worlds that are either kept separate or explored through dialectical movements. However, dialectics is not a solution:

> Linking the two poles of nature and society by as many arrows and feedback loops as one wishes does not relocate the quasi-objects or quasi-subject that I want to take into account. On the contrary, dialectics makes the ignorance of that locus still deeper than in the dualist paradigm since it feigns to overcome it by loops and spirals and other complex acrobatic figures. Dialectics literally beats around the bush....Quasi-objects are much more social, much more fabricated, much more collective than the "hard" parts of nature, but they are in no way the arbitrary receptacles of a full-fledged society. On the other hand they are much more real, nonhuman and objective than those shapeless screens on which society — for unknown reasons — needed to be "projected." [Latour 1993, p.55]

Latour proposes "quasi-objects" and a constitution that retains elements of pre-modernism, modernism, and postmodernism (1993, p. 66). We have paraphrased this constitution and amended it with respect to IS development:

- the non-separability of the common production of Information Technology and organizational work/context;
- the inseparable objectivization of Information Technology and subjectivization of organizational work/context;
- freedom is a capacity for sorting and recombining sociotechnical imbroglios;
- the replacement of the clandestine proliferation of technological/organizational hybrids by their regulated and commonly-agreed-upon production.

The modernist division between nature and society has scientists speaking on behalf of things which cannot speak for themselves (mutes) and sovereigns speaking on behalf of subjects. The scientist represents nature faithfully and the sovereign represents what the subjects would have said if they had all been able to speak at once. In terms of system development there are developers who represent "things," such as software, and users who represent their communities (often known as "key" users). However, there is the possibility of a double betrayal: the developers might be talking about themselves rather than the technology that they represent and the key user might be pursuing his/her own interests rather than those of the user community at large. How can we know whether the developers and user representatives translate or betray? Latour argues that it is our attempt to separate nature and society that is the problem (1993, pp. 142-145). Representing nature and representing society are not two problems of representation but one. The "parliament of things" is a place where technology is present with its representatives (suppliers and developers of IT) who speak in its name; society (users) is present, but with the objects that form its ballast. Latour argues that this view need not lead to a revolution since all that it requires is a ratification of what we have always done, albeit clandestinely.

We now turn to the question of how these technical/organizational hybrids are combined and how black boxes of hard(*ened*) fact emerge.

2.2   Networks and Black Boxes

Rather than posit that science and technology and society are separable, Latour proposes that we are faced by a "gamut of weaker and stronger associations" (1987, p. 259), where to understand what facts and machines are is the same task as understanding who the people are. Adopting this approach, we see IT not as diffusion of technology but as translation carried out through networks. These networks will be shorter or longer, with weaker and stronger associations, possibly containing obligatory passage points (strongholds in the network, such as the law of gravity). IS development is concerned with transforming a "lash-up" (Law 1986) of heterogeneous, disorderly, and unreliable allies into an automaton, which, once it resembles an organized whole, can be considered as a black box. Thus, we can picture a sophisticated word-processor, such as Microsoft's Word for Windows, as a black box that hides many complicated parts and is supported by a complex commercial network of sales, support, marketing, and product development. Whether we are concerned with scientific facts or with technical artefacts:

> The problem of the builder of "fact" is the same as that of the builder of "objects": how to convince others, how to control their behavior, how to gather sufficient resources in one place, how to have the claim or the object spread out in time and space. In both cases, **it is the others who have the power to transform the**

claim or the object into a durable whole. [Latour 1987, p. 131, emphasis added]

Latour outlines a number of strategies for enrolling others in the creation of a black box: to appeal to the other's explicit interests; to get the others to follow our interests; to suggest a short detour (this is particularly strong when their road is blocked); to reshuffle interests and goals by tactics such as inventing new goals, inventing new groups; by becoming indispensable to the others. To build a black box, others have to be enrolled so that the black box is bought and spread across time and space; once enrolled, they need to be kept in line so that what is disseminated remains broadly the same.

In the next section consideration is given to how the motivations of *the others* might be described, providing a basis for an analysis of interests and goals.

3. INTERESTS

The generation of black boxes through networks raises a particular issue: who are the *others* and what are their *interests*. Latour seems to assume that the identification of others and understanding their interests is not especially problematic. Interests are defined as *inter-esse*, lying between actors and their goals. Latour argues that resources will "jump" at the chance to translate claims and technical artefacts that further their goals (1987, p. 109) and that the formation of black boxes is promoted when interests move in the same direction. In our opinion, Latour's view of interests and goals is problematic insofar as it supports a view that goals have an objective existence, act as the motivation for the actions of the others, and thereby impact the formation, strengthening, and weakening of networks. Rather than see goals as determining action, it is perhaps tempting to argue that goals are socially constructed through action. However, all this achieves is the establishment of another binary opposition, goals as objective entities and goals as social constructs, and if it is not appropriate to nature and society then why should it be appropriate to actions and goals?

Viewing goals and actions as outcomes of the mediation of interests accords with the concept of quasi-objects described above: goals and actions are the outcomes of a process of purification rather than goals causing actions or actions creating goals. This view of goals and interests has parallels with structuration theory (Giddens 1984), in which there are three dimensions of structure and interaction: signification/communication, domination/power, and legitimation/sanction, mediated by an interpretative scheme, facility, and norm respectively. Structuration theory has been used by Walsham (1993) to provide a link between the context and content of change with the process of change; considerable attention is given in Walsham's analysis to the interests of those involved. In our opinion, the adoption of a structurational view of interests makes it possible to view actions and goals as co-present, mediated through interests, thereby allowing a symmetrical approach to interests to be taken that parallels the symmetry of technology and organizational work. In such a view, interests represent a mediation between goals (structure) and action by the others. This implies that action is constrained by goals and at the same time can result in changes to goals. The meaningfulness of the goals is mediated through an interpretive scheme that addresses interests. Structuration theory provides a powerful framework for understanding the implementation of IT through the dispensation of power (control over resources) and the legitimation of action (appeal to norms). In this paper we focus on understanding the goals and the interests of the others, but we are aware that the ways in which interests are pursued in actuality can be understood through further dimensions of structuration theory.

In analyzing the goals and interests of significant others we draw from work on stakeholder analysis, soft systems thinking, and multiple perspectives.

3.1 Stakeholder Identification and Representation

One task for the implementors of IT is to identify in a specific problem situation who the others are. The rich picture is a Soft Systems Methodology (SSM) technique that allows a complex and messy problem situation (Ackoff 1974) to be expressed informally, including relationships and value judgements (Checkland and Scholes 1990; Lewis 1994; Stowell and West 1994). Rich pictures are helpful in gaining a heterogeneous understanding of a situation and can be used to represent human and non-human allies. There is no formal notation for a rich picture, although some diagrammatic conventions, such as crossed swords to indicate conflict and an eyeball to represent a concern, have been used widely. The rich picture has been used to identify the involved parties who have a stake in a problem situation (Vidgen 1994; Wood, et al. 1995) and we propose here that rich pictures can be used to provide a static analysis of actor networks.

Stakeholder analysis is a well-established technique, which in its evolved form states that: "Stakeholders are any individual, group, organization, institution that can affect as well as be affected by an individual's, group's, organization's, or institution's policy or policies" (Mitroff and Linstone 1993, p. 141).

An organization comprises the entire set of relationships it has with itself and its stakeholders (Mitroff and Linstone 1993, p. 142) and, as these relationships change over time, then so the organization changes, becoming in effect a different entity. This view of organization is sympathetic with Vickers' notion of appreciation and a concern with relationship-maintaining and judgement rather than the "poverty-stricken notion of goal-seeking" (Checkland and Casar 1986). However, this is very much a social view of stakeholders and organizations. To bring in non-human allies requires a new definition of *stakeholder*. We propose that:

> *Stakeholders are any human or non-human organization unit that can affect as well as be affected by a human or non-human organization unit's policy or policies.*

In the above definition, organization unit is used to cater for individuals through institutions and, for example, a computer chip through the interNet. We use the word organization in the tradition of cybernetics where the organization of a system defines the identity of the system (Beer 1981; Maturana and Varela 1980), as well as reminding the analyst of the recursive properties of organization units in a systems approach.

In different situations there might be further non-human stakeholders. For example, in the aerospace industry real-time flight control systems must be able to cope with the low temperatures associated with high altitudes; in such a case, the weather can be thought of as a stakeholder. As these stakeholders cannot speak for themselves, representatives need to be appointed. In one sense this is no different from the task of identifying representatives of human stakeholder groups, since assumptions need to be made and therefore the analyst is likely to be faced with the same difficulties: is the representative faithful to the interests of the stakeholder group? It is unlikely that it will be possible for each and every member of a stakeholder group to be involved, hence the need to appoint a "sovereign" to represent the interests of the subjects. Similarly there is a need to appoint a representative for the non-human stakeholders. Having identified human and non-human stakeholders/actors, we now consider how interests can be understood in practice.

3.2   Understanding Stakeholder Interests

Habermas' (1972) work on knowledge interests provides a framework for exploring stakeholder interests. These knowledge interests are technical, practical, and emancipatory, and have been described by Dahlbom and Mathiassen (1993) and Flood and Jackson (1991) as follows: the technical interest is concerned with control and labor and can be characterized by the metaphor of the engineer; the practical interest is concerned with interpretation and language (the facilitator); the emancipatory interest is concerned with criticism and power (the emancipator). The multiple perspective approach (Linstone 1989; Mitroff and Linstone 1993) also draws upon the idea of different domains of knowledge. Mitroff and Linstone consider three perspectives: Technical, Organization, and Personal. The Technical perspective is concerned with a scientific world-view, logic, rationality, modeling and analysis, and a claim of objectivity. The Organization perspective is concerned with social entities, politics, and the establishment of shared understandings. The Personal perspective addresses individuals and factors such as power, influence, prestige, learning, values, and experience. In order to understand stakeholder interests we propose that multiple perspectives/different knowledge interests will need to be considered: no single perspective will, by itself, be sufficient in gaining an understanding of complex and messy situations.

A multiple perspective approach is adopted in this paper for the purposes of gaining a rich understanding of interests and concerns. We have defined the following categories: the *Rational* perspective is used to reflect a logical view of interests (which need not be the rationality of science); the *Organizational* perspective is concerned with social and political interests; the *Individual* perspective allows personal concerns, such as status, career progression, job security, to be included. This model is referred to as ROI. The presence of an R perspective does not mean that the O and I perspectives are irrational, nor that the R perspective should necessarily be privileged with respect to the other perspectives.

In the next section, the ideas developed in sections 2 and 3 are applied to a case study of technology implementation.

4. CASE STUDY

The case study concerns the implementation of an innovative car park system, which is both an information system and an access control system. It has been chosen because it involves IT (and thus a data component), physical equipment, and heterogeneous allies. The choice and justification of research method is presented first, followed by the background to the case study.

4.1   Research Method

We are primarily concerned with gaining understanding of a particular problem situation and the assessment of the potential value of using the ideas described in sections 2 and 3 above in the implementation of IT. According to Zmud, Olson and Hauser (1989), case studies may be a highly appropriate medium. Case studies offer a holistic (as opposed to a reductionist) view of the processes involved (Gummesson 1988) and a high level of "richness of worldly realism" (Mason 1989). There are however disadvantages, in that case studies have an inherent predisposition to weak internal and external validity (Zmud Olson and Hauser (1989), or as Mason puts it, a lack of control and a corresponding difficulty in generalizing the results. Gummesson disputes this when he says that it is no longer obvious that a limited number of observations cannot be used for the basis of generalization, any more than it is still obvious that large numbers of observations will lead necessarily to more meaningful generalizations (1988, p.78-79). In a similar vein, Walsham describes an interpretivist (soft) approach to case study in which he argues that generalization from an individual case or cases is not a matter of statistical validity but the "plausibility and cogency of the logical reasoning used in describing the results from the cases, and in drawing conclusions from them" (1993, p. 15). We use the ideas developed in sections 2 and 3 as a way of understanding the case study presented here.

4.2   Background to the Case Study

In 1993, an institute of higher education in the UK purchased a new automatic access control system (AACS) for each of its three main car parking areas. The system has a number of unconventional features including proximity cards, retractable steel bollards, and an "invisible" card reader, which we briefly describe.

Proximity card technology. These are cards which resemble "magic wands" in the sense that they need only be waved around close to the "reader" rather than inserted into a slot in order to operate the system. The cards each contain a unique code which has been allocated to the card holder. When this is presented to the system, a check is made against a database image which is downloaded periodically from a personal computer (PC) to the car park site computer, via modem links, for validation. The system also includes a more conventional "slot," into which a token may be inserted, for casual users or visitors. Tokens may be purchased from vending machines that are located in the entrances of a number of campus buildings. Information held on the database includes car registration and make, owner's name, department and status (e.g., staff, student). Information concerning usage of the system, either collectively for the three sites, from individual sites, or indeed for individual use, can be uploaded and processed as required. The times individuals enter and leave car parks can be monitored, the identities of those (registered users) who are in the organization at any given time can be ascertained, and many other ways of statistically manipulating such data for management or other purposes is possible. In this respect we can describe the system as an information system that utilizes IT.

Retractable steel telescopic bollards. These are unusual compared with the more conventional "arm" type wooden barrier with which most drivers are familiar. When retracted, these bollards are flush with the ground. Associated with the bollard are three induction loops, embedded in each of the access roads, designed to detect the presence of motor vehicles in the system. These are critical to the safe operation of the system. If a vehicle were unfortunate enough to stall over the bollard, for example, its detection on the loop ensures that the bollard remains retracted.

Hidden card reader. The card reader is housed within a brick structure, and is therefore not visible to the user. There is a metal plate on the brick housing which indicates where the proximity card should be generally waved about, but there is no direct access to the reader, which picks up the code programmed into each card. The system has other unusual features, but those which we have described are most relevant for our purposes, since they are obvious to the car park users, and are therefore of some significance, as we shall see.

4.3   Implementation Problems Arise

Within four weeks of implementing this system, there were four accidents which involved vehicles colliding with the bollards, causing damage to the vehicles. Following the final accident the systems were shut down by the organization's managers and they have remained so since then.

Accident Number 1. The first accident happened during the testing period following installation of the system. The car park capacity variable had been set to ten and, on entering, the tenth car triggered the "car park full" sign, as indeed it should, but it also triggered the bollard to rise despite the fact that a car following was also "in" the system. This resulted in a minor collision. A small software change was all that was necessary to correct this, so that even if the car park is full, if there is a car in the system, then the bollard will not rise.

Accident Number 2. The next accident also occurred during the testing phase. Someone entered the car park through the entry road, but realizing he/she would have to "pay" to leave, made a sharp U-turn and tried to exit through the entry road, not realizing that the bollard, which had been retracted during entry, was now on its way back up. There was a minor collision. The system has now been modified so that even if a car drives the wrong way through the entrance route, when the induction loop detects the vehicle the bollard will retract. This has compromised security to some extent.

Accidents 3 and 4. The next two accidents are more difficult to explain, since both people claim (in separate incidents) to have presented their proximity cards, received a green "go" light, and attempted to leave the car park. As they approached the bollard, it began to rise and they collided with it. They each tell the same story but one difference, which may be significant, is that one happened on the first day that the system became operational, the other approximately four weeks later. It was after the fourth accident that the system was shut down.

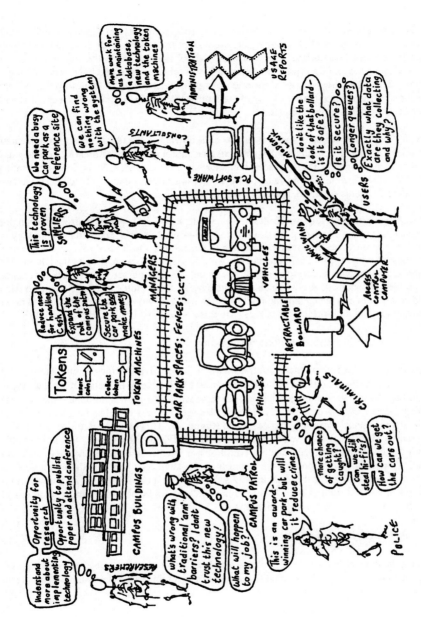

Figure 1. A Rich Picture

After the third accident, the designers looked for every conceivable way to explain how this could have happened. They concluded that the only remote possibility was that there had been some "crosstalk" between the induction loops controlling the exit bollard, where the accident occurred, and the induction loop on the nearby entrance road, over which a car could have been passing at the time. The odds, they say, were enormously against this, but it did seem to offer the only explanation. They adjusted the sensitivity of the loops accordingly, so that such an event is now (it is claimed by the suppliers) impossible.

Following the fourth accident, the system was shut down and the management brought in an independent technical consultancy firm to examine thoroughly the hardware, software and operations of the system. They concluded that the system was sound, safe and in good working order. They furthermore tried to recreate the conditions under which it was claimed the two unexplained accidents occurred, but they were unable to do so.

The AACS was turned off four weeks after it was commissioned for production use. The campus management are now considering what action to take — whether to abandon the technology or to attempt to re-introduce it. At this point, one of the authors was invited to conduct a review of the problems with the implementation of the AACS. As will be seen, despite the adoption of interpretive case study as a research method, we do not consider ourselves to be wholly outside of the problem situation and we have included ourselves as a stakeholder group. Our motivation for this is that, while investigating the politics of the case study organization, we wish to make explicit our identity and surface our beliefs (Knights and Murray 1994, p. 16).

4.4   Investigating the Problem Situation

Figure 1 is a rich picture representation of the situation, as perceived by the current authors. We have placed the car park and AACS at the center of the rich picture, reflecting its role as a way of organizing our thoughts about the situation. In some ways, the more significant issues emerge from the periphery, such as the strained relationship between campus patrol and managers. Using the rich picture, a stakeholder map was developed (Figure 2). This map shows a number of non-human stakeholders: the AACS, vehicles, the physical car park, and the campus. It is not possible for each and every car park user, campus patrol officer, etc. to be involved, hence the need to appoint a "sovereign" to represent the interests of the subjects. Similarly there is a need to appoint a representative for the machines. As the map in Figure 2 contains human and non-human stakeholders, it forms a basis for constituting a "parliament of things" and a symmetrical approach to technology and organizational work.

4.5   Investigating Interests

In Table 1, the interests and goals of the human stakeholders have been analyzed using the ROI approach described above. The symbol ☺ represents a favorable response, ☻ ambivalence, and ☹ resistance.

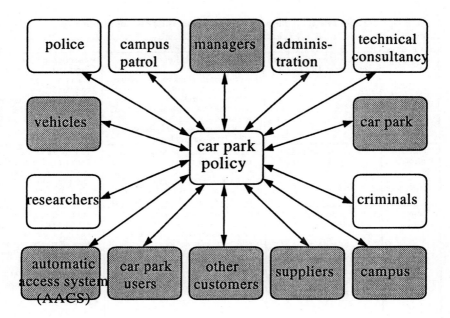

Figure 2: Stakeholder Map

The analysis in Table 1 represents assumptions about the stakeholder's interests goals and does not necessarily reflect the interests of actual stakeholders. For example, the view of "criminals" records the assumptions of the campus management and police officers (as interpreted by the researchers) and as such reflects the biases and prejudices of these parties as much as it does any interests of the criminals themselves. The stakeholder assumptions generated through ROI analysis can be mapped in terms of the degree of importance and certainty and those assumptions that are rated as important and uncertain should be explored further (Mitroff and Linstone 1993, p. 144; Vidgen 1994).

In Table 2, we have attempted to articulate the interests and goals of the non-human allies. We have drawn upon the ideas of systems thinking and catered for the different ways that non-human resources can be combined to form *component* objects with emergent properties. *Interests* have been analyzed in one dimension as we felt uncomfortable about assigning anthropomorphic properties to non-human resources, especially from an individual perspective. Rather, we consider that it is the interests of the *potential representatives* of non-human resources that we should be concerned with. The analysis of interests of technology gives a view of the situation that is complementary to the interests of human stakeholders. One benefit of the technology view is that it can surface human stakeholders that would be otherwise overlooked, such as architects, vehicle manufacturers, and vehicle insurers.

The next section looks at what we have learnt about the car park case study through the application of the ideas described in sections 2 and 3 above.

Table 1: ROI Analysis of Stakeholder Interests and Concerns

	Rational	Organizational	Individual
Managers	• increased security of the car park and the campus ☺	• car park usage statistics become available ☺ • redeployment of car park attendants to campus patrol duties ☺ • increased control over car park related activity through deployment of a reliable ally (AACS) ☺ • exploitation of revenue producing potential of car parking ☺	• career-enhancing - impressive to Institution's senior management and to peers ☺ • career-limiting if the implementation fails ☹
Administrators	• efficient administration of car park authorizations ☺	• significant change in working practice: manual system to computerized ☺ • maintenance of token machines ☺ • analysis of car park activity; administration of car park user database ☺	• fear of new technology ☹ • fears about increases in work load due to new technology ☺
Campus patrol	• increased security of the car park and the campus ☺	• change in role from car park attendants to security patrol ☺ • loss of power through erosion of self-determination ☹	• more time to be spent patrolling the campus and less in a warm hut ☹ • fears about new technology - retractable bollard ☹ • reduction in social contact with car park users ☺ • fears about unemployment through automation of security activity ☺
Car park users	• increased security of vehicle and person ☺		• possibility of monitoring of movements - surveillant properties ☺ • queues to enter and leave car park ☹ • fear of damage to vehicle by retractable bollard L
Suppliers	• a prestigious reference site for a new technology ☺	• important sale for the future of the supplier ☺	• kudos derived by salesperson ☺
Police	• a reduction in car-related crime reported ☺	• high-profile system with gold award ☺ • improved knowledge of what works in car park security ☺	• increased respect - if it works ☺
Researchers	• an opportunity to conduct research ☺	• an opportunity to publish papers and attend conferences ☺	• understand more about IT implementation issues ☺ • enhance careers through publication ☺
Criminals	• a more secure car park ☹	• vandal-proof system makes retaliation difficult ☹ • the Institution appears to be getting serious about car-related crime ☹	• higher risk of being caught ☹ • new opportunities to impress peers ☺
Other customers	• demonstration of AACS technology working effectively in a large car park ☺	• reduction in "post-purchase dissonance" ☺ • survival of supplier ☺	• successful implementation confirms "rightness" of choice and adds to job security ☺
Technical consultancy	• ascertain the technical correctness of the AACS ☺	• income from customer and potential of more AACS assignments ☺	• recognition of role of "expert" ☺

Table 2. Analysis of Non-Human Stakeholder Interests and Goals

	Components	Interests	Potential representatives
AACS	• retractable bollard • hidden card reader • induction loops • IT support - database of users, usage data • data communications • token dispensers • cash • magic wands	• to be used and maintained in accordance with manufacturers instructions • to be used for a fit purpose • security of cash proffered for tokens	• suppliers • technical consultancy • police
Vehicle	• bodywork • parts (e.g., wheels) • accessories (e.g., hi-fi) • contents (e.g., personal possessions of driver)	• to be kept in a secure situation whilst not in use (in part and in whole)	• users • vehicle manufacturers, repairers • police • insurers
Car park and campus	• location of buildings • location of car park • CCTV • car park perimeter fences • car park capacity • access roads to car park	• efficient use of car park space • efficient use of campus space • sufficient space between vehicles	• managers • architects/surveyors • public liability insurers

5. DISCUSSION

5.1 AACS: Success or Failure?

In one way the installation of this automatic access system (AACS) must be counted unequivocally a failure since the network associations were not strong enough for the AACS to be maintained as a black box in this organizational context. The campus management may have believed that it was buying a black box technology, but in the situation described in the case study the technology unraveled: the AACS is no longer a black box since its component parts have become painfully visible as different parties question whether there is a fault in the software, the induction loops, the way the car park users interact with the AACS, and so on. Should the AACS technology remain unraveled at this site and become so at further sites, then it would be reasonable to expect that, at some point, the technology will be abandoned in its entirety. Although the suppliers and other stakeholders are putting considerable effort into strengthening the associations that they believe will make the AACS successful, such an effort is constrained by time and available resources. Uniform products do not necessarily behave uniformly in different contexts and considerable and sustained effort might be needed to maintain the network of associations.

From a relativist stance, one might argue that the degree of success or failure depends upon the perception of a stakeholder (Markus 1983); for the criminal, the implementation of the AACS might be considered a "success." Although the quasi-object view allows one to make more definite judgements about success/failure, it provides little scope for debating value judgements about "good" and "bad." To make value judgements, one must consider the interests of the stakeholders and the norms that they draw upon (norms are a mediator between structures of legitimation and sanction in structuration theory). Implementation success/failure from a quasi-object perspective depends upon the ability to create and sustain black boxes; from an interest perspective, success is assessed with reference to norms. These views are not separate and exclusive and we believe that both are needed since, although it is difficult to deny the "success" of a particular black box, for example motor cars and atomic bombs, we can (and must) investigate the norms that have been drawn upon to create and sustain the network that gave rise to the black box.

5.2 AACS: The Same Technology or Different?

The AACS technology is in one sense unchanged as a result of the implementation: it still contains basically the same programs and physical components as it did before installation in this car park. In another, arguably more interesting sense, the technology has changed significantly through being *translated*. The suppliers of the AACS wish to disseminate the AACS through time and space by enrolling others. We can conceptualize that their aim is to spread the AACS through lengthening the network, while at the same time exercising control over the form of the AACS, that is over the translations that occur. In this case, the AACS has been translated in such a way that its progress through time and space has been slowed and now runs a risk of being halted altogether. There are inter-relationships between the number of people to be convinced, the angle at which claims clash with other claims, the hardening of facts, and the number of allies that have to be fetched. The failure to implement the AACS in the situation described by the case study has resulted in new claims, a hardening of facts that weaken the network, and claims that now meet at a wider angle. The AACS has been translated and, from a quasi-object point of view, is certainly not the same technology now as the AACS that the campus management bought originally.

5.3 Automation: An Unmanned Car Park?

One aim of the installation of the AACS was to allow the car park to operate unmanned. Successful implementation would have resulted in a car park that was more heavily manned than when there was a manual system. Black boxes are accompanied by many more people, as becomes evident when it fails and the allies become readily visible: the supplier (including sub-contractors who supply specialist components), campus management, campus patrol, car park users. Accordingly, there are more people involved in an unmanned car park than in a manned one, implying that there will be more associations to manage. The implication for IT is that it is erroneous to assume that automation involves fewer people; this is only true in a superficial sense, since the automation is supported by longer and more complex networks of human and non-human allies.

5.4 Automating and Informating

The AACS in becoming a black box takes on the properties of an automaton. In a manual system it would be possible, in theory, for human attendants to record the vehicle registration, time of entry, and time of departure of each and every car. The introduction of the AACS makes it possible to automate the collection of this data through a non-human car park attendant that has a more direct interest in collecting such data. The primary task of the AACS is to control entry and exit and to record these transactions; its interest is direct, whereas human attendants might be tired, uninterested, bored and disenchanted with the (often) wet weather. Even if a human attendant can collect this data, it will still need to be converted to a machine-readable form for the purposes of statistical analysis, reports and enquiries.

A successful implementation of the AACS results in the automation of the process and the AACS itself becoming an automaton with black box properties. Zuboff recognizes that there is a duality of IT — "its capacity to automate and to informate" (1988, p.390). Zuboff argues that automating is a necessary but not sufficient condition for informating and that, although IT development can proceed without consideration of the informating potential of IT, informating will still occur, but as an unintended consequence. The AACS has yet to be implemented successfully and it is therefore not possible to comment on the informating implications of the new technology. We can speculate that, for example, the availability of data that shows the time people arrive and leave could be used to analyze individual and departmental working patterns of staff and students. If the technology was extended to include movements of people around the campus, then rather more complete records of activity could be maintained. Knights and Murray argue that Zuboff gives insufficient attention to power and politics. They argue that Zuboff adopts a determinist approach in which IT is viewed as inherently progressive, leading to "less hierarchical and unequal, yet more dynamic and innovative, organizations capable of continuous learning and adaptability" (1994, p. 9). Analysis of the car park suggests that there might well be informating aspects of automation, but that these affects might not necessarily be beneficial and need to be considered in the context of power.

5.5 Impact on Organizational Work

From the perspective of the campus management, the introduction of the AACS should allow management at a distance. The creation of distance from the center has been recognized as a theme in total quality management, with accounting data being used to overcome the distance created by delegation (Munro 1995). The data capture facilities of the AACS allow the campus management to distance the car parking operations while at the same time gaining more control through the enrollment of a reliable ally — the AACS. For the campus patrol officers, the impact is not just a limited change to duties; they are being asked to transform their role from car park attendants into campus patrol officers who will work to increase and maintain the security of the campus. The campus patrol representative on the AACS implementation committee was not sufficiently strong to voice the concerns of his group, which allowed the campus management to push through the implementation of new technology in the car park. In this instance, the interests of an important stakeholder group were not represented faithfully, contributing to the failure of the implementation. Other stakeholders are also impacted. Car park users see car parking as a means to an end: it is something one does to get to work, to get to a meeting. While car parking is working, it is a black box that is *ready-to-hand* (Winograd and Flores 1986). A *breaking down*, such as the retractable bollard damaging a car or long queues to enter or leave the car park, results in the car park becoming *present-at-hand*. A successful implementation for car park users will result in a car park that is once again ready-to-hand, that is a black box. Such stakeholders are subject to second-order effects insofar as they will only come to reflect upon the technology in the event of a break-down, whereas campus patrol officers, for example, are affected directly by changes to their working practices brought about by the introduction of the AACS and will reflect actively upon the implications of the changes.

6. CONCLUSIONS AND FUTURE DIRECTION

We have argued, following Latour (1987, 1993), that a dualism of object/nature and subject/society is an artificial distinction which results in either social construction or technological determinism being privileged. A quasi-object approach focuses attention on a collective that produces things and people and a process of mediation. This view can be contrasted with the socio-technical approach (Emery and Trist 1969; Mumford and Weir 1979; Eason 1988) to Information Technology implementation in which it is assumed that object and subject worlds are different and separable and the aim is to bring together the worlds of organizational work and Information Technology. If we follow Latour's arguments, then we need to start from the premise that technical and social systems are inseparable and that any perceived separateness is a temporary outcome of purification rather than a starting point. Similarly, the assumption of separability can be found in the literature concerned with combining "hard" and "soft" approaches to information system development, as in the "grafting and embedding" distinction described by Miles (1988). However, the grafting of an interpretivist method, such as Soft Systems Methodology (SSM) (Checkland 1981; Checkland and Scholes 1990), onto a deterministic method for building computer systems is beset by practical difficulties of making the paradigmatic shift from an organizational context orientation to a technology orientation. Embedding hard methods in a soft framework has the practical advantage of privileging the soft perspective over the hard, but depends upon a dialectical relationship for its success. A quasi-object approach needs to keep subjects and objects together such that paradigm shifts that result from the artificial separation of context and technology are ameliorated. One area for future research is symmetrical information system development methods that is, methods that are based upon a duality of organizational work and Information Technology. In one sense, we are arguing that IS development methods should reflect the practice of IS development, where practice is characterized by the clandestine proliferation of technological/organizational hybrids. The theoretical basis of IS development methods needs then to be concerned more with the regulation of the production of hybrids and less with paradigms and paradigmatic incommensurability. Although considerable work is needed to explore the implications for IS development methods, a small contribution in this area is the inclusion of human and non-human stakeholders on a stakeholder map.

Through the creation and strengthening of network associations, claims and technologies, such as Information Technology, become black boxes, that is, they become hard*ened* facts. For an Information Technology implementation to take on the properties of a black box and to be disseminated through space and time, allies (human and non-human) need to be enrolled and their interests taken into account. We described how multiple perspectives can be used to gain a richer understanding of a problem situation. The case study also contained a description of a sequence of accidents that appeared to lead to the shutting down of the AACS. A simplistic explanation of the case study is to see the accidents as causing the system to be shut down — a series of technology-related failures that inexorably lead to an implementation failure. An alternative explanation is to see the accidents as resources that can be enrolled to legitimate actions. The campus management were experiencing difficulties with the changes to the working practice of the campus patrol officers brought about by the introduction of new technology and could enroll the accidents in order to legitimate the decision to suspend the operation of the AACS. The campus patrol officers were unhappy about the changes in working practices and the way the changes were being introduced and could also use the accidents to further their interests. Although the supplier denied that the technology malfunctioned in accidents 3 and 4, they could not bring enough weight to bear on the situation to gain control of the interpretation placed on the accidents. The ways in which power is exercised to influence the meaning attributed to events needs to be considered and would go some way to countering the critique of Knights and Murray, who have commented upon the failure of actor network theorists to analyze power.

There would appear to be parallels between the work of Latour on quasi-objects and networks and the structuration theory of Giddens. By viewing goals and actions as outcomes mediated by interests, we have sought to avoid assuming that interests and goals have a real-world existence or that goals and interests are purely social constructs. Using the ideas of Latour and Giddens in concert is a fertile area for research and will be developed in the next stage of the car park research, in which we will be using action research (Susman 1983; Checkland 1991) in a bid to assist the re-implementation of the AACS. Elsewhere we have suggested the use of a communication strategy drawing upon marketing concepts and techniques for the support of Information Technology implementation (McMaster and Vidgen 1995); this is one means of enrolling others in the creation of a black box and will be adopted for the re-implementation project. The use of marketing concepts and techniques is a practical response to Latour's analysis of strategies for enrolling others in the creation of a black box (see section 2.2 above).

We are not comfortable with technological determinism as a basis for IS research; neither are we comfortable with social constructivism. Furthermore, we do not see a solution in dialectics, preferring to consider organizational context and technology as inseparable. In our opinion, the distinctive nature and strength of IS research is the potential to treat context and technology symmetrically, thus differentiating IS research from context-oriented disciplines, such as management, and technology facing disciplines, such as computer science.

7. ACKNOWLEDGMENTS

The authors would like to thank the editor, Geoff Walsham, and the anonymous referees for their constructive comments and suggestions for improvements to an earlier version of this paper.

8. REFERENCES

Ackoff, R. *Redesigning the Future.* New York: Wiley, 1974.

Beer, R. *The Brain of the Firm*, Second Edition. Colchester: Wiley, 1981.

Berger, P. L., and Luckman, T. *The Social Construction of Reality.* GardenCity, New York: Doubleday, 1966.

Boehm, B. "Software Engineering." *IEEE Transactions on Computers*, Volume 25, Number 12, 1976, pp. 1226-1241.

Budde, R.; Kautz, K.; Kuhlenkamp, K.; and Züllighoven, H. *Prototyping: An Approach to Evolutionary Systems Development.* Berlin: Springer Verlag, 1992.

Burrell, G., and Morgan, G. *Sociological Paradigms and Organizational Analysis.* London: Heinemann Educational Books, 1979.

CCTA. *SSADM Version 4 Reference Manual.* Oxford: NCC Blackwell, 1990.

Checkland, P. *Systems Thinking, Systems Practice.* Chichester: Wiley, 1981.

Checkland, P. B. "From Framework through Experience to Learning: The Essential Nature of Action Research." In H.-E. Nissen, H. K. Klein, and R. Hirschheim (Editors), *Information Systems Research: Contemporary Approaches and Emergent Traditions.* Amsterdam: Elsevier Science Publishers (North Holland), 1991.

Checkland, P., and Casar, A. "Vickers' Concept of an Appreciative System: A Systemic Account." Journal of Applied Systems Analysis, Volume 13, 1986.

Checkland, P., and Scholes, J. *Soft Systems Methodology in Action.* Chichester: Wiley, 1990.

Dahlbom, B., and Mathiassen, L. *Computers in Context.* Oxford: NCC Blackwell, 1993.

Eason, K. *Information Technology and Organisational Change.* London: Taylor and Francis, 1988.

Emery, F. E., and Trist, E. L. "Socio-technical Systems." In F. E. Emery (Editor), *Systems Thinking.* New York: Penguin Books, 1969, pp. 281-296.

Flood, R., and Jackson, M. *Creative Problem Solving, Total Systems Intervention.* Chichester: Wiley, 1991.

Giddens, A. *The Constitution of Society.* Cambridge: Polity Press, 1984.

Gummesson, E. *Qualitative Methods in Management Research.* Stockholm: Studentlitteratur, 1988 (Chapter 4).

Habermas, J. *Knowledge and Human Interests.* London: Heinemann, 1972.

Hirschheim, R. A., and Klein, H. K. "Four Paradigms of Information Systems Development." *Communications of the ACM*, Volume 32, Number 10, 1989, pp. 1199-1216.

Knights, D., and Murray, F. *Managers Divided: Organisation Politics and Information Technology Management.* Chichester: Wiley, 1994.

Latour, B. *Science in Action.* Cambridge: Harvard University Press, 1987.

Latour, B. *We Have Never Been Modern.* Harvester Wheatsheaf, 1993.

Law, J. "On the Methods of Long-Distance Control: Vessels, Navigation and the Portuguese Route to India." In J. Law (Editor), *Power, Action and Belief: a New Sociology of Knowledge?* Sociological Review Monograph Number 32 (University of Keele). London: Routledge, 1986.

Lewis, P. *Information Systems Development.* London: Pitman, 1994.

Linstone, H. A. "Multiple Perspectives: Concept, Applications, and User Guidelines." *Systems Practice*, Volume 2, Number 3, 1989, pp. 307-331

McMaster, T., and Vidgen, R. "Implementation Planning for Information Systems: Promoting the Transition with a Communication Strategy." In J. Pries-Heje, P. Fowler, and K. Kautz (Editors), *Diffusion and Adoption of Information Technology.* Proceedings of the first IFIP WG8.6 Conference, 14-17 October 1995, Oslo. Amsterdam: North Holland, 1995.

Mason, R. "Field Experimentation in MIS Research." In I. Benbasat (Editor), *The Information System Research Challenge: Experimental Research Methods*, Volume 2. Cambridge: Harvard Business School Research Colloquium, 1989.

Markus, L. "Power, Politics and MIS Implementation." *Communications of the ACM*, Volume 26, Number 6, 1983, pp. (6): 430-444.

Maturana, H., and Varela, F. "Autopoiesis: The Organization of the Living." In H. Maturana and F. Varela (Editors), *Autopoiesis and Cognition.* Dordrecht, Holland: D. Reidel, 1980.

Miles, R. "Combining 'Soft' and 'Hard' Systems Practice: Grafting or Embedding?" *Journal of Applied Systems Analysis*, Volume 15, 1988, pp. 55-60.

Mitroff, I., and Linstone, H. *The Unbounded Mind: Breaking the Chains of Traditional Business Thinking.* New York: Oxford University Press, 1993.

Mumford, E., and Weir, M. *Computer Systems in Work Design - The ETHICS Method.* London: Associated Business Press, 1979.

Munro, R. "Governing the New Province of Quality: Autonomy, Accounting and the Dissemination of Accountability." In A. Wilkinson and H. Willmott (Editors), *Making Quality Critical.* London: Routledge, 1995.

Stowell, F., and West, D. *Client-led Design.* Maidenhead, UK: McGraw-Hill, 1994.

Susman, G. "Action Research: A Sociotechnical System Perspective." In G. Morgan (Editor), *Beyond Method: Strategies for Social Research.* Newbury Park, California: Sage, 1983.

Vidgen, R. "Research in Progress: Using Stakeholder Analysis to Test Primary Task Conceptual Models in Information Systems Development." *Proceedings of the Second Annual Conference on Information System Methodologies.* Edinburgh: BCS IS Methodologies Specialist Group, August 31 - September 2, 1994.

Walsham, G. *Interpreting Information Systems in Organizations.* Chichester: Wiley, 1993.

Willmott, H. "Beyond Paradigmatic Closure in Organizational Enquiry." In J. Hassard and D. Pym (Editors), *the Theory and Philosophy of Organizations: Critical Issues and New Perspectives.* London: Routledge, 1990.

Winograd, T., and Flores, F. *Understanding Computers and Cognition: A New Foundation for Design.* Ablex, Norwood, New Jersey: Ablex, 1986.

Wood, J. R. G.; Vidgen, R. T.; Wood-Harper, A. T.; and Rose, J. "Business Process Redesign: Radical Change or Reactionary Tinkering?" In J. Peppard (Editor), *Examining Business Process Reengineering: Current Perspectives and Research Directions.* Kogan Page., 1995.

Woolgar, S. "Rethinking Requirements Analysis: Some Implications of Recent Research into Producer-Consumer Relationships in it Development." In M. Jirotka and J. Goguen (Editors), *Requirements Engineering: Social and Technical Issues.* London: Academic Press, 1994, pp. 165-200.

Zmud, R. W.; Olson, M.; and Hauser, R. "Field Experimentation in MIS Research." In I. Benbasat (Editor). *The Information System Research Challenge: Experimental Research Methods*, Volume 2. Cambridge: Harvard Business School Research Colloquium, 1989.

Zuboff, S. *In the Age of the Smart Machine: The Future of Work and Power.* Oxford: Heinemann, 1988.

About the Authors

Richard Vidgen joined the University of Salford as a lecturer in Information Systems in 1992. Having obtained a first degree in Computer Science and Accounting and an M.Sc. in Accounting, he worked for a software company where he was involved in developing and supporting financial applications. This was followed by a number of years working as a freelance consultant, designing and implementing IT solutions for the banking and insurance industries. Current research interests include IS development methodologies, IS quality (which is the subject of his doctoral research), business process reengineering, and data and object modeling. In 1995, he co-authored the book *Data Modeling for Information Systems*.

Tom McMaster joined the University of Salford in 1993, where he teaches in Information Systems. He previously spent a number of years providing IT training in local government, and the subject of his doctoral research (systems development in public sector organizations) reflects a continued interest in that sector. Other research interests include the transfer and implementation of technology in organizations and, related to this, he was a founding member of IFIP WG 8.6 (concerned with the Diffusion, Transfer and Implementation of Information Technology) in Pittsburgh in 1993.

17

Embodying Information Systems

J. C. Mingers
Warwick Business School
University of Warwick

Abstract

This paper presents a case for embodying information systems. That is, for recognizing the fundamental importance of the body in human cognition and social action, and exploring the consequences for information systems and artificial intelligence. Current work within philosophy, biology, cognitive science, and social theory demonstrates that the Cartesian dualism of mind and body is no longer tenable and points to the embodied and enactive nature of thought and language. Sections of the paper cover a philosophical and biological framework for embodied cognition; the main arguments in favor of the approach; a range of work within social theory on embodiment; and the implications for information systems and artificial intelligence.

1. INTRODUCTION

It is the purpose of this paper to argue the case for *embodying* information systems, that is for recognizing the fundamental position that the body plays in human cognition, and exploring the implications of that for information systems and artificial intelligence. Under the influence of Cartesian dualism, cognition and the mind has long been split from action and the body, and IS has not merely adopted this approach, but actually extended it through a tendency to *disembody* work practices (Zuboff 1988). This tendency can actually be seen as part of the larger terrain of post-modernity and post-modernism in which the individual('s) body disappears in favor of discursive and linguistic constructions of fashion, deconstruction, signification, and virtual reality (Hayles 1992). However, recent work within philosophy, cognitive science, and social theory has argued persuasively that the body cannot be ignored but must be seen as intimately involved in processes of cognition and social activity.

The structure of this paper is that section 2 will outline the history of dis/embodiment within information systems and the related area of artificial intelligence.[1] Section 3 presents a framework at the levels of philosophy (critical realism), biology (autopoiesis), and semiotics (the relations between information and meaning) from which the importance of the body and embodied cognition naturally emerges, while section 4 makes the primary case for recognizing that cognition is embodied. Section 5 presents a selection of recent work on embodiment within social science in order to stimulate research and, finally, section 6 highlights some of the possible implications for information systems.

2. HISTORY

This section will sketch the history of information systems (IS) and artificial intelligence (AI) in three periods that differ in terms of their assumptions about the nature of human cognition. The first, and still the dominant paradigm, is Cartesian representationalism based on a split between mind and body, and a model of cognition as the processing of representational information. The second, which can be marked by the publication of Winograd and Flores' *Understanding Computers and Cognition*,[2] saw a recognition of the context-bound and situated nature of human activity, and the linking of language and action with cognition. The third, and the main focus of this paper, undermines still further the mind/body dichotomy by focusing on cognition as an essentially *embodied* activity, seeing purely *conceptual* processes as the tip of a large iceberg. This approach will be explored through the work of Varela (Varela, Thompson and Rosch 1991) on *embodied cognition* and *enaction*.

2.1 Cartesian Representationalism

Cartesian representationalism formed the backbone of the main cognitivist period which started with meetings between Simon, Chomsky, Minsky and McCarthy in 1956 and continues, to this day, to be the "normal" paradigm within IS and AI. Cognitivism forms around the hypothesis that (human) intelligence is, like a computer, *computational*. In particular, that the brain processes symbols which are related together to form *representations* of the world outside. Thus, according to this view, cognition occurs by taking in information provided by the environment, forming this into representations which can then be processed to provide logical responses by way of activity. The metaphor is clearly that of the sequential, humanly-programmed computer or information-processing machine.

This computational paradigm has been enormously influential in several other disciplines — e.g., psychology, neurobiology and psychoanalysis — but I shall discuss it mainly in terms of AI. For a more detailed discussion see West and Travis (1991a, 1991b). It has formed the basis of mainstream (sometimes known as "formalist") AI where the effort has been in producing rationalistic algorithms for performing supposedly intelligent actions. It is based on four principles: that there is a Cartesian separation between mind and body; that thinking consists of

---

[1] Although AI and IS have different goals, they share sufficient assumptions (about cognition) and tools (computers) for them to be considered together.

[2] Although arguably it was initiated by Dreyfus' critique in 1972.

manipulating abstract representations; that these manipulations can be expressed in a formal language; and that this is deterministic enough to be embodied in a machine. In practice, this has two requirements: forms of *representation* and methods of *search*. Thus, it is first necessary to find some way of formally representing the domain of interest (whether it be, for example, chess, problem-solving or vision), and then to find some method of sequentially searching the resultant multi-dimensional space.

AI has been very successful in certain, well-defined, domains. Probably the best known is chess, where a computer can now play at grandmaster level. However, cognitive AI systems do not attempt to mimic the way the brain actually works, but try to reformulate situations into something capable of resolution by an efficient search. They assume (following Turing) that the successful performance of "intelligent" actions *is intelligence*, no matter *how* it is performed. In recent years, however, the hegemony of cognitive AI has been breaking down in the face of continued failure in the majority of domains which have been addressed, and attacks on the philosophy of AI (Dreyfus and Dreyfus 1988; Graubard 1988; Searle 1990; Denning 1990). From expert systems through natural language to robotics, performance at the level of human beings has been the exception rather than the rule. Interestingly for the argument of this paper, it is the most basic human abilities, such as perception, physical manipulation, and speech that have proved the hardest to mimic. Any PC can play a reasonable game of chess but ask it to set up the pieces out of the box and you are, literally, in another world.

2.2   Winograd and Flores' Language/Action Approach

A major critique from within AI came from the work of Flores and Winograd (Flores and Ludlow 1981; Winograd and Flores 1987; Kensing and Winograd 1991). In *Understanding Computers and Cognition,* Winograd and Flores assimilate the phenomenology and hermeneutics of Heidegger (1962) and Gadamer(1975), Searle's (1969) theory of speech acts, and Maturana's (1978; Maturana and Varela 1987) cognitive theories to produce a critique of the traditional objectivist, rationalist approach to computer systems design and AI. In its place, they suggest an approach based on *conversations* and *commitments*, which they generally refer to as the "language/action approach."[3]

The main outlines are, first, that cognition and thought is not an isolated, separate mental function but our normal everyday activity — our "being-in-the-world." It is embodied in the patterns of behavior which are triggered by our interactions and which have developed through our *structural coupling* (Maturana and Varela 1980). "Thinking" is not detached reflection but part of our basic attitude to the world — one of continual purposeful action. Second, knowledge does not consist of representations, in individuals' heads, of objective independent entities. Rather, we make distinctions through our language in the course of our interactions with others, continually structuring and restructuring the world as we coordinate our purposeful activities. Third, that

---

[3]However, this name is also used by a group of mainly Scandinavian writers (Goldkuhl and Lyytinen 1982, 1984; Lyytinen and Klein 1985; Lehtinen and Lyytinen 1986; Lyytinen, Klein and Hirschheim 1991) who do not base their ideas on Maturana but rather on Habermas (1979, 1984, 1987). There is, however, considerable similarity in the emphasis on language, language as action, and speech act theory.

which is said does not occur *de novo*, but is grounded in our past experiences and tradition — the history of our structural couplings.

Fourth, the most important dimension of our actions as humans is language, but we must change our view of language away from seeing it as representational and denotative toward seeing it as (social) action through which we coordinate our activity. Languaging takes place in conversations which become the central unit of analysis. Such conversations are networks of distinctions, requests and commitments, valid in respect of their acceptance by others rather than their correspondence to an external reality. Finally, the view of "problems" which computers can help "solve" must change. Problems are not objective features of the world, but the result of breakdowns within our structural coupling to objects or to others. When our activities do not succeed or our coordinations fail, our routine operation is disrupted and a "problem" occurs. This is always against a particular background, for a particular individual or group and the nature of the problem only becomes defined through the attempts to repair it.

These ideas lead to a distinctive view about both about the development of information systems in Organizations and about the nature of computers and artificial intelligence (Smith 1991). Organizations are seen as networks of recurrent and recursive conversations between individuals and groups of individuals. The conversations consist of speech acts mainly involving requests, promises, commitments and declarations coordinating general activities and the conversations themselves. Information systems should be designed to be part of and facilitate this communicative and coordinating process. They must be open and flexible, reflecting the changing distinctions and conversations generated within a domain rather than imposing an external and unchanging straitjacket.

Although the Winograd and Flores book is well known, there has been little substantive work developed from autopoiesis. Stephens and Wood (1991) presented a general description of a constructivist approach to information systems, and Harnden (1990; Harnden and Mullery 1991) has outlined ideas for what he calls Enabling Network Systems (ENS). Harnden and Stringer are currently incorporating some of these ideas into an architecture for multimedia systems and the design of hypermedia (Harnden and Stringer 1993a, 1993b).

2.3 Embodied/Enactive Cognition

The cognitivist program of representationalism, and indeed much of Western philosophy of mind, has been guided by the Cartesian dualism between mind and body — mind being a disembodied realm of pure ideas. However, the thrust of Varela's (and Maturana's) work is in the opposite direction — showing how our cognition and thought is inextricably bound to our *embodied* selves. This is a reversal that has also occurred in phenomenology, beginning with the difference between Husserl's (1964, 1977) analysis of pure consciousness and Heidegger's focus on concernful, day-to-day, activity. This trend was continued by Merleau-Ponty (1962, 1963), who took phenomenology down to the level of action and perception, emphasizing the embodied nature of cognition. Section 4 will expand on this theme, drawing on Merleau-Ponty and also Varela's theory of enaction, but first, in section 3, a general framework will be presented as a context for the study of embodiment. Finally, section 5 will show that the importance of the body has recently been recognized in several other disciplines.

3. A PHILOSOPHICAL AND BIOLOGICAL FRAMEWORK

The importance, and role, of the body and embodiment for information systems can be appreciated within a framework developed by Mingers (1993, 1994, 1995). This framework synthesizes the work of a number of writers and consists of an underlying philosophy based on critical realism (Bhaskar 1978, 1979, 1989); a biological explanation of the nature and limitations of the observer and cognition (Maturana and Varela 1980, 1987); and a semiotic analysis of the nature of information and its relationship to meaning (Stamper 1973; Dretske 1981; Habermas 1979, 1984, 1987). It is illustrated in Figure 1. Only a brief sketch can be given here.

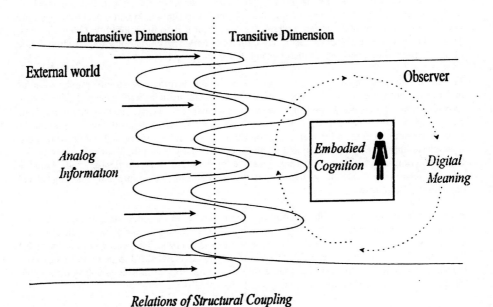

Figure 1. A Framework for Embodied Cognition

At the philosophical level, critical realism provides a post-empiricist ontology and epistemology. It is accepted that we can have no objective, observer-independent, access to reality but against constructivism it is maintained that there is an independent external world constituted by structures or entities with causal powers (the domain of the *real*). These are seen as generative mechanisms responsible for the events which actually occur, or which may not because of countervailing tendencies (the domain of the *actual*). A subset of these events may impinge on humans: the domain of the *empirical*. Epistemologically, science proceeds by hypothesizing potential generative mechanisms that, if they did exist, would account for our observations and experiences. A distinction is drawn between the *transitive* and *intransitive* dimensions of science. The intransitive (ontological) dimension is the domain of the real objects of scientific knowledge, the transitive (epistemological) dimension is the domain of humanly-constructed cognitive objective of science such as theories, experiments and concepts.

At the biological level, autopoiesis provides an explanation of our interactions with the world. As living systems, we have a closed (autopoietic) organization, but are interactively open to our environment or medium. The nature and limitations of such interactions are determined primarily by our own physical structure (structure-determined) rather than by the environment. External stimuli provoke or trigger a response, but the nature of the response is determined by the structure of the organism at that instant, not by the stimuli. Moreover, it is the structure that determines what can or cannot be a stimulus for the organism — organisms without eyes or the equivalent cannot be triggered by light. Given this under-determination of the organism by its environment, how is it in fact that responses in particular situations are generally appropriate? This is answered through the concept of structural coupling. The maintenance of autopoiesis through recurrent interactions with the environment or other organisms will lead to the generation of mutually adapted structures that can be said to be structurally coupled.

Moving to the level of information and meaning, events or signs in the empirical world, especially symbolic and linguistic ones, can be said to carry information about their origins, the causal mechanisms giving rise to them. Such signs will be triggers or perturbations for the nervous systems of organisms or human observers but, as shown above, cannot determine or control the reaction or internal compensation that it provokes. We can see this process as one in which the *information*, carried in analog form by the sign, is transformed into *meaning*, expressed in digital form for the observer. The information is objective in the sense of being independent of the observer, but the meaning that it generates is (inter-)subjective and observer-dependent. It is precisely this process of the digitalization of the analog that is the main focus of this paper as it is carried out, largely unconsciously, by the body and its nervous system. This *is* embodied cognition.

4. EMBODIMENT

This section will argue for the importance of considering embodied cognition through the work of Merleau-Ponty and Varela. In considering perception, and cognition in general, Merleau-Ponty critiqued both what he called empiricist (realist) and intellectualist (idealist) modes of explanation (Merleau-Ponty 1962; Hammond, Howarth and Keat 1991). The empiricist simply takes the world as objectively given and sees cognition as a reflection of the world. Intellectualism recognizes that the subject is involved in constituting the experienced world, but is too disembodied and mentalistic. For Merleau-Ponty, cognition is embedded in our body and our nervous system. It is the body which "knows how to act" and "knows how to perceive" on the basis of pre-formed readiness and habits developed through its structural coupling with the environment. This is what Varela (1991) means by "embodiment": the idea that cognition necessarily occurs through and within our bodily structures which are themselves coupled to biological and social contexts.

Merleau-Ponty also analyses the relationship between the perceiver and the world, which he sees as a reciprocal relationship: the world does not determine our perception, nor does our perception constitute the world.

> "The properties of the object and the intentions of the subject...are not only intermingled; they constitute a new whole." When the eye and the ear follow an animal in flight, it is impossible to say "which started first" in the exchange of stimuli and responses. Since all the movements of the organism are always

conditioned by external influences, one can, if one wishes, readily treat behavior as an effect of the milieu. But, in the same way, since all the stimulations that the organism receives have in turn been possible only by its preceding movements which have culminated in exposing the receptor organ to the external influences, one could also say that the behavior is the first cause of all the stimulations.

it is the organism itself...which chooses the stimuli in the physical world to which it will be sensitive. "The environment (Umwelt) emerges from the world through the actualisation or being of the organism — [granted that] can exist only if it succeeds in finding in the world an adequate environment. [Merleau-Ponty 1963, p. 13; quoted in Varela 1991, p. 441]

This is the basis of Varela's theory of enactive cognition which has two aspects:

i)   that perception consists in perceptually guided actions;

ii)   that cognitive structures emerge from the recurrent sensory-motor patterns that enable action to be perceptually guided. [Varela 1991, p. 441]

The first point is that perception is neither objectivist nor purely constructivist — pace Maturana (Varela 1992, p. 254) Rather, it is co-determined by the linking of the structure of the perceiver and the local situations in which it has to act to maintain its self.

As seen in Figure 2, there can be no fixed point independent of the organism, nor can the organism construct its own closed world. The organism's activity conditions *what can be perceived* in an environment, and these perceptions, in turn, condition future actions. Varela (1992; Varela, Thompson and Rosch 1991, Chapter 8) assembles various neurophysiological evidence for this. For instance, in the area of perception, it is clear that color and smell are by no means simple mappings of external characteristics. Rather, they are co-creations, dependent on the color and smell "spaces" constituted by a particular organism's nervous system, and only triggered by external stimulation. Equally, our perception depends for its effectiveness on movement, as shown by Held and Hein's (1958) kittens. Two groups of kittens shared the same, artificial, light conditions, but one group were allowed to be active while the other group were passively moved around. When released, the active ones were normal while the passive one acted as if they were blind even though their visual system was unimpaired.

The organism must interact with its environment for its self-continuation and so the question becomes, how does it happen that the world it carves out is one which permits its continuance? The answer lies not in the world, but in the relations between the sensory and motor surfaces of the nervous system. How is it that these are such as to enable effective, perceptually-guided action in a perception-dependent world? This brings us to the second of Varela's points: how action is selected and how the process generates higher cognitive structures.

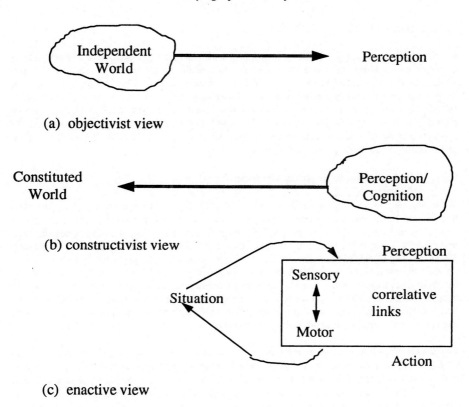

(a) objectivist view

(b) constructivist view

(c) enactive view

Figure 2. Perceptually-Guided Action

Our behavior is seen as a constant switching from one task or activity to another according to our readiness for action. How is it that one is chosen rather than another? This seems to occur as the result of what might be thought of as a competition between different sub-nets or "agents" in the brain. Brain studies have shown that there are bursts of fast activity followed by more stable patterns as activities stop and new ones start. At each choice-point or breakdown there are many possibilities available, but eventually the historically conditioned structure leads to a selection and a new stability. It is next argued that this dynamic interplay linking sensor and motor activity gives rise to the higher cognitive structures. It does not determine them, but does both enable and constrain the more conceptual and abstract modes of thought. The key here is the emergence of the symbol or sign, and thus language itself, as a new domain of neuronal activity. Varela points here to the work of Piaget (1954), and particularly of Johnson (1987) and of Lakoff (1987; Lakoff and Johnson 1980), which will be discussed in the next section.

5. OTHER CONTRIBUTIONS

Having argued from a particular philosophical and biological perspective that much human cognition is essentially embodied, the purpose of this section of the paper is to demonstrate that similar conclusions have been reached within the social sciences. This is both to support the earlier conclusions and to provide a range of interesting perspectives and theories to stimulate further research into embodied cognition within information systems and AI. The first section considers the complex relations between the body and its social context; the second points to the specific concerns of feminist perspectives on the body; and the third reviews the work of Lakoff and Johnson on the bodily basis of language.

5.1   The Social Body or the Body Social

Within the social sciences, especially sociology, it has been the case until recently that the body has largely been ignored. Cognition, action, and language have been seen as essentially mentalistic phenomena. Since the early 1980s, however, the social relevance of the body has been recognized (Turner 1984; 1992; Featherstone, Turner and Hepworth 1991; Hayles 1992; Synnott 1993). Shilling (1993) suggests that there are three broad theoretical approaches: the traditional, *naturalistic* approach that views the body as an essentially given, biological and genetic substrate for society; the *social constructionist* approach that emphasizes the extent to which the social and cultural context constructs the form and representation of the body; and the *embodied* approach that recognizes both the social construction of the body and the biological constitution of cognition and language, in short, the *embodiment of the self.* I shall discuss the latter two.

The social constructionist approach can be exemplified by Goffman and Foucault. Goffman (1963, 1969) focuses on the way that individuals present themselves in their daily interactions, paying particular attention to the role of the body. For Goffman, our bodily appearance and gestures can be managed so as to contribute to the impression that we wish to give. In so doing, they are part of a social context of meanings and idioms: our behavior, dress, and manners convey the messages that they do because of the shared social meanings that they embody. We must remember, of course, that our bodies and appearance convey much information that is not consciously controlled and may well not be that which we would intend. This unconscious and unintended generation of meaning links up to Giddens' (1984) process of structuration in the reproduction of social structure. Goffman's analysis also points to the extent to which our bodily appearance contributes to our construction of *self-identity* through a process of internalization. This is particularly obvious in people with unusual features or stigma (Goffman 1968).

Foucault (1977, 1981, 1982) develops a much more radical view of the relations between society and the body in which the body comes to be viewed as almost entirely constructed by the repressive regimes of a disciplinary society. For Foucault, the body is very much an object of study: it is seen as the essential link between daily practices and interactions and the wider power structures of society. Foucault undertook detailed historical studies of particular types of institution (such as prisons and asylums) and particular arenas of bodily activity (such as sexuality) as they changed in the transformation to modernity. In broad terms, Foucault sees this transition in terms of society's need for an increased control of its population and he sees the body as the major medium through which this exercise of power is enacted. Beginning with fairly crude physical modes of control — imprisonment, surveillance, regimentation, and punishment — power is now exercised more sophisticatedly and minutely through knowledge, desire, and *self*-regulation. Our most intimate and individual desires become structured in such a way that they instantiate power relations — sexuality becomes nothing other than the effect of power — and we thus become implicitly self-regulated (Grosz 1994).

While Foucault has many important insights that have been developed, particularly by feminists but also to a limited extent in information systems (Zuboff 1988), his work over-emphasizes the extent to which the body is simply a blank slate to be inscribed by society. In Hayles' terms, he is concerned only with *the body,* as an abstract universal cultural construct, rather than with *embodiment,* the personal, contextual, experience of having a body. It has been argued that the body is not infinitely malleable, but provides both possibilities and limitations for social action. This move toward a more dialectical view of *embodiment* can be seen in Turner's (1992) later work, where he has tried to integrate Foucauldian analyses together with a more biological and anthropological appreciation of the body. Drawing on philosophical anthropology (Honneth and Joas 1988), the human body is contrasted with more primitive animals that are highly specialized and determined, only able to exist in a specific environment. Humans, however, are particularly flexible and under-determined by their genetic characteristics. The body is born an "unfinished project" that must be completed through social construction and that must, in the same process, generate a meaningful world to inhabit.

Other writers whose work can be seen to contribute toward this embodied view are Connell (1987), Freund (1982), and Hochschild (1983). Connell and Freund focus, in different ways, on how the body is enmeshed and transformed by social relations in ways that produce and reproduce established structures of inequality. Connell analyses the formation of *gendered* bodies and the interaction between the physical and social experience of gender. This process works in three stages: first, through social categories that define male and female bodies in particular, culturally and temporally relative, ways; second, through social practices that actually lead to the transformation of bodies toward these categories or stereotypes; and, finally, through the mutually reinforcing interaction of the social images and the physical experiences. Freund is concerned with the social structuring of health and illness. He argues that good health requires both the physical body functioning well and there being a good integration between our body and our "self." This integration is crucially linked to our social situation through our emotional well-being which, itself, is socially differentiated. Hochschild has studied the effect of work on bodily health for people who have to perform what she calls *emotion work*: that is, where the management of emotion and feeling in order to generate specific bodily displays and gestures is an inherent part of the work. A particular example is that of airline stewardesses who are required to continually project feelings of warmth, calmness, and helpfulness.

5.2   The Body and Feminism

Clearly the body is of central importance for many feminist writers and their work could not be covered at all adequately in a few paragraphs. Feminist theory also ranges across the three approaches outlined above: for example, Orbach (1988) and Chernin (1983) can be seen as *naturalistic* in accepting that the body has some natural state (although differing on what this might be) that society then distorts, while Delphy (1984) and Wittig (1982) are *constructionist* in arguing that the biological is not a separate domain, but a manifestation of the social. I shall just mention a recent work by Grosz that does seek to explore what she calls *corporeal feminism,* an approach to embodiment that seems consonant with that outlined in section 4 above. She aims to develop a multi-faceted approach to the relations between self and body that *enables subjectivity to be understood as fully material and for materiality to be extended to include and explain the operations of language, desire, and significance* (Grosz 1994, p. 210). Such an approach needs to eschew dualisms such as mind/body or, for that matter, sex/gender, recognizing that while the body is, indeed, a site of political, cultural, and social production and transformation, it is also historically and biologically conditioned. It inevitably channels meanings and inscriptions that are projected upon it in sexually specific ways.

5.3   Bodily Metaphors

Lakoff and Johnson are concerned to show how language emerges from and reflects our bodily structure and functioning. For example, much of language can be seen as either direct metaphor, or as developing from metaphor, and at base most metaphors stem from bodily activity (Lakoff and Johnson 1980). These metaphors are so deeply sedimented that they are not seen as such. Many of the most basic stem from our experience of space (e.g., *up/down* — "get *up*," "wake *up*," "my spirits *sank*"); of objects (e.g., "I'm running out *of steam*," "I'm a little *rusty*"); or of containers (e.g., "he's *in* love," "we're *out of* trouble," "she's *getting into* shape").

Equally, many of the categorizations that we use in language, especially the most fundamental ones, arise in relation to our habitual perceptual and motor activities, not as some direct reflection of the world (Lakoff 1987). For example, in hierarchic taxonomies, such as *furniture: chair: rocker,* there is a most basic category which will generally be in the middle of the taxonomy. It will be the highest level at which all members have a similar shape, there can be a single representative mental image, and with which there can be a single form of motor interaction. In this case, the basic category is *chair* and this is learned first, is the quickest to be identified, the first to enter a language, and is the most commonly used. As Johnson (1987, p. 206) concludes:

> Shared understanding is not merely a matter of shared concepts and propositions.
> It is also a matter of embodied structures of understanding...which constitute a
> large part of what we mean by form itself in our experience. Such structures...
> emerge in our bodily functioning.

6. IMPLICATIONS FOR AI/IS

The argument so far has stressed the importance of recognizing the embodied and situated nature of human cognition and action in general. This section considers the implications for information systems and AI in particular. It is interesting to note that there is very little work within the IS/AI literature, apart from the area of HCI, that considers the body explicitly at all. The only examples discovered are Dreyfus (1972), Zuboff (1988), Varela, Thompson and Rosch (1991) and Beeson (1994), and, from a more cultural perspective, Hayles (1992).

6.1   Artificial Intelligence

To understand the implications for artificial intelligence, it is first necessary to consider what AI is trying to achieve. There are broadly two aims: the achievement of a genuinely intelligent "being" by artificial means and research to aid understanding of human intelligence. With regard to the latter, the argument of this paper suggests that the traditional, representationalist, AI paradigm will shed little light on human intelligence as it is based on quite a different mode of operation. With regard to the former, strong program in AI, it again seems most unlikely that intelligence could be generated through a top-down, formalist approach. Instead, I would suggest that any AI research program aiming at either of the above objectives (although especially the first) needs to develop systems that have, as a minimum, the following conditions:

i)   The equivalent to a neural structure having an architecture functionally equivalent to at least the higher mammals. That is, it should possess the potentials for both perception and action, and their correlation; and it should possess the necessary structures for symbolic, linguistic and self-descriptive interactions.

ii)   This nervous system should be structurally plastic — that is, able to modify its own interconnections in response to environmental disturbance.

iii)   It should be organizationally closed in an autopoietic sense — that is, it must be able to be self-referential. For example, a neural network whose inputs are connected to its outputs is organizationally closed.

iv)   The nervous system should be embedded within a "body" that in turn interacts within an environment. The environment should have stable patterns within it that are relevant to the "survival" of the system as a whole.

v)   The system must undergo a prolonged period of interaction within its environment in order to become structurally coupled to its environment and other intelligences within it.

Even if these very demanding conditions were met, it is interesting to speculate on the extent to which any resulting "intelligence" would be similar to a human, or indeed whether we should even be able to communicate with it. The theory predicts that communication would only be possible to the extent that a consensual domain of interactions were possible. That is, that we and it share sufficient interactions within a context, and similarity of structure (both body and nervous system) to be able to become structurally coupled and coordinate our interactions.

Another aspect relevant to AI, particularly expert systems, is the nature of knowledge. The embodied paradigm suggests that much that we "know," in the sense that we are able to undertake particular actions and activities, is essentially tacit, habitual, and beneath our consciousness. Such knowledge is always performative, i.e., action-oriented; learned through practice and habituation (a process of incorporation rather than inscription, to use Hayles' terms) and is not algorithmic nor able to be formalized or made explicit and discursive. Such embodied knowledge actually defines the boundaries of our consciousness rather than the other way round. This type of knowledge can be illustrated most simply by our mastery of language. In language, we have a system that is incredibly elaborate, flexible, and sophisticated yet we can use it expertly without being able to consciously formulate any of its rules or categories.[4] The implications of this for AI are similar to the conclusions above concerning intelligence. It is unlikely that such embodied knowledge can be successfully reconstituted in a top-down, representationalist manner. Rather systems will have to "learn" it through their own interactions within a domain relevant for their continued existence.

6.2   Information Systems

I shall take information systems as a discipline in its widest sense, concerned not simply with producing more effective organizational information systems, but also with studying the general relations and interactions between information technology/systems and the social and organizational world.

First, it is clear that in terms of the three stages outlined in section 2, IS is locked into the first — that of disembodied Cartesianism. Indeed IS is currently precisely epitomized by such an approach since what it sets out to do is to capture that, *and only that,* which can be represented by an abstract symbolism suitable for electronic storage and processing. IS is premised on the assumption that cognition and thought are essentially abstract representations since that is what computers are good at handling. However, if it is *in fact* the case that most human cognition is embodied, then IS are working against rather than with humans' natural abilities. Indeed, IS are not just doing this by default but, as Zuboff documents well, deliberately supplanting the skilled bodily experience of, say, plant operators, with abstract computer-based models: that is, replacing the need for action-centered skills with intellectual skills. It might be argued that the computer models are better than humans, but this contention is far from proved, particularly in complex, judgmental domains. The problem can be illustrated with the demise of expert systems. It soon became clear that expert systems could work well in clearly defined areas where the rules and relationships were well-known and explicit. However, in fuzzier domains, or exceptional situations, the intuitive judgements of experts was far superior.

We must recognize that computers and brains work in different ways and are good at different things. Computers are good at carrying out repetitive operations faultlessly and quickly, at storing and recalling large amounts of essentially arbitrary data, and at reacting extremely quickly to well-specified events. In comparison, human are relatively poor in these areas, but are excellent at motor and perceptual tasks, synthesizing diverse types of information and sensation, interpreting poorly defined situations and events, and making complex judgements. Note that most of these skills rely on embodiment. We should accept this situation and, rather than try to

---

[4]Similar arguments are put forward by sociologists such as Bourdieu (1977), with his concept of the *habitus* as a set of embodied practices and dispositions to act, and Giddens' (1984) multi-level conceptualization of the acting subject.

force computers to do that which they inherently cannot, we should aim to maximize the fruitful coordination of the two together.

Part of this process is better forms of HCI and this means enhancing the flexibility of output modes to make more use of peoples bodies. This is, in fact, already happening but in rather a haphazard way. The advent of graphical interfaces such as Windows is clearly a step in this direction as it brings in sight, through graphical objects, and touch, through a mouse. There is clearly a long way to go, although the destination can already be seen in the example of virtual reality (VR). At first sight, this technology might appear to be disembodying in that it actually does away with the necessity of real physical interactions and, as reported by Hayles, subjects have experienced the effect as de-actualizing or de-materializing their body. However, it is actually confirming the importance of embodiment but merely replacing the feedback between sensor and motor neurons that normally happens through the environment with a computer simulated one. The success of VR will depend on the extent to which it can mimic a response to all the nervous system's sensory modalities. How useful it will be is another matter. While there are obvious applications, for example in situations that are hazardous or difficult to reach, or over long distances, or in learning new skills, I personally would not expect that it would replace actual physical interaction in everyday situations.

A related aspect of current developments in IT is that of computer-based telecommunications — i.e., computer-mediated communications and decision-making at a distance through the Internet or group decision support software (GDSS). While such technologies have obvious benefits, their disembodied nature clearly limits the quality and depth of the conversations that they support. One piece of research (Rocco and Warglien 1995) compared experimentally face-to-face with electronically-mediated decision making in a Prisoner's Dilemma type situation. The general findings were that the electronic groups found it much harder to establish cooperation through group cohesion: all the face-to-face groups established stable, high-return patterns of behavior, while none of the electronic groups did, although there was evidence that the electronic groups were better at pure, calculative, problem-solving. While this is only one, small-scale, study its interesting results point to the need for much more research on the effects of increasing disembodiment.

Another development is that of multimedia or hypermedia systems that synthesize a variety of different modes of interaction, for example, traditional computer displays, sound, photos, videos, simulations, and also allow access to be structured by, rather than imposed upon, the user. *Theseus*, developed by Harnden and Stringer (1993a, 1993b) is an interesting example. This is a generic system for generating different learning environments. It sees the computer not as a *tool* with predefined functions, but as a *medium* of linked multimedia objects within which users can actively explore particular domains, generating their own paths and links, and in the process altering the underlying connectivity of the media base. The quality of experience of the user is enhanced by the use of dramatic (e.g., computer-gaming and theater[5]) and aesthetic effects in order to generate greater engagement and participation. The approach is based in part on

---

[5]See, for example, Laurel (1991).

insights into cognitive processes in terms of *embodied knowledge*....the focus of research has shifted from the problem of "representation," to the issue of "effective action" in an historically grounded process....Relevance or not ...is not pre-given, but *enacted* or *brought-forth*, in an ongoing process of selection and punctuation. [Harnden and Stringer 1993a, p. 234, emphasis in original]

We also need to look from the opposite perspective, being concerned not with more effective IS, but the effects of IT and IS on humans and human society in general. Here again, as the review in section 5 showed, these effects occur not simply at the abstract level of the availability of more information, surveillance, and control. They also occur at the level of the body, which provides the nexus both between our biological inheritance and our cognitive and social development, and between the external world of signs and information and the internal world of meaning. I would suggest that there is much scope here for interdisciplinary research concerning the effects that the process of disembodiment has already had, as well as those that are still to come. This is of major significance since developments in IS/IT are likely to determine the shape of human communication and, indeed, cognition in the future. Hayles, for example, argues that developments in technology, particularly information technology, are one of the most important means by which our embodied, incorporated practices change over time, and that these changes in our embodiment in turn generate changes within the discursive realm of society.

7. CONCLUSION

This paper has put forward the argument that the disciplines of IS and AI need to become *embodied*. That is, they must move beyond the dualism of mind and body to recognize that human cognition and social action are inherently embodied. The body is a nexus for the interaction of both the individual and society, and action and cognition, and is, therefore, of central importance both for developing more effective information-based systems and for observing the effects of such systems on people and society.

Research in this area needs to develop in a number of directions:

i) Within AI, aiming to develop systems that actually learn and are cognitive in a similar way to human beings, that is, in a way that is embodied, experiential, activity-based, implicit, and non-representational.

ii) Improving the effectiveness of IS by recognizing the divergent but complementary nature of human and computer processes, and explicitly considering the importance of embodiment at both the interactive level, e.g., interfaces, virtual reality, and multimedia, and at the decision-making level, e.g., communications and GDSS systems.

iii) Examining the effects on individuals and society of the way that IS/IT has, so far, resulted in the *disembodiment* of much skilled and unskilled work, and particularly how technology is the fulcrum of changes to society's practices.

8. ACKNOWLEDGMENT

I would like to thank the referees and the editor for helpful comments and references.

9. REFERENCES

Beeson, I. "The Body in the Information System." *Philosophical and Logical Aspects of Information Systems*, University of the West of England, April 1994.

Bhaskar, R. *A Realist Theory of Science*, Second Edition. Sussex: Harvester Press, 1978.

Bhaskar, R. *Reclaiming Reality*. London: Verso, 1989.

Bhaskar, R. *The Possibility of Naturalism*. Sussex: Harverster Press, 1979.

Bourdieu, P. *Outline of a Theory of Practice*. Cambridge: Cambridge University Press, 1977.

Chernin, K. *Womansize: the Tyranny of Slenderness*. London: Women's Press, 1983.

Connell, R. *Gender and Power*. Cambridge: Polity Press, 1987.

Delphy, C. *Close to Home: A Materialist Analysis of Women's Oppression*. London: Hutchinson, 1984.

Denning, P. "The Science of Computing: Is Thinking Computable?" *American Scientist*, Volume 78, 1990, pp. 100-102.

Dretske, F. *Knowledge and the Flow of Information*. Oxford: Blackwell, 1981.

Dreyfus, H. *What Computers Can't Do: A Critique of Artificial Reason*. New York: Harper and Row, 1972.

Dreyfus, H., and Dreyfus, S. "Making a Mind Versus Modeling the Brain: Artificial Intelligence Back at a Branchpoint." In S. Graubard (Editor), *The Artificial Intelligence Debate*. Cambridge: MIT Press, 1988.

Featherstone, M.; Turner, B.; and Hepworth, M. (Editors). *The Body: Social Process and Cultural Theory*. London: Sage, 1991.

Flores, F., and Ludlow, J. "Doing and Speaking in the Office." In G. Fick and R. Sprague (Editors), *DSS: Issues and Challenges*. London: Pergamon Press, 1981, pp. 95-118.

Foucault, M. *Discipline and Punish: The Birth of the Prison*. London: Penguin, 1977.

Foucault, M. *The History of Sexuality, Vol. 1: An Introduction*. Harmondsworth: Penguin, 1981.

Foucault, M. "The Subject and Power." In H. Dreyfus and P. Rabinow (Editors), *Michel Foucault: Beyond Structuralism and Hermeneutics*. New York: Harvester Press, 1982.

Freund, P. *The Civilized Body: Social Domination, Control, and Health*. Philadelphia: Temple University Press, 1982.

Gadamer, H. *Truth and Method*. New York: Seabury Press, 1975.

Giddens, A. *The Constitution of Society*. Cambridge: Polity Press, 1984.

Goffman, E. *Behavior in Public Places: Notes on the Social Organization of Gatherings*. New York: The Free Press, 1963.

Goffman, E. *The Presentation of Self in Everyday Life*. Harmondsworth: Penguin, 1969.

Goffman, E. *Stigma: Notes on the Management of Spoiled Identity*. Harmondsworth: Penguin, 1968.

Goldkuhl, G., and Lyytinen, K. "A Language Action View of Information Systems." In M. Ginzberg and K. Ross (Editors), *Proceedings of the Third International Conference on Information Systems*, Ann Arbor, Michigan, 1982, pp. 13-29.

Goldkuhl, G., and Lyytinen, K. "Information: Systems Specification as Rule Reconstruction." In T. Bemelmans (Editor), *Beyond Productivity: Information Systems for Organizational Effectiveness*. Amsterdam: North Holland, 1984, pp. 79-94.

Graubard, S. (Editor). *The Artificial Intelligence Debate*. Cambridge: MIT Press, 1988.

Grosz, E. *Volatile Bodies: Towards a Corporeal Feminism*. Bloomington: Indiana University Press, 1994.

Habermas, J. *Communication and the Evolution of Society*. London: Heinemann, 1979.

Habermas, J. *The Theory of Communicative Action Volume 1: Reason and the Rationalization of Society*. London: Heinemann, 1984.

Habermas, J. *The Theory of Communicative Action Volume 2: Lifeworld and System: A Critique of Functionalist Reason*. Oxford: Polity Press, 1987.

Hammond, M.; Howarth, J.; and Keat, R. *Understanding Phenomenology*. Oxford: Blackwell, 1991.

Harnden, R. The Languaging of Models: The Understanding and Communication of Models with Particular Reference to Stafford Beer's Cybernetic Model of Organization Structure." *Systems Practice*. Volume 3, Number 3, 1990, pp. 289-302.

Harnden, R., and Mullery, G. "Enabling Network Systems (ENS)." *Systems Practice,* Volume 4, Number 6, 1991, pp. 579-598.

Harnden, R., and Stringer, R. "Theseus: The Evolution of a Hypermedium." *Cybernetics and Systems,* Volume 24, 1993a, pp. 255-280.

Harnden, R., and Stringer, R., "Theseus: A Model for Global Connectivity." In F. Stowell, D. West, and J. Howell (Editors), *Systems Science: Addressing Global Issues.* New York: Plenum Press, 1993b.

Hayles, N. "The Materiality of Informatics." *Configurations,* Volume 1, 1992, pp.147-170.

Heidegger, M. *Being and Time.* Oxford: Blackwell, 1962.

Held, R., and Hein, A. "Adaption of Disarranged Hand-Eye Coordination Contingent upon Re-afferent Stimulation." *Perceptual-Motor Skills,* Volume 8, 1958, pp. 87-90.

Hochschild, A. *The Managed Heart: Commercialization of Human Feeling.* Berkeley: University of California Press, 1983.

Honneth, A., and Joas, H. *Social Action and Human Nature.* Cambridge: Cambridge University Press, 1988.

Husserl, E. *Cartesian Meditations.* The Hague: Martinus Nijhoff, 1977.

Husserl, E. *The Idea of Phenomenology.* The Hague: Martinus Nijhoff, 1964.

Johnson, M. *The Body in the Mind: The Bodily Basis of Imagination, Reason, and Meaning.* Chicago: University of Chicago Press, 1987.

Kensing, F., and Winograd, T. "The Language/Action Approach to Design of Computer-Support for Cooperative Work: A Preliminary Study in Work Mapping." In R. Stamper, P. Kerola, R. Lee, and K. Lyytinen (Editors), *Collaborative Work, Social Communications and Information System.* Amsterdam: Elsevier North Holland, 1991, pp. 311-332.

Lakoff, G. *Women, Fire and Dangerous Things: What Categories Reveal about the Mind.* Chicago: University of Chicago Press, 1987.

Lakoff, G., and Johnson, M. *Metaphors We Live By.* Chicago: Chicago University Press, 1980.

Laurel, B. *Computers as Theater.* Reading, Massachusetts: Addison-Wesley, 1991.

Lehtinen, E., and Lyytinen, K. "Action Based Model of Information Systems." *Information Systems,* Volume 11, 1986, pp. 299-317.

Lyytinen, K., and Klein, H. "The Critical Theory of Jurgen Habermas as a Basis for a Theory of Information Systems." In E. Mumford, R. Hirschheim, G. Fitzgerald. A. T. Wood-Harper (Editors), *Research Methods in Information Systems*. Amsterdam: North-Holland, 1985, pp. 219-236.

Lyytinen, K.; Klein, H.; and Hirschheim, R. "The Effectiveness of Office Information Systems: A Social Action Perspective. *Journal of Information Systems*, Volume 1, 1991, pp. 41-60.

Maturana, H. "Biology of Language: The Epistemology of Reality. In G. Millar and E. Lenneberg (Editors), *Psychology and Biology of Language and Thought: Essays in Honor of Eric Lenneberg*. New York: Academic Press, 1978, pp. 27-63.

Maturana, H., and Varela, F. *Autopoiesis and Cognition: The Realization of the Living*. Dordrecht: Reidel, 1980.

Maturana, H., and Varela, F. *The Tree of Knowledge*. Boston: Shambhala, 1987.

Merleau-Ponty, M. *Phenomenology of Perception*. London: RKP, 1962.

Merleau-Ponty, M. *The Structure of Behavior*. Boston: Beacon Press, 1963.

Mingers, J. "An Examination of Information and Meaning." Systemist, Volume 15, Number 1, 1993, pp. 17-27.

Mingers, J., 1994, An evaluation of theories of information with regard to the semantic and pragmatic aspects of information systems, Warwick Business School Research Papers 136, University of Warwick, Coventry, UK.

Mingers, J. "Information and Meaning: Foundations for an Intersubjective Account." *Information Systems Journal*, forthcoming 1995.

Orbach, S. *Fat is a Feminist Issue*. London: Arrow Books, 1988.

Piaget, J. *The Construction of Reality in the Child*. New York: Basic Books, 1954.

Rocco, E., and Warglien, M. "Computer Mediated Communication and the Emergence of 'Electronic Opportunism'." Working Paper 1/95, Dipartimento di Economia e Direzione Aziendale, Universita degli Studi di Venezia, 1995.

Searle, J. "Is the Brain's Mind a Computer Program?" *Scientific American*, Volume 262, Number 1, 1990, pp. 26-31.

Searle, J. *Speech Acts*. Cambridge: Cambridge University Press, 1969.

Shilling, C. *The Body and Social Theory*. London: Sage, 1993.

Smith, B. "The Owl and the Electronic Encyclopedia." *Artificial Intelligence*, Volume 47, 1991, pp. 251-288.

Stamper, R. *Information in Business and Administrative Systems*. London: Wiley, 1973.

Stephens, R., and Wood, J. "Information Systems as Linguistic Systems: A Constructivist Perspective." In M. Mackson, G. Mansell, R. Flood, R. Blackham, and S. Probert (Editors), *Systems Thinking in Europe*. London: Plenum, 1991, pp. 469-474.

Synnott, A. *The Body Social: Symbolism, Self and Society*. London: Routledge, 1993.

Turner, B. *The Body and Society*. Oxford: Blackwell, 1984.

Turner, B. *Regulating Bodies: Essays in Medical Sociology*. London: Routledge, 1992.

Varela, F. "Making it Concrete: Before, During and after Breakdowns." *Revue Internationale de Psychopathologie*, Volume 4, 1991, pp. 435-450.

Varela, F. "Whence Perceptual Meaning? A Cartography of Current Ideas." In F. Varela and J. Dupuy (Editors), *Understanding Origins: Contemporary Views on the Origin of Life, Mind and Society*. Dordrecht: Kluwer Academic, 1992, pp. 235-263.

Varela, F.; Thompson, E.; and Rosch, E. *The Embodied Mind: Cognitive Science and Human Experience*. Cambridge: MIT Press, 1991.

West, D., and Travis, L. "The Computational Metaphor and Artificial Intelligence: A Reflective Examination of a Theoretical Falsework." *AI Magazine*, Spring 1991a, pp. 64-79.

West, D., and Travis, L. "From Society to Landscape: Alternative Metaphors for Artificial Intelligence." *AI Magazine*, Summer 1991b, pp. 69-83.

Winograd, T. "A Language/Action Perspective on the Design of Cooperative Work." *Human-Computer Interaction*, Volume 3, 1987, pp. 3-30.

Winograd, T., and Flores, F. *Understanding Computers and Cognition*. New York: Addison Wesley, 1987.

Wittig, M. "The Category of Sex." *Feminist Issues*, Fall 1982, pp. 63-68.

Zuboff, S. *In the Age of the Smart Machine: The Future of Work and Power*. New York: Basic Books, 1988.

About the Author

John Mingers is a Senior Lecturer in Operational Research and Systems at Warwick Business School, Warwick University.   He is Director of the M.Sc. in Management Science and Operational Research.

He began his career working in Information Systems and Operational Research for companies such as Unilever and British Leyland.   He then attended Lancaster University and undertook postgraduate studies in Systems, and particularly Soft Systems Methodology, with Professor Peter Checkland.

Dr. Minger's teaching career included Ealing College of Higher Education and Southbank Polytechnic before starting work at Warwick University in 1987.

His research interests are in the areas of philosophical aspects of Information systems and particularly the nature of Information; the use of Soft and Critical Methodologies within Information Systems and Operational Research; and applications of Autopoiesis.

PART FOUR

Reflections of Research: Inscription

18

Social Theory and the Study of Computerized Work Sites

Bruno Latour
Centre de Sociologie de l'Innovation
Ecole Supérieure des Mines de Paris

Abstract

This paper is a meditation written by an ignorant trying to understand what has changed in his field, social theory, because of the development of information technology and because of the analysis of sociologists, specialists of labor relations, of organizations, of situated cognition, etc. It starts with a simple example of practice and tries to analyze it by following new concepts which seem to derive from the redistribution of humans and non-humans due to the pervasiveness of computerized work sites. It then tries to list the services rendered to social theory by the studies made by much more knowledgeable colleagues. Finally, it tries to show, with a very clumsy vocabulary, how we could account in better terms than networks, for a social theory redistributed by information technology and its students.

1. PROLOGUE

"Let us meet at 12:30 at the Eurotunnel Gate at Waterloo Station," I had told Adam on the phone from Paris. "All right. I will be there," he had said, approving this quasi contract with the telephonic equivalent of a hand shake or of a signature. I could have asked him to send a confirmation fax to make doubly sure that we had agreed on the same information in spite of the one hour lag that England insists on having over the Continent (to feel closer, I guess, to the United States). But since we are friends and not business partners, our word is our bond. While I am sitting on the train, the sentence we have both uttered a few hours before has changed its position quite a bit. It is now hovering over me (and, I hope without being certain, over him as well) to offer both of us a *program of action* which allocates roles to two individual designated by the same first name "Adam" and "Hélène," and to make these individuals circulate in a space and time trajectory marked by land marks — Paris, London, Waterloo Station (not such a nice label, by the way, for welcoming a French woman) — and by other types of marks like gate names or numbers and hands of clocks indicating 12:30 (of course I did not mention that it was p.m. and not a.m., relying on his implicit knowledge of what is "of course" and goes without saying, but of this I am no longer completely sure while I am fretting on the comfortable seat).

Reading through the Chunnel, I go through a sort of out-of-body experience, a very common one, since there are now at least two Hélène s, the one sitting there and the other one anticipated by the agreed upon program of action and which is due to meet Adam at the expected time and place an hour from now (twenty minutes if the bloody Brits had managed to modernize their line as speedily as the French!). When we meet one another, I will not only be reunited with Adam, but the Adam-of-the-script will coincide with the Adam-in-the-flesh and the Hélène-of-the-script will meet Hélène at the Eurotunnel Gate which will be, if everything goes well, the same as the gate-of-the-script. The coincidence is a risky one, though. The train might be delayed — possible — Waterloo debaptised to please the French and renamed "Austerlitz" — quite unlikely — Adam might be late — more likely. It is only when all the conditions of felicity will have been fulfilled that we will forget about the script hovering over us and, after a friendly kiss, head for the National Gallery.

2. DIFFERENT TYPES OF DELEGATES

What does this anecdote have to do with natural or artificial intelligence, information technology and with organizations? A lot as we will see later, but we need to analyze it first by unfolding its various threads.

Over the phone, Hélène and Adam have told each other a *story* about London, trains, stations, Waterloo and about visiting the National Gallery, a story which, by itself, is no different from daydreaming or novels. They have together, one pushing the other, invented a possible world in which they could meet, be friends again (see, for instance, Pavel 1986). In the course of the story they delegated characters also called "Adam" and "Hélène" which could do things, and meet and talk and follow a certain path inside a background of land marks which were also called "London," "Waterloo" and "Trafalgar Square." In such a way they went through another out-of-body experience since they lent to their story characters, in part similar to them in part different, who were doing new and impossible things in this other frame of reference. As in the Allen film, where Bogart takes over the conversation of the too clumsy Woody, they duplicated themselves, adding a set of clones to their own selves.

The story, however, took a completely different meaning when they decided over the phone that it was no longer a possible world that they had populated until then with similes of their own bodies, but that, on the contrary, they were binding themselves to a program of action, a script which was, from now on, delegating roles and trajectory *to them*.[1] They were organizing a joint trip to London. The script has become the dispatcher of their future activity, and they had now to fulfill the roles allocated to them, although, a few minutes ago, they were sending characters resembling them in another space and time. Without changing much of its material content, the story which they were telling each other has become an *organization*. They could change it at

---

[1] See, for instance, Taylor (1993). See also the work of Barbara Czarniawska on organizations as peculiar forms of discourse.

will, but now that the telephone has been put down, and that they have no way to ring one another, the script takes over and limits their ability to maneuver. Hélène and Adam in the flesh are now the delegated characters of their own story — but that's the point, the story is no longer their own.

Characters in the story may change, and it is because they change so much, shifting quickly out to other times, spaces and actants that they deploy so many possible worlds, worlds which were not even envisioned a few minutes ago. Characters in the script dispatch roles, appointments, performances in a space and time trajectory which is also going to produce novelty but not of the same kind as that of the story. Instead of possible worlds, the dispatching is going to actualize *one* world, the one where Adam in the flesh meets Hélène in the flesh at 12:30 in London by distributing agents and functions in a spatial and temporal trajectory.

The script that dispatches activity to make one possible world actual is too weak in itself to *bind* its delegated characters to it. The bonds of legal ties have to be added to transform this script into a quasi-contract that will make sure that the personality and wishes of Adam and Hélène will be stable over the period of time and the span of space that separates them from their kissing each other. The characters of the story and of the script are now tied up with chains that cross beyond the limits of space and time. Of course, since they are friends they do not need to instrument these ties with so many faxes, signatures, attorneys at law, lawyers and paperwork. An "all right" on the phone is all it takes to insure the isotopy of all those characters through time and space. Hélène is confident in Adam; she recognized the sincerity of his voice and his tone of indisputable engagement; his track record so far has been impeccable. Friendship and confidence are enough to carry the will through space and time without too much deformation. Lawyers and paperwork could become visible, however, if things went wrong, trains crashed, homicide were committed, Hélène kidnapped, etc. Traces of this informal quasi-contract would be elicited from telephone companies, Eurotunnel computers, wiretapping, and so on, to prove that they had planned a meeting (detectives are good at finding the most implausible traces of informal exchanges and turn out evidence no one expected).

To the story, to the script, to the bonds of quasi-contracts, Adam and Hélène have added references to places and times like Waterloo Station or the Eurotunnel Gate. They do not bring those actants in their scripts, they allude to them through a form, a name, a description that carries no resemblance whatsoever with what they talk about but carries information about them. More delegates *standing for* Waterloo Station and London and which circulate in such a way that some path is thus established through space and time could retie those forms back to what they refer.[2] Hélène, who has never been to Waterloo Station, will not be able to recognize the station but will be able to *read* the large letter signs that are written all over the platform of her destination, W-A-T-E-R-L-O-O. She will know she is at the right place because of the correspondence between the piece of information she has jotted down and the big signs she can now see through the window. Correspondence but not resemblance is what will lead both of them through those blind referential chains. (Adam, however, being a Londoner, will not even look at the labels but will simply fall back on an old embodied routine and walk through the

---

[2]For an example in a science field, see Latour (1995).

streets from his studio to the Station, adjusting from time to time, without even thinking, to the few roadblocks along the path, just doing next what comes naturally).[3]

Who talks over the phone? Who travels to London? Not Adam and Hélène only. Talking from Paris to London would require a very loud voice and walking and swimming from one point to the other would require quite a good breath and an athletic body, and a lot of time, and Hélène will age quite a bit through this strenuous effort and may drown along the way. Adam, Hélène, and electrons, and digits and telephone companies are doing the talking. Hélène and the trains and SNCF and Eurotunnel are doing the traveling. Delegates again by the millions which are taking over the tasks of talking and traveling and afford, allow, permit, authorize Adam and Hélène to rejoin. Not, to be sure, this Hélène and this Adam, but *an* Adam and *a* Hélène among the many they have statistically anticipated and for whom they have designed telephones and seats and fares and week-end packages — breaking down consumers in small socio-professionnal categories through fine tuned marketing, averaging out body sizes and weights through clever ergonomics. For *this* Hélène, the millions of delegates count for naught: she just boards the sleek train, but they act all the same; as for the Eurotunnel, it is Hélène who is just one passenger among (they hope) millions of others, one user's input at the ticket counter keyboard (although the hostess has been asked, in a training program set up by a public relations outfit, to smile so as to "personalize" the anonymous relation).

The rail tracks, the telephone lines, the software, the beautiful umbrella of Waterloo Eurostar Station, the seats are reliable and steady not because they form the outside world in which Hélène's human interaction with Adam takes place but because each of them rely on other actants which have a different timing.[4] The silicone of the chips, the steel of the dome, the plastic foam of the seats, are coming from far away in space and time and continue to act, dislocated, rearranged, recombined, offering a steady background to the fleeting interaction where these two youngsters kiss one another for a fraction of a second at the Eurotunnel Gate. The couple can change their plans or cancel their trips, but the chips, the steel frame, the carriage will last a bit longer, if, that is, inspectors, engineers, and maintenance crews keep them up according to schedule. To the intersubjectivity of their relations, one should add the *interobjectivity* of all these folded delegates they rely on so much (Latour 1994b).

We met the Hélène-on-the-phone, which we called "in the flesh" to simplify, then the Hélène character in the story who was going to London, then the Hélène delegated by the script which was supposed to fulfill the role expected from her, then the Hélène stabilized through time and space by the bonds of contracts and engagements, then the many statistical Hélène-like customers and consumers inscribed in the systems, marketing and fares of the telephone and railways companies. Quite a lot of Hélènes! And all this without mentioning those Hélènes anticipated by Adam who might bear much more resemblance with idols of dreams and flesh conjured, through crystallization and condensation, out of a vast array of mothers, bodies, animals and djinns, than with the beautiful, fleeting and unsteady Hélène walking out of the train in her red coat smiling through her deep blue eyes.

---

[3]On the routine nested inside an organization, see the classic book by Suchman (1987).

[4]On the notion of technical delegates, see Latour 1994a.

Then we had the many delegates that travel back and forth through the referential chains allowing places, actants and times to be carried over in the various forms and accounts and then back again to where they came from — and this was without counting the metrology that makes possible, at great expense, to connect the clocks all over Europe so that the large mechanical one of Big Ben, across the River Thames, coincides with the high-tech digital clock over the gate and with Adam's own watch, at which he is nervously glancing. Present through the steady mediations of bricks, steel, software, door closers, counters and elevators, hundreds of engineers, workers, designers, architects, bureaucrats, and millions of past parts are *sharing* the interactions with the couple, present, *hic et nunc*, and now reunited. Present and absent, silent and meaningful, those other kinds of delegates organize in advance, indicate, force, forbid, afford, allow the zigzagging path that the two friends are now drawing over the white lobby floor to exit Waterloo station.

3. IN WHAT KIND OF WORLD DO COMPUTERIZED WORK SITES EXIST?

The kind of world I tried so clumsily to describe, by following the paths of delegation instead of its components resembles the two former ones in which computing has been successively, and somewhat successfully, inserted but it also differs from them in a few crucial features. The first one took the humans as irrelevant; the second tried to circumscribe the non-humans as much as possible. The third follows, as far as possible, and in all its consequences the impossibility of allocating humanity and non-humanity in the first place.[5]

The first world was that of efficient machines, accurate facts, and profitable markets that were produced by human subjects almost entirely reducible to calculations, to the point where no one could distinguish a calculation made inside a human machine from an automatic human outside of a body. In such a world, to be sure, there subsisted a few pockets of disorder, passion, feelings, and politicking, but they were just that, pockets, which should, like ponds after a storm, dry up under the warm and clear sun of Reason. Dreams of clarity proliferated from the principle of universal calculability, to automated factories, transparent communication, cybernetic feedback, robots finally embodying the disembodied conceptions of reason devised by so many philosophers who did not know that they were, long before chips and silicon, talking about computers when they reformed minds, mores, societies and mathematics.[6] For a moment, in the fifties and sixties, the coincidence of philosophy, brain sciences, social reforms, world markets and the advent of computers seemed so powerful that this dream of absolute clarity was shared by everyone (I mean the few who believed they counted for everyone).

Dreams of clarity are dreams all the same: that is, fuzzy and blurred. Fuzziness seemed soon to creep in and "softies" took over introducing us to a second picture of the world. Computers have bugs; software engineers are a rather unmanageable lot; organizations are so flaky and so fickle that many big systems crashed; human experts seemed to have at the tips of their fingers many things that could not easily pass through the keyhole of the keyboard; lawyers have an uncanny

---

[5]As usual novelists, once on the right track, do much better than social theorists, as can be witnessed in reading the extraordinarily subtle book by Powers (1995). I thank Geff Bowker for this reference and for many others.

[6]This is made clear in Gardner (1985), as well as in many articles by Phil Agre.

ability to get back into the lines of software with litigation and copyright laws; clients obstinately refused to clearly state the specifications they wanted implemented or, believing in the ease and transparence that was so much trumpeted around, constantly asked for changes and new features. The picture, like in a background/foreground Gestalt shift, was suddenly reversed and computer technologies, expert systems, and information sciences appeared as little pockets, tiny microtheories, small and fragile experiments, inside a human, organizational, social and political mess which gave no sign of slowly fading away. Opacity grew instead of transparence. All those black boxes piled on top of one another inside soft organizations and shifting markets, made for an even more obscure imbroglio.

The human dimension had been forgotten, it was said.[7] The subjective, intentional, interactive human was said to be back (for an impressive study, see Lave 1988). Organizations and political forces have to be taken into account, it was argued, since they offered the background and logistics of those computer systems. After the triumph of engineers in the first world, were we witnessing the revenge of sociologists, psychologists, ethnographers, hermeneuticians, management experts, organizational scientists and other "softies" to give us a picture of the second?

I do not think so. The field is already much further than the defense of humanity inside microchips. The works by Susan Leigh Star on computerized work sites (see, for instance, Star 1989), of Ed Hutchins on cognitive anthropology (Hutchins 1995), of Lucy Suchman and Charles Goodwin on coordination into work sites,[8] of Laurent Thévenot (1994) on familiar courses of action, in addition to the studies by social historians of science,[9] and sociologists of science turned to organization like John Law (see, in particular, Law 1993), point to a complete redefinition of the divide between the two worlds. In the following statement, "information science and artificial intelligence in human organizations," only the two couplers "and" and "in" have remained unscathed! Each of the six other words have been reformatted beyond recognition. Neither the first nor the second picture of the world seems to be able to handle those changes. The paradox is that there are still people who advocate — or fear — the development of those terms although the practical result of their introduction has been to completely dismantle each of them.[10]

Take the human, for instance. Of course, it is no longer a calculating entity which could easily be morphed into silicon chips. But it is certainly not a subjective, reflexive, intentional, embodied unity either. Not only has its cognition been distributed, situated, but it is now shared with many intellectual technologies to the point where studying a human is studying a field of forces and transfers of documents, instruments, ideographies, through a collective of similarly distributed fellows, some of them look anthropomorphic but many don't. The engineering dream was to morph the human into a rational machine. The humanist counterdream was to recover an

---

[7]For the general public, at least, this position is well represented by Dreyfus (1992).

[8]See, for instance, the marvelous piece on cognitive group work in an oceanography ship by Goodwin (1995).

[9]Among which that of Simon Schaffer stands as particularly compatible with those of sociologists of labor and computerized work sites; see among, Schaffer 1994.

[10]As can be seen in reading Collins (1990), who tries to patrol a boundary as fractal as that of Bosnia.

intentional, reflexive and coherent carrier of values. The result is a rather bizarre cyborg that resembles neither the machine nor the human.[11]

Intelligence has undergone changes which are as drastic. With so many intellectual technologies being introduced from writing to laboratories, from rulers to pebbles, from pocket calculators to material environments, the very distinction between natural, situated, tacit intelligences and artificial, transferable, disembodied ones has been blurred. Intelligence no longer seems a psychological or even a cognitive property, but something more akin to heterogeneous engineering and world making, a distributed ability to link, associate, tie, fragments of reasoning, stories, action routines, subroutines, and to hang them to many holders; some of them look like neurone nets, other like software, other like graphics, still other like conversations and rituals.

Artefacts themselves have changed to the point where neither engineers nor sociologists would recognize them any more. Machines, automatisms, material components were supposed to be asocial and ahistorical. This is why they fascinated so much the engineers dreaming to delegate to them the flesh and blood of the disorderly bodies and why social scientists and humanists worried so much about their barbaric introduction into the civilized world. But artefacts, in turn, have become active social actants endowed with a history and a collective career, shifting competencies and affordances back and forth between one another and between the (by then deeply) redistributed human agents (Latour 1992). They enter the collective, not because they close the mouth of intentional humans, stop the controversies of squabbling scientists, bring passive resources to the inventive mind, offer a convenient receptacle for social values, but, on the contrary, because they *add* intentions, controversies, activities, meanings to programs of action that would be, without them, too limited and narrow.

For political reason, science had offered, for several centuries, the common blueprint to picture the human mind, its natural intelligence, and that of matter and artefacts. But what is left now of the former vision of an asocial, ahistorical science, hovering away and above the collective brew of passions and politics? The sciences too have been reformatted beyond recognition without losing the reality and objectivity they were so much boasting about. Many new realities and objects are brought in through the referential chains launched by fragile disciplines inside narrow, local, tiny, expensive and blind networks of practice which establish connections with totally unexpected entities which, from now on, have a different history and form a different society (for one example of this complete change, see Smith and Wise, 1989). Clever delegates, sophisticated instruments, tiny non-human observers are now populating those relativistic networks *animating* society and history with fresh actants. Being real and objective in addition no longer makes them so many foreign bodies in the social fabric. They simply add to its complication, to the intricacies of its political representation.

Information takes a different meaning if the sciences are thus reconfigured. A form cannot be what it is the form of. The words "Waterloo Station" are not Waterloo Station any more than a map is the territory, but it is what allows Hélène in Paris to establish at a distance some connection between Paris and the place of her rendezvous. It does not bridge the distance

---

[11]As can be witnessed in reading Haraway (1992).

because it would carry nothing from the Station to her flat since nothing that resembles the building would travel in such a way. But it is not a conventional or mnemonic sign standing arbitrarily for the real Station either. It is only one transformer into a long chain of similar transformers that will cross through the various matters of expression allowing a *constant* to be maintained through the continuous shift of delegates and translators. Words never face the world, they never mirror nor conventionally relate to "it." Worlds may be shaped in such a way that many types of expression, including words, may trace a referential path within it, allowing action at a distance. Information does not draw a virtual world added to the first; it is deeply rooted in it, part of it, risky paths linking entities to one another through the peculiar grasp of reference.

Organizations, finally, no longer look the same now that to their local interactions, and to their dispatchers, has been added so many computers and data banks, so many artefacts and intellectual technologies, so many stories, so many centers of calculation and information processing rooms, so much distributed and situated cognition. It is no longer clear if a computer system is a limited form or organization or if an organization is an expanded form of computer system. Not because, as in the engineering dreams and the sociologists nightmares, complete rationalization would have taken place, but because, on the opposite, the two monstrous hybrids are now coextensive. If instead of Hélène going to London to meet Adam, I had told the story of a GOTO function in BASIC programming language — the only one I know to my great shame — we would have encountered as many legal, material, social, and referential features. Exactly as following Hélène forced us to get out of her interaction with Adam to take into account many other paths through many other types of delegations, following the realization of software instructions will have taken us out of chips and gates through many heterogeneous paths.

Thus, if I am correct in recapitulating all those changes, to follow "information science and artificial intelligence in human organizations" no longer means to try to expand rationality everywhere, nor does it mean to try to limit its expansion by insisting on the human dimension of all personal interactions and on the irreducible irrationality of work sites. The world in which computing occurs has too many unexpected features, many of which have been revealed to social theory and philosophy by the attempts to develop computer systems according to the politics of reason and by the failures to do so.

4. TYING THE FRAGMENTS BACK TOGETHER

One description of this third world into which the study of computerized work sites has introduced us, is to say that computer systems are no more embedded in human organizations than human organizations can be embedded in computer systems. Embedding is not a good metaphor to follow the many *displacements* that have modified beyond recognition definitions of labor, expert, information, communication, computing, simulation and institutions. But how to follow those displacements?

One way of talking about displacements without using structures and essences is, of course, to consider that *fragments* are the only thing we have to consider: fragments of intelligence distributed through machines, fragments of machines dispersed through bodies, fragments of organizations morphed into software lines, fragments of codes sticking into institutions, fragments of subjects floating into virtual space. Much of the cyborg literature looks to me as an appeal to the inevitable fragmentation of bodies, organizations, subjects, science, artefact, markets and stories.

Are fragments, however, so different from the structuralist position they wish to disseminate? This is not certain. The fragment has the same differential property as the element of the bygone structure. In the same way as an item in a structure is defined only by its difference in a list of substitutable items, a fragment takes its meaning only from its position in the system of transformations it alludes to. The only difference between the construction of structuralism and its deconstruction into fragments is that there is no longer any structure to compose the list of substitutions. Thus, fragments are structural features without structure! This might be a way of accumulating the disadvantages of the rationalism that has been criticized without keeping any of its enlightening features.[12] If we accept the deconstruction metaphor, the relish in fragmentation, so pervasive in postmodern writings, is simply, under the guise of modesty, a way of prolonging modernism a bit longer without running the risk of shaping a vast and fragile system.

This is, of course, why we talked so much of networks (or better rhyzomes in order to avoid the technical connotation of the word).[13] First because it was a way, as powerful as structures, to fight essences. A new software package, a new computer site, a new chip, a new anti-trust policy, a new electronic forum will not be seen as having to do with technology, or labor organization, or culture, or law but as the heterogeneous branching out of a rhyzome. This is a useful way of talking since it does not require, at the beginning, a definition of what it is to be a skilled human worker, or an efficient organization, or a body of expertise, or an automaton, or an enterprise. Each element in the network is simply defined by the heterogeneous list of its associates. A consumer of bank services is redefined by "its" association with the automatic bank teller exactly as the definition of an Intel chip is modified by being associated with a new software or an Army weapon system. An expert knowledge is simply reformatted and reconfigured once it has been in part written down in an expert system inside a stock management package. A fuzzy logic gate, once inserted into a washing machine in a Korean factory to win through advertise-ment a new market share, is simply another heterogeneous connection that reformats fuzzy logic as much as Korean markets. Essence is existence, and existence is association.

The second advantage of a network is that it radically differs from a structure — fragmented or not — since it defines entities not by the substitutability of other differential positions but by the list of *unsubstitutable* and wholly specific associations of elements that make it up. Instead of being composed out of differentials — following the linguistic metaphor that held structuralism together — a network is made up of actants, each endowed with its unique specificity, hence its use in following historical and local trajectories to a degree of precision unknown in the

---

[12]As Serres (1995) puts it, "The larger is the [vase] the more fragile it is. If you break it, the smaller the fragment is, the more resistant it is. Consequently, when you create a fragment, you seek refuge in places, in localities, which are more resistant than a global construction....The philosophy of fragments brings together the philosophy of the museum and the museum of philosophy; thus, it is doubly conservative" (p. 120).

[13]For a recent analysis, see Callon (1992). The word "rhyzome" being, of course, from Deleuze and Guattari (1972/1983). Deleuze being certainly the most interesting philosopher, in that respect, since he always lived in this third world. For an excellent presentation, see Zourabichvili (1994).

structuralist literature.[14] In a network, each item is, so to speak, an independent *mediator* instead of a differential at the intersection of paradigmatic and syntagmatic lists, a mediator being defined as an event which is neither completely a cause nor a consequence.

Rhyzomes and heterogeneous networks are thus powerful ways of avoiding essences, arbitrary dichotomies, and to fight structures. But if they provide the analyst with a degree of freedom and with an agnosticism as large as those he or she is following around, their limit is to define entities only through association. Their flexibility is at once their main advantage and their main disadvantage. Powerful against structures as well as essences and moralizing, they become empty when asked to provide policy, pass judgement or explain stable features. Talk of rhyzomes allows the analyst to avoid revolution talks, technological fix talks, hypes of many sorts and is good at showing, for each innovation, the ordinary bricolage which makes it up. It also allows us to connect fragments together in the freest way. However, this is precisely where the weakness of rhyzomes lies: they are critical of every move, including of course the denunciatory tone of the critique, but they remain critical tools, good only at distributing, undoing, deploying, disseminating. Their dissolving power is so great that after having dissolved the illusions of critical postures, there is not much that is left and they even may turn into a somewhat perverse enjoyment of the diversity, perversity, heterogeneity and multiplicity of the unexpected associations they deploy so well.

This is why something else has to be added to the network to make them useful in following displacements without seeing them as so many fragments, something which they always had in practice but not explicitly — certainly not in so called actor-network theory anyway.[15] This supplement cannot of course be a return either to essences or to structures, nor can it be a specification of the types of associations in which entities are entangled, since, by definition, the number of types will be as large as the multiplicity of associations. The power of networks would be lost if one had to embark on the impossible dream of listing what kind of linkages are allowed and which are forbidden or impossible. A mad socio-logic would succeed the former mad dream of logicians.

Anne-Marie Mol and John Law (1994) have offered the useful notion of *fluid* to name this supplement which sticks firmly to the steel frame of networks but adds movement to it. Essences are not redefined only by the list of their associations but also by the fluid that distributes through them. Michel Callon (1995) proposes to reuse the economists' expression of *modes of coordination* in order to follow, not what is above or beneath the networks, but what traces them. In the prologue and the first section I tried, very tentatively, to introduce different *regimes of delegation* in order to follow at once the dissemination of an indefinite number of entities and the limited number of ways in which they grasp one another. Whatever the expressions, the attempt is the same: to keep the freedom of rhyzomes — against the modernist urge at rationalization and the postmodernist delight in fragments — but to overcome the limits of actor-networks in specifying the trajectories traced by those free associations.

---

[14]This is also what explains the virtual merging, in science studies at least, between social history and sociology of scientists at work.

[15]I would also apply this critique to my own work (Latour 1988).

I might have exaggerated the impact of information technology on social theory and the needs for revision. Rationality, humanism, structures, fragments, networks, all of those might be useful in describing some of the computerized work sites with which we are faced. I just wanted to explore another possibility: if we had to describe those imbroglios of computer chips, organizations, subjectivity, software, legal requirements, routines, and markets without using modernist or postmodernist idioms, how would we proceed?

5. REFERENCES

Callon, M. "The Dynamics of Techno-Economic Networks." In R. Coombs, P. Saviotti, and V. Walsh (Editors), *Technical Change and Company Strategies*. London: Academic Press, 1992.

Callon, M. *Réseaux et coordination* (in preparation). "Representing Nature, Representing Culture." Opening Address of the Center for Social Theory and Technology, University of Keele, March 1995.

Collins, H. *Artificial Experts: Social Knowledge and Intelligent Machines*. Cambridge: MIT Press, 1990.

Deleuze, G., and Guattari, F. *Anti-Oedipus, Capitalism and Schizophrenia*. Minneapolis: University of Minnesota Press, 1972, 1983.

Dreyfus, H. L. *What Computers Still Can't Do*. Cambridge: MIT Press, 1992.

Gardner, H. *Mind's New Science*. New York: Basic Books, 1985.

Goodwin, C. "Seeing in Depth." *Social Studies of Science*, Volume 25, Number 2, 1995, pp. 237-284.

Haraway, D. "The Promises of Monsters: A Regenerative Politics for Inappropriate/d Others." In C. N. L. Grossberg and P. A. Treichler (Editors), *Cultural Studies*. New York: Routledge, 1992, pp. 295-337.

Hutchins, E. *Cognition in the Wild*. Cambridge: MIT Press, 1995.

Latour, B. *Aramis, ou l'amour des techniques*. Paris: La Découverte, 1992. Translated by C. Porter, Cambridge: Harvard University Press, 1996.

Latour, B. *Irreductions part II of The Pasteurization of France*. Cambridge: Harvard University Press, 1988.

Latour, B. "On Technical Mediation." *Common Knowledge*m Volume 3, Number 2, 1994a, pp. 29-62.

Latour, B. "The 'Pédofil' of Boa Vista: A Photo-Philosophical Montage." *Common Knowledge*, Volume 4, Number 1, 1995, pp. 144-187.

Latour, B. "Une sociologie sans objet? Note théorique sur l'interobjectivité." *Sociologie du travail*, Volume 36, Number 4, 1994b, pp. 587-607.

Lave, J. *Cognition in Practice, Mind, Mathematics and Culture in Everyday Life.* Cambridge, England: Cambridge University Press, 1988.

Law, J. *Organizing Modernities.* Cambridge, England: Blackwell, 1993.

Mol, A., and Law. J. "Regions, Networks, and Fluids: Anaemia and Social Topology." *Social Studies of Science*, Volume 24, Number 4, 1994, pp. 641-672.

Pavel, T. *Fictional Worlds.* Cambridge: Harvard University Press, 1986.

Powers, R. *Galatea 2.2.* New York: Farrar, Strauss and Giroux, 1995.

Schaffer, S. "Babbage's Calculating Machines and the Factory System." *Des manufactures à la facture des connaissances.* Paris: INSERM, 1994.

Serres, M. *Conversations on Science, Culture and Time (with Bruno Latour).* Ann Arbor: The University of Michigan Press (Translated by Roxanne Lapidus), 1995.

Smith, C., and Wise, N. *Energy and Empire: A Biographical Study of Lord Kelvin.* Cambridge, England: Cambridge University Press, 1989.

Star, S. L. "The Structure of Ill-Structured Solutions: Boundary Objects and Heterogeneous Distributed Problem Solving." In L. Gasser and M. N. Huhns (Editors), *Distributed Artificial Intelligence.* London: Pitman, 1989, pp. 37-54.

Suchman, L. *Plans and Situated Actions: The Problem of the Human Machine.* Cambridge, England: Cambridge University Press, 1987.

Taylor, J. R. *Rethinking the Theory of Organizational Communicatoin: How to Read an Organization.* Norwood, New Jersey: Ablex Publishing, 1993.

Thévenot, L. "Le régime de familiarité. Des choses en personne." *Genèses*, Volume 17, 1994.

Zourabichvili, F. *Deleuze, une philosophie de l'événement.* Paris: PUF, 1994.

About the Author

Bruno Latour was trained as a philosopher and an anthropologist. After field studies in Africa and California, he specialized in the analysis of scientists and engineers at work. He has written *Laboratory Life and Construction of Scientific Facts* (Princeton University Press), *Science in Action* and *The Pasteurization of France* (both at Harvard University Press). He recently completed a new field study on an automatic subway system, *Aramis or the Love of Technology* (to be published by Harvard), and an essay on symmetric anthropology, *We Have Never Been Moderns* (Harvard University Press). He has just published *La clef de Berlin*, a series of essays on science and techniques. He is professor at the Centre de sociologie de l'Innovation in the Ecole nationale supérieure des mines in Paris.

19

From Work to Activity: Technology and the Narrative of Progress

Richard J. Boland, Jr.
Ulrike Schultze
Weatherhead School of Management
Case Western Reserve University

Abstract

Information technology transforms work in all its variety into uniform inscriptions that are combinable across time and space. Its digitized codings and classifications are immutable mobiles which claim to represent the true form of work to management and workers alike. Activity based costing is an accounting technology that produces such immutable mobiles. It promises to capture the essence of work and transport it unchanged from the factory floor to the manager's suite. We use this accounting technology as an exemplar to trace the rhetoric of how new worlds and new logics of work are created with the inspiration of information technology. We do so by analyzing a central story with which activity based costing justifies itself and makes its truth claims, and by identifying the kind of world, organization and work it creates. By expanding and extending the plot of the story told by the principal proponents of activity based costing, we expose some contradictions of this powerful system of representation and locate it within a larger narrative that promises progress through information technology.

1. INTRODUCTION

As managers and technicians develop ever more precise methods of gathering data at a distance, they are able to make representations of the world to themselves in ways that claim to be ever more real. Their motto could well be "the greater the accuracy, the greater the reality." Advances in information networks and representational technologies promise to transport particulars of local situations to managerial centers where they can be combined into a universalized knowledge-at-a-distance, enabling managerial knowledge to make ever stronger truth claims. The data used to construct such representations are what Latour (1990) refers to as immutable mobiles: inscriptions that claim to resist change and depict the same essence though communicated widely through space and time. Even the networked organization, in which strong centralized control is replaced by dispersed pockets of autonomous managers, relies upon immutable mobiles being available to each local manager, directly revealing the "form" of the world to them (Boland 1987; Latour 1987). As these digitized representations strengthen in their claims to accuracy and universalized truths, factory work is transformed. The logic of the factory shifts from one that assesses local efficiency to one that connects the micro movements of workers to global competitive consequences for the firm (Miller and O'Leary 1994).

In this paper we explore some aspects of how new systems for inscribing organizational work and representing it to ourselves are constructed and installed. As an exemplar of such a system we will consider activity based costing (Cooper and Kaplan 1988), which has come to dominate images of accounting for factory work over the last ten years. This is a computing intensive cost accounting system whose rise to prominence has been made possible by the development of microprocessor technology (Johnson 1992). Put simply, activity based costing replaces traditional methods for averaging costs across products with techniques for tracing a cost to the specific product it helped produce. Traditional cost accounting methods accumulated costs in a few overhead accounts and then spread those costs across products by various rules of thumb. Activity based systems use data processing to identify each detailed cost with a specific product. Activity based costing is a good exemplar for our purposes because its proponents make exceptionally strong claims that it is a more truthful representation than prior systems of cost accounting, and because it is a central feature in the redesign of factory work. Robert Kaplan and Robin Cooper are the most visible and vocal advocates of activity based costing, and they characterize it as:

- the first real management information system,
- the essential core of just-in-time manufacturing,
- a prerequisite for total quality management,
- and the underlying logic of any successful attempt at business process reengineering. [Kaplan 1992]

In other words, activity based costing has been put forward through the eminence of the *Harvard Business Review* as the mother of all information systems.

Activity based costing systems are an exemplar of information technologies that not only transform work but also transform the organizations, logics, ethics, aesthetics and worlds in which certain representations of work are claimed to be true. In an activity based costing system, work is replaced by the notion of activity. Work is a job to be accomplished or a function to be performed that has a local, self-contained quality. Activity, in contrast, is a more abstract notion in which mental or physical actions of a person are identified not as a job-of-work in their own terms, but as one element in the complex assemblage of a particular product or service, produced for a specific customer (Miller and O'Leary 1994). Activity based costing systems link the inscription of a person's mental and physical effort through complex paths within the organization to the product that "caused" them to happen. The immutable mobiles of an activity based costing system are a chain of digitized representations that trace from the need of a customer through the product that satisfies that need, to each of the elements that contributed to that product, and finally to the individual person whose activity created that element. With activity based costing, the individual who formerly did a job that was well-bounded in a local space and immediate time is now a mediated and essential piece of an enterprise-wide logic that could conceivably be global in scope.

When work becomes an activity it is transformed from overhead to direct product cost. What was a job to do and part of a general overhead of the firm, allocated to products by a rule of thumb, becomes an immediate element in the extended logic of the product. Work takes place in a local space that is reflexive in its own terms (humble as they may be). Activity, in contrast, takes place in an exposed global space, extended and linked directly to products and distant outcomes in an enterprise-wide form of reflexivity. Work is localized, passive and contained. Activity is abstract, global and extended.

We will develop our study of activity based costing by drawing inspiration from Latour's analysis of how truth claims for new images of the world and new techno science practices are made. First, we will explore briefly how the qualities of immutable mobiles are manifest in activity based costing, so that we may understand better how truth claims are constructed and strengthened with information technologies. We will then analyze the rhetorical processes through which activity based costing proponents have created persuasive arguments that their system represents a progress toward truth that it is superior to that of other cost accounting systems. With these persuasive rhetorics, they have enrolled companies worldwide to change work practices and install activity based information systems.

For this rhetorical analysis we will present the central narrative used by the principal proponents of activity based costing and will show why we believe it is such a powerful and convincing story to support their claims of truth and progress. Then, we will play with their narrative in order to undermine its claims. We will do this by telling an alternative but equally compelling story, and also by extending the original story and telling it further — to see what happens next. In both cases we will show how a narrative constructs alternative possible worlds, and how a technology and its logics of action depend upon the plausibility of the world that the narrative creates. As our analysis of activity based costing will reveal, the power of a narrative to provide worlds, logics, ethics, aesthetics and motivations to restructure work with information technologies depends on controlling what is read into the story, on stopping rival counter-stories from being told, and on terminating its own tale before the story goes too far.

2. THE RHETORIC OF TRUTH MAKING WITH INFORMATION TECHNOLOGY: CAPTATION OF THE READER

Presenting a narrative of life in the factory is an important rhetorical device for making activity based costing so believable; Latour (1987) refers to this as the process of *captation* through which the reader of an activity based costing proposal is carried along to its author's desired conclusions. The reader can be expected to raise objections to the line of argument in a text. A reliable reader is a skeptical one, but the successful truth maker skillfully anticipates a reader's objections and develops a "captation" to control the reader's possible meandering. As Latour stresses, if the author is to succeed as a truth maker, the reader must freely reach the desired conclusion, but only that one. The problem is "how to leave someone completely free and have them at the same time completely obedient" (Latour 1987, p. 57).

Captation refers to the way a truth maker can develop a persuasive line of argument that, like a river valley, allows readers to flow freely yet will succeed in "moving readers far away from what they were ready to accept at first" (p. 57). In the case of activity based costing, we see a narrative — the story of two factories (Cooper and Kaplan 1988) — playing the crucial role in its successful process of captation. Cooper and Kaplan use the story of two ballpoint pen factories as a principle vehicle in presenting a compelling case for activity based costing as opposed to traditional cost accounting. The story of the two factories will be presented, countered and extended below as we analyze how narrative enables truth making within particular kinds of worlds and their logics for the design of work.

Adopting Latour's vocabulary, we can approach activity based costing as a technology that has been made true and has been established as a widespread practice through a process of translation in which allies have been enrolled, black boxes have been constructed and stacked, and arguments have been built-up into many layered defenses against adherents of the traditional cost accounting techniques. Activity based costing is a kind of jump shift in the progress of cost accounting as a center of calculation, promising to collect data and enable managers to see and act from a distance with a dramatic increase in precision and truth in cost representations. Accounting has been inscribing business transactions into texts and providing authoritative readings of them since the time of ancient Mesopotamia (Hoskin 1993). Accounting is perhaps one of the first "immutable and combinable mobiles" with its use of clay tablets in hollow balls to transmit details of business transactions along the earliest caravan trade routes. Cost accounting has always promised managers to present the factory to them in a way that enabled them to analyze and manipulate it for purposes of control. Activity based costing promises a kind of hyper-realism in that form — a realism that offers a new, more penetratingly accurate truth, one that exposes and corrects the lies generated by cost accountings of the past.

Adherents of activity based costing are leading a revolution intent on overthrowing ideas of accounting for factory work that have been firmly in place for over a century and replacing them with an utterly new set of ideas and guiding images. Their claim is that all cost accounting theories and practices which have gone before are wrong. For over a hundred years, accountants have thought that any cost of running a factory department that did not arise from directly touching the product during its manufacture (such as the materials in a product or the labor that shaped these materials) was to be classified as an indirect cost or overhead. This overhead was to be assigned to products with various rules of allocation that had been developed through decades of cost accounting practice. Indirect costs generated by support activities such as engineering changes or parts maintenance were thus allocated to products in proportion to material or direct labor costs assigned to them, or in proportion to the square footage in the factory dedicated to their manufacture, or a myriad of other cost allocation rules.

Activity based critics of this traditional allocation practice have denounced it, claiming that it creates a false image of the product, its costs and its potential for profit (Cooper and Kaplan 1988, 1991; Johnson 1992). Traditional costing, they claim, arbitrarily assigns overhead expenses to individual units of manufactured product. Cost allocations that divide overhead by the number of units produced naively assume that indirect costs vary with units of output. Instead, activity based costing makes visible the degree to which a particular product was "touched" by activities anywhere in the firm and traces the cost of the activity to that product. A cursory brush with an activity does not cost a product as much as a significant encounter with it, and activity based costing promises to use information technologies to characterize every activity in the firm as a touching and thereby a cost of some product.

The advocates of activity based costing thus argue that the practice of averaging costs across many product classes based on materials or labor consumed in their manufacture have created blurred pictures. These have deceived managers and have led them to think and act in foolish ways. Because product costs calculated by cost allocation systems were not correct, the managers could easily sell items at the wrong price, creating losses rather than profits by mistake. Activity based costing proponents, inspired by the capacity of computers to collect, store and process seemingly infinite amounts of information (Johnson 1992) called for redesigning accounting systems in the factory so that any activity anywhere in the organization would be traced directly to the particular product that had "caused" that activity to happen.

All costs in the factory therefore become direct costs, just like the materials in the product and the labor that shaped it. They become direct costs because information technology can monitor micro movements anywhere in the factory and can provide a trace from every product at each and every moment of its manufacture back to the activities that sustain that product, no matter how distant, complicated, or indirect that path might be. Activity based costing proponents hold that the only limit to tracing through these complex paths is the limit of computational ability in today's computer systems. As computer power increases and as computer prices decrease, the dream of completely tracing every activity, no matter where it takes place, back to a product on the factory floor that caused it, edges closer and closer to reality.

One can see even before we explore the rhetoric of captation for activity based costing that its claims of progress and truth are part of a larger myth of information technology shared by many application systems. This is the myth that managers can see the world clearly through numbers, can grab onto it, and can shape it with a logic of efficiency revealed through the numbers (Boland 1987; 1989). Computers and related information technologies are intertwined with and feed into a belief in progress toward an enlightened future state. Activity based costing has been positioned as the factory accounting system that embodies that hope. It will save the manager from error because it will make visible the true state of affairs as well as the road forward.

3. THE STORY OF TWO BALL-POINT PEN PLANTS

In setting the stage for their discussion of how traditional costing systems generate distorted product costs and how activity based costing systems, by contrast, can produce accurate ones, Cooper and Kaplan (1988, pp. 97-98) tell "The Story of Two Plants." Both plants are identical in size and equipment, and both manufacture one million ball point pens per year. Plant I makes only blue pens, while Plant II makes a wide variety of pens. As Cooper and Kaplan describe it, "In a typical year, Plant II produces up to 1,000 product variations with volumes ranging between 500 to 100,000 units" (p. 97).

Plant II, although having the same standard labor and materials costs, has a much larger production support staff than Plant I: more product variation requires more people for scheduling, designing, negotiating with vendors, and so on. There is also more idle time, overtime, inventory and scrap in Plant II. Using traditional cost allocation methods, these overheads are distributed equally to every unit of output. Hence, blue pens, which represent 10% of Plant II's production will carry about 10% of factory costs and low-volume specialty pens, like lavender ones, will have only a small fraction of factory costs apportioned to them. The accounting system will report equal costs for lavender and blue pens "even though lavender pens, which are ordered, fabricated, packaged, and shipped in much lower volumes, consume far more overhead per unit" (1988, p. 98). The moral of their story of Plant I and Plant II is told by Cooper and Kaplan as follows:

> Think of the strategic consequences. Over time, the market price for blue pens, as for most high-volume products, will be determined by focused and efficient producers like Plant I. Managers of Plant II will notice that their profit margin on blue pens is lower than on their specialty products. The price for blue pens is lower than for lavender pens, but the cost system reports that blue pens are as expensive to make as the lavender.
>
> While disappointed with the low margins on blue pens, Plant II's managers are pleased they're a full-line producer. Customers are willing to pay premiums for specialty products like lavender pens, which are apparently no more expensive to make than commodity-type blue pens. The logical strategic response? De-emphasize blue pens and offer an expanded line of differentiated products with unique features and options.
>
> In reality, of course, this strategy will be disastrous. Blue pens in Plant II are cheaper to make than lavender pens – no matter what the cost system reports. Scaling back on blue pens and replacing the lost output by adding new models will further increase overhead. Plant II's managers will simmer with frustration as total costs rise and profitability goals remain elusive. An activity-based cost system would not generate distorted information and misguided strategic signals of this sort. [Cooper and Kaplan 1988, p. 98]

The story of Plant I and Plant II is a compelling narrative. Upon hearing it we can almost see the blue pens in Plant I, flowing smoothly through a continuous production process untouched by the Plant's limited production support staff. We can imagine an equally smooth flow of blue pens in Plant II. But the Plant II picture is marred by the stops and starts caused by specialty pens, the jolts in production seen in idle time and overtime, the messiness of surplus inventory and the waste of scrap associated with these non-blue pens. *We* can see the difference between the two plants, but the managers of Plant II are oblivious to it. Their inability to see what we as readers can see gives a suspense to this story. It makes us wish we could intervene and stop the strategic blunders that are sure to befall Plant II.

Reading (or listening) is an important source of the power of narrative, because we don't just read a story — we also of necessity read into a story. The story as told or written is always sketchy.

More details can and will be added by the reader because a story is never a complete telling of all the motivations, histories or circumstances of the characters or the setting. Bruner (1990) refers to this as the subjunctive quality of narrative. To get the "whole story" the reader's imagination is always at work completing the whole characters, the whole situation, the whole set of possible consequences and meanings that the events and plot suggest. Readers are always "writing" a virtual text as they "appropriate" a text's meaning for themselves (Ricoeur 1981). This subjunctive quality is an important part of the captation at work in the two plant story. Because we actively read into it and complete the story, its compelling logic is in part our own.

The story of Plant I and Plant II, simple as it may be, displays the essential elements of narrative structure (Bruner 1990, p. 77). First of all, it involves events that occur in a sequence and have a beginning, middle and end. We could tell the story with flashbacks so that the events appear out of sequence in the actual telling, but the underlying chrono-logical structure would remain undisturbed. The reader would, in effect, write its proper chrono-logic for herself. Second, the story involves intentional agents whose action is directed toward goals. The plot involves the seeking of the goals and the sequence of events builds a dramatic tension toward the denouement. Third, the story draws upon, questions and ultimately speaks to what we in the management community take to be canonical behavior. The intentionality of the characters is judged in terms of this sense of canonicality. The story dramatizes how the decisions and actions of Plant II's management violate the norms of expected behavior. It does so by contrasting it to the canonical behavior of Plant I, and this contrast relies upon the fourth element of narrative, the narrator's perspective. As the teller of this story, the narrator externalizes himself from the action and can therefore see both Plant I and Plant II in a way that neither of their managers can. It is the narrator's perspective that makes us as readers privy to how the managers of Plant II are oblivious to violating our (and their) standards of canonicality.

Chatman (1978) presents an elaborate framework for diagraming narrative structure and we can use some of his techniques in a simplified form to portray the structure of Cooper and Kaplan's two plant story (see Figure 1). In diagramming the structure of events in a story plot, Chatman distinguishes between major and minor events. He calls major events kernels and shows each kernel as a square. Minor events are satellites and are shown as dots. Satellites are events which enrich the story aesthetically, but are not crucial to the plot. Satellite events "necessarily imply the existence of kernels, but not vice versa" (Chatman 1978, p. 54).

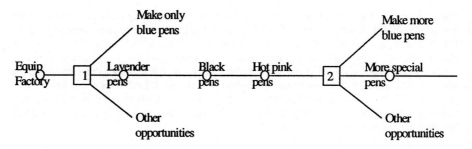

Figure 1. Diagram of the Plant II Story

Adapting Chatman's technique for depicting the narrative structure of the story of the two plants results in a diagram with a striking resemblance to the kind of river valley which Latour (1987) uses to describe the process of captation. Just as the narrator highlights some satellite events while deliberately keeping quiet about others so as to make the plot coherent and arrive at a certain moral, so the truth maker must set up a line of argument that prevents the reader from straying off the path up a tributary into a side valley. If the narrative is strong enough it can lead even the most skeptical dissenter to the desired conclusion.

In our diagram of its narrative structure, we identify two kernels in Kaplan and Cooper's story. The first is when Plant II chooses to produce other pens in addition to just blue ones. Details of how many different colors and sizes they developed (is it 1,000 or 1,500) are satellite events which elaborate upon but are not crucial to the plot. The second kernel comes when the management of Plant II bases its decision to pursue a specialty pen strategy on traditional cost accounting reports, once again failing to choose the path of pure blue pens. These two kernels as seen from the narrator's perspective are the crux of the non-canonical behavior by Plant II's managers. The story then subjunctively promises that canonicality could be restored, if an activity based costing system were used instead of a traditional one. Management would then have made a different choice at the second kernel and avoided their strategic blunders. That is how the story first disturbs, then promises to restore canonicality and how it helps the reader to construct a world in which activity based costing is needed.

But what is the moral of the story? What are the lessons to be learned from it beyond the desirability of activity based costing? In our reading of it, the moral of the story is found in the kind of world it constructs. Beyond activity based costing, the story of the two plants is presenting a world in which a certain type of plant is preferred. It is a world with a certain type of ethic and sense of value embodying ideas about the identity of a firm and its products, the nature of work, and the responsibility of a manager.

The moral of the story is that variety and small volumes breed inefficiency, which is costly and therefore bad. Treating products and customers as commodities in a mass market helps management reduce the variety it faces, which is good. Traditional cost allocations hide this true reality from us and induce us to first indulge in variety and then eventually to pursue it blindly. Activity based costing is not the moral of the story. It is a practice which promises to align us with the moral, which is to seek a world in which it is possible to be a low cost, high volume producer of commodity products to a consumer mass market. The moral is that true blue is beautiful, ordered and pure but multi-colored variety is messy, disorganized and noisy. Activity based costing is an information technology for restoring the beautiful world of order and truth. Why resist it?

4. ANTI-STORIES OF OTHER COST ACCOUNTINGS

Even though narratives are a powerful mechanism for convincing an audience of the correctness of an argument, they are also fragile. Seeing a story as an incident or an example, allows us to challenge it by a counter example, keeping in mind that for stories to be effective in the communication of morals, the narrator and the reader must share a sense of coherence and canonicality. By appealing to the reader's common sense view of the world (Linde 1993), we can renarrate this story and guide the reader's subjunctivizing toward a differently charted course.

Below we present two different approaches to renarrating and undermining Kaplan and Cooper's two plant story. First, we will resist the "facts" or kernels as presented in their telling of the story. Instead, we will move up a tributary and chart an alternative course by adding events and creating an anti-narrative with a reverse canonicality. After that retelling, we will undermine their narrative in another way, by picking it up where they left off, and telling the *rest* of the story.

4.1   The Two Plant Story: The Anti-Narrative

Shortly after Plant II begins producing specialty pens, several events in the environment combine to create a radical shift in consumer preferences. Elements in the background include an increased use of color graphics in personal computer displays, a series of popular press reports on psychological research showing that color is an effective communication tool, and a number of popular novels and multimedia experiences published with text of various colors — each color of text denoting different qualitative elements in the story. Against this background, leading companies in the business community begin a "reengineering" of corporate communications in which colored pens are used to highlight written documents and increase their "communication power." Packets of pens with an individual's preferred set of communicating colors become the new rage. Soon, pen packets are a symbol of professionalism and creativity for workers at every level of the corporate hierarchy.

At first, Plant I does not responds to these events, treating it as a fad that will go away. They continue their strategy of producing only blue pens, but consumer fascination with using color to communicate persists. Demand for standard blue pens decreases sharply. Plant I's management responds by lowering its price to keep market share. Unfortunately, many other pen manufactures have adopted activity based costing and have followed the low variety, single color strategy chosen earlier by Plant I. They also have been cutting prices, leaving Plant I with continually declining sales.

At this same time, Plant II finds its sales booming because they are able to produce multi-color pen packets with ease. They can offer their pens in an unlimited number of color combinations, almost customized for each customer's preference. As fashions in colors and their meanings change, Plant II is able to smoothly shift its production in response.

After a while, Plant I's management is forced to produce pens in different colors. Finding new suppliers, testing their quality and establishing relations with them is an expensive and difficult process. Variations in ink of different colors requires subtle changes in pre-mixing and machine adjustment. Plant I finds that it lacks the support staff with the expertise to handle these new tasks.

Because the management of Plant I desires to avoid a large production support group, consultants are hired to redesign their pens, find new suppliers, test the new inks, reformulate their mixing procedures and recalibrate their machines. Plant I's workers perceive these changes as a threat and fear being made redundant because of the different skills that are needed to produce multi-color pens. The few engineers that Plant I does have on its staff resent the dependence on consultants and become as demoralized and alienated as the production workers. Nonetheless, Plant I's management is eventually able to get multi-colored pen packets produced and shipped. They breathe a small sigh of relief as the plant slowly begins bringing its production volume back up.

Meanwhile, Plant II had anticipated that customers would soon go beyond wanting a pen packet with multiple colors and would demand packets in which each pen had the same feel in use and wrote with the same texture and thickness of line, no matter which color they were using. The sense of aesthetics of Plant II engineers dictated that the writing on a multi-color document should be identical in every respect except color. All the pens should have the same properties of line thickness, drying time, smudge resistance, fade resistance, bleed through, and so on.

This refinement in consumer tastes made Plant II's pen packets the most desirable on the market. Plant I tried to develop a similar feel and look in its pens by once again hiring consultants, but the skills and knowledge to achieve the needed consistency were beyond the consultants' ability and the workers and staff at Plant I had a very limited capacity for learning. After a short while, Plant I's sales of pen packets decreased sharply and management wondered what to do next.

4.2   The Moral of the Anti-Narrative of the Two Plants

In the version of the two plant story presented above, the moral is not one of purity and order, but one of networked interdependence and requisite variety. The moral goes something like this: only organizations with a sufficient capacity for complex interaction and coping with the variety presented by their environment will survive. As for the nature of the world presumed by these stories, we might say that the original two plant story presumed a world in which things will not change (except slowly and predictably), whereas our second version presumes a world in which things can and will change, and often quickly.

In the first kind of world, wisdom is something you achieve after learning about the world very well, just once. After something has been learned, the goal is to perfect it through repetition. Exact measures and comparisons against established norms are used to ensure high performance. "Pay attention only to that which is measured" is the operant logic in this world. In the second kind of world, wisdom is something you achieve when you realize that you must learn about the world over and over again, without end. "Learning is never wasted" is the motto that captures the ethic of this world. Knowledge and wisdom have blurred boundaries and are therefore hard to confine with activity/product traces. They are more like an accumulation of a resource that is available for drawing upon later. In a sense, this accumulation of experience as learning is an overhead, but a desirable one. In the first kind of world, a learning capacity beyond what is needed for perfecting the manufacture of one product is a luxury and an indication of waste and inefficiency; in the second kind of world, it is a necessity and a sign of an organization's fitness.

One implication for information technologies such as activity based costing is that the appropriateness of the logic of a given system is dependent on the type of world in which it is to operate. The way Cooper and Kaplan (1988) narrativize a manager's experience clearly makes activity based costing a compelling choice. Another implication is that the way we narrativize our experience and the kinds of information systems we select is also in part a making of our world. In the original two plant story, the customer is seen through the eyes of product costing. The desirable customer becomes a commodity, like the desirable product. Costs attach to the customer as they do to any other element of production, and the best customer is a low variety customer that does not demand high discounts, frequent delivery of small lots or expensive sales and technical resources (Cooper and Kaplan 1991, p. 134). If customers demand too much, i.e., become too costly, "fire them" (Kaplan 1992, pp. 62-63).

It turns out that in the second version of the two plant story, the canonicality of traditional allocation based costing and activity based costing are reversed. Traditional allocation based costing would have generated signals that encouraged the development of specialty pens and positioned management well for the coming changes in consumer tastes. It is not our purpose to prove that any one cost system is *the* true one, but rather to unpack the narratives that construct the worlds associated with different deployments of information technology.

Still, the question of learning raised by the second version seems to pose a difficulty for activity based costing in almost any circumstance, except that of a stable world. Learning is tangled and messy, transferring with surprise from one product to another. Solving a difficulty with red pens can result in knowledge that transfers to pink or purple ones. Building relations with a vendor while negotiating for green ink may affect relations with that vendor for all other inks. The design team that learns to reconfigure one line of pens builds skills and develops knowledge that can transfer to all future design projects.

Plant II did well in version two of the story because it had developed the capacity to learn and the costs associated with learning were not attached to any one product or activity. It is in the interrelations among persons, products and departments that an apparently localized act of learning can reveal its greater organizational benefit. Activity based costing isolates the linkages between discrete actions and products. It compartmentalizes persons, products and departments and thereby ignores the interrelations where learning can create value.

Activity based costing suffers from the reductionist fallacy in an extreme form; it is like saying we can study the individual members of a group separately and understand all we need to about their functioning as a team. Activity based costing, by teasing out separately traceable cost elements, sharpens the edges and outlines of the production process but cuts out the richness of interrelations and network of interdependencies that gives value to organizational learning.

4.3   Extending the Narrative Structure of the Original Two Plant Story

Stories have a beginning, middle and end. Coherence and plausibility are dependent upon relating events to the narrative's ending. The beginning and end provide a frame within which characters and incidents can be evaluated. It is this frame that enables both the narrator and the reader to moralize about the story. Thus the story can be fundamentally changed by ending it at a different place. "Reframing" the story in this way implies that the significance of events changes, that its plausibility needs to be reassessed and that a different moral may be drawn.

We will now change the ending of the two plant story, as a reframing strategy. In the first alternative story presented above, we created a different world by traveling up a "forbidden" tributary. Now we do so by staying within the river's valley but not stopping at the vista to which Cooper and Kaplan's story has led us. Instead, we will go further along the valley and arrive at a new moral. We thus continue the story line of the original "Two Plant Story" by following the major plot beyond its current ending point to see where it leads. The plot we will follow further is the implication of tracing the mental activity in production support to the specific product being thought about.

In activity based costing, products that are the focus of attention of engineers preparing change orders, or staff handling customer queries are, identified through "drivers," and the cost of that mental work is attached to its focus of attention. Accountants have always wanted to trace costs this way, the story goes, but couldn't do so because of record keeping and computational impracticality. Now, however, computers are able to do the amount of information processing required to make activity based systems possible. In principle, as the power and ubiquity of computers grow, the scope of mental work attached to products will also grow. As Cooper and Kaplan (1988, pp. 101-102) express it, only the costs of excess capacity and new product R&D would be excluded from an ideal activity based costing system. This is the direction in which we will expand the narrative structure of activity costing. We assume that by the year 2000, computers will have become so powerful, small and inexpensive that wholly new domains of mental activity will be opened for direct tracing to product costs. The kernel event we will add to the original activity based costing story is the invention in 2001 of the "Executive Jacket."

4.4 Capturing the Cost of Management Attention: The Executive Jacket

Plant I, after being forced to recognize the change in consumer tastes described above and to manufacture multi-colored pen packets, feels it is more important than ever to expand the scope of activity based costing to include all mental work in the company, including that of top management. Low-cost microprocessors have made new data collection devices possible that were unthinkable just a few years before. Cost accountants have used them to develop novel systems for tracking the mental activity of managers and tracing the costs of management directly to the products they focus their attention on during the day. One such device, called "The Executive Jacket," has been incorporated into the activity based costing system of Plant I.

The Executive Jacket is a fine quality suit coat with microprocessors, data storage, and "wireless" infrared communications, as well as location sensors, bar code readers, sound recording and high resolution video cameras woven into the lining of the jacket. Each manager in Plant I, including the CEO, wears an Executive Jacket and in so doing allows much of his or her mental attention to be recorded and allocated as costs of production.

Through the day, each manager's spoken words are recorded, transcribed, and key word indexed. All reading and writing is recorded by the video camera or gyroscopic pens and similarly indexed. Every second of a manager's time is then allocated to the product or project being discussed or written about. Each Executive Jacket comes with a pair of executive glasses in the breast pocket. These glasses have a bar code reader, a scanner and a gyroscopic tracker built into them, and managers wear their executive glasses whenever they read a document or report. Each page of every company document is bar coded and calibrated with grid lines readable by the glasses' scanner. As a manager turns to a new page on a cost report or budget, the glasses record which page is being looked at and where on that page the manager's attention is focused. This on-line tracking of their mental attention is transmitted to mass storage devices and entered into the cost file for the relevant product or project.

When several managers are together in a meeting, location sensors in their jackets allow the central computer to capture and allocate the costs of all managers present. As the director of cost accounting systems explains it, "When one manager in a meeting is speaking, we assign the cost of the other managers at the meeting to the product or project being discussed. It isn't perfect of course, since not everyone is really paying attention and some may even be having private thoughts, but it will take a big leap in technology to deal with those shortcomings."

The Executive Jacket system is not without problems. Managers have discovered that discussing a given product in a group meeting with ten or twelve executives can dramatically shift the cost structure for that product. "Twelve executives plus their support staffs can easily run $100,000 per hour, so discussing a product's cost per unit for more than just a few seconds can change the cost enough to invalidate their decision," explained the director of cost systems. "It seems that each refinement of the Executive Jacket enabling us to improve our cost tracing for management just makes the problem worse," he continued. "Hopefully, they will learn to think about things less and keep our products more cost competitive," he joked. Managers have now requested a real time costing system with interactive displays in their meeting rooms so they can track the changing costs of a product as it is being discussed. As one of the consultants hired by Plant I put it, "They have discovered the Heisenberg Uncertainty Principle of activity based costing — the harder they look at exactly where the cost is, the faster it moves."

4.6   The Moral of the Story of the Executive Jacket

The moral of this version of the two plant story is something like "beware of what you wish for — you just might get it" which is in some way analogous to the notion that we often mistakenly transfer the accuracy of the medium to the accuracy of the message (Latour 1990). By shrinking the distance in space and time between cost incurrance and its representation to the actors, the edges of action are sharpened leaving little room for people to talk, negotiate and maneuver. With the Executive Jacket, managers look into the computer display and see a mirror image of themselves. Action and the accounting of that action becomes instantaneous, leaving no place for the actor to be alone or even to stand.

We can imagine two main story lines that Plant I and its Executive Jacketed management team might follow from this point on. In the first story line, a question as to the value of management would be raised by workers and their unions as well as by the company's Board of Directors. The question would be: "How can we justify the cost of this management attention? Can't the workers and staff closest to the problem deal with it most effectively?" In this story line, the very information technology that gave management the power to make the mental processes of production support visible and traceable to products comes back later and is applied to them. With their mental work, they touch the product in much the same way as the shopfloor workers do. Activity based costing turns this work into a direct, visible cost. The result is a questioning of the value and efficiency of management itself, leading for a call to "fire the manager," instead of "fire the customer" as in the original story. Through a concerted effort of the Board and the Unions, management ranks are reduced to a mere few residual area coordinators. Over time, the managerless Plant I becomes even less able to sense, interpret and respond to the environment than before. The company moves slowly but surely to bankruptcy.

The problem of advanced information systems in this story is once again a failure to account for (or allow for) learning. Hopefully, learning was taking place in those management meetings and when they discussed an issue concerning hot pink pens they were learning about similar issues related to other colors and styles of pens. Similarly, when managers talked about a consumer reaction to a new pen packet line, they were learning about consumers in ways that would improve their knowledge of the market generally, including competitors, economic conditions and broader consumer preferences.

By directly linking mental activity to the immediate object of thought, an activity based system ignores relationships among objects, ignores the capacity for abstraction, and in short ignores learning. We could imagine that the managers of Plant I would themselves come to see this, which suggests a second story line that the tale of the Executive Jacket could follow.

In this story line, management begins to install the Executive Jacket system for management activity accounting, but stops abruptly, declaring that they have just had an insight: they have come to see that when they think about something they never *just* think about that one thing — they also are always *self-reflecting*, or thinking about their thinking (Bateson 1972). Self-reflection, in contrast to the apparent product or problem focus on their surface level speaking, reading and writing, is a meta-level activity that shapes and guides their thought. Self-reflection is what gives their thinking its value, and self-reflection is fundamentally about monitoring a focused activity in light of its full context of relationships. "No wonder activity based costing gave such distorted results of our management deliberations," the President of Plant I said after achieving this insight about self-reflection.

This story line has a kind of happy ending you might enjoy hearing. The management of Plant I revised their cost accounting and created a "Learning Account." Most of the cost of their deliberations were put into this new account. The cost accumulated in this account was then allocated to products based on broad indicators, such as labor hours, machine hours or materials cost. Management's insight on reflection soon grew to include the realization that production support staff also self-reflect during their work. As a result, a majority of the cost of the production support staff was also being assigned to "Learning Accounts" and allocated to products on the same broad indicators as managements'.

5. CONCLUDING THOUGHTS

The narrative of information technology as exemplified by activity based costing is a narrative of progress toward clarity, simplicity and purity. Information technology has a kind of magical power attributed to it for sharpening edges that were dull, making clear what was blurred and purifying what was contaminated. The world of work has become messy and inefficient over the last few decades as overheads grew and inventories proliferated. We long for the simple days when products were made directly for familiar customers in stable local communities. Information technology is intimately bound up with a kind of dream wish for restoring that simple past, and activity based costing is an exemplar of how information systems promise to fulfill that dream.

Information systems like activity based costing promise to replace free-floating and ethereal overheads of work with direct connections between activities and products, enterprise wide. They do so by cutting the edges of representations ever more exactly and precisely in the writing of globally reflexive texts. But the progress of return that they promise is just as false as the representations they replace.

The mental work of production support and management is a kind of organizational tapestry. By picking apart separate strands of thought-object linkages, activity based systems begin a process of unraveling the tapestry. Activity based systems claim to be more complex than the simplified traditional systems they are to replace. However, as a knowledge structure, activity based accounting is itself a progressive simplification — a systematic ignoring of relationships and sharpening of boundaries between activities (Star 1983).

Traditional cost allocation systems may appear simple to proponents of activity based costing, but by not pushing too far to sharpen the outlines of objects and processes, traditional systems allow a space for the complexity of interrelations in mental work. The allocations of traditional systems result in a blurring of the linkage between production support and products, but that blur allows for the possibility that learning and interrelationships can persist, safe from inscription.

Our conclusion is not to argue for yet another new kind of costing as the truly "unbiased" one, but instead to suggest that more appreciation be given to the narratives which underlie our technologies and the worlds which they create. More attention should be paid to narratives that emerge from the shop floor and the production support staffs themselves. Consideration for multiple narratives that give voice to and allow the construction of multiple worlds will not give us any one representation of work that is enduringly true, but they may give us more interesting ways to think about the organization, ethics and aesthetics of work than the search for such true systems has.

6. ACKNOWLEDGMENTS

The authors gratefully acknowledge helpful conversations with Keith Hoskin in developing this manuscript.

7. REFERENCES

Bateson, G. *Steps to an Ecology of Mind.* New York: Ballantine, 1972.

Boland, R. J. "The In-formation of Information Systems." In R. J. Boland, Jr., and R. A. Hirschheim (Editors), *Critical Issues in Information Systems Research.* Chichester: Wiley, 1987, pp. 363-379.

Boland, R. J. "Metaphorical Traps in Developing Information Systems for Human Progress." In H. K. Klein and K. Kumar (Editors), *Systems Development for Human Progress*. New York: North Holland, 1989.

Bruner, J. S. *Acts of Meaning*. Cambridge: Harvard University Press, 1990.

Chatman, S. *Story and Discourse in Fiction and Film*. Ithaca, New York: Cornell University Press, 1978.

Cooper, R., and Kaplan, R. S. "Measure Costs Right: Make the Right Decisions." *Harvard Business Review*, September-October 1988, pp. 96-103.

Cooper, R., and Kaplan, R.S. "Profits Priorities from Activity-Based Costing." *Harvard Business Review*, May-June 1991, pp. 130-135.

Hoskin, K. "Technologies of Learning and Alphabetic Culture: The History of Writing as the History of Education." In B. Green (Editor), *The Insistence of the Letter: Literacy Studies and Curriculum Theorizing*. London: Falmer Press, 1993.

Johnson, H. T. "It's Time to Stop Overselling Activity-Based Costing." *Management Accounting*, September 1992, pp. 26-35.

Kaplan, R. S. "In Defense of Activity-Based Cost Management." *Management Accounting*, November 1992, pp. 58-63.

Latour, B. "Drawing Things Together." In M. Lynch and S. Woolgar (Editors), *Representation in Scientific Practice*. Cambridge: MIT Press, 1990.

Latour, B. *Science in Action*. Cambridge: Harvard University Press, 1987.

Linde, C. *Life Stories: The Creation of Coherence*. New York: Oxford University Press, 1993.

Miller, P., and O'Leary, T. "Accounting, 'Economic Citizenship' and the Spatial Reordering of Manufacture." *Accounting, Organizations and Society*, Volume 19, Number 1, 1994, pp. 15-44.

Ricoeur, P. (Edited and translated by J. Thompson). *Hermeneutics and the Human Sciences*. Cambridge: Cambridge University Press, 1981.

Star, S. L. "Simplification in Scientific Work: An Example from Neuroscience Research." *Social Studies of Science*, Volume 13, 1983, pp. 206-228.

About the Authors

Richard Boland joined Case Western Reserve University in 1989 after thirteen years as Professor of Accounting at the University of Illinois in Urbana-Champaign. His research interests include qualitative analysis of the design and use of information systems and he is particularly interested in organization and human consequences of information technologies. Dr. Boland is Editor-in-Chief of the research journal *Accounting, Management and Information Technologies* and is Co-Editor of the "Series in Information Systems" for John Wiley & Sons. He currently serves on the Editorial Boards of *Accounting, Organizations and Society, Information Systems Research*, and *Information Systems Journal.*

Ulrike Schultze is a Ph.D. Candidate at Case Western Reserve University. Her dissertation investigates whether and how soft information is hardened in a groupware-mediated environment. This topic is borne out in her research in sociology of science and the role that technology plays in the creation of information and knowledge. Ulrike employs the concepts of narrative and paradigmatic modes of cognition to distinguish between different kinds of information and the social processes by which they are generated.

20

Social Shaping of Information Infrastructure: On Being Specific about the Technology

Eric Monteiro
Department of Informatics
University of Trondheim

Ole Hanseth
Norwegian Computing Center

Abstract

In this paper, we discuss conceptualizations of the relationship between IT and organizational issues. To move beyond an "IT enables/constrains" position, we argue that it is necessary to take the specifics of an information system (IS) more seriously. A theoretical framework called actor-network theory from social studies of science and technology is presented as promising in this regard. With respect to new organizational forms, the class of ISs which needs closer scrutiny is information infrastructures (INIs). They have characteristics which distinguish them from other ISs, namely the role and pattern of diffusion of standards. These standards are neither ready-made nor neutral: they inscribe organizational behavior deeply within their "technical" details. Diffusion and adoption of standards depart from other kinds of ISs by requiring the coordination of the surrounding actors, institutional arrangements and work practices.

1. INTRODUCTION

The theme of this paper is theorizing the relationship between technological and organizational issues, focusing on one such theory called actor-network theory (ANT), and contrasting it with

Giddens' structuration theory. This analysis is then extended to the more restricted relationship between information infrastructure (INI)[1] and new organizational forms.

We are witnessing a rapidly increasing number of theoretical, speculative or empirical accounts dealing with the background, contents and implications for a restructuring of private and public organizations. The sources of these accounts mirror the complex and many-faceted issues raised of an economical (OECD 1992), social (Clegg 1990), political (Mulgan 1991) and technological (Malone and Rockart 1993; Malone, Yates and Benjamin 1991) nature. A comprehensive account of this is practically prohibitive; the only feasible strategy is to focus attention on a restricted set of issues. To explain how we intend to approach this, it is necessary to make certain assumptions explicit and indicate how we position our work relative to other accounts.

As our point of departure, we embrace the fairly widespread belief that IT is a, perhaps the, crucial factor as it simultaneously enables and amplifies the trends for restructuring of organizations (Applegate 1994; Orlikowski 1991). The problem, however, is that this belief does not carry us very far; it is close to becoming a cliche. To be instructive in an inquiry concerning current organizational transformations, one has to supplement it with a grasp of the interplay between IT and organizations in more detail. We need to know more about how IT shapes, enables and constrains organizational changes. Faced with such a situation, there are in principle two possible strategies: (i) a more proper understanding should emerge as the result of an appropriate theoretical framework (Orlikowski and Robey 1991, p. 144) or (ii) through the accumulation of more empirical material (Smithson, Baskerville and Ngwenyama 1994, p. 10). Obviously, we neither want to argue against more suitable theoretical constructs nor empirical evidence per se, but we do suggest that what is lacking most is a satisfactory account of the interwoven relationship between IT and organizational transformations. More specifically, we argue that we need to learn more about how this interplay works, not only that it exists. This implies that it is vital to be more concrete with respect to the specifics of the technology. As an information system (IS) consists of a large number of modules and inter-connections, it may be approached with a varying degree of granularity. We cannot indiscriminatingly refer to it as IS, IT or computer systems. Kling (1991, p. 356) characterizes this lack of precision as a "convenient fiction" which "deletes nuances of technical differences." It is accordingly less than prudent to discuss IS at the granularity of an artefact (Pfaffenberger 1988), the programming language (Orlikowski 1992a), the overall architecture (Applegate 1994) or a medium for communication (Feldman 1987). To advance our understanding of the interplay it would be quite instructive to be as concrete about which aspects, modules or functions of an IS enable or constrain which organizational changes — without collapsing this into a deterministic account (Monteiro, Hanseth and Hatling 1994).

The remainder of the paper is organized as follows. In section 2, we elaborate the argument sketched above, namely that scholarly studies need to be more specific about the various components of an IS. We critically discuss contributions to the conceptualizations of IT and organizations based on Giddens' structuration theory and argue that these studies are lacking in

---

[1]INI is not a homogeneous concept. It is related to a number of concepts, some of which denote existing technologies (communication technology, inter-organizational systems [IOSs] and electronic data interchange [EDI]) and some do not (information or electronic highways). In particular, INI is currently being developed and shaped.

precision regarding the specifics of the IS. An alternative, theoretical framework borrowed from the field of social studies of science and technology called actor-network theory (ANT) is presented. ANT is on a fairly general and theoretical ground argued to offer a more promising way to account for the specifics of an IS. From this theoretical discussion concerning the appropriate way to conceptualize IT and organizations, in section 3, we turn to the issue of new organizational forms. The line of thought, developed above, here takes on the following shape: even brief reviews of arguments and evidence for new organizational forms motivate the need for a firmer understanding of the interplay with IT. The need to be specific and concrete regarding IT, in this context, amounts to describing how minute, technical design decisions embodied in the standards which constitute the information infrastructure are interwoven with organizational issues. The relevant class of IT to study is what during the last couple of years has been called information infrastructure. Its technical back-bone is standards. We accordingly study the social construction of standards. Our approach is based on two assumptions: (i) these standards are not ready-made, they are currently being shaped through complex, social processes, and (ii) these standards, contrary to most accounts, are anything but neutral: buried deep in "technical" details, they inscribe anticipations of individual, organizational and inter-organizational behavior. Extending the more general argument of section 2, we suggest that ANT is quite useful in accounting for how standards acquire stability, how they become increasingly "irreversible." Section 4 presents empirical illustrations from two cases of how ANT, in a quite concrete manner, may be used to describe important and neglected aspects of INI. In section 5 we make a few comments on important aspects of the interplay between technical and non-technical elements of INIs which ANT cannot properly account for. Section 6 contains concluding remarks.

2. CONCEPTUALIZATIONS OF THE RELATIONSHIP BETWEEN IT AND ORGANIZATIONS

The problem of how to conceptualize and account for the relationship between, on the one hand, IT development and use and, on the other hand, organizational changes is complex — to say the least. A principal reason for the difficulty is due to the contingent, interwoven and dynamic nature of the relationship. There exists a truly overwhelming body of literature devoted to this problem. We will discuss a selection of contributions which are fairly widely cited and which we consider important. (Consult, for instance, Coombs, Knights and Willmott 1992; Kling 1991; Orlikowski and Robey 1991; Walsham 1993 for a broader discussion.) Our purpose is to motivate a need to incorporate into such accounts a more thorough description and understanding of the minute, grey and seemingly technical properties of the technology and how these are translated into non-technical ones.

2.1. The Duality of IT

The selection of contributions we consider all acknowledge the need to incorporate, in some way or another, that subjects interpret, appropriate and establish a social construction of reality (Galliers 1992; Kling 1991; Orlikowski 1991; Orlikowski and Robey 1991; Smithson, Baskerville and Ngwenyama 1994; Walsham 1993). This alone enables us to avoid simple-minded, deterministic accounts. The potential problem with a subjectivist stance is how to avoid the possibility that, say, an IS could be interpreted and appropriated completely freely, that one interpretation would be as reasonable as any other. This obviously neglects the constraining effects the IS have on the social process of interpretation (Akrich 1992; Bijker 1993; Orlikowski and Robey 1991). A particularly skillful and appealing elaboration of this insight is the work done by Orlikowski, Walsham and others building on Giddens' structuration theory (Orlikowski 1991, 1992a, 1992b; Orlikowski and Robey 1991; Walsham 1993).

Despite the fact that these accounts, in our view, are among the most convincing conceptualizations, they have certain weaknesses. These weaknesses have implications for the way we in later sections approach the question of the relationship between information infrastructure and new organizational forms. Our principal objection to conceptualizations (such as Orlikowski 1991, 1992a; Orlikowski and Robey 1991; Walsham 1993) is that they are not fine-grained enough with respect to the technology to form an appropriate basis for understanding or to really inform design. Before substantiating this claim, it should be noted that the studies do underline an important point, namely that "information technology has both restricting and enabling implications" (Orlikowski and Robey 1991, p. 154). We acknowledge this, but are convinced that it is necessary to push further: to describe in some detail how and where IT restricts and enables action. At the same time, we prepare the ground for the alternative framework of ANT describing the social construction of technology. To this end, we briefly sketch the position using structuration theory.

The aim of structuration theory is to account for the interplay between human action and social structures. The notion of "structure" is to be conceived of as an abstract notion; it need not have a material basis. The two key elements of structuration theory according to Walsham (1993, p. 68) are (i) the manner in which the two levels of actions and structure are captured through the duality of structure and (ii) the identification of modalities as the vehicle which links the two levels. One speaks of the duality of structure because structure constrains actions but, at the same time, human action serves to establish structure. This mutual interplay is mediated through a linking device called modalities. As modalities are what link action and structure, and their relationship is mutual, it follows that these modalities operate both ways. There are three modalities: interpretative scheme, facility and norm. An interpretative scheme deals with how agents understand and how this understanding is exhibited. It denotes the shared stock of knowledge that humans draw upon when interpreting situations; it enables shared meaning and hence communication. It may also be the reason why communication processes are inhibited. In applying this to IT, Orlikowski and Robey (p. 155) note that "software technology conditions certain social practices, and through its use the meanings embodied in the technology are themselves reinforced." Facility refers to the mobilization of resources of domination, that is, it comprises the media through which power is exercised. IT, more specifically, "constitutes a system of domination" (p. 155). Norms guide action through mobilization of sanctions. As a result, they define the legitimacy of interaction. They are created through continuous use of sanctions. The way this works for IT is that IT "codifies" and "conveys" norms (pp. 155-156).

Given this admittedly brief outline of the use of structuration theory for grasping IT, we will proceed by documenting in some detail how these accounts fail to pay due attention to the specifics of IT. Orlikowski and Robey (p. 160) point out how "tools, languages, and methodologies" constrain the design process. The question is whether this lumps too much together, whether this is a satisfactory level of precision with regard to the specifics of IT. There are, after all, quite a number of empirical studies which document how, say, a methodology fails to constrain design practice to any extent; it is almost never followed (Curtis, Krasner and Iscoe 1988). Referring to Orlikowski (1991), Walsham (p. 67) notes that "the ways in which action and structure were linked are only briefly outlined." This is hardly an overstatement of Orlikowski, as opposed to what one might expect from examining "in detail the world of systems development" (Orlikowski 1991, p. 10), maintains that the CASE tool — which is never described despite the fact that such tools exhibit a substantial degree of diversity (Vessey, Jarvenpaa and Tractinsky 1992) — was the "most visible manifestation" of a strategy to "streamline" the process (Orlikowski 1991, p. 14). In her later work, Orlikowski (1992a) suffers from exactly the same problem: organizational issues are discussed based on the introduction of Lotus Notes, which is never explained in any detail beyond referring to it as "the technology" or "Notes," the functions of the applications. This is particularly upsetting considering that Lotus Notes is a versatile, flexible application level programming language.

In instructive, in-depth case studies, Walsham does indeed follow up his criticism cited above by describing in more detail than Orlikowski (1991, 1992a) how the modalities operate. But this increased level of precision does not apply to the specifics of the technology. The typical level of granularity is to discuss the issue of IBM vs. non-IBM hardware (Walsham 1993, pp. 92-94), centralized versus decentralized systems architecture (p. 105) or top-down, hierarchical control vs. user-control (p. 136-138).

Not distinguishing more closely between different parts and variants of the elements of the IS is an instance of the aforementioned "convenient fiction" (Kling 1991, p. 356). An unintended consequence of not being fine-grained enough is removing social responsibility from the designers (p. 343). It removes social responsibility in the sense that a given designer in a given organization obliged to use, say, a CASE tool, may hold that it is irrelevant how she uses the tool; it is still a tool embodying a certain rationale beyond her control.

2.2   Actor-Network Theory

What is required, then, is a more detailed and fine-grained analysis of the many mechanisms, some technical and some not, which are employed in shaping social action. We are not claiming that structuration theory cannot deliver this (cf. Walsham 1993, p. 67). But we are suggesting that most studies conducted so far (Korpela 1994; Orlikowski 1991, 1992a; Orlikowski and Robey 1991; Walsham 1993) are lacking in describing, with a satisfactory level of precision, how specific elements and functions of an IS relate to organizational issues. We also suggest that the framework provided by actor-network theory (ANT) is more promising in this regard. We proceed to give an outline of the basics of ANT based on Akrich (1992), Akrich and Latour (1992), Callon (1991), and Latour (1987) before discussing what distinguishes it from the position outlined above.

Key concepts, for the present purposes, are actor-network, translation, alignment, inscription and irreversibility. We explain them in order. ANT, like structuration theory, recognizes that establishing and changing a social order relies on a tight interplay between social and technical means: one speaks of society as a socio-technical web. The difference lies in how they describe this web. According to ANT, humans and non-humans are linked together into actor-networks.

Further, ANT assumes that (a section of) society is inhibited by actors pursuing interests. An actor's interest can be translated into technical or social arrangements, for instance an IS or organizational routines. A basic question it attempts to answer is how a diverse group of actors reach agreement at all, that is, how a social order establishes a certain degree of stability or exhibits structural properties. According to ANT, stability is the end-result of the social process of aligning an initially diverse collection of interests to "one"; acceptance, "truth" or stability is the result of reaching a certain degree of alignment of interests (Callon 1991). The solution reached is constituted by an aligned actor-network. To achieve this, it is vital, as actors' interests from the outset are non-aligned, that one is successful in translating, that is, representing or appropriating the interests of others to one's own (Latour 1987). The strength of ANT is very much related to exactly this point: ANT provides a language for describing how this translation takes place on a quite specific and concrete level. This takes us to the notion of an inscription (Akrich 1992; Akrich and Latour 1992).

An inscription is the result of the translation of one's interest into material form (Callon 1991, p. 143). In general, any component of the heterogeneous network of skills, practices, artefacts, institutional arrangements, texts and contracts establishing a social order may be the material for inscriptions. There are four especially interesting aspects of the notion of inscriptions: (i) what is inscribed: which anticipations of use are envisioned, (ii) who inscribes them, (iii) how are they inscribed: what is the material for the inscriptions, and (iv) how powerful are the inscriptions: how much effort does it take to oppose an inscription.

The inherent difficulty in changing an actor-network — removing an inscription — can nicely be captured by Callon's concept of the (possible) irreversibility of an aligned network. This concept describes how translations between actor-networks are made durable, how they can resist assaults from competing translations. Callon (p. 159) states that the degree of irreversibility depends on (i) the extent to which it is subsequently impossible to go back to a point where that translation was only one among many, and (ii) the extent to which it shapes and determines subsequent translations.

2.3   Actor Networks Meet Structuration Theory

Having given an outline of ANT, let us see what is achieved *vis-à-vis* structuration theory. The principal improvement, as we see it, is the ability ANT provides to be more specific and concrete with respect to the functions of an IS. It is not the case, in our view, that ANT in every respect is an improvement over structuration theory. We only argue that it applies to the issue of being specific about the technology. For instance, we consider the important issue of the structuring abilities of institutions to be better framed within structuration theory than within ANT. Let us explain why we consider it so. We first compare the two theories on a general level, partly relying on pedagogic examples. Then we attempt to reinterpret Orlikowski (1991) in terms of ANT.

Inscriptions are given a concrete content because they represent interests inscribed into a material. The flexibility of inscriptions vary: some structure the pattern of use strongly, others quite weakly. The power of inscriptions, whether they must be followed or can be avoided, depends on the irreversibility of the actor-network they are inscribed into. It is never possible to know before hand, but by studying the sequence of inscriptions we learn more about exactly how and which inscriptions were needed to achieve a given aim. To exemplify, consider what it takes to establish a specific work routine. One could, for instance, try to inscribe the required skills through training. If this inscription was too weak, one could inscribe into a textual description of the routines in the form of manuals. If this still is too weak, one could inscribe the work routines by supporting them by an IS.

Latour provides an illuminating illustration of this aspect of ANT. It is a constructed example intended for pedagogic purposes. Hotels, from the point of view of management, want to ensure that the guests leave their keys at the front desk when leaving. The way this may be accomplished, according to Latour, is to inscribe this desired pattern of behavior into an actor-network. The question then becomes how to inscribe it and into what. This was impossible to know in advance, so management made a sequence of trials to test the strength of the inscriptions. First, they tried to inscribe it into an artifact in the form of a sign behind the counter requesting all guests to return the key when leaving. This inscription, however, was not strong enough. Then one tried having a manual door-keeper with the same result. Management then inscribed it into a key knob. What they did was to use a metal knob of some weight. By stepwise increasing the weight of the knob, the desired behavior was finally achieved. Through a succession of translations, the hotels' interests were finally inscribed into a network strong enough to impose the desired behavior on the guests.

ANT's systematic blurring of the distinction between the technical and the non-technical extends beyond the duality of Orlikowski and Robey and of Walsham. The whole idea is to treat situations as essentially equal regardless of the means; the objective is still the same. Within ANT, technology receives exactly the same (explanatory!) status as human actors; the distinction between human and non-human actors is systematically removed. ANT takes very seriously the fact that, in a number of situations, technical artefacts in practice play the same role as human actors: the glue that keeps a social order in place is a heterogeneous network of human and non-human actors. A theoretical framework that makes an a priori distinction between the two is less likely to manage to keep its focus on the aim of a social arrangement regardless of whether the means for achieving this are technical or non-technical. The consequence of this is that ANT supports an inquiry which traces the social process of negotiating, redefining and appropriating interests back and forth between an articulate, explicit form and a form where they are inscribed within a technical artefact. With reference to the small example above, the inscriptions attempting to establish the work routine were inscribed in both technical and non-technical materials. They provide a collection of inscriptions — all aimed at achieving the same effect — with varying power. In any given situation, one would stack the necessary number of inscriptions which together seem to do the job.

We believe that the empirical material presented by Orlikowski (1991) may, at least partially, be reinterpreted in light of ANT.[2] Her primary example is the development and use of a CASE tool in an organization she calls SCC. The control (and productivity) interests of management are inscribed into the tool. The inscriptions are so strong that the consultants do as intended down

---

[2]Doing this in any detail would, of course, demand access to the empirical material beyond the form in which it is presented in the article. We have no such access.

to a rather detailed level. The only exceptions reported are some senior consultants saying that they, in some rare instances, do not do as the tool requires.

What is missing, then, in comparison with ANT is to portray this as more a stepwise alignment than the kind of all-in-one character of (Orlikowski 1991). In ANT terms, management's control interests are inscribed into the CASE tool in forms of detailed inscriptions of the consultants' behavior. The inscriptions are very strong in the sense that there is hardly any room for interpretive flexibility. The CASE tool is the result of a long process where management's control and productivity interests have been translated into a larger heterogeneous actor-network encompassing career paths, work guidelines, methodologies and, finally, the CASE tool. Together these elements form an actor-network into which consultants' behavior is inscribed. Just like Latour's example presented above, the inscriptions become stronger as they are inscribed into a larger network. This network is developed through successive steps where inscriptions are tested out and improved until the desired outcome is reached. It is only when, as a result of a long sequence of testing and superpositioning of inscriptions, that one ends up in situations like the one presented by Orlikowski. If one succeeds in aligning the whole actor-network, the desired behavior is established. Analytically, it follows from this that if any one (or a few) of the elements of such an actor-network is not aligned, then the behavior will not be as presented by Orlikowski. Empirically, we know that more often than not the result is different from that of Orlikowski's case (Curtis, Krasner and Iscoe 1988; Vessey, Jarvenpaa and Tractinsky 1992).

We end this section by merely pointing out another issue we find problematic with Orlikowski (1992b). She states,

> The greater the spatial and temporal distance between the construction of a technology and its application, the greater the likelihood that the technology will be interpreted and used with little flexibility. Where technology developers consult with or involve future users in the construction and trial stages of a technology, there is an increased likelihood that it will be interpreted and used more flexibly. [p. 421]

We agree on the importance of user participation in design. According to ANT, however, the interpretive flexibility of a technology may increase as the distance between designers and users increases. Interpretive flexibility means unintended use, i.e., using the technology differently than what is inscribed into it. When the designers are close to the users, the network into which the intended user behavior is inscribed will be stronger and accordingly harder for the users not to follow. An important aspect of ANT is its potential to account for how restricted interpretative flexibility across great distances can be obtained (Law 1986).

3. NEW ORGANIZATIONAL FORMS AND INFORMATION INFRASTRUCTURE

3.1   Some of the Arguments — and the Evidence

New organizational forms are assumed to be important in order to achieve enhanced productivity, competitiveness, flexibility, etc. New organizational forms are usually of a network type positioned between markets and hierarchies. The discussions about new organizational forms borrow from a number of sources. We briefly review some of these.

From economics, basically relying on transaction-cost considerations, there is a growing pressure to accommodate to the "information economy" (Ciborra 1992; OECD 1992). Transaction-cost considerations fail to do justice to the dynamically changing redivision of labor and functions which are two important aspects of new organizational forms (Ciborra 1992). Within business policy literature, the arguments focus on issues of innovation processes as facilitated through strategic alliances and globalization which emerge pragmatically from concerns about maintaining competitiveness in a turbulent environment (Porter 1990; von Hippel 1988). In organizational theory, one emphasizes the weaknesses of centralized, bureaucratic control in terms of responsiveness to new situations (Clegg 1990). Ciborra sees new organizational forms as rational, institutional arrangements to meet the increased need for organizational learning. Technological development within information and communication technology are identified by some scholars as the driving force for the restructuring of organizations (Malone, Yates and Benjamin 1991; Malone and Rockart 1993).

Even such a brief exposition of theoretical considerations should make it evident that the issue of new organizational forms is vast. When we turn to what exists of empirical evidence, the picture gets even more complicated. This is because the empirical material document a far less clear-cut picture as it contains numerous contradicting trends (Applegate 1994; Capello and Williams 1992; Orlikowski 1991; Whitaker 1992). In line with the argument above, we intend to approach matters in a highly selective manner. As in the more general case discussed in section 2, the principal challenge is to account convincingly for the interwoven relationship between new organizational forms and their IT-based backbone, that is, INI. We are, therefore, led to consider in more detail the specifics of an INI.

3.2 Information Infrastructure

INIs have a number of characteristic features which serve to distinguish them from other kinds of ISs. These differences are not only of contrived interest. They have strong repercussions on the way INIs are developed, spread and used. We point out and discuss a few of the characteristics which need a deeper understanding.

A principal difference, related to the fact that an INI is a systemic technology that regulates communicative behavior, is the role and status of standards. For most technologies, including the bulk of other ISs, standards evolve gradually as the technology matures. What makes INIs different is the absolute requirement that all involved parties have to adhere to a standard at any given moment. The INI simply ceases to exist if communication does not follow the standard (Besen and Saloner 1989).

Another characteristic of INI, related to that above, is the way it acquires its stability. Because any modifications of the standards need to be coordinated and organized to avoid collapsing the communicative behavior, modifying a standard grows increasingly more difficult as the standard diffuses. In economic vocabulary, this property of an INI produces "network externalities" (Antonelli 1993): a situation where the value for the users increases with the diffusion of the technology creating lock-ins and self-reinforcing effects. Expanding the installed base of a standard gives rise to an accumulated "momentum" of the standard. This aspect is nicely captured by the notion in ANT of "irreversibility" (Callon 1991), thus providing an additional and different motivation for ANT than the ones already given.

4. INFORMATION INFRASTRUCTURE AS ACTOR-NETWORK

Intuitively, as ANT's primary objective is to describe technological systems and non-technical structures as single units, i.e., as socio-technical networks, it should be well suited for describing interrelations between network organizations and network technologies.

We describe what we think are important aspects of INIs and show how ANT can help us understand and deal with them. These aspects are:

1. Standards, being the essence of INIs, are not just neutral technological components. Rather they inscribe their use, i.e., interorganizational communication patterns, as well as actions that have to take place locally in user organizations.

2. Technological and non-technological elements are linked, implying (among other things) that which organizations are involved in the standardization/INI design process shape the standard, as well as the standard having implications for which organizations need to participate in the design process. The actor-networks of INIs and INI standardization easily turn into unmanageably complex ones.

3. A standard is more that just a technical system, it is a socio-technical network.

4. As standards become realized INIs, they easily turn into irreversible actor networks.

The examples we are using to illustrate these aspects are primarily chosen from the development of an INI for the Norwegian health care sector. The examples are exchange of drug prescriptions and laboratory orders and results. Our presentation is based on a study of historical material (minutes, reports, proposed standards), interviews, and experience obtained by one of the authors engaged by one of the involved software vendors for a period of two years. Developing Norwegian standards for the health sector takes place in close connection with the development of European standards organized by CEN.[3]

4.1 Inscribing Inter-Organizational Behavior into Standards

The definition of the Norwegian standard for drug prescription exchange was organized as a project where those considered relevant participated. The main task of the project was the definition of an EDI message representing a prescription. An important part of such a message is the definition of how the prescribed drugs are identified. Early in the project, the pharmacies

---

[3]CEN is the European branch of ISO (the International Standardization Organization).

expressed their wish to use the same drug identification numbers in the electronic drug prescription message as the ones they were using in their existing systems. The pharmacies wanted these identification numbers because they could then integrate the system receiving prescriptions with their existing applications for inventory control and electronic ordering from The Norwegian Drug Medication Depot (NMD).

No one objected to the suggestion to include this number in the message. All agreed because this information did not seem to conflict with anyone's interest. The problem was only that the GPs made no use of it and hence had no access to it in their work. Neither the GPs nor their applications were aware of which identifiers corresponded to which drugs. The initially straightforward and technical issue of how to code and represent a prescribed drug identification number — a six digit number — in the message had thus been translated into another issue: how should one inscribe this into the message in such a way that the GPs will provide this number as part of the prescription without creating additional work for the GPs? If using the drug identifiers as intended turns out to be inconvenient for the GPs, they will probably not do it properly. Proper use of the identifiers may be supported by the GPs' information system. This support may be offered by installing the drug item list as a part of the GPs information system. An alternative solution would be the drug item list integrated with the Common Catalogue (in Norwegian: Felleskatalogen). These two alternative technical solutions represent two alternative translations of the pharmacies' interests.

The pharmacies' drug item list is provided by the NMD and they make it available to the pharmacies via their application supplier. The list contains information useful for the GPs, for instance price and synonymous drugs. The GPs' representative argued that this list had to be made available for the GPs' applications. Today the GPs use their own drug lists which are either typed in by themselves or installed with the application (as a supplier's service). In either case, the GPs themselves have to update their drug list.

As everyone agreed that the GPs need the drug item list, the focus has been on whether or not the GPs should pay for access to the drug item list and, if so, at what price. The Pharmacies' Association has recognized the GPs' need for the list. They have no principal objections against offering relevant parts of it to the GPs. The NMD, however, who is responsible for the drug item list, has not yet decided what to do. NMD is not represented in the project and will probably not offer the list free of charge. The pharmacies are not willing to let the GPs have access to the drug item list as it is at the present, because the list also contains information which the pharmacies want to keep for themselves (for instance about profit margins on pharmaceutical products). The list thus has to be tailored to the needs of the GPs. The drug item list is updated every month; each time, the version used by GPs has to be produced. The GPs' medical record systems need to be adapted to make use of the list. The lists can be distributed to GPs directly from NMD or through the vendors of the GPs' systems.

The GPs also have available a paper based catalogue, called the Common Catalogue, containing information about all registered drugs in Norway. It also contains other important and practical information about treatment of acute poisoning, drug interactions, a register of drug producers and a register of all pharmacies in Norway. Having access to this catalogue as a part of their information systems would be very useful when the GPs are specifying a drug prescription. This catalogue is provided by yet another organization, an organization not part of the drug prescription project. The catalogue is printed once a year, but additions are printed during the year as drugs are introduced or disappear. The Common Catalogue now exists electronically as well. Work is being done to integrate the catalogue with the GPs' drug list to ease the work for the GPs. This is seen as a possible solution to the problem above: how to offer something to the GPs which makes it acceptable for them to register the proper prescribed drug identification number. This integration work requires the cooperation of GPs, suppliers of GP systems, the NMD and the organization responsible for the Common Catalogue. All these parties have commercial interests in this area and their motivation must be combined with the GPs' actual need for integration of drug information. This work has just started and in the mean time the drug prescription exchange project has to solve the problem of how to make the item prescription number available for the GPs.

This example illustrates how rather complex inter-organizational behavior related to the updating and distribution of a list of identifiers are inscribed into the definition of one single element of a standardized message. Defining identifiers of this kind is usually considered a mere "technical detail." This example illustrates that this is not always the case. The technical design represents translated interest, in particular that of the pharmacies. The identifier list is linked to a number of organizations, constituting an actor-network. This network must be aligned, i.e., each of the organizations must do as prescribed if the drug prescription exchange system is to work. The definition of identifiers presupposes a certain organizational behavior, but this inscription may be too weak. To really make the GPs behave as intended, the inscriptions of their behavior were strengthened by offering additional services as part of the system.

4.2   The Interdependencies Between Standards and Standardization Process

The example above also illustrates the interdependencies between standards and standardization process. Those involved tried to translate their interests into the standard just like the pharmacies did. A specific solution proposal may affect others in ways making it necessary to involve them in the process as happened with NMD.

A commonly applied criterion for evaluating technical solutions is that they should be as simple as possible. From an ANT perspective, this means that not only the technical system but rather the actor-network of which it is a part should be as simple as possible. The more complex an actor-network, the more complex it is to align. We believe that the actor-networks representing INIs may often be very complex, in fact almost too complex to be aligned. This will be illustrated by the development of EDI systems for exchange of lab results from labs to GPs.

The development of an INI for exchange of lab information in Norway started when Dr. Fürst's Medisinske Laboratorium, a privately owned chemical-clinical laboratory, developed a system enabling their customers (GPs) to receive the test results electronically. Fürst had for a long time been a competitive, service oriented lab and advanced in the use of technology. They saw a strategic opportunity and developed a simple system. They paid the patient record vendors to adapt their products to it and offered it free of charge to GPs (even paid their expenses for modems). Receiving electronic reports from clinical-chemical labs makes the work of GPs significantly easier as each GP receives approximately twenty reports a day, which take quite some time to register manually in their medical record system. Fürst was very successful as the INI helped them attract a large number of new customers.

The competitive advantage Fürst obtained by means of their INI created a problem for other labs. Most are hospital labs and their expenditures are paid for by the owners: the county authorities. The county also pays when a GP orders a test at a private lab. The profit margins were significant so the counties soon saw the need to respond by providing similar services. Most of them did that. The systems supporting the services were to a large extent copies of Fürst's.

Those involved in the development of these smaller INIs recognized that they should be considered parts of a larger INI for the health sector. This demands shared standards. Working out and spreading a stable standard amounts to successfully aligning the heterogeneous network of involved actors, institutions and work practices into a "convergent" network (Callon 1991). The effort of aligning such a network grows dramatically as the complexity, that is the number of elements, of the network grows. Fürst's solution was simple and tailor-made to their needs. In particular, it involved a relatively small number of elements in the network. A general, standardized solution, however, would be considerably more complex. Figure 1 indicates this by connecting the elements in addition to Fürst's solution with dashed lines. It follows from this that aligning the network for the standardized solution is radically more difficult than for Fürst's.

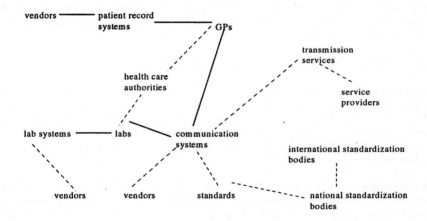

Figure 1. The Actor-Network of Lab Information Exchange

The increased complexity of a standardized solution is due to the presence of a large variety of labs (for instance, clinical-chemical, micro-biology, pathology and allergy), the ambition of also enabling transmission of information among other institutions within health care (for instance, hospitals, various governmental institutions and health insurance authorities), and because it was decided that the Norwegian standardization work should follow European standardization work. It has been decided, for instance, that lab results should be exchanged as EDIFACT messages.

This implies that the specific messages should fulfil the requirements of messages set by the EDIFACT standardization bodies and that these bodies (at both the national and European level) will be involved in the standardization work as well.

4.3   Designing a Socio-Technical Network

The definition of a standard is more than designing a technological system. It is the design of a socio-technical network. The standard is just one element, an element linked to a number of other elements, technical and non-technical, in this network. This can be illustrated by the proposed systems for exchange of lab orders. One crucial issue here is to ensure that the electronic order is linked to its proper physical specimen at the lab. Today the paper order is physically connected to the specimen container and they are sent together from the GP to the lab. A unique number is glued to both. Lists of pairs of adhesive labels containing unique numbers are pre-produced by the labs and given to GPs. These lists are produced in a way minimizing the probability of mixing up the labels on the order and the specimen container. Finding an equally safe procedure when the order is transmitted electronically will not be easy and will certainly include the design of specific technological as well as organizational arrangements. This amounts to recognizing that design of a solution for lab orders invariably involves the design of a large collection of associated work routines as well as computer systems. The solution must include label producing machines (bar code printers), label reading machines, manual routines and new computer applications. The standardized message will reflect the working routines; they will be inscribed into the message. For instance, what kind of information is necessary for carrying out the control routines depends on how these routines are defined. This information must, of course, be represented in the message.

4.4   The Irreversibility of the Installed Base

INIs and their standards must, just as any information system, change to adopt to local needs, changed needs, and to improve according to use experience (Hanseth, Thoresen and Winner 1993, Monteiro, Hanseth and Hatling 1994). Callon (1991, p. 159) states that an actor-network may turn irreversible depending on (i) the extent to which it is subsequently impossible to go back to a point where that translation was only one among many and (ii) the extent to which it shapes and determines subsequent translations.

We believe that INIs may easily become irreversible as they grow. This is because everybody communicating has to use the same standard. A standard may be changed by developing a new version which is compatible with the old one in the sense that all implementations of the old version may communicate with installations of the new as if they were equal. In this case, individual users can switch to the new version independently. However, using this strategy, the kind of changes that can be introduced into the new version is significantly limited. Defining a new incompatible version removes this constraint. On the other hand, switching to the new version is more difficult. One alternative is that all users switch over to the new version at the same time, at a so-called "flag day." Coordinating such a change, however, becomes difficult as the number of installations grows. A second strategy for switching to a new incompatible version may be to develop and install gateways between the old and the new. The difficulties in doing this depend on the degree of incompatibility between the two versions. A third strategy is to build up a new separate INI based on the new version. The drawback with this alternative is that the usefulness of an INI depends on the number of users connected. Accordingly, all users would prefer the old INI with many users rather than new one with very few.

To our knowledge, the INI for the Norwegian health care sector has not yet reached a state where its (possible) irreversibility has appeared as a problem. However, considering the difficulties in developing the first versions of the various standards, we assume that defining new versions will be harder as a large number of installed standardized systems in itself put additional constraints on what can be a suitable solution. In the Internet world, work has been going on since 1990 to develop a new version of the IP protocol. A new version with only modest changes from the existing one is expected to be settled late this year (RFC 1952). This new version requires changes in 58 other Internet standards and a vast number of implementations of these Internet standards must be modified.

A number of more substantial changes are necessary if Internet is to be able to support, for instance, multimedia information and mobile communication properly. Necessary changes for these purposes were intended to be a part of the ongoing revision. The modest changes obtained during a five year period indicates that Internet is approaching a state of irreversibility (Monteiro, Hanseth and Hatling 1994).

4.5   Beyond Actor-Networks

ANT cannot account for all relevant aspect of INIs. For instance, it cannot properly deal with institutions: how they shape actions at the same time as the very same actions shape the institutions — what we see as the primary contribution of structuration theory. The institutional framework of standardization and INI development is an important part of these processes.

Another important aspect of INIs which ANT cannot account for properly is their openness. An INI is open in the sense that, whatever its scope is, several user organizations would prefer the INI extended to other areas which they see as tightly connected with those areas where they are using it. In the case of lab communication, the GPs communicate with several different kinds of labs. The labs are not only communicating with GPs but with hospitals, other labs, etc. GPs also communicate, in a similar way as with labs, with X-ray clinics, hospitals, etc. Each of these institutions communicate with others, and so on indefinitely. Defining a unified, compatible set of standards for all is impossible. What is needed is a conceptual framework for developing flexible standards and INIs for limited areas which can be linked together in one way or another. In terms of ANT, what is needed is concepts for dealing with not only one, but larger numbers of actor-networks and how they connect and interact. Star and Griesemer's (1989) concept of boundary objects is a step in this direction.

5. CONCLUSION

There is, in 1995, a widespread agreement among scholars in the field that "IT enables/constrains action." It seems that the time is ripe to push further and learn more about how this operates on a concrete level. We argue that a firmer grasp of the interplay between IT and organizational issues has to take the specifics of an IS quite seriously. This is, in particular, necessary for informing design and increasing social responsibility (Kling 1991, p. 343).

Even highly praised accounts (we have only considered a few which build on structuration theory but believe that it holds more generally) fail in this crucial regard. This should not be read as a claim that structuration theory, in principle, is not capable of supporting this kind of concrete and specific description. We do argue that ANT quite immediately provides a language for doing this; its overall rationale is geared toward this. There are, however, other aspects that seem to be better captured within structuration theory than ANT (for instance, the role of institutions). Given the premise that we need to be more specific, it strikes us as a more promising strategy to employ ANT than to await an elaboration of the notion of modalities, in ways not entirely clear to us, before proceeding.

With regard to new organizational forms, this implies that we need a thorough understanding of the characteristics of the relevant class of ISs, namely INIs and their underlying standards. This amounts, we argue, to a study both of how organizational behavior is inscribed into "technical" details of the standard and how adoption and diffusion of a standard involves making it irreversible by aligning the surrounding, heterogeneous network of institutional arrangements and work practices.

6. REFERENCES

Akrich, M. "The De-scription of Technical Objects." In W. E. Bijker and J. Law (Editors), *Shaping Technology/Building Society*. Cambridge: MIT Press, 1992, pp. 205-224.

Akrich, M., and Latour, B. "A Summary of a Convenient Vocabulary for the Semiotics of Human and Nonhuman Assemblies." In W. E. Bijker and J. Law (Editors), *Shaping Technology/ Building Society*. Cambridge: MIT Press, 1992, pp. 259-264.

Antonelli, C. "The Dynamics of Technological Interrelatedness: the Case of Information and Communication Technologies." In D. Foray and C. Freeman (Editors), *Technology and the Wealth of Nations: The Dynamics of Construed Advantage*. New York: Pinter Publications, 1993, pp. 194-207.

Applegate, L. "Managing in an Information Age: Transforming the Organization for the 1990s." In R. Baskerville, S. Smithson, O. Ngwenyama, and J. I. DeGross (Editors), *Transforming Organizations with Information Technology*. Amsterdam: North-Holland, 1994, pp. 15-94.

Besen, S.M. and Saloner, B. "The Economics of Telecommunication Standards." In R. W. Crandall and K. Flamm (Editors), *Changing the Rules. Technological Change, International Competition, and Regulation in Communication."* The Brookings Institute, 1989.

Bijker, W. E. "Do Not Despair: There Is Life after Constructivism." *Science, Technology, and Human Values*, Volume 18, Number 1, 1993, pp. 113-138.

Callon, M. "Techno-Economic Networks and Irreversibility." In J. Law (Editor), *a Sociology of Monsters. Essays on Power, Technology and Domination.* London: Routledge, 1991, pp. 132-161.

Capello, R., and Williams, H. "Computer Network Trajectories and Organizational Dynamics: A Cross-National Review." In C. Antonelli (Editor), *the Economics of Information Network.* Amsterdam: North-Holland, 1992, pp. 347-362.

Ciborra, C. *"Innovation, Networks and Organizational Learning."* In C. Antonelli (Editor), *the Economics of Information Network.* Amsterdam: North-Holland, 1992, pp. 91-102.

Clegg, S. R. *Modern Organizations.* Newbury Park, California: Sage, 1990.

Coombs, R.; Knights, D.; and Willmott, H. C. "Culture, Control and Competition: Towards a Conceptual Framework for the Study of Information Technology in Organizations." *Organization Studies*, Volume 13, Number 1, 1992, pp. 51-72.

Curtis, B.; Krasner, H.; and Iscoe, N. "A Field Study of the Software Design Process for Large Systems." *Communications of the ACM*, Volume 31, Number 11, 1988, pp. 1268-1287.

Feldman, M. S. "Electronic Mail and Weak Ties in Organizations." *Office, Technology and People*, Volume 3, 1987, pp. 83-101.

Galliers, R. "Choosing Information Systems Research Approaches." In R. Galliers (Editor), *Information Systems Research: Issues, Methods and Practical Guidelines.* Oxford: Blackwell Scientific Publications, 1992.

Hanseth, O.; Thoresen, K.; and Winner, L. "The Politics of Neworking Technology in Health Care." *Computer Supported Cooperative Work*, Volume 2, Number 2, 1993.

Kling, R. "Computerization and Social Transformations." *Science, Technology and Human Values*, Volume 6, Number 3, 1991, pp. 342-367.

Korpela, E. "Path to Notes: A Networked Company Choosing its Information Systems Solution." In R. Baskerville, S. Smithson, O. Ngwenyama, and J. I. DeGross (Editors), *Transforming Organizations with Information Technology.* Amsterdam: North-Holland, 1994, pp. 219-242.

Latour, B. *Science in Action.* Cambridge: Harvard University Press, 1987.

Latour, B. "Technology Is Society Made Durable." In J. Law (Editor), *a Sociology of Monsters: Essays on Power, Technology and Domination.* London: Routledge, 1991, pp. 103-131.

Law, J. "On the Methods of Long-distance Control: Vessels, Navigation and the Portuguese Route to India." In J. Law (Editor), *Power, Action and Belief.* London: Routledge and Kegan Paul, 1986, pp. 234-263.

Malone, T. W., and Rockart, J. F. "How Will Information Technology Reshape Organizations? Computers as Coordination Technology." In S. P. Bradley, J. Hausman, and R. L. Nolan (Editors), *Globalization, Technology, and Competition: The Fusion of Computers and Telecommunications*. Cambridge: Harvard Business School Press, 1993, pp. 37-56.

Malone, T. W.; Yates, J.; and Benjamin, R. I. "Electronic Markets and Electronic Hierarchies." In T. J. Allen and M. S. Scott Morton (Editors), *Information Technology and the Corporation of the 1990s: Research Studies*. New York: Oxford University Press, 1991, pp. 61-83.

Monteiro, E.; Hanseth, O.; and Hatling, M. "Standardization of Information Infrastructure: Where Is the Flexibility?" Technical Report, Science and Technology Studies, University of Trondheim, 1994. Presented at the annual conference of The Society of Social Studies of Science (4S), New Orleans. Submitted for review.

Mulgan, G. *Communication and Control. Networks and the New Economics of Communication*. London: Polity Press, 1991.

OECD. *Information Networks and New Technologies: Opportunities and Policy Implications for the 1990s. Information Computer Communication Policy*. Paris, 1992.

Orlikowski, W. J. "Integrated Information Environment or Matrix of Control? The Contradictory Implications of Information Technology." *Accounting, Management and Information Technology*, Volume 1, Number 1, 1991, pp. 9-42.

Orlikowski, W. J. "Learning from Notes: Organizational Issues in Groupware Implementation." In *Proceedings of CSCW'92*, 1992a, pp. 362-369.

Orlikowski, W. J. "The Duality of Technology: Rethinking the Concept of Technology in Organizations. *Organization Science*, Volume 3, Number 3, August 1992b, pp. 398-427.

Orlikowski, W. J., and Robey, D. "Information Technology and the Structuring of Organizations." *Information Systems Research*, Volume 2, Number 2, 1991 pp. 143-169.

Pfaffenberger, B. "Fetisched Objects and Humanised Nature: Towards an Anthropology of Technology." *Royal Anthropological Institute*, Volume 23, 1988.

Porter, M. "The Competitive Advantage of Nations." *Harvard Business Review*, March-April:, 1990, pp. 73-93.

RFC 1995. "The Recommendation for the IP Next Generation Protocol". RFC 1752, IAB and IESG, January 1995.

Smithson, S.; Baskerville, R.; and Ngwenyama, O. "Perspectives on Information Technology and New Emergent Forms of Organizations." In R. Baskerville, S. Smithson, O. Ngwenyama, and J. I. DeGross (Editors), *Transforming Organizations with Information Technology*. Amsterdam: North-Holland, 1994, pp. 3-14.

Star, S. L., and Griesemer, J. R. "Institutional Ecology, 'Translations,' and Boundary Objects: Amateurs and Professionals in Berkeley's Museum of Vertebrate Zoology, 1907-39." *Social Studies of Science*, Volume 19, 1989, pp. 387-420.

Vessey, I.; Jarvenpaa, S. L.; and Tractinsky, N. "Evaluation of Vendor Products: Case Tools as Methodology Companions." *Communications of the ACM*, Volume 35, Number 4, 1992, pp. 90-105.

von Hippel, E. *The Sources of Innovation*. New York: Oxford University Press, 1988.

Walsham, G. *Interpreting Information Systems in Organizations*. London: John Wiley and Sons, 1993.

Whitaker, A. "The Transformation in Work: Post-Fordism Revisited." In M. Reed and M. Hughes (Editors), *Rethinking Organization: New Directions in Organization Theory and Analysis*. Newbury Park, California: Sage, 1992, pp. 184-206.

About the Authors

Eric Monteiro graduated from the Norwegian Institute of Technology in 1987. He received his Ph.D. in information from the University of Trondheim in 1992. Prior to that, he worked five years as an applied researcher at the Norwegian Computing Centre. His current research interests include spelling out the socio-technical web of systems development. Of particular interest is a firmer grasp of the standardization procedure — broadly conceived — of communication technologies.

Ole Hanseth is currently Research Director at the Norwegian Computing Centre where he has been employed since 1982 with a two year break working for a software company in Oslo. His current research interests include the development of inter-organizational systems and information infrastructures, in particular understanding the interrelationships between technical and non-technical issues.

21

Infrastructure and Organizational Transformation: Classifying Nurses' Work

Geoffrey C. Bowker
Graduate School of Library and Information Science
University of Illinois

Stefan Timmermans
Department of Sociology
Brandeis University

Susan Leigh Star
Graduate School of Library and Information Science
University of Illinois

Abstract

This paper describes an evolving classification system for understanding the nature of nursing work, the Nursing Interventions Classification (NIC) developed at the University of Iowa. We describe the balancing act inherent in maximizing three dimensions of the system: comparability, control and visibility. As part of a series of studies on the relationship between classification, infrastructure, work and knowledge, we link NIC with other classification systems such as the International Classification of Diseases (ICD) and its role in organizational coordination. We analyze some of the features of evolving infrastructure, and its potential impact on organizations and practice.

"It's not always suitable to view work as production of information" — Bjerknes and Bratteteig 1987a, p. 323

1. INTRODUCTION: INFRASTRUCTURE, CLASSIFICATION AND ORGANIZATION

Very large information systems such as the Internet or global databases carry with them a politics of voice and value which is often invisible, embedded in layers of infrastructure. The "politics of artifacts" of a nuclear bomb or a genetically reengineered organism are more available for public debate then those of information interchange protocols or how insurance data are encoded. Yet these latter decisions and standards may affect markets, differential benefits from particular technologies, and the visibility of constituencies, among other important public goods. They are important in organizing work, and are often used explicitly as vehicles for professional and organizational transformation, via accounting and legitimation processes. They appear, as parts of accounting schemes, in technologies of organizational change such as business process reengineering and total quality management; in addition to record keeping and accounts, they also classify people and their importance in organizations.

For several years we have been investigating this "quiet politics" of voice and values in information infrastructure, seeking to clarify how it is that values, policies and modes of practice become embedded in large information systems (Bowker and Star 1994; Star 1995a, 1995b, 1995c; Bowker 1994a, 199b). In this paper, we focus on a classification system directed at nursing work and develop some theoretical notions about the relationship between classification, information systems, work and organizations. We primarily take the point of view of design: what are the problems designers of the system face from their constituency? Further work will examine the implementation of the system in various field sites and its direct impact on nursing work. Here, we examine the "upstream" implications.

Classification systems are a kind of crucible for organizations and occupations; they are at once the place where distinctions in knowledge are made, and the raw stuff of knowledge-based systems (explicit or tacit). They are a good venue for investigating

- the role of new information technologies in restructuring fields of practice and knowledge production;

- the ways in which global schemes are modulated locally so as to fit into pre-existing practices and beliefs (e.g., in the medical case, Western medicine and acupuncture);

- the multiple use of classification systems in variably integrated infrastructures;

- a pragmatic view of how moral and ethical conflicts are resolved by designers and administrators of classification systems.

The information sciences have this century grappled with new ways of configuring, storing and retrieving information, as fundamentally novel as was the printing press in its day (see Eisenstein 1983). This new infrastructure has powerful ramifications, comparable to the railroads (Schivelbusch 1986; Friedlander 1995) or electricity (Hughes 1983); infrastructures that respectively accompanied the first industrial revolution and drove the second. Because new information infrastructures fundamentally change both work practice and knowledge, they also inscribe a moral order. They do this by allocating resources (e.g., Where will the railroad go? Which cities and towns are the most important?); structuring markets (e.g., the public versus private ownership of electricity); and affecting the rhythms of daily life. In the case of information technologies, which traffic in representations, they also advantage some voices and values over others, make some things visible and others invisible.

How does one *make* a successful, practically workable classification scheme while balancing out these differential advantages? The problem is an old one in philosophy of knowledge, from Occam's razor to Quine's objects. Blurring categories mean that existing differences are covered up, blurred, merged, or removed altogether, while distinctions construct new partitions or reinforcement of existing differences. This mutual process of constructing and shaping differences through classification systems is crucial in our conceptualization of any reality; it is the core of much taxonomic anthropology. The case studies in Douglas and Hull (1992) point to the ways in which a category can be non-existent (distributed out of existence) until and unless it is socially created. Thus Hacking (1986) talks about the creation of "child abuse" this century: it is not that there was nothing in the nineteenth century that we call child abuse, but rather

- that category did not exist then and so tended to go by a disaggregated host of other names;

- once the category was declared a legal and moral one at a particular historical juncture, then people who abused children could learn socially how to be a child abuser; reports in the press would teach them what was expected of the abuse personality (see also Becker [1953-54] on how to become a marijuana user).

The result is a shifting of balances of distinctions, a change in the architectural relationships. Every newly constructed difference, or every new merger, changes the workability of the classification in the ecology of the workplace. As with all tools and all knowledge, such classification schemes are entities with consequences to be managed, negotiated, and experienced all at once (see Clarke and Casper 1992 for an excellent exposition of this in the relationship between cancer, classification and laboratory techniques).

"Difference" is the prime negotiated entity in the construction of a classification system, and it enters the workstream in a subtle and complex fashion. The work to be classified doesn't go away with new classification schemes, but the *work* of classifying itself may cause shifts which in turn present challenges to both the designers of the scheme (faced with decisions about how fine-grained it should be) and to users (filling out forms and encoding diagnoses) and consumers (assessing the viability of the scheme). In this process, work itself is neither created nor destroyed, yet may be radically reshaped to fit into the emerging matrix. Commonly, the larger contexts within which these classification shifts occur include professionalization, automation and informatization, and the creation of international research and record keeping procedures.

There are three main areas of challenge in crafting a classification scheme that will fit the workstream and agendas created by these larger contexts:

1. *Comparability.* A major purpose of a classification system is to provide good comparability across sites, to ensure that there is a regularity in semantics and objects

from one to the other, thus enhancing communication. If "injection" means giving medication by needle in one country and enema in another, there is no use trying to count the number of injections given worldwide until some equivalence is reached by negotiation. The more intimate the communication setting, the less necessary are such negotiations for a variety of reasons, including that they may already exist historically, or by convention; or they are more private and less subject to regulatory scrutiny.

2. *Visibility*. How does one differentiate areas of work which are invisible? While they are invisible, they are by definition unclassifiable except as a residual category: other. If work "just gets done" according to some, it has found no voice in the classification scheme. Invisibility is not only erasure, although, on this view, it can come from intimacy, as with a team which has worked together for so long they no longer need to voice instructions or classify activities.

3. *Control*. No classification system, any more than any representation, may specify completely the wildness and complexity of what is represented. Therefore any prescription contains some amount of control to be exercised by the user, be it as small as in the most Taylorist factory or prison, or as large as the most privileged artists' retreat. Control, like visibility, has good and bad elements, depending on one's perspective. Freedom trades off against structurelessness; being able to exercise a wide range of judgment is only worthwhile if one has the power and resources to do so safely and effectively. Too much freedom for a novice or a child may be confusing, or lead to breakdowns in comparability across setting, thus impairing communication. Judgment about how differentiated to make the classification must revolve in due consideration of this factor. This balance can never be fully resolved (as indeed novices and strangers are always entering the field of work); the managerial trick is to measure the degree of control required to get the job done well, for most people, most of the time.

From the point of view of design, the creation of a perfect classification scheme ideally preserves common sense control, enhances comparability in the right places, and makes visible what is wrongly invisible, leaving justly invisible discretionary judgment. It has, simultaneously, intimacy, immutability/standardization, and is manageable. A manageable classification system works in practice, is not too fine-grained or arcane in its distinctions, and fits with the way work is organized. It is standard enough to appear the same in every setting, and is stable over time as well.[1] Intimacy means that the system acknowledges common understandings that have evolved among members of the community.

---

[1] Although it may seem at first sight that comparability and standardization are the same thing, we see an important difference between the two concepts. An example might explain this. Two things can be comparable but not standardized: thus, you can compare an education at Harvard with an education at Local Community College because you know that, in general, a lot more resources are pumped into Harvard and outcomes tend to be different because of the homogeneity of backgrounds. In that case, one would be high on the "comparability" side of standardization, but low on the "visibility" side: no one spells out exactly what the difference is. If you then subject all students to a single standardized test, you have to match comparability with visibility to provide standardization (and, of course, in the case of comparing educational systems, this is both politically and organizationally complex and fraught).

However, such a perfect scheme does not really exist, since these areas trade off against each other in a real world setting. Maximizing visibility and high levels of control threaten intimacy; comparability and visibility pull against the manageability of the system; comparability and control work against standardization. In order for a classification system to be standardized, it needs to be comparable across sites and leave a margin of control for its users. However both requirements are difficult simultaneously to fulfill. A manageable classification system (for whomever) doesn't only require that the system classifies the same things across sites and times but also that it uncovers invisible work; this impacts recording of data. The combination of those two thus require compromise. Finally, to keep a level of intimacy in the classification system control is to trade off against the requirement to make everything visible. These tradeoffs become the areas of negotiation, sometimes of conflict.

Because one cannot optimize all three parameters at once to produce simultaneously perfect degrees of intimacy, manageability, and standardization, a real-life classification scheme encompasses a thorough, pragmatic understanding of these tradeoffs in their historical context. It places them, as we have said above, in the workstream. In the next part of this article, we situate this process in our observations of the building of a classification system in progress, NIC.

2. THE NURSING INTERVENTIONS CLASSIFICATION

The Nursing Interventions Classification (NIC) aims to depict the range of activities that nurses carry out in their daily routines. The classification system consists of a list of some 336 interventions each comprised of a label, a definition, a set of activities, and a short list of background readings. Each of those interventions is in turn classified within a taxonomy of six domains and 26 classes. For example, one of the tasks nurses commonly perform is getting a patient emotionally ready for a risky or painful treatment. The nursing intervention "Preparatory Sensory Information"[2] is defined as describing "both the subjective and objective physical sensations associated with an upcoming stressful health care procedure/treatment." (McCloskey and Bulechek 1993, p. 253). This intervention is followed by a list of activities which are related to the assessment of patients, situations, and care provision. The intervention is then further classified in the class of "Coping Assistance" that in turn is classified under the domain of "Behavioral."

NIC is being developed at the University of Iowa, with Joanne McCloskey and Gloria Bulechek, experienced and well-respected nursing researchers, as principal investigators. The NIC researchers built up their system of nursing interventions inductively. They surveyed compilations of discrete nursing activities and created a preliminary list that distinguished between nursing interventions and activities. Expert surveys of nurses with master's degrees and focus groups narrowed the preliminary list of interventions to the original 336 published in Nursing Interventions Classification (McCloskey and Bulechek 1993). These interventions were further validated via surveys sent to specialist nursing organizations. Based on a hierarchical cluster analysis and similarity analysis, the different interventions were grouped and reviewed to assure clinical relevance and significance (Iowa Intervention Project 1993). The taxonomy was then validated through surveys with nurse experts in theory development and a coding

---

[2]This is what sociologists have called "sentimental work" (Strauss et al. 1985).

scheme was developed (Iowa Intervention Project forthcoming). The classification system is thus growing slowly through a wide-scale cooperative process, with nurses in field sites trying out categories and suggesting new ones as well as refinements in a series of regional and specialist meetings. Since 1992, the group of nursing researchers has added over fifty interventions to their original list.

The nursing investigators modeled NIC after the classification system of NANDA (North American Nursing Diagnosis Association) which was established in the early 1970s (Gebbie and Lavin 1975). NANDA brought about a major change in the nursing profession by establishing nursing-specific diagnoses. The nursing profession used the diagnosis classification system to promote the claim that nurses diagnose patients in certain domains of care. They are thus not solely dependent on physician's orders. Along similar lines, the NIC investigators want to further the professional struggle for autonomy by creating a list of all nursing interventions. The list is intended to make the invisible work of nursing visible via a detailed representation of the range of nursing tasks. NIC makes a historical connection between diagnoses and outcomes. Having listed nursing interventions, another group of researchers will make a list of possible nursing outcomes to measure the impact of nursing interventions. This will provide classification systems for the full range of nursing work and responsibility.

NIC, although still relatively young, promises to be a major rallying point for nurses in the decades to come. Since its first workable version in 1992, NIC has been taken up by a major medical publisher, formally used to organize nursing training, endorsed by the major hospital accrediting agency, adopted by two main nursing reference indexes, and added to the National Library of Medicine's Metathesaurus for the Unified Medical Language System (UMLS). It has sold its translation rights in different languages and is currently being tested in five field sites across the United States.

So, what is NIC? As a set of interventions it provides a list of what nurses do and therefore what nursing is. Although NIC might look like a straightforward organizational tool, it is much more than that. It merges scientific knowledge, practice, bureaucracy and information systems. NIC coordinates bodies, impairments, charts, reimbursement systems, vocabularies, patients, and health care professionals. Ultimately, it provides a manifesto for an organized occupation: a domain of living scientific knowledge, a highly specialized practice, and an important element of cost and cost-containment in health care.

Creating and establishing NIC means balancing the ideals of visibility, comparability and control against an ongoing backdrop of struggle and change in the domain of nursing autonomy. The past few decades have seen the emergence of nursing science and the general processes of professionalization. It also occurs against the backdrop of a changing classification arena in the American state.[3] In the following sections, we explore how the NIC researchers negotiated the different requirements in the construction of the classification. We evaluate the intentions and rhetoric of the NIC researchers as a process of defining the characteristics of their object and the world in which it functions. With Akrich (1992) and Latour (Akrich and Latour 1992), we see

---

[3]This is made more urgent by potential changes to the national health care system under the current administration and by the widespread increase in medical informatic and multimedia electronic imaging systems for remote medical diagnosis and testing ("telemedicine").

this process as "inscribing" their vision of what nursing is and should be in the technical content of the classification system. A close analysis of the negotiations allows us to understand how nurses are balancing the need for distinct categories with other organizational demands. The empirical material for this analysis consists of all the minutes of NIC team meetings and publications of the NIC group since 1987, eighteen open-ended in-depth interviews with principal investigators, co-investigators, and research associates, and observations of team meetings.

3. INFRASTRUCTURE AND ORGANIZATIONS

There is no simple way to tell the story of the complex theoretical and practical work that goes into the development of an information infrastructure. Star and Ruhleder (submitted for publication, p. 6) argue that an infrastructure has six key properties

- *Embeddedness* ("it is 'sunk' into other structures"). NIC is embedded into various information practices and tools, used by hospitals and insurance companies for costing and coding reimbursements, and by medical librarians for accessing medical literature. NIC is used in clinical decision making software, hospital accounting systems and nursing information systems.

- *Transparency* ("it does not have to reinvented each time"). NIC is oriented to standard scientific and working practical knowledge and to being "ready to hand" for the practitioner. Instead of applying idiosyncratic or new labels to diseases, practitioners are asked to turn to classification systems to fill out forms, assign values, and compare results.[4]

- *Having reach or scope* (it is not a "one-off event or one-site practice"). NIC aims to cover US nursing with a slow growth currently into the European nursing community. Interest has been shown by groups of social workers, occupational therapists and pharmacists in adapting it.

- *It is learned as part of membership* ("associated with communities of practice). NIC is increasingly present in nursing education programs. Because of the ways in which it is propagated, it is closely tied with what it means to *be* a nurse.

- *It is linked with conventions of practice* ("both shapes and is shaped by the conventions of its communities of practice"). For NIC, the informatic conventions are young, but a key design issue is the fit with the conventions of nursing practice. One aspect of NIC user meetings is the developer's insistence that NIC integrate with work practice and that NIC users share common conventions about the system's use. They are currently encouraging the development of clusters of interventions (invisible to the classification system) to represent local practice at specific institutions , e.g., at nursing homes.

---

[4]The NIC principal investigators maintain that at present time there is effectively *no* scientific nursing knowledge; it is only with the creation and maintenance of a stable classification system that the groundwork will have been laid to make such knowledge attainable.

• *Multifunctionality*("as with electricity, supports several functions"). NIC supports a wide range of functions, from data collection and basic epidemiological research to accounting by insurance firms and legitimation of work practices.

These definitions are touchstones to order discussion here and to help guide the construction of a useful model for organizational analysis. Although there is a rich body of research on computerization, impact, values and workplace politics, as yet theories of information infrastructure and its evolution, meaning, and values implications are not well developed.

We know that over the years many innovative applications in information technology have failed due to insufficient consideration of the projected users. However, when developing new information infrastructures, the scope of "usage" is murky. Users may not know, prior to experience, what they want from the new system and how they will use it. The success of France's "Minitel Rose" is a prime example, where, much to the designers's surprise, personal messages and not official information sold the system (Taylor and Van Every 1993). New infrastructures do more than support work which is already being done — they change the very nature of what it is to *do* work and what work will count.

In this sense, NIC is an actively developing infrastructure. It is fed into a clinical decision support system, directs nurses on which activities to perform, and is fed into a hospital accounting system. It lays claim to a professional territory for nursing; as part of ongoing research programs, current nursing interventions (fluctuating at present) become stabilized. Since research is built around these categories, a feedback loop is set up which stabilizes the current set. We saw a similar set of events in the development of the International Classification of Diseases (ICD), a larger and older global epidemiological information system (Bowker and Star 1994). Political, cultural, ethical, social, religious, economic and institutional factors each play a role in its development. Thus, for example, the definition of "stillbirth" has been a site of conflict between states with different religious constituencies and epidemiologists argue that it is still highly variably diagnosed depending on the beliefs of the attending physicians. Similar coding problems have been documented in the case of AIDS and its associated illnesses, especially during the early 1980s (see Verghese 1994).

With the ICD, as with NIC, apparently precise, measurable qualities often prove much more fuzzy when looked at closely. Yet as classification systems, they present knowledge in a form that is transportable and usable in a wide range of different infrastructural technologies — databases, decision support systems and so forth. They are complementary, in that NIC concentrates on work practice/information technology and the ICD on information technology/domain specific knowledge (although clearly all three factors are significant for each). NIC is associated with the traditionally "invisible work" which is often gender and status-linked (Star 1991), the ICD with highly visible medical knowledge — and yet each is being merged into seamlessly integrated infrastructures.

In science studies, Latour's work calls attention to the power of inscriptions, and the relationship between inscriptions, work practice and standards. In *Science in Action* (1987), he developed the concept of *immutable mobiles* to explore the ways in which scientific knowledge gets to move from a local, messy field site into the laboratory and out into textbooks. (The development of NIC displays the force of both of his analytic points: indeed the work of holding classifications stable and enrolling allies in their use has been central.) This emphasis on scientific work practice and culture has been developed in collections by Pickering (1992); Clarke and Fujimura (1992); and Star (1995a, 1995b).

Foucault, in *The Order of Things* (1970), explored the political and philosophical power of classification systems. He drew analytic attention to the epistemic consequences of trying to classify all of knowledge in a given domain. His work on "governmentality" (compare Porter 1994) discusses the rise of statistics as a new mode of government. Following this, Ewald (1986) examined the rise of the welfare state as form of government of the body and soul. A similar theme arises in the work of Rose (1990), whose argument that accounting systems reflect a moral order and help define the self has been widely adopted in social studies of accounting (see, for example, the journal *Accounting, Management and Information Technologies*). Central here is the recognition that statistics and other numbers (invariably based on classification systems — and recognized by WHO and the NIC designers as a key product of their own systems) are socially and politically charged actors. One question posed by the collection of medical statistics has been the role of the state in the physical welfare of its citizens. For instance, the classification of death from being "worn out" disappeared from the ICD early this century. After that, death could only result from something having gone wrong — a potentially avoidable accident or curable disease and thus a site for state intervention (Fagot-Largeault 1989). The equation can be direct and brutal — one doctor suggested in 1984 that statistics on missed diagnoses (about 10% of all cases subjected to autopsy) be tabulated according to the number of functional units affected — viz. the number of productive work-years lost (Anderson 1984, p. 492). Tort (1989) has extended Foucault's work through the nineteenth century, to the rise of universal classification systems in the 1880s and 1890s to cover labor, disease, criminal physiognomies and race.

The problems discussed by Hacking (1995), as noted, have produced an archeology of the classification of child abuse and of multiple personality disorder. He notes some problems for classification systems relevant to both NIC as a vehicle for organizational transformation. A contemporary classification based on current best theory and understanding cannot necessarily be projected back into the past or forward into the future (did "child abuse" exist before the category?). And yet, in order to produce a body of stable knowledge, a classification system must be held steady over time. Therefore doctors often, consciously or not, work together with their patients to make symptoms and category converge.

As information technologies become better able to integrate across a range of places and times, these problems are exacerbated. Kirk and Kutchin's work (1992) on the history and sociology of the diagnostic and statistical manual (DSM) calls attention to both the centrality of the development of a classification scheme to the professionalization of psychiatry (a sentiment shared by many nurses with respect to NIC) and the range of people and organizations that influence the development of such a scheme. They argue that for DSM-3, validity became subordinate to reliability via many sorts of gatekeeping, infrastructural, and power politics.

In a related argument, Berg (1995) takes the example of a medical expert system for dealing with cardiac arrest patients introduced into a number of hospitals in Europe, and Forsythe of the design of a medical diagnostic AI system (1993). They demonstrate that the expert system, often considered universal, only operates successfully if it is accompanied by a disciplining of local work practice. Thus, paradoxically, the system is only universally true if it is locally imposed. This paradox is one discussed at length by Latour with respect to networks of scientific knowledge.

Below, we discuss the three dimensions of classification systems that form pragmatic challenges for designers and users.

4. COMPARABILITY: THE NEED FOR STANDARD DESCRIPTIONS IN RESEARCH

A man and a woman sit in a kitchen. It is early in the morning. He is reading the newspaper intently; she is putting away last night's dishes and preparing breakfast. She pours a cup of coffee and puts it in front of him, carefully avoiding the angle of turning of the newspaper pages. After a moment, he takes a sip of the beverage. "Cold." From this single word, she infers the following: he is still angry over the squabble they had last night; he is feeling apprehensive about his upcoming work review; the dinner they ate together which precipitated the squabble sat heavily on his stomach and he slept less well than usual. Correctly, she predicts that he will be a little snippy with his secretary in the office and forget to bring his second cup of coffee in the car with him on the way to work, a practice he has recently adopted. This omission will result in a late-morning headache.

Psychologist Gail Hornstein[5] analyzes this snippet of conversation as a means to understanding the relationship between intimacy and language: the more intimate the relationship, the more seemingly telegraphic may language become with no loss of meaning.

The construction of a nursing interventions classification implies a drive to abstract away from the local, the particular — to make "nursing" the same entity wherever it may appear. Ideally, local language, the idiosyncrasies of each ward and each staff nurse, should change immediately through an adoption of NIC in hospital administration. Those making the classification examine variability in order to either eliminate or translate it across settings. This is the strategy of moving toward universality: rendering things comparable so that each actor may fit their allotted position in a standardized system and comparisons may be communicated across sites. Julius Roth (1963) has described this process for the operation of tuberculosis sanatoria (rendering patients equivalent); Marc Berg (forthcoming) for the development of medical protocols (rendering treatment equivalent); Geof Bowker and Leigh Star (1991, 1994; Star and Bowker submitted for publication) for the development of the International Classification of Diseases (rendering statistics equivalent); and Stefan Timmermans (1993) for resuscitation techniques (rendering life saving equivalent).

For the nursing interventions classification, the urge to erase the particular and communicate equivalents is apparent in several strategies the group adopts to further their cause. The developers consider NIC a basis for curriculum development: they reason that only with a

---

[5]Personal communication.

complete classification system can one guarantee thorough, standardized and cross-site comparability in professional training. The nursing interventions classification is being integrated into model course development efforts at the University of Iowa and elsewhere. The basic interventions are part of undergraduate nursing curricula, while the more advanced interventions will be taught to master's students. But NIC is ultimately as well a standardized language for comparability. As one respondent said: "The classification is an aspect that makes it a tool, more useable, but it is the standardized language that is really critical." According to the NIC researchers, "a standardized language for nursing treatments is a classification about nursing practice that names what nurses do relative to certain human needs to produce certain outcomes." (McCloskey and Bulechek 1994b, p. 57). In the eyes of the NIC creators, the classification system provides such a standardized language for nursing treatments that can be used across units, across health care settings, and across health care disciplines. A classification alone would be useful for costing, record keeping, and teaching, but the linguistic aspect is necessary for research and comparability. This was clearly expressed in several interviews:

> Certainly we are aiming at standardizing nursing languages. So that when we talk among other nurses and other health professionals, we all know what we talk about. Because what one nurse might be talking about is very different [from another nurse]. What is the difference between therapeutic play and play therapy? And then we need to communicate with parents, consumers, patients, physicians and other health professionals and knowing that they are talking the same language. It is really important that we talk in a language that is not foreign to other groups. Maybe we like to be unique, but sometimes we need to bend so that we talk the same language as families, consumers, and medical professionals.

> A hospital administrator told me a couple of years ago, "If nursing could just tell us what they do." You can't say "the nursing process" because everyone does nursing assessment, intervention. That is a model that everyone can apply. Physical therapy can say what they do: muscles and bones. Respiratory therapy can define their tasks. But nurses do all that. Nursing is so broad. The only thing that they know is that they can't work without us. NIC is extremely helpful because it provides a language to communicate what we do with a firm scientific base.

The Unified Medical Language System, among others, is indicative of the drive for a standardized language in new developments of health care information systems. To study the effectiveness of nursing care, the nursing profession proposed the uniform and routine collection of essential nursing information or a Nursing Minimum Data Set (NMDS) (Werley and Lang 1988; Werley, Lang and Westlake 1986). "The purpose of the NMDS is to foster comparability of nursing care across patient populations, with the ultimate goal the improvement of health care" (McCloskey and Bulechek 1994b, p. 56). This data set consists of sixteen data elements including four nursing care elements: nursing diagnoses, nursing interventions, nursing outcomes, and nursing intensity. NIC is promoted by its creators as providing the nursing intervention variable for the NMDS. A standardized language is also necessary to communicate with extant information systems.

Ironically, NIC's biggest critics come from the same information systems world. Criticism has been directed against NIC's standardized language ambitions. Susan Grobe, a nurse and information scientist at the University of Texas, Houston, criticizes the attempts at creating an universal standardized system as scientifically outmoded and inflexible. Instead, Grobe proposes her own nursing intervention system, the Nursing Intervention Lexicon and Taxonomy (NILT) which consists of eight broad categories of nursing interventions. According to Grobe, in NILT "the burden of standardized language is resident in the automated systems and not dictated to practicing professionals for their memorization and adoption" (Grobe 1993, p. 94). Where NIC expects nurses to learn and use a standardized terminology, Grobe believes that nurses should keep their natural language and computers should be used to standardize language. She argues that having computers decide how terms will be standardized is inevitable and cites researchers who are working on this in health care documentation.

NIC researchers defend themselves against Grobe's criticism by specifying how a standardized language increases comparability (for more on NIC and NILT, see Bowker, Neumann, and Timmermans forthcoming). They note that, although the advent of computers was an impetus for standardized languages, different organizations and agencies developed their own system "with the result that we cannot collect comparable data from multiple agencies, or even within agencies from one unit to the next." They further quote Sherrer, Cote, and Mandil:

> intelligent documentation systems cannot totally discard classifications. Moreover, the availability of at least one classification is a necessary condition for a good documentation system. Classifications are not a necessary evil but a very effective way of representing knowledge about the domain of discourse" [McCloskey and Bulechek 1994b, p. 59; see also Bulechek and McCloskey 1993]

Thus, since a "natural language" is at this moment lacking in nursing, the NIC researchers claim that their classification system fills the void and at the same time achieves the goal of comparability.

In their newsletter, the NIC investigators summarize their vision about a standardized language to achieve comparability across sites and professions:

> Norma Lang has often been quoted as saying, "If we cannot name it, we cannot control it, finance it, teach it, research it, or put it into public policy." We would like to be quoted as saying: "Now that we have named it, we can control it, finance it, teach it, research it, and put it into public policy." [*NIC Newsletter* 1994]

Striving for comparability in a standardized language across settings conflicts with the need for visibility within local settings. The nursing intervention architects want their entire system to be adopted by health care institutions. As a language, its entire vocabulary needs to be available to nursing professionals. However, certain institutions will most likely only need part of the NIC taxonomy. For example, nurses in a geriatric hospital will probably not require "Newborn Care" as an intervention. The results of validation studies with different nursing specialties suggests that between 20% and 80% of the terminology would be routinely used by several nursing specialties. This raises the issue of how to limit each institution's modifications. Too much flexibility would obviously undermine the birth of a standard language, but too much control makes a system user unfriendly especially in such a safety critical and busy line of work. As a rule of thumb, the NIC group decided that an institution should adopt the whole classification system at the level of the copywritten interventions, definitions, and labels but that activity-level descriptions could be modestly changed. However, control and enforcement of this rule ultimately rests with the publisher.

This "central tension" between standards on the one hand and local, tailorable systems on the other is a familiar one in information systems (Trigg and Bødker 1994). It remains a tradeoff — that is, a tension not resolved by resorting to either a lowest common denominator, a universal algorithm, or an appeal to universal positivist knowledge (Star 1992).

5. VISIBILITY AND LEGITIMACY

Literary critic Alice Deck[6] relates the following anecdote:

> *In the 1930s, an African-American woman travels to South Africa. In the Capetown airport, she looks around for a toilet. She finds four, labeled: "White Women," "Colored Women," "White Men," and "Colored Men." (Colored in this context means Asian.) She is uncertain what to do; there are no toilets for "Black Women" or "Black Men," since Black Africans under the apartheid regime are not expected to travel, and she is among the first African Americans to visit South Africa. She is forced to make a decision which will cause her embarrassment or even police harassment.*

Comparability rests on the management and mobility of differences and equivalencies across sites. The issue becomes, what is local and particular or what do all nurses have in common that can be rendered equivalent across settings and nursing specialties? Then, what does this commonality render invisible? The nursing classification designers employ a definition of nursing interventions as a guideline. "A nursing intervention is any direct care treatment that a nurse performs on behalf of a client. These treatments include nurse-initiated treatments resulting from nursing diagnoses, physician-initiated treatments resulting from medical diagnoses, and performance of the daily essential functions for the client who cannot do these" (Bulechek and McCloskey 1989). Here, the emphasis is on direct care: that which nurses do to increase the well-being of a patient at the bedside. Direct care is separated from care which only indirectly benefits the patient — e.g., coordinating treatment schedules, discharge planning, and patient supervision. One step further removed from the bedside is administrative care, activities for creating an environment for direct and indirect care. This includes coordinating administrative units and supervising nurses. Initially, the NIC group concentrated on direct care interventions. The researchers deliberately supported an image in the classification of nursing as a clinical discipline. This was a political decision, as several NIC team members noted in interviews: "Nurses think that laying hands on patients is nursing. We would not have had the attention of the nursing community if we had not begun there."

---

[6]From a talk given at the Program for Cultural Values and Ethics, University of Illinois, December 1993.

However, questions arose in the course of the project about the distinction between direct and indirect care. For instance, if nurses must check the resuscitation charts with every shift, and this is not included in NIC, these activities will not be reimbursed when NIC is implemented. Time spent on this task will be invisible and thus fiscally wasted. Over the course of the project, indirect interventions grew in importance and will be included in the second edition of the NIC book. The researchers even adapted their initial definition of a nursing intervention to include the indirect interventions.

However, nurses themselves are somewhat ambivalent about how to account for indirect care time. Statistical analyses based upon different validation studies reveal that several of the indirect care interventions are indeed considered in a different category by nurses responding to the surveys.

Administrative care is even more controversial. In interviews, some of the NIC collaborators, whose main tasks are administrative, expected that NIC would eventually also contain those kind of interventions:

> Nursing is very different in that when you make changes it involves many people, so the need for managers and supervision and coordination of planned change is so much more a part of nursing, there are so many more people that are a part of changing nursing. I think anything that reflects nursing needs to reflect those kind of things.

However, a majority of the design team and consulting group was not sure whether administrative care was typical for nurses and thus whether it belonged in a nursing classification. "The administrators are not actually nursing. When they are not, there the nursing continues without them." Or, in the words of Gloria Bulechek, "Management science is a different discipline: all managers have to manage people and it is not unique to nursing." For the latter group, the need to make administrative care visible is not as urgent as the need to differentiate nursing as a hands-on discipline. Although the nursing researchers are aware that the boundaries between direct, indirect and administrative care are not firm, administrative care is not part of NIC nor is it scheduled to be part of the revised edition of NIC. This dilemma about the encoding of administrative work points to a practical limit on the visibility-discretion tradeoffs. In order to fully abstract from the local, everything must be spelled out; in order to avoid resistance from nurses and nursing administrators, some work must be left implicit. What is left implicit becomes doubly invisible: it is the residue left over when other sorts of invisible work has been made visible (Strauss et al. 1985; Star 1991). That is, where claims are made for the completeness of an accounting system, that which is not accounted for may be twice overlooked. We are noting this here as both a formal and a practical challenge for the classification designers and users.

The tension between visibility and control became apparent when several group members noted that the classification of the system's developers is strong, and maybe too strong, within the nursing specialties such as the complex physiological domain. However, it is still underdeveloped in other nursing areas such as community health and social-psychological nursing. Social-psychological caregiving is one of the areas where the control/visibility dilemma is very difficult to grasp. For example, NIC lists as one nursing intervention "humor." How can one capture humor as a deliberate nursing intervention? Does sarcasm, irony, or laughter count as a nursing intervention? How to reimburse humor, how to measure this kind of care? No one would dispute its importance, but it is by its nature a situated and subjective action. Since NIC does not contain protocols and procedures for each intervention, a grey area of common sense remains for the individual staff nurse to define whether some of the nursing activities can be called nursing interventions or are worth charting. Of course, this same grey area remains for more clinical interventions such as "Cerebral Edema Management" or "Acid-Base Monitoring."[7] But because the classification is modeled after a clinical model of nursing, the team felt it easier to define and include those more clinical interventions.

Not only in the interventions themselves but also in the decisions underlying NIC, the borderland between professional control and the urge to make nursing visible is fraught with difficult choices and balances. Team members recalled discussions where interventions were so singular and demarcated as to warrant inclusion, but they ended up not being included. For example, one will not find "Leech Therapy" as an intervention in the classification, although there was enough research literature to support this intervention as typical nursing in many parts of the world (Neumann 1995).[8] Also the advanced statistical analysis of the validation studies was located in what the design team members typified as "common sense." One could have a coefficient of .73, but if it didn't respond to a visible or controllable enough nursing reality, it became an outlier, a non-result, or resulted in a residual category. As with all statistical analyses, a link with theory and practice must precede testing or the results are meaningless.

In other cases, the criteria for inclusion and control are themselves contested. One research member confided in an interview that her intervention was rejected because it was not supported with research evidence. Her plan was to first publish a paper about the intervention in a research journal and then resubmit the intervention for consideration with her own reference as research evidence.

In these examples, the goal of making as much visible as possible clashes with what should remain taken for granted. The nursing researchers temper their quest to make nursing visible with the image of what nursing is or should be about. Again, there is no final answer or algorithm but a complex balance of experience and rules. Visibility is tempered by common practice, contingency, and legitimacy.

6. CONTROL, DISCRETION AND RELIABILITY

> *The movie "A Few Good Men" hinges on an anecdote about several soldiers who perform a "code red" on another soldier, during which he dies. A "code red" is an illegal informal punishment/harassment in the manner of a rough fraternity joke. The death of the soldier causes an investigation; the command-*

---

[7] See Michael Lynch's work (1984) on "turning up signs" for an example of the inexhaustible discretion and improvisation in every human activity — the study of which has been the major contribution of ethnomethodology and phenomenology.

[8] This was the situation during our interview round. According to Joanne McCloskey, Leech Therapy probably will be included in the next edition of the NIC book.

ing officer is suspected of deliberately ordering the code. The harassing soldiers defend themselves by saying that they could not have been ordered to perform a code red because that was forbidden by the manual of conduct. The denouement of the film has the prosecuting attorney closely questioning one defendant in a truly ethnomethodological moment:

"Does he do everything by the book?"

"Yes."

"Does the book contain all knowledge about how to conduct oneself in military life?"

"Yes."

"Did he have breakfast this morning?"

"Yes."

"Does the manual specify how to get to the mess hall, or where it is located?"

"No."

"QED — the manual does not contain all knowledge."

There is a continuing tension within NIC, as we have noted, between abstracting away from the local and rendering "invisible work" visible. Nurses' work is often quintessentially invisible for a combination of good and bad reasons. Nurses have to ask mundane questions, rearrange bedcovers, move a patient's hand so that it is closer to a button, and sympathize about the suffering involved in illness (Olesen and Whittaker 1968). Bringing this work out into the open and differentiating its components has encountered problems from the nurses themselves. In naming and differentiating someone's work, there is a fine line between being too obvious and being too vague, once one has decided to take on naming as a central task. If the task that is brought under the glare of enlightenment is too obvious and mundane, then some nurses who are testing the system find it insulting. To tell a veteran nurse to shake down a thermometer after taking a temperature puts him or her into a childlike position. Some experienced nurses, encountering interventions they felt were too obvious, have called them an NSS or "No Shit, Sherlock" intervention. That is, it really doesn't take a Sherlock Holmes to realize that nurses have to do this! Creating difference by cutting up the continuum of duties that make up "looking after the patient's welfare" is thus sociologically, as well as phenomenologically and philosophically, very difficult. One must be explicit enough for the novices and not insulting to the veterans. Reading the NIC minutes, one is frequently reminded of ethnomethodological texts: just how much "common sense" can be taken for granted is a perpetually open question, and to whom it is in fact common sense is not always so obvious (e.g., Sacks 1975). But ethnomethodology alone will not solve the political and organizational controversies and dilemmas of discretion. We see a link here with all previous attempts to rationally reconstruct the workplace, especially those modeling work for information systems; as Schmidt and Bannon (1992) point out, the management of real-time contingencies ("articulation work") never goes away but, if ignored, will be costly in many ways.

One of the battlefields where comparability and control appear as opposing factors is in linking NIC to costing. NIC researchers assert that the classification of nursing interventions will allow a determination of the costs of services provided by nurses and planning for resources needed in nursing practice settings. Currently, nursing treatments "are lumped in with the room price." In our interviews with them, team members noted that although nurses fill in for physical therapists during weekends, the nursing department is not always reimbursed for this service. Sometimes the money flows back to the hospital at large, to the physical therapy department, or these treatments are simply not reimbursed. According to the NIC researchers, NIC will allow hospital administrators to determine nursing costs and resource allocation and stop such apparent "freeloading." Until it is made explicit exactly what nurses do on a daily basis, administrators have trouble rationally allocating tasks. Similarly, NIC is used in the development of nursing health care systems and communication with the classification systems of other health care providers. This coordination provides a safety net and planning vehicle for untracked costs.

The horizon is not fully clear, however. Wagner (forthcoming; Egger and Wagner 1993); Robinson (Gray, Elkan and Robinson 1991; Strong and Robinson 1990); and Bjerknes and Bratteteig (1987a, 1987b) have studied the implementation of similar measures in Europe. While they have the effect of making nursing work visible and differentiated, it may also become a target for social control and surveillance of nursing work, working against control in the sense of discretionary judgment and common sense. Wagner notes that:

> Nurses' striving for a higher degree of professionalization contains a contradictory message. Nurses might gain greater recognition for their work and more control over the definition of patients' problems while finding out that their practice is increasingly shaped by the necessity to comply with regulators' and employers' definitions of "billable categories." [Wagner forthcoming, p. 10)]

She states that while computerization of care plans in French and Austrian hospitals is partly designed to give nurses greater scope of responsibility, and legitimize their care giving in some detail, it also has another side:

> The idea of computerized care-plans, as put forward in nursing research, is to strengthen the focus on nurses' own pre-planned nursing "projects." Like "the autonomous profession," nurses are seen as setting apart time for specialized activities, irrespective of ad-hoc-demands...the reality of computerized care plans — even when nurses themselves have a voice in their development — may lag far behind this idea, given the authority structures in hospitals. With management focusing on care plans as instruments that may help them with their legal and accreditation issues, and nurses having to continue documenting their work on the KARDEX and other forms as well, care plans cannot unfold their potential. [Wagner forthcoming, p. 8]

Once designed, a classification system is then not a "black box" before it becomes part of nursing practice. The balancing act of the designer team needs to continue on every ward of every hospital.

7. PROFESSIONALIZATION, CLASSIFICATION SYSTEMS, AND NURSING AUTONOMY

Since the focus of the Nursing Interventions Classification is on making nursing visible, along with balancing out control and comparability, it is interesting to compare the strategies chosen by the NIC researchers in order to fully professionalize nursing to the range of strategies discussed by Abbott (1988) in *The System of Professions*. Abbott puts the struggle for jurisdiction in central place and his model of "the cultural machinery of jurisdiction" (p. 59) characterizes professional work in terms of diagnosis, treatment, inference and academic work. The very words are drawn from the medical profession; staking out a jurisdictional claim within that profession is particularly difficult. What is specific in a "nursing diagnosis" that differentiates it from "medical diagnosis"? He does not describe any other case where a central tool has been the creation of a classification system. Yet within the medical system as a whole, having access to one's own classification has long been a control strategy. Kirk and Kutchins, for example, discuss jurisdictional disputes between the ICD and the DSM and show convincingly that the DSM became a tool for a particular theory of psychiatry, empowering more physiologically-based models at the expense of psychological models. There is such a "Tower of Babel" of classification systems within medicine,[9] that a major thrust now is the creation of a Unified Medical Language System (UMLS), which will allow a cross translation between the various classifications. NIC has been recognized by the UMLS as a valid nursing classification. This is a major victory for the development group.

In sum, in order to gain equity with the medical profession (where they have often been seen as subordinate), nursing research is an important aspect of legitimation. In turn, classification of work is a cornerstone of research. Nursing classification creates the possibility of equivalence on the research end. Because nursing had long been defined as the undifferentiated other (everything that doctors don't do with respect to the treatment of patients), it was impossible to create precise arguments for professionalization based on research results.

However, as nursing differentiates and becomes more autonomous, it too creates its own undifferentiated other. In what sense? As Abbott emphasized, professionalization depends upon the scope of the professions' jurisdiction. For NIC, this implies that if nurses define a number of activities as specifically nursing activities, they also claim only these activities. Although the researchers mean to include all the activities which nurses do, it is impossible to be totally inclusive, as we have demonstrated. Regional variations, and those activities which cut across professional domains, cannot be articulated in a interventions classification system. Some may be left in residual categories, or left for other health care groups such as licensed vocational

---

[9]Including occupational classifications, disability, geographical and regional, and specialty-based systems, among others. Looming on the horizon as well is a territorial dispute between allopathic and complementary ("alternative" or traditional) approaches to medicine, which both the WHO and the NIH have acknowledged in the establishment of directives and committees to study the problem (Karnik 1994).

nurses and technicians. Implicit in the physician's classification systems was the assumption that nurses would perform any unaccounted work that would allow the fit between the doctors' prescription and the patient's health.[10] Now that nurses are creating their own classification system, they too might rely in a changed fashion on the invisible and unaccounted work of others.

The NIC group hopes that their classification system will sensitize the entire health care sphere to the contribution that nurses make to the well-being of patients. The road to such an outcome is a difficult (and potentially even dangerous) one for nurses as a group, as Wagner has shown for the European example. For instance, it is possible that NIC might be used against nursing professionalization in some computerization and surveillance scenarios. Imagine a hospital administrator who has implemented NIC and evaluates what the nurses are doing. In an effort to curtail costs and adequately allocate resources, the administrator might prescribe nursing activities that are more cost efficient. When asked about this issue, one of the principal investigators, Joanne McCloskey, emphasized that is more important that nurses deal with those questions instead of leaving them tacit. "It may create some problems, but it forces nursing into the mainstream and forces nurses to be responsible, accountable, health care providers. Then, of course, you have to deal with the questions that physicians have had to deal with for a long time. And we ought to be able to deal with that and find a good new solution" (see also McCloskey and Bulechek 1994a).

A classification system is an important tool in the struggle for professional recognition. When the tensions between visibility, comparability, and control are skillfully managed in the construction of the classification system itself, the same processes need to be balanced at the level of users and policy makers. NIC's goal is to promote the work of nurses by communicating newly-visible (in the sense of inscribed and legitimated) work practices and by leaving enough space for controllable action. But even if the designers succeed in creating an equilibrium at the information system level, there are potential utilization problems in the political arena. Professionalization through visibility alone may have latent consequences: constant surveillance in the name of the panopticon of cost containment (Foucault 1979). In this era of information infrastructure shifts, the gravity of this scenario is enormous.

8. CONCLUSION

Classification activity is a very basic form of infrastructural work. It is pervasive within the world of medicine. In order to maintain a good system of medical records, a state needs to classify a huge amount of information about not only its own citizens, but about citizens of countries that it is in contact with. The need for information — and thence the burden of classificatory activity — is effectively infinite. A wish list from 1985 for a national medical information system in the United States of America included "all factors affecting health... genetic and biological; environmental, behavioral, psychological, and social conditions which precipitate health problems' complaints, symptoms and diseases which prompt people to seek medical care; and evaluation of severity and functional capacity, including impairment and handicaps" (Rothwell 1985, p. 169-170).

---

[10]Strauss et al. (1985) call this activity "articulation work."

There is no foretelling what information will be relevant:

> To classify a chisel, a hand drill, and a spanner together as "hand tools," or the first two as "cutting and piercing instruments" may be obscurantist, or even misleading. Whereas to one accident researcher it is significant that a chisel is edged, a drill pointed, and a spanner neither, to another it may be more important that the chisel is pushed, the spanner turned and the drill operated by rotary motion.

Here is Spinoza's problem as bureaucratic nightmare: in order to properly record information about a given disease at a given time, you need to know everything about the social, economic, personal and physical conditions of the patient.

The state in a sense pits itself against the passage of time and tries, in its own interest, to legislate bureaucratic immortality for its citizens (Desrosières and Thévenot 1988). It is a hungry organizational device, squirreling away detail after detail of its people's lives where they touch on any aspect of health, the body, life — and death. At the same time, the bureaucracies of medical intervention have themselves grown exponentially and fractured, so that we are faced with ever-increasing numbers of medical and paramedical activities, each needing an often-overlapping classification system for its record keeping work. Classification schemes are needed to keep this work manageable. They provide both a living organizational memory (Walsh and Ungson 1991) and a means for bureaucratic control. Suchman (1994) says: "Categorization device are devices of social control involving contests between others' claims to the territories inhabited by persons or activities and their own, internally administered forms of organization." The ramified lists of concepts which build up a classification system reflect an attempt, at the larger scale, to create a displacement of interests — the genesis of the state or a discipline.

A classification system is then a political actor in the attempts to establish power on broad institutional and historical levels. When a classification system intends to promote a professional group, the challenges are geared toward their ability to enhance professionalization. In the best case, classification systems hold a memory of work that has been done (laboratory, organizational, epidemiological, sociological) and so permit the recommendation of a reasonable due process for future work (Gerson and Star 1986).

It is difficult to retrace these processes after the classification is black boxed. We have been fortunate to observe an effort to classify work in its early days, coordinated by a group of American nursing researchers, which is beginning to spread to other locations as well. Their work exemplifies a profoundly skilled "balancing act" revolving around managing the tradeoffs outlined above. The NIC project team has a global strategy of balanced classification through a series of sophisticated moves of differentiation and dedifferentiation. This strategy assumes that the work of producing equivalence (making other things equal) will reduce on the overall amount of effort: retraining when a nurse needs to move into a new situation, introducing the nurse to the medical information system in a new hospital, and so on. It is linked with the strategy of the creation of a single information infrastructure to facilitate hospital operation.

A favorite metaphor of NIC members to describe their task is "to make the invisible work visible." As the layers of complexity involved in its architecture reveal, however, a light shining in the dark illuminates certain areas of nursing work, but may cast shadows elsewhere: the whole picture is a very complex one. NIC is at once an attempt at a universal standardized tool, with a common language, and, at the same time, its development and application proceeds by managing and articulating local language and particulars. It is in that sense a boundary object between communities of practice, with a delicate cooperative structure (Star and Griesemer 1989). At the same time, it is balanced in a workflow and historical period which makes it a potential target for control. The fact that NIC researchers are carefully involving a huge web of nurses and nursing researchers, and building slowly over time, with revisions, is key to this. The conservation of work inscribed in the static list of concepts and activities which form a classification system will be inserted in a field of ongoing practices, negotiations, and professional autonomy disputes. These practices, at the political field in which they occur, form the architecture of intimacy, manageability, and standardization. The local and macro contexts of the classification system and its attendant practices (Berg forthcoming) determine in final instance the extent of the displacement of nursing work. In classification systems, differentiation and dedifferentiation emerge as a continuous and negotiated accomplishment over time. It is not a question of map or territory, but map *in* territory.

9. ACKNOWLEDGMENTS

We are very much indebted to the members of the Nursing Interventions Project at the University of Iowa. In particular, Joanne McCloskey and Gloria Bulechek provided many helpful suggestions during conversations. We would further like to thank the following Iowa team members who have graciously allowed us to interview them: Laurie Ackerman, Sally Blackman, Gloria Bulechek, Joan Carter, Jeanette Daly, Janice Denehy, Bill Donahue, Chris Forcucci, Orpha Glick, Mary Kanak, Vicki Kraus, Tom Kruckeberg, Meridean Maas, Joanne McCloskey, Barbara Rakel, Marita Titler, Bonnie Wakefield, and Huibin Yue. We would also like to thank our colleagues on the Classification Project, University of Illinois: Theresa Chi Lin, Niranjan Karnik, and Laura Neumann (who assisted with the interviews) for ongoing discussions and insight; the Advanced Information Technologies Group; and the Graduate School of Library and Information Science at the University of Illinois for support. Comments by Annemarie Mol, Marc Berg, Isabelle Baszanger and Pauline Cochrane were most helpful, and we thank our anonymous referees for helpful comments as well.

10.   REFERENCES

Abbott, A. *The System of Professions: An Essay on the Division of Expert Labor*. Chicago: University of Chicago Press, 1988.

Akrich, M. "The De-Scription of Technical Objects." In W. E. Bijker and J. Law (Editors), *Shaping Technology/Building Society: Studies in Sociotechnical Change*. Cambridge: MIT Press, 1992, pp. 205-224.

Akrich, M., and Latour, B. "A Summary of a Convenient Vocabulary for the Semiotics of Human and Non-human Assemblies." In W. E. Bijker and J. Law (Editors), *Shaping Technology/Building Society: Studies in Sociotechnical Change*. Cambridge: MIT Press., 1992.

Becker, H. S. "Becoming a Marihuana User." *American Journal of Sociology*, Volume 59, 1953-54, pp. 235-242.

Berg, M. *Rationalizing Medical Work: A Study of Decision Support Techniques and Medical Practices*. Ph.D. Dissertation, University of Limburg, Maastricht, Netherlands, 1995.

Berg, M. "Order(s) and Disorder(s): Of Protocols and Medical Practices." In Marc Berg and Annemarie Mol (Editors), *Differences in Medicine: Unraveling Practices, Techniques, and Bodies*, forthcoming.

Bjerknes, G., and Bratteteig, T. "Florence in Wonderland: System Development with Nurses." In G. Bjerknes, P. Ehn, and M. Kyng (Editors), *Computers and Democracy: A Scandinavian Challenge*. Avebury, UK: Aldershot, 1987a, pp. 281-295.

Bjerknes, G., and Bratteteig, T. "Perspectives on Description Tools and Techniques in System Development." In P. Docherty (Editor), *System Design for Human Development and Productivity: Participation and Beyond*. Amsterdam: Elsevier-North Holland, 1987b, pp. 319-330.

Bowker, G.; Neumann, L.; and Timmermans, S. "NIC and NILT: Two Approaches to Nursing Interventions Classification." Working Paper, Graduate School of Library and Information Science, University of Illinois, forthcoming.

Bowker, G. *Science on the Run: Information Management and Industrial Science at Schlumberger, 1920-1940*. Cambridge: MIT Press, 1994a.

Bowker, G. "Information Mythology and Infrastructure." In L. Bud-Frierman (Editor), *Information Acumen: The Understanding and Use of Knowledge in Modern Business*. London: Routledge, 1994b, pp. 231-247.

Bowker, G., and Star, S. L. "Of Lungs and Lungers: The Classified Story of Tuberculosis." Submitted to *Configurations*.

Bowker, G., and Star, S. L. "Knowledge and Infrastructure in International Information Management: Problems of Classification and Coding." In L. Bud-Frierman (Editor), *Information Acumen: the Understanding and Use of Knowledge in Modern Business*. London: Routledge, 1994, pp. 187-213.

Bowker, G., and Star, S. L. "Situations vs. Standards in Long-Term, Wide-Scale Decision-Making: The Case of the International Classification of Diseases." In *Proceedings of the Twenty-Fourth Hawaiian International Conference on Systems Sciences*. Anaheim, California: IEEE Computer Society Press, 1991, pp. 73-81.

Bulechek, G. M., and McCloskey, J. C. "Nursing Interventions: Treatments for Potential Diagnoses." In R. M. Carroll-Johnson (Editor), *Proceedings of the Eighth NANDA Conference*. Philadelphia: J. B. Lippincott, 1989, pp. 23-30.

Bulechek, G. M., and McCloskey, J. C. "Response to Grobe." In *Canadian Nurses Association, Papers from the Nursing Minimum Data Set Conference.* Edmonton, Alberta: Canadian Nurses Association, 1993, pp. 158-160.

Clarke, A. E., and Casper, M. "From Simple Technology to Complex Arena: Classification of Pap Smears, 1917-1990." Working Paper, University of California, San Francisco, 1992.

Clarke, A. E., and Fujimura, J. H. (Editors). *The Right Tools For The Job: At Work in Twentieth-Century Life Sciences.* Princeton, New Jersey: Princeton University Press, 1992.

Desrosières, A., and Thèvenot, L. *Les catégories socio-professionnelles.* Paris: Découverte, 1988.

Douglas, M., and Hull, D. L. *How Classification Works: Nelson Goodman among the Social Sciences.* Edinburgh: Edinburgh University Press, 1992.

Egger, E., and Wagner, I. "Negotiating Temporal Orders: The Case of Collaborative Time Management in a Surgery Clinic." *Computer Supported Cooperative Work*, Volume 1, 1993, pp. 255-275.

Eisenstein, E. L. *The Printing Revolution in Early Modern Europe.* Cambridge, England: Cambridge University Press, 1983.

Ewald, F. *L'sEtat providence.* Paris: B. Grasset, 1986.

Fagot-Largeault, A. *Causes de la mort: histoire naturelle et facteurs de risque.* Paris: Librairie philosophique J. Vrin, 1989.

Forsythe, D. "Engineering Knowledge: The Construction of Knowledge in Artificial Intelligence." *Social Studies of Science*, Volume 23, 1993, pp. 445-477.

Foucault, M. *Discipline and Punish: The Birth of the Prison.* Translated by Alan Sheridan. New York: Vintage Books, 1979.

Foucault, M. *The Order of Things: An Archaeology of the Human Sciences.* London: Tavistock Publications, 1970.

Friedlander, A. *Emerging Infrastructure: The Growth of Railroads.* Reston, Virginia: Corporation for National Research Initiatives, 1995.

Gebbie, K. M., and Lavin, M. A. *Classification of Nursing Diagnoses. Proceedings of First National Conference.* St. Louis, Missouri: Mosby Co., 1975.

Gerson, E., and Star, S. L. "Analyzing Due Process in the Workplace." *ACM Transactions on Office Information Systems*, Volume 4, 1986, pp. 257-270.

Gray, A.; Elkan, R.; and Robinson, J. *Policy Issues in Nursing*. Milton Keynes, England: Open University Press, 1991.

Grobe, S. J. "Response to J. C. McCloskey's and G. M. Bulechek's Paper on Nursing Intervention Schemes." In *Papers from the Nursing Minimum Data Set Conference*. Edmonton, Alberta: The Canadian Nursing Association, 1993.

Hacking, I. *Rewriting the Soul: Multiple Personality and the Sciences of Memory*. Princeton, New Jersey: Princeton University Press, 1995.

Hacking, I. "Making Up People." In T. C. Heller, et al. (Editors), *Reconstructing Individualism*. Stanford: Stanford University Press, 1986, pp. 222-236.

Hughes, T. P. *Networks of Power: Electrification in Western Society, 1880-1930*. Baltimore: Johns Hopkins University Press, 1983.

Iowa Intervention Project. "The NIC Taxonomy Structure." *IMAGE: Journal of Nursing Scholarship*, Volume 25, Number 3, 1993, 187-192.

Iowa Intervention Project. *Validation and Coding of the NIC Taxonomy Structure*. Forthcoming.

Karnik, N. "Western and Traditional Medicine in India." Working Report, Illinois Research Group on Classification, 1994.

Kirk, S. A., and Kutchins, H. *The Selling of the DSM: The Rhetoric of Science in Psychiatry*. New York: Aldine de Gruyter, 1992.

Latour, B. *Science In Action: How To Follow Scientists And Engineers Through Society*. Cambridge: Harvard University Press, 1987.

Lynch, M. "Turning Up Signs in Neurobehavioral Diagnosis." *Symbolic Interaction*. Volume 7, Number 1, 1984, pp. 67-86.

McCloskey, J. C., and Bulechek, G. M. *Nursing Interventions Classification*. St. Louis, Missouri: Mosby Year Book, 1993.

McCloskey, J. C., and Bulechek, G. M. "Standardizing the Language for Nursing Treatments: An Overview of the Issues." *Nursing Outlook*, Volume 42, Number 2, 1994a, pp. 56-63.

McCloskey, J. C., and Bulechek, G. M. "Response to Edward Halloran." *IMAGE: Journal of Nursing Scholarship*, Volume 26, Number 2, 1994b, pp. 93.

Neumann, L. "What about Leech Treatment? Nursing Classification and Professionalization," Working Paper, Illinois Research Group on Classification, 1995.

Olesen, V. L., and Whittaker, E. W. *The Silent Dialogue: A Study in the Social Psychology of Professional Socialization*. San Francisco: Jossey-Bass, 1968.

Pickering, A. (Editor). *Science as Practice and Culture*. Chicago: University of Chicago Press, 1992.

Porter, T. M. "Information, Power and the View from Nowhere," In L Bud-Frierman (Editor), *Information Acumen: The Understanding and Use of Knowledge in Modern Business*. London: Routledge, 1994, pp. 214-246.

Rose, N. S. *Governing the Soul: The Shaping of the Private Self*. London: Routledge, 1990.

Roth, J. A. *Timetables: Structuring the Passage of Time in Hospital Treatment and Other Careers*. Indianapolis, Indiana: Bobbs-Merrill, 1963.

Rothwell, D. J. In R. Cote (Editor), *Requirements of a National Health Information System*. 1985, pp. 169-178.

Sacks, H. "Everyone Has to Lie." In M. Sanches and B. G. Bount (Editors), *Sociocultural Dimensions of Language Use*. New York: Academic Press, 1975, pp. 57-80.

Schivelbusch, W. *The Railway Journey : The Industrialization of Time And Space in the 19th Century*. Berkeley: University of California Press, 1986.

Sherrer, J. R.; Cote, R. A.; and Mandil, S. H. *Computerized Natural Medical Language Processing for Knowledge Representation*. North Holland: Elsevier Science Publishers B.V., 1989.

Star, S. L. (Editor). *The Cultures of Computing*. Sociological Review Monograph Series. Oxford: Basil Blackwell, 1995a.

Star, S. L. (Editor). *Ecologies of Knowledge: Work and Politics in Science and Technology*, Albany, New York: SUNY Press, 1995b.

Star, S. L. "Invisible Work And Silenced Dialogues In Representing Knowledge." In I. V. Eriksson, B. A. Kitchenham, and K. G. Tijdens (Editors), *Women, Work and Computerization: Understanding and Overcoming Bias in Work and Education*. Amsterdam: North Holland, 1991, pp. 81-92.

Star, S. L. "The Politics of Formal Representations: Wizards, Gurus, and Organizational Complexity." In S. L. Star (Editor), *Ecologies of Knowledge: Work and Politics in Science and Technology*. Albany, New York: SUNY Press, 1995c, pp. 88-118.

Star, S. L. "The Trojan Door: Organizations, Work, and the 'Open Black Box'." *Systems/Practice*, Volume 5, 1992, pp. 395-410.

Star., S. L., and Bowker, G. "Of Lungs and Lungers: The Classified Story of Tuberculosis." Submitted to *Configurations*.

Star, S. L., and Griesemer, J. R. "Institutional Ecology, 'Translations' and Boundary Objects: Amateurs and Professionals in Berkeley's Museum of Vertebrate Zoology, 1907-39." *Social Studies of Science*, Volume 19, 1989, pp. 387-420.

Star, S. L., and Ruhleder, K. "Steps toward an Ecology of Infrastructure: Borderlands of Design and Access for Large Information Spaces." Submitted to *Information Systems Research*.

Strauss, A.; Fagerhaugh, S.; Suczek, B.; and Wiener, C. *Social Organization of Medical Work*. Chicago: University of Chicago Press, 1985.

Strong, P., and Robinson, J. *The NHS — Under New Management*. Bristol, England: Open University Press, 1990.

Suchman, L. "Do Categories Have Politics? The Language/Action Perspective Reconsidered" *Computer Supported Cooperative Work*, Volume 2, 1994, pp. 177-190.

Taylor, J. R., and Van Every, E. J. *The Vulnerable Fortress: Bureaucratic Organization and Management in the Information Age* (with contributions from H. Akzam, M. Hovey, G. Taylor). Toronto: University of Toronto Press, 1993.

Timmermans, S. "From 'Out Goes the Bad Air...' to 'ABC': A Sociological Analysis of the Development of Resuscitation Techniques." Paper presented at the Social Studies of Science (4S) Conference, Purdue University, November 1993.

Tort, P. *La raison classificatoire: les complexes discursifs: quinze etudes*. Paris: Aubier, 1989.

Trigg, R., and Bødker, S. "From Implementation to Design: Tailoring and the Emergence of Systematization in CSCW." In *Proceedings of ACM 1994 Conference on Computer-Supported Cooperative Work*. New York: ACM Press, 1994, pp. 45-54.

Verghese, A. *My Own Country*. New York: Simon and Schuster, 1994.

Wagner, I. "Technology and Women's Voice: The Case of Nursing Information Systems." *AI & Society*, forthcoming.

Walsh, J. P., and Ungson, G. R. "Organizational Memory." *Academy of Management Review*, Volume 16, 1991, pp. 57-91.

Werley, H. H., and Lang, N. M. *Identification of the Nursing Minimum Data Set*. New York: Springer, 1988.

Werley, H. H.; Lang, N. M.; and Westlake, S. K. "The Nursing Minimum Data Set Conference: Executive Summary." *Journal of Professional Nursing*, Volume 2, pp. 217-224.

About the Authors

Geoffrey Bowker is Assistant Professor, Graduate School of Library and Information Science, University of Illinois at Urbana-Champaign. His recent book on information science and the sociology of science, *Science on the Run: Information Management and Industrial Geophysics at Schlumberger, 1920-1940*, was published by MIT Press in 1994. He is currently writing a book on classification and information infrastructure with Susan Leigh Star and researching in the field of organizational memory.

Stefan Timmermans received his Ph.D. in 1995 from the University of Illinois, Urbana. He is an Assistant Professor in the Sociology Department at Brandeis University. His research interests include medical technology and interpretive sociology and the historical and ethnographic study of the development and usage of resuscitation technology. He is interested in issues of universality and standardization. Dr. Timmermans' future research plans include classification systems and telemedicine. He has published articles in "Social Studies of Science" and "Sociology of Health and Illness," as well as several book chapters.

Susan Leigh Star is Associate Professor of Library and Information Science and Women's Studies at the University of Illinois, Urbana-Champaign. Her recent research centers on the social and organizational aspects of large information systems, including digital libraries and medical classification. She has edited two volumes, *Ecologies of Knowledge: Work and Politics in Science and Technology* (SUNY Press, 1995) and *The Cultures of Computing (Sociological Review Monograph)* (Basil Blackwell 1995). Recent papers include "Steps Toward an Ecology of Infrastructure: Design and Access for Large Information Spaces" (with Karen Ruhleder), *Proceedings of CSCW'94* (ACM Press 1994).

22

Madness and Organization: Informed Management and Empowerment

Brian P. Bloomfield
Christine McLean
Centre for Research on Organisations
Management and Technical Change
Manchester School of Management

Abstract

Empowerment has become a popular and alluring concept associated with ideas of emancipation, participation, and the delegation of decision making. It is seen as a way of enabling individuals, organizations, or even nations to exert a greater degree of control over their destinies. In addition, information technology (IT) is seen as an enabling medium through which empowerment can be realized. Yet, in some cases technology is also viewed as the source of oppression and control, while empowerment is regarded as a myth. This paper addresses the relationship between IT and empowerment in the context of recent developments within the management and delivery of care in mental health services. Drawing upon research in an NHS psychiatry department, it examines the process by which individuals (both mental health service professionals and patients) are constituted as empowered through specific discursive practices centered on information and information management.

1. INTRODUCTION

As we come to the end of the current millennium, it is clear that many see developments in information technology (IT) as an indicator of modernization, or even post modernity (Poster 1990). Visions of the modernized organization revolving around notions of managers empowered by information, flattened hierarchies, network organizational designs, not to mention the "virtual" organization, all presuppose an IT infrastructure both to help bring about, and then to sustain, such changes. But further, beyond the advertising copy and the case studies of how IT *changed the world*, there is also a sense in which, for some at least, IT provides the focus for a more basic expression of hope for the future. In particular, the Internet global communications network has become a repository for a wide variety of goals and imaginings: while the view of the computer as Big Brother still lurks in the background, in certain quarters the image of the empowered citizen brandishing a "PC plus a modem" has come to represent an icon of egalitarianism and democratic participation.[1]

For individuals, organizations (Peters 1989; Zuboff 1989), and sovereign states (Porter 1990; Toffler 1980), the future is seen to be characterized by empowerment through IT.[2] In part because of the belief that everything can be conceived in information-theoretic terms, IT is regarded as a technology that will reach into every interstice of social life while at the same time transforming social, educational, professional, and other working practices beyond recognition. In particular, to the extent that IT provides the lure of increased organizational control, visibility, efficiency and flexibility, organizations and management are increasingly constituted around information processing and information management. In this regard the UK National Health Service (NHS) is no exception. Rising demand for health care and constraints on financial resources, coupled with the notion that, historically speaking, the NHS has been under-managed, have provided a potent concoction for which IT is seen as the antidote. The hope being that IT would enable the connection between service activity and its costs to become visible and thus assist the search for greater efficiency.

In this paper we reflect upon some recent developments in the management and delivery of care in mental health services where one finds that notions of empowerment through IT — for managers, practitioners, and patients — circulate alongside (muted) fears of increasing central control, cutbacks and a commercially-minded search for efficiency. The concept of empowerment raises many difficult issues.[3] For though the equation of computers with power is almost taken for granted, what remains in dispute is whether the exercise of that power is ultimately enslaving or emancipating. We specifically avoid trying to solve the empowerment conundrum *per se*, or indeed evaluate particular instances of empowerment, for to do so would require some Archimedean position or neutral standpoint against which it could be judged. Rather, we aim to consider how subjects are *constituted* as empowered, in particular through the institution of IT mediated practices which open up a space for thought and action centered on information and information management (Bloomfield and Coombs 1992).

Our starting point is a brief discussion of some recurrent themes in studies of the social *impact* of technology, in contrast to which we develop an alternative line of enquiry focussed on the relationship between thought, information, information management and users of information systems. We will then consider the case of mental health services and go on to present a case study of the development of information management practices in a mental health department of

---

[1]Although many would challenge the individualist and free market values often embodied in the political agenda among some Internet groups, not to mention its effective exclusion of women.

[2]To a degree, this hope is paralleled by a fear that those who let the opportunities afforded by IT pass them by will be reduced to, or remain, an underclass: for example, as the notion of computer literacy threatens to erect a new barrier of access to employment and even citizenship.

[3]For two different approaches, see Clement (1994) and Eccles (1993). For a critical discussion of empowerment within the context of corporate culturalism, see Willmott (1993).

an NHS Trust hospital. In particular, we are interested in the changing conceptualization of patients, mental health workers, and managers, which are mediated and reinforced by recent moves to improve the management of health care delivery and to empower patients and health professionals.

2. TECHNOLOGY: BEYOND GOOD AND EVIL

Discussions of the social *impact* of IT frequently revolve around a set of now familiar questions: does IT deskill or enskill, enslave or empower, is it an instrument of managerial (class) control or does it represent the potential for worker autonomy (Bloomfield and Vurdubakis 1992)? The fears about control stem from the surveillance potential associated with IT, and in this connection the (dis)empowering effects have been explored through the Foucauldian metaphor of the panopticon — in this case the *electronic panopticon* (Webster and Robbins 1989; Sewell and Wilkinson 1992). In contrast, for Zuboff (1989) the electronic panopticon represents a manifestation of an outdated modality of managerial control, one which should be superseded by networked organizations populated by knowledge workers empowered through their access to, and use of, IT. For Zuboff, then, IT is seen to have the capacity both to empower and disempower, this depending on the way that it is applied within the organization.

Rather like any other technology, IT serves as a object to which all manner of familiar views and their underlying problem become assigned. In Turkle's analogy, computers are rather like the ink blots of the Rorschach Test: all manner of virtues and vices can be read off them (Turkle 1984: 5). However, although IT cannot be thought of as either good or bad in *itself*, neither can it be considered to be politically neutral. Every technology is developed for a particular context, with specific users in mind, and is envisaged as a contribution to specific purposes or goals (of course, these may well be subverted as a result of the unintended consequences of an innovation). In studying technology, we need to be sensitive to the exercise of power as well as issues of distribution (Law 1991) but we must do so without *reducing* technological developments to either managerial or technical imperatives.

Thus, rather than considering the *impact* of IT on mental health services, we wish to consider the changes in the relationships between, for example, mental health workers and patients, or practitioners and managers, which are presupposed and modified by current initiatives centered on IT. In the terminology of Akrich (1992), we seek a "de-scription" of technology: that is, we aim to unravel the "script" of technological practice which users are called upon to play and which is "inscribed" in technology. Hence the term "de-scription" or "de-inscription" — that is, to reverse the process of inscription and thus reveal or deconstruct the user script. In our case, we endeavor to illuminate the scripts presumed for users (be they managers, other health professionals, or patients) and inscribed in the subsequent information systems.[4] Similarly, we aim to elucidate the moral order represented in the user scripts for technological practice. In terms of IT, this order constitutes the information-related activities of users, making sense of their practice and justifying its dissemination as a new hallmark of professional responsibility and

---

[4]By which we mean the whole heterogeneous network of machines (hardware/software, etc.), human beings, and discursive practices of data gathering, etc.

accountability. This necessitates that we discuss the changing view of mental health expertise, the enhanced role of information in service management, and the subjectivity of the mental health patient.

3. RECONCEPTUALIZING THE WORLD THROUGH IT

In contrast to studies of IT and the labor process, or the political shaping of technology more generally (Winner 1980; MacKenzie and Wajcman 1985), rather less attention has been paid to the cognitive aspects of IT: for instance, to the ways in which thinking about the world in terms of information and information processing changes our conceptualization of ourselves and the world around us. Examples in this vein (though admittedly from a variety of different theoretical and political perspectives) include Weizenbaum's (1976) argument about instrumental reason in the realm of computing, and Artificial Intelligence research in particular; Turkle's (1984) socio-psychologically oriented study of children's and hackers' affinities with personal computers; and Heim's (1987) philosophical discussion of writing in the context of the development of word processing. The latter is of particular interest here because of the centrality of discursive practices within the information management procedures which are increasingly part-and-parcel of the delivery of mental health care. Heim's argument draws upon Walter Ong's transformative hypothesis which (very simply, and crudely) sees an intimate connection between the human psyche and the prevailing technologies of representation and communication. Among other things, the change from oral to print-based cultures marked a shift in human consciousness: from an acoustic to a visual means of information transmission, from an aural to a visual sensitivity toward reality. While we are not pursing an argument of such broad scale and historical sweep here, it is nonetheless interesting to speculate about the possible analogous changes within mental health services. More specifically, what can be made of those changes in the assessment and management of patient needs which increasingly center on the processing of forms and lists; where talking and listening to the patient is mediated by the need to complete a form — for administrative purposes of information management, to identify patient's needs, and to plan their future care? Lists and forms may appear as mundane features of administrative/managerial practice but they are a key to much broader issues than such a designation allows. "Large-scale decision making is impossible without lists. These in turn entrain whole series of substantive political and cognitive changes in the classes they inventory" (Bowker and Star 1991, pp. 74).

While we do not have the space here to attempt a substantive answer to the question outlined above, it does serve a useful purpose in signaling the distance between conventional treatments of computers and power and the sort of research questions we seek to pursue.

Studies have also been done on the work of specific professional groups. For instance, Mathiassen and Andersen (1983) have attempted to explore the changing semiotics of communication in nursing practice resulting from a move from paper-based to computer-based patient records on wards. Put simply, they argue that the change from a situation in which information was formulated by nurses and hand-written on cards (this being backed-up orally during shift change-overs), to one in which nurses recorded patient details by making selections from predetermined menus on a computer screen, represents a shift from cognition centered on interpretation to one revolving around classification. Similarly, Wagner (1993) has sought to explore the role of computers in the cultural transformation of nursing, with particular reference to questions of gender.

Here we are interested in the changing conceptions of the expert-patient relationship, the subjectivity of mental health professionals (including psychiatrists and psychiatric nurses) and of patients, and the specific role now allocated to information and information technology in mental health services. In short, we seek to elaborate the mutual interdependence between the conceptualization of the "empowered" subjects of modern psychiatric practice — be they managers, psychiatric professionals, or patients — and the role given to information and information systems in enabling that empowerment.

4. THE SUBJECT IN PSYCHIATRY: INFORMATION AND EMPOWERMENT

The history of psychiatry is a large and contentious topic which has been periodically marked by a series of radical critiques regarding orthodox knowledge and practice. The late nineteenth century and early twentieth century was seen to be a period of revolution with major advances in clinical treatment, the development of new approaches by psychiatric and psychological experts, new technology in the form of drugs, the legal status of the mentally ill, and state-run programs of welfare policies. Further, in the last fifty to sixty years there has been a dramatic shift in the conceptualization of the psychiatric patient. As Armstrong notes, for some considerable time "the patient was viewed essentially as a passive object in which was contained interesting pathology." (Armstrong 1982, pp. 119) However, increasingly (in many Western societies), the view of the patient-as-object has now given way to a more holistic perspective: the patient is a *person* rather than an object with a diseased mind. They have rights and with appropriate assistance may (re)gain their autonomy as self-directing individuals. The majority of approaches developed within this period seem to have encouraged a process of self-reflection and analysis including client-centered therapy (Rogers 1951), Gestalt Therapy (Perls, Hefferline and Goodman 1951), Transactional Analysis (Harris 1969), Primal Therapy (Janov 1970), and Bioenergetics (Lowen 1975), while a more radical political program was envisaged by the anti-psychiatry movement of the 1960s (Cooper 1974; Laing 1960 1967). (For more recent reviews of psychiatry, see Miller and Rose 1986; Sedgwick 1982; Szasz 1992).

The issue of self-advocacy and user rights should not, however, be seen as a recent development. For instance, groups such as the John Percival Alleged Lunatics Friendly Society date back to the nineteenth century (Conlan 1992). It was not until the 1960s and 1970s that the civil rights movement took hold, with various campaigns against psychiatric oppression, while during the 1980s several local pressure groups were formed and later developed into national organizations (Conlan 1992). More recently these groups have received an increased level of recognition and funding which has enabled them to participate to a greater extent in training, research, and planning initiatives that serve to promote the issues surrounding self-advocacy and user empowerment.

In the UK, the aim of patient empowerment received its greatest expression with the launch of the care in the community program (Department of Health and Social Security 1989). No longer is the patient to be captured within the structure of the hospital environment — the total institution according to Goffman (1968) — which governs the patient's eating habits, the administration of drugs, close supervision and a network of support. Although not completely abandoned, the in-patient scenario has been largely replaced by the community setting which is seen by some as a more suitable environment for patient rehabilitation and care.

The concept of empowering patients has taken specific form in moves to increase their participation in the derivation of care plans — that is, agreed programs of care — and the assessment of their needs. These have come about not only because of pressure on the part of various user and advocacy groups, but have also been promoted by Department of Health directives and guidelines associated with community care. The Department's moves in this direction present an interesting and complex topic that would take us beyond the scope of the argument here. However, it is useful to note that, in addition to the increased recognition of the rights and sovereignty of the mental health patient, there has also been a powerful impetus to reduce the burgeoning costs of service provision. The costs of maintaining hospital beds (of which nursing represents the greatest factor) — the so-called "hotel costs" — tie up a significant proportion of NHS resources, so any reorganization which envisaged a move away from such provision would have seemed welcome.

The documents associated with *care in the community* tend to highlight the need for patient participation in a "needs-led" approach to care.

> For the last thirty years since the Royal Commission on Mental Health and the Mental health act, the philosophy and emphasis has been on helping people help themselves to lead more fulfilled lives — "an enabling approach." [Browning 1992, p. 40]

This approach involves a greater recognition of the role the patient can play in the determination of care and the definition of needs through a process of consultation and involvement. Although these documents and papers often support the concept of patient participation in the process of care planning and assessment, in practice it is questionable whether it has actually attained the high profile intended for it.

> People receiving community care are not "cases" in need of being managed; they are citizens with rights to privacy, dignity and self determination. Issues of user advocacy and user involvement have to be taken seriously if community care services are not to repeat the patterns of stigmatizing institutionalization which have inadvertently worked to block individual independence and the growth of mutual support and solidarity among mental health service users. [Conlan 1992, p. 62]

Thus, some feel that although major steps have been taken in terms of advocacy and patients' needs, this area still requires further development and a greater level of awareness (see also Barker and Peck 1987).

The concept of empowerment can also be tackled on a more philosophical level by considering further the relationship between psychiatry, conceived as a discourse, and the conception of patients, or, in other words, the subjectivity of the patient. For Foucault, the historical objectification of the mentally ill by psychiatry was closely linked to a form of cruelty: "It might be said that all knowledge is linked to the essential forms of cruelty. The knowledge of madness is no exception" (1970, p. 73).

Indeed, the institutionalized abuse of patients provided much of the impetus behind movements such as that of the anti-psychiatrists during the 1960s. Further, the shifting conceptions of the patient, and the competing discourses on which these depend, indicate the changing constitution of subjectivity rather than the discovery of the "truth" of mental illness.

> In scrutinizing the consequences and implications of accepting the patient-as-person, the discourse has fabricated that same patient. This "whole person" is therefore the product of a series of smaller discourses (on compliance, communication, etc.) which, though intertwined with one another, have contributed separate elements to the final perception of the patient: a "subject" imbued with personal meanings, constructs, feeling, subjectivity, etc. The whole person is a multi-dimensional rather than a unitary being. [Armstrong 1982, p. 119]

This line of argument is crucial to any debate about empowerment. Put starkly, does it remove the repressive controls on an otherwise free subject, the inner essence of the human being, or does it presuppose and also constitute a new form of subject — the empowered patient? Any assessment of empowerment has to question the assumed ontological status of the subject to be released from the repressive regime. Is the patient to be liberated by modern mental health services or constituted by them? In Foucault's terms, we cannot speak of empowerment *per se*, of emancipating the subject as such, but only of the shift from one regime of "truth" to another.[5]

The assumed subjectivity of the patient within different discourses has been complemented by the development of the techniques of clinical practice deemed appropriate to each. "The clinical examination was a device for ordering bodies which, in doing so, constituted them; the medical interview and relationship has become a comparable mechanism for analyzing, and thereby constituting, idiosyncratic patients" (Armstrong 1982, p. 119).

Thus the discipline of psychiatry has developed a whole battery of technologies for inspecting, calculating, controlling, and even operating on the human psyche. This is similarly illustrated by the case of psychological models for diagnosis and assessment:[6]

> They enabled human powers to be transformed into material that could provide the basis for calculation. The examination formed the model for all psychological inscription devices...[and] combined the exercise of surveillance, the application of normalizing judgement and the technique of material inscription to produce

---

[5]However, the extent to which these developments reverse the great exclusion so long carried out in the name of psychiatry and thus allow the reconciliation between reason and unreason remains an open question.

[6]It may be objected that psychiatry and psychology cannot be equated. However, while they are certainly not the same, neither are they easily separable.

calculable traces of individuality....The psychological assessment is not merely a moment in a epistemological project, an episode in the history of knowledge: in rendering the subjectivity calculable it makes persons amenable to having things done to them — and doing things to themselves — in the name of their subjective capacities. [Rose 1990, p. 7]

The development of the different forms of technologies within psychiatry can be seen as devices not only for inscribing and codifying individual attributes, but also as systems for conceptualizing and calculating human subjectivity. They render the subject open to calculation and classification through various strategies and complex mechanisms of power.

We contend that recent changes in the management of mental health services represent interesting developments as far as this line of argument is concerned. In addition to the subjectivity of the patient, we wish to consider management as a disciplinary body of knowledge and techniques, one which increasingly revolves around information and the management of information, the subjectivity of managers and other health professionals, and also the role allotted to IT as a condition of possibility for empowerment — either for management or patients. To the extent that the efficient and effective provision of mental health services have come to be seen as problems of information, then those services have become constituted as objects of information management. Conceiving of mental health services in such terms opens up a space for managers and other health professionals to seek to intervene and exert some control over the nature of those services — precisely through the management of information.[7] Moreover, to the extent that the patient participates in their own assessment, they thereby help initiate important information processing and decision making procedures constitutive of their case.

5. CARE IN THE COMMUNITY: INFORMATION, MANAGEMENT, AND ACCOUNTABILITY

The development toward care in the community was accompanied by a general feeling of apprehension within the Department of Health and other agencies regarding accountability and "control" associated with the behavior of out-patients who may have previously been admitted as in-patients (and therefore securely locked away from the general public). Thus the concepts of control and accountability were presented as fairly important features associated with good clinical practice within the literature associated with community-based systems of care. These include approaches and systems that have increasingly inscribed the patient within an informational context — through encoding, categorizing, and representing — as a result of the introduction of varying technologies for out-patient care, care planning techniques, and information systems that maintain documentary records of patient details. For instance, the management of out-patients includes the diagnosis of certain patients as having complex and long term mental health needs in the form of access to rehabilitation programs, the continued prescription of certain drugs and medication, psychotherapy techniques, and residential units.

---

[7]There is a complex history pertaining to the relationship between medical practice, health care and computers. For instance, Kaplan (1995) explores this relationship in terms of dreams and visions that are tied into a "mythical charter" which is instrumental in gaining support for particular programs of computerization and which shape how these are subsequently developed and implemented.

In particular, the Care Programme Approach (CPA) is a mandatory and binding requirement launched by the Department of Health (Department of Health 1990).[8] It calls for a "system to ensure that in future patients treated in the community receive the health and social care they need." It also states that the aims of the CPA involve

> Introducing more systematic arrangements for deciding whether a patient referred to the specialist psychiatric services can, in the light of available resources and the views of the patient and, where appropriate, his/her carers, realistically be treated in the community...ensuring proper arrangements are then made, and continue to be made, for the continuing health and social care of those patients who can be treated in the community. [Department of Health 1990, p. 23]

The CPA is acknowledged to have played an important role in discussions regarding the reorganization of the management and delivery of mental health services:

> In addition to establishing systematic arrangements for assessing health and social care and ensuring that the relevant services are provided, the care programme approach initiative has acted as a catalyst for discussion and evaluation of a wide variety of related issues. These include multi-disciplinary and inter-agency working, the role of users, carers and voluntary agencies, the impact of the organization of health services (for example sectorization) on discharge planning and the role of computerized information systems. [North and Ritchie 1992, p. 108]

One of the factors widely seen as central to care in the community is IT. Thus a number of documents have stressed the importance of developing computerized information systems to ensure the successful implementation of the CPA (Challis et al. 1990; Cambridge 1992; Onyett 1992). "In a recent study on the implementation of the care programme approach, delays in the installation of computerized systems to deal with the information collected was a barrier, particularly in the monitoring process"(North West Regional Health Authority 1993, p. 14).

Some of the underlying themes associated with this desire for a greater level of information include the feeling that with the right policies and technologies, resources will be distributed more fairly according to patients' needs. This is supported by Cambridge (1992) who suggests that

> departments are recognizing the need to build good service utilization and cost management information systems, which will help formulate answers to equity questions at the client and service levels, and provide information for cost-effective individual service planning and community care planning more generally. [Cambridge 1992, p. 19]

---

[8]Health Circulars are part of the documentation provided by the Department of Health. They contain directives and guidelines which aim to ensure that each hospital follows a particular way of introducing new measures or initiatives in the prescribed way.

Such developments include the deployment of information systems for use in the process of coordinating and allocating resources to patients by selecting from a wide range of options in a preset menu (Onyett 1992, p. 9). The needs assessment form (see appendix) provides a good illustration of preset options in the way that the selection of needs are restricted to those defined within the form. The process assumes that by establishing which of these needs are unmet, resources can be allocated more efficiently, while the task of resource rationing provides an image of an effective and equitable system of assessment and allocation.

A major contributor to the needs assessment process is the *keyworker*. This role has been created within the CPA to ensure that needs are assessed and suitable care plans are produced using a multidisciplinary approach and in accordance with the patient's wishes. Therefore, the allocation of the keyworker role to the professional group, such as a community psychiatric nurse or a social worker, will depend on the case in hand. One of the goals of the information system within this process is to enable the needs assessed by the keyworker and the patient to be categorized and represented in a graphical form (Onyett and Cambridge 1992). This is meant to ensure that unmet needs which require additional funding and support are highlighted. Specifically, unmet needs are derived from the concept of the *needs-led* approach to clinical care: if the "actual" needs of the patient as revealed by assessment cannot be addressed within the multidisciplinary approach to care, then these needs are recorded as unmet. The importance associated with the need to document unmet needs reflects the increased level of accountability and efficiency associated with the allocation of resources within the internal market and the perceived need to argue for additional resources.

Moreover, the issue of accountability has extended the role of monitoring and reviewing patient care and supervision to an "at risk" register (NHS 1994). Implemented as an information system, the official purpose of the register is to form an electronic "safety net," to prevent patients within the care in the community program from escaping the control of mental health professionals and either harming themselves or others. In practical terms this has put pressure on psychiatry departments to prove that their systems satisfy the national requirements — that is, that their safety net is in place.

6. INFORMATION AND NEEDS: EMPOWERMENT AND PARTICIPATION IN PRACTICE

The psychiatry department in which our research is based is located within a large teaching hospital which operates as an NHS Trust (that is, it is self-governing). The research has been ongoing over the past two years. In addition to the analysis of texts — including official government White Papers, mental health acts, policy directives, research studies, care models, and internal documents — it has also involved interviews and participant observation. In particular, one of the authors became a member of the CPA Audit Team within the psychiatry department and took on the responsibility for producing an audit report to assess the "efficient" and "effective" operation of CPA within the hospital.

Until the advent of the CPA, the main information system within the department had been a database of patient records. This system records all patients in contact with the psychiatric services and is updated each time the care setting of the patient changes.

> A range of patient specific information is essential to any understanding of the effectiveness of treatment....Analysis of the data collected is also important in enabling staff to think more coherently about the services offered and to plan and evaluate new provision effectively. [Psychiatry Department *Information Systems Overview*]

However, this system was viewed by those involved in assessing the information requirements of the department (principally the Information Manager) to be unsuitable because of technical problems associated with providing a system that would support community care, and in particular a needs-led approach to clinical care. This was thought to be particularly problematic in the light of the CPA and the need to implement the supervision register. Moreover, other initiatives were beginning to place increasing demands for information, for example, in the area of medical costing, research, joint planning with social services (in line with the Department of Health directives) and medical audit. While a stand alone system was required to support the CPA initiative, the department was also going through a process of selecting another clinical and management information system based around the principles of the CPA and case management techniques. Here we will refer to this information system as the Care Manager system.

While the general feeling within the department reflects a positive view toward the CPA and the proposed Care Manager system, some have expressed reservations: could the CPA unite the services and what role would it play in terms of clinical care? As one Consultant Psychiatrist expressed the matter:

> The good thing about the system is that the clinicians seem to feel that the information is useful so you are more likely to get reliable information at the end of the day. I'm not so sure how useful the information really is for clinicians though as it seems more appropriate to administration and monitoring than clinical care. [Interview with Consultant Psychiatrist, September 1994]

Consequently, although the CPA and the Care Manager systems were presented as a way of integrating the care of patients in a systematic and coordinated way within the whole program of care planning and management, some questioned the assumption that any approach or system has the ability to determine and perform this form of integration within the network of clinical practice. "There is the expectation that pieces of paper (the CPA and the information systems) will weld together a service that is structurally disparate" (Interview with Consultant Psychiatrist, September 1994).

7. NEEDS ASSESSMENT

There were also numerous claims and expectations linked to the notion of empowering both patients and mental health workers through accountability and support, needs-led assessment and informed choice. These were expressed both in official documents (Department of Health and Social Security 1989) and in CPA meetings at the hospital. In accordance with the needs-led community based system of care, there had been a feeling that the style of treatment associated with asylums and institutions should be replaced with individualized care. This was to be provided on a continual basis and with the participation of patients in the assessment of their needs. The latter forms a major component in the derivation of care plans. While the assessment of the in-patient's needs can be performed within a pre-discharge meeting attended by a multidisciplinary team, or prior to this meeting by the ward nurse, the out-patient procedure is different. In this case, the location of the needs assessment may be carried out in a variety of settings: in the patient's home, a day hospital, a rehabilitation center, or a consulting room. Whatever the location or the status of the patient (in-patient or out-patient), the keyworker should perform the needs assessment evaluation in association with the patient and then transfer the information onto the needs assessment form, which (in this department) is generated by the CPA system. The needs assessment form (see appendix) is designed to encourage the adoption of a needs-led approach through the continual monitoring of patients' requirements: by separating and then codifying their needs into a range of categories. Thus, the needs assessment form contains basic details about the patient, keyworker, and the general practitioner etc. It also provides a list of over twenty different categories of needs, including social, cultural, day care, support, accommodation, and advocacy needs.

The central rationale underpinning the needs assessment is the idea that the needs of the patients go beyond "clinical" needs and include those associated with their "social," "cultural" and "practical" requirements (for example, in terms of income, accommodation, domestic and social support, carer's needs, and training). Once the needs assessment form is completed, it is sent to the CPA coordinator and the information is transferred onto a database which enables the identification of the unmet needs.[9] This information system has the facility to identify future review dates (when patients' cases are reconsidered) and it also provides graphical representations of unmet needs. It is seen to be useful to management not only for identifying the specific needs that are unmet but also the services that are seen to be under funded.

> The CPA can be used to inform the planners where more resources are required. For example, in the case of rehabilitation certain services are seen as very effective ways of improving the quality of life of the chronically ill, but they need more funding. [Consultant Psychiatrist, CPA Audit Meeting, August 1994]

The procedure for generating and processing information associated with care planning and needs assessment has been met with a variety of reactions from mental health and social service workers. Some view it merely as a paper-pushing exercise that appears to provide no real benefit for the service: "I'll continue to go through each of the unmet needs with the patient and tick the relevant boxes on the form, but I don't see the point in it" (Acute Psychiatric Nurse, CPA Audit Interview, August 1994).

Others see the process of determining needs in this way as problematic because it is entangled within a web of very difficult issues concerning diagnosis and clinical care. Thus within the needs assessment process the role of the patient is further complicated by the divergence of opinion regarding the role of the "expert" in the assessment of needs, as opposed to the participation of

---

[9]In other departments at hospitals elsewhere, additions and variations to the assessment have included a scoring system attached to determine the need for care management — these having been criticized for conflicting with clinical judgment. Other areas have been keen to develop a "common dependency assessment" which would provide assessment criteria that could be used by a wide range of professionals from both health and social services.

the patient in the construction of their care plans. When does the view of the individual become superseded by the opinion of the "professional" and who should have responsibility over the coordination of services for patients? As one manager expressed the matter:

> There can always be conflict in decisions concerning the care and treatment of the patient. We have one case here where there is a disagreement over whether a patient should receive psychotherapy....Ultimately, you have to rely on the judgement of the expert....It's a bit like when you take your car to be serviced and you have to rely on the mechanic for their advice on what needs fixing. [Service Manager, CPA Audit Interview, September 1994]

The issues involved here came to a head during a departmental review of the CPA in August 1994, when a hypothetical case was raised in order to flesh out the problems of determining patients' needs. One consultant psychiatrist felt that in certain situations a variety of interpretations concerning the needs of the individual could be produced depending on the judgment of the person assessing the unmet needs: "What would happen if you had to assess the needs of an individual living alone in a flat and surrounded by neighbors who are seen as a threat to them (that is, the patient) in some way?"

In order to provide some form of documentary evidence based on the situation above, it was accepted that an assessment of the patient's *real* needs would be required. From the patient's perspective, they may view their problems as deriving from their housing needs — that is, they needed rehousing. However, if they were diagnosed as schizophrenic, their feelings about their neighbors may be seen as delusional and so in this case the *real* unmet need could be seen from a more clinical perspective. Accordingly, a second consultant psychiatrist at the meeting suggested that "It wouldn't be possible to rehouse every patient with delusions about their neighbors and anyway this wouldn't address their real needs, which isn't housing."

This line of argument was supported by a ward manager who felt that "addressing the issue of accommodation as an unmet need merely reinforces the patients delusional fears of their neighbors. Rehousing would not help the patient deal with these delusions and it could actually make the situation worse."

Thus within the process of interpreting unmet needs there appear to be major obstacles concerning the diagnosis of *real* needs. While some supported the view that in this case the patient's view of their needs was based on delusions and should therefore be ignored, others present at the meeting took an opposite position. The latter felt that in this case the assessment should be based on the patient's perspective — this being the hallmark of patient-centered care. The belief that the patient's perception of the situation should be followed was neatly summed up in the following comment a Community Social Worker: "Even if the assessor feels that the patient's perception of the neighbors as a threat is based on a delusion, the need for new accommodation is a real one to them and should therefore be treated in that way."

The interchanges and issues arising in this episode stress the variety of interpretations associated with the role of the patient and that of the experts (that is, the health and social services professionals) in the assessment of needs. What must also be highlighted is the role of the specific discursive practices within the whole process — namely, the completion of the needs assessment form. We need to consider how the *writing* of the form, and the wider information system which it feeds, may shape clinical practice and relationships between patients and experts within psychiatric care (Smith 1978). In this particular case, this involves examining the notion of empowerment in relation to the way that the needs assessment forms are constructed in such a way as to facilitate the categorization of unmet needs within the overall information system, as well as the monitoring role delegated to this technology.

8. THE SUBJECT AS PATIENT

The aims and objectives of the purchasing Health Authority, in which the psychiatric department operates, states that individuals and communities should be empowered so that they can take action to improve their own health.

> By empowered individuals we mean individuals who: have the appropriate information on health and health services; can make informed choices; are consulted about the health care options available to them; feel as though they are in control over their own lives. [Health Authority *Aims and Objectives Plan* 1994]

Both the CPA and the subsequent implementation of information systems that contain patient and service information are seen to support these claims of patient empowerment: by facilitating an increased level of patient participation in the determination of needs and by the provision of a continual and coordinated service of clinical care. Hence, this presupposes that a more *accurate* and *true* representation of the patient's needs can be achieved through an increased level of participation in the needs assessment process. In turn, this is based on the problematic assumption that the patient has the capacity to make "informed" and therefore (by implication) rational "choices." We are not dealing here with the sovereign subject of rational choice theory — indeed the patient is assisted by the keyworker in the exercise of choice. Nonetheless, the assumption of "informed choice" and feeling "in control of their own lives" still relies upon a notion of rationality within the needs assessment process. A central problem here is that such rationality is not a *condition* of participation but, rather, is *constituted* by it (see also Mullender and Ward 1991). Of course rationality in a wider sense is also presupposed by participation. That is, a patient who declares them self to be a Martian in response to every utterance of the health service professionals would presumably be deemed unable to participate in the needs assessment process and therefore could not be empowered.

What we are dealing with here is a technology of needs assessment; a technology based on a specific discursive practice that — in the terminology of Akrich (1992) — contains an implicit script. This applies both to the patient, whose needs are to be determined, and the mental health professional, who is to intermediate between the patient and the wider system of care. As regards the patient, this script calls for an informed individual able to make choices and this provides the key to understanding the nature of participation and empowerment in this context. We are not dealing with participation and emancipation *per se* but the constitution of these terms in the specific way afforded by the practice involved. This is not a condemnation of these varieties of empowerment and participation so much as an articulation of their particular character. To put things simply, a patient might wish to be better and to express this during the needs assessment exercise; however, this is not a *choice* which is open to them in the sense of a deliberate action that they might take. In other words, the assumption and constitution of rationality through the exercise of choice operates through pre-given categories over which the patient has no influence. Their sense of "control over their own lives" may extend to the sorts of choices they can make within the range of options on offer, but it does not include the discretion to exert control over their illness. It is also worth pointing out that the notion of empowerment sits uneasily with that of case management which is similarly seen as central to the management and delivery of care. Following the publication of the *Caring For People* (Department of Health and Social Security 1989), the term "case management" was felt by some patient groups to be an inappropriate way of addressing individuals in the community insofar as it appears to reinforce the position of the patient as merely a *case* to be worked on by mental health and social service employees — as opposed to an empowered subject (Onyett and Cambridge 1992). As a consequence, there was a general move within the mental health services to adopt the term *care* management rather than case management.

The increased visibility of patients' actions as constituted through their participation in the formulation of care plans and the definition of unmet needs can also be seen to impose a degree of accountability on the individual. That is, having participated in the needs assessment process, with the implicit rationality of choice defining a sort of logic of their situation, they can later be called to account should their behavior or future expression of needs conflict with their earlier choices. That is, changes which cannot be accounted for may thus come to indicate a lack of reason.

Additional problems pertaining to the needs assessment exercise have also been identified in relation to patients' perceptions of the keyworker role in satisfying their needs. Where the role is seen as powerful one, the patient may feel that their views are sometimes not acknowledged or taken into account and, therefore, they tend to withdraw from participating fully in the process. A role perceived as weak, however, may project an image of token backing and the feeling that nothing has changed regarding user involvement and support.

> For the service user the stark choice of heads I lose and tails you win, is all too familiar one in a world where information, like power and resources, is a very scarce commodity. The right to make informed choices more often belongs to the world of rhetoric than reality. [Conlan 1992, p. 65]

This sentiment was also echoed by one of the department's service managers:

> Information is knowledge but not power, as power is still in the hands of the establishment....We are merely agents of social control....We never provide patients with power we just provide them with more information. It's a bit like saying that you could offer the criminal fraternity more information about different courts, types of judges and prisons, because at the end of the day you are still going to detain them against their will. [Service Manager, informal discussion, January 1995]

The option of caring for patients in the community and allowing them to participate in the derivation of their care plans is presented as a move toward a more preferable process of clinical care — and indeed, who would defend the system of incarceration of the asylum? However, we have to recognize how the changing practices of clinical care still represent a particular regime of truth, one which constitutes subjects and renders them visible and open to calculation in a specific way.

9. THE SUBJECT AS INFORMATION MANAGER

Turning now to the professionals who work with the mentally ill, we find that the CPA system is also seen as a means to empower keyworkers. In particular, this empowerment is seen to reside in the provision of a system of procedures that provides a standard and structured way of assessing the needs of the patient within a framework of informed choice. This presupposes that by providing keyworkers with a comprehensive list of services, they would be able to make informed decisions regarding the aftercare of the patient and would subsequently ensure the provision of a more effective service for them. While some feel that the systematic and standardized design of the needs assessment form limits the flexibility and interpretive ability of psychiatric workers — for instance, by restricting the choice of categories in which to assess patients' needs — others believe that the assessment form could actually expand the interpretative skills of the mental health or social service worker. In particular, it could provide them with a greater appreciation of different needs and services through informed choice. "The keyworker is empowered not only through informed choice, but also in the way that the needs assessment process and the care plan provide a well documented and structured approach to care planning" (Care Plan Coordinator, CPA Audit Meeting, January 1995).

Therefore, although the format of the needs assessment exercise may be viewed by some as a desirable way of recording patients' details to enable the information to be processed and classified in a way that will facilitate analysis and accountability, it can also be seen to play a role in constructing practice. Specifically, a keyworker may be a nurse, a consultant psychiatrist, or indeed someone from social services, but whatever their professional background, keyworkers have something else in common — namely, they are constituted as information managers. The conceptualization of what they do is mediated by the demands of information processing — both in terms of needs assessment, in order to carry out their role as keyworker, and in terms of documenting accountability and the effective discharge of their role.

One issue particularly emphasized by those involved in the introduction of the CPA system is the subsequent impact this approach has had on the administrative duties of the workers involved. This has been felt from both sides of the mental health and social services division and in particular by the social workers, community psychiatric nurses and consultant psychiatrists. For example, consultant psychiatrists feel that the increased level of paperwork and workload involved in completing forms, assessing patient needs, arranging team meetings, and the general increase in organizational responsibilities, has restricted the time available to actually care for the patient. "There is an opportunity cost. As we spend more time filling in forms there is less time available for patient care" (Consultant Psychiatrist, CPA Audit Meeting, October 1994).

Underlying administrative regimes such as the CPA are a variety of assumptions related to the concepts of accountability, communication and coordination. For example, in the case of the managers of this information there is the presupposition that by making themselves more accountable in terms of patient care and the provision of services they also open up a whole new space for action. Indeed, changing practices and the implementation of the CPA system have led to the creation of new positions — including the keyworker. A major part of this role, together with that of the care plan coordinator, is the management of information including patient care plans, the assessment and recording of client needs and the coordination of multidisciplinary teams. Upon inspection of the needs assessment form, one observes that the process of identifying unmet needs appears as a checklist: for each category, the needs are either unmet or not. Note that upon identification of an unmet need, no specific action or solution is represented in this form; the information is gathered in order to reveal an overall picture of unmet needs within the population for which the department has service contracts with purchasing health authorities. Rather, the actions which follow the identification of unmet needs are mediated and reinforced by another writing instrument — namely, the care plan. Although the information on unmet needs feeds into, as it were, the formulation of the care plan, the discursive separation of the two procedures reinforces the importance of information and information gathering within organizational practice.

10.   DISCUSSION

This paper has sought to address the relationship between empowerment and IT in the specific context of the management and delivery of mental health services. We have not aimed to show the *impact* of IT on either organizational practice or mental health patients. Rather, the analysis of the developments in our case study psychiatry department indicate that the roles assumed for the keyworkers and patients are a *condition* for the operation of technology, not a consequence of it. Thus empowerment — either of patients or health professionals — is not a consequence of the introduction of IT but is constituted through the development and implementation of this technology in specific ways. For patients, empowerment is a matter of making informed choices: the subject is not liberated by technology but constituted as an empowered subject to the degree that they "participate" in the needs assessment exercise and formation of care-plans. For the health professional, empowerment centers on the increased organizational visibility and span of control/accountability opened up by practices of information gathering and management. In each case, the discourse of empowerment is pitched at the level of individual subjects but, following the line of argument developed here, it should be apparent that particular forms of organizational life are being promoted and reinforced: empowerment for individuals presupposes a world of rational organization dominated through, and on, paper in the shape of the forms central to needs-assessment and care-planning.

Moreover, the various actors involved at our case study hospital have been actively engaged in shaping the construction of the technology — for instance, the needs assessment form and the care plan form. It was almost inevitable that new IT systems would be introduced, not only because of Department of Health directives but also because management in the psychiatry department had been proactive in the area of IT for some time. However, the actual characteristics of the IT systems when implemented, and thus in live operation, not to mention their ongoing maintenance and extension, are not predetermined by any technological imperative. Similarly, although keyworkers have become managers of information — a role inscribed in the IT system — the matter of what counts as information, as well as the meaning of the changed organizational/health service practices which it mediates and reinforces, is not pre-given but actively constituted. Thus the implementation of the Care Programme Approach differs between different mental health service provider units. As the exchange of views regarding the needs assessment form indicates, its meaning even within one site is subject to interpretative flexibility.

Finally, one role that needs further consideration is that of the information systems — the CPA system and the Care Manager. What is of particular interest here is that in parallel to the notion that keyworkers are empowered through their access to, and use of, the IT systems, it is also evident that certain aspects of organizational control have been "delegated" to those systems (Latour 1992). The task of monitoring the care planning process — such as highlighting review dates, recording the responsibilities and duties of all those associated with the patient's care, and displaying warnings when workers have failed to meet target dates or information requirements — has been automated. This implies that there will be less direct management of the operational information by the keyworker and care plan coordinator. The onus on psychiatry departments to establish systems of control *vis-à-vis* patients in the community depends on the cooperation of the keyworkers and other staff in playing the roles inscribed for them in the information system, but the responsibility for such control has been delegated to the IT system. The future implications of this for organizational practice — both in terms of management and psychiatry — will be interesting to follow.

11.   ACKNOWLEDGMENTS

We would like to thank Wanda Orlikowski, Hugh Willmott, Theo Vurdubakis and the anonymous referees for their helpful suggestions regarding the ideas addressed in this paper.

12.   REFERENCES

Akrich, M. "The De-Scription of Technical Objects." In W. Bijker and J. Law (Editors), *Shaping Technology/Building Society.* Cambridge: MIT Press, 1992, pp. 205-224.

Armstrong, D. "The Doctor-Patient Relationship: 1930-1980." In P. Wright and A. Treacher (Editors), *The Problem of Medical Knowledge.* Edinburgh: Edinburgh University Press, 1982, pp. 109-122.

Barker, I., and Peck, E. *Power in Strange in Places: User Empowerment in Mental Health Services.* London: Good Practices in Mental Health, 1987.

Bloomfield, B. P., and Coombs, R. "Information Technology, Control and Power: The Centralization and Decentralization Debate Revisited." *Journal of Management Studies*, Volume 29, Number 4, 1992, pp. 459-484.

Bloomfield, B. P., and Vurdubakis, T. "A Note of the Role of Technology in Accounts of the Labor Process." Tenth Annual International Conference on Organization and Control of the Labor Process, Aston University, 1-3 April, 1992.

Bowker, G. and Star, S. L. "Situations vs. Standards in Long Term, Wide Scale Decision-Making: The Case of the International Classification of Diseases." *Proceedings of the Twenty Fourth Annual Hawaiian International Conference on Systems Science*, Volume 4, 1991, pp. 73-81.

Browning, D. "Looking to the Future." In S. Onyett and P. Cambridge (Editors), *Case Management — Issues in Practice*. Canterbury: University of Kent, 1992, pp. 40-43.

Cambridge, P. "Questions for Case Management II." In S. Onyett and P. Cambridge (Editors), *Case Management — Issues in Practice*. Canterbury: University of Kent, 1992, pp. 13-21.

Challis, D. "Looking to the Future." In S. Onyett and P. Cambridge (Editors), *Case Management — Issues in Practice*. Canterbury: University of Kent, 1992, pp. 22-31.

Challis, D. et al. *Case Management in Social and Health Care: The Gateshead Community Care School*. Canterbury: University of Kent, 1990.

Clement, A. "Computing at Work: Empowering Action by 'Low Level Users'." *Communications of the ACM*, Volume 37, Number 1, 1994, pp. 53-63.

Conlan, E. "Case Management and Advocacy Issues in Mental Health." In S. Onyett and P. Cambridge (Editors), *Case Management — Issues in Practice*. Canterbury: University of Kent, 1992, pp. 62-67.

Cooper, D. *The Grammar of Living*. Harmondsworth, Middlesex: Penguin Books, 1974.

Department of Health and Social Security. *Caring For People: Community Care in the Next Decade and Beyond*. London: Department of Health and Social Security, 1989.

Department of Health. *The Care Programme Approach for People with a Mental Illness Referred to the Specialist Psychiatric Services*. Department of Health, Circular HC(90)23/LASSL(90)11, 1990.

Eccles, T. "The Deceptive Allure of Empowerment." *Long Range Planning*, Volume 26, Number 6, 1993, pp. 13-21.

Foucault, M. *Mental Illness and Psychology*. London: Harper and Row, 1970.

Goffman, E. *Asylums*. Harmondsworth, Middlesex: Penguin Books, 1968.

Harris, T. A. *I'm OK, You're OK*. New York: Harper and Row, 1969.

Heim, M. *Electric Language*. London: Yale University Press, 1987.

Janov, A. *The Primal Scream: Primal Therapy - The Cure for Neurosis*. New York: Putnam, 1970.

Kaplan, B. "The Computer Prescription: Medical Computing, Public Policy, and Views of History." *Science, Technology and Human Values*, Volume 20, Number 1, 1995, pp. 5-38.

Laing, R. D. *The Divided Self*. London: Tavistock, 1960.

Laing, R. D. *The Politics of Experience and the Bird of Paradise*. Harmondsworth, Middlesex: Penguin Books, 1967.

Latour, B. "Where Are the Missing Masses?" In W. Bijker and J. Law (Editors), *Shaping Technology/Building Society*. Cambridge: MIT Press, 1992, pp. 225-258.

Law, J. "Introduction: Monsters, Machines and Sociotechnical Relations." In W. Bijker and J. Law (Editors), *A Sociology of Monsters: Essays on Power, technology and Domination*. London: Routledge, 1991, pp. 1-23.

Lowen, A. *Bioenergetics*. New York: Coward, McCann and Geoghegan, 1975.

MacKenzie, D., and Wajcman, J. *The Social Shaping of Technology*. Milton Keynes, UK: Open University Press, 1985.

Mathiassen, L., and Andersen, P. B. "Nurses and Semiotics: the Impact of EDP-Based Systems upon Professional Languages." *The Sixth Scandinavian Research Seminar on Systemeering*, 1983, pp. 227-260.

Miller, P., and Rose, N. (Editors). *The Power of Psychiatry*. Cambridge: Polity Press, 1986.

Mullender, A., and Ward, D. *Self-Directed Groupwork: Users Taking Action for Empowerment*. London: Whiting and Birch, 1991.

NHS Management Executive. "Introduction of Supervision Registers for Mentally Ill People from 1 April 1994." *Health Service Guidelines*, HSG(94)5, 1994.

North, C., and Ritchie, J. *Factors Influencing the Implementation of the Care Programme Approach*. London: HMSO, 1992.

North Western Regional Health Authority. *The Care Programme Approach Operational Guidance*. Manchester, England: Community Care Services, 1993.

Onyett, S., and Cambridge, P. *Case Management — Issues in Practice*. Canterbury: University of Kent, 1992.

Perls, F. S.; Hefferline, R. F.; and Goodman, P. *Gestalt Theory: Excitement and Growth in the Human Personality.* New York: Julian Press, 1951.

Peters, T. *Thriving on Chaos.* London: Pan Macmillan, 1989.

Porter, M. *The Competitive Advantage of Nations.* New York: Free Press, 1990.

Poster, M. *The Mode of Information.* Oxford: Polity Press, 1990.

Rogers, C. R *Client-Centered Therapy: Its Current Practice Implications and Theory.* London: Constable, 1951.

Rose, N. *Governing the Soul: The Shaping of the Private Self.* London: Routledge, 1990.

Sedgwick, P. *Psycho-Politics: Laing, Foucault, Goffman, Szasz and the Future of Mass Psychology.* New York: Harper and Row, 1982.

Sewell, G., and Wilkinson, B. "Someone to Watch over Me: Surveillance Discipline and the JIT Labor Process." *Sociology*, Volume 26, Number 2, 1992, pp. 271-289

Smith, D. "'K is mentally Ill' The Anatomy of a Factual Account." *Sociology*, Volume 12, Number 1, 1978, pp. 23-53.

Szasz, T. *A Lexicon of Lunacy — Metaphoric Malady, Moral Responsibility and Psychiatry.* New Brunswick: Transaction Publishers, 1992.

Toffler, A. *The Third Wave.* New York: Morrow, 1980.

Turkle, S. *The Second Self.* London: Granada, 1984.

Wagner, I. "Women's Voice: The Case of Nursing Information Systems." *AI and Society*, Volume 7, 1993, pp. 295-310.

Weizenbaum, J. *Computer Power and Human Reason.* Harmondsworth: Penguin, 1976.

Webster, F., and Robbins, K. "Towards a Cultural History of Information Society." *Theory and Society*, Volume 18, 1989.

Willmott, H. "Strength is Ignorance; Slavery is Freedom: Managing Culture in Modern Organizations." *Journal of Management Studies*, Volume 30, Number 4, 1993, pp. 515-552.

Winner, L. "Do Artifacts Have Politics?" *Daedalus*, Volume 109, 1980, pp. 121-136.

Zuboff, S. *In the Age of the Smart Machine.* New York: Heinemann Professional, 1989.

About the Authors

Brian P. Bloomfield is a Senior Lecturer in Management Information Systems and Technology Management at Manchester School of Management, UMIST. He has published articles in the areas of sociology of science and the sociology of technology. His research interests include issues of power and knowledge in relation to the development and use of information systems; connections between social order and concepts of risk and blame in the context of technological failures; social aspects of the development and public reception of new reproductive technologies.

Christine McLean is a research student at Manchester School of Management, UMIST. Her research interests include the sociology of science and technology and the role management information systems play within organizations and society. She is in the final stages of completing her Ph.D., which examines the relationship between power, knowledge and information technology within psychiatry, with a particular focus on issues of accountability and control

APPENDIX: EXAMPLE NEEDS ASSESSMENT FORM

no: ▨▨▨▨   ⬛⬛⬛   No: Today:

Ward/Team_no: Date on caselink:

                                       Date last change:

Client details
First names: ▨▨▨▨▨▨
Surname:
Address:

Postcode:

Date of Birth:
Age Band:
Gender:
Ethnic Origin: N/K
Locality:
Social Services Area:
Date last care plan:
Date last review:
Date next review:
SECTION 1177:   N/K
Client agreed:

Over 70?: NO

Over 65?: NO

Source of info:
Any needs unmet?:   N/K
Does this person have a Key Worker?:

Telephone no.:
Address:

Postcode:

2nd contact:
Telephone no.:

Address:

Postcode:

Discharged?: NO   Date:
Discharge reason:
Discharge detail:

G.P. Name.:

Consultant:

Memo:

UNMET KEY WORKER:
UNMET PERSONAL CARE:
UNMET CULTURAL NEEDS:
UNMET INFORMATION NEEDS:
UNMET MEDICATION NEEDS:
UNMET COMMUNICATION NEEDS:
UNMET TECHNICAL AIDS NEEDS:
UNMET CARERS NEEDS:
UNMET RESPITE NEEDS:
UNMET ACCOMM. CHANGE:
UNMET ACCOMM. SUPPORT:
UNMET DOMESTIC SUPPORT:
UNMET TRAINING/EDUCATION:
UNMET SUPPORT:
UNMET EMPLOYMENT:
UNMET COUNSELING:
UNMET ADVOCACY:
UNMET SOCIAL:
UNMET FINANCIAL:
UNMET THERAPY:
UNMET TRANSPORT:

PART FIVE

Reflections of Research: Learning

23

Disassembling Frames on the Assembly Line: The Theory and Practice of the New Division of Learning in Advanced Manufacturing

Claudio U. Ciborra
Università di Bologna – Instiţut Theseus

Gerardo Patriotta
Università di Bologna – Institut Theseus

Luisella Erlicher
Isvor – Fiat

Abstract

Car assembly plants have changed dramatically over the last twenty years, after the Kalmar model, lean production, semi-autonomous work groups and kanban. Or have they? By auditing the complex and intertwined learning processes taking place in a brand new assembly plant where the Punto, 1995 European "Car of the Year," is manufactured, it turns out that radical changes in work organizations and operations have been implemented, but their impact stops halfway. The reason is due to the subtle influence that the Fordist "formative context" still exert on the way the plant is designed, and especially the way management knowledge is divided. By analyzing how bottlenecks and breakdowns are tackled by operators and managers, it is shown how the new division of labor requires a rethinking of the kind of know-how operators should master in order to cope with an advanced production system. The paper includes two important tools that were used during the analysis: a conceptual model of the learning organization, called the learning ladder, and the main steps of the learning audit methodology.

1. INTRODUCTION

Traditionally, changes in work organization have been carried out relying on the analysis of procedures, data flows, activities, "objects," transactions and processes, assuming that "work" can be ultimately decomposed in such constituent elements. Technology is then harnessed to streamline processes, make transactions more efficient, and better govern and store data flows (Davenport 1993). However, the study of situated work practices has pointed out, in a variety of office and manufacturing settings, that work is more than a bunch of analytical abstractions and models to be rationalized (Wynn 1979; Suchmann 1987; Brown and Duguid 1991; Zuboff 1988). Rather, it is a complex bundle of situated actions and interpretations aimed at making sense of resources and structures, and maintaining the identity of the members and the working community confronted by both routine and breakdown events. One important design challenge that remains for specialists, users and scholars today is to identify the role of information technology (IT) in supporting work, understood according to those perspectives which emphasize the crucial role of human action and interpretation (Barley 1986; Winograd and Flores 1986; Orlikowski 1992; Walsham 1993; Ciborra and Lanzara 1994; Boland, Tenkasi and Te'eni 1994).

We tackle this challenge in the light of Zuboff, who suggests that the design of computer-mediated work should be centered on the idea of learning as "the new form of labor": "The informated organization is a learning institution, and one of its principal purposes is the expansion of knowledge...knowledge that comes to reside at the core of what it means to be productive" (Zuboff 1988, p. 395). This perspective requires the development of an appropriate methodology, as the existing ones are oriented to data flow, decision making or transaction analysis. In short, we need a "compact" way to understand how learning is typically divided in a firm. Our study must clearly be of an interdisciplinary nature, since learning processes have been the subject of recent economic literature (Nelson and Winter 1982; Williamson 1985); sociology, anthropology and social psychology (Argyris and Schön 1978; Lave and Wenger 1991); and management literature (Huber 1990; March 1991; Fiol and Lyles 1985). In particular, recent studies in the resource based view of strategy (Grant 1991) and structuration theory (Giddens 1984; Orlikowski 1992; Walsham 1993) can improve our understanding and be a new platform for work and systems redesign.

In our perspective, the processes through which resources and routines become part of the core capabilities of the firm and of its structure should be looked at as the key learning "tasks" carried out by members of the organization from the shopfloor to top management (Andreu and Ciborra 1994).

A new methodology should identify the key processes of knowledge production (Nonaka 1994) and accumulation in an organization, their inefficiencies, and point out how IT can meet the needs for improving the existing division of learning. We develop and apply such a methodology, called "the learning audit," while evaluating work design and patterns of computer usage in one of the most advanced car manufacturing plants in Europe: Fiat's Melfi car factory. This factory features a lean production organization; work flow based on assembly lines and teams; advanced applications of IT to production management and control; and extensive reliance on total quality management. Since our study was carried out during the first year of operation of the green-field plant, we could observe in detail how the new organization was performing in facing a variety of minor and major breakdowns, by enacting different sorts of problem solving, computer-mediated communication and learning strategies. We found that the cognitive and information resources that support the division of learning in the new plant were not fully appropriate and that, as a result, the traditional assembly line concept (or formative context [Ciborra and Lanzara 1990]) still exerted a subtle, far-reaching influence on the interpretive schemes and organizational routines applied by workers and managers in the Melfi factory. In positive terms, we could also identify new frames and new routines (i.e., the new formative context) needed to better run the process, intervene in breakdowns, use IT and learn.

In section 2, we present a model of the firm as a learning organization, called the learning ladder. The model draws on key ideas of the resource based view of strategy and, in part, from the theory of structuration. The "learning audit" methodology is briefly described, in section 3, as a way of capturing the dynamics of the learning processes identified by the learning ladder. In section 4, the case of the *avant garde* plant is presented, where the learning audit methodology has been tested. In section 5, the results of the analysis indicate the points of failure of a few, main learning processes dedicated to the control of breakdowns and bottlenecks. The analysis further suggests what interventions (both technological and instructional) would be needed to ameliorate the lean manufacturing operations. More general conclusions on cognition and the organization of work in advanced manufacturing follow.

2. THE LEARNING LADDER: A MODEL FOR THE LEARNING ORGANIZATION

In any economic organization, there are a variety of learning processes at work. For example, in highly situated ways, people learn by doing (Williamson 1975; Nelson and Winter 1982); they learn by using systems and technologies (Rosenberg 1982; von Hippel 1988); at times, they engage in double-loop or radical learning (Argyris and Schön 1978); and, more generally, they are busy creating new knowledge by socializing the results of learning and converting explicit into tacit knowledge and vice versa (Nonaka 1994). Our aim is to build a "compact" model of the main learning processes in an economic organization. Such a model is useful as a "backbone" reference scheme for investigating strengths and weaknesses of actual learning processes.

To begin with, consider the recent strategy literature, specifically the resource-based view of strategy. At the heart of the firm's competitive strength is a process that develops distinctive, core capabilities (Prahalad and Hamel 1990), i.e., capabilities that differentiate a company strategically and deliver competitive advantage (Leonard-Barton 1992; Barney 1991). Core capabilities develop through a fundamental *transformation process*, by which standard resources available in open markets (where all firms can acquire them) are used and combined, within the organizational context of each firm, to produce capabilities, which in turn can become the source of competitive advantage, especially if they are rare and difficult to imitate or substitute. We look at such a transformation as a *situated learning process*, i.e., a learning process whose unfolding is highly contingent upon the interaction among people, resources and routines present in a given situation. Situated learning plays a strategic role for the firm because (1) it implies path — dependency and specificity in the resulting core capabilities, and (2) consequently, it causes their inimitability, a crucial characteristic for obtaining competitive advantage. In order to build our model of the learning organization, we propose to analyze in more detail the major stages of the learning/transformation process through which the firm's core capabilities are generated.

A first step in the transformation consists in the emergence of generic capabilities from standard resources (see Figure 1).

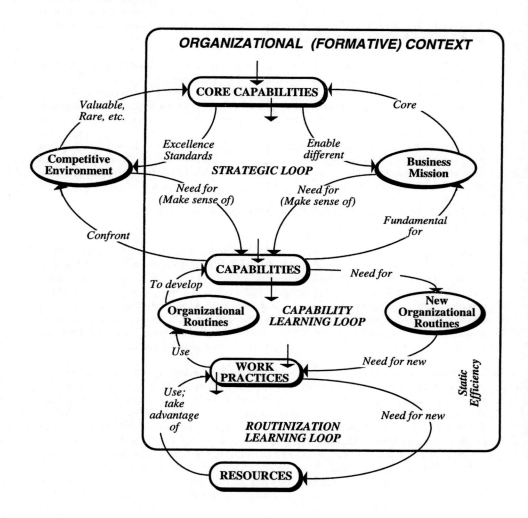

Figure 1. The Learning Ladder

Two different types of learning take place at this stage. One deals with mastering the use of standard resources, and produces what we can call efficient work practices (Lave and Wenger 1991). Individuals and groups (or communities of practice) in the firm learn how to use resources in a given organizational situation. The quest for better work practices may trigger a search for new resources, more appropriate to the practices under development. Or, the appearance of new resources (say technological innovations) may motivate individuals and groups to "take advantage of them" through new work practices. We call such a learning loop between resources and work practices the *routinization learning loop*, since its outcome are repertoires of constrained, routinized and interdependent actions (Pentland and Reuter 1994). Mastering the usage of a spreadsheet by an individual or a team in a specific department is an example of this type of learning.

A second learning process "abstracts" capabilities from existing work practices. Several characteristics connote this learning process: it involves combining emerging work practices and organizational routines; its outcome has a strong potential connotation, as capabilities convey knowledge which can be put to work in a variety of organizational contexts (non-situated knowledge). That is capabilities are more abstract than work practices: they are "skills without a place" that can be transferred across the organization (such as a quality control capability). Finally, capabilities can be easily described in terms of *what* they do and *how* they do it, but *why* they do it is taken for granted, not necessarily well defined and rarely challenged. We call this the *capability learning loop*. To summarize, learning at this level results in a continuously improving set of capabilities — specialized and idiosyncratic ways of using resources for given purposes. These purposes are functionally well defined and stable over time (e.g., cutting production costs), although how they are attained may change drastically, for example with the emergence of a radically new technology (resource), or a revolutionary new use of an old resource (Penrose 1959). The driving force for continuous capability improvement is static efficiency (Ashby 1966; Klein 1977; Ghemawat and Ricart 1993). Such learning processes tend to occur spontaneously, but the organizational climate and context, the incentive, power and motivational systems, and, last but not least, the technology are ultimately responsible for the learning styles that can be observed in different organizations.

At a higher level, capabilities can evolve into core capabilities which differentiate a company strategically (Grant 1991). There are two main elements against which capabilities can be checked for their potential to become core: the competitive environment and the business mission of the firm. When faced with its competitive environment, a firm learns whether some capabilities have strategic potential (they are valuable, rare, etc.). A converse influence, from core capabilities to capabilities, also exists through the competitive environment, as (1) core capabilities of different firms competing in an industry define the "standards of excellence" for that industry. Hence, they can elicit which capabilities a firm should develop in order to compete effectively. (2) It is when confronted with a given environment that capabilities acquire a sense of *why* they are important: we are in the realm of dynamic efficiency (Klein 1977). For example, changes in the environment can make a highly efficient (in the static sense) capability worthless, because it is useless for competing under new circumstances (Langlois 1985).

A firm's business mission is also relevant for identifying the core capabilities, since it sets priorities in the alignment between them and the current mission. In turn, core capabilities can enable new business missions which, if accepted, may trigger new "capabilities — core capabilities" transformations. These interrelationships are captured by the *strategic learning loop* which links capabilities and core capabilities.

The environment in which learning occurs is an organizational context, which influences the learning process and is in turn influenced by its result (i.e., new working practices become part of the context, thus increasing the knowledge base of the organization [Giddens 1984; Orlikowski 1992]). Such an organizational context has the characteristics of a formative context (Ciborra and Lanzara 1990).[1]

Also, the strategic loop takes place within the firm's organizational (formative) context and so it is "structured" by it. In turn, its outcome — core capabilities — can reshape the context itself (Giddens 1984). In this respect, consider the role of organizational inertia and the limits to learning (Argyris and Schön 1978; Kim 1993). To drastically change the context in which learning takes place is a difficult endeavor, although sometimes necessary — for example, in order to respond to radical shifts in the environment and/or business mission. However, drastic changes in the business mission are not likely to occur, as its definition and meaning correspond closely to a given organizational context. Revolutionary changes in organizational context or business mission require radical learning, i.e., becoming aware of what the context is and explicitly stepping out of it in order to innovate (Argyris and Schön 1978).[2]

3. THE LEARNING AUDIT METHODOLOGY

Learning occurs through situated knowledge creation and accumulation processes. The learning ladder indicates that knowledge is created on four different levels: routines, capabilities, core capabilities, and formative context. The learning audit methodology is aimed first at evaluating the effectiveness of each learning loop. Specifically, we look at how people at work engage in individual and collective actions and reflections, which lead to the transfer of existing knowledge and the production of new one. Starting from the assumption that knowledge is embodied in praxis (Pentland 1992), we have operationalized our theoretical framework by means of a qualitative/inductive methodology. In other words, we conduct an ethnographic inquiry on the learning processes of individuals and work teams based on participant observation and a "thick description" of everyday practices and routines (Geertz 1973). The methodology elicits from the surface content of objects and behaviors the implicit beliefs embodied in them. It uses grids as

---

[1]A formative context is defined as "the set of preexisting institutional arrangements, cognitive frames and imageries that actors bring and routinely enact in a situation of action" (Ciborra and Lanzara 1994; Unger 1987). It comprises both the interpretive schemes and the organizational routines that influence problem solving in organizations (Dougherty 1992). However, the explicit reference to the notion of context points out that a formative context shapes routines and frames: it is their background and active mold. Learning new routines is a single-loop process. Restructuring a context implies double-loop learning (Argyris and Schön 1978).

[2]In this paper, we omit the analysis of how the learning ladder is situated in the broader social context, i.e. , how does learning within firms contribute to changes in the broader social context and, conversely, how broader social institutions shape the ladder (Powell and Di Maggio 1991).

guidelines which provide a general framework for observation and interviews (see Tables 1 through 4).

Table 1. Where is Knowledge Situated? Flows and Systems

FLOWS & SYSTEMS	EVIDENCE
ORGANIZATIONAL STRUCTURE	organizational units, tasks and roles
WORK FLOW	production cycle, work operations, production lines
INFORMATION SYSTEM	e-mail, computerized production control, "radar" system
QUALITY CONTROL SYSTEM	quality control procedures, quality indicators and certificates

Table 2. Where is Knowledge Situated? Actions and Events

ACTIONS & EVENTS	EVIDENCE
MEETINGS	analysis of interaction patterns, language, idiosyncracies, attitudes
COACHING	analysis of transferred values, skills, behaviors, coaching styles, attitude toward errors
INFORMAL COMMUNICATIONS	face to face interaction, conversations
BREAKDOWNS	local case phenomenology
WORK PRACTICES	organizational routines, rituals, patterned activities
LEADERSHIP STYLES	language, gestures, management of individuals, groups and resources, leader background

Table 3. Where is Knowledge Situated? Objects and Artefacts

OBJECTS & ARTEFACTS	EVIDENCE
VISUAL CONTROL TOOLS	notice boards, panels on the line, kanban, error messages
ORGANIZATIONAL MEMORIES	anomaly cards, problem solving procedures, customer feedback diaries, informal memos, charts
ORGANIZATIONAL SYMBOLS	writings, signs, metaphors
WORK TOOLS	machinery, equipment

Table 4. The Learning Outcomes

Learning Loops / Observed Items	ROUTINES	CAPABILITIES	CORE CAPABILITIES	FORMATIVE CONTEXT
FLOWS & SYSTEMS				
ACTIONS & EVENTS				
OBJECTS & ARTEFACTS				

The study concerns two levels of analysis. The first level addresses the issue: "Where is knowledge situated?" Specifically, it observes relevant events, visible behaviors and artefacts, and the organizational action system, i.e., how people interact in and with the situation. We selected features of a situation, such as flows and systems, actions and events, objects and artefacts, which constrain or induce intentional performances or at least fall into the scope of attention of the actors in the situation. The situation sets the stage where people engage in processes of interpretation and sense-making (Daft and Weick 1984). Thus, two types of phenomena stand out: observed behaviors and interpretations provided by the actors. The second level deals with the "institutional" dimension of knowledge (Douglas 1986). Its purpose is to trace back from the observation of visible behaviors and artefacts, the "theories in use" (Argyris and Schön 1978) or interpretive schemes (Orlikowski 1992) informing them, together with the organizational routines and contexts that shape them. The framework in which action takes place consists of specific institutional arrangements and the stock of background knowledge (formative context) which actors take for granted. Such a context emerges only in situations of breakdowns and critical circumstances, when the obviousness of daily routines becomes problematic. The actors' perceptions and interpretations can also be integrated with the concepts inferred by the researchers. Table 4 shows the main items which should be collected in the field for this purpose.

The study, which included the test of the learning audit methodology, was conducted during 1994. Data was gathered during six one-day visits to the plant and a five day period of immersion in the work environment. Thirteen people were observed while they were working in the plant and interviewed at their workplace. They included a variety of profiles ranging from generic workers to those responsible for the work teams and managers of various functions. Twenty hours of interviews were recorded on tape. Additional informal conversations took place throughout the plant and were not recorded. Four meetings were held as group interviews with production and systems managers. After the first report was delivered, three further meetings were held with the same group of managers to discuss and validate the results.

4. THE MELFI PLANT: FROM TOTAL AUTOMATION TO THE "INTEGRATED FACTORY"

The Melfi plant produces the latest Fiat model, the Punto, today the best selling car in Europe. The plant can assemble 1,600 cars a day (450,000 per year) at full production speed, employing 7,000 people on three shifts. The factory, situated in the south of Italy between Naples and Bari, is a "green field" site, set up at the end of 1993 and, after an experimental phase, opened officially in October 1994. Inside the Melfi industrial district are the plants of sixteen suppliers. Their location, close to the main assembly plant, makes possible the reduction of suppliers' lead times. Lean production and, in part, Just In Time (JIT) are applied as methods to organize the work cycle. The workforce belongs to a homogeneous cultural and geographical background. Workers, managers and employees are young and mostly from the south, often at their first job. The core group of first-hired workers is composed of skilled personnel with a good level of education (engineers or high school degree). The local identity is quite strong: they are highly motivated with a great sense of pride and enthusiasm (the region where the plant is located, like the rest of the south of Italy, has very high unemployment).

At the beginning of the 1980s, Fiat embarked resolutely into the so-called high-tech factory concept, which privileged intense automation to yield high productivity and quality, while reducing the role of human work drastically. Results, however, were deceptive, and the lessons learned from "lean production" (Womack, Jones and Roos 1990) have led to the implementation of a different strategy. The Melfi plant is the first example of the new production concept adopted by Fiat in the 1990s: the *integrated factory*. The apparent shift from automation to integration was due to management's newly acquired awareness that quality cannot be the outcome of a sophisticated technology only, with little involvement of the workforce. The new philosophy of integration tries to reconcile a high-tech infrastructure and the rigid synchronization of the assembly line with elements typical of the job shop (such as working in teams). To use an analogy, as in the building industry, the finishing jobs are entrusted to skilled carpenters in order to increase the added value of the building. Today, for the finishing work on a car, one relies much more on human work, rather than sheer automation, in order to raise the *quality* of the final product. Integration means *tighter coordination* through a variety of means. The great amount of paper as a means of communication, the highly sophisticated production and control information system, the frequent meetings and face to face interactions support the multiple facets of both formal and informal coordination. On the other hand, the distributed capability of managing breakdowns and problem solving, the importance of intuition, the coaching/training routines based on imitation emphasize the key role played by human resources and the presence of a capability for improvisation and bricolage. Such a capability is typical of *craftsmen*. The workers are able to react to the frequent breakdowns without going into a panic (Weick 1993). The action-centered skills ("fire fighting," "hands on" attention of the workforce) and the role of the "body" seem to prevail upon the intellectual skills and the capacity to abstract from action (Foucault 1980; Zuboff 1988).

4.1   The "Crystal Pipeline"

The factory is divided into four operating units (OU) responsible for the different stages of the production process: Pressing, Body Welding, Painting and Assembly. The four OUs cooperate in defining the daily production plan, monitoring the advancement of production, and managing the critical situations/problems. The longer term production plans are defined in Fiat's head office in Turin (in the north of Italy). The production process can be described as an incremental one. The essence of the process is to build the car *bit by bit* by having workers perform the same task on each car as it moves through their workstation on a conveyor system. The average time for each operation is about thirty seconds per car. Inside the Assembly unit, most of the tasks are performed by workers, while the other units are almost completely automated.

Each OU is divided into a number of UTEs (Elementary Technical Unit). The UTE, which comprises from twenty to forty workers and supervisors, is the basic production structure of the integrated factory. It can be defined as a semi-autonomous work team that manages a technical subsystem with its distinctive product and production process. Specific objectives and results are assigned to each UTE such as productivity, quality, budget, mix, and quantity. A UTE has a leader supported by a staff of technical specialists for maintenance tasks (the "technologists"). Typically, a UTE controls one or more production lines that are split into a varying number of workplaces occupied by one or two workers (or robots in the automated OUs). The number of workplaces depends on the number of elementary operations that have to be carried out in order to complete a given production sequence. UTEs also have a small "office" (often located alongside the line), which can be considered an information point, and a work group base. Here we find desks, PCS, terminals, and a number of notice boards that contain different signs and charts. The UTEs report to other management functions (Production Engineering, Quality, Personnel, etc.) from which they receive guidelines, and instructions, so they are not in a position to close the feedback loop (i.e., to influence the choices of these functions). In other words, a UTE is expected to solve (or contribute to solving) all problems that may hinder production, to control many quality aspects, but it cannot contribute to the overall development of (or have an explicit influence on) its immediate environment. UTEs can be seen as self-contained minifactories managing a whole segment of the production process. The modular organization fosters fluidity and integration of production processes and ensures a high degree of flexibility. The various units composing the organizational structure are linked according to a *customer-supplier model*, which means that each UTE must think of the next process as its "customer." More generally, the whole production system is organized as a customer-driven market, in which activities are structured as a network of flows and transactions between semi-autonomous units. The lean production logic implies producing only the amount required by the customer, at high quality, at low cost, and at the time needed. The production lines are organized in a way that allows every work place (and therefore UTE) to receive and pass on a "finished product" that can be judged for its quality. Bonazzi (1993) has described the integrated factory model by using the metaphor of a "crystal pipeline." The pipeline represents the continuous flow as it was originally conceived: a simple, linear structure in which work-in-process flows. The pipeline is open to market demand and the work flow is structured through a rigid orders schedule which is imposed from Fiat headquarters according to the production mix required by demand.

The image of the pipeline that portrays lean production indicates a rigid synchronization of all the processes occurring inside it and a high level of collaboration between the different units. But the pipeline is made of crystal, material that evokes the idea of transparency and fragility. Transparency means first eliminating waste and defects. Second, avoiding informal stocks and slack, and thus curbing shirking and other forms of opportunistic behavior. Third, making all available knowledge explicit: work is made transparent and "textualized" (Zuboff 1988) by representing all relevant aspects of the work flow through the *visual control system* (see below the "radar system"). The fragility of the pipeline is related to the rigid synchronization of the work flows and to the lean production concept. Since bottlenecks and the piling up of inventories can disrupt the flow and break the pipeline at any moment, everything in the plant has been synchronized with the purpose of avoiding bottlenecks, work-in-process inventories and buffers.

4.2 Breakdowns and Bottlenecks

In the best of all worlds, the line never stops. Unfortunately, the lean production concept is a source of unexpected and risky events. In fact, this concept is associated with a complex system of relations which is not always possible to fully control. At any moment, the mechanical synchronization of the operations can collapse for various, unpredictable reasons: absence of supplies, machine breakdowns, human errors, and so on. As the line stops, work-in-process piles up quickly, bottlenecks may emerge, and UTEs can be kept on hold, unless they intervene. In some cases, the causes of bottlenecks can be very complex, since they are related to the constantly changing product mix and not to a specific breakdown. That is, even if the factory as a whole might have enough capacity, there may be a mismatch between the line balance and the product mix being pushed through. Such bottlenecks highlight the key role of capacity planning (Schmenner 1990).

Bottlenecks are the most frequent manifestation of both local and systemic breakdowns. At the end of each line, there is an inventory where the car bodies, waiting to pass to the next process, are stored. These inventories can be seen as buffers. If a line stops as a result of a breakdown, the upstream processes keep going until the inventory closer to the problem is full. At this point, a bottleneck arises and the upstream lines must be stopped (thus creating work-in-process inventory). The downstream processes, in turn, stop receiving cars and, once their upstream inventory is emptied, they must be halted too. When the problem causing the bottleneck is solved, the line is able to receive the bodies and the flow can restart. If it is solved before the formation of bottlenecks along the line, it will remain at a local level. Otherwise, it will affect the whole system. The longer the duration of the halt, the higher the number of parts accumulated and the imbalance created to the flow.

In car manufacturing, the main *sources of bottlenecks* can be caused by process/product anomalies, line imbalance, machine breakdown, lack of materials, quality problems and lack of workforce (Suzaki 1987).

But bottlenecks may also have a more "abstract" origin related to problems of coordination, of which capacity planning is one. Another is due to the opacity of human behavior, to the tendency to focus on individual interests and to "manage one's own position" (Senge 1990). For example, the customer-supplier concept implies that UTEs coordinate activities between them as transactions between semi-autonomous units (Williamson 1985). In this "coordination game," instances of "local suboptimization" and opportunistic behavior may arise; that is, activities are executed in order to optimize a given UTE's performance rather than the overall production. In turn, local suboptimization may lead to the build-up of inventories along the lines. Often opportunistic behavior may be fostered unwittingly by a company's values. For example, in Melfi, *quality* is a pervasive concept crossing all production processes and is displayed through multiple organizational artefacts. Quality is both a *technical requirement* (absence of defects; reduction of waste and demerits) and a *cultural value* (responsibility; collaboration; commitment and motivation; identification with the customer, the product, and the company). In order to "measure" it, quality has been defined in terms of "demerits" (i.e., number of defects). The demerits system sets visible targets for continuous improvement and enhances the level of care and attention to the product and the process. However, as each demerit is ascribed to a UTE (or better, a work station), which is supposed to be at the origin of that demerit, the negative measurement may be perceived as a punishment and be frustrating for particular individuals and UTEs. The demerits system, possibly inherited from the conventional Fordist model, may represent a barrier to the achievement of full transparency of behaviors, since it induces workers to enact defensive behaviors, face saving, scapegoating and other tactics that ultimately interfere with effective problem solving and learning (Argyris 1993).

Finally, bottlenecks can be traced back to the coupling between the sheer complexity of the production system and the actors' bounded rationality. The new assembly line and the system of exchanges between customers and suppliers can be compared to a network of concurrent events, which is impossible to fully control, as opposed to the traditional, sequential assembly line. Sometimes a corrective action performed in one point of the system can generate a problem in another (distant) station along the line. As the complexity of relationships between different processes is very high and cannot be properly handled, bottlenecks can be generated unknowingly as a result of a lack of "systems thinking" (Senge 1990). To conclude, bottlenecks represent opportunities for problem solving and learning. Effective intervention requires an ability to discern their sources and causes, lest corrective routines are adopted that may lead to further propagation of mistakes and disruptions, and to very little learning.

5. THE MAIN FINDINGS

In what follows, we report the analysis of the learning processes observed in connection with a variety of breakdowns and bottlenecks, using the four main levels (learning loops) of the learning ladder presented in section 2. A first empirical finding regards the discrepancy between those problem solving procedures which are successful, and lead to higher levels of learning and competence building, and those interventions which are less successful and do not contribute to any further learning or competence enhancement. A second finding is that the same problem solving routine is applied to most breakdowns along the line, no matter what their cause. Data collected on the learning loops allowed us to identify the reasons for which workers and managers were showing good levels of competence and learning when dealing with certain situations, while they were not so competent in other circumstances, typically when system-wide disturbances occurred. The learning ladder shows that the origins of such discrepancies lie in the formative context that has subtly influenced the design and implementation of the Melfi plant. The same model, coupled with the audit methodology, can point out the positive reforms that could be introduced in management and worker training programs and information systems design, in order to increase the variety of the problem solving repertoire and help change the extant formative context. We present the findings by describing first the generalized problem solving routine that is applied daily throughout the plant. Next, we consider the different situations for which the routine in question is more or less effective. Then, we look at the cognitive and organizational dynamics of the main learning processes related to the application of the routine. Finally, we suggest a number of interventions to address the failures of the learning processes.

5.1   Trouble-Shooting in Melfi

The problem solving routine most frequently observed in the plant operations is based on an incremental feedback model. Whatever the breakdown, the routine seems to consist of the following "moves" (Pentland 1992):

- "see " a problem (e.g., building up of work-in-process inventory);

- mentally "search" for the station where the cause of the problem may originate, based on the previous knowledge of past bottlenecks; work stations and relevant operations characteristics; information received or gathered from other points on the line;

- "go to" the station held responsible for the breakdown, or communicate with operators there (depending on proximity of the station);

- "disassemble/re-assemble" a part or a component of the car or the production machine in order to fix the problem;

- register intervention and solution for future memory;

- take care *ex post* and on *ad hoc* way of inventory pile-ups or stock outs as minor side effects to be fixed (since the main cause has now been dealt with). If such side effects persist, wait for the flow to settle down to the normal pace of operation (no significant learning seems to take place at this stage).

The striking characteristics of such a problem solving procedure, which we have called the "Disassembly/Assembly" (D/A) problem solving routine, besides its "routinized" or repetitive nature (Pentland and Reuter 1994), are its ubiquity, concreteness, "situatedness," and high consistency.   Namely, we found instances of its application even in areas distant, at least conceptually, from the car manufacturing process: *"When we started to work in the new plant, we didn't even have desks for the UTE's offices.*   We built them *with pieces of iron that were laying around"* (Head of UTE A).   Problem solving must be concrete, "hands on" a machine. *"It is more effective to hold a meeting in front of a problem than in front of a desk....To start reasoning in front of a drawing is one thing.   To be directly in front of the machine is a totally different thing....We need to transfer the problem* [solving procedure] *from the desk to the operations point....We need to work as a team in front of the problem* [the machine]" (Head of UTE B).   And, although a strong need for a "global vision" of the production flows is strongly needed, the way suggested by the UTE's leaders as to how to acquire such a vision is pretty concrete: *"We convey a global vision by having workers learn something new all the time through job rotation.   The worker acquires more confidence with different production phases and operations....He learns to "see" new things and gets a global vision of the process"* (Head of UTE C).

The computer-based information system reinforces this way of solving problems.   In each UTE's office, a PC shows screens which portray the relevant segments of the production lines, listing for each work station the number of semi-finished cars entering and exiting the station, together with the levels of in-process-inventories.   Other screens offer the data in a more aggregate form, identifying the quantitative flows between UTEs.   The same network feeds into the big electronic boards (the so called "radar" system) which show production data for each UTE and all the related alarms.   The radar boards reproduce at a higher level the idea that you have to *"see"* and *"feel"* a problem in order to make it *"really true,"* and amenable to a "go to" and "hands on" solution.

Finally, the routine allows for variations, although within the boundaries set by the D/A metaphor. At a cognitive level the whole production process is perceived and thought of as a sequence of operations.   Although sometimes knowledge of the global process is necessary to solve "local" problems, or take care of the ramifications of local breakdowns, the procedure followed consistently implies the decomposition of global problems into lower level ones, capable of being resolved through a local D/A intervention.   We have observed various instances when a breakdown occurs, or a bottleneck is perceived, in which the worker or the supervisor goes back mentally through the working cycle and through a *gedanken* experiment disassembles the car in order to search for and identify the potential source of the default, i.e., what *operation* might not have been carried out in the proper way.   It is implicitly assumed that the source of the default is always unique.   If the mental and physical search is successful the problem is visualized, a local intervention is proposed, tried out and learned: [background noise; line-stop alarm ringing because of an inventory build up] "It's four screws.   You slam it down, re-screw and streamline [the body of a car].   *You know it better than I do!   It is just four screws!"* (Head of the UTE A to a technologist).   To conclude, an analogy emerges between the *physical* layout and workflow in the integrated factory, and the *cognitive* strategies present in the problem solving routines.   The way operators think is linear and sequential, thus reflecting the organization of the physical flow of cars along the line.

5.2 Mixed Success

Our empirical observations of breakdowns and the ways they are tackled indicate that the D/A problem solving routine works efficiently for the large majority of technical breakdowns occurring along the lines. That is, workers have acquired and internalized the procedural skills and competencies necessary for dealing with most breakdowns. As wished by Fiat's new vision of the integrated factory, workers in the Melfi plant appear to be "smart artisans" and good "mechanics," able as "bricoleurs" to make effective use of the resources available in their work environment. We noticed, however, situations during which a lack of competence seemed to emerge at various levels of the organization, starting from the lower ones. In general, such situations are related to the build-up of in-process-inventories. Their causes are often of a "second order" nature. They may stem from local sub-optimization strategies carried out by some UTEs, or unintended side-effects due to the application of a local D/A routine to fix a problem somewhere along the line, or "systemic" causes linked to the production mix, capacity load, etc.

Picture two sharply different scenarios: A proactive one, where for disturbances for which a "local" cause, whether real or imagined, has been figured out, and the worker "sees," "goes to" and "intervenes hands on"; and a passive one where, in the face of systemic breakdowns, workers simply wait for the line to restart. In the latter scenario, although a line stoppage and the ensuing waiting time are regarded as a form of waste within the lean production context, we found that it was an accepted behavior "to take a break and smoke a cigarette" if an inventory pile-up occurs for which causes cannot be easily discerned and fixed locally. But it is not only a matter of line slow-down or stoppage. Learning is impaired too. The linear mental map of the assembly line, seen as a rigid sequence of operations, does not work as a cognitive resource at hand for effective problem solving. On the other hand, no appropriate mental map of the concurrent events which lead to the stochastic in-process-inventories is available throughout the organization. Hence, there is no ground on which to accumulate knowledge about how similar problems have been solved previously. Instead of learning, then, and competence building, a conviction takes over whereby the complexity of the process overwhelms the decision makers. Bottlenecks seem to pop up in an unpredictable way (*"Every day there is something new happening"*). They seem to require always new, *ad hoc* solutions (*"Bottlenecks do not happen to have always the same solutions"*), or choosing between doing nothing or applying the D/A routine, just to "keep busy" in front of the unknown (Weick 1993). The generalized D/A routine is consistent with both the concept of the "mechanical," rigid sequence of operations on the traditional assembly line and the role of the worker as a mechanic-bricoleur. However, the lean production concept as applied in the Melfi plant generates an integrated, dynamic system connecting interdependent stations, which have a certain degree of autonomy in carrying out operations (the customer-supplier model). The repertoire of problem solving routines should be molded to a great extent by the latter design concept, too. But this is not the case. Why?

5.3 The Learning Ladder Unveiled

We believe that the D/A routine is so powerful in shaping problem solving and learning throughout the plant, because it embeds the "archetype" of mass production, and the assembly line in particular (Greenwood and Hinings 1988). The D/A metaphor appears to have been transferred almost intact from the slaughter houses in Chicago, where Ford had the first idea of the assembly line, to the *avant garde* plant in Melfi. Based on our interviews, we suggest that such a transfer occurred during the one-year long, intensive training period (carried out in the old assembly plant of Mirafiori in Turin), where the capabilities of the future workforce were developed and fine-tuned, especially during the hands-on sessions that included building off the line a real car "bit by bit." *"A smart idea during our basic training was to disassemble, re-assemble and disassemble again and again a few cars. Can you imagine? These cars are still laying around somewhere in the new plant"* (Head of UTE A). The D/A metaphor stays at the heart of the "assembly line" formative context and exerts a strong influence on the vast array of learning processes which take place in the plant. Here, the learning ladder can reveal how pervasive this influence is:

- *work practices*, both individual and team based, are aimed at building the car, or deconstructing it in case of breakdowns, bit by bit;

- *capabilities*: the D/A work practice becomes a generalized problem solving capability in use across the whole plant. It is applied to whatever problem emerges along the line. Where distance impedes a direct presence "in front of the machine," appropriate communication and information mechanisms are set up to handle the problem in a distributed way, while preserving the basic approach;

- *core capabilities*: the strategic value of quality of the final product is also supported by the D/A capability. For one thing, analytical attention to the detail is paramount to the implementation of quality management throughout the plant (*"Quality is there in the smallest assembly operation....Quality is not something pompous; it is doing things well according to the rule, and doing them in the same way over and over again"* Head of UTE B).

- *the formative context*: Ford's concept of the assembly line is very much alive in the design of the new plant. It is present in the split between task execution and task directional, though in a modified form, whereby all knowledge necessary to carry out D/A operations is widely distributed, so as to support the partial self management of each UTE and the coordination between them. However, production planning and control and, more generally, a systems view of the flows remain with a few functions at a higher level.

- the *computer-based information system* is designed to convey and register all the quantitative data regarding actual versus planned production, with the smallest detail for each work station along the line.

The consistency found along the learning ladder, and in the information system that supports it, has both strengths and weaknesses. Namely, the learning audit points out that accumulation of knowledge which fits the basic metaphors and practices embedded at the various levels of the ladder takes place smoothly. In other words, problems involving fixing the car along the line are solved with dexterity and speed; solutions are stored and made accessible for the work teams; artefacts are available to capture in written form such solutions and the network infrastructure is used to communicate in relation to such activities. However, problems which do not fit the existing formative context are dealt with in a much more nebulous way. No cognitive maps, individual or shared, help the operators to represent the disturbances and identify a solution space, and even less to store the causal links between errors detected and problem solving routines. Hence, no memory and competence are built up; learning does not take off from the *ad hoc* work practices, and capabilities are not generated. On the other hand, the formative context which enforces the separation between task execution and task direction prescribes that knowledge (frames, routines, know how) be relegated to those specialized and managerial functions, which deal with the design of the plant, its computer system and the management and control of production (following, then, the principles of Scientific Management [Taylor 1911]). The audit highlighted a strong departmentalization and hierarchization in the way production management knowledge and learning were divided. For example, only those specialists in Turin, who designed the Melfi plant, knew the simulation programs for capacity planning and the flows layout design. These programs were developed by a separate subsidiary. The Production department did not use the simulation programs, and only a few managers of the plant were taught scheduling programs. Finally, line managers did not have enough resources to go beyond troubleshooting and firefighting when bottlenecks occurred. All this reinforces the following conclusion: the old and the new production concepts clash with one another, despite attempts at reconciling them in the original design of the Melfi plant and operations. The old kept task direction strictly separated from execution, but endowed it with resources (production programmers and managers). The new concept, instead, delegates part of decision making and problem solving to the UTEs and, at the same time, subtracts resources from the managerial structure (aiming at a leaner organization). The audit shows that the learning ladder regarding the control of complex production events is consistent with the old concept. Hence, distributed learning about the management of production flows is not obtained. The widely available network infrastructure does not help either, since the systems do not support the running of any simulation of the production flows. They compute inputs and outputs for each work station, but not rates, flows, and probabilities data that would enable UTEs' members to simulate on their office PCS the potential consequences of their interventions at a plant-wide level.

5.4   Some Redesign Suggestions

A number of positive design ideas have emerged from our study. First, we recommend that exposure to the concepts of systems dynamics could be a way for UTEs' members to learn more effective strategies to cope with complex breakdowns and bottlenecks. Second, learning new frames and routines, such as the distributed control over flows at the UTE level, which belong to a formative context where the institutional separation between task direction and execution is challenged in a deeper way than it actually is, could support the development of the new capabilities. Such capabilities might reveal themselves as strategic, i.e., of benefit to the operations as a whole, although we do not have enough data from the study to reach a firm conclusion on this issue. Finally, the computer-based system could be practically redesigned according to the new formative context: as a platform for simulation exercises and distributed control routines. At the end of our study, a simulation prototype of a segment of the Welding line was built and presented to management as a candidate training tool. The prototype helped to make our point about the need for broadening the skill base of the workforce more concrete.[3] During the follow

---

[3]Our recent team played the "concreteness game," espousing the prevailing attitudes we discovered in the plant. We built a software object that could be looked at and touched in order to make our conclusions better understood by factory management.

up discussions, the Production manager of the Welding line wondered: *"What is the population of workers, supervisors and managers who would need to be trained on the new tool and be exposed to the principles of systems dynamics?"* The very fact that this issue was raised as a question meant that the old division of labor was not considered taken for granted, especially given the puzzles experienced daily in the plant. It is by asking these kind of questions that management can start inquiring into the existing formative context, and possibly trigger the discovery of a new division of learning, more consistent with the principles and organization of advanced manufacturing.

6. CONCLUSIONS

We can consider the various UTEs as "communities of knowing" (Boland 1995), engaged in learning and problem solving about minor and major breakdowns of production. Our analysis, based on the application of the learning audit methodology has shown that each time a breakdown occurs, the existing formative context triggers interpretive schemes and organizational routines that are driven by the D/A metaphor. In other words, when facing a problematic event, both improvisations and planned interventions are performed by members of the community taking a special perspective, present both in the traditional concept (and technology) of the assembly line and in the new concept of "artisanal, quality work": *building the car bit by bit*. The existing information systems support this kind of "perspective taking." We have also seen that individual and collective learning processes are heavily influenced by such a perspective. Specifically, we have discussed the variety of breakdowns that plague the production process, pointing out those for which the perspective taken by the teams is effective and those for which it is dysfunctional. In the latter situation, the pervasiveness of the D/A metaphor does not lead to a rapid and effective "learning by trial and error." We conclude that UTE members, and the plant management, should engage in "making" operational another perspective, the one of *systems dynamics*, for which the interdependencies among the production events and operations are more visible. Such a perspective can help members construct new understanding and response routines and, most importantly, unleash learning on how to improve the distributed control of operations. Consistent with such a perspective, simulation applications could be made available through the information systems, (a) to be used off-line as a complementary training tool for managers, supervisors, and key members of the UTEs, and (b) to enable the on-line exploration and evaluation of alternative modes of operations.

7. REFERENCES

Amit, R., and Schoemaker, P. J. H. "Strategic Assets and Organizational Rent." *Strategic Management Journal*, Volume 14, 1993, pp. 33-46.

Andreu, R., and Ciborra, C. *Core Capabilities and Information Technology: An Organizational Learning Approach*. Seventh International Conference on Socio-Economics, Paris, 1994.

Argyris, C. *Knowledge for Action*. San Francisco: Jossey-Bass, 1993.

Argyris, C., and Schön, D. *Organizational Learning: A Theory of Action Perspective*. Reading, Massachusetts.: Addison-Wesley, 1978.

Ashby, W. R. *Design for a Brain*. London: Science Paperbacks, 1966.

Barley, S. R. "Technology as an Occasion for Structuring: Evidence from Observations of CT Scanners and the Social Order of Technology Departments." *Administrative Science Quarterly*, Volume 31, 1986, pp. 78-108.

Barney, J. "Firm Resources and Sustained Competitive Advantage." *Journal of Management*, Volume 17, Number 1, 1991, pp. 99-120.

Boland, R. J. "Perspective Making and Taking." *Organization Science*, forthcoming 1995.

Boland, R. J.; Tenkasi, R.V. ; and Te'eni, D. "Designing Information Technology to Support Distributed Cognition ." *Organization Science*, Volume 5, Number 3, August 1994, pp. 456-475.

Bonazzi, G. *Il tubo di cristallo*. Bologna: Il Mulino, 1993.

Brown, J. S., and Duguid, P. "Organizational Learning and Communities of Practice: Toward a Unified View of Working, Learning and Innovation." *Organization Science*, Volume 2, Number 1, 1991, pp. 40-57.

Ciborra, C., and Lanzara, G. F. "Formative Contexts and Information Technology: Understanding the Dynamics of Innovation in Organizations." *Accounting, Management and Information Technology*, Volume 4, Number 2, 1994, pp. 61-86.

Ciborra, C., and Lanzara, C. F. "Designing Dynamic Artifacts: Computer Systems as Formative Contexts." In P. Gagliardi (Editor), *Symbols and Artifacts: Views of the Corporate Landscape*. Berlin: De Gruiter, 1990.

Daft, R. L., and Weick, K. E. "Toward a Model of Organizations as Interpretation Systems." *Academy of Management Review*, Volume 9, Number 2, 1984, pp. 284-295.

Davenport, T. H. *Process Innovation: Re-engineering Work through Information Technology*. Cambridge: Harvard Business School Press, 1993.

Dougherty, D. "Interpretive Barriers to Successful Product Innovation in Large Firms." *Organisation Science*, Volume 3, Number 2, 1992, pp. 179-202.

Douglas, M. *How Institutions Think*. London: Routledge, 1986.

Fiol, C. M., and Lyles, M. A. "Organizational Learning." *Academy of Management Review*, Volume 10, Number 4, 1985, pp. 803-813.

Foucault, M. *The History of Sexuality*, Volume I. New York: Vintage Books, 1980.

Geertz, C. *The Interpretation of Cultures*. New York: Basic Books, 1973.

Gemawhat, P., and Ricart, J. E. *The Organizational Tension between Static and Dynamic Efficiency.* Research Paper 225, Barcelona: IESE, 1993.

Giddens, A. *The Constitution of Society.* Berkeley: University of California Press, 1984.

Grant, R. M. "The Resource-Based Theory of Competitive Advantage: Implications for Strategy Formulation." *California Management Review*, 1991.

Greenwood, R., and Hinings, C. R. "Organizational Design Types, Tracks and the Dynamics of Strategic Change." *Organization Studies*, Volume 9, Number 3, 1988, pp. 293-316.

Huber, G. P. "A Theory of the Effects of Advanced Information Technologies on Organizational Design, Intelligence, and Decision Making." *Academy of Management Review*, Volume 15, 1990, pp. 47-71.

Kim, D. H. "The Link between Individual and Organizational Learning." *Sloan Management Review*, Fall 1992, pp. 37-50.

Klein, B. H. *Dynamic Economics.* Cambridge: Harvard University Press, 1977.

Kogut, B., and Zander, U. "Knowledge in the Firm, Combinative Capabilities, and the Replication of Technology." *Organization Science*, Volume 3, August 1992.

Langlois, R. N., Editor. *Economics as a Process: Essays in the New Institutional Economics.* Cambridge: Cambridge University Press, 1985.

Lave, J., and Wenger, E. *Situated Learning: Legitimate Peripheral Participation.* Cambridge: Cambridge University Press, 1991.

Leonard-Barton, D. "The Factory as a Learning Laboratory." *Sloan Management Review*, Fall 1992.

March, J. G. "Exploration and Exploitation in Organizational Learning." *Organization Science*, Volume 2, Number 1, February 1991, pp. 71-87.

Nelson, R. R., and Winter, S. G. *An Evolutionary Theory of Economic Change.* Cambridge, Massachusetts: Belknap, 1982.

Nonaka, I. "A Dynamic Theory of Organizational Knowledge Creation." *Organization Science*, Volume 5, Number 1, 1994, pp. 14-37.

Orlikowski, W. I. "The Duality of Technology: Rethinking the Concept of Technology in Organizations." *Organization Science*, Volume 3, Number 2, 1992, pp. 398-427.

Penrose, E. *The Theory of the Growth of the Firm.* London: Basil Blackwell, 1959.

Pentland, B. T. "Organizing Moves in Software Support Hot Lines." *Administrative Science Quarterly*, Volume 37, 1992, pp. 527-548.

Pentland, B. T., and Reuter, H. "Organizational Routines as Grammars of Action." *Administrative Science Quarterly*, Volume 39, 1994, pp. 484-510.

Powell, W. W., and Di Maggio, P. J. *New Institutionalism in Organizational Analysis*. Chicago: University of Chicago Press, 1991.

Prahalad, C. K., and Hamel, G. "The Core Competence of the Corporation." *Harvard Business Review*, Volume 68, Number 3, 1990.

Rosenberg, N. *Inside the Black Box*. Cambridge: Cambridge University Press, 1982.

Schmenner, R. W. *Production/Operations Management*. New York: MacMillan, 1990.

Senge, P. M. *The Fifth Discipline: The Art and Practice of The Learning Organisation*. New York: Doubleday, 1990.

Suchmann, L. *Plans and Situated Actions*. Cambridge: Cambridge University Press, 1987.

Suzaki, K. *The New Manufacturing Challenge*. New York: Free Press, 1987.

Taylor, F. W. *The Principles of Scientific Management*. New York: Harper, 1911.

Unger, R. M. *False Necessity*. Cambridge: Cambridge University Press, 1987.

von Hippel, E. *The Sources of Innovation*. Cambridge: MIT Press, 1988.

Walsham, G. *Interpreting Information Systems in Organizations*. Chichester: Wiley, 1993.

Weick, K. E. "The Collapse of Sensemaking in Organizations: The Mann Gulch Disaster." *Administrative Science Quarterly*, Volume 38, 1993, pp. 628-652.

Williamson, O. E. *Markets and Hierarchies: Analysis and Antitrust Implications*. New York: Free Press, 1975.

Williamson, O. E. *The Economics Institutions of Capitalism*, New York: Free Press, 1985.

Winograd, T., and Flores, F. *Understanding Computers and Cognition: A New Foundation for Design*. Norwood, New Jersey: Ablex, 1986.

Womack, J. J. D.; Jones, D. T.; and Roos, D. *The Machine that Changed the World: The Triumph of Lean Production*. New York: Rawson, 1990.

Wynn, E. *Office Conversation as an Information Medium.* Unpublished Ph.D. Dissertation, University of California, Berkeley, 1979.

Zuboff, S. *In the Age of the Smart Machine.* New York: Basic Books, 1988.

24

PANEL

The Social Organization of Tele-Learning in Companies

Participants

Werner Beuschel (Chair)
Brandenburg State University
Brandenberg, Germany

Peter van den Besselaar
University of Amsterdam
Amsterdam, The Netherlands

Lars Krogh
Finnmark Research Centre
Alta, Norway

Rosalie Gowlland
Berlitz School
London, United Kingdom

1. INTRODUCTION

The system of learning in organizations is about to change. Computer supported tele-learning provides new opportunities for training and further education of individuals as well as groups. While long-existing traditional forms of tele-learning were considered "dull," the new technical option of transferring video, audio and text by broad bandwidth channels puts new attention on distance learning processes. A variety of synchronous and asynchronous forms of teaching and learning wait to be explored.

Viewed from either the organizational, the economical, or the didactic-methodological perspective, tele-learning incorporates a vast potential for application within a medium time range.

Especially for small and medium enterprises and in regions with weak infrastructure, tele-learning promises advantages compared to the usual system of skill development: it can be used at the discretion of individual learners, employees can stay in-house, saving costs of traveling and fees this way, and they may expect up-to-date learning packages to take on skill deficits. Thus, experts predict the breakthrough of tele-learning applications not so much in domains such as schools or universities, but in companies.

Closer observation of the tele-learning scenery reveals that there is a gap between technical possibilities and concepts of uptake and use. The enabling technology, based on ISDN, mailboxes, teleconferencing and now widely available satellite and networking facilities, is indeed developing at a considerable pace. Not so much attention is paid to the social and organizational side of tele-learning. Requirements for "best" arrangements of tele-learning are not yet clear. The appropriateness of areas for tele-learning, where current forms of education should be replaced, is also not much investigated. A framework for evaluating learning effects is missing in many cases.

A number of pilot projects involving companies across Europe are underway, trying to find answers. Many of them are funded from money in the programme area of "Telecooperation" of the European Union. Beyond this realm, individual companies interested in tele-learning face many ambiguities. For them, it is still unclear which strategy they should follow and which steps they should take.

2. IMPORTANT ISSUES IN TELE-LEARNING

If a company decides to introduce tele-learning, it is wise to know who is willing to take on the leadership of implementing and maintaining the system. Questions arise around issues such as organizational requirements for access, control, and coordination. Depending on synchronous or asynchronous learning situations, organizational precautions have to be taken.   The coordination of access rights and the exchange of material seems crucial. Also, the interests of a company, of end-users and of the providers of learning material have to be brought into a balance. Since few traditional relationships are available in this area, new alliances have to be built.

The main question from an economic angle usually centers on basic and ongoing costs. If a company wants to implement tele-learning, the current hardware and software situation has to be considered thoroughly. A good knowledge of technology and of the market is necessary to select the appropriate equipment. Since most systems supporting tele-learning functions are in their early marketing stages, it can be expected that costs will go down; this would indicate postponement of the implementation process. On the other hand, criteria are not available for assessing when the right time has come for a company to enter the field.

Tele-learning in its general version can be characterized by the permanent spatial separation between teaching and learning persons. Viewed from the didactic-methodical level, computer support not only adds new multimedia features, it creates potential areas of interaction. Teaching materials can be co-developed by exchanging ideas and requirements between educational institutions and learners. What is most important, synchronous interaction between tutor/teacher and learner can be arranged by means of teleconferencing. Thus, one main requirement for all learning situations — immediate response — can now be reconstructed in new ways.

It is obvious that the systems currently being tested do not supply us with answers to all these questions. So far the field of tele-learning is very open, many players are not yet known, and a balance of needs has still to be found. As this process of reorganization of knowledge transfer in companies is just about to start, it seems helpful to reflect current experiences with tele-learning and to explore opportunities for appropriate social organization.

3. GOAL OF THE PANEL

The panel wants to address these social, organizational and economic questions in the area of tele-learning. The goal is to share experiences and to generate guidance on directions we should take or avoid in the development and use of tele-learning.

The following five themes should help to structure the discussion:

- Organizational context: How is tele-learning embedded in an organization? Who does it and when? What are the incentives? Who has/who gains control over access or usage profiles? Who designs and who provides? What are the new coordination requirements? How can a balance of needs be managed in the process?

- Social organization and technical infrastructure: Bandwidth of tele-learning environments; discrepancies in the social and technical structure; comparability; adaptation of organization to the technology; group-learning processes; cross-company or cross-country uses.

- Economics of tele-learning: Advantages over traditional learning; economic consequences on the company and individual level; cost factors of different tele-learning environments.

- Learning theories and actual achievements: Learning theories adopted or assumed; evaluation dimensions; changes in learning practices; requirements for supporting existing practices.

- Next steps to take: Any success factors recognizable? Do we agree on evaluation dimensions? What do we learn from earlier/similar learning technologies? What are the most controversial issues? Which problem should be solved next?

The panelists are from four different European countries and provide both industrial and academic experiences. Their professional backgrounds cover a variety of relevant areas in tele-learning:

for instance, regional and infrastructural prerequisites, company strategies, approaches to system development, support of learning practices, and organizing further education for small and medium companies.

In an opening statement, each panelist will provide an overview of his/her perspective on tele-learning, research, empirical data, and experiences. After that, the audience will have the opportunity to discuss the issues in the field of tele-learning with the panel participants.

PART SIX

Reflections of Research: Participation

25

Designing for Freedom in a Technical World

Enid Mumford
Emeritus Professor
Manchester University

Abstract

This paper discusses the notion of freedom and relates this to the processes and outputs of systems design. It focuses on the ideas of Mary Parker Follett, an American administrator, who lectured and wrote in the 1920s and 1930s. Follett had revolutionary ideas on industrial democracy and on how employee involvement in problem solving and decision taking could be used to improve the efficiency and success of American industry. Follett's ideas are compared with those of the Human Relations Movement and with socio-technical design.

The author describes how she tries to apply the ideas of Mary Parker Follett and socio-technical design in her own work. She also discusses how Follett's philosophy compares with the management principles being put forward by modern management gurus such as Vickers and Handy.

1. THE LIFE OF MARY PARKER FOLLETT

Most academic papers have a theoretical basis which underlies the argument and provides hypotheses that can be critically examined and discussed. Many of the weightier theories have been derived from earlier academics, now dead, whose thoughts have become received wisdom. Almost all of these sources of wisdom are men. The author of this paper decided that she would base her writing on the theories of someone who has had a great influence on her thinking over the years. This person was not an academic nor a man. She was an American social worker who was born in Boston in 1868 and died in 1933. Her name is Mary Parker Follett.

Mary Parker Follett was a highly educated woman. In 1890, she spent a year at Newnham College, Cambridge, England where she read political science, history and law. She followed this with six years at Radcliffe College, Cambridge, Massachusetts, graduating in 1898 after studying philosophy, economics and government. This led to further graduate study in Paris.

She regarded herself as a political scientist and her first major interest was the study of American public life. She contributed to the improvement of this by pioneering a network of evening classes for the young people of Boston and, in 1909, she produced her first important publication. This was called *The Speaker of The House of Representatives*. Prior to this publication, she had become interested in vocational guidance as a result of a visit to Edinburgh in 1902 where she had seen some pioneer work on this subject and, in 1912, she became a member of the Boston Placement Committee, which later became the Boston Department of Vocational Guidance. This took her into industry and she began researching working conditions in different sectors while, at the same time, she became increasingly interested in the problems of management and industrial relations.

In 1920, she produced her main work. This was called *The New State: Group Organization the Solution of Popular Government* (Follett 1920). In this book, she advocated the replacement of bureaucratic institutions by group networks in which the people themselves analyzed their problems and implemented their own solutions. This book was followed in 1924 by a second influential book called *The Creative Experience* (Follett 1924). In this work, she discussed the possibility of accepting and using conflict as a positive and enriching experience.

Follett was now famous as a political scientist. *The New State* was reviewed in journals throughout the world and brought her international recognition. It led to her becoming a friend of the British Lord Haldane and of many other distinguished philosophers and political scientists. But gradually, through her increasing contacts with industry, she moved away from political science and the problems of government to social administration and business management.

She gave many lectures to interested audiences. On visits to England, in 1926 and 1928, she spoke at the Rowntree Lecture Conferences in Oxford and to the National Institute of Industrial Psychology. In 1929, after the death of the friend with whom she lived in Boston, she moved to England and stayed there until 1933.

While living in England she continued her studies of management, explaining to an audience at the London School of Economics that she did this "because industry is the most important field of human activity and management is the fundamental element in industry." She died in December 1933, when on a brief return visit to the United States.

During her early studies in the United States Mary Parker Follett met Dr. H. Metcalf and he later published many of her lectures. It was he, together with a British management consultant, Colonel L. Urwick, who, in 1941, assembled her lectures in a book called *Dynamic Administration* (Metcalf and Urwick 1941). Many years ago, the author of this paper had the good fortune to secure a copy of this book. In the introduction the chocolate magnate and philanthropist B. S. Rowntree wrote:

> The principles which she outlined are fundamental to all human progress. They should be widely known and acted upon, particularly at the present time, when good organization is of supreme importance to national survival. They will be found more necessary when the war is over and humanity is faced with the almost

superhuman task of fashioning a new and better world. [Metcalf and Urwick 1941]

Despite her international fame, Follett's writing and influence vanished from the American scene after her death. In a new book, *Mary Parker Follett: Prophet of Management*, Peter Drucker in his introduction tries to find an explanation (Graham 1995). He describes how when, in 1941, he asked management experts to help him compile a reading list of important management books, no one mentioned her name. It was when he met Colonel Urwick in 1951 that he first heard of her. Drucker claims that there was no reference to her in any American management book until he published his *Practice of Management* (Drucker 1954). Even here, when this author checked, she found that the only reference there was the title *Dynamic Administration* in a selected bibliography. Follett did not appear in the index.

Drucker discounts the suggestion that she was neglected because she was a woman, claiming that there were many prestigious women around at the time, for example, Lilian Gilbreth, the time and motion study expert. He argues that she was pushed into obscurity because her ideas were regarded as subversive in the 1930s and 1940s. Running industry after the last war was seen as a battle between management and unions. Her ideas on communication, conflict resolution and joint problem solving had no legitimacy. Contemporary management believed that the route to success was control not consensus. And so Mary Parker Follett became a nonperson. She might never have existed. However, Rosabeth Moss Kantor, who provides a preface to the new book, does not agree with Drucker that there was no sexism in her rejection. She believes that Follett's gender did play an important part in her neglect.

Like many prophets who are neglected at home, her star continued to shine in other countries. The Japanese embraced many of her ideas and through Dr. Metcalf and Colonel Urwick her work was kept alive in Britain. In the 1970s and 1980s, many British books on organizational theory and management had chapters on Follett. All used the Metcalf and Urwick book as their information source.

2. THE IDEAS OF MARY PARKER FOLLETT

Mary Parker Follett had many highly innovative ideas and theories. As the subject of this paper is "freedom" the focus will be on those that contribute to this subject.

First, she believed that freedom required order. But order must be integral to the situation and must be recognized as such. Even though different groups with different interests would have different views, all should agree on the nature of the problems that had to be solved. Order should be the agreed "law of the situation," but order and orders must be the composite conclusion of those who give and those who receive them. In her view, freedom comes from efforts to achieve a consensus and it is the freedom of the individual and the group, not the individual alone.

Follett took a holistic view of business and business organizations. She believed in integration. She tells us:

The first test of good business organization is whether you have a business with
all its parts so coordinated, so moving together in their closely knit and adjusted
activities, so linking, interlocking, interrelating, that they make a working unit —
that is not a congeries of separate pieces. [Follett 1926]

Successful integration leads to freedom because it encourages face-to face communication,
personalization and self assertion. It is not remote and bureaucratic. It takes account of the fact
that situations are always evolving and that discussions and decisions must be circular, not linear.

In her view, the undue influence of leaders is one of the main obstacles to integration. Orders and
organization should not be a result of domination but come from a recognition by all parties of
the problems that have to be tackled. Order and control then emerge from a common
understanding and accepted "law of the situation."

Follett recognized that freedom is often associated with power. The more power an individual
has, the more he or she is likely to be free from constraints. She believed that what was required
was not "power over" but "power with" or joint power. She says: "One of the tests of a
conference or committee should be: are we developing joint power or is someone trying unduly
to influence the others?" (Follett 1926).

In her view, attempts must be made to reduce "power over." She asked:

How do we reduce power over? Individual freedom can lead to coercive
exploitation. We want group freedom. Circular behavior is the basis of
integration. You influence another while they influence you. If both sides obey
the law of the situation no person has power over another. [Follett 1926]

She continued:

Our first approach should always be to discover the law of the situation. We
should try to reduce power over even if we cannot get rid of it.

She believed that power over could be reduced through integration, through recognizing that all
should submit to the law of the situation and through making the business more and more of a
functional unity. Function should equal capacity and there should be the authority and
responsibility to go with the function.

When differences of opinion arise, she suggested that there are three ways of dealing with these:
domination, compromise and integration. With domination, only one side got what it wanted.
With compromise, neither side got what it wanted. But through integration, it is possible to find
a way in which both sides get what they want.

She pointed out that many think they are losing freedom and independence through joining with
others but this is a false perception of freedom. Mangers do not give up their freedom when they
give their workers a share in management. On the contrary they are freeing themselves from
strikes, sabotage and indifference. Employers are not free when these occur.

Follett translated these ideas from the individual firm to national and international level. She anticipated the Common Market by asking for the organization of markets: "Nations cannot be free while struggling for markets. We want the organization of markets."

She saw no conflict between planning and freedom. In her view good planning could provide more freedom by providing opportunities for personal initiative. "Individualism and collective control should equal collective self control."

Follett saw freedom in work as problem solving and decision taking in which all played a part. To achieve this she suggested four fundamental principles of organization (Pugh, Hickson and Hinings 1971). These were:

- **Coordination by direct contact.** All employees must be in direct contact regardless of their position in the organization. Horizontal communication is as important as vertical chains of command in achieving coordination.

- **Coordination in the early stages.** Employees should be involved in policy or decisions while these are being formed and not simply brought in afterwards. In this way, the benefits of participation will be obtained in increased motivation and morale.

- **Coordination as the "reciprocal relating" of all factors in a situation.** All factors should be related to one another, and these interrelationships must themselves be taken into account.

- **Coordinating is a continuous process.** "An executive decision is a moment in a process." So many people contribute to the making of a decision that the concept of final or ultimate responsibility is an illusion. Combined knowledge and joint responsibility take its place. Authority and responsibility should derive from the actual function to be performed, not from place in the hierarchy.

Follett accepted the traditional concepts of power, authority and leadership but redefined these as "power *with*," "*joint* responsibility" and "*multiple* leadership."

She did, however, recognize that achieving this kind of freedom would not be easy. Problems that would have to be solved included facilitating communication among all interested groups. At a later date, Jurgen Habermas makes the same plea. Planning, whether local or national has to be flexible enough to encourage initiative and experiment. Collective control and decentralized responsibility have to be made compatible. There is no place for regulation or coercion; every thing should emerge from discussion and agreement.

Follett presents us with an ideal to strive for even though it may be difficult to attain. She believed strongly in rational thinking so that problems are fully understood, in effective planning and organization of a kind that is generally agreed, and in working through discussion and consensus.

Her definition of freedom is "freedom for the individual and the group," with the one supporting and enhancing the other. This kind of freedom comes from knowledge, discussion and integration. It requires continuous and close communication, a recognition of common interests and a willingness to participate in solving problems. All conflicts can be solved given an understanding of their nature and a desire for a solution. Goodwill and good relations are the routes to freedom for all.

3. RELATED THEORIES

This theoretical approach, although utopian, is not very different from Jurgen Habermas' theory of communicative action. This too is a theory of social interaction with the objective of creating an "ideal speech situation." This is a situation in which there is undistorted communication with participants who are free and equal in their dialogue roles and can arrive at a rational consensus. This is in contrast to distorted forms of communication which are characterized by social domination, authoritarianism etc. (Gould 1988). But, despite the similarity of their theories and despite living in the U.S. during the last war, like Drucker, Habermas appears not to have heard of Follett.

All ideas have a past as well as a future and Mary Parker Follett is no exception. She had studied political science and philosophy at Newnham and Radcliffe and in her early days she called herself a political scientist. It is most probable that her ideas were influenced by the thinking and writing of a number of classical philosophers although we can only guess at which. Like her, many have taken as their point of departure the premise of an underlying unity and symmetry that could be uncovered through reason. William James called the proponents of these ideas the "tender minded." Some, including Aristotle, favored the decentralization of authority and the encouragement of pluralism with many different interest groups. The sixteenth century philosopher Althusius believed in a community of communities as did more recent thinkers such as Burke, Weber and Durkheim.

All of these saw freedom associated with function. Each group or community within the larger community should have the greatest possible autonomy consistent with the performance of its function and with the performance of other groups and communities it associated with. The emphasis of these philosophers was on the small and the local — the family, neighborhood, local association and work group.

Edmund Burke in the eighteenth century detested what he called "arbitrary power." He saw society as a contract, or partnership founded on kinship, neighborhood or social group. Hegel, too, in the nineteenth century viewed society as plural with many centers of authority. These included the church, local community, profession and occupational association. He describes freedom as "being with oneself in another," that is, actively relating to something other than oneself in such a way that this other becomes integrated into one's projects, completing and fulfilling them so that it counts as belonging to one's own action. This means that freedom is possible only to the extent that we act rationally and in circumstances where the objects of our action are in harmony with our reason (Wood 1991).

De Tocqueville, the nineteenth century French philosopher, carried on the intellectual pursuit of democratic communities in which all men are equal. Pluralism had now taken a number of different forms. There was "conservative" pluralism, which saw its mission as the reinforcement of traditional groups such as the family and the church. There was also "liberal" pluralism, which was concerned with the relationships between a democratic state and a structure of social organization that provided the highest degree of individual freedom. And there was "radical" pluralism, which was Marxist in inspiration and envisaged a totally new society.

Follett appears to fit in the tradition of "liberal" pluralism which aims to provide individual freedom within the context of group freedom. She restricted her philosophy to the business organization, although she thought the principles could also be applied to national and international trade. If she lived in Britain today, she would probably be a supporter of the Liberal Democrat party.

4. WHAT IS FREEDOM TODAY?

In the twentieth century, there have been many definitions of freedom, not all the same as Mary Parker Follett's. Liberal individualism has tended to see freedom as an absence of constraints. It has seen the welfare of society, and even the welfare of its most deprived members, as being served by the pursuit of individual self interest and by the efficiency of a free market. In England for ten years this was the dominant set of values of the Thatcher government.

Daniel Bell has argued for a recognition of the complexity and variety of modern society. He sees Western industrial society as divided into different sectors, each guided by its own principle. There is the techno-economy, whose guiding principle is efficiency; the political sphere, whose legitimacy is based on the concept of free and equal citizens; and the culture, increasingly dominated by the ideal of unlimited self expression. Bell (1974) suggests that these apparently incompatible realms of society are a source of many of today's conflicts. Can people who want self development and fulfilment achieve this in an industrial society where roles and specialization still rule to a high degree? Will today's movement toward flatter hierarchies, multi-skilling, total quality and reengineering bring the freedom and power sharing Follett desired or are these new names for old bureaucracies?

For most of us, freedom today means the capacity for choice and its exercise, the absence of constraining conditions and the availability of means. It means equal opportunity for self-development in association with one's fellows, enabling conditions and the encouragement and motivation to take this route (Galston 1991). Self-development involves the creation of new capacities and the enrichment of existing ones; in other words, a general enhancement in the quality of individual, group and organizational life (Gould 1988). Follett would be in agreement with all of these things.

However, individualism and diversity for all require some generally agreed values. For example, an acceptance of the work ethic which requires personal independence to be associated with the desire to do a job well, and a restriction on untrammeled self-indulgence so that the needs of the group are in harmony with the needs of the individual.

5. WHO HAS FOLLOWED FOLLETT?

How close have we come to achieving these things? Have there been any serious and successful moves toward the kind of freedom for which she strove? The answer to this question is "yes" although progress has been patchy, sporadic and, up to now, not greatly influenced by technology.

6. HUMAN RELATIONS

The American "human relations" movement of the 1950s, 1960s, and 1970s had many ideas similar to those of Follett although there is no acknowledgment of her in their writings. Elton Mayo was the founding father of the human relations school of thought and his experiments in the Hawthorne plant of the Western Electric Company made industry more aware of the fact that workers and managers must first be understood as human beings (Roethlisberger and Dickson 1949). Frederick Herzberg, Chris Argyris, Rensis Likert and Douglas McGregor all followed in his footsteps. Herzberg (1966) spoke for them all when he said: "The primary function of any organization, whether religious, political or industrial, should be to implement the needs of men to enjoy a meaningful existence."

Mayo found that workers who were consulted, given responsibility for choosing their pace of work, and treated as partners rather than subordinates, responded with high motivation and high production. Mayo (1949) came to believe that an important task for management was to create situations where this spontaneous cooperation could develop and grow.

Argyris' objective was to help people to attain freedom through developing their potential. He believed this kind of self-actualisation benefits not only the individual but also those around as well as the employing organization. Again, better communication is a means for achieving this. Managers must be prepared to show their real feelings to those above and below them (Argyris 1957). Herzberg, too, was interested in assisting the development of human potential. In his view, job satisfaction came, not from money alone, but from achievement, recognition and responsibility. Jobs must be "enriched" to provide these motivating factors (Herzberg, Mausner and Snyderman 1959).

Rensis Likert and Douglas McGregor had similar philosophies. Supervisors must be "employee centered" and able to build effective work groups which have high achievement goals. They must regard their jobs as dealing with human beings rather than with work. Their role is to "help" people to work efficiently, to exercise general but not detailed supervision, and to allow maximum participation in decision taking. Likert's System 4 participative group management approach would also have delighted Follett. Communication now flows downwards, upwards and sideways; workers and bosses are psychologically close, decision taking is through group processes with each group linking to the next through a "linking pin" individual who is a member of more than one group.

Likert was an admirer of Follett and her notion of "the law of the situation." He believed that the greater amount of objective information available to modern management enabled problems to be depersonalized and dealt with rationally and participatively (Likert 1961).

McGregor followed on from these ideas with his Theory X and Theory Y management. Theory X is control and coercion, Theory Y is the development of "supportive" relationships that enable employees to have self-actualisation, responsibility, self direction and self control (McGregor 1966).

A considerable amount of American industry responded to these ideas and they were increasingly accepted as good management practice. They were seen as enabling the needs and objectives of the individual and of the company to come together in a harmonious relationship. This was exactly what Follett wanted to achieve.

7. SOCIO-TECHNICAL SYSTEMS

Europe did not have a human relations movement. In England, for example, management and workers looked at each other across a big divide with each side regarding the other as "the enemy." The workers were usually backed by strong trade unions and the climate was more like a war game than a series of supportive relationships. But there were some new groups with ideas similar to those of Mary Parker Follett. One of the strongest of these was the socio-technical movement which emerged from the ideas of Eric Trist and the Tavistock Institute from the 1950s onward (Trist and Murray 1991, 1993).

Interestingly, although the Tavistock group came together soon after *Dynamic Administration* was published and from its inception the ideas of the group have been close to those of Follett, there is no reference to her in the socio-technical literature. (See, for example, the two historical works edited by Trist and Murray.)

Whereas the Americans focused on changing attitudes, the British and later European groups believed the answer to organizational health was in the new forms of work structure that would improve efficiency but also create a good quality work environment and high job satisfaction. These new work structures were based on logically connected groups of tasks that enabled employees to acquire a number of skills, to do a whole job, to take decisions and to solve problems. They would also offer opportunities for working as members of integrated teams, for supportive relationships and personal development. Many of these ideas came from biology and the notion of "open" systems (von Bertalanffy 1968).

Early experiments with these semi-autonomous group structures were first carried out in the British Coal Industry and then moved to India, Scandinavia and the United States. Socio-technical design is still flourishing, although its scope and influence seem not to be known to the new proponents of Business Process Reengineering. It has a sound theoretical basis and a well-tested methodology. It takes a process and open system perspective, recognizing the dependencies between different parts of the work situation and between the work situation and the external environment.

The author is now a Council member of the Tavistock Institute and so closely in touch with its philosophy and approach. She first came into contact with it when she was asked to join the International Quality of Working Life Committee which consisted of STS practitioners from different parts of the world. Powerful figures at the time were Lou Davis in the United States,

Hans Van Beinum in Canada, Federico Buttero in Italy, Einar Thorsrud in Norway, Fred Emery in Australia and, of course, the person who started it all, Eric Trist, who later moved to the United States and became a professor at the Wharton School. Although the STS pioneers were interested in both theory and practice, Mary Parker Follett was never a subject for discussion. One reason for this may have been that the early interest in STS came principally from Scandinavia. With the exception of Professor Lou Davis at the University of California, Los Angeles, and one or two others, socio-technical design in the U.S. was slow to start.

8. THE AUTHOR'S EXPERIENCE

The author became interested in, and aware of, the ideas of Mary Parker Follett in the 1960s when she was fortunate enough to acquire a copy of *Dynamic Administration*. In the 1970s, she became a member of the International Committee for the Quality of Working Life. Since then, she has tried to apply the philosophies and principles of both Follett and socio-technical systems design. One of her objectives has always been to increase the user group's freedom to choose the organizational and technical system that they preferred. She has done this by using participative approaches that, whenever possible, involved all affected users in the design process.

She began to do this in the early 1970s when she was asked by different companies to help groups of staff design and implement new computer systems. These groups were not computer specialists. They were often clerks who participated in the systems design task by identifying their information needs, choosing the best system to fit these needs and designing an effective organization of work around the new technology. Usually the selected new form of work organization included important socio-technical design principles (Mumford and Weil 1979).

This early work in firms such as ICI, Rolls Royce and many banks tried to achieve the socio-technical objective of optimal use of both technology and people, with employees being given the Follett freedom to analyze their own problems and agree and implement acceptable and viable solutions and, in this way, exerting some influence on their future working conditions (Mumford and Henshall 1979). Humanistic technology was a desired output but technology was not used to assist the design process.

This changed in the 1980s, when the author undertook a large project with the Digital Equipment Corporation in Boston to assist the design of XSEL, one of Digital's first expert systems (Mumford and MacDonald 1989). XSEL was a configuring aid directed at helping the Digital sales force to make fewer errors when they prepared financial estimates for customers and sent orders to the manufacturing plants. These errors were expensive and cost Digital a great deal of money through lawsuits and compensation payments.

Because XSEL was intended for all sales offices throughout the world and the sales force was a powerful group, it was decided that the expert system must be designed participatively with the active involvement of the sales force. Digital believed that if the sales force were not given the freedom to do this, they would respond by refusing to use the system. Freedom now was a necessity rather than an ideal.

The problem was how to do this when the sales force was so large. The answer was a representative design group of sales people together with the use of electronic mail. An iterative design approach was used with the sales force specifying their needs, the knowledge engineers building a prototype to this specification, and the sales force testing this out and commenting on their experience. This specify, build, and test process continued until a system good enough to release for general use was produced. This took about three years.

During this period, there were regular meetings of the design group and after each meeting an account of what had taken place was sent to each U.S. sales office for discussion and comments. If questions were raised at the meeting that could not be easily answered, or decisions were difficult to make, the sales office staff were asked to send their views to the design group by e-mail. In this way a continuing dialogue concerning the design and implementation of XSEL took place. Through the use of e-mail, all sales staff could participate in this until the system became operational. Here then was a real world attempt at Follett's integrated communication using a new electronic aid.

Discussion of the technical quality of XSEL was also assisted by building a comments facility into the machine. Salespeople could use this to express their approval or dismay as they tested the system.

XSEL was implemented throughout the United States and worked fairly successfully for a number of years. The design group and the use of e-mail for communication continued during this period. This assisted the solution of technical problems and guided further development of the system.

9. DESIGNING TO ASSIST FREEDOM

If we accept that Mary Parker Follett's ideas are ethically and practically of value, what can we do about it? One thing we can do is to try and implement her ideas in the groups with which we work closely. If we are systems designers or other kinds of computer specialists, we will be in constant touch with users. Here is the opportunity for a new approach with a humanistic and moral content.

The author explained earlier that she tried to use the philosophy of Follett and the objectives of the socio-technical school when helping users to design new systems. This is true whether these users are clerks, specialist groups or senior managers.

Following are some of principles she finds most useful and relevant in her areas of activity.

Principles Derived Mainly from Mary Parker Follett

* **Participation.** Users are always given a major role in the design process so that they can play an important part in the selection and design of systems that will improve their own efficiency, effectiveness, job satisfaction and quality of working life.

Giving users the freedom to take on this role enables them to have some control over the degree of freedom they can exercise in their new work situations.

- **Representation**. All user interests need to be represented in a design group, irrespective of status, age or gender. Direct users of the new system should play a major role in systems design; indirect users should be consulted whenever factors that affect them are discussed.

- **Joint problem solving**. Once the design group is operational, the first step is to get agreement on the problems and needs that have to be addressed through change. This is coming to a consensus on the Law of the Situation. The group must agree that during meetings everyone is regarded as of equal status. The views of a junior clerk must be given as much weight as those of a senior manager. No single individual must be allowed to dominate the meeting. This point is particularly applicable to the technical specialists who may have favorite technical solutions they want to press on the participants.

- **Freedom of speech**. There must be face-to-face communication, honest exchange of views and freedom of speech. Following Follett's advice, differences of opinion should be dealt with through integration rather than domination or compromise. Integration means striving to achieve a "win, win" solution. This is a solution from which all parties with a major interest in the new system feel that they have gained something.

- **Gaining power**. The design group must recognize that by working together to ensure agreement on needs and solutions they can gain considerable power. They may need this power to ensure that their preferred solution is accepted by other powerful groups in the company. There needs to be a recognition that power is being increased, not lost, through the participation process. The technologists must believe that they are not losing power by sharing design with users. Senior management also must feel that they are not losing power by allowing lower level groups to take decisions. The accepted view should be that all are gaining power as good, well conceived systems are introduced that users want, understand and own.

- **Integrating all factors**. The design group must also take account of all relevant factors in the situation they want to change. It is not unusual for design groups to identify benefits and forget about costs. For example, a system that reduces staff numbers can greatly reduce costs but this reduction may be offset by the costs of overworked and over stressed staff who take time off from work because they cannot manage the additional work load.

- **Staying together**. The design group may wish to continue working together over a considerable period of time and this can have advantages. The XSEL design group met over many years, handling first the design process, next implementation and evaluation and, finally, planning for the future development of XSEL.

Principles Derived Mainly from Socio-Technical Design

- **Quality of working life**. The most important principle is that an improvement in user quality of working life should be given as much importance as an improvement in efficiency.

- *Multi-skilling.* Every effort should be made to design interesting, challenging and significant jobs for individuals and groups. However, challenge should not create high levels of stress.

- *Boundary Management.* All new designs, whether associated with hierarchies or processes, will include the movement across boundaries. As most serious problems occur on the boundary between one group or activity and another, careful attention must be paid to designing for good boundary management.

- *Information flow.* Information systems should be designed so that information goes directly to the place where action is to be taken or to the source that originated it.

- *Continuing design.* It must be recognized that the design task is never completed. It is a continuous, ongoing process.

10.   ARE FOLLETT'S IDEAS RELEVANT TODAY?

Today's management gurus are arguing forcibly that hierarchical and functional organizations are no longer working and will not work in the fiercely competitive world of the future (Hammer and Champy 1993). They emphasize the need for change to improve efficiency and recommend panaceas such as business process reengineering, total quality, performance related pay and short term contracts. They also stress the importance of information technology as a means for stimulating and ensuring the success of this kind of change.

This is still an engineering view of the world. In 1903, Frederick Winslow Taylor (1947) was recommending a not too dissimilar kind of approach. He wanted the optimum use of machines, a narrow division of labor, tight work standards and individual pay incentives. Yet people are the most important input to business success and few of these new and old remedies pay much attention to their needs for participation, motivation, job satisfaction and creativity.

Follett saw the achievement of business success coming as much from enabling the individual and the group to contribute their skills and knowledge freely and without constraints. This kind of freedom came from motivated individuals working together in small group situations within a close and integrated work environment. We now have to ask the question, "How relevant are her ideas today?" Can we still apply them in work situations where face-to-face communication is replaced or enhanced by video-conferencing, voice mail and telework and where electronic networks are expanding to engulf every type of industrial and commercial activity.

First let us remind ourselves of the ideas of Mary Parker Follett. She wanted freedom and responsibility for the individual and the group. This required group membership, communication, participation, joint problem solving and joint decision making. All of these have to take place both within groups and between groups. She believed in power and control but it was "power with" not "power over." Power sharing of this kind requires common values and agreement on the cause and nature of problems. This she called "the Law of the Situation." She also believed in multiple leadership so that no single individual or group was able to dominate the others. Similar ideas are still being propagated. In England, a distinguished social scientist, Geoffrey Vickers has written:

> We must abandon the idea that political and economic life is primarily the interaction of individuals, each pursuing their own self-interest....We shall have to conceive ourselves as maintaining a number of institutional systems which are essential to our significance and survival but which depend completely on our capacity to resolve or contain the conflicts which they engender....This requires intelligence, tolerance, wisdom, acceptance of common constraints and assurances of membership. [Vickers 1973]

Vickers believed that organizations can only survive if they are able to contain and resolve their conflicts and that communication and debate make a major contribution to this resolution. These provide a shared view of the problem and an understanding of the special interests of each party.

Handy, another influential British writer on management supports this view, saying:

> If we want to reconcile our humanity with our economics, we have to find a way to give more influence to what is personal and local, so that we each can feel that we have a chance to make a difference, that we matter, along with those around us....A formal democracy will not be enough. We have to find another way, by changing the structure of our institutions to give more power to the small and to the local. [Handy 1994]

Handy sees the answer in what he calls "federalism." Federalism is an old idea which had as one of its objectives the creation of a balance of power within an institution. Federal organizations are both small and large. They aim to be small and local in their appearance and in many of their decisions, but national, even global, in their scope. Like the Chinese philosophy of Yin and Yang, they are built on contradictions. They endeavor to maximize independence while maintaining a degree of interdependence. Also, like Yin and Yang, the secret of doing this successfully is achieving the right balance for the organization and the situation between things big and small. Individuals recognize and accept that they are members of both groups and that control is a shared activity.

Handy associates federalism with what he calls "subsidiarity": the individual parts retain as much independence as they can handle but give some power to the center because they know the center can do some things better. The center is not necessarily large; it may be quite small but it has a view of the whole. Today this view is assisted by communications technology which provides it with the information it needs to survey the whole. Handy points out that subsidiarity is not empowerment. Empowerment implies that someone is giving away power. Subsidiarity means that power belongs lower down where most of the action takes place.

This form of organization requires small units with real power. The members of each unit are constantly in touch with other units, recognize and accept common rights and duties and work together in a climate of mutual trust. Handy points out that "organizations are nothing if they are not communities of people....A community has members, not employees, and it belongs to its members."

11.   PROBLEMS WITH THE CONCEPT OF FREEDOM

One problem is that freedom is very hard to achieve. Handy admits that the "federal organiza-tion" is messy, untidy and always a little out of control. Nevertheless. he says, "there is no real alternative in a complicated world."

An important factor that can be an enhancer or reducer of freedom is current attitudes. Handy believes that human progress, as defined by Follett, is at present inhibited by our pursuit of efficiency and economic growth in the conviction that these are the necessary ingredients of progress. He believe that efficiency, like technology, should be a means not an end in itself.

Technology is, of course, another factor that can reduce or increase freedom. The history of technology is that its consequences have always been mixed. The more powerful have usually gained from its use, while the weaker have lost. One early group of sufferers were women clerks who found that they had lost what was often quite interesting manual work and become data input operators. This new job required concentration, was deadly boring and, to add insult to injury, the speed at which the women worked could be monitored by the computer and reported to management (Baker 1964).

A group that constantly comes under attack for causing technology to dehumanize work and remove freedom are the engineers. They are seen to be disciples of Taylor and, by writers such as David Noble, to be tools of the capitalist system using technology to reduce the human being to a machine component (Noble 1979).

Hopefully, we have now passed this stage and the versatile computer is being used to enhance, not degrade, skills. Vickers points out that technology always makes ethical demands in what it requires people to expect of each other and therefore of themselves. In many fields today, the effect of technology is very positive for the computer is an instrument of great variety that can be used in many different ways.

Let us hope this is true in its communication role where it may help us to realize the democratic organization sought by Follett. Computers and networks can help us to communicate with people located far away, to take decisions based on accurate knowledge, to plan strategies with the alternatives clarified, to write joint papers and reports, and to pass around innovative ideas.

In theory this is splendid. The question is, will it work in the desired and desirable way? We are only just learning how to handle this new telefreedom and beginning to realize that the desired results are not so easy to achieve.

Mary Parker Follett's ideas give us something to aim for and provide a vision that many see as relevant to today's and tomorrow's urgent problems.

12.   REFERENCES

Argyris, C. *Personality and Organization.* New York: Harper and Row, 1957.

Baker, E. F. *Technology and Woman's Work.* New York: Columbia University Press, 1964.

Bell, D. *The Coming of a Post-Industrial Society.* London: Heinemann, 1974.

Drucker, P. *The Practice of Management.* New York: Harper, 1954.

Follett, M. P. *Creative Experience.* London: Longmans, 1924.

Follett, M. P. *The New State.* London: Longmans, 1920.

Follett, M. P. "The Psychological Foundations of Business Administration." In H. C. Metcalf (Editor), *The Scientific Foundations of Business Administration.* London: Williams and Wilkins, 1926.

Galston, W. A. *Liberal Progress.* Cambridge, England: Cambridge University Press, 1991.

Gould, C. *Rethinking Democracy.* Cambridge, England: Cambridge University Press, 1988.

Graham, P. *Mary Parker Follett: Prophet of Management.* Cambridge: Harvard Business Press, 1995.

Hammer, M., and Champy, J. *Reengineering the Corporation: A Manifesto for Business Revolution.* London: Nicholas Brealey, 1993.

Handy, C. *The Empty Raincoat.* London: Hutchinson, 1994.
Herzberg, F. W. *Work and the Nature of Man.* New York: World Publishing Company, 1966.

Herzberg, F.; Mausner, B.; and Snyderman, B. *The Motivation to Work.* New York: Wiley, 1959.

Likert, R. *New Patterns of Management.* New York: McGraw-Hill, 1961.

Mayo, E. *The Social Problems of an Industrial Civilisation.* London: Routledge and Kegan Paul, 1949.

McGregor, D. *Leadership and Motivation.* Cambridge: MIT Press, 1966.

Metcalf, H. C., and Urwick, L. *Dynamic Administration.* London: Management Publications Trust, 1941.

Mumford, E., and Henshall, D. *A Participative Approach to Computer Systems Design.* Manchester: Associated Business Press, 1979.

Mumford, E., and MacDonald, B. *XSEL's Progress.* New York: Wiley, 1989.

Mumford, E., and Weir, M. *Computer Systems in Work Design: The ETHICS Method.* Manchester: Associated Business Press, 1979.

Noble, D. *America by Design.* New York: Knopf, 1979.

Pugh, D. S.; Hickson, D. J.; and Hinings, C. R. *Writers in Organizations.* New York: Penguin, 1971.

Roethlisberger, F. J., and Dickson, W. J. *Management and the Worker.* Cambridge: Harvard University Press, 1949.

Taylor, F. W. *Scientific Management.* New York: Harper and Row, 1947.

Trist, E., and Murray, H. *The Social Engagement of Social Science. Volume 1: The Socio-Technical Perspective.* Philadelphia: University of Pennsylvania Press, 1991.

Trist, E., and Murray, H. *The Social Engagement of Social Science. Volume 2: The Socio-Technical Perspective.* Philadelphia: University of Pennsylvania Press, 1993.

Vickers, G. *Making Institutions Work.* Manchester: Associated Business Programs, 1973.

Von Bertalanffy, L. *General System Theory.* London: Braziller, 1968.

Wood, A. W. *Hegel.* Cambridge, England: Cambridge University Press, 1991.

About the Author

Enid Mumford is an Emeritus Professor of Manchester University, England; a Visiting Senior Fellow at the Manchester Business School; and a Consultant with the Consulting Services Group in the Netherlands. She is a Companion of the British Institute of Personnel Management and a Fellow of the British Computer Society. She chairs the BCS Working Party on Sociotechnical Systems Design.

Dr. Mumford is also a Council Member of the Tavistock Institute of Human Relations in London. It was the Tavistock Institute which first developed and implemented the notions of team work, multi-skilling, and self-management, which are increasingly popular today.

In 1983, Dr. Mumford won the American Warnier gold medal for her contributions to Information Science. She is the author of twenty-six books and many papers. Her current interest is developing tools and methods to assist the management of technical and organizational change. She works both in the Netherlands and in the United Kingdom.

INDEX OF CONTRIBUTORS

Printed in the United Kingdom
by Lightning Source UK Ltd.
9556600001B